U.S. Supreme Court Precedents on Arbitration

# International Litigation in Practice



VOLUME 14

The titles published in this series are listed at *brill.com/inli*

# U.S. Supreme Court Precedents on Arbitration

## *Shaping the American Arbitration Law and Practice*

*Edited by*

Kabir Duggal, Yasmine Lahlou, Carlos Alberto Carmona, and Gustavo Favero Vaughn

BRILL | NIJHOFF

LEIDEN | BOSTON

Library of Congress Cataloging-in-Publication Data

Names: Duggal, Kabir, editor. | Lahlou, Yasmine, editor. | Carmona, Carlos Alberto, editor. | Vaughn, Gustavo Favero, editor.
Title: U.S. Supreme Court Precedents on Arbitration : Shaping the American Arbitration Law and Practice / edited by Kabir Duggal, Yasmine Lahlou, Carlos Alberto Carmona, and Gustavo Favero Vaughn.
Other titles: US Supreme Court precedents on arbitration
Description: Leiden ; Boston : Brill/Nijhoff, 2025. | Series: International litigation in practice | Includes bibliographical references and index. | Summary: "In the United States, arbitration - international and interstate alike - is a federal law subject. However, the U.S. law governing international arbitration is based on a century-old statute, the Federal Arbitration Act (FAA, which has not been meaningfully amended since its enactment nearly 100 years ago, except for the addition of two chapters, implementing the New York and Panama Conventions on the recognition and enforcement of international arbitral awards.
Identifiers: LCCN 2024046069 | ISBN 9789004715813 (hardback) | ISBN 9789004715820 (ebook)
Subjects: LCSH: Arbitration and award–United States. | Stare decisis–United States. | United States. Supreme Court–Decision making.
Classification: LCC KF9085 .U55 2025 | DDC 347.73/9–dc23/eng/20241008
LC record available at https://lccn.loc.gov/2024046069

Typeface for the Latin, Greek, and Cyrillic scripts: "Brill". See and download: brill.com/brill-typeface.

ISSN 1874-0502
ISBN 978-90-04-71581-3 (hardback)
ISBN 978-90-04-71582-0 (e-book)
DOI 10.1163/9789004715820



This book is printed on acid-free paper and produced in a sustainable manner.

# Contents

# Notes on Contributors

*Rafael Francisco Alves*

is a Partner at Souto Correa Advogados and Professor at FGV São Paulo Law School (FGV DIREITO SP). He is also a Member of the Board of Directors of the International Institute for Conflict Prevention and Resolution (CPR) and Officer of the Brazilian Arbitration Committee (CBAr). He holds a Ph.D, Master of Laws and Bachelor of Laws from University of São Paulo (USP) and also an LL.M. from New York University (NYU), where he was an Arthur T. Vanderbilt Scholar. He regularly sits as arbitrator.

*Rafael Stefanini Auilo*

holds Ph.D. e M.Sc. degrees from the University of São Paulo Law School, Brazil. Rafael is trained in Brazilian law and holds an LLB (hons) from the São Paulo Catholic Pontifical University Law School. Rafael acted as visiting-professor and visiting-scholar at University of Messina Law School, Italy (2013). Rafael is a partner at Yarshell Advogados and has handled several domestic and international arbitrations, both as lawyer and arbitrator, across a broad range of sectors, including energy, mining, insurance, construction, pulp and paper, aviation, and food and beverages.

*Zeinab Bailoun*

is an associate at Baker Botts LLP, with a focus on high-stakes, complex commercial litigation and international arbitration.

*Jessica Beess und Chrostin*

is a Partner in King & Spalding's International Disputes Group. Jessica's practice focuses on complex international dispute resolution, with particular expertise in high-stakes commercial, investor-state, construction, and global award enforcement disputes. Jessica regularly represents clients in international disputes in the infrastructure, oil and gas, mining, construction, and renewable energy sectors, and has significant experience in consumer goods, real estate, and telecommunications disputes. Jessica has been recognized by IFLR Americas as a Rising Star in Commercial Arbitration and by CPR as a Rising Star in Alternative Dispute Resolution. She is also ranked by Who's Who Legal as a Future Leader in International Arbitration.

*Andrew Behrman*
is a partner at Baker Botts LLP in New York. His practice focuses on international disputes with a particular emphasis on international arbitration. Andrew advises clients on a wide range of matters and claims covering a broad spectrum of industries before international tribunals such as the ICC and AAA/ICDR.

*Yining Bei*
is an associate at Baker Botts LLP, with a focus on high-stakes, complex commercial litigation and international arbitration.

*Gary L. Benton*
C.Arb, F.CIArb, F.CollArb, is an internationally recognized Arbitrator based in Palo Alto, California. He focuses on U.S. and international business, corporate investment, technology, IP and emerging growth matters. He is qualified as a U.S. lawyer (NY, CA and DC) and an English solicitor, and serves on the Adjunct Faculty at Santa Clara University Law School. https://garybentonarbitration.com.

*Caetano Berenguer*
is a Partner at Sergio Bermudes Advogados. With more than twenty years of practice as both lawyer and arbitrator in high-value litigation and commercial arbitration, Caetano has been recognized by various market-leading legal rankings, such as Chambers & Partners, Legal 500 Latin America, Leaders League, Benchmark Litigation, and the Best Lawyers. He is a guest lecturer at the Brazilian Institute of Capital Markets (Ibmec), in Sao Paulo, and holds an LL.M. degree from Columbia Law School.

*George A. Bermann*
is the director of the Center for International Commercial & Investment Arbitration at Columbia Law School. He is a world-renowned authority on comparative law, EU law, international trade contracts, WTO dispute resolution, and transnational litigation and arbitration. For more than four decades, he has been an active international arbitrator in commercial and investment disputes in all sectors, including general commercial contract, construction, intellectual property, energy, oil and gas, competition law, insurance, telecommunications, pharmaceuticals, distributorship and franchising, transportation, and employment. He also serves regularly as an expert witness before international arbitral tribunals as well as before courts in arbitral-related cases. Bermann joined the Columbia Law School faculty in 1975. He founded both

the *Columbia Journal of European Law* and the European Legal Studies Center, where he serves as the director. In addition to teaching full-time at the Law School, he is an affiliated faculty member of the School of Law of Sciences Po in Paris and the MIDS Masters Program in International Dispute Settlement in Geneva. Bermann was the chief reporter for the American Law Institute (ALI) for its *Restatement of the Law, The U.S. Law of International Commercial and Investor-State Arbitration*, a 12-year project that was completed in 2019; it was the first ALI Restatement on this area of the law.

*João Lucas Bevilacqua*
is a Partner at Sergio Bermudes Advogados. He is a dual-qualified lawyer admitted to practice in New York and in Brazil. He holds an LL.B. from Pontifícia Universidade Católica de São Paulo (PUC-SP) and an LL.M. from the New York University School of Law.

*Preeti Bhagnani*
is a Partner in the International Arbitration practice of White & Case, based in New York. With nearly two decades of experience, she represents private companies and sovereign States in commercial and investor-state disputes in all major arbitral fora. She has handled dozens of arbitrations across a broad range of sectors, including energy, mining, insurance and life sciences. She formerly served as in-house counsel at a global energy company. Preeti is trained in New York, Singapore and English law, and holds an LLB (Hons) from the London School of Economics, and an LL.M. from Columbia Law School.

*R. Doak Bishop*
is a partner in King & Spalding's Houston office and a founding member of the firm's International Disputes Practice Group. The firm's International Disputes Practice Group has been ranked numerous years as No. 1 Worldwide by Global Arbitration Review, International Practice Group of the Year by Law360. Mr. Bishop specializes in international arbitration, with a focus on Latin America. With extensive experience in litigation and international arbitration, Mr. Bishop has served both as an arbitrator and counsel. He represents clients in disputes concerning oil and gas and energy, renewable energy, power plant and turbine generator, public utilities and infrastructure, mining, aviation, IT, data processing and software, foreign investment, construction and environmental matters. Doak has served on the boards of directors of the major arbitral institutions such as the Institute of Transnational Arbitration. American Arbitration Association (AAA) and as a member of the U.S. delegation to the North American Free Trade Act (NAFTA) Advisory Committee

on Private Commercial Disputes. As an arbitrator, Doak has led or participated in more than 100 arbitrations under the auspices of the International Centre for Settlement of Investment Disputes (ICSID), International Chamber of Commerce (ICC), London Court of International Arbitration (LCIA), UN Commission on International Trade Law (UNCITRAL), International Centre for Dispute Resolution (ICDR), AAA, the Inter-American Commercial Arbitration Commission (IACAC) and the Center for Public Resources (CPR), as well as in ad hoc arbitrations. A frequent author with major publications in the field, and keynote speeches, Doak is listed by Chambers USA in Tier 1 as a top seven U.S. arbitration counsel, and by Chambers Global in Tier 1 of the top 11 international arbitration counsel globally. He is also listed as a top 20 arbitration specialist by Cross-Border Quarterly, published in the UK.

*Jonathan I. Blackman*
is senior counsel at Cleary Gottlieb Steen & Hamilton LLP in New York. His practice focuses on litigation, including international litigation and arbitration, banking, and insurance law. He has participated in numerous international arbitrations involving both public international law and complex commercial disputes, litigation involving the immunity of foreign states and their agencies under the U.S. Foreign Sovereign Immunities Act, and commercial litigation in a variety of U.S. federal and state courts.

*Michael B. Carlinsky*
is the Co-Global Managing Partner, Global Head of Complex Litigation, Co-Chair of Insurance Litigation and Co-Head of Brazil Practice at Quinn Emanuel Urquhart & Sullivan.

*Carlos Alberto Carmona*
is a Professor of Procedural Law and Arbitration at the University of Sao Paulo. He is a lawyer registered in the Brazilian Bar Association, São Paulo section, since 1981. Expert in civil procedure, litigation and arbitration, Carmona is a Partner of Marques Rosado, Toledo Cesar & Carmona Advogados. He is also a member of the *Associação dos Advogados de São Paulo* (Association of Lawyers of São Paulo) and former President of the *Instituto Brasileiro de Direito Processual* (Brazilian Institute of Procedural Law). Carmona was part of the Commission responsible for the drafting of the Brazilian Arbitration Law.

*Peter E. Carzis*
is an Associate at Cleary Gottlieb Steen & Hamilton LLP in New York in the litigation and arbitration practice group.

*Felipe Conrado*
is an associate at Tannuri Advogados, a distinguished boutique law firm in Brazil specializing in high-value complex arbitration and litigation. He holds a bachelor degree from the school of law of FGV-SP.

*Eduardo Damião Gonçalves*
is a partner at Mattos Filho, Veiga Filho, Marrey Jr. e Quiroga Advogados. He represents clients in domestic and international arbitration matters related to mergers and acquisitions, corporate disputes, infrastructure, and particularly in conflicts arising from construction agreements and public concessions. He also represents clients in complex litigation in the areas of environmental law, information technology, infrastructure, and arbitration-related disputes. Eduardo has been the vice president of the International Chamber of Commerce's (ICC) International Court of Arbitration since 2018, and a member of the International Council for International Arbitration's (ICCA) governing body since 2022. He was a founder and former president of the Brazilian Arbitration Committee, and remains a board member. Eduardo was also previously the vice president of the Latin American Arbitration Association (ALARB) and the International Bar Association's (IBA) Arbitration Committee. He holds an LL.B degree from Universidade de São Paulo (USP), an LL.M degree from Université de Paris II, and a Ph.D degree from USP.

*Erico Bomfim de Carvalho*
is a partner at Advocacia Velloso. He is specialized in international arbitration and in litigating high-profile cases before the Brazilian Supreme Court (STF) and the Superior Court of Justice (STJ). Erico holds an LL.M. from Columbia Law School, where he was a Harlan Fiske Stone Scholar and a recipient of the Parker School Certificate of Achievement in Foreign and Comparative Law.

*Katharine Menéndez de la Cuesta*
is a partner of Holland & Knight's Miami office. Clients rely on her experience to represent them in international arbitration proceedings in English and Spanish, and in litigation matters before U.S. federal and state courts in New York and Florida. Ms. Menéndez de la Cuesta has handled international arbitrations applying the laws of New York, Florida, Illinois, Spain, France, United Kingdom, Namibia, Saudi Arabia, Hong Kong, Venezuela, Colombia, and Guatemala, among other jurisdictions, and administered by the main arbitral institutions. She has acted as administrative secretary of arbitral tribunals and been appointed as arbitrator. She was a representative for North America of the ICC's Young Arbitrators Forum (YAF) for its 2019–2021 mandate.

Ms. Menéndez de la Cuesta has been involved in disputes arising out of mergers and acquisitions (M&A), energy (including LNG and mining disputes) and transportation matters (airport and rail industries).

*Kabir Duggal*
is a Senior Fellow at the Center for International Commercial and Investment Arbitration at Columbia Law School (CICIA) and an attorney in Arnold and Porter's New York office, focusing on international arbitration and public international law matters, serving both as arbitrator and mediator. He is recognized as a "Chartered Arbitrator" (the highest ranking for arbitrators) by both the Chartered Institute of Arbitrators and the Asian Institute of Alternative Dispute Resolution. He is also a Lecturer-in-Law at Columbia Law School, an adjunct Professor at Fordham Law School, and a Course Director and a Faculty Member for the Columbia Law School-Chartered Institute of Arbitrators Comprehensive Course on International Arbitration.

*Marcel Engholm*
is an associate with Chaffetz Lindsey LLP in New York. Marcel handles arbitration and litigation disputes in contractual, construction, oil & gas, and reinsurance matters. Marcel is experienced in civil and common law systems, having practiced law in Brazil and in New York. Marcel has represented clients from North America, Latin America, Europe, Africa, and Asia in matters under the ICC, SCC, UNCITRAL, CCBC, and FIESP rules, as well as in various courts in the U.S. and in Brazil. He holds a law degree from Pontifical Catholic University of Sao Paulo, a Master's degree from the University of Sao Paulo and an LL.M. from New York University.

*John Fellas*
is full-time arbitrator at Fellas Arbitration; adjunct professor of law, New York University School of Law; honorary professor of law, Durham Law School.

*Michael A. Fernández*
is a Partner at Cozen O'Connor and Adjunct Professor of Law at Fordham University School of Law whose practice is focused on complex and cross-border commercial litigation, international commercial and investor-state arbitration, and corporate internal investigations.

*Andrew Finn*
is a partner in Sullivan & Cromwell's Litigation Group and the head of S&C's International Arbitration and Global Dispute Resolution Practice. His practice

focuses on multi-jurisdictional and international disputes, both in arbitration and U.S. state and federal courts. Andrew has litigated a wide variety of cases, from commercial and investor-state arbitrations, to securities class actions and other significant contractual, bankruptcy and competition cases. He has worked with clients in a wide-range of industries, including finance and banking, transportation, mining, energy, software, entertainment and health care. Andrew also has advised on corporate monitorships and other large-scale government settlement compliance matters.

*Peter Fox*
is a partner at the law firm of Scoolidge Peters Russotti & Fox LLP, where his practice focuses on international commercial arbitration and transnational litigation, among other areas of dispute resolution. He is admitted to practice, and has filed briefs, in the U.S. Supreme Court.

*Elliot Friedman*
is a Partner at Freshfields Bruckhaus Deringer U.S. LLP.

*James Fullmer*
is an attorney admitted to the bar of Massachusetts, United States. He is a graduate of the University of California, Berkeley and of Harvard Law School. Prior to entering private practice, he served as a law clerk to the Honorable G. Murray Snow of the U.S. District Court for the District of Arizona.

*Katie L. Gonzalez*
is a senior associate at Cleary Gottlieb Steen & Hamilton LLP in New York. Her practice focuses on international litigation and arbitration, with an emphasis on Latin America. Katie has significant experience representing sovereign and private entities in commercial and investor-state arbitration matters, as well as in state and federal courts. Katie is also an adjunct professor at Cardozo Law School, where she teaches a course on international arbitration. Who's Who Legal has recognized Katie as a "Future Leader in International Arbitration."

*Surya Gopalan*
is an Associate in the International Arbitration practice of White & Case, based in New York. He advises and represents sovereign states and private clients in high-stakes disputes around the world involving a range of industries. Surya has an LL.M from Columbia University and a LL.B / B.Ec. from the University of Sydney. He is a member of the bars of New York and New South Wales (Australia).

*Grant Hanessian*
is an independent arbitrator in New York, specializing in international, investor-state and complex commercial disputes. Prior to July 2020, he was a partner at Baker McKenzie, where he served as global co-head of the firm's International Arbitration Practice. He has had leadership roles in several international arbitration institutions and was U.S. member on the ICC's International Court of Arbitration from 2015 to 2021. Mr. Hanessian is an Adjunct Professor of Law at Fordham University School of Law in New York, where he teaches the International Commercial Arbitration and LL.M. International Arbitration Practicum courses. He has edited six books on international arbitration subjects and authored more than fifty articles and book chapters. He is a frequent speaker at arbitration conferences and law schools around the world and annually recommended as an arbitrator by Chambers and other publications.

*Samaa Haridi*
is a Partner at King & Spalding LLP, based in New York. Samaa is common and civil law trained and has significant experience representing clients in multi-jurisdictional international commercial and investment arbitration proceedings under the arbitration rules of all the major arbitral institutions. Samaa also frequently sits as an arbitrator in international commercial and investment disputes. Samaa is currently serving as an officer in a number of arbitral organizations, including as Vice-President of the ICC International Court of Arbitration, and Member of ICCA's Governing Board. Samaa has been recognized by clients and peers and repeatedly listed in Chambers USA and Chambers Global for International Arbitration. She is also recognized by The Legal 500, and by Who's Who Legal: Global Elite Thought Leaders—Arbitration 2023. She is a member of the bars of New York, California, and England & Wales and is fluent in French and Arabic.

*Stephen Hogan-Mitchell*
is an associate in the International Arbitration practice of White & Case, based in New York. His practice focuses on complex commercial disputes across a variety of sectors, including technology, energy, insurance, and life sciences. Stephen holds a JD from Columbia Law School and is admitted to practice in New York.

*James Hosking*
originally from New Zealand, is a founding partner of New York-based Chaffetz Lindsey LLP and leads the firm's international arbitration practice. He has acted as counsel in disputes under all the leading rules, and sat as an arbitrator

in some 60 commercial or investor-state cases. A significant part of James' practice involves disputes arising out of global political and economic crises, particularly in Latin America. He is a member of the Governing Board of the International Council for Commercial Arbitration, a Fellow of the Arbitrators and Mediators Association of New Zealand, and Vice President of the Court of the Saudi Center for Commercial Arbitration. James has also published widely on international arbitration, including as the co-author of the leading commentary on the ICDR International Rules, and is an adjunct professor at NYU School of Law.

*Pedro José Izquierdo*
is a special counsel in Sullivan & Cromwell's Litigation Group and a member of the Firm's International Arbitration and Latin America practices, where he focuses on complex international disputes under civil law, common law, and public international law. His practice encompasses commercial, investment and construction disputes in English and Spanish under the major international arbitration rules (ICC, ICDR, ICSID, LCIA, UNCITRAL, etc.), acting both as counsel and in the preparation of legal expert reports for disputes in various jurisdictions.

*Zachary Kady*
is a senior associate in Gibson Dunn's International Arbitration Group. He has 10 years of experience representing clients in commercial arbitrations as well as investor-state disputes before several arbitral institutions, including the ICC, SIAC, AAA, JAMS, LCIA, ICSID, ICDR, and more. Mr. Kady also has extensive experience litigating disputes in United States courts related to arbitration, including the enforcement of agreements to arbitrate, discovery related to arbitration, and disputes concerning the enforcement and vacatur of arbitration awards.

*Sherman Kahn*
with the law firm Maschoff Brennan. He is an arbitrator and represents clients in international arbitrations presenting complex technical and commercial issues. He has arbitrated under the ICC, AAA, ICDR, CPR, JCAA, HKIAC, UNCITRAL rules as well as other rules and pure ad hoc. He has sat as chair, sole arbitrator, and wing arbitrator in international and domestic arbitrations on subjects including IT outsourcing, software development, biotechnology and pharmaceuticals, mining, patent infringement, standard essential patents, trademark licensing, unfair competition and trade disparagement, and commercial issues. He has also provided advice regarding clause drafting and

pre-dispute issues in connection with major construction and infrastructure projects. He is on the International Centre for Dispute Resolution (ICDR) Panel of Arbitrators, the American Arbitration Association Roster of Commercial Arbitrators and the CPR Distinguished Panel of Neutrals and the Korean Commercial Arbitration Board (KCAB) Panel of International Arbitrators. He is a Fellow of the Chartered Institute of Arbitrators (FCIArb) and a member of the Silicon Valley Arbitration and Mediation Center Tech List. He also acts as a mediator. Mr. Kahn has more than twenty-five years of experience in patent litigation including matters involving biotechnology, DAN and protein constructs, semiconductors, programmable logic devices, microprocessors and controllers, memory devices, construction equipment, medical devices, supercomputers, LCD & PDP display devices, LED Lighting, computer software, and networking technologies. He also litigates and arbitrates outsourcing, trade-secret, trademark, copyright, and antitrust matters.

*Mark Kantor*
is a retired partner of Milbank, Tweed, Hadley & McCloy (now Milbank LLC), an international arbitrator in investment and commercial disputes, Adjunct Professor at the Georgetown University Law Center and Editor-in-Chief of the online journal Transnational Dispute Management. He was a member of the World Bank Group Sanctions Board (term ended Fall 2021). He is a former member of the American Arbitration Association Board of Directors and the Council of the American Arbitration Association, and former Chair of the DC Bar International Investment Committee and the DC Bar International Dispute Resolution Committee. He has authored numerous works, including Reports of Overseas Private Investment Corporation Determinations (eds. Mark Kantor, Michael D. Nolan and Karl P. Sauvant), Valuation for Arbitration: Compensation Standards, Valuation Methods and Expert Evidence (OGEMID Best Book 2008) and "A Code of Conduct for Party-Appointed Experts in International Arbitration—Can One be Found?" 26 Arbitration International 323 (2010) (OGEMID Best International Dispute Resolution Article 2010).

*Lea Haber Kuck*
is an independent arbitrator with more than three decades of experience in international and domestic dispute resolution under various arbitration rules and in the United States courts. Prior to launching her full-time arbitrator practice in 2022, she was a partner at Skadden, Arps, Slate, Meagher and Flom LLP in the international litigation and arbitration group advising clients from around the world on the resolution of complex disputes arising out of international business transactions.

*Yasmine Lahlou*

Partner, Chaffetz Lindsey. Yasmine Lahlou, who is fluent in English, French and Italian and proficient in Portuguese, has over 20 years of experience in international arbitration, representing clients in energy, mining, construction, pharmaceutical, telecommunications, infrastructure, real estate, aviation, corporate disputes, among others, and has a leading foreign award and foreign judgment enforcement practice. Initially trained in Paris and admitted in Paris and New York, Yasmine is experienced in civil and common law systems. Yasmine has been counsel in dozens of arbitrations conducted under the ICC, ICDR, LCIA, UNCITRAL and ad hoc rules. She has acted as a presiding, sole and co-arbitrator in ICC, ICDR/AAA, SCC, CRCICA (in Cairo) and LCIA arbitrations. Yasmine has been named one of 23 "Global Elite Thought Leaders" in North America—a title reserved for the top 2.5% of ranked practitioners considered the "very best by peers and clients, achieving the highest number of recommendations in the research"—by Who's Who Legal 2024 Arbitration report, and she has been recognized by Legal 500, Chambers, and Super Lawyers—including her Latin America expertise.

*Laura Lambert da Costa*

is a senior associate at Mattos Filho, Veiga Filho, Marrey Jr. e Quiroga Advogados. Her practice focuses on complex court litigation, arbitration and pre-litigation negotiations involving cross-border disputes in the areas of product liability, mergers and acquisitions, technology and environmental law. Laura has practiced at Latham & Watkins in New York and was a member of the Columbia International Arbitration Association in New York. She holds an LL.B degree from Universidade de São Paulo (USP) and an LL.M degree from Columbia Law School, where she graduated with James Kent Scholar honors.

*Andre Luis Monteiro*

is Of Counsel at Quinn Emanuel Urquhart & Sullivan. Visiting Scholar at the School of International Arbitration at Queen Mary, University of London (2018–2019). Junior Academic Visitor at the University of Oxford (2015–2016). PhD (2013–2017) and Master's (2009–2012) degrees from Pontifical Catholic University of São Paulo, Brazil.

*Alex Lupsaiu*

is an associate at Chaffetz Lindsey LLP in New York representing clients in international commercial arbitrations, commercial litigations, and bankruptcy matters across a variety of industry sectors including construction, energy, and real estate. He is a graduate of NYU School of Law, where he served as Notes Editor on the Annual Survey of American Law.

*Dana MacGrath*
is a full-time arbitrator based in New York. Previously she acted as counsel in domestic and international arbitrations with several leading law firms. She is an adjunct professor at Fordham University School of Law where she teaches international arbitration. Her arbitrator practice focuses on commercial disputes. She is co-chair of the International Committee of the ABA Dispute Resolution Section and co-chair of the Large Complex Case Committee of the American Arbitration Association. She is the immediate past President of ArbitralWomen and currently co-chair of the Equal Representation in Arbitration Pledge USA Subcommittee.

*Ari D. MacKinnon*
is a partner at Cleary Gottlieb Steen & Hamilton LLP in New York. His practice focuses on international arbitration matters in Latin America, with a focus on the oil and gas, energy, mining, infrastructure, and paper and pulp sectors. Ari has experience conducting arbitrations in both English and Spanish. Ari has been recognized as a banded lawyer for international arbitration by *Chambers Latin America*, *Chambers Global* and *Chambers USA*.

*Peter J. Messitte*†
was a United States District Judge for the District of Maryland for 30 years. He was Adjunct Professor of Comparative Law and Director of the Brazil-US Legal & Judicial Studies Program at American University Washington College of Law and Senior Advisor to the American Bar Association Rule of Law Initiative for Latin America and the Caribbean.

*Rahim Moloo*
is a partner and global co-chair of Gibson Dunn's International Arbitration Group. His practice focuses on complex commercial and investor-state disputes before courts and arbitral tribunals around the world. Mr. Moloo has been recognized as a global thought leader in international arbitration and has been recognized for his advocacy skills and expertise in handling international disputes by several publications and institutions, including Chambers Global, Law 360, Who's Who Legal and Global Arbitration Review. Mr. Moloo is also an adjunct professor at Columbia Law School and has published several books and articles on a wide range of topics in the field of international disputes.

*Boaz S. Morag*

is a counsel at Cleary Gottlieb Steen & Hamilton LLP in New York. His practice focuses on international commercial litigation and arbitration matters involving private as well as foreign sovereign parties. He is active in the New York City Bar Association and most recently Chaired the City Bar Working Group that published an extensive report on the Hague Convention on Choice of Court Agreements, Hague Convention on the Recognition and Enforcement of Foreign Judgments in Civil or Commercial Matters and the U.N. Convention on International Settlement Agreements Resulting from Mediation.

*Caline Mouawad*

is a partner at Chaffetz Lindsey LLP in New York, Caline Mouawad has over 20 years of experience representing clients in international commercial arbitrations and investment treaty disputes, as well as related litigation matters, across the globe and in a variety of industry sectors. She acts as counsel in arbitrations conducted in English and French before all major arbitral institutions, and regularly serves as an arbitrator. Among other leadership roles, Caline serves as Vice-Chair of the ICC Commission on Arbitration and ADR and Vice-Chair of the IBA Arbitration Committee.

*Arthur Gonzalez Cronemberger Parente*

is a partner at Mattos Filho, Veiga Filho, Marrey Jr. e Quiroga Advogados, where he focuses on international and domestic arbitration, litigation, and pre-litigation negotiations involving M&A, securities, and commercial disputes. He regularly advises shareholders, boards of directors and executives on corporate governance conflicts, drawing on his extensive experience as a corporate lawyer in corporate and M&A transactions. He has also practiced at Freshfields Bruckhaus Deringer in Paris and at Boies Schiller Flexner in New York. He founded and presided over the Columbia International Arbitration Association in New York. He holds an LL.B degree from Universidade do Estado do Rio de Janeiro (UERJ) and an LL.M degree from Columbia Law School.

*Laura França Pereira*

an associate at Three Crowns LLP, specializes in international commercial and investor-State arbitration. She has experience acting in complex and high-value disputes across a range of sectors, including banking and finance, energy, oil and gas, infrastructure, and retail. Laura has acted in proceedings under a number of arbitration rules, including ICC, ICSID, UNCITRAL, LCIA, and AAA-ICDR. Laura holds an LLM from Harvard Law School and an LLB from University of São Paulo, where she graduated first in her class.

*Rekha Rangachari*
is the Executive Director of the New York International Arbitration Center (NYIAC). Rekha is actively engaged with the arbitration community, including as Board Member of ArbitralWomen (AW) and leads its Cooperation and Global Events Committees. In parallel, Rekha maintains an active connection to academics as Adjunct Professor at Fordham Law School and Cardozo School of Law.

*Fabiano Robalinho*
holds an LL.M from Harvard Law School. He is a professor at the Fundação Getúlio Vargas School of Law (FGV-RJ), a partner at Sergio Bermudes Advogados and a member of the ICC International Court of Arbitration.

*Cameron Russell*
is a Senior Associate at Freshfields Bruckhaus Deringer U.S. LLP

*Peter B. Rutledge*
the holder of the Talmadge Chair of Law, became dean of the University of Georgia School of Law on January 1, 2015. He has written two books and over fifty articles on a wide array of topics, including international dispute resolution. He is the author of the book Arbitration and the Constitution and co-author with Gary Born of the book International Civil Litigation in United States Courts, the leading book in the field. His works have been published by the Yale University Press, the Oxford University Press and the Cambridge University Press, and his articles have appeared in a diverse array of journals such as The University of Chicago Law Review, the Vanderbilt Law Review and the Journal of International Arbitration.

*Matheus Soubhia Sanches*
is a partner at Tannuri Advogados, a distinguished boutique law firm in Brazil specializing in high-value complex arbitration and litigation. He holds an LL.M. degree from Columbia Law School and a master's degree in civil law from the Pontifical Catholic University of São Paulo. In late 2023, he worked as an International Temporary Associate in the litigation department at Davis Polk and Wardwell LLP in New York.

*Ank Santens*
is a Partner in the International Arbitration practice of White & Case, based in New York. She serves as counsel or arbitrator in commercial, investment, and construction arbitrations around the world in a broad range of industries. Ank

holds leadership positions in several arbitration organizations, including Chair of the Executive Committee of the Foundation for International Arbitration Advocacy (FIAA), Court Member of the London Court of International Arbitration, and Board member of the International Institute for Conflict Prevention & Resolution (CPR). She is top-ranked by Chambers, Who's Who Legal, and Legal 500, and two-time recipient of the "Best in Commercial Arbitration" award (Euromoney's Americas Women in Business Law Awards). Ank has an LL.M from Columbia University and a Master in Law and Bachelor in Philosophy from KU Leuven, and is a member of the New York bar and a Solicitor of England and Wales. She handles matters in English, Spanish, French, and Dutch.

*Daniel Schimmel*

leads the International Litigation & Arbitration practice of Foley Hoag's New York office. Daniel has served as Chair, Sole Arbitrator, Co-Arbitrator, Emergency Arbitrator, Appellate Arbitrator, and counsel in over 70 arbitrations arising from a broad range of contracts and transactions. He has served as Chair and emergency arbitrator in a number of disputes in excess of $350 million and as sole arbitrator in many expedited arbitrations. Daniel also represents clients, including the Republic of France, ministère des Armées, and French and European companies in litigation in the United States. Daniel has been ranked by Chambers and Partners or Chambers USA since 2017. He is a Board member and the Vice-President of the Chartered Institute of Arbitrators, NY Branch, a Board member of NYIAC, and a member of the National Academy of Distinguished Neutrals. He was the first law clerk to the Hon. Jed S. Rakoff in the Southern District of New York and worked as an assistant de justice at the Tribunal de Grande Instance de Bobigny (France). He graduated from Columbia Law School (JD, LLM), University of Paris Law School (Paris II), and ESSEC Business School.

*Peter C. Sester*

CIArb (New York/Singapore). Head of Arbitration at Warde Advogados (São Paulo) and Professor of Law at Foundation Getúlio Vargas (Rio de Janeiro). He is a dual qualified lawyer in Germany and Brazil. From 2002 to 2020 he was a tenured professor in Germany and Switzerland. He was the director of the Institute for Law & Finance at Goethe University Frankfurt (Germany) and of counsel at a global law firm (2002–2020). He is the author of *Contract Law in International Commercial Arbitration* published in Kluwer's International Arbitration Law Library Series (Volume 66, 2023) and *Business and Investment in Brazil: Law and Practice* published by Oxford University Press (2022).

*Steven Skulnik*
is an international commercial arbitrator. He is on the roster of arbitrators for the AAA/ICDR, CPR, SIAC, and other major providers. He is also a senior legal editor in the litigation and arbitration services of Thomson Reuter's Practical Law division. In that capacity he writes and edits legal know-how resources that help law firm lawyers, in-house counsel, and arbitrators perform more effectively and efficiently. Steve co-chaired the Arbitration Committee of the New York State Bar Association's Dispute Resolution Section and chaired the New York City Bar Association's Arbitration Committee. He also sits on the City Bar's International Commercial Disputes Committee and the ICDR's Publications Committee. He is a member of or affiliated with: Silicon Valley Arbitration & Mediation Center, International Arbitration Club of New York, New York International Arbitration Center (NYIAC), and the National Academy of Distinguished Neutrals. He is a fellow of the Chartered Institute of Arbitrators and the College of Commercial Arbitrators.

*Liz Snodgrass*
a partner at Three Crowns LLP, has more than twenty-five years of experience as an advocate and adviser in international disputes. She acts in commercial and investment treaty arbitrations in the United States and around the world, with a focus on the upstream energy, power, technology and mining sectors. Liz has particular expertise handling disputes involving States and State entities, including investment treaty cases, fiscal disputes under long-term contracts, disputes that implicate both contract and treaty protections, and disputes that involve parallel domestic and international proceedings.

*Rodrigo Tannuri*
is the naming partner at Tannuri Advogados, a distinguished boutique law firm in Brazil specializing in high-value complex arbitration and litigation. He holds an LL.M. degree from Columbia Law School and a master's degree in civil law from the Pontifical Catholic University of São Paulo. In 2008, he worked as an International Lawyer in the arbitration department at White & Case LLP in Washington DC.

*Shrutih Tewarie*
is a Partner at Foley Hoag, where she is the Co-Chair of the firm's International Trade & National Security practice. She has extensive experience representing U.S. and foreign companies as well as foreign sovereign governments and their instrumentalities in a variety of high stakes disputes and has obtained victories for clients before U.S. courts and international tribunals. She also

defends clients in government and internal investigations and counsels them in regulatory compliance matters involving international trade and national security matters. She has been published nationally and internationally, and interviewed by various media outlets including Bloomberg Law, the Wall Street Journal, the American Lawyer, the Boston Globe, and Law360.

*Marcio Vasconcellos*
is an associate in King & Spalding's New York office and a member of the International Disputes Practice Group. The firm's International Disputes Practice Group has been ranked numerous years as No. 1 Worldwide by Global Arbitration Review, International Practice Group of the Year by Law360. Marcio's practice focuses on commercial and investor-state arbitration, and he has a particular focus on disputes involving mergers and acquisitions, mining, energy, and financial sectors, as well as broad experience in matters involving Latin America and Brazil. He holds an LLB and an LLM from the Federal University of Rio Grande do Sul and an LLM in International Arbitration from Pepperdine University's Straus Institute for Dispute Resolution. Marcio was the Chair of the Los Angeles Chapter for the Chartered Institute of Arbitrators and a lecturer in law at the University of Southern California (USC) and an adjunct professor at Pepperdine University teaching classes on international arbitration. Marcio is admitted to practice law in Brazil, California, Illinois, and New York and he is ranked in Chambers Global and Chambers Brazil as an associate to watch.

*Gustavo Favero Vaughn*
is a Partner at Cesar Asfor Rocha Advogados, a boutique with offices in São Paulo and Brasília, in Brazil, specializing in high-value and complex litigation, as well as commercial arbitration. He has an LL.M. degree from Columbia Law School, and a master's degree on civil procedure from the University of São Paulo School of Law. After pursuing his LL.M. degree, Gustavo spent nine months working as an International Lawyer at Cleary Gottlieb Steen & Hamilton's office in New York City. Gustavo is an Alumni Advisor at the American Review of International Arbitration (ARIA) and Academic Coordinator at Arbitration Channel. He has been appointed to serve as an auditor of the Brazilian Superior Court of Sports Justice for Football, basead in Rio de Janeiro, and as an administrative judge of the São Paulo Bar Association's Ethics and Disciplinary Court. Lecturer-in-law at IDP Online.

*Carlos Mário da Silva Velloso*

served as Chief Justice of the Brazilian Supreme Court (STF) and the Brazilian Superior Electoral Court (TSE). He is an Emeritus Professor at the University of Brasília (UnB) and the Pontifical Catholic University of Minas Gerais (PUC/MG), where he was a tenured professor in Constitutional Law and General Theory of Public Law. He also served as a professor of Constitutional Tax Law at the Brazilian Institute of Public Law (IDP). Justice Carlos Velloso holds honorary doctorate degrees from The University of Craiova (Romania) and Santa Úrsula University (Rio de Janeiro).

*João Carlos Banhos Velloso*

has been a partner at Advocacia Velloso since 2018. Before that, he served as a lawyer at the renowned law firm Barroso Fontelles, Barcellos, Mendonça Advogados. His expertise lies in handling intricate court cases at the Brazilian Supreme Court (STF) and the Superior Court of Justice (STJ). Joao obtained his LL.M. degree from the University of California, Berkeley, in 2019.

*Gretta Walters*

is a partner with Chaffetz Lindsey LLP in New York. Her extensive experience as an arbitrator and counsel spans a diverse range of commercial and investment disputes in domestic and international arbitration and state and federal courts, including concerning construction/infrastructure projects; energy projects (oil & gas, wind, solar, coal-fired, hydroelectric); licensing and distribution agreements; banking and finance in developed and emerging markets; and mergers & acquisitions. Gretta is also an adjunct professor at NYU Law School, where she teaches international arbitration. Prior to joining Chaffetz Lindsey, Gretta was legal counsel at the SCC Arbitration Institute and a visiting lecturer at Stockholm University, where she also earned an LLM in International Commercial Arbitration Law.

*Flávio Luiz Yarshell*

is a Full Professor at University of São Paulo Law School, Brazil, and is the founding partner of Yarshell Advogados. Yarshell is trained in Brazilian law, and holds LLB, M.Sc. and Ph.D degrees from the University of São Paulo Law School. Yarshell has handled several domestic and international arbitrations, both as lawyer and arbitrator, across a broad range of sectors, including energy, mining, insurance, construction, pulp and paper, and transportation. Yarshell was appointed as an Electoral Judge, a highly prestigious position in Brazil occupied by only a limited number of state and federal judges and lawyers (2006). Yarshell is a member of the editorial boards of two publishers which specialize in law.

## Editors' Note

Despite the complicated federal structure within the United States, the Supreme Court reigns as the highest court in the United States, presiding over a common law jurisdiction where the doctrine of stare decisis holds sway. As the ultimate arbiter for those seeking justice under the Constitution or federal laws, it wields the authority of judicial review, scrutinizing not only the constitutionality of laws and government actions but also defining the parameters of governmental powers.

SCOTUS, as it is popularly known, was first convened in 1790. Since then, it has grappled with a myriad of legal issues, some of which have deeply divided the nation along political lines, notably contentious issues like abortion and gun rights. An area of particular scrutiny by the Supreme Court has been arbitration, evident by its frequent granting of certiorari petitions on arbitration-related matters over the years, showcasing its proactive role in shaping arbitration law in the United States.

The U.S. has a long tradition of arbitration and the arbitration law in the U.S. is among the most developed worldwide. But anyone reading the Federal Arbitration Act, the primary Federal law dealing with arbitration which Congress adopted nearly 100 years ago in 1925, quickly realizes that the statute alone is insufficient to understand arbitration law in the U.S. As such, the Supreme Court's rulings on arbitration law, the other key pillar of arbitration, are foundational and touch upon crucial matters such as the allocation of power between the courts and arbitral tribunals to decide so called gateway issues of consent to arbitration, the interplay between the Federal Arbitration Act and state laws, or an arbitrators' duty to disclose or even what subject matters can be arbitrated. Collectively, the arbitration precedents explored in this book underscore the Supreme Court's unwavering endorsement of arbitration as a preferred method of dispute resolution.

The genesis of this book traces back to 2022, at an international arbitration conference in New York City hosted by the Brazilian-American Chamber of Commerce, in collaboration with Columbia Law School, NYU School of Law, and Arbitration Channel. During this event, a shared sentiment among us—the four editors of this book—that the SCOTUS decisions on arbitration warrant further scholarly analysis, led to its conception. We recognized a notable gap in the editorial market—a lack of a comprehensive book addressing what we deemed the most relevant SCOTUS cases on arbitration.

Therefore, we embarked on this endeavor with Brill to fill that void. In pursuit of this goal, we have selected a diverse group of leading international dispute resolution practitioners—arbitrators, scholars, experts, or attorneys—who have contributed their invaluable insights and extensive experience to provide a valuable resource to the legal community for navigating the intricate terrain of U.S. arbitration law.

Crafted with the dual purpose of serving as a comprehensive guide and a prospective textbook for law schools, this book seeks to enhance understanding and foster appreciation for U.S. arbitration jurisprudence.

We sincerely hope our readers find value and enjoy reading this book.

*Kabir Duggal, Yasmine Lahlou, Carlos Alberto Carmona and Gustavo Favero Vaughn*
June 19, 2024
New York/São Paulo

CHAPTER 1

# Supreme Court Case Law on Arbitration through a Restatement Lens

*George A. Bermann*

## 1 Introduction

In the United States, arbitration – international and interstate alike – is a federal law subject. However, the U.S. law governing international arbitration is based on a century-old statute, the Federal Arbitration Act (FAA), which has not been meaningfully amended since its enactment nearly 100 years ago, except for the addition of two chapters, implementing the New York and Panama Conventions on the recognition and enforcement of international arbitral awards. As such, it has not kept up with the profound changes that have taken place over this period, much less responded to the countless questions that make their way to the courts.

The U.S. law of international arbitration is thus the accretion of judicial decisions rendered over an exceptionally long period. The great bulk of the cases making their way to the courts concern three subjects: (a) enforcement of agreements to arbitrate, (b) involvement of U.S. courts in the conduct of arbitral proceedings, and (c) post-award actions either for the annulment or the enforcement of an arbitral award. It goes nearly without saying that the burden of developing international arbitration law falls chiefly to the federal district courts and the courts of appeal and that the resulting case law is less than systematic or comprehensive. Moreover, only an exceedingly small fraction of international arbitration cases ever make their way to the U.S. Supreme Court.

It is under these circumstances that the American Law Institute (ALI) took the step of commissioning a first Restatement of the U.S. Law of International Commercial and Investor-State Arbitration (Restatement). The general purpose of Restatements is precisely to bring a measure of coherence and consistency to fields of law that have been subject to different and often inconsistent court decisions, whether at the state or federal level. Although drafters of the Restatement enjoy wide discretion to develop the law, and deviate from what may be the prevailing position among the courts on international arbitration issues, they are bound by what the U.S. Supreme Court has had to say on the

 | DOI:10.1163/9789004715820_002

subject. U.S. Supreme Court case law on international arbitration, and arbitration more generally, is of paramount importance.

It is tempting to consider and determine whether a court's ruling on any given issue can fairly be described as "pro-arbitration" in the sense that it ultimately promotes the purposes that arbitration is meant to serve or better enables it to do so. As is widely appreciated, a ruling may be viewed as favoring arbitration in some respects but not doing so in others.[1] Nevertheless, this chapter attempts as it best it can determine whether, on the whole, the U.S. Supreme Court has taken positions that are fundamentally pro-arbitration.

## 2 How Has the U.S. Supreme Court Supported the Foundations of International Arbitration?

Many of the Court's rulings may be viewed as favorable to arbitration because they basically affirm principles generally viewed as fundamental to arbitration. Such rulings may be described as definitionally pro-arbitration. The best examples are those that reinforce such basic notions as the fact that arbitration's legitimacy is founded on the basis of party consent,[2] that arbitration agreements are to be enforced absent a recognized defense to enforcement,[3] and that courts may decline to enforce any arbitration agreement they consider to be contrary to public policy.[4]

Other of the Court's rulings are favorable to arbitration in ways that are more precise and determinate. Of these the best examples are those dealing with arbitrability, with the scope of agreements to arbitrate and with the preemption of state law.

According to the Supreme Court, claims are presumptively arbitrable, i.e., legally capable of being arbitrated, and that presumption can be overcome only if Congress expressly declares them to be non-arbitrable. The leading case are most certainly Scherck v. Alberto Culver Co.[5] and Mitsubishi Motors Corp. v. Soler Chrysler-Plymouth, Inc.[6] which held that, despite their importance from a public interest point of view, securities act and antitrust claims, respectively,

1 George A. Bermann, *What Does it Mean to be Pro-Arbitration*?, 34 ARB INT'L 341 (2018).

2 Volt Info. Svcs., Inc. v. Bd of Trs. Of Leland Stanford Junior Univ., 498 U.S. 468, 485 (1989); AT&T Techs., Inc. v. Commc'ns Workers of Am., 465 U.S. 643, 648–649 (1986).

3 Gilmer v. Interstate/Johnson Lane Corp., 500 U.S. 20, 24 (1991).

4 United Paperworkers Int'l Union v. Misco, Inc., 484 U.S. 29, 42 (1987).

5 417 U.S. 506 (1974).

6 473 U.S. 614 (1985).

are arbitrable.[7] Because Congress in fact has only very rarely expressly declared statutory claims to be non-arbitrable, the presumption in favor of arbitrability is scarcely ever overcome. There can be little doubt that this body of case law is fundamentally pro-arbitration. In addition, the Court has ruled that where a given dispute involves claims that are both arbitrable and non-arbitrable, and those claims are closely intertwined, the arbitrable claims must be severed and sent to arbitration, while the non-arbitrable claims go to court.[8] In so holding, the Court allowed its commitment to arbitration to outweigh the efficiencies of having these closely intertwined claims adjudicated together.

In much the same vein, the Supreme Court has repeatedly affirmed that, when an arbitration agreement may fairly be viewed as covering a given claim or not covering it, the former interpretation is to be preferred. As the Court stated in the leading case of Moses H. Cone Memorial Hospital v. Mercury Construction Corporation, "as a matter of federal law, any doubts concerning the scope of arbitrable issues should be resolved in favor of arbitration, whether the problem at hand is the construction of the contract language itself or an allegation of waiver, delay or a like defense to arbitrability."[9] If courts, in case of doubt, treat a claim as encompassed by an arbitration agreement, rather than not encompassed by it, they are clearly enhancing arbitration's place in the world of international dispute resolution. Relatedly, the Court has ruled that, at least presumptively, claims arising under or related to a contract containing an arbitration clause are subject to arbitration even after the contract has been terminated.[10]

A third way in which the Supreme Court may be viewed as promoting arbitration has been to find a substantive federal law principle favoring arbitration and treat state laws that curtail the availability of arbitration as a dispute resolution method as contrary to that principle and accordingly unconstitutional from a federalism viewpoint. The Court first laid down that position in the case of Hines v. Davidow,[11] but reiterated it prominently in Southland Corporation v. Keating,[12] which has been followed by a striking number of subsequent

7 See also Rodriguez de Quijas v. Shearson/Am. Express, Inc., 490 U.S. 477, 483 (1989); Vimar Seguros y Reaseguros, S.A. v. M/V Sky Reefer, 515 U.S. 528 (1995).

8 Dean Witter Reynolds, Inc. v. Byrd, 470 U.S. 213, 217 (1985). See also KPMG LLP v. Cocchi, 565 U.S. 18, 22 (2011).

9 460 U.S. 1, 24–25 (1983). See also Drake Bakeries, Inc. v. Local 50, American Bakery & Confectionery Workers, 370 U.S. 254, 257–260 (1962); United Steelworkers of Amer. V. Warrior & Gulf Nav. Co., 363 U.S. 574, 582 (1960).

10 Nolde Bros., Inc. v. Bakery & Confectionery Workers Union, 410 U.S. 243, 255 (1977).

11 312 U.S. 52, 67 (1941).

12 465 U.S. 1, 16 (1984).

Supreme Court rulings.[13] Through this jurisprudence, the Court has consistently barred U.S. states, even when legislating within their constitutional sphere of authority, from declaring the statutory claims that they create to be non-arbitrable. The Court has also barred parties to an arbitration agreement from obtaining relief from a state agency. "When parties agree to arbitrate all questions arising under a contract, the FAA supersedes state laws lodging primary jurisdiction in another forum, whether judicial or administrative."[14]

More generally, the "preemption" doctrine bars states from imposing on arbitration agreements constraints that do not apply to contracts generally or otherwise substantially interfering with the efficacy of arbitration. A leading example is the Court's decision in Mastrobuono v. Shearson Lehman Hutton, Inc.,[15] denying effect to New York state case law denying tribunals the authority to impose punitive damages.

The Supreme Court case law on the "preemption" of state laws that hinder the enforceability of arbitration agreements is accordingly both solid and emphatic. Preemption is not merely a federalism principle. In the case of EEOC v. Waffle House, Inc.,[16] the Court barred the Equal Employment Opportunity commission, an administrative agency, from seeking damages from the defendant company on behalf of a worker for injuries suffered at work when the worker's employment contract with the company provided for arbitration of such claims. It elsewhere held that the "mere involvement of an administrative agency in the enforcement of a statute does not limit private parties' obligation to comply with their arbitration agreements."[17]

## 3 How Has the Supreme Court Further Promoted the Efficacy of International Arbitration?

These three large sets of rulings hardly exhaust the list of those that may fairly be looked upon as pro-arbitration. The Supreme Court has been unflagging in

13 *See, e.g.*, Kindred Nursing Centers, L.P. v. Clark, *581 U.S.* 246, 250 (2017); Nitro-Lift Techs., L.L.C. v. Howard, 568 U.S. 17 (2012); Marmet Health Care Ctr., Inc. v. Brown, 565 U.S. 530, 532–533; (2012); Preston v. Ferrer, 552 U.S. 346, 362–363 (2008); Allied Bruce Terminix Cos. v. Dobson, 513 U.S. 265, 272 (1995); Perry v. Thomas, 482 U.S. 483, 492 (1987).

14 Preston v. Ferrer, 552 U.S. 346 (2008).

15 514 U.S. 52, 58 (1995). *See also* DirectTV, Inc. v. Imburgia, 577 U.S. 47 (2015); Doctor's Associates, Inc. v. Casarotto, 517 U.S. 681 (1996).

16 534 U.S. 279, 289 (2002).

17 Gilmer v. Interstate/Johnson Lane Corp., 500 U.S. 20, 28–29 (1991).

its support of other principles on which the efficacy of arbitration depends. Of these, another five are of considerable importance.

Foremost among them is the principle of separability, which ensures that a claim remains subject to arbitration, even if the underlying contract is claimed to be invalid; only a challenge to the validity of the arbitration agreement itself will justify a court in making that determination before referring the parties to arbitration. The Court prominently announced this principle in the case of Prima Paint v. Flood & Conklin Manufacturing Co.,[18] and has emphatically maintained it.[19] Separability ensures that challenges to the validity of contract are treated as merits matters and reserved to a tribunal.

Second, the Court has also repeatedly recognized that some threshold issues are to be treated as non-gateway or admissibility matters, and therefore left primarily for decision by a tribunal rather than a court. It first announced this principle in 1964 in the case of John Wiley & Sons, Inc. v. Livingston,[20] but later confirmed it both in commercial cases, notably Howsam v. Dean Witter Reynolds, Inc.,[21] and in investor-State cases, notably BG Group, PLC v. Republic of Argentina.[22] In the latter decision, the Court asserted that the requirement that an investor litigate in the host State court for 18 months prior to pursuing arbitration was essentially a procedural provision applicable to an arbitral proceeding rather than a jurisdictional requirement. This position too reserves for tribunal determination matters that, if viewed as jurisdictional, would have been for judicial determination.

Third, the Supreme Court has further strengthened the decisional freedom of arbitrators by assimilating them to judges and thereby according them the same absolute immunity from suit enjoyed by judges, provided the action they took falls within the scope of their authority as arbitrators.[23] Such protection from litigation and liability affords arbitrators an immunity enjoyed by virtually no other service provider.

Fourth, the Supreme Court has also been reliably amenable, under appropriate circumstances, to treating non-signatories to arbitration agreements as if they were parties to those agreements. Under such circumstances they may

18 388 U.S. 395, 405 (1967).

19 See, e.g., Buckeye Check Cashing, Inc. v. Cardegna, 546 U.S. 440, 445 (2006).

20 376 U.S. 543, 555–559 (1964).

21 537 U.S. 79, 85 (2002) (statute of limitations).

22 572 U.S. 25, 33 (2014) (exhaustion of remedies requirement).

23 Burns v. Reed, 500 U.S. 478, 499–500 (1991); Stump v. Sparkman, 435 U.S. 349, 357 (1978). In the case of Butz v. Economou, 438 U.S. 478, 511–512 (1978), the Court had extended absolute immunity to administrative officers who perform adjudicatory functions analogous to those performed by judges.

both invoke[24] and be bound by[25] an arbitration agreement to which they were not signatories. Arbitration is thereby extended to a significant number of disputes for which it would otherwise be unavailable. The Court has seen fit to broaden the definition of commerce for purposes of the FAA than it otherwise might have been, thereby expanding its scope of application.[26]

Fifth, in the case of Hall St. Associates LLC v. Mattel, Inc.,[27] the Court was faced with a split among the lower courts on the question whether parties may by agreement expand beyond those enumerated in the FAA the grounds upon which an award made in the U.S. might be vacated. The Court thereby ruled out in principle that possibility under the FAA, thereby ensuring, for example, that awards could not be vacated on grounds of error of fact or error of law.

There remain still less prominent means by which the Court has helped render arbitration at least marginally more effective. Arguably, international arbitration benefits from falling within the scope of federal subject-matter jurisdiction in suits for the recognition or enforcement of New York and Panama Convention awards under FAA Chapter 2.[28] The Court has gone on to recognize federal subject-matter jurisdiction, even in cases falling under FAA Chapter 1, by allowing them to "look through" to the underlying claim advanced in the arbitration, and exercise jurisdiction if that claim itself fell within the scope of federal subject-matter jurisdiction.[29] It is fair to assume that federal judges are more familiar with and knowledgeable about international arbitration than their state court counterparts. Even actions to enforce domestic awards may readily be heard in federal court if the underlying action is one that, absent an arbitration agreement, could have been heard in federal courts. The Court has also ruled that, although FAA Section 9 and 204 identify, as the venue for confirmation or vacatur of an award, the court chosen by the parties for that purpose or, if none, the court in whose district the award was made, in fact these venue provisions are permissive. Relief may be sought in any venue allowable under the general venue statute.[30]

---

24 GE Energy Power Conversion France SAS v. Outokumpu Stainless USA LLC, 140 S. Ct. 1637, 1644 (2020).

25 Andersen LLP v. Carlisle 556 U.S. 624, 631 (2009).

26 The Court has given an expansive application to the term commerce (see Citizen's Bank v. Alafabco, 539 U.S. 52, 56 (2003)), for example, by bring employment contracts within the scope of the FAA (see Circuit City Stores, Inc. v. Adams, 532 U.S. 105 (2001)).

27 552 U.S. 576, 578 (2006).

28 9 U.S.C. ___.

29 Vaden v. Discover Bank, 556 U.S. 49, 59 (2009).

30 Cortez Byrd Chips, Inc. v. Bill Harbert Constr., 529 U.S. 193, 198 (2000).

## 4 How Might Individual Supreme Court Decisions Promote International Arbitration in Some Ways, while Failing to Do So in Others?

The discussion up to now has suggested that the judgments cited are all to be viewed as pro-arbitration due to their enhancing arbitration's capacity to serve the purposes for which it is intended and to do so efficaciously. In so doing, it has not allowed for the very real possibility that a Supreme Court ruling might be pro-arbitration in some respects and not pro-arbitration in others. We have several very important examples.

A first example of this reality arises out of the *Mitsubishi* decision discussed earlier. That decision can safely be characterized as favorable to arbitration insofar as it enables parties to submit antitrust claims to arbitration rather than to court, expanding importantly the scope of arbitrable disputes. However, in order to reach that outcome, the Court felt it necessary to invite a plaintiff disappointed in the result of an antitrust arbitration to come afterwards to a U.S. court, asking that the court deny recognition to the award on the ground that it failed to give effect to U.S. anti-trust l complaining that the tribunal had failed to give effect to U.S. antitrust law. Under the Court's so-called "second look doctrine," a court may inquire into whether the tribunal "took cognizance" of the antitrust laws.

> Having permitted the arbitration to go forward, the national courts of the United States will have the opportunity at the award-enforcement stage to ensure that the legitimate interest in the enforcement of the antitrust laws has been addressed. The Convention reserves to each signatory country the right to refuse enforcement of an award where the "recognition or enforcement of the award would be contrary to the public policy of that country." While the efficacy of the arbitral process requires that substantive review at the award-enforcement stage remain minimal, it would not require intrusive inquiry to ascertain that the tribunal took cognizance of the antitrust claims and actually decided them.[31]

Depending on the standard of review employed in that situation, a court may substantially reexamine the merits of an award, which is contrary to the general understanding in U.S. arbitration law that merits review of an award is off the table.

31 473 U.S. at 638.

A second example of how a Supreme Court decision may serve arbitration's purposes in some respects, while disserving them in others concerns the notion of "delegation." It has been well established in U.S. law that a party denying the existence[32] or validity[33] of an arbitration agreement is entitled to a judicial ruling on that matter. The leading case, First Options of Chicago., Inc. v. Kaplan,[34] the Court insisted that parties may not be required to arbitrate absent their prior consent to do so and have access to a court, either before or after arbitration, to demonstrate that they did not in fact agree to arbitrate. In so doing, the Court reinforced the fundamental notion that the foundation of arbitration is party consent. On the other hand, the Court determined that, in the interest of party autonomy, parties could agree to forego independent judicial determination of their consent to arbitrate, provided they do so "clearly and unmistakably." In that event, it is the tribunal, not the court, that will have primary authority to determine whether a party in fact agreed to arbitrate. In so holding, the Court evidently sought to strike a balance between the principles of party consent and party autonomy, both of which are fundamental tenets of arbitration. The Court reinforced its commitment to delegation by ruling in the case of Henry Schein, Inc. v. Archer & White Sales, Inc.[35] that, once a delegation is made, a court must respect it even if it considers the challenge to enforceability of an arbitration agreement to be "wholly groundless." And in Rent-A-Center, West, Inc. v. Jackson,[36] the Court assumed that the parties had in fact made a delegation when their agreement to arbitrate stated that "[t]he Arbitrator, and not any federal, state, or local court or agency, shall have exclusive authority to resolve any dispute relating to the interpretation, applicability, enforceability or formation of this Agreement including, but not limited to any claim that all or any part of this Agreement is void or voidable."

In the cases that followed, lower federal courts have held that parties signify their clear and unmistakable assent to a delegation merely by incorporating by reference into their arbitration agreement a set of procedural rules containing a Competence-Competence clause. But since Competence-Competence clauses are ubiquitous, the practical effect of treating such clauses as clear and unmistakable evidence of a delegation is that parties will almost invariably be found to have foregone their fundamental right to an independent judicial determination of whether they did in fact consent to arbitration of their

32 Granite Rock Co. v. Int'l Bhd. Of Teamsters, 561 U.S. 287, 295–297 (2010).

33 First Options of Chicago., Inc. v. Kaplan, 514 U.S. 938, 944 (1995).

34 *Id.* at 944.

35 586 U.S. 63 (2019).

36 561 U.S. 63 (2010).

dispute. Viewed in this light, it is now much less clear than it was when *First Options* was decided that it was in fact a pro-arbitration ruling by the Court.

A third example concerns the question whether parties to a commercial or investment arbitration may invoke the provision of U.S. law (28 USC § 1782), which allows interested parties to request the aid of a U.S. federal court in obtaining evidence for use in a foreign or international court or tribunal. In the consolidated cases of ZF Automotive U.S., Inc. v. Luxshare, Ltd. and AlixPartners, LLP v. Fund for Protection of Investors' Rights in Foreign States,[37] counsel on both sides argued that the interests of arbitration would best be served by the position on the issue that they took. Proponents of the availability of Section 1782 in arbitral proceedings argued that arbitration, as a dispute resolution mechanism, would benefit from the parties and the tribunal having access to as much relevant evidence as possible, while opponents argued that allowing parties in arbitration to resort to a U.S. court for discovery would interfere with the freedom of the tribunal to ensure that arbitrations proceed in the fairest and most efficient way possible, unaffected by interventions by national courts. The Court ultimately found Section 1782 to be unavailable in arbitration, though on a different ground altogether, namely that Section 1782 was designed strictly to assist proceedings of bodies imbued with governmental authority, and neither commercial nor investment tribunals fit that description.

A fourth example relates to the doctrine of manifest disregard of the law as a ground for annulment of an award. The FAA purports to set out the exclusive bases for annulment of an award made in the U.S. The Supreme Court is nevertheless understood to have recognized an additional non-statutory ground for annulment, namely manifest disregard of the law, which the Court has unfortunately never defined.[38] In the view of most commentators, recognition of manifest disregard for these purposes as an annulment ground is inimical to arbitration, not only because it goes above and beyond the grounds ostensibly set out exclusively in the FAA, but also because it improperly allows courts to enter into merits issue in an annulment proceeding. However, one may argue that, on the contrary, it is in arbitration's best interests for arbitral awards that manifestly disregard the applicable law should be annulled.

A fifth and perhaps best example of disagreement over whether a Supreme Court ruling is or is not favorable to arbitration arises in the highly controversial context of class arbitration. Not only has the compatibility of class

---

37 596 U.S. ___ (2022).

38 Wilko v. Swan, 346 U.S. 427 (1953).

arbitration with the FAA and the federal policy in favor of arbitration sharply divided the Court, but both sides of the Court insist that their position, and their position alone, is pro-arbitration. A majority of the Court has held that arbitration conducted on a class basis is not the kind of arbitration contemplated by the FAA, so much so that an arbitration agreement should not be interpreted as permitting class arbitration unless the agreement positively so states.[39] It has also upheld the enforceability of class arbitration waivers on the ground that respect for the arbitration agreements requires that they be enforced as written, thus disallowing state courts or legislatures to declare such waivers unconscionable and for that reason unenforceable.[40] The majority considers that, in both respects, it is being fundamentally faithful to the principles that undergird arbitration in the U.S. The minority does not share the view that class arbitration is inimical to the purposes of arbitration or that arbitration agreements should be interpreted with so strong a bias against class arbitration. It also believes that, since the FAA expressly subjects arbitration agreements to principles of state contract law, a state legislature or court should be permitted to declare waivers of class arbitration unenforceable as unconscionable under state law, just as they have declared waivers of class action litigation to be unenforceable, inasmuch as class adjudication may be prohibitively expensive and the only way in which individuals can in practice pursue low-value claims. The majority has expressly rejected that argument.[41]

## 5 Conclusion

There can be no doubt that the U.S. Supreme Court has lent powerful and steadfast support to international arbitration over the years. It has done so in myriad ways. On some occasions it has championed international arbitration by anchoring its most basic foundations in U.S. law. On others, it has addressed international arbitration more discretely and operationally, seeking simply to enhance its efficacy in practice. The Restatement has captured as many of the Court's such contributions as it possibly could. Needless to

39 Lamps Plus, Inc. v. Varela, 139 S. Ct. 1407, 1417–1418 (2019): Oxford Health Plans LLC v. Sutter, 569 U.S. 564, 571–573 (2013); Stolt-Nielsen S.A. v. AnimalFeeds Int'l Corp., 559 U.S. 662, 673–675 (2010). These decisions appear to abandon the position previously taken by the Court in Green-Tree Financial Corp. v. Randolph, 531 U.S. 79 (2000).

40 AT&T Mobility LLC v. Concepcion, 563 U.S. 333, 343 (2011); Epic Sys. Corp. v. Lewis, 138 S. Ct. 1612, 1626–1629 (2018).

41 Am. Express Co. v. Italian Colors Rest., 570 U.S. 228, 243 (2013).

say, for the Restatement, the decisions of the Court are givens around which revolve rulings of lower federal courts and state courts – rulings from which the Restatement can more legitimately and comfortably distance itself.

Still, there are occasions, on which the Supreme Court, while promoting arbitration in some ways, is simply unable to promote it in others. This is not a reflection on the Supreme Court. Rather it is a manifestation of arbitration's multivalence, and more particularly of the multiplicity of ways in which a policy's or practice's pro-arbitration character may be gauged.[42] Those ways are so many and diverse that positions cannot be viewed as arbitration-friendly in terms of them all at the same time. This chapter would further be incomplete and misleading if it failed to acknowledge that situations, however rare, may arise in which the Court cannot allow maximization of international arbitration's efficacy to eclipse or take precedence over other values. A prime example are those decisions in which the Court has found that, where Congress has expressly afforded individuals the right to bring suit in federal court to protect certain fundamental constitutional or statutory rights, those proceedings are not subject to either *res judicata* or collateral estoppel on the basis of a prior arbitral award. Only in the rarest of circumstances would the Court conclude that arbitration cannot provide an adequate substitute for proceedings in a judicial forum.[43]

The drafters of the Restatement were struck by the sheer number of international arbitration issues to which the Court has agreed to speak. International arbitration cases figure disproportionately in the Supreme Court's docket as compared to the docket of virtually any other U.S. court, including the federal courts sitting in New York and the District of Columbia. So far international arbitration does not appear to have raised doubts, concerns or misgivings among the Justices of the Supreme Court. This is due in no small measure to the Court's own steady contributions to the enterprise.

---

42 *See* Bermann, *supra* note 1.

43 McDonald v. City of West Branch, 466 U.S. 284 (1984); Barrentine v. Arkansas-Best Freight System, Inc., 450 U.S. 728 (1981); Alexander v. Gardner-Denver Co., 415 U.S. 36 (1974).

CHAPTER 2

# The Evolution of Arbitration in Light of Supreme Court Decisions

*Peter J. Messitte†, Carlos Mário da Silva Velloso, Erico Bomfim de Carvalho and João Carlos Banhos Velloso*

## 1 Introduction

Before the emergence of arbitral institutions[1] and the enactment of the Federal Arbitration Act (FAA) in 1925, arbitration had already been widely used in the United States for almost three centuries.[2] Colonies such as Maryland utilized arbitration as a regular method of dispute resolution well before contemporary arbitration laws existed.[3] By 1750, the importance of arbitration was already acknowledged to such an extent that certain jurisdictions enacted their own statutes.[4] At the time, however, U.S. courts would only enforce final arbitration awards; they refused to compel arbitration by enforcing contractual agreements to arbitrate future disputes. The FAA changed that landscape by providing that arbitration agreements should be enforced.[5] Since then, the U.S. Supreme Court's stance has been one of full deference to the terms of arbitration agreements.[6] This article briefly explores the evolution of arbitration in the United States through an analysis of the Supreme Court's decisions, both

1 *See* MIKAËL SCHINAZI, THE THREE AGES OF INTERNATIONAL COMMERCIAL ARBITRATION 41 (2021) (explaining that from 1780s to the 1920s, the extensive use of arbitration around the world was not based on structured rules of arbitral institutions, which only came into existence after the 1920s).

2 Bruce L. Benson, *An Exploration of the Impact of Modern Arbitration Statutes on the Development of Arbitration in the United States*, 11 J. L. ECON. & ORG. 479, 481 (1995).

3 James Oldham & Su Jin Kim, *Arbitration in America: The Early History*, 31 L. & HIST. REV. 241 (2013) (indicating that arbitration had been a part of the United States legal culture since the early 1600s).

4 Paul L. Sayre, *Development of Commercial Arbitration Law*, 37 YALE L.J. 595, 612 (1928).

5 9 U.S.C. § 2.

6 *See* Peter J. Messitte, Arbitration in the U.S. 3 (Aug. 24, 2021) (unpublished manuscript) (on file with author). (stating that "*parties make their agreement and the courts hold that most live by them. Pacta sunt servanda, as the well-established principle provides: 'Agreements must be kept*'") (Emphasis added).

 | DOI:10.1163/9789004715820_003

before and after the enactment of the FAA. A compelling story emerges of how arbitration has matured over the last two centuries to become a ubiquitous method for the resolution of disputes.

## 2 Pre-FAA Supreme Court Case Law

### 2.1 *Early Years*

Given the lack of clarity between arbitration proceedings and other dispute resolution methods such as mediation and conciliation, almost a century before the enactment of the FAA, the Supreme Court in one of its first decisions, was called upon to address what constituted an arbitral award[7] and also to establish more sophisticated rules for arbitration proceedings, such as applying the common law doctrine of "functus officio" to arbitration.[8] These early decisions laid the foundation for the current legal framework governing arbitration and continue to influence practice today.

In this period, an arbitration agreement had "no binding effect,"[9] as U.S. Courts generally "would not specifically enforce arbitration agreements"[10] to compel arbitration,[11] only the resulting award itself.[12] Given the courts' refusal to order specific performance of agreements to arbitrate, the party seeking to submit the dispute to an arbitrator could only resort to an action seeking to

---

7 *See* Holker v. Parker, 11 U.S. (7 Cranch) 436, 452, 3 L. Ed. 396, 402 (1813) (establishing that a settlement agreement fashioned as an arbitral award "[was] not the judgment of the arbitrators in the cause, but a compromise[] between the attorneys, taking the form of an award").

8 Black's Law Dictionary defines "functus officio" (of an officer or official body) "without further authority or legal competence because the duties and functions of the original commission have been fully accomplished." *Functus Officio*, BLACK'S LAW DICTIONARY (11th ed. 2019); *see also* Bayne v. Morris, 68 U.S. (1 Wall) 97, 99, 17 L. Ed. 495, 496 (1863) ("Arbitrators exhaust their power when they make a final determination on the matters submitted to them. They have no power after having made an award to alter it; the authority conferred on them is then at an end").

9 M. M. B., Editorial, *Arbitration under the Modern Statutes*, 23 MICH. L. REV. 881, 883 (1925).

10 Roger J. Perlstadt, *Article III Judicial Power and the Federal Arbitration Act*, 62 AM. U. L. REV. 201, 210 (2012).

11 *See* Red Cross Line v. Atlantic Fruit Co., 264 U.S. 109, 120, 44 S. Ct. 274, 276, 68 L. Ed. 582, 585 (1924) ("The federal courts—like those of the States and of England—have, both in equity and at law, denied, in large measure, the aid of their processes to those seeking to enforce executory agreements to arbitrate disputes").

12 M. M. B., *supra* note 9, at 883.

recover damagesfor the contractual breach by the recalcitrant party,[13] a remedy that was often inadequate.[14]

Even so, courts did enforce limited executory arbitration agreements restricted to the calculation of damages or losses while leaving the general question of liability for the courts to decide.[15] Additionally, while litigation was pending, courts were disposed to enforce executory arbitration agreements pursuant to a "rule of court"[16] if and when parties had expressed their clear intention to move the dispute to arbitration.[17] In the latter case, arbitrators were required to submit the resulting award to the court where the action was

13 Hamilton v. Home Insurance, 137 U.S. 370, 385, 11 S. Ct. 133, 138, 34 L. Ed. 708, 713 (1890).

14 Sidney P. Simpson, *Specific Enforcement of Arbitration Contracts*, 83 U. PA. L. REV. 160 (1934–1935) (highlighting the inadequacy of the available "legal remedy for the breach of an arbitration contract," since the plaintiff could "recover only nominal damages at law").

15 *See* Hamilton v. Liverpool, London & Globe Ins. Co., 136 U.S. 242, 255, 10 S. Ct. 945, 949, 34 L. Ed. 419, 423 (1890) ("Such a stipulation [limited executory arbitration agreement], not ousting the jurisdiction of the courts, but leaving the general question of liability to be judicially determined, and simply providing a reasonable method of estimating and ascertaining the amount of the loss, is unquestionably valid").

16 This "rule of court" was a widespread practice in colonial courts. *See* Oldham & Kim, *supra* note 3, at 246 ("The seventeenth century custom took the form of what was called a 'reference': the consensual removal of pending litigation from the court docket and the referral of the dispute to arbitration. This practice emerged in both England and the American colonies in the mid-1600s").

17 *See* Thornton v. Carson, 11 U.S. (7 Cranch) 596, 599, 3 L. Ed. 451, 451 (1813) (refusing to set aside awards deemed to be "uncertain, not final, unreasonable, conditional, and void," that originated from two actions that "were referred by consent under a rule of Court to arbitrators"); Alexandria Canal Co. v. Swann, 46 U.S. (5 How.) 83, 88, 12 L.Ed. 60, 62 (1847) (holding that "a trial by arbitrators, appointed by the court with the consent of both parties, is one of the modes of prosecuting a suit to judgment as well established and as fully warranted by law as a trial by jury"); Heckers v. Fowler, 69 U.S. (2 Wall) 123, 131, 17 L.Ed. 759, 761 (1865) (recognizing that the practice of referring pending actions under a rule of court, by consent of parties, was well known at common law); Newcomb v. Wood, 97 U.S. (7 Otto) 581, 583, 24 L.Ed. 1085, 1086 (1878) ("The power of a court of justice, with the consent of the parties, to appoint arbitrators and refer a case pending before it, is incident to all judicial administration, where the right exists to ascertain the facts as well as to pronounce the law"); Red Cross Line v. Atlantic Fruit Co., 264 U.S. 109, 120–21, 44 S.Ct. 274, 275–76, 68 L.Ed. 582, 585 (1924) (holding that an executory arbitration agreement may be enforced by a rule of court); Kimberly v. Arms, 129 U.S. 512, 9 S. Ct. 355, 32 L. Ed. 764 (1889) (establishing that an award resulting from a dispute referred to a master under a rule of court cannot be set aside or disregarded at the mere discretion of the reviewing court); Wellness Int'l Network, Ltd. v. Sharif, 575 U.S. 665, 674, 135 S. Ct. 1932, 1942, 191 L. Ed. 2d 911, 921 (2015) (stating that during the early years of the Republic, federal courts, with the consent of the litigants, regularly referred adjudication of entire disputes to non-Article III referees, masters, or arbitrators).

pending. The reviewing court would then decide whether to accept, reject, or recommit the award for further review.[18]

But in general U.S. courts not only deemed arbitration agreements unenforceable; they also held that arbitration submissions could be revoked at any time before an award was made, except when the reference was pursuant to a rule of court.[19] Some states, however, enacted statutes imposing limitations on the possibility of parties revoking submissions to arbitration,[20] but none of them established that arbitration agreements were irrevocable.[21]

### 2.2 *Pro-arbitration Sentiments*

Despite this reticence to enforce executory arbitration agreements, Supreme Court decisions before the enactment of the FAA were highly deferential towards arbitral awards.

*Burchell v. Marsh*,[22] decided in 1854, symbolized a pivotal moment in the Supreme Court's attitude toward arbitration. For the first time, the Supreme Court recognized that resolving disputes through arbitration should "receive every encouragement from courts" and that the standard of court review of an award should be very narrow.[23] The Court also held that arbitrators are "judges chosen by the parties" and that an impartial decision, within the scope of the submission and upon a fair hearing, should not be set aside "for error, either in law or fact," even if the reviewing court believes it could have reached a different conclusion.[24] *Burchell* highlighted the Supreme Court's commitment to curtailing any potential abuse of judicial review. The decision also articulated a narrow scope of review for arbitration awards and laid important groundwork for the delicate balance between judicial intervention and arbitration autonomy.

---

18 Interestingly, the Supreme Court in *Heckers v. Fowler* upheld the validity of a different procedure to accommodate the parties' true intentions. Given that the parties had agreed that the "report of the referee should have the same force and effect as a judgment of the court," judgment was automatically entered upon the filing of the award with the clerk of court, without further review by an Article III judge.

19 *See* Pizzini v. Hutchins, 127 N.Y.S. 1043, 70 Misc. 94 (Sup. Ct. 1910).

20 *Id.* at 1044, 70 Misc. at 95 (noting that a Virginia statute provided that an arbitration submission was not revocable except with leave of court and that a New York statute established that the submission was not revocable after final submission to the arbitrators).

21 Simpson, *supra* note 14, at 165 (explaining that all but two states enacted arbitration statutes prior to 1920, but that none established that arbitration agreements were binding).

22 Burchell v. Marsh, 58 U.S. (17 How.) 344, 15 L. Ed. 96 (1855).

23 *Id.* at 349, 15 L. Ed. at 99.

24 *Id.* at 349, 15 L. Ed. at 99.

In *Kimberly v. Arms*,[25] the Supreme Court addressed the authority and weight of findings made by a special master in chancery. The Court distinguished between a master's findings pursuant to a general "rule of court" and a master's findings when the parties have consented to entrust him with the task of hearing and deciding all the issues, both of fact and of law.[26] The Court held that, while courts cannot abdicate their duty to issue a judgment if parties have selected and mutually agreed upon a special master, "though not strictly a submission of the controversy to arbitration," the findings of that tribunal should be treated with as much weight as the court's own findings.[27] Such findings by the special master were accordingly not subject to being set aside except for "manifest error in the consideration given to the evidence, or in the application of the law."[28,29]

Other pro-arbitration decisions followed. For example, the Supreme Court held that an award should be considered binding even if the submission agreement did not expressly mandate future compliance with the arbitrator's decision.[30] In another case, the Court upheld the validity of an award by a divided panel of arbitrators despite the absence of a provision in the agreement authorizing a non-unanimous decision.[31] In both cases, the Court gave a broad and permissive interpretation of the arbitration agreements with the clear intention of upholding the binding nature of the resulting arbitration awards—an unequivocal demonstration of its support for arbitration as a method of dispute resolution.[32]

---

25 Kimberly v. Arms, 129 U.S. 512, 524, 9 S. Ct. 355, 359, 32 L. Ed. 764, 768 (1889).

26 *Id.*, 9 S. Ct. at 359, 32 L. Ed. at 768.

27 *Id.*, 9 S. Ct. at 359, 32 L. Ed. at 768.

28 *Id.*, 9 S. Ct. at 359, 32 L. Ed. at 768.

29 The Supreme Court adopted that same rationale in *Crawford v. Neal*, 144 U.S. 585, 596, 12 S. Ct. 759, 762, 36 L. Ed. 552, 557 (1892), *Furrer v. Ferris*, 145 U.S. 132, 134, 12 S. Ct. 821, 821, 36 L. Ed. 649, 651 (1892), and *Davis v. Schwartz*, 155 U.S. 631, 39 L. Ed. 289, 15 S. Ct. 237, at 637 (1895).

30 Smith v. Morse, 76 U.S. (9 Wall.) 76, 82, 19 L.Ed. 597, 599 (1869) ("The law implies an agreement to abide the result of an arbitration from the fact of submission").

31 Hobson v. Heirs of M'Arthur, 41 U.S. (16 Pet.) 182, 188, 10 L. Ed. 930, 932 (1842) (confirming the validity of the majority award while interpreting the arbitration agreement provision for the appointment by the parties of two arbitrators who were to name a third if they could not reach an agreement); *see also* Colombia v. Cauca Co., 190 U.S. 524, 528, 23 S. Ct. 704, 706, 47 L. Ed. 1159 (1903) (upholding as "sufficient and effective" a majority award resulting from the resignation of one of the arbitrators).

32 *But see* Chas. Wolff Packing Co. v. Court of Indus. Rels., 262 U.S. 522, 43 S. Ct. 630, 67 L. Ed. 1103 (1923); Dorchy v. Kansas, 264 U.S. 286, 44 S. Ct. 323, 68 L. Ed. 686 (1924); Chas. Wolff Packing Co. v. Court of Indus. Rels., 267 U.S. 552, 45 S. Ct. 441, 69 L. Ed. 785 (1925) (a trilogy

### 2.3 *Grounds for Setting Aside Arbitral Awards*

More than two hundred years ago, the Supreme Court embarked upon the task of establishing the grounds for judicial review of arbitral awards.

Its early decisions aimed to preserve party autonomy by ensuring that an arbitrator had the authority to decide only those matters specifically included in the arbitration agreement. In *Carnochan & Mitchel v. Christie*,[33] the Supreme Court decided that an arbitral award must be certain, final, and conclusive, addressing all matters within the submission. The Court later established that an award would only be set aside on such a ground (*i.e.*, failure to decide all the matters in the arbitration agreement) if the parties could "distinctly show" that they had notified the arbitrators of all the matters not addressed in the final award.[34] Beyond determining that arbitrators could not refrain from dealing with all the issues the parties had agreed to arbitrate, the Supreme Court ruled in *York & Cumberland Railroad v. Myers*[35] that arbitrators could not exceed their mandate and rule on issues not explicitly stipulated in the arbitration agreement. In that case, the final award contained a single ruling encompassing matters not included in the arbitration agreement; in consequence, the Supreme Court set the award aside, where it was impossible to distinguish the issues properly submitted from those that were not.[36] Still, the Court recognized in multiple decisions the possibility of a partial vacatur,[37] *i.e.*, the partial setting aside of the award, where the arbitrator exceeded the scope of the arbitration agreement if—and only if—the void part was separable from the remainder of the award.[38]

---

of cases holding unconstitutional a Kansas statute imposing "compulsory arbitration" of disputes between employers and employees in designated industries).

33 Carnochan & Mitchel v. Christie, 24 U.S. (11 Wheat.) 446, 6 L. Ed. 516 (1826).

34 Karthaus v. Yllas y Ferrer, 26 U.S. (1 Pet.) 222, 227, 7 L. Ed. 121, 121 (1828).

35 York & Cumberland R.R. Co. v. Myers, 59 U.S. (18 How.) 246, 15 L. Ed. 380 (1856).

36 *Id.* at 252, 15 L. Ed. at 383 ("If an arbitrator embraces in his award matter not submitted, and includes the result in a single conclusion, so as to render it impossible to separate the matters referred from those which have not been, the award is bad").

37 Currently, § 4.33(d) of the Restatement (Third) of the U.S. Law of International Commercial Arbitration admits partial vacatur relief, while Article V(1)(c) of the New York Convention also contemplates the partial recognition and enforcement of a foreign award.

38 *See* Lyle v. Rodgers, 18 U.S. (5 Wheat.) 394, 409, 5 L. Ed. 117, 121 (1820) ("That an award may be void in part, and good for the residue, will be readily admitted; but if that part which is void be so connected with the rest as to affect the justice of the case between the parties, the whole is void"); De Groot v. United States, 72 U.S. (5 Wall.) 419, 18 L. Ed. 700, 703 (1867) ("If the part which is in excess can be clearly separated from the remainder which is within the submission, the latter may stand"); McCormick v. Gray, 54 U.S. (13 How.) 26, 39, 14 L.Ed. 36, 41 (1851) ("There are cases in which, after rejecting part of an award, the residue is sufficiently final, certain, and in conformity with the submission, to stand; but it is'

After this first group of decisions dealing with the scope of the arbitrator's authority, the Supreme Court proceeded to establish other grounds for vacatur. In *Lutz v. Linthicum*,[39] the Court held that the integrity of arbitration lies in its adherence to due process and procedural fairness, such that failure to give proper notice to one of the parties about the hearing of the case would also be a ground for setting an award aside.[40] In *United States v. Farragut*,[41] the Court decided that an award could be set aside "for fraud, and for all the reasons on which awards are set aside in courts of law or chancery,"[42] and that a "manifest mistake of law" was also an independent ground for vacatur.[43] Interestingly, the *Farragut* decision was cited almost eighty years later in *Wilko v. Swan*[44] to support the Court's conclusions regarding the availability of a "manifest disregard" review.[45]

---

indispensable that the part thus allowed to stand should appear to be in no way affected by the departure from the submission").

39 Lutz v. Linthicum, 33 U.S. (8 Pet.) 165, 178–79, 8 L.Ed. 904, 909 (1834) ("Without question, due notice should be given to the parties of the time and place of hearing the cause; and, if the award was made without such, notice, it ought, upon the plainest principles of justice, to be set aside").

40 *See also* Omaha v. Omaha Water Co., 218 U.S. 180, 194, 30 S. Ct. 615, 616, 54 L. Ed. 991, 997 (1910) ("An arbitration implies a difference, a dispute, and involves ordinarily a hearing and all thereby implied. The right to notice of hearings, to produce evidence and cross-examine that produced is implied when the matter to be decided is one of dispute and difference").

41 United States v. Farragut, 89 U.S. (22 Wall.) 406, 22 L. Ed. 879 (1874).

42 *Id.* at 420, 22 L. Ed. at 883.

43 *Id.* at 420, 22 L. Ed. at 883. The ruling in *Farragut* apparently contradicted the Supreme Court's previous *Burchell* decision forbidding the set aside of awards "for error, either in law or fact." However, in *Burchell* the Supreme Court also remarked, citing the 1791 decision of Lord Thurlow in *Knox v. Symmonds*, that vacatur was available if the arbitration award contained "something more than an error of judgment, such as ... gross mistake, either apparent on the face of the award, or to be made out by evidence." Burchell v. Marsh, 58 U.S. (17 How.) 344, 350, 15 L. Ed. 96, 99(1854).

44 Wilko v. Swan, 346 U.S. 427, 74 S. Ct. 182, 98 L. Ed. 2d 168 (1953).

45 The "manifest disregard of law" standard is not listed in the Federal Arbitration Act, enacted in 1925, as one of the grounds for vacatur of an arbitral award. However, the *Wilko* Court established that "manifest disregard of law" should be understood as a non-statutory vacatur ground, a much controversial ruling that has received ambiguous treatment in later Supreme Court decisions. *See* Hall St. Assocs., LLC v. Mattel, Inc., 552 U.S. 576, 128 S. Ct. 1396, 170 L. Ed. 2d 254 (2008) (holding that the standards set forth in the FAA are exclusive and cannot be expanded by private arrangements); Stolt-Nielsen S. A. v. AnimalFeeds Int'l Corp., 559 U.S. 662, 130 S. Ct. 1758, 176 L. Ed. 2d 605 (2010) (refusing to decide whether the "manifest disregard" standard set forth in *Wilko* survived the decision in *Hall Street* as an independent ground for review).

Taken together, these decisions represent the Supreme Court's first attempts to safeguard the binding nature of an award,[46] establishing vacatur grounds that were later incorporated into the FAA.[47]

## 3 Post-FAA Supreme Court Decisions

### 3.1 *The Federal Arbitration Act*

While earlier arbitration statutes only covered agreements for submission of existing controversies,[48] the New York Arbitration Act of 1920 was the first to provide that an agreement to arbitrate an existing or future dispute should be valid, irrevocable, and enforceable by courts.[49]

Five years later, after persistent advocacy by the American Bar Association and the American Arbitration Association,[50] the enactment of the Federal Arbitration Act (FAA) represented a turning point in the judicial treatment of arbitration within the United States,[51] declaring written arbitration agreements to be "valid, irrevocable, and enforceable,"[52] and providing an authoritative list of grounds upon which an arbitration award could be "vacated, modified, or corrected."[53]

Despite early—and isolated—criticism,[54] the FAA undoubtedly altered the arbitration landscape in the United States. Its enactment was a legislative

46 Citigroup Global Mkts. Inc. v. Bacon, 562 F.3d 349, 351 (5th Cir. 2009) (Noting that "even before the enactment of the United States Arbitration Act in 1925, courts of equity would set aside an arbitration award only in narrowly defined circumstances").

47 Except for the "manifest mistake of law" standard, these narrow grounds came to be included years later in the FAA.

48 Wesley A. Sturges and Richard E. Reckson, *Common-Law and Statutory Arbitration: Problems Arising from Their Coexistence*, 46 MINN. L. REV. 819, 822 (1961).

49 Lyden Macassey, *International Commercial Arbitration—Its Origins, Development and Importance*, 24 A.B.A. J. 518, 522 (1938); *see also* Preston D. Wigner, *The United States Supreme Court's Expansive Approach to the Federal Arbitration Act: A Look at the Past, Present, and Future of Section 2*, 29 U. RICH. L. REV. 1499, 1503 (1995) (stating that the 1924 Supreme Court decision in *Red Cross Line v. Atlantic Fruit Co.* "opened the door for Congress" to enact the FAA one year later).

50 Macassey, *supra* note 48, at 522.

51 Wilko v. Swan, 346 U.S. 427, 431, 74 S. Ct. 182, 185, 98 L. Ed. 2d 168, 173 (1953) (expressing that the FAA established by statute "the desirability of arbitration as an alternative to the complications of litigation").

52 9 U.S.C. § 2.

53 9 U.S.C. §§ 9–11.

54 Philip G. Phillips, *The Paradox in Arbitration Law: Compulsion as Applied to a Voluntary Proceeding*, 46 Harvard L. Rev. 1258, 1267 (1933) ("The commencement of an arbitration

response to arbitration's "increasing popularity"[55] and "centuries of judicial hostility to arbitration agreements."[56]

### 3.2 *Arbitration as a Matter of Consent*

The Supreme Court has consistently articulated, since the enactment of the FAA, that arbitration is fundamentally a matter of contract and that arbitrators derive their authority solely from the parties' mutual agreement.[57] As with virtually any other form of contract, parties can structure their arbitration

proceeding by court compulsion means a vanishing of its voluntary nature, and a spirit of litigation prevails. Enforced arbitration is not arbitration").

55 M. M. B., *supra* note 9, at 886 ("Arbitration as a substitute for litigation is rapidly increasing in popularity, due in large measure to its proven efficiency in actual operation").

56 Scherk v. Alberto-Culver Co., 417 U.S. 506, 510, 94 S. Ct. 2449, 2452, 41 L. Ed. 2d 270, 276 (1974); *see* Gilmer v. Interstate/Johnson Lane Corp., 500 U.S. 20, 24, 111 S. Ct. 1647, 1651, 114 L. Ed. 2d 26, 36 (1991) (stating that the FAA purpose was to "reverse the longstanding judicial hostility to arbitration agreements that had existed at English common law and had been adopted by American courts, and to place arbitration agreements upon the same footing as other contracts"); *see also* Epic Sys. Corp. v. Lewis, 584 U.S. ___, 138 S. Ct. 1612, 1621, 200 L. Ed. 2d 889, 898 (2018) (holding that the FAA was enacted "in response to a perception that courts were unduly hostile to arbitration").

57 *See* United Steelworkers v. Warrior & Gulf Navigation Co., 363 U.S. 574, 582, 80 S. Ct. 1347, 1353, 4 L. Ed. 2d 1409, 1417 (1960) ("[A]rbitration is a matter of contract and a party cannot be required to submit to arbitration any dispute which he has not agreed so to submit"); Gateway Coal Co. v. United Mine Workers, 414 U.S. 368, 374, 94 S. Ct. 629, 635, 38 L. Ed. 2d 583, 590 (1974) ("The law compels a party to submit his grievance to arbitration only if he has contracted to do so"); Nolde Bros., Inc. v. Local No. 358, Bakery & Confectionery Workers Union, 430 U.S. 243, 250, 97 S. Ct. 1067, 1071, 51 L. Ed. 2d 300, 308 (1977) ("[T]he arbitration duty is a creature of the collective-bargaining agreement and ... a party cannot be compelled to arbitrate any matter in the absence of a contractual obligation to do so"); First Options of Chicago, Inc. v. Kaplan, 514 U.S. 938, 943, 115 S. Ct. 1920, 1924, 131 L. Ed. 2d 985, 992 (1995) ("[A]rbitration is simply a matter of contract between the parties; it is a way to resolve those disputes—but only those disputes—that the parties have agreed to submit to arbitration"); Buckeye Check Cashing, Inc. v. Cardegna, 546 U.S. 440, 443, 126 S. Ct. 1204, 1207, 163 L. Ed. 2d 1038, 1042 (2006) ("Section 2 [of the FAA] embodies the national policy favoring arbitration and places arbitration agreements on equal footing with all other contracts"); Rent-A-Center, West, Inc. v. Jackson, 561 U.S. 63, 67, 130 S. Ct. 2772, 2776, 177 L. Ed. 2d 403, 410 (2010) ("The FAA reflects the fundamental principle that arbitration is a matter of contract"); AT&T Mobility LLC v. Concepcion, 563 U.S. 333, 351, 131 S. Ct. 1740, 1752, 179 L. Ed. 2d 742, 758 (2011) ("Arbitration is a matter of contract, and the FAA requires courts to honor parties' expectations"); Am. Express Co. v. Italian Colors Rest., 570 U.S. 228, 233, 133 S. Ct. 2304, 2309, 186 L. Ed. 2d 417, 424 (2013) (Describing "the overarching principle that arbitration is a matter of contract").

agreements as they see fit,[58] which courts must "rigorously enforce" according to their terms,[59] unless the FAA's mandate has been "overridden by a contrary [C]ongressional command."[60]

In interpreting the FAA, the Supreme Court has established that arbitration is a matter of consent, not coercion, meaning that the parties' intentions are the ultimate governing factor in determining the scope of an arbitration agreement.[61] Accordingly, no one can be compelled to submit to arbitration a dispute—or matter—that they have not explicitly agreed to. As the Supreme Court recently reaffirmed: "consent is essential under the FAA because arbitrators wield only the authority they are given."[62]

The Supreme Court has long recognized and enforced a "liberal federal policy favoring arbitration agreements."[63] The FAA's policy favoring arbitration must be interpreted to ensure the enforcement of private arbitration agreements according to their terms[64] and the aspirations of the contracting parties,[65]

---

58 Volt Info. Scis, Inc. v. Bd. of Trs., 489 U.S. 468, 479, 109 S. Ct. 1248, 1256, 103 L. Ed. 2d 488, 500 (1989) ("Arbitration under the Act is a matter of consent, not coercion, and parties are generally free to structure their arbitration agreements as they see fit").

59 Dean Witter Reynolds Inc. v. Byrd, 470 U.S. 213, 221, 105 S. Ct. 1238, 1242, 84 L. Ed. 2d 158, 165 (1985) ("The preeminent concern of Congress in passing the [Federal Arbitration] Act was to enforce private agreements into which parties had entered, and that concern requires that we rigorously enforce agreements to arbitrate").

60 Shearson/American Express Inc. v. McMahon, 482 U.S. 220, 226–27, 107 S. Ct. 2332, 2337, 96 L. Ed. 2d 185, 194 (1987).

61 *See* Mitsubishi Motors Corp. v. Soler Chrysler-Plymouth, Inc., 473 U.S. 614, 626, 105 S. Ct. 3346, 3354, 87 L. Ed. 2d 444, 455 (1985) ("[A]s with any other contract, the parties' intentions control"); Mastrobuono v. Shearson Lehman Hutton, Inc., 514 U.S. 52, 57, 115 S. Ct. 1212, 1216, 131 L. Ed. 2d 76, 84 (1995) ("[T]he FAA's proarbitration policy does not operate without regard to the wishes of the contracting parties"); Stolt-Nielsen S. A. v. AnimalFeeds Int'l Corp., 559 U.S. 662, 684, 130 S. Ct. 1758, 1775, 176 L. Ed. 2d 605, 624 (2010) (highlighting the "foundational FAA principle that arbitration is a matter of consent").

62 Lamps Plus, Inc. v. Varela, 587 U.S. __, 139 S. Ct. 1407, 1416, 203 L. Ed. 2d 636, 646 (2019).

63 Moses H. Cone Mem'l Hosp. v. Mercury Constr. Corp., 460 U.S. 1, 24, 103 S. Ct. 927, 941, 74 L. Ed. 2d 765, 785 (1983) ("Section 2 is a congressional declaration of a liberal federal policy favoring arbitration agreements, notwithstanding any state substantive or procedural policies to the contrary"); *see also* Southland Corp. v. Keating, 465 U.S. 1, 10, 104 S. Ct. 852, 858, 79 L. Ed. 2d 1, 12 (1984) (stating that the FAA established a "national policy favoring arbitration and withdrew the power of the states to require a judicial forum for the resolution of claims which the contracting parties agreed to resolve by arbitration").

64 *See* Prima Paint Corp. v. Flood & Conklin Mfg. Co., 388 U.S. 395, 407 n. 12, 87 S. Ct. 1801, 1086 n.12, 18 L. Ed. 2d 1270, 1277 n.12 (1967) ("[T]he purpose of Congress in 1925 was to make arbitration agreements as enforceable as other contracts, but not more so").

65 Volt Info. Scis., Inc. v. Bd. of Trs., 489 U.S. 468, 476, 109 S. Ct. 1248, 1254, 103 L. Ed. 2d 488, 498 (1989) ("There is no federal policy favoring arbitration under a certain set of procedural

and any ambiguities or doubts "must be resolved in favor of arbitration."[66]

Since the enactment of the FAA, the Supreme Court has issued many key rulings ranging from (i) the need for arbitrators to disclose any dealings that might signal bias;[67] (ii) the exhaustive nature of the statutory grounds for vacating or modifying an arbitration award under the FAA;[68] (iii) the ability of non-signatories to compel arbitration under the domestic doctrine of equitable estoppel;[69] (iv) the unavailability of discovery in private foreign and international arbitrations;[70] (v) the necessity for a district court to halt proceedings during an interlocutory appeal based on a question of arbitrability;[71] and (vi) judicial recognition that waiver of the right to arbitrate is not conditioned on a showing of prejudice.[72]

While these rulings have addressed certain unique issues, it is worthwhile to consider the evolution of the Supreme Court decisions on a few prominent recurring arbitration themes—*e.g.*, allocation of authority between the arbitrators and the courts, the arbitrability of statutory claims, the significance of choice-of-law clauses, and classwide procedures.

---

rules; the federal policy is simply to ensure the enforceability, according to their terms, of private agreements to arbitrate").

66 *Lamps Plus*, 587 U.S.at ___, 139 S. Ct. at 1418, 203 L. Ed. 2d at 649 ("ambiguities about the scope of an arbitration agreement must be resolved in favor of arbitration"); *see also Mitsubishi Motors Corp.*, 473 U.S. at 626, 105 S. Ct. at 3353, 87 L. Ed. 2d at 454 (1985) ("any doubts concerning the scope of arbitrable issues ... be resolved in favor of arbitration").

67 Commonwealth Coatings Corp. v. Cont'l Cas. Co., 393 U.S. 145, 150, 89 S. Ct. 337, 340, 21 L. Ed. 2d 301, 305 (1968) ("[A]ny tribunal permitted by law to try cases and controversies not only must be unbiased but also must avoid even the appearance of bias").

68 Hall Street Associates, L.L.C. v. Mattel, Inc., 552 U.S. 576, 584, 170 L. Ed. 2d 254, 128 S. Ct. 1396 (2008) ("[9 U.S.C.] §§ 10 and 11 respectively provide the FAA's exclusive grounds for expedited vacatur and modification").

69 GE Energy Power Conversion Fr. Sas, Corp. v. Outokumpu Stainless USA, LLC, 590 U.S. ___, 140 S. Ct. 1637, 1644, 207 L. Ed. 2d 1, 11 (2020) ("[T]he New York Convention does not conflict with the enforcement of arbitration agreements by nonsignatories under domestic-law equitable estoppel doctrines").

70 ZF Automotive U.S., Inc., et al. v. Luxshare, Ltd., 596 U.S. ___, 142 S. Ct. 2078, 2091–92, 213 L. Ed. 2d 163, 178 (2022) ("[O]nly a governmental or intergovernmental adjudicative body constitutes a 'foreign or international tribunal' under 28 U.S.C. § 1782").

71 Coinbase, Inc., v. Bielski, 599 U.S. ___, 143 S. Ct. 1915, 1918, 216 L. Ed. 2d 671, 676 (2023) ("[A] district court must stay its pre-trial and trial proceedings while the interlocutory appeal is ongoing").

72 Morgan v. Sundance, Inc., 596 U.S. ___, 142 S. Ct. 1708, 1714, 212 L. Ed. 2d 753, 760 (2022) ("prejudice is not a condition of finding that a party, by litigating too long, waived its right to stay litigation or compel arbitration under the FAA").

### 3.3 *Allocation of Authority to Determine Arbitrability*

In deciding who has the authority to determine the enforceability of arbitration agreements—arbitral tribunals or courts—the Supreme Court has distinguished between "gateway issues" and "non-gateway issues" as a guiding principle.[73] Gateway issues, also called "questions of arbitrability,"[74] touch upon the parties' consent to arbitrate and, thus, typically warrant judicial determination.[75] Examples include examination of whether a "valid arbitration agreement" exists,[76] whether it "applies to a certain type of controversy,"[77] and whether it extends to disputes concerning "contract formation."[78] On the other hand, parties would likely expect for an arbitrator to decide non-gateway issues, *i.e.*, "procedural questions which grow out of the dispute and bear upon its final disposition,"[79] involving, in general, the interpretation of contracts and the application of procedural provisions.[80]

But the Supreme Court has held that parties may also agree that an arbitrator will have exclusive authority to resolve gateway issues, provided there is "clear and unmistakable" evidence of an agreement to arbitrate the question of arbitrability.[81] However, the Court clarified that challenges must be directed

---

73 George A. Bermann, *After First Options: Delegation Run Amok*, 32 AM. REV. INT'L ARBITRATION 15 (2021).

74 Moses H. Cone Mem'l Hosp. v. Mercury Constr. Corp., 460 U.S. 1, 24, 103 S. Ct. 927, 941, 74 L. Ed. 2d 765, 785 (1983).

75 George A. Bermann, *supra* note 73.

76 Green Tree Fin. Corp. v. Bazzle, 539 U.S. 444, 452, 123 S. Ct. 2402, 2407, 156 L. Ed. 2d 414, 422 (2003).

77 *Id.*

78 Granite Rock Co. v. Int'l Bhd. of Teamsters, 561 U.S. 287, 296, 130 S. Ct. 2847, 2855, 177 L. Ed. 2d 567, 577 (2010) (stating that if there is a genuine dispute about whether an arbitration agreement was ever formed between the parties, that gateway question is for the courts to decide).

79 Howsam v. Dean Witter Reynolds, Inc., 537 U.S. 79, 84, 123 S. Ct. 588, 592, 154 L. Ed. 2d 491 (2002).

80 *See Green Tree Fin. Corp.*, 539 U.S. at 452–53, 123 S. Ct. at 2407, 156 L. Ed. 2d at 422 (establishing that the interpretation of whether a contract forbids class arbitration, a discussion that "concerns neither the validity of the arbitration clause nor its applicability to the underlying dispute between the parties," is for an arbitrator to decide); BG Group, PLC v. Republic of Argentina, 572 U.S. 25, 134 S. Ct. 1198, 188 L. Ed. 2d 220 (2014) (holding that the interpretation and application of procedural provisions involving conditions precedent to arbitration are primarily for the arbitrators to decide); *Howsam*, 537 U.S. at 84 123 S. Ct. at 592, 154 L. Ed. 2d at 497 (holding that the applicability of the National Association of Securities Dealers—NASD time limit rule is a matter presumptively for the arbitrator, not for the judge to decide).

81 First Options of Chicago, Inc. v. Kaplan, 514 U.S. 938, 944, 115 S. Ct. 1920, 1924, 131 L. Ed. 2d 985, 994 (1995) ("Courts should not assume that the parties agreed to arbitrate arbitrability

only to the "delegation provision" of the arbitration agreement, not the arbitration agreement as a whole.[82] Otherwise, the matter of enforceability would be for the arbitrator to decide.[83] In a recent decision on the issue, the Supreme Court has held that, even in the presence of a delegation provision, courts, not arbitrators, should decide the threshold issue of whether an exception under Section 1 of the FAA—rendering the arbitration agreement invalid—applies.[84]

### 3.4 *Arbitration of Statutory Claims*

The Supreme Court has consistently confirmed the enforceability of arbitration agreements involving statutory claims, absent a Congressional command prohibiting arbitration or evidence that arbitration would deprive a party of

---

unless there is 'clear and unmistakable' evidence that they did so"); *see also* Henry Schein, Inc. v. Archer & White Sales, Inc., 586 U.S.___, 139 S. Ct. 524, 202 L. Ed. 2d 480 (2019) (holding that when the parties delegate the question of arbitrability to an arbitrator, a court may not override that delegation, even if it considers the claim of arbitrability to be "wholly groundless").

82 Rent-A-Center, West, Inc. v. Jackson, 561 U.S. 63, 130 S. Ct. 2772, 177 L. Ed. 2d 403 (2010) (holding that unless the party opposing arbitration can specifically demonstrate that the delegation clause—as opposed to the arbitration agreement as a whole—is unconscionable, the matter of enforceability should be decided by the arbitrator).

83 The decision in *Rent-A-Center* further expanded the Supreme Court's holding in *Prima Paint* to create another level of "separability" between the "arbitration agreement" and the "delegation clause." In *Prima Paint Corp. v. Flood & Conklin Mfg. Co.*, 388 U.S. 395, 87 S. Ct. 1801, 18 L. Ed. 2d 1270 (1967), the Supreme Court had ruled that an arbitration agreement is "separable" from the main contract in which it is inserted, what became known as the "separability doctrine." In essence, the arbitration agreement is treated as an independent contractual agreement that survives even if the underlying contract is found to be invalid. Therefore, under the holding in *Prima Paint*, a claim of fraud in the inducement of the main contract, rather than the arbitration agreement itself, is to be referred to arbitrators, not courts. *See also* Buckeye Check Cashing, Inc. v. Cardegna, 546 U.S. 440, 445–46, 126 S. Ct. 1204, 1209, 163 L. Ed. 2d 1038, 1044 (2006) ("Unless the challenge is to the arbitration clause itself, the issue of the contract's validity is considered by the arbitrator in the first instance").

84 New Prime Inc. v. Oliveira, 586 U.S. ___, 139 S. Ct. 532, 202 L. Ed. 2d 536 (2019). There is a strong rationale behind this decision. Section 1 of the FAA excludes "contracts of employment of seamen, railroad employees, or any other class of workers engaged in foreign or interstate commerce" from the FAA's scope. Therefore, if Section 1 exception applies, there is no valid arbitration agreement under the FAA, and this threshold issue must be decided by courts, not arbitrators, even in the presence of a "delegation provision." *See also* Southwest Airlines Co. v. Saxon, 596, U.S.___, 142 S.Ct. 1783, 213 L. Ed. 2d 27 (2022) (holding that airline ramp supervisors, who train and supervise teams of agents who load and unload cargo on and off airplanes, belong to a "class of workers engaged in foreign or interstate commerce," are covered by the Section 1 exemption and therefore are exempt from the FAA's coverage).

substantive rights. As an example, the Court upheld the enforceability of arbitration agreements compelling arbitration of claims involving the Sherman Antitrust Act,[85] the Age Discrimination in Employment Act (ADEA),[86] the Credit Repair Organizations Act (CROA),[87] the Securities Act of 1933,[88] the Carriage of Goods by Sea Act (COGSA),[89] the Securities Exchange Act of 1934 and the Racketeer Influenced and Corrupt Organizations Act (RICO).[90]

Some critics, however, say that the Supreme Court has "grossly erred"[91] in interpreting the FAA to allow arbitration of statutory claims, since the FAA was created to deal with the private resolution of commercial disputes, rather than be extended to a wide range of disputes.[92]

---

85 Mitsubishi Motors Corp. v. Soler Chrysler-Plymouth, Inc., 473 U.S. 614, 105 S. Ct. 3346, 87 L. Ed. 2d 444 (1985) (holding that claims arising under the Sherman Act and encompassed within a valid arbitration clause in an agreement embodying an international commercial transaction are arbitrable under the FAA); *see also* Am. Express Co. v. Italian Colors Rest., 570 U.S. 228, 231, 133 S. Ct. 2304, 2307, 186 L. Ed. 2d 417, 422 (2013) (upholding the enforceability of a class action waiver within an arbitration agreement, even though it would compel the arbitration of antitrust claims under the Sherman Act).

86 Gilmer v. Interstate/Johnson Lane Corp., 500 U.S. 20, 111 S. Ct. 1647, 114 L. Ed. 2d 26 (1991) (holding that a claim under the Age Discrimination in Employment Act of 1967—ADEA can be subjected to compulsory arbitration).

87 CompuCredit Corp. v. Greenwood, 565 U.S. 95, 132 S. Ct. 665, 181 L. Ed. 2d 586 (2012) (holding that a claim under the Credit Repair Organizations Act—CROA does not preclude the enforcement of an arbitration agreement).

88 Rodrigues de Quijas v. Shearson/American Express, Inc., 490 U.S. 477, 109 S. Ct. 1917, 104 L. Ed. 2d 526 (1989) (asserting the enforceability of a predispute agreement to arbitrate claims under the Securities Act of 1933).

89 Vimar Seguros y Reaseguros, S.A. v. M/V Sky Reefer, 515 U.S. 528, 115 S. Ct. 2322, 132 L. Ed. 2d 462 (1995) (holding that the Carriage of Goods by Sea Act—COGSA did not preclude a forum selection clause in a bill of lading requiring arbitration to be conducted in a foreign country).

90 Shearson/American Express Inc. v. McMahon, 482 U.S. 220, 107 S. Ct. 2332, 96 L. Ed. 2d 185 (1987) (holding that claims brough under the Securities Exchange Act of 1934 and the Racketeer Influenced and Corrupt Organizations Act must be referred to arbitration in accordance with the terms of the arbitration agreement); *see also* Pacificare Health Systems, Inc. v. Book, 538 U.S. 401, 406, 123 S. Ct. 1531, 1535, 155 L. Ed. 2d 578, 583 (2003) (compelling arbitration of claims arising under RICO given that courts should not, "on the basis of mere speculation," conclude that an arbitrator would incorrectly interpret an ambiguous remedial limitation in the arbitration agreement); Scherk v. Alberto-Culver Co., 417 U.S. 506, 94 S. Ct. 2449, 41 L. Ed. 2d 270 (1974) (ordering arbitration, pursuant to a provision embodied in an international agreement, of a claim arising under the Securities Exchange Act of 1934).

91 Imre Stephen Szalai, *Exploring the Federal Arbitration Act Through the Lens of History*, 2016 J. DISP. RESOL. 115, 117 (2016).

92 David S. Clancy & Matthew M.K Stein, *An Uninvited Guest: Class Arbitration and the Federal Arbitration Act's Legislative History*, 63 BUS. LAW. 55, 61 (2007) (clarifying that

### 3.5 *Choice-of-Law Clauses*

The Supreme Court has frequently been called upon to address the applicability of choice-of-law clauses within arbitration agreements, especially when the FAA and state law appear at odds.

In *Volt Information Sciences, Inc. v. Board of Trustees*, the Court held that where parties have agreed that their arbitration contract would be governed by California law—a law that allowed courts to stay arbitration during related litigation—this state provision was not preempted by the FAA, even though it conflicted with it.[93] As indicated elsewhere, arbitration under the FAA is rooted in the principle of consent rather than coercion. The FAA mandates the enforcement of arbitration agreements "according to their terms" but does not require arbitration to proceed only according to "a certain set of procedural rules."[94] Therefore, if parties decided to be governed by California law, which allows for a stay of arbitration, their choice was deemed to align with the FAA's foundational emphasis on honoring the terms of private agreements to arbitrate.[95]

Elaborating on this notion in *Mastrobuono v. Shearson Lehmon Hutton, Inc.*, the Supreme Court discussed the differences between a general choice-of-law provision and an arbitration clause.[96] The Court held that, although parties could choose to incorporate specific provisions of state arbitration laws into their contracts—possibly fending off a preemption challenge—courts should not interpret general choice-of-law clauses as implicit agreements to apply limitations on arbitration that might apply according to varying state laws. There, the Court held that a general choice-of-law provision indicating that the contract should be governed by New York law did not automatically incorporate a New York rule prohibiting arbitrators from awarding punitive damages.[97]

---

during a Congressional session in 1931, the Chairman of the House Judiciary Committee, Representative George Graham, explained the main objective behind the enactment of the FAA: "This bill simply provides for one thing, and that is to give an opportunity to enforce an agreement in commercial contracts and admiralty contracts—an agreement to arbitrate, when voluntarily placed in the document by the parties to it").

93 Volt Info. Scis., Inc. v. Bd. of Trs., 489 U.S. 468, 109 S. Ct. 1248, 103 L. Ed. 2d 488 (1989).

94 *Id.* at 476, 109 S. Ct. at 1254, 103 L. Ed. 2d at 498.

95 *Id.* at 479, 109 S. Ct. at 1256, 103 L. Ed. 2d at 500 ("Where, as here, the parties have agreed to abide by state rules of arbitration, enforcing those rules according to the terms of the agreement is fully consistent with the goals of the FAA, even if the result is that arbitration is stayed where the Act would otherwise permit it to go forward").

96 Mastrobuono v. Shearson Lehman Hutton, Inc., 514 U.S. 52, 115 S. Ct. 1212, 131 L. Ed. 2d 76 (1995).

97 *Id.* at 63–64, 115 S. Ct. at 1219, 131 L. Ed. 2d at 88 ("We think the best way to harmonize the choice-of-law provision with the arbitration provision is to read 'the laws of the State of New York' to encompass substantive principles that New York courts would apply, but

### 3.6 *Classwide Arbitration*

There is considerable controversy surrounding the Supreme Court decisions restricting the availability of classwide arbitration and the enforcement of class action waivers in consumer contracts and employment agreements.

In a first set of decisions, the Supreme Court established that class arbitration is only available when there is explicit consent of the parties. In *Stolt-Nielsen S. A. v. AnimalFeeds International Corp.*, the Court held that parties cannot be compelled to submit a dispute to class arbitration without an explicit agreement allowing for class proceedings.[98] The Court deemed class arbitration so inherently different from individual arbitration that "it cannot be presumed the parties consented to it by simply agreeing to submit their disputes to an arbitrator."[99] Three years later, in *Oxford Health Plans LLC v. Sutter*, the Court reaffirmed that "class arbitration is a matter of consent" and that "an arbitrator may employ class procedures only if the parties have authorized them."[100] *Lamps Plus Inc. v. Varela*, the last case of the trilogy, solidified that approach. There the Court held that arbitration agreements that are silent or ambiguous cannot be interpreted as to allow class arbitration.[101] In other words, "courts may not infer from an ambiguous agreement that parties have consented to arbitrate on a classwide basis."[102]

In a second group of cases, the Supreme Court upheld the legality of class action waivers in consumer and employment contracts. For example, the Court established in *AT&T Mobility LLC v. Concepcion* that the FAA preempts state laws that held class action waivers in consumer contracts were unconscionable.[103] The Court reasoned that a California statute treating as unconscionable arbitration agreements prohibiting all forms of collective litigation or arbitration was essentially in conflict with the "liberal federal

---

not to include special rules limiting the authority of arbitrators. Thus, the choice-of-law provision covers the rights and duties of the parties, while the arbitration clause covers arbitration; neither sentence intrudes upon the other").

98 Stolt-Nielsen S. A. v. AnimalFeeds Int'l Corp., 559 U.S. 662, 684, 130 S. Ct. 1758, 1775, 176 L. Ed. 2d 605, 624 (2010) ("[A] party may not be compelled under the FAA to submit to class arbitration unless there is a contractual basis for concluding that the party agreed to do so").

99 *Id.* at 685, 130 S. Ct. at 1775, 176 L. Ed. 2d at 624.

100 Oxford Health Plans LLC v. Sutter, 569 U.S. 564, 565–66, 133 S. Ct. 2064, 2066, 186 L. Ed. 2d 113, 117 (2013).

101 Lamps Plus, Inc. v. Varela, 587 U.S. ___, 139 S. Ct. 1407, 1417, 203 L. Ed. 2d 636, 647 (2019) ("Neither silence nor ambiguity provides a sufficient basis for concluding that parties to an arbitration agreement agreed to undermine the central benefits of arbitration itself").

102 *Id.* at ___, 139 S. Ct. at 1419, 203 L. Ed. 2d. at 649.

103 AT&T Mobility LLC v. Concepcion, 563 U.S. 333, 131 S. Ct. 1740, 179 L. Ed. 2d 742 (2011).

policy favoring arbitration"[104] that requires courts to enforce arbitration agreements "according to their terms so as to facilitate streamlined proceedings."[105] In the Court's view, the informality of arbitration trumped class action procedures which were "slower, more costly, and more likely to generate procedural morass than final judgment."[106] In *American Express Co. v. Italian Colors Restaurant,* the Court also upheld the enforceability of an arbitration clause in an AmericanExpress merchants' agreement, which explicitly ruled out the possibility of arbitration "on a class action basis."[107] The issue there was whether the waiver was enforceable under the FAA even when the cost of individually arbitrating a federal statutory claim exceeded potential recovery. The Court found "no contrary [C]ongressional command" capable of making the waiver unenforceable.[108] Additionally, the Court was unswayed by the argument supporting the applicability of the "effective vindication" doctrine—a judicial exception to the FAA designed to invalidate arbitration agreements that make it impractical for plaintiffs to vindicate federal statutory rights—given that the parties were not barred from taking their antitrust claims to an arbitrator; they found it, however, economically impracticable to do so.[109]

In *DirecTV, Inc. v. Imburgia*, the Supreme Court reversed a California Court of Appeals judgment holding a class action waiver in DirecTV's service agreement unenforceable.[110] The agreement provided that the entire arbitration agreement would be "unenforceable" if the "law of your state," in this case, California, made the waiver of class arbitration unenforceable.[111] When the contract was drafted, California law made class arbitration waivers unenforceable, but the statute was later held invalid in the *Concepcion* case. Ignoring the ruling in *Concepcion*, the California Court of Appeals held that state law, even if invalidated, should render the arbitration agreement unenforceable. The U.S. Supreme Court reversed. In deciding that reliance on an invalid state law was inconsistent with the broader objectives of the FAA, the Court held that the California Court of Appeals failed to place arbitration contracts "on equal footing with all other contracts."[112] The Supreme Court also sustained,

104 *Id.* at 346, 131 S. Ct. at 1749, 179 L. Ed. 2d at 755.
105 *Id.* at 344, 131 S. Ct. at 1748, 179 L. Ed. 2d at 754.
106 *Id.* at 348, 131 S. Ct. at 1751, 179 L. Ed. 2d at 756.
107 Am. Express Co. v. Italian Colors Rest., 570 U.S. 228, 231, 133 S. Ct. 2304, 2308, 186 L. Ed. 2d 417, 423 (2013).
108 *Id.* at 233, 133 S. Ct. at 2309, 186 L. Ed. 2d at 424.
109 *Id.* at 235, 133 S. Ct. at 2310, 186 L. Ed. 2d at 425.
110 DirecTV, Inc. v. Imburgia, 577 U.S. 47, 136 S. Ct. 463, 193 L. Ed. 2d 365 (2015).
111 *Id.* at 49, 136 S. Ct. at 466, 193 L. Ed. 2d at 369.
112 *Id.* at 58, 136 S. Ct. at 471, 193 L. Ed. 2d at 375.

in *Epic Systems Corp. v. Lewis*, the legality of arbitration agreements containing class action waivers[113] on the basis that arbitration agreements "must be enforced as written," dismissing the argument that such agreements would amount to a violation of employees' rights under the National Labor Relations Act (NLRA).[114]

The Supreme Court decision in *Viking River Cruises, Inc. v. Moriana* continued this line of precedents. At issue was whether the FAA preempted a California precedent[115] invalidating contractual waivers of the right to assert representative claims under California's Labor Code Private Attorneys General Act (PAGA).[116] Writing for the majority, Justice Alito declared that the prohibition on PAGA waivers "violates the fundamental principle that 'arbitration is a matter of consent,'" and thereby "unduly circumscribes the freedom of parties to determine 'the issues subject to arbitration' and 'the rules by which they will arbitrate.'"[117] The Court also found that the FAA preempted the California rule barring the division of PAGA actions into individual and non-individual claims,[118] holding that "Viking is entitled to compel arbitration of Moriana's individual claim."[119]

In all but one of the Supreme Court decisions involving the availability of classwide arbitration, the Justices have been conspicuously divided.[120] The dissenting voices in these cases have been far from subdued, raising significant critiques of the majority opinions as potentially undermining consumer

113 Epic Sys. Corp. v. Lewis, 584 U.S. ___, 138 S. Ct. 1612, 200 L. Ed. 2d 889 (2018).

114 *Id.* at ___, 138 S. Ct. at 1632, 200 L. Ed. 2d at 915; *id.* at ___, 138 S. Ct. at 1619, 200 L. Ed. 2d at 897 ("Congress has instructed in the Arbitration Act that arbitration agreements providing for individualized proceedings must be enforced, and neither the Arbitration Act's saving clause nor the NLRA suggests otherwise").

115 Iskanian v. CLS Transp. Los Angeles, LLC, 59 Cal. 4th 348, 380, 327 P.3d 129, 146 (2014).

116 Viking River Cruises, Inc. v. Moriana, 596 U.S. ___, 142 S. Ct. 1906, 213 L. Ed. 2d 179 (2022).

117 *Id.* at ___, 142 S. Ct. at 1906, 213 L. Ed. 2d at 198 (citing *Lamps Plus, Inc. v. Varela*, 587 U.S. ___, 139 S. Ct. 1407, 203 L. Ed. 2d 636 (2019)).

118 *Id.* at ___, 142 S. Ct. at 1912, 213 L. Ed. 2d at 187 ("[S]tate law cannot condition the enforceability of an arbitration agreement on the availability of a procedural mechanism that would permit a party to expand the scope of the arbitration by introducing claims that the parties did not jointly agree to arbitrate").

119 *Id.* at ___, 142 S. Ct. at 1925, 213 L. Ed. 2d at 200. The Court also noted that when an individual claim is sent to arbitration, the individual loses the standing to maintain non-individual claims and, as a result, "Moriana lacks statutory standing to continue to maintain her non-individual claims in court."

120 The non-unanimous decisions include *Stolt-Nielsen* (5–3); *Lamps Plus* (5–4); *Concepcion* (5–4); *Italian Colors* (5–3); *DirecTV* (6–3); *Epic Systems* (5–4); and *Viking River Cruises* (8–1). The only unanimous decision was in *Oxford Health Plans*.

and employee protections.[121] Commentators have also argued that these decisions represent "an unconstitutional evisceration of statutory and common law rights"[122] which would ultimately lead to the "extinction of most class actions."[123]

## 4 Conclusion

Contrary to conventional wisdom, in the years prior to the enactment of the FAA, courts were not entirely hostile to arbitration. True, they took an unfavorable view of agreements to arbitrate, but to arbitration agreements only. At the same time, this view stood in marked contrast to the judiciary's strong encouragement of arbitration as an alternative method of dispute resolution and a general understanding that courts should typically enforce arbitration awards.

The FAA represented a turning point, establishing written arbitration agreements to be "valid, irrevocable, and enforceable."[124] In the years that followed, the Supreme Court embraced a "liberal federal policy favoring arbitration agreements,"[125] declared that arbitration agreements should be enforced "according to their terms,"[126] and determined that any ambiguities in the agreement "must be resolved in favor of arbitration."[127] Despite criticism from some quarters, the Court further interpreted the FAA to allow the arbitration of statutory claims,[128] as well as to allow the enforceability of class action waivers

---

121 *See* DirecTV, Inc. v. Imburgia, 577 U.S. 47, 67, 136 S. Ct. 463, 476, 193 L. Ed. 2d 365, 380 (2015) (Ginsburg, J., dissenting) (noting that the FAA has been routinely invoked to deny employees and consumers "effective relief against powerful economic entities").

122 Judith Resnik, *Diffusing Disputes: The Public in the Private of Arbitration, the Private in Courts, and the Erasure of Rights*, 124 YALE L.J. 2804 (2015).

123 JOHN C. COFFEE, ENTREPRENEURIAL LITIGATION 2971 (Harvard Univ. Press, Kindle Ed. 2015).

124 9 U.S.C. § 2.

125 Moses H. Cone Mem'l Hosp. v. Mercury Constr. Corp., 460 U.S. 1, 24, 103 S. Ct. 927, 941, 74 L. Ed. 2d 765, 785 (1983); *see also* Southland Corp. v. Keating, 465 U.S. 1, 10, 104 S. Ct. 852, 858, 79 L. Ed. 2d 1, 12 (1984).

126 Volt Info. Scis., Inc. v. Bd. of Trs., 489 U.S. 468, 476, 109 S. Ct. 1248, 1254, 103 L. Ed. 2d 488, 498 (1989).

127 Lamps Plus, Inc. v. Varela, 587 U.S. ___, 139 S. Ct. 1407, 1418, 203 L. Ed. 2d 636, 648 (2019); *see* also Mitsubishi Motors Corp. v. Soler Chrysler-Plymouth, Inc., 473 U.S. 614, 626, 105 S. Ct. 3346, 3353, 87 L. Ed. 2d 444, 455 (1985).

128 *See Mitsubishi Motors Corp.*, 473 U.S. at 626, 105 S. Ct. at 3353, 87 L. Ed. 2d at 455; Am. Express Co. v. Italian Colors Rest., 570 U.S. 228, 133 S. Ct. 2304, 186 L. Ed. 2d 417 (2013); Gilmer v. Interstate/Johnson Lane Corp., 500 U.S. 20, 111 S. Ct. 1647, 114 L. Ed. 2d 26 (1991); CompuCredit Corp. v. Greenwood, 565 U.S. 95, 132 S. Ct. 665, 181 L. Ed. 2d 586 (2012);

in consumer contracts and employment agreements.[129] The post-FAA era has also marked a significant increase in the complexity of arbitration issues. No longer are legal concerns confined to the grounds upon which an arbitration award should be vacated. The Court now regularly faces a highly complicated set of issues—ranging from the allocation of authority between courts and arbitrators, the enforceability of statutory claims within arbitration, the significance of choice-of-law clauses, and the availability of classwide actions.

In sum, the Supreme Court's attitude toward arbitration has evolved significantly over the last two centuries: from skepticism toward agreements to arbitrate but deference to arbitral awards—to today's vigorous endorsement of both agreements to arbitrate and arbitral awards.[130]

---

Rodrigues de Quijas v. Shearson/American Express, Inc., 490 U.S. 477, 109 S. Ct. 1917, 104 L. Ed. 2d 526 (1989); Vimar Seguros y Reaseguros, S. A. v. M/V Sky Reefer, 515 U.S. 528, 115 S. Ct. 2322, 132 L. Ed. 2d 462 (1995); Shearson/American Express Inc. v. McMahon, 482 U.S. 220, 107 S. Ct. 2332, 96 L. Ed. 2d 185 (1987); Pacificare Health Systems, Inc. v. Book, 538 U.S. 401, 123 S. Ct. 1531, 155 L. Ed. 2d 578 (2003); Scherk v. Alberto-Culver Co., 417 U.S. 506, 94 S. Ct. 2449, 41 L. Ed. 2d 270 (1974).

129 *See* Stolt-Nielsen S. A. v. AnimalFeeds International Corp., 559 U.S. 662, 130 S. Ct. 1758, 176 L. Ed. 2d 605 (2010); Oxford Health Plans LLC v. Sutter, 569 U.S. 564, 133 S. Ct. 2064, 186 L. Ed. 2d 113 (2013); *Lamps Plus, Inc.*, 587 U.S. at ___, 139 S. Ct. at 1407, 203 L. Ed. 2d at 636; AT&T Mobility LLC v. Concepcion, 563 U.S. 333, 131 S. Ct. 1740, 179 L. Ed. 2d 742 (2011); Am. Express Co. v. Italian Colors Rest., 570 U.S. 228, 133 S. Ct. 2304, 186 L. Ed. 2d 417 (2013); DirecTV, Inc. v. Imburgia, 577 U.S. 47, 136 S. Ct. 463, 193 L. Ed. 2d 365 (2015); Epic Sys. Corp. v. Lewis, 584 U.S. ___, 138 S. Ct. 1612, 200 L. Ed. 2d 889 (2018); Viking River Cruises, Inc. v. Moriana, 596 U.S. ___, 142 S. Ct. 1906, 213 L. Ed. 2d 179 (2022).

130 That explains the high percentage of voluntary compliance (80% according to the American Arbitration Association) of arbitration awards in the U.S. *See* Messitte, *supra* note 6 at 6. (adding that "parties recognize that not only is there apt to be needless expense in trying to vacate the award; the court may well impose additional monetary sanctions—attorney fees and cost—when the efforts to undo the arbitration award are deemed frivolous or merely for purposes of delay").

CHAPTER 3

# The Importance of the U.S. Supreme Court in Shaping U.S. Arbitration Law & Practice

*Daniel Schimmel, Shrutih Tewarie and James Fullmer*

The Federal Arbitration Act ("FAA") is the essential federal statute relating to arbitration in the United States. Among other things, the FAA states that a written agreement to arbitrate "in any maritime transaction or a contract evidencing a transaction involving commerce ... shall be valid, irrevocable, and enforceable, save upon such grounds as exist at law or in equity for the revocation of any contract."[1] The Supreme Court has said that this "is a congressional declaration of a liberal federal policy favoring arbitration agreements, notwithstanding any state substantive or procedural policies to the contrary" which "create[s] a body of federal substantive law of arbitrability, applicable to any arbitration agreement within the coverage of the [FAA]."[2] The reach of the FAA extends beyond domestic arbitration; in 1970, the FAA was amended[3] to implement the Convention on the Recognition and Enforcement of Foreign Arbitral Awards (also known as the New York Convention),[4] with the Supreme Court subsequently noting that the "federal policy in favor of arbitral dispute resolution" thus "applies with special force in the field on international commerce."[5]

The Supreme Court's role in interpreting the FAA and in shaping arbitration law and practice in the United States has evolved with developments in Supreme Court jurisprudence as a whole. The FAA was enacted in 1925. This was the pre-New Deal era, more than a decade before the famous "switch in time that saved nine."[6] At that time, Congress's power to legislate on matters

1 9 U.S.C. § 2.

2 Moses H. Cone Mem'l Hosp. v. Mercury Constr. Corp., 460 U.S. 1, 24 (1983).

3 9 U.S.C. §§ 201–208.

4 Convention on the Recognition and Enforcement of Foreign Arbitral Awards, June 10, 1958, 21 U.S.T. 2517, T.I.A.S. No. 6997.

5 Mitsubishi Motors Corp. v. Soler Chrysler-Plymouth, 473 U.S. 614, 631 (1985).

6 According to Professor John Q. Barrett, this humorous description of Justice Roberts's sudden switch to upholding the constitutionality of New Deal legislation, which came shortly on the heels of President Roosevelt's threat to increase the size of the Supreme Court, was originally coined by newspaper columnist Cal Tinney. *See John Q. Barrett, Attribution Time: Cal Tinney's 1937 Quip, "A Switch in Time'll Save Nine"*, 73 OKLA. L. REV. 229, 238–39 (2021).

 | DOI:10.1163/9789004715820_004

affecting "commerce" was limited to only those matters which *directly* affected *interstate* commerce.[7] This raises the question of what Congress meant when it defined the reach of the FAA as extending to contracts "evidencing a transaction involving commerce."[8] As Justice Souter noted in his dissent in *Circuit City Stores v. Adams*,[9] the scope of this phrase can be read in "two quite different ways." One could argue that the FAA "extends only to those contracts 'involving commerce' that were understood to be covered in 1925" or, alternatively, one could argue for an "elastic view" where the statutory power is meant to extend "as far as Congress could go, whatever that might be over time." It was the second view that the Court adopted.

Whatever the FAA may have meant to Congress in 1925, the expansion of federal law and regulation in the wake of the New Deal, and the exponential development of arbitration as a method of dispute resolution, have given the Supreme Court many opportunities to weigh in and shape the law applicable to aspects of arbitral proceedings in the United States, ranging from the formation of the agreement to the judicial enforcement and ultimate effect of an arbitral award. Nearly one hundred years on, the Supreme Court has created a body of law that guides practice, but also raises many open questions: What is the underlying principle guiding the Court's jurisprudence? How far does the "liberal federal policy favoring arbitration agreements" extend? And how might the Court decide the open questions that remain about the FAA and about arbitration law and practice in the United States?

The following decisions of the U.S. Supreme Court on topics ranging from formation of the arbitration agreement to the enforcement of arbitral awards provide a flavor of the Court's role in the development of arbitration law and practice.

## 1 The Agreement to Arbitrate

As the Supreme Court noted in several decisions, arbitration "is strictly a matter of consent."[10] In another oft-repeated formulation, "arbitration is a creature

7 *See, e.g.*, United States v. Lopez, 514 U.S. 549, 554–55 (1995) (citing A.L.A. Schechter Poultry Corp. v. United States, 295 U.S. 495, 546 (1935)).

8 For an exploration of this point, see generally Christopher R. Drahozal, *In Defense of* Southland*: Reexamining the Legislative History of the Federal Arbitration Act*, 78 NOTRE DAME L. REV. 101, 127–30 (2002).

9 532 U.S. 105.

10 *See, e.g.*, Viking River Cruises, Inc. v. Moriana, 142 S. Ct. 1906, 1918 (2022) (internal quotation marks omitted).

of contract."[11] But what principles determine if a valid arbitration agreement exists? The answer comes in the form of another well-known phrase: "ordinary state-law principles that govern the formation of contracts."[12] On the face of it, this might suggest that the Supreme Court has little to say about the formation of arbitration agreements. But the underlying rationale for these statements shows quite the opposite. In *Perry v. Thomas*,[13] the Court considered a California law that guaranteed employees the right to litigate wage disputes in court "without regard to the existence of any private agreement to arbitrate." The Court found this statute preempted by the FAA because the requirement of a judicial forum to resolve the dispute was at odds with the FAA's requirement, in Section 2 of the statute, that courts enforce arbitration clauses. The Court also noted that a court "may not ... in assessing the rights of litigants to enforce an arbitration agreement, construe that agreement in a manner different from that in which it otherwise construes nonarbitration agreements under state law." Applying these preemption principles from the Supreme Court, some lower courts, both state and federal, have found that state laws barring mandatory arbitration clauses in consumer contracts are preempted by the FAA.[14]

The formulation, therefore, that "ordinary state-law principles that govern the formation of contracts" apply is not a signal of deference to state-law principles, whatever they may be. While state contract law principles do govern the formation of arbitration agreements, they do so against the backdrop of federal arbitration law as construed by the Supreme Court.

What does this mean for the analysis of an arbitration agreement that is contained within a broader contract? Is the validity of that agreement dependent on the validity of the contract as a whole, just as arbitration agreements are analyzed using general contract law principles? Or does the federal policy in favor of arbitration require a separate analysis of the arbitration agreement? The Supreme Court answered this question in *Prima Paint Corp. v. Flood and Conklin Manufacturing Co.*[15]—specifically, whether "arbitration clauses as a matter of federal law are 'separable' from the contracts in which they are embedded" and whether, therefore, a claim that a contract *as a whole* was

---

11 *See, e.g.*, Hall St. Assocs., L.L.C. v. Mattel, Inc., 552 U.S. 576, 585 (2008).

12 First Options of Chi., Inc. v. Kaplan, 514 U.S. 938, 944 (1995).

13 482 U.S. 483 (1987).

14 *See, e.g.*, Andersen v. Walmart Stores, Inc., No. 16-CV-6488 CJS, 2017 U.S. Dist. LEXIS 22862, at *22–23 (W.D.N.Y. Feb. 17, 2017); Lobel v. Ccap Auto Lease, No. 53753/2021, 2022 NYLJ LEXIS 383, at *20–21 (Westchester Cty. Sup. Ct. Apr. 8, 2022).

15 388 U.S. 395 (1967).

induced by fraud will be ordered to arbitration if there is no claim that the arbitration provision specifically was induced by fraud.

The Supreme Court held that, in such a situation, the arbitration agreement would be enforced (assuming, of course, that there was no evidence that the arbitration agreement itself was procured by fraud). Does this indicate, then, that (*contra Perry v. Thomas*) arbitration agreements *are* different from other contracts, and should get special treatment pursuant to a pro-arbitration federal policy? Certainly, there are no shortage of scholars who argue that courts have developed a sort of "arbitration favoritism" based on the Supreme Court's pronouncements in this area of law.[16] But the Court in *Prima Paint* did emphasize that its holding was based on the language of the FAA itself:

> Under § 4 [of the FAA], ... the federal court is instructed to order arbitration to proceed once it is satisfied that "the making of the agreement for arbitration or the failure to comply [with the arbitration agreement] is not in issue." Accordingly, if the claim is fraud in the inducement of the arbitration clause itself—an issue which goes to the "making" of the agreement to arbitrate—the federal court may proceed to adjudicate it. But the statutory language does not permit the federal court to consider claims of fraud in the inducement of the contract generally.

In a legal world where, in the words of Justice Kagan, "we are all textualists now,"[17] it is worthwhile to understand the ways in which the Supreme Court's arbitration jurisprudence does derive from the text of the FAA itself.

The cases above have addressed situations where state law may arguably impinge upon the FAA's mandate relating to the enforceability of arbitration agreements. What about the opposite scenario—where state law principles are what provides the basis for the arbitrability of a dispute? This question, again, was answered by a close look at the statutory text.

In *Arthur Andersen LLP v. Carlisle*,[18] the Supreme Court looked at a situation that is not uncommon under state law: where a non-signatory to an arbitration agreement is nevertheless asserted to be bound by that agreement. The

16 *See, e.g.*, Richard Frankel, *The Arbitration Clause as Super Contract*, 91 WASH. U. L. REV. 531, 532–33 (2014) (arguing that prior Supreme Court case law has led to "arbitration favoritism" in which courts put arbitration clauses on a "pedestal").

17 Harvard Law School, The Antonin Scalia Lecture Series: A Dialogue with Justice Elena Kagan on the Reading of Statutes, YouTube at 08:28 (Nov. 25, 2015), https://www.youtube.com/watch?v=dpEtszFToTg.

18 556 U.S. 624 (2009).

question was whether a party seeking to enforce the arbitration agreement in federal court could enforce it against a non-signatory, given that the FAA allows litigants to obtain a stay of any action that is "referable to arbitration under an agreement in writing." The argument that the FAA did not apply was based on the assertion that because a non-signatory had not signed the contract containing the arbitration clause, the dispute involving them was not referable to arbitration under the contract but rather under a state law principle extending the obligation beyond the contract. The Supreme Court disagreed after a careful parsing of the statutory text:

> "[T]raditional principles" of state law allow a contract to be enforced by or against nonparties to the contract through "assumption, piercing the corporate veil, alter ego, incorporation by reference, third-party beneficiary theories, waiver and estoppel[.]" ...
>
> Respondents argue that, as a matter of federal law, claims to arbitration by nonparties are not "referable to arbitration *under* an agreement in writing," ... because they "seek to bind a signatory to an arbitral obligation *beyond* that signatory's strictly contractual obligation to arbitrate[.]" ... Perhaps that would be true if § 3 mandated stays only for disputes between parties to a written arbitration agreement. But that is not what the statute says. It says that stays are required if the claims are "referable to arbitration under an agreement in writing." If a written arbitration provision is made enforceable against (or for the benefit of) a third party under state contract law, the statute's terms are fulfilled.

Once again, in *Arthur Andersen LLP v. Carlisle*, the Supreme Court issued a decision favoring arbitration, but it grounded this analysis in a close textual read of the statute that placed the arbitration agreement at issue on the same playing field as any other contract.

More recently, the Supreme Court emphasized the limits of the supposed "policy favoring arbitration" embodied in the FAA. In *Morgan v. Sundance*,[19] the question was the validity of an Eighth Circuit rule requiring a party asserting that the other party had waived its right to arbitrate demonstrate not only that the other party (a) knew of its right and (b) acted inconsistently with its right (as must be demonstrated for any claim of waiver), but also (c) prejudiced the first party by its actions (the last being a judicially-created element applicable

19 142 S. Ct. 1708 (2022).

only in the arbitration context). The Supreme Court rejected this rule in an emphatic paragraph:

> [T]he FAA's "policy favoring arbitration" does not authorize federal courts to invent special, arbitration-preferring procedural rules. ... Accordingly, a court must hold a party to its arbitration contract just as the court would to any other kind. But a court may not devise novel rules to favor arbitration over litigation. ... The federal policy is about treating arbitration contracts like all others, not about fostering arbitration.

It remains to be seen how *Morgan v. Sundance* will apply to issues other than waiver.

Recall that this discussion began with the well-settled principle that state contract law governs the formation of arbitration agreements. Far from representing an abdication of the Supreme Court's role in crafting the federal law of arbitration, the cases discussed so far demonstrate the influence the Supreme Court has had in applying federal arbitration law to guide the application and understanding of enforceability of the agreement to arbitrate.

## 2 The Scope of the Agreement and Arbitrability

Federal law, as construed by the Supreme Court, informs not just the principles by which consent to arbitrate is determined, but also the presumptions that go into the substance and scope of consent, addressing not just the question of whether there has been consent but who has the primary authority to decide the question of arbitrability and what has been agreed to—indeed, what can be agreed to.

A key Supreme Court case addressing arbitrability was *First Options of Chicago, Inc. v. Kaplan*.[20] In that case, the Court addressed whether arbitrators or courts have the primary power to determine whether the merits of a dispute are arbitrable. The Court noted that there was a "certain practical importance" to this "narrow" question: If an arbitrator decides in the first instance whether a dispute is arbitrable, a court will review that determination deferentially, while a court making the decision in the first instance will make up its mind independently. This, the Court noted, could "make a critical difference to a party resisting arbitration."

20 514 U.S. 938 (1995).

The Court held, therefore, that the answer to the question depended on the parties' agreement, stating that "a court must defer to an arbitrator's arbitrability decision when the parties submitted that matter to arbitration." But it added an "important qualification"; courts "should not assume that the parties agreed to arbitrate arbitrability" absent clear and unmistakable evidence of such an agreement. And this, as the Court acknowledged, meant that the general presumption in favor of arbitration was actually reversed on the specific question of who has the primary responsibility to decide arbitrability. Under *First Options*, when it comes to the topic of arbitrating arbitrability, the presumption is against arbitration. In the 2010 case of *Rent-A-Center, West, Inc. v. Jackson*, the Supreme Court found that explicit contractual language stating that an arbitrator "shall have exclusive authority to resolve any dispute relating to the interpretation, applicability, enforceability or formation of this Agreement" was sufficient to overcome that presumption and demonstrate that the parties had agreed to arbitrate arbitrability.

Another issue relating to the scope of arbitrability involves class arbitration. Although the prototypical image of an arbitration proceeding involves a relatively small number of parties on each side, arbitration can also be used in a class context. A series of decisions over the past decade-plus have restricted the circumstances under which courts will permit class arbitration.

In *Stolt-Nielsen S.A. v. AnimalFeeds International Corp.*,[21] the Court held that where an arbitration clause was silent as to classwide arbitration, the parties could not be compelled to submit to classwide arbitration. In so holding, the Court noted "just some of the fundamental changes brought about by the shift from bilateral arbitration to class-action arbitration." These included that (a) class arbitration "no longer resolves a single dispute … but instead resolves many disputes between hundreds or perhaps thousands of parties"; (b) the "presumption of privacy and confidentiality" is not present; (c) class arbitration "adjudicates the rights of absent parties as well"; and (d) the "commercial stakes" are far higher.

In *AT&T Mobility LLC v. Concepcion*,[22] the parties' agreement explicitly waived the right to class arbitration, which directly conflicted with a state law effectively barring such waivers by declaring them unconscionable. How did the Supreme Court address the interplay between the parties' agreement, state law, and the federal presumption in favor of arbitrability?

---

21 559 U.S. 662 (2010).

22 563 U.S. 333 (2011).

> The overarching purpose of the FAA, evident in the text of §§ 2, 3, and 4, is to ensure the enforcement of arbitration agreements according to their terms so as to facilitate streamlined proceedings. Requiring the availability of classwide arbitration interferes with fundamental attributes of arbitration and thus creates a scheme inconsistent with the FAA.

*Concepcion* thus touches on several principles. One principle, explicitly stated, is this: State laws that conflict with the FAA are preempted—a principle that proceeds straightforwardly from the Supremacy Clause of the Constitution. But this raises the question of why, precisely, a state law barring class arbitration waivers conflicts with the FAA. Is it because the FAA ensures that parties' arbitration agreements will be enforced as written, including with respect to the type of arbitration proceeding, without undue interference from state law? Or because the FAA itself elevates a specific type of arbitration proceeding—individual, not classwide—as presumptively valid? Or is it both? The language of *Concepcion*, citing both the "enforcement of arbitration agreements according to their terms" as well as the "fundamental attributes of arbitration," suggests it might be both.

Subsequently, in *Lamps Plus, Inc. v. Varela*,[23] the Supreme Court addressed whether classwide arbitration was permissible when the parties' agreement did not unambiguously provide for it. The Court began with the principle that arbitration "is a matter of consent" and then discussed whether consent could be inferred from ambiguity. The answer, according to the Court, was no. Because of the "crucial differences" between individual and class arbitration, as identified in *Stolt-Nielsen*, the Court found that there was a presumption that parties would not agree to "sacrifice[] the principal advantage of arbitration" without clear evidence of that agreement. The majority decision did not cite the legislative history of the FAA or the understanding of arbitration at the time the FAA was drafted, although one can imagine buttressing the Court's presumption against class arbitration by arguing that class arbitration was not common at the time of the FAA's enactment.

The nature of arbitration proceedings—what types of disputes are suitable for arbitration—is an inquiry that has given rise to another line of cases dealing with an important question: When, if ever, can parties waive their right to pursue statutory claims in litigation and agree to pursue them in arbitration instead?

---

23 139 S. Ct. 1407 (2019).

An early case addressing this was *Wilko v. Swan*.[24] There, a customer brought claims in court under federal securities law against a securities brokerage firm; the brokerage firm argued that these claims must be referred to arbitration under the agreements between the customer and the firm. The Supreme Court found the arbitration agreements unenforceable citing, among other things, the possibility that arbitrators may not be qualified to interpret the applicable law; the fact that arbitrators could in this case issue a decision without adequately explaining their findings; and the difficulty in reviewing and vacating a deficient arbitral award. This, to the Court, went against Congress's intent in "enact[ing] the Securities Act to protect the rights of investors."

*Wilko* survived for several decades, but it was overturned in the late 1980s. First came *Shearson/American Express v. McMahon*,[25] which undercut the rationale for *Wilko* without expressly overruling it. The *McMahon* case addressed a pair of federal statutes (the Exchange Act and RICO) but began the analysis of whether claims arising under those statutes could be arbitrated with the FAA:

> The [FAA], standing alone, therefore mandates enforcement of agreements to arbitrate statutory claims. Like any statutory directive, the [FAA's] mandate may be overridden by a contrary congressional command. The burden is on the party opposing arbitration, however, to show that Congress intended to preclude a waiver of judicial remedies for the statutory rights at issue. …
>
> To defeat application of the [FAA] in this case, therefore, the McMahons must demonstrate that Congress intended to make an exception to the [FAA] for claims arising under RICO and the Exchange Act, an intention discernible from the text, history, or purposes of the statute.

Under this analysis, therefore, the question did not begin with Congress's intent in creating the statute under which the claim was brought (as in *Wilko*); it began with the FAA's presumption in favor of the enforcement of arbitration agreements. Citing *McMahon*, the Court explicitly overruled *Wilko* two years later.[26] Since that time, the Court has consistently held that federal statutory claims can be arbitrated in the absence of statutory language precluding arbitration.[27]

---

24 346 U.S. 427 (1953).

25 482 U.S. 220 (1987).

26 *See* Rodriguez de Quijas v. Shearson/American Express, Inc., 490 U.S. 477 (1989).

27 *See, e.g.*, Epic Sys. Corp. v. Lewis, 138 S. Ct. 1612 (2018) (Fair Labor Standards Act); CompuCredit Corp. v. Greenwood, 565 U.S. 95 (2012) (Credit Repair Organizations

## 3 Enforcing the Agreement and Intervening in the Arbitration Process

Given the disputes over consent and scope discussed above, it is not surprising that courts will often encounter questions relating to arbitration when parties dispute whether arbitration is appropriate. If one party asks a court to enforce an arbitration agreement, and the other party argues that the dispute belongs in court, what procedures apply? What latitude do courts have to allow the dispute to proceed in a judicial forum instead of an arbitral forum? And what latitude do courts have to become involved in ongoing arbitration proceedings?

The text of the FAA provides a relatively straightforward answer to the question of whether courts must order a dispute to arbitration if a valid arbitration agreement exists, or if they merely may do so. In *Dean Witter Reynolds Inc. v. Byrd*,[28] the Court found that courts have no discretion to refrain from enforcing a valid arbitration agreement, noting that the FAA uses the imperative "shall" in the relevant statutory provisions.

In some cases, of course, a court may find that an arbitration agreement is invalid or does not apply to a particular dispute, and may allow a litigation to proceed in court even if one side has sought to compel arbitration instead. The losing party—that is, the party that unsuccessfully argued the dispute should be arbitrated—has a right to an interlocutory appeal.[29] Does the litigation proceed during the pendency of the appeal? Or must the litigation be stayed until the appeal is decided? It was not until 2023 when this issue was decided, in *Coinbase, Inc. v. Bielski*,[30] with the Court ruling that a stay of litigation is mandatory when a party takes an interlocutory appeal from a denial of a motion to compel arbitration.

Another recent development in the Supreme Court's ongoing shaping of arbitration law in the United States came in 2022 and related to foreign arbitral proceedings. U.S. courts have statutory authority to assist foreign or international tribunals in collecting evidence located within the jurisdiction of the U.S. courts. In *ZF Automotive U.S., Inc. v. Luxshare, Ltd.*,[31] the Court addressed whether an international commercial arbitration proceeding is the type of "foreign or international tribunal" that U.S. courts are empowered to assist

Act); Gilmer v. Interstate/Johnson Lane Corp., 500 U.S. 20 (1991) (Age Discrimination in Employment Act).

28 470 U.S. 213 (1985).

29 *See* 9 U.S.C. § 16.

30 143 S. Ct. 1915 (2023).

31 142 S. Ct. 2078 (2022).

pursuant to 28 U.S.C. §1782, which permits U.S. district courts to order testimony or production of evidence for "for use in a proceeding in a foreign or international tribunal." The Court analyzed this question with respect to two proceedings: one before a commercial arbitration panel and one before an ad hoc investor-state arbitration panel. The answer shed light not only on the role of U.S. courts in the broader international community but also on the nature of arbitration proceedings in general:

> These consolidated cases require us to decide whether private adjudicatory bodies count as "foreign or international tribunals." They do not. The statute reaches only governmental or intergovernmental adjudicative bodies, and neither of the arbitral panels involved in these cases fits that bill. …
>
> [With respect to the commercial arbitration panel,] [p]rivate parties agreed in a private contract that DIS, a private dispute-resolution organization, would arbitrate any disputes between them. … By default, DIS panels operate under DIS rules, just like panels of any other private arbitration organization operate under private arbitral rules. The panels are formed by the parties—with each party selecting one arbitrator and those two arbitrators choosing a third. No government is involved in creating the DIS panel or prescribing its procedures. This adjudicative body therefore does not qualify as a governmental body. …
>
> [With respect to the investor-state dispute, a] sovereign is on one side of the dispute, and the option to arbitrate is contained in an international treaty rather than a private contract. [But] a body does not possess governmental authority just because nations agreed in a treaty to submit to arbitration before it. The relevant question is whether the nations intended that the ad hoc panel exercise governmental authority. And here, all indications are that they did not.

The holding of *ZF Automotive U.S.* means that the power of U.S. courts to assist in foreign and international litigation does not extend to international commercial arbitration. This reflects the broader principles that when a dispute is subject to arbitration rather than litigation, U.S. law as promulgated by the Supreme Court emphasizes the separation between the two forums. After the arbitral tribunal has rendered an award, however, the judiciary takes on a greater role once again, as discussed in the next section.

## 4 After the Arbitral Award Is Rendered

The FAA provides a mechanism for victorious parties in an arbitration to seek judicial confirmation of an award, but it also provides recourse for the losing side. Specifically, the FAA allows a party to seek vacatur, modification or correction of an arbitral award.

This raises the question of the grounds on which an arbitral award may be vacated, modified, or corrected. Take the case of vacatur. Section 10 of the FAA[32] lists four specific grounds for vacatur:

(1) where the award was procured by corruption, fraud, or undue means;
(2) where there was evident partiality or corruption in the arbitrators, or either of them;
(3) where the arbitrators were guilty of misconduct in refusing to postpone the hearing, upon sufficient cause shown, or in refusing to hear evidence pertinent and material to the controversy; or of any other misbehavior by which the rights of any party have been prejudiced; or
(4) where the arbitrators exceeded their powers, or so imperfectly executed them that a mutual, final, and definite award upon the subject matter submitted was not made.

The text of the FAA is clear enough, therefore, that an arbitral award rendered as a result of bribes being paid to the arbitrators would be subject to vacatur. But what about situations that do not fall within these enumerated reasons for vacatur? Consider, for example, if the arbitral panel misunderstood an applicable legal principle and, based on this mistake of law, rendered a decision that was incorrect under a correct interpretation of the law. If a trial court did this, it would surely be reversed by an appellate court. But does the same principle apply to an arbitral tribunal? Or does the interest in the finality of an arbitral award override this?

The Supreme Court, in 2008, addressed whether parties by contract could expand the grounds for vacatur (as well as for modification of an award under Section 11 of the FAA) by contract, or if the FAA provided the exclusive such grounds. The case was *Hall Street Associates, L.L.C. v. Mattel, Inc.*[33] The Court ruled that parties cannot by contract expand the scope of review of an arbitral award allowed under the FAA. In so doing, it noted that the provisions

32 9 U.S.C. § 10.
33 552 U.S. 576 (2008).

"substantiat[e] a national policy favoring arbitration with just the limited review needed to maintain arbitration's essential virtue of resolving disputes straightaway," and that "[a]ny other reading opens the door to the full-bore legal and evidentiary appeals."

What *Hall Street* did not do, though, was define exactly the scope of review permitted by the FAA itself. Recall the hypothetical posed a couple paragraphs above—whether a court has the power to overturn an arbitral award founded on an egregious mistake of law. Certainly, in light of *Hall Street*, parties cannot *confer* that power on a court in their agreement to arbitrate. But there is still an open question as to whether the FAA itself permits that type of review. The various federal circuit courts have come to divergent conclusions as to whether, in the words of the case law, an arbitrator's "manifest disregard of the law" constitutes an appropriate ground for vacatur.[34] And the Supreme Court has explicitly left the question open, at least for now.[35]

Regardless of how *Hall Street* is applied, finality is an important virtue in arbitration. How far does that finality extend? If an arbitral award is final, does this mean it has claim preclusive or issue preclusive effect in other proceedings? The Supreme Court addressed this question in *McDonald v. West Branch*.[36] This case involved a lawsuit brought under Section 1983,[37] the federal statute providing a cause of action for certain civil rights violations. The arbitral award at issue came in a labor arbitration pursuant to a collective bargaining agreement, a distinct context with nuances not applicable to other types of arbitration that have been at issue in many of the Supreme Court's arbitration cases. Nevertheless, the analysis sheds further light on the Court's understanding of the nature of arbitration in the dispute-resolution system.

Ultimately, the Supreme Court determined that an arbitration award did not have preclusive effect in a subsequent Section 1983 action. The Court cited three particular considerations: first, that an arbitrator may not "have the expertise required to resolve the complex legal questions" at issue; second, that the arbitrator would be obligated to enforce the collective bargaining agreement,

34 *Compare, e.g.*, Schwartz v. Merrill Lynch & Co., 665 F.3d 444, 451–52 (2d Cir. 2011) ("This Court, in the wake of Hall Street Associates, 'concluded that manifest disregard remains a valid ground for vacating arbitration awards,' and we have continued to recognize that standard as a valid ground in the wake of the Supreme Court's decision in Stolt-Nielsen." (internal citations omitted)), *with* Frazier v. Citifinancial Corp., LLC, 604 F.3d 1313, 1324 (11th Cir. 2010) (finding manifest disregard standard "no longer valid" after *Hall Street Associates*).

35 Stolt-Nielsen S.A. v. AnimalFeeds Int'l Corp., 559 U.S. 662, 672 n.3 (2010).

36 466 U.S. 284 (1984).

37 42 U.S.C. § 1983.

rather than applicable legislation, in the event of a conflict; and third, that arbitration may not have the same procedural protections as litigation.

It is interesting to note that the reasoning in *McDonald* at least echoes the reasoning in *Wilko*, discussed above, although *McDonald* did not rely on *Wilko*. And perhaps because the preclusive effect of an arbitral award does not directly affect the availability of arbitration in the first place, unlike in *Wilko*, the *McDonald* principles remain relevant and valid in what the Court apparently sees as a case-by-case inquiry. A year after *McDonald*, the Court emphasized that "courts may directly and effectively protect federal interests by determining the preclusive effect to be given to an arbitration proceeding" and that "in framing preclusion rules in this context, courts shall take into account the federal interests warranting protection."[38]

## 5 Concluding Notes

The preceding pages are, of course, only a sample of the Supreme Court's decisions in the arbitration field. Of that sample that makes up this chapter, each issue addressed by the Court could merit its own chapter. And as the citation of cases from 2022 and 2023 demonstrates, this is still an evolving area of law, with many loose ends yet to be tied up. (And, of course, many questions have been addressed, with great nuance and variation, by the lower federal courts, making a thorough study of applicable law beyond Supreme Court rulings a necessity for effective practice.)

Nevertheless, certain key themes are clear even from these few examples and will remain central to the Court's still-developing jurisprudence—among these, the FAA's presumption in favor of arbitration and the Court's sensitivity to the unique benefits (but also limitations) of arbitration. Also clear is the sheer reach of the Court's decisions in this area. Arbitration may be a creation of private contracts between private parties; and it may be governed in part by "ordinary state-law principles"; but the Supreme Court nevertheless has exerted and continues to exert an enormous influence on arbitration law and practice in the United States.

---

38 Dean Witter Reynolds Inc. v. Byrd, 470 U.S. 213, 223 (1985).

CHAPTER 4

# *Prima Paint Corporation v. Flood & Conklin Mfg. Company* (1967)

*R. Doak Bishop and Marcio Vasconcellos*

## 1 Introduction

PRIMA PAINT CORPORATION VERSUS FLOOD & CONKLIN MANUFACTURING COMPANY ("*Prima Paint v. Flood & Conklin Mfg. Co.*") is one of the foundational arbitration cases by which the U.S. SUPREME COURT helped define and shape the law of arbitration in the United States. This case and its progeny were paramount to the definition and application of the "separability principle" in the United States. This chapter will begin with a primer on the "separability principle" in the United States, as applied under the UNITED STATES FEDERAL ARBITRATION ACT ("*FAA*"). Next, this chapter will summarize the factual background of the case, the parties' positions, the Court's opinion, and the dissent. Finally, this chapter will address the impact of this paradigmatic decision on U.S. arbitration law and practice and its main takeaways. The "separability principle" is an essential concept to arbitration practice and the road to understanding it in full necessarily goes through *Prima Paint v. Flood & Conklin Mfg. Co.*

## 2 A Primer on the "Separability Principle"

The "separability principle" or "severability principle" or "separability doctrine"[1] may be described as a legal fiction[2] according to which the arbitration agreement in a contract is treated as being autonomous from the main contract of which it is a part.[3] Another approach to understanding the same phenomenon

1 In other legal systems this concept is referred to as the autonomy of the arbitration clause (*l'autonomie de la clause compromissoire*).

2 Jan Paulsson, 'Separability demystified', *in The Idea of Arbitration* (Oxford University Press, 2013), ch. 3, sec. 1(c).

3 *See* Nigel Blackaby, Constantine Partasides, et al., *Redfern and Hunter on International Arbitration (Seventh Edition)*, (© Kluwer Law International; Oxford University Press 2023), ¶2.107.

 | DOI:10.1163/9789004715820_005

is the analysis that there are in fact two separate contracts: *the main contract*, which contains the commercial obligations of the parties; and a *secondary contract*, which contains the obligation to arbitrate disputes arising from the main contract.[4] Under either prism, the result is identical and the agreement to arbitrate survives the breach or termination of the main contract.[5]

While this may be a "fantastic" outcome, to borrow from Justice Black's dissent, it is a logical and indeed necessary solution to a potential attempt to defeat the agreement to arbitrate. Imagine a hypothetical scenario in which one of the parties, having agreed to arbitrate, no longer wishes to honor that agreement, and instead wishes to litigate in some other forum. Worse, imagine a hypothetical scenario in which having participated in the arbitration and lost, the disgruntled loser now wants to avoid the outcome of the arbitration altogether. The easiest approach would be to argue that the principal contract was void or invalid (for example, because the party did not sign it, or the person who signed it lacked capacity or authority) and that its invalidity would result in the invalidity of the agreement to arbitrate contained therein, forcing the parties to go to court.[6]

The first court to resolve this problem was the French Court of Cassation in *Société Gosset v. Société Carapelli* (1963), which ruled that the agreement to arbitrate is autonomous from the main contract, and therefore cannot be affected by the invalidity of the latter.[7] This same solution has been adopted in the United Kingdom in *Harbour Assurance v Kansa General International Insurance*[8] (1993) and in the United States in *Prima Paint v. Flood & Conklin Mfg. Co.* (1967). This is the context in which this essential decision is inserted and at its core is the fundamental principle of separability.

---

4 *See* Nigel Blackaby, Constantine Partasides, et al., *Redfern and Hunter on International Arbitration (Seventh Edition)*, (© Kluwer Law International; Oxford University Press 2023), ¶2.109.

5 It is possible for contracting parties to enter into an agreement to arbitrate that is a standalone document, physically separate from the main contract. Perhaps the visualization of a separate instrument titled "agreement to arbitrate" may be helpful in internalizing the doctrine of separability. However, the main point of the separability doctrine is that it will still treat the agreement to arbitrate as an autonomous undertaking from the main contract even if it is included in the same document.

6 This is what the late, great professor Emmanuel Gaillard described as one of the "*Seven Dirty Tricks in International Arbitration*," lecture available at: https://www.youtube.com/results?search_query=dirty+tricks+arbitration.

7 *Société Gosset v. Société Carapelli*, Judgment of May 7, 1963, Cass. Civ. 1re, Fr. [1963] D. Jur. 545.

8 *Harbour Assurance v Kansa General International Insurance* [1993] 1 Lloyd's Rep 455.

## 3 The Case

### 3.1 *Background of the Case*

On October 7, 1964, FLOOD & CONKLIN MANUFACTURING COMPANY, a New Jersey corporation ("*Flood & Conklin*"), entered into a consulting agreement ("*Consulting Agreement*") with PRIMA PAINT CORPORATION, a Maryland corporation ("*Prima Paint*").[9] The Consulting Agreement was executed less than three weeks after the execution of another contract by which Prima Paint purchased the entirety of Flood & Conklin's business ("*Purchase Agreement*").[10] The Consulting Agreement provided for a period of six years in which Flood & Conklin would furnish advice and consultation "in connection with the formulae, manufacturing operations, sales and servicing of Prima Trade Sales accounts."[11] These services were to be performed personally by Flood & Conklin's chairman, Mr. Jerome K. Jelin, except in the event of his death or disability. Flood & Conklin also undertook not to compete with Prima Paint.[12] The agreement contemplated the possibility that Prima Paint might encounter financial difficulties, including bankruptcy, but made no reference to possible financial problems.[13] Essential to the analysis here, the Consulting Agreement included a broad arbitration clause, which read in part:[14]

> 8. Arbitration. Any controversy or claim arising out of or relating to this Agreement, or the breach thereof, shall be settled by arbitration in the City of New York, in accordance with the rules then obtaining of the American Arbitration Association, by three arbitrators, one of whom shall be an attorney-at-law and one of whom shall be a certified public accountant, and judgment upon the award rendered may be entered in any Court having jurisdiction thereof. The costs of arbitration shall be shared equally by Prima & F&C.

Prima Paint was obligated to make the first payment to Flood & Conklin on September 1, 1965, but no payment was made.[15] Instead., Prima Paint made the payment 17 days later into an escrow account alleging that Flood & Conklin

9 *Prima Paint Corp. v. Flood & Conklin Mfg. Co.*, 388 U.S. 395, 397, (1967) ("*Prima Paint v. Flood & Conklin Mfg. Co.*").

10 *Prima Paint v. Flood & Conklin Mfg. Co.*, at 397.

11 *Prima Paint v. Flood & Conklin Mfg. Co.*, at 397.

12 *Prima Paint v. Flood & Conklin Mfg. Co.*, at 397.

13 *Prima Paint v. Flood & Conklin Mfg. Co.*, at 397.

14 *Prima Paint v. Flood & Conklin Mfg. Co.*, 1967 WL 113916 (U.S.), 6–7 (U.S., 2004) ("Brief for the Petitioner").

15 *Prima Paint v. Flood & Conklin Mfg. Co.*, at 398.

had breached several provisions of both the Consulting Agreement and the earlier purchase agreement by failing to disclose its state of insolvency.[16] Prima Paint's contention was that Flood & Conklin had fraudulently represented that it was solvent and able to perform its contractual obligations, but the company was in fact insolvent. Prima Paint further alleged that, at the time of contracting, Flood & Conklin already intended to file a petition under Chapter 11 of the BANKRUPTCY ACT. Flood & Conklin filed such a petition on October 14, 1964, one week after the contract had been signed.[17]

In response to Prima Paint depositing the funds in escrow, on October 25, 1964 Flood & Conklin filed a "notice of intention to arbitrate" and, in response to that "notice," on November 12, 1964 Prima Paint filed suit in the United States District Court for the Southern District of New York seeking "rescission of the consulting agreement on the basis of alleged fraudulent inducement."[18] The parties filed cross-motions from Prima Paint to enjoin Flood & Conklin from proceeding with the arbitration and to stay the court action pending arbitration.[19] The arguments of the parties centered on the issue of whether fraud in the inducement of the Consulting Agreement was an issue for the arbitrators or for the District Court.[20]

The District Court sided with Flood & Conklin and granted the motion to stay the action pending arbitration, holding that a charge of fraud in the inducement of a contract containing an arbitration clause as broad as the one contained in the Consulting Agreement was a question for the arbitrators and not for the Court.[21] The Court of Appeals for the Second Circuit[22] dismissed Prima Paint's appeal and held that because the contract in question evidenced a transaction involving interstate commerce, in accordance with its controlling precedents, "a claim of fraud in the inducement of the contract generally—as opposed to the arbitration clause itself—is for the arbitrators and not for the courts; and that this rule—one of 'national substantive law'—governs even in the face of a contrary state rule."[23]

As addressed in more detail below, the U.S. Supreme Court took the case in order to resolve a circuit split on the issue of whether a claim of fraud in the

16 *Prima Paint v. Flood & Conklin Mfg. Co.*, at 398.

17 *Prima Paint v. Flood & Conklin Mfg. Co.*, at 398.

18 *Prima Paint v. Flood & Conklin Mfg. Co.*, at 398.

19 *Prima Paint v. Flood & Conklin Mfg. Co.*, at 399.

20 *Prima Paint v. Flood & Conklin Mfg. Co.*, at 399. Section 3.2, below, will address the parties' contentions in more detail.

21 *Prima Paint v. Flood & Conklin Mfg. Co.*, at 399.

22 The Second Circuit exercises federal appellate jurisdiction over the federal courts sitting in the states of Connecticut, New York, and Vermont.

23 *Prima Paint v. Flood & Conklin Mfg. Co.*, at 399–400.

inducement of a contract as a whole that includes an arbitration clause is an issue for courts or for arbitrators. While the Second Circuit concluded that the issue of fraud in the inducement of the contract as a whole was an issue for the arbitrators to decide, the Court of Appeals for the First Circuit[24] decided that the question of "severability" of the arbitration agreement from the contract of which it is a part "is one of state law, and that where a State regards such a clause as inseparable, a claim of fraud in the inducement must be decided by the court."[25] The U.S. Supreme Court then had to determine who decides a challenge to the contract as a whole and whether Congress intended to control the issue under the FAA or whether Congress intended for states to regulate this matter on an individual basis.

Taking a step back from the mantras the readers may have recited in arbitration classes around the globe, the question is a valid and sensible one: *how can the arbitration agreement survive if the entire contract, which includes the arbitration clause, has been procured by fraud?* The answer, while perhaps counterintuitive, is equally sensible: *it survives because it must, otherwise arbitration becomes essentially impossible because every disgruntled party can simply allege fraud as an excuse to circumvent the agreement to arbitrate.* A less cynical answer, which is perhaps even more sensible, is that a case having been referred to arbitration does not mean an arbitrator will become an accessory to fraud. If indeed the contract was procured by fraud, that is an argument that will be made to the arbitral tribunal, who may agree or disagree with the party making that allegation.

Nevertheless, it is against this background that the U.S. Supreme Court granted certiorari in *Prima Paint v. Flood & Conklin Mfg. Co.* to decide which Circuit was correct: the Second Circuit, the First Circuit (joined by the Ninth Circuit and the Sixth Circuit), or neither.

### 3.2 *Issue and Parties' Contentions*

At issue in *Prima Paint* was whether a federal court or an arbitrator should resolve a claim of fraud in the inducement of a contract that contains a broad arbitration clause governed by the FAA.[26] As discussed above, broad arbitration

24 The First Circuit exercises federal appellate jurisdiction over the federal courts sitting in the states of Maine, Massachusetts, New Hampshire, Puerto Rico and Rhode Island.

25 *Prima Paint v. Flood & Conklin Mfg. Co.*, at 402–03.

26 The elements of a claim for fraudulent inducement are typically articulated in some version of: (1) a false representation of material fact, (2) known by the utterer to be untrue, (3) made with the intention of inducing reliance and forbearance from further inquiry, (4) that is justifiably relied upon, and (5) results in damages. For examples under New York law, *see Schumaker v. Mather*, 133 N.Y. 590, 595, 30 N.E. 755 (1892) and *MBIA Ins.*

clauses are those that, like the clause in *Prima Paint v. Flood & Conklin Mfg. Co.*, refer to "[a]ny controversy or claim arising out of or relating to"[27] the agreement for arbitration. Before deciding the fraud issue, the Court first had to address the issue of whether the Consulting Agreement was indeed governed by the FAA, and if it was, whether the FAA requires that this issue be resolved under federal law or state law.[28]

Prima Paint argued that its claim for fraud in the inducement of the Consulting Agreement, despite containing an arbitration clause, should be referred to federal courts, not arbitration, for four main reasons:

1. *First*, the Consulting Agreement was not a contract "evidencing a transaction involving interstate commerce" because it did not contemplate "substantial interstate activity."[29] Instead, Prima Paint argued that the Consulting Agreement was merely an agreement for personal or managerial services, and therefore the FAA was inapplicable.[30]
2. *Second*, when jurisdiction arises solely by virtue of diversity of citizenship, federal courts are required to apply state substantive law, and therefore the Second Circuit's declaration that the FAA created a "national substantive law" under the maritime and commerce powers of Congress, which also applies to diversity cases, was flawed.[31] Prima Paint also noted that the Ninth Circuit, the Sixth Circuit and the First Circuit all contradict the Second Circuit's position on this issue.[32]
3. *Third*, an arbitration clause in a contract does not exist as a separable, special agreement and that whether parties intended to arbitrate are matters to be decided under the applicable state rules. Prima Paint's position would essentially negate the doctrine of separability.[33]
4. *Finally*, before referring the parties to arbitration, courts should rule on the validity of that undertaking on the basis of traditional contract law principles, such as equitable rescission, cancellation, and unclean hands. This, in petitioner's view, would have resulted in the conclusion that when the parties have not assented to all the promises as a single whole,

---

*Corp. v Credit Suisse Sec. (USA) LLC*, 32 Misc 3d 758, 773 [Sup Ct 2011], on reconsideration, 33 Misc 3d 1208(A) [Sup Ct 2011], revd, 102 AD3d 488 [1st Dept 2013].

27 *Prima Paint v. Flood & Conklin Mfg. Co.*, at 398.

28 While there is a lot to unpack regarding these issues, the below analysis of the Court's opinion in item 3.3 includes explanations and additional contextualization.

29 Brief for the Petitioner, at 9–11.

30 Brief for the Petitioner, at 12.

31 Brief for the Petitioner, at 12–13.

32 Brief for the Petitioner, at 13.

33 Brief for the Petitioner, at 23.

there would be no bargain, and all undertakings (including the arbitration agreement) would be voided.[34]

Flood & Conklin took the contrary position, that the dispute should be referred to arbitration pursuant to the broad arbitration agreement contained in the Consulting Agreement. Essential to its argument was that "no charge is made by Prima [Paint] that the agreement of the parties to arbitrate disputes, referred to above, was fraudulently induced."[35] Respondent also advanced four arguments:

1. *First*, Congress created a "new body of federal substantive law affecting the validity and interpretation of arbitration agreements."[36] This new body of federal substantive law established a federal right to enforce arbitration agreements in contracts involving "maritime transactions" and "transactions involving interstate commerce."[37] Crucial to Flood & Conklin's position was the argument that Congress has "plenary power over interstate commerce" and therefore is empowered by the U.S. Constitution to regulate interstate commerce through the FAA.[38]
2. *Second*, the interpretation and effect of an arbitration provision governed by the FAA should be decided under federal law, not state contract law, which would result in "even greater frustration of Congressional intent than would a decision that the [FAA] has no application to diversity cases."[39] Flood & Conklin's position was that federal courts will apply federal law, and that "if Congress intended no more than a federal law which would defer to local law, the [FAA] would have been meaningless."[40]
3. *Third*, a claim of fraudulent inducement of the principal contract was an issue "referable to the arbitrators if encompassed by the particular arbitration agreement."[41] Flood & Conklin's position was that the broad arbitration agreement entered into by the parties is broad enough to encompass disputes involving fraudulent inducement,[42] and that the nature of the remedy sought should not affect the validity of the

34 Brief for the Petitioner, at 26.
35 Brief for the Petitioner, at 6.
36 *Prima Paint v. Flood & Conklin Mfg. Co.*, 1967 WL 113917 (U.S.), 16 (U.S., 2004) ("*Brief for the Respondent*").
37 Brief for the Respondent, at 13–15.
38 Brief for the Respondent, at 16.
39 Brief for the Respondent, at 21–22.
40 Brief for the Respondent, at 22.
41 Brief for the Respondent, at 23.
42 Brief for the Respondent, at 25.

arbitration agreement because arbitrators are free to grant the same remedies that Prima Paint seeks from a court.[43]

4. *Finally*, and in any event, Prima Paint failed to demonstrate any substance supporting its claim of fraud, did "not come forward with any facts which would give substance either to its charge of fraud or to its request for rescission,"[44] and, therefore, waived any right it may have had to rescind the Consulting Agreement.[45]

In addition to the positions of the parties, the American Arbitration Association ("AAA") filed an amicus brief in support of Flood & Conklin's position in favor of arbitration.[46] In essence, the AAA advanced two arguments:

*First*, the FAA enacted "substantive" federal law meant to apply to an arbitration agreement contained in a "contract evidencing a transaction involving interstate commerce" when jurisdiction exists solely by diversity of citizenship.[47] According to the AAA's interpretation of the legislative history of the FAA, the Congressional intent was to provide a "new remedy"[48] in an area of "congressional substantive power."[49]

*Second*, the FAA requires arbitration of fraud in the inducement disputes under a broad clause, such as the one contained in *Prima Paint v. Flood & Conklin Mfg. Co.*, because the extent of the parties' agreement to arbitrate is contained in the arbitration clause.[50] The AAA emphasized that "what is relevant is that the parties intended to exclude the judiciary, for reasons which apply equally as well to 'fraud in the inducement' disputes as to any others."[51]

As is pertains to the separability doctrine more directly, the AAA offered an educational explanation, which began with the premise that "unless the arbitration clause is treated as separable, a claim that the entire transaction was induced by fraud requires that the arbitration provision necessarily falls with the rest of the contract."[52] However, a rule that disregards the doctrine

43 Brief for the Respondent, at 28.

44 Brief for the Respondent, at 35.

45 Brief for the Respondent, at 37.

46 *Prima Paint v. Flood & Conklin Mfg. Co.*, 1967 WL 113919 (U.S.) (U.S., 2004) ("Brief for the Amicus Curiae").

47 Brief for the Amicus Curiae, at 4.

48 Brief for the Amicus Curiae, at 8.

49 Brief for the Amicus Curiae, at 9. At footnote 5, the AAA further noted that the FAA contained the support of 122 organizations and that a law with 'minimal impact' would not have drawn as much interest from the market, so the goal was to have a substantial impact.

50 Brief for the Amicus Curiae, at 13.

51 Brief for the Amicus Curiae, at 16–17.

52 Brief for the Amicus Curiae, at 17.

of separability "cannot be accepted" because "it inherently disregards the single fundamental question at issue," which is: "[d]id the parties intend that the dispute of fraudulent inducement be arbitrated?"[53] Of course, if the parties intended to arbitrate a dispute of fraudulent inducement, then logically the arbitration agreement would have had to survive the allegation of fraudulent inducement in order for the arbitral tribunal to have the authority to resolve that dispute.

The AAA then concluded that "the separability rule … might properly be described as a rule of legal necessity, designed to give effect to the intentions of the parties."[54]

### 3.3 *The U.S. Supreme Court's Opinion*

In a 6-3 decision, the U.S. Supreme Court held that a claim of fraud in the inducement of the contract as a whole is an issue for the arbitrators, not courts, to decide where the parties agreed to a broad arbitration clause that provides for reference of 'any controversy or claim arising out of or relating to' the agreement to arbitrate. In addition, and recognizing the contractual, voluntary nature of arbitration, the majority opinion emphasized the absence of evidence that the parties intended to withhold the issue of fraud in the inducement from the jurisdiction of the arbitral tribunal. The majority opinion may be summarized in four findings, discussed below.

*First*, the majority held that the Consulting Agreement evidenced a transaction involving interstate commerce, which triggered the application of the FAA.

This issue relates to the balance between the rights of states to regulate conduct which occurs within its borders and the rights of the federal government to regulate interstate commerce.[55] Maintaining this balance is further complicated by the fact that many states have their own arbitration statutes, which are not always identical to the federal statute on point. Pursuant to Sections 1 and 2 of the FAA, the federal statute applies to two sets of cases. First, disputes involving "maritime transactions," defined as charter parties, bills of lading of water carriers, agreements relating to wharfage, supplies furnished vessels or repairs to vessels, collisions, or any other matters in foreign commerce fall within the category of admiralty jurisdiction.[56] Second, disputes arising out

53 Brief for the Amicus Curiae, at 17–18.

54 Brief for the Amicus Curiae, at 18.

55 *See*, e.g., Lawrence Meir Friedman, *Law in America: a short history*, 10–12 (2002).

56 FAA, 9 U.S.C.A. § 1.

of contracts "evidencing a transaction involving commerce," defined as "commerce among the several States or with foreign nations."[57]

The first question the majority addressed was whether the Consulting Agreement evidenced interstate commerce and therefore triggered the application of the FAA.[58] Because Prima Paint acquired Flood & Conklin Mfg. Co., a New Jersey paint business that served at least 175 wholesale clients in a number of States and arranged for the transfer of manufacturing operations from New Jersey to Maryland, the Court concluded that the Consulting Agreement was "inextricably tied to this interstate transfer" of assets and to "the continuing operations of an interstate manufacturing and wholesaling business."[59] In fact, the majority concluded that "there could not be a clearer case of a contract evidencing a transaction in interstate commerce."[60]

*Second*, the majority held that, because of the broad arbitration agreement, a claim of fraud in the inducement of the entire contract is to be referred to arbitration rather than federal court.

The majority opinion described this as the "central issue" in this case and noted that different federal courts of appeals reached different conclusions on this issue, which triggered the U.S. Supreme Court's intervention to resolve the circuit split. The view of the Second Circuit was that, except when the parties otherwise intend, "arbitration clauses as a matter of federal law are 'separable' from the contracts in which they are embedded" and that "where no claim is made that fraud was directed to the arbitration clause itself, a broad arbitration clause will be held to encompass arbitration of the claim that the contract itself was induced by fraud."[61] In contrast, the First Circuit held that the question of 'severability' of the arbitration agreement from the contract of which it is a part "is one of state law, and that where a State regards such a clause as inseparable, a claim of fraud in the inducement must be decided by the court."[62] In other words, the Second Circuit was prepared to embrace the "separability principle" as a necessary doctrine embedded in the FAA, while the First Circuit (joined by the Ninth Circuit and the Sixth Circuit) was not.

---

57 FAA, 9 U.S.C.A. §§ 1 and 2.

58 *Prima Paint v. Flood & Conklin Mfg. Co.*, at 401.

59 *Prima Paint v. Flood & Conklin Mfg. Co.*, at 401.

60 *Prima Paint v. Flood & Conklin Mfg. Co.*, at 401.

61 *Prima Paint v. Flood & Conklin Mfg. Co.*, at 402.

62 *Prima Paint v. Flood & Conklin Mfg. Co.*, at 402–03. In addition to the First Circuit, Prima Paint cites to cases in the Ninth Circuit and the Sixth Circuit that followed the same "non-separability" approach.

Furthermore, for those cases involving "maritime transactions" and contracts "evidencing a transaction involving commerce" the majority opinion held that Section 4 of the FAA provides an "explicit answer" as to who should resolve a claim of fraud in the inducement.[63] Pursuant to Section 4 of the FAA, "[a] party aggrieved by the alleged failure, neglect, or refusal of another to arbitrate under a written agreement for arbitration may petition any United States district court which … would have jurisdiction … for an order directing that such arbitration proceed in the manner provided for in such agreement."[64] Section 4 of the FAA further states that the court, "upon being satisfied that the making of the agreement for arbitration or the failure to comply therewith is not in issue … shall make an order directing the parties to proceed to arbitration in accordance with the terms of the agreement."[65] Therefore, the court's inquiry is limited to satisfying itself that the making of the agreement to arbitrate is not at issue and, provided that is the case, directing the parties to proceed to arbitration.

The majority further analyzed the interplay between Section 4 of the FAA, which authorizes a court to issue an order compelling the parties to arbitrate their disputes, with Section 3 of the FAA, which allows a stay of litigation while the parties comply with the order compelling arbitration. Under Section 3 of the FAA, if a dispute is brought to court despite containing an arbitration agreement, once the court is "satisfied" that "the issue involved in such suit or proceeding is referable to arbitration under such an agreement," the court shall "stay the trial of the action until such arbitration has been had in accordance with the terms of the agreement, provided the applicant for the stay is not in default in proceeding with such arbitration."[66]

In reviewing Sections 3 and 4 of the FAA, the majority opinion concludes that "a federal court may consider only issues relating to the making and performance of the agreement to arbitrate" and not the making and performance of the contract as a whole.[67] The majority further held that this interpretation honors both the "plain meaning" of the FAA and the "congressional purpose" that arbitration be "speedy and not subject to delay and obstruction in the courts."[68]

---

63 *Prima Paint v. Flood & Conklin Mfg. Co.*, at 403.

64 FAA, 9 U.S.C.A. § 1.

65 FAA, 9 U.S.C.A. § 4.

66 FAA, 9 U.S.C.A. § 3.

67 *Prima Paint v. Flood & Conklin Mfg. Co.*, at 404.

68 *Prima Paint v. Flood & Conklin Mfg. Co.*, at 404.

The majority concludes that "if the claim is fraud in the inducement of the arbitration clause itself—an issue which goes to the 'making' of the agreement to arbitrate—the federal court may proceed to adjudicate it" but that the FAA "does not permit the federal court to consider claims of fraud in the inducement of the contract generally."[69] This is the most crucial finding of the *Prima Paint v. Flood & Conklin Mfg. Co.* case and the crux of the separability principle in the United States.

*Third*, the majority held that Congress may prescribe how federal courts are to conduct themselves in cases involving the FAA.

This issue relates to which rules federal courts should apply when the basis for their jurisdiction is diversity rather than federal question. By way of background, federal courts[70] in the United States base their authority on one of two grounds: diversity jurisdiction, pursuant to 28 U.S.C. § 1332(a), when the amount in controversy exceeds $75,000 and complete diversity of citizenship exists (*i.e.*, no plaintiff and defendant are domiciled in the same state, which includes foreign parties); or federal question jurisdiction, pursuant to 28 U.S. Code § 1331, when the cause of action arises under federal law.[71] For cases arising under federal question jurisdiction, the federal rules of decision that give rise to the federal question will apply. However, for cases involving diversity jurisdiction, federal courts are required to follow state rules of decision in matters which are "substantive" rather than "procedural" or where the matter is "outcome determinative."

For a more complete discussion on this issue, the authors refer the readers to the case of *Erie R. Co. v. Tompkins*,[72] which established the "Erie Doctrine," a

---

69 *Prima Paint v. Flood & Conklin Mfg. Co.*, at 403–04.

70 In the United States, state courts are typically referred to as courts of "general jurisdiction," meaning that state courts can hear almost any state of federal claim, with some exceptions. Federal courts, conversely, are typically referred to as courts of "limited jurisdiction," meaning that federal courts can hear cases only of a particular subject matter.

71 This is significant because in the United States contract law is generally a matter of state law, not federal law. There is an argument to be made in favor of federalizing contract law and developing more uniform federal law such as the Uniform Commercial Code, but these efforts do not negate the overwhelming conclusion that in the United States contract law is primarily a matter of state, not federal law. As a result, not often will a commercial contract give rise to a federal question that would permit the exercise of jurisdiction via 28 U.S. Code § 1331, and diversity jurisdiction is likely to continue to be the primary cause for the exercise of federal oversight over commercial contracts that contain arbitration clauses. Therefore, what law governs and how the process unfolds in diversity jurisdiction cases was (and continues to be) essential to the development of arbitration law in the United States.

72 *Erie R. Co. v. Tompkins*, 304 U.S. 64, 58 S. Ct. 817, 82 L. Ed. 1188 (1938).

set of rules to determine which rules of decision federal courts are required to apply in diversity jurisdiction cases. While an in-depth discussion of the Erie Doctrine exceeds the scope of this commentary, some context is helpful. *Erie* came about at a moment when U.S. courts were concerned with discouraging "forum-shopping" between state and federal courts and avoiding the "inequitable administration of the laws." These goals, which guide the application of *Erie*, require the same outcome for the same set of facts regardless of whether it is adjudicated by a federal or state court. The U.S. Supreme Court resolved this problem by requiring federal courts to follow state rules of decision in matters which are "substantive" rather than "procedural," or where the matter is "outcome determinative."[73] Easier said than done.[74]

This discussion is significant because *Prima Paint v. Flood & Conklin Mfg. Co.* was in federal court solely on the basis of diversity of citizenship, which would ordinarily result in the application of state law as opposed to federal law. However, as discussed in the first finding of the majority opinion above, the Court concluded that this was a case involving interstate commerce, and therefore that the FAA governed the question of whether the arbitration clause is separate from the underlying contract of which it forms a part. Therefore, because the underlying dispute involves interstate commerce, the FAA governs, and Congress may prescribe how federal courts are to conduct themselves in this instance. This is a technical argument that is closely linked to the majority's first finding on the applicability of the FAA.

Justice White, who joined the majority, asked counsel for Prima Paint at oral argument[75] what he would think "*if the state statute said arbitration agreements shall not be enforceable*" and whether in that circumstance counsel would still support the argument that this is a matter for state law rather than federal law. Counsel replied that he "would say that, that is a policy of the state and its citizens." Perhaps unbeknownst to counsel at the time, that response may have been the *coup de grâce* to a Court that was already convinced of the utility and necessity of arbitration. Conversely, counsel for amicus curiae AAA provided a succinct and compelling conclusion to the issue:

> The doctrine of separability is one of constructive intent that must be followed, and we hardly recommend that the view endorsed by [the Second

73 *See*, e.g., *Guaranty Trust Co. v. York*, 326 U.S. 99 (1945).

74 As moot court competitions so often explore, the distinction between "substantive" and "procedural" is seldom portrayed in bright lines and the Erie Doctrine has become a notorious headache among U.S. students.

75 Oral argument available at: https://supreme.justia.com/cases/federal/us/388/395/.

> Circuit], if commercial arbitration is to exist in this country the way the businessmen desire it. It is a voluntary contract between two parties, to go to arbitration. There is no requirement but they put this clause in, they may narrow it in any way they like, we're not saying to the Court to use this clause or interpret it this way if it's narrow, only where the party is saying, as we claim they say here, as if it was said in *haec verba* the parties intend to arbitrate everything including fraudulent inducement of the contract, but not fraudulent inducement of the arbitration clause.

Finally, the majority held that Prima Paint advanced no argument of fraud in the inducement of the agreement to arbitrate, only that the alleged fraud induced Prima Paint to enter into the agreement as a whole. This issue brings all previous conclusions from the Court together in that: (i) federal courts are bound to apply rules enacted by Congress with respect to matters involving interstate commerce; (ii) Congress enacted the FAA to determine which claims are to be decided by courts and which claims are to be decided by arbitrators, and; (iii) the question that Prima Paint asked the federal courts to adjudicate exceeded the scope of what Congress intended for Section 3 of the FAA to accomplish.[76] As a result, Prima Paint's position could not prevail.

### 3.4 *The Dissent's Rebuke of Arbitration and of the Separability Principle*

Three Justices dissented from the majority and railed against the separability doctrine, and indeed against arbitration in general. The dissent is slightly longer than the majority opinion and begins with the characterization of the majority opinion as "fantastic," in the sense of legitimating fanciful arguments.[77] This characterization stems from the dissent's incredulity that the "legal issue of a contract's voidness" could be decided by persons designated to arbitrate disputes arising out of a valid contract, not a potentially invalid one.[78] Indeed, the "separability" doctrine is a strange and "fantastic" concept in the sense that it is not intuitive, but it is a necessary one because without it, the role of arbitration as a final and binding dispute resolution mechanism would be substantially diminished. Next, the dissent turns to a rebuke of arbitration as a whole:

> [T]he arbitrators who the Court holds are to adjudicate the legal validity of the contract need not even be lawyers, and in all probability will be

---

76 *Prima Paint v. Flood & Conklin Mfg. Co.*, at 406.
77 *Prima Paint v. Flood & Conklin Mfg. Co.*, at 407.
78 *Prima Paint v. Flood & Conklin Mfg. Co.*, at 407.

> nonlawyers, wholly unqualified to decide legal issues, and even if qualified to apply the law, not bound to do so. I am by no means sure that thus forcing a person to forgo his opportunity to try his legal issues in the courts where, unlike the situation in arbitration, he may have a jury trial and right to appeal, is not a denial of due process of law. I am satisfied, however, that Congress did not impose any such procedures in the Arbitration Act. And I am fully satisfied that a reasonable and fair reading of that Act's language and history shows that both Congress and the framers of the Act were at great pains to emphasize that nonlawyers designated to adjust and arbitrate factual controversies arising out of valid contracts would not trespass upon the courts' prerogative to decide the legal question of whether any legal contract exists upon which to base an arbitration.[79]

While the dissent's criticism of arbitration seems harsh and misplaced in today's arbitration-friendly environment, the world was different in the 1960s and several other courts engaged in discussions regarding whether arbitration provides a suitable replacement for court-supervised due process of law. In fact, some jurisdictions around the world are still debating these issues. Context aside, the dissent evaluates briefly the three findings of the majority and reaches opposing conclusions. We discuss the dissent's analysis below.

First, the dissent would have held that in accordance with the legislative history of the FAA, Congress intended to limit arbitration to "contracts between merchants for the interstate shipment of goods," not all contracts "affecting" interstate commerce.[80] In support of its contention, the dissent argued that Congress normally uses the language "affecting commerce," as oppose to "involving commerce," and that this distinction should mean that the latter formulation is narrower than the former. As a result, the dissent concluded that the FAA does not apply to the Consulting Agreement and that "whether the making of the arbitration agreement is in issue is to be determined by reference to state law, not federal law."[81]

Second, the dissent would not have found Section 4 of the FAA to provide an "explicit answer" to the question of whether the arbitration clause is "separable" from the rest of the contract in which it is contained.[82] The dissent took the view that when Section 4 of the FAA calls for a court to be "satisfied that the

79 *Prima Paint v. Flood & Conklin Mfg. Co.*, at 407–08.
80 *Prima Paint v. Flood & Conklin Mfg. Co.*, at 409.
81 *Prima Paint v. Flood & Conklin Mfg. Co.*, at 423.
82 *Prima Paint v. Flood & Conklin Mfg. Co.*, at 410.

making of the agreement for arbitration or the failure to comply therewith is not in issue," this only posed further questions as to what kinds of allegations would put the making of the arbitration agreement in issue.[83] Here, the dissent noted that "a person who attacks a contract on the ground of fraud and seeks to rescind it has to seek rescission of the whole, not tidbits, and is not given the option of denying the existence of some clauses and affirming the existence of others."

Finally, the dissent further takes issue with the majority's use of a federal statute to displace state substantive law and the lack of analysis of the Erie Doctrine, discussed above. The dissent considers that there exists a "serious constitutional problem"[84] because at the time arbitration clauses were not considered "separable" from the main contract under the applicable New York law,[85] and the majority's interpretation of the FAA "would require the federal court to enforce an agreement to arbitrate which the state court across the street would not enforce." This is precisely one of *Erie's* twin aims, preventing the "inequitable administration of the laws" and divergent results between federal and state courts. As a result, the dissent concludes that "had this identical contract dispute been litigated in New York courts under its arbitration act, Prima [Paint] would not be required to present its claims of fraud to the arbitrator if the state rule of non-separability applies."

While some of the points on dissent spring from an older prejudice against arbitration, evidenced by the conclusory statement in the beginning that the dissenting justices are "by no means sure that ... arbitration ... is not a denial of due process of law," some of the more technical points regarding the interplay between federal and state law are fair points to be raised. However, the majority opinion was simply more forward-looking and expressed "neither the desire nor the warrant"[86] to limit the application of the FAA solely to the interstate shipment of goods, and had a different understanding of the legislative history of the FAA, which included "that '[the] control over interstate commerce (one of the bases for the legislation) reaches not only the actual physical interstate shipment of goods but also contracts relating to interstate commerce.'"[87]

Therefore, despite the dissent's general rebuke of arbitration, incredulity as to the "separability doctrine," and rejection of Congress' authority to pass legislation "relating" to interstate commerce, the majority opinion prevailed.

---

83 *Prima Paint v. Flood & Conklin Mfg. Co.*, at 410.

84 *Prima Paint v. Flood & Conklin Mfg. Co.*, at 411.

85 *Prima Paint v. Flood & Conklin Mfg. Co.*, at 421.

86 *Prima Paint v. Flood & Conklin Mfg. Co.*, at 401, footnote 7.

87 *Prima Paint v. Flood & Conklin Mfg. Co.*, at 401, footnote 7.

### 3.5 *Key Takeaways*

The key takeaway from *Prima Paint* is the holding that "arbitration clauses as a matter of federal law are 'separable' from the contracts in which they are embedded, and that where no claim is made that fraud was directed to the arbitration clause itself, a broad arbitration clause will be held to encompass arbitration of the claim that the contract itself was induced by fraud." This new national substantive law shaped the law of arbitration in the United States by limiting the "dirty tricks" (to borrow an expression from the late Professor Gaillard) that a party who has had a change of heart would employ to try to excuse itself from arbitration.[88] Thus, a party who has agreed to arbitrate its disputes will not be able to excuse itself from that commitment, or from a resulting adverse award, by alleging some invalidity in the making of the agreement as a whole. Instead, only challenges that go to the making of the arbitration agreement itself would excuse a party from arbitration, a much narrower inquiry.

Another key takeaway from *Prima Paint v. Flood & Conklin Mfg. Co.* is the conclusion that for contracts evidencing "transactions involving interstate commerce," the FAA will govern and will limit the issues that a federal court may consider in determining whether to order the parties to arbitrate their disputes.[89] Pursuant to Sections 3 and 4 of the FAA, once the court is "satisfied" that there is a valid arbitration agreement, then the court shall stay the trial of the action and refer the parties to arbitration.[90] This conclusion further limits the ability of state courts and legislatures to enact laws that would curtail the practice of this "new national policy" of enforcing arbitration agreements. In addition, the phrasing in Sections 3 and 4 of the FAA, pursuant to which a court must be "satisfied" that "the issue involved in such suit or proceeding is referable to arbitration under such an agreement," leaves a door open for courts to intervene in the extreme cases.

That is the beauty of the framework established under the FAA: for the vast majority of cases, the most likely scenarios, which is a party's change of heart, Sections 3 and 4 of the FAA offer an "explicit answer," to borrow language from the majority.[91] And yet, the same sections also leave the door open for courts to intervene when they are not "satisfied" that the issue is referable to arbitration. This flexibility and clarity as to how to address these types of cases are among the great legacies of *Prima Paint v. Flood & Conklin Mfg. Co.* for the law of arbitration in the United States.

---

88 *See* footnote 10, above.

89 FAA, 9 U.S.C.A. §§ 1 and 2.

90 FAA, 9 U.S.C.A. §§ 3 and 4.

91 *Prima Paint v. Flood & Conklin Mfg. Co.*, at 403.

## 4 The Impact of *Prima Paint v. Flood & Conklin Mfg. Co.* on U.S. Arbitration Law

As of the time of this writing, in late 2023, *Prima Paint v. Flood & Conklin Mfg. Co.* has been cited over 18,000 times on Westlaw and Lexis Nexis, of which 3,696 are cases. Literally thousands of cases have been resolved in accordance with the "separability" doctrine, from which several implications flow. We discuss some of these implications below.

*First*, because the arbitration agreement is independent from the other terms of the contract, it survives termination or invalidity of the main contract and provides a basis on which the arbitral tribunal may decide its own jurisdiction even if the main contract is subject to a claim that it is null and void.[92] This is typically referred to as the "competence-competence" principle, inspired by the French *compétence de la competence* and the German *Kompetenz-Kompetenz*. While this concept will be addressed more fully in other chapters of this publication, there is a necessary interrelationship between the "separability" doctrine (*i.e.*, the notion that the agreement to arbitrate is separate from its underlying contract) and the "competence-competence" principle (*i.e.*, the notion that arbitrators shall decide the limits and the scope of their jurisdiction first). Precisely because the agreement to arbitrate may survive the termination or invalidity of the main contract, arbitrators must retain the authority to decide that contract's validity. Otherwise, without the "separability" doctrine, how could arbitrators have the authority to say that a contract is invalid if it was that same contract that gave them the authority to say it in the first place?

*Second*, because termination or invalidity of the main contract does not necessarily affect the validity of the arbitration agreement, a decision by an arbitral tribunal that the main contract is null and void does "not entail *ipso jure* the invalidity of the arbitration clause."[93] In fact, some legal systems take a

---

92 *See*, e.g., Article 23(1) of the UNCITRAL Arbitration Rules (2021): "The arbitral tribunal shall have the power to rule on its own jurisdiction, including any objections with respect to the existence or validity of the arbitration agreement. For that purpose, an arbitration clause that forms part of a contract shall be treated as an agreement independent of the other terms of the contract. A decision by the arbitral tribunal that the contract is null shall not entail automatically the invalidity of the arbitration clause."

93 *See*, e.g., Article 16(1) of the UNCITRAL Model Law on International Commercial Arbitration (1985 with amendments as adopted in 2006): "The arbitral tribunal may rule on its own jurisdiction, including any objections with respect to the existence or validity of the arbitration agreement. For that purpose, an arbitration clause which forms part of a contract shall be treated as an agreement independent of the other terms of the

step further from negating an *ipso jure* inference and provide that the invalidity of the main contract shall not influence or serve as a basis upon which disputing parties may argue that the arbitration agreement itself is invalid. One example is the private international law act of Switzerland, which provides that: "[t]he validity of an arbitration agreement *may not* be contested on the grounds that the main contract is invalid or that the arbitration agreement concerns a dispute which has not yet arisen."[94]

*Third*, because the arbitration agreement is autonomous from the main contract, another implication of the "separability" doctrine is that the arbitration agreement could be governed by a different legal regime than the main contract.[95] But if different laws governing the arbitration agreement and the main contract are possible, in the absence of an express agreement by the parties should courts give a preference to the law of the main contract, the law of the seat of arbitration, or take some other approach? Some scholars and practitioners take the position that there is "a very strong presumption" in favor of applying the law governing the substantive agreement to the arbitration agreement"[96] because the latter is included in the former and they are not totally independent. Another possible solution, as adopted by mainland Chinese courts, is to apply the law of the seat to the arbitration agreement instead of the substantive law of the main contract.[97] Yet another possible solution, of which perhaps France is the best example, is for courts to adopt a different model that analyzes the existence and scope of an arbitration agreement exclusively by reference to the parties' common intention as a substantive rule (*règle materiale*) of international arbitration without any reference to national law.[98] Different jurisdictions may offer different solutions to identical

---

contract. A decision by the arbitral tribunal that the contract is null and void shall not entail ipso jure the invalidity of the arbitration clause."

94 *See* Swiss Private International Law Act, s. 178(3), emphasis added.

95 *See* Nigel Blackaby, Constantine Partasides, et al., *Redfern and Hunter on International Arbitration (Seventh Edition)*, (© Kluwer Law International; Oxford University Press 2023), ¶3.09.

96 Julian DM Lew KC, *The law applicable to the form and substance of the arbitration clause* (1999) 9 ICCA Congress Series 114, at 143.

97 *See* Nigel Blackaby, Constantine Partasides, et al., *Redfern and Hunter on International Arbitration (Seventh Edition)*, (© Kluwer Law International; Oxford University Press 2023), ¶3.14: "Mainland Chinese law looks first for any expressly stated choice by the parties, but, in the absence of any express choice—and unlike English or French law—there is no search for the parties' implied choice. Instead, a court will apply the law of the seat of the arbitration, or, if even that is not stipulated, the law of the place of the relevant arbitral institution."

98 *See, e.g.*, *Municipalité de Khoms El Mergeb c/Sté Dalico*, Cass. Civ. 1ere, 20 December 1993, [1994] Rev Arb 116, p. 117, as translated by Professor Gaillard in Savage and Gaillard (eds)

legal issues, which makes the selection of the seat of arbitration one of the most impactful decisions when drafting an arbitration agreement.

In the United States, in the absence of an express agreement by the parties, courts may apply the law of the main contract or the law of the seat to arbitration agreements.[99] Although the FAA controls arbitrations seated in the United States involving interstate or foreign commerce,[100] the defenses that are generally available to defeat enforcement of an agreement to arbitrate international disputes are governed by the body of law that results from the forum's choice-of-law principles.[101] As a result, the forum's choice-of-law rules may lead to the application of domestic or foreign law to whether a defense to the enforcement of an arbitration agreement has been established.[102]

Because the arbitration agreement can be governed by a different legal regime than the main contract, and because of the various different approaches courts can take to determine which law applies to the arbitration agreement, parties should consider selecting the law governing the arbitration agreement in addition to the law governing the main contract. While in the authors' experience this selection is uncommon, some institutional rules provide that, in

---

Fouchard, Gaillard, Goldman on International Commercial Arbitration (Kluwer Law International, 1999), p. 437: "[B]y virtue of a substantive rule of international arbitration, the arbitration agreement is legally independent of the main contract containing or referring to it, and the existence and effectiveness of the arbitration agreement are to be assessed, subject to the mandatory rules of French law and international public policy, on the basis of the parties' common intention, there being no need to refer to any national law." This rule has been recently restated by the Paris Court of Appeal in *Kabab-Ji (Lebanon) v Kout Food Group (Kuwait)*, cour d'appel de Paris, Pôle 1—chambre 1, 23 June 2020, Case No. 17/22943), pp. 5, 8.

99 *See* Restatement (Third) U.S. Law of Int'l Comm. Arb. § 2.7, comment (f).

100 FAA, 9 U.S.C.A. §§ 1 and 2. The FAA also implements the New York Convention on the Recognition and Enforcement of Foreign Arbitral Awards.

101 *See* Restatement (Third) U.S. Law of Int'l Comm. Arb. § 2.9, comment (g): "Depending on the applicable choice-of-law rule, a court may apply some body of U.S. law to determine whether a defense to the enforcement of the arbitration agreement is established. That may be because the parties subjected their agreement to a body of U.S. law, or because a U.S. jurisdiction has the strongest connection to the case or the greatest interest in having its law applied to a particular defense, or because the court considers a particular defense to be most appropriately subject to forum law, for example, because procedural or jurisdictional in nature. In that case, the question whether a given ground for refusing to enforce an arbitration agreement has been established will depend on U.S. law."

102 *See, e.g., Motorola Credit Corp. v. Uzan*, 388 F.3d 39, 50 (2d Cir. 2004) ("We have applied a choice-of-law clause to determine which laws govern the validity of an agreement to arbitrate."). *See also* Restatement (Third) U.S. Law of Int'l Comm. Arb. § 2.9, comment (g), compiling cases in which U.S. courts have applied choice-of-law rules to determine which legal regime governs the arbitration agreement.

the absence of an express agreement by the parties, the law of the seat shall govern the arbitration agreement.[103] Thus, by virtue of their selection of institutional rules including such a provision, the parties would likely be deemed to have selected the law applicable to the arbitration agreement.

Following his oral argument on behalf of amicus curiae AAA, Mr. Gerald Aksen wrote an article recognizing the many implications of *Prima Paint* to U.S. arbitration law. In his article, Mr. Aksen characterized the decision as "undoubtedly the most significant judicial opinion ever rendered concerning agreements to arbitrate commercial controversies"[104] and provided a summary of its impact on U.S. arbitration law:

> In addition to resolving a conflict in the circuit courts of appeals concerning the appropriate approach to [the question of whether an arbitrator or a federal court decides if the principal contract has been fraudulently induced], the opinion dealt with such questions as the scope to be accorded the broad arbitration clause, the concept of the "separate" arbitration agreement, the test of "commerce" applicable to evidence a transaction under the Act, the uniform treatment that federal district courts will apply to motions to compel or stay arbitration whether under sections 3 or 4 of the Act, the meaning of federal jurisdiction save for the arbitration agreement, the characterization of arbitration as "substantive" rather than procedural for *Erie* purposes thus disposing of constitutional limitations, the effect of seeking "rescissional" relief, the attempts to define the area of contracts to which the rule applies, and the difference in result from [Second Circuit precedent], all of which are affected by this decision.

Mr. Aksen's conclusions highlight the significance and the impact of *Prima Paint* on U.S. arbitration law. While many of the consequences of the "separability" doctrine have been subject to intense debate and litigation since *Prima Paint*, the U.S. Supreme Court has consistently reaffirmed that, regardless of

103 *See*, e.g., the London Court of International Arbitration (LCIA) Arbitration Rules effective 1 October 2020, Article 16.4: "Subject to Article 16.5 below, the law applicable to the Arbitration Agreement and the arbitration shall be the law applicable at the seat of the arbitration, unless and to the extent that the parties have agreed in writing on the application of other laws or rules of law and such agreement is not prohibited by the law applicable at the arbitral seat."

104 Gerald Aksen, *Prima Paint v. Flood & Conklin—What Does It Mean?*, 43 ST. JOHNS L. REV. 1 (1968), at 2.

whether brought in federal or state court, "a challenge to the validity of the contract as a whole, and not specifically to the arbitration clause, must go to the arbitrator."[105]

## 5 Conclusions

*Prima Paint* is one of the foundational cases on U.S. arbitration law because it unequivocally recognized that the Federal Arbitration Act created a national substantive law upholding Congress' policy of enforcing arbitration agreements in commercial transactions involving interstate commerce and admiralty. In addition, the U.S. Supreme Court affirmed that Congress eliminated the previous judicial hostility to arbitration and placed arbitration agreements on an equal footing with all other contractual undertakings. Finally, *Prima Paint* cemented the concept of a "separate" arbitration clause, which means that disputing parties can have their disputes determined by the arbitrators of their choice with limited court interference. These decisions paved the way for the development of arbitration law and practice in the United States—and, as the Ninth Circuit later definitively put it, "we have become an arbitration nation."[106]

---

105 *Buckeye Check Cashing, Inc. v. Cardegna*, 546 U.S. 440, 449, (2006). *See also* Alan Scott Rau, *Everything You Really Need to Know About "Separability" in Seventeen Simple Propositions*, 14 Am. Rev. Int'l Arb. 1 (2003).

106 *Aspic Eng'g and Constr. Co. v ECC Centcom Constructors LLC*, 913 F3d 1162, 1169 [9th Cir 2019].

CHAPTER 5

# *Commonwealth Coatings Corp. v. Continental Cas. Co.* (1968): The Supreme Court's Fractured Interpretation of "Evident Partiality" under the Federal Arbitration Act and Its Legacy

*Ank Santens, Surya Gopalan and Stephen Hogan-Mitchell*

## 1 Introduction

Faith in arbitration as a dispute resolution mechanism hinges on the parties' confidence in the fairness of the proceedings. Fair proceedings, in turn, require impartial decision-makers. A partial arbitrator, in contrast, threatens the integrity of the arbitral process and ultimately the enforceability of any award rendered by the tribunal of which that arbitrator is a member. In the United States, this principle is codified in 9 U.S.C. § 10 (the Federal Arbitration Act ("FAA")), which includes among the limited grounds for vacating an arbitral award "where there was evident partiality or corruption in the arbitrators, or either of them."[1]

The Supreme Court has addressed the meaning of "evident partiality" only once—in the 1968 decision *Commonwealth Coatings Corp. v. Continental Cas. Co.*[2] Unfortunately, the Court's judgment in that case produced more questions than answers. In the more than five decades since that judgment, lower courts have diverged in interpreting and applying it, giving rise to a circuit split which prevails today.

In this chapter, we provide a summary of the Supreme Court's decision in *Commonwealth Coatings* and comment on its legacy in U.S. arbitration law and practice.

1 9 U.S.C. § 10(a)(2).

2 *Commonwealth Coatings Corp. v. Continental Cas. Co.*, 393 U.S. 145 (1968).

 | DOI:10.1163/9789004715820_006

## 2 The Case

### 2.1 *Factual Background and the Arbitration*

Commonwealth Coatings Corp. ("Commonwealth Coatings") was a subcontractor performing painting services for multiple construction projects in Puerto Rico.[3] The general contractor for the projects, A.C. Samford Overseas, Inc. ("Samford"), alleged that Commonwealth Coatings abandoned the projects prior to completing work. Samford terminated Commonwealth Coatings' engagement as a subcontractor on that basis and initiated *ad hoc* arbitration seeking damages for breach of contract.[4]

Commonwealth Coatings, for its part, brought suit in the United States District Court for the District of Puerto Rico against Samford's two sureties on the projects, Continental Casualty Company and Fireman's Fund Insurance Company, alleging that Samford had failed to pay Commonwealth Coatings for its services and seeking payment from the sureties.[5] The sureties successfully moved to stay that action pending the outcome of the arbitration between Commonwealth Coatings and Samford.[6]

In the arbitration, Commonwealth Coatings and Samford each appointed one arbitrator to serve on the tribunal, and the parties' respective appointees jointly selected Mr. Jose L. Capacete as the presiding arbitrator.[7] Mr. Capacete was eminently qualified for the role. He was one of the top professional consulting engineers in Puerto Rico, taught engineering at the University of Puerto Rico, and was associated with prominent engineering consulting and architecture firms in Puerto Rico.[8]

Following extensive arbitration proceedings, spanning more than a year and including ten days of hearings, the tribunal issued a unanimous written award partially granting Samford's breach of contract claim and awarding Samford almost $16,000 in damages.[9] The tribunal rejected Commonwealth Coatings'

3 *See* Brief of Petitioner, *Commonwealth Coatings Corp. v. Continental Cas. Co.*, 393 U.S. 145, 1968 WL 129387, at *4.

4 *See* Brief of Respondents, *Commonwealth Coatings Corp. v. Continental Cas. Co.*, 393 U.S. 145, 1968 WL 112587, at *2–3.

5 *See* Brief of Petitioner, *Commonwealth Coatings Corp. v. Continental Cas. Co.*, 393 U.S. 145, 1968 WL 129387, at *4.

6 *See* Brief of Respondents, *Commonwealth Coatings Corp. v. Continental Cas. Co.*, 393 U.S. 145, 1968 WL 112587, at *2–3.

7 *Commonwealth Coatings Corp. v. Continental Cas. Co.*, 393 U.S. 145, 146 (1968).

8 *See* Brief of Respondents, *Commonwealth Coatings Corp. v. Continental Cas. Co.*, 393 U.S. 145, 1968 WL 112587, at *10.

9 *Id.* at *14.

counterclaim against Samford for non-payment of its painting services fees.[10]

### 2.2 *The U.S. District Court for the District of Puerto Rico Confirms the Award, Which the First Circuit Affirms*

After the tribunal issued its award, Commonwealth Coatings petitioned the U.S. District Court for the District of Puerto Rico to vacate the award under 9 U.S.C. § 10(a)(2), alleging that Mr. Capacete had shown "evident partiality."[11] The basis for this allegation was Commonwealth Coatings' discovery after the arbitration that Samford was a regular customer of the engineering consulting business in Puerto Rico of which Mr. Capacete was an officer and part-owner.[12] While the business relationship between Samford and Mr. Capacete's firm was sporadic, and there had been no dealings between them for nearly a year before the arbitration, Samford was nonetheless a repeat and significant customer of Mr. Capacete's business, spending about $12,000 dollars over a period of four or five years.[13] The services rendered even involved the very projects at issue in the arbitration.[14]

The U.S. District Court for the District of Puerto Rico rejected Commonwealth Coatings' arguments and confirmed the underlying arbitration award, finding that the non-disclosure was not sufficient to demonstrate evident partiality. In affirming the District Court's finding, the First Circuit acknowledged that, regarding potential arbitrator conflicts, there was "a difficult line between what should, in good faith, be volunteered, and what may be left for inquiry."[15] The First Circuit further acknowledged that where there is a "disturbingly close relationship" between an arbitrator and a party "the very failure to make disclosure could be evidence of partiality," and that "it would have been far better if there had been disclosure here."[16] Nonetheless, the First Circuit concluded that the relationship between Capacete and Samford was not close enough to demonstrate "evident partiality" as a matter of law, emphasizing that the payments themselves were "a very small part of Capacete's income."[17] The

10 *Id.*
11 *Commonwealth Coatings Corp. v. Continental Cas. Co.*, 393 U.S. 145, 146 (1968).
12 *Id.*; *see also* Brief of Respondents, *Commonwealth Coatings Corp. v. Continental Cas. Co.*, 393 U.S. 145, 1968 WL 112587, at *10.
13 *Commonwealth Coatings Corp. v. Continental Cas. Co.*, 393 U.S. 145, 146 (1968).
14 *Id.*
15 *Commonwealth Coatings Corp. v. Continental Cas. Co.*, 382 F.2d 1010, 1011 (1st Cir. 1967), *rev'd*, 393 U.S. 145 (1968).
16 *Id.* at 1011–12.
17 *Id.*

First Circuit also noted that the District Court was "well warranted" in concluding that there had been no actual prejudice or bias during the arbitration proceedings.[18]

Commonwealth Coatings appealed the First Circuit's decision and the Supreme Court granted certiorari. Commonwealth Coatings' primary argument before the Supreme Court was that Capacete's failure to disclose his "disturbingly close" business relationship with Samford was a breach of the "evident partiality" standard, regardless of whether any actual bias resulted from that relationship.[19] In support of its argument, Commonwealth Coatings argued that Capacete should be held to a higher standard of impartiality and disclosure given that he was "the third or 'neutral' arbitrator," as opposed to a party-appointed arbitrator.[20] Commonwealth Coatings further argued that the public interest in the fairness of arbitration proceedings and the impartiality of arbitrators weighed in favor of its position.[21]

Samford and the sureties argued in turn that the relationship between Samford and Capacete was "remote, casual, insignificant, and isolated" and therefore a failure to disclose such a relationship did not demonstrate "evident partiality."[22] They argued that proof of actual bias was necessary to demonstrate "evident partiality," which they argued was "a much greater showing than of the mere existence of a non-disclosed past relationship."[23] Samford and the sureties pointed out that, in the circumstances of this case, there was no evidence of actual bias, and that the lower courts found that the proceedings were in fact fair and impartial.[24] They argued that Capacete was under no general duty to disclose and that instead Commonwealth Coatings had a duty to make "reasonable and prudent inquiry" into potential conflicts if they wished to rely on them as grounds for vacating the award.[25] Finally, they also appealed to public policy, emphasizing that U.S. policy in favor of ensuring the "validity" and "finality" of awards weighed in favor of affirming the award to strengthen arbitration as "a practical contractual remedy."[26]

---

18 *Id.*

19 *See* Brief of Petitioner, *Commonwealth Coatings Corp. v. Continental Cas. Co.*, 393 U.S. 145, 1968 WL 129387, at *17.

20 *Id.* at *24.

21 *Id.* at *28–30.

22 *See* Brief of Respondents, *Commonwealth Coatings Corp. v. Continental Cas. Co.*, 393 U.S. 145, 1968 WL 112587, at *33.

23 *Id.* at *63–64.

24 *Id.* at *34.

25 *Id.* at *35.

26 *Id.* at *35–37.

### 2.3 *The Supreme Court's Opinion*

In a 6–3 decision, the Supreme Court reversed the First Circuit's decision and granted Commonwealth Coatings' petition to vacate the award. Justice Hugo Black, writing the opinion of the Court, found that Mr. Capacete's failure to disclose his business relationship with Samford demonstrated "evident partiality," even though Justice Black agreed that there was no allegation or evidence that Mr. Capacete had acted with actual bias.[27]

Justice Black's opinion adopted a strict view of an arbitrator's obligation of impartiality, reasoning that it was just as stringent—if not more stringent—than the constitutional standard applied to judges.[28] He explained that if a judge were shown to have a similar relationship to a party as Capacete had to Samford, any judgment rendered would certainly be "subject to challenge."[29] He cited to the Court's earlier decision in *Tumey v. State of Ohio*,[30] where the Court overturned a conviction when it was shown that "a small part of the judge's income consisted of court fees collected from convicted defendants."[31] Justice Black disagreed with the First Circuit that the size of the payments mattered, since the Court held in *Tumey* that a decision should be set aside even where there existed the "'slightest pecuniary interest' on the part of the judge."[32]

Justice Black extended this "constitutional principle" as expressed in *Tumey* to arbitration, setting out a rule requiring arbitrators to disclose any dealings which "might create even an impression of possible bias."[33] He also found support for his conclusion in the rules of the American Arbitration Association at the time (even though they did not apply to the underlying arbitration) as well as in the 33d Canon of Judicial Ethics, both of which stated that arbitrators should disclose all potential conflicts to avoid "even the *appearance* of bias."[34]

Justice Byron White authored a concurring opinion, joined by Justice Thurgood Marshall. Though Justice White opened his concurrence by stating that he was "glad to join" Justice Black's opinion, his opinion has since been read as articulating a different standard for arbitrator impartiality.[35] Justice

27 *Commonwealth Coatings Corp. v. Continental Cas. Co.*, 393 U.S. 145, 146 (1968).
28 *Id.* at 148–49.
29 *Id.* at 148.
30 *Tumey v. State of Ohio*, 273 U.S. 510 (1927).
31 *Commonwealth Coatings Corp. v. Continental Cas. Co.*, 393 U.S. 145, 148 (1968).
32 *Id.* (citing *Tumey v. State of Ohio*, 273 U.S. 510, 524 (1927)).
33 *Id.* at 149.
34 *Id.* at 149–50 (emphasis added).
35 *Commonwealth Coatings Corp. v. Continental Cas. Co.*, 393 U.S. 145, 150 (1968) (White, J., concurring).

White was clear that "[t]he Court does not decide today that arbitrators are to be held to the standards of judicial decorum of Article III judges, or indeed of any judges."[36] And while Justice White agreed that in this case Mr. Capacete's failure to disclose his ties to Samford warranted vacating the award, he clarified that a business relationship between a party and an arbitrator was not automatic grounds for disqualification where the parties were "informed of the relationship in advance" or the relationship was "trivial."[37]

Justice White agreed that arbitration was best served by "an atmosphere of frankness" that included full disclosure of "any financial transactions" between arbitrators and the parties.[38] Such disclosures, he reasoned, would minimize the risk of any future challenge to an award and help ensure the effectiveness of arbitration as a method of dispute resolution. Justice White further commented that "[t]he judiciary should minimize its role in arbitration as judge of the arbitrator's impartiality."[39] That role, he stated, was "best consigned to the parties, who are the architects of their own arbitration process, and are far better informed of the prevailing ethical standards and reputations within their business."[40] Ultimately, Justice White concluded that "it is enough for present purposes to hold, as the Court does, that where the arbitrator has a substantial interest in a firm which has done more than trivial business with a party, that fact must be disclosed."[41]

Justice Abe Fortas, joined by Justices Potter Stewart and John M. Harlan, dissented. Justice Fortas agreed with the lower courts that, where the award was unanimous and there was no allegation of *actual* bias or an *intentional* failure to disclose a relationship, there was no basis for setting aside the award.[42] While Justice Fortas acknowledged that "failure of an arbitrator to volunteer information about business dealings with one party will, prima facie, support a claim of partiality or bias," he concluded that where there is no evidence that the nondisclosure was "calculated" or led to bias or misconduct, "the presumption is clearly overcome."[43]

Justice Fortas also disagreed with Justice Black and Justice White on the meaning of "evident partiality," finding that it required "conduct—or at least

36 *Id.*

37 *Id.*

38 *Id.* at 151.

39 *Id.*

40 *Id.*

41 *Id.* at 151–52.

42 *Commonwealth Coatings Corp. v. Continental Cas. Co.*, 393 U.S. 145, 152–53 (1968) (Fortas, J., dissenting).

43 *Id.* at 154.

an attitude or disposition—by the arbitrator favoring one party rather than the other," which the parties agreed was not present in this case.[44] Justice Fortas also cited the fundamental principles of arbitration as a practical and flexible means of dispute resolution based on party consent, observing that these principles limited the circumstances where a final award should be overturned and weighed in favor of applying a lower standard for disclosure of potential conflicts of interest than that applied to judges.[45]

### 2.4 *Key Takeaways*

While Justice White joined Justice Black's opinion, many lower courts have considered that there was a split between Justice White's concurrence and the opinion of the Court, which left open a major question: what standard must courts apply to determine whether an arbitrator who has failed to disclose a potentially problematic relationship with a party has demonstrated "evident partiality" within the meaning of the FAA? Justice Black's opinion would suggest a low evidentiary threshold requiring no proof of actual bias and requiring disclosure from arbitrators of "any dealings that might create an impression of possible bias."[46] In that context, any failure by an arbitrator to disclose such dealings could, by itself, satisfy the "evident partiality" standard. While one might read Justice White's concurrence as hewing to the basic standard set forth in Justice Black's opinion, one might also read the concurrence—while strongly favoring disclosure—as being limited more closely to the facts of the case and leaving open the possibility that something more substantial must be shown in order to demonstrate evident partiality.[47] In other words, an arbitrator's failure to disclose past or current dealings with a party may not by itself satisfy the "evident partiality" standard, unless that past (undisclosed) dealing amounts to a "substantial interest in a firm which has done more than trivial business with a party," which is a higher evidentiary threshold than the test articulated by Justice Black.

In the years since the Supreme Court's decision, many lower courts have recognized an apparent tension between Justice Black's and Justice White's opinions and have noted that this tension leaves courts with little guidance on how to apply the "evident partiality" standard to cases of non-disclosure.[48]

---

44 *Id.*

45 *Id.* at 154–55.

46 *Commonwealth Coatings Corp. v. Continental Cas. Co.*, 393 U.S. 145, 149 (1968).

47 *Id.* at 151–152 (White, J., concurring).

48 *See, e.g., Positive Software Solutions, Inc. v. New Century Mortg. Corp.*, 476 F.3d 278, 281–82 (5th Cir. 2007) (noting that, like many "plurality-plus" decisions, *Commonwealth Coatings* "is not pellucid" before proceeding to contrast the opinion of the Court and the

Some have read Justice Black's opinion as a true majority opinion (and therefore controlling on lower courts), while others have read it as more akin to a plurality opinion (and therefore not controlling on lower courts) because they interpret Justice Black's opinion as seemingly irreconcilable with Justice White's concurrence.[49]

As discussed in greater detail in the following section, courts' differing interpretations of Justice White's concurrence has led to divergence among lower courts on when the "evident partiality" standard is satisfied.

## 3 *Commonwealth Coatings'* Impact on U.S. Arbitration Law and Practice

### 3.1 *Interpretations of* Commonwealth Coatings

The confusion generated by the differing interpretations of *Commonwealth Coatings* has culminated in a circuit split on the meaning of "evident partiality" in the FAA and the standard applicable when an arbitrator fails to disclose a potentially compromising relationship.

The Ninth and Eleventh Circuits have adhered more closely to Justice Black's opinion and adopted a lower evidentiary standard for "evident partiality" whereby an award may be vacated where there is evidence of an undisclosed relationship creating a "reasonable impression of partiality."[50] This

concurrence); *Morelite Const. Corp. v. N.Y.C. Dist. Council Carpenters Benefit Funds*, 748 F.2d 79, 82–83 (2d Cir. 1984) ("[M]uch of Justice Black's opinion must be read as dicta, and we are left in the dark as to whether an 'appearance of bias' will suffice to meet the seemingly more stringent 'evident partiality' standard of 9 U.S.C. § 10.").

49 *Compare Schmitz v. Zilveti*, 20 F.3d 1043, 1047 (9th Cir. 1994) ("Given Justice White's express adherence to the majority opinion in *Commonwealth Coatings*, it is clear that the majority opinion, including its 'appearance of bias' language, received at least five votes. Even so, the majority did not articulate a succinct standard."), *with Morelite Const. Corp. v. N.Y.C. Dist. Council Carpenters Benefit Funds*, 748 F.2d 79, 83, n.3 (2d Cir. 1984) ("It might be thought that Justice Black's opinion represents the views of six members of the Court, for Justice White wrote that he was 'glad to join my Brother Black's opinion.' … Because the two opinions are impossible to reconcile, however, we must narrow the holding to that subscribed to by both Justices White and Black.").

50 *See, e.g., Schmitz v. Zilveti*, 20 F.3d 1043, 1047 (9th Cir. 1994) ("'Reasonable impression of partiality' … is the best expression of the *Commonwealth Coatings* court's holding."); *Lifecare Int'l, Inc. v. CD Med., Inc.*, 68 F.3d 429, 433 (11th Cir. 1995), *opinion modified and supplemented*, 85 F.3d 519 (11th Cir. 1996) ("In order to vacate on the ground of evident partiality in a nondisclosure case, the party challenging the arbitration award must establish that the undisclosed facts create a 'reasonable impression of partiality.'") (internal citations omitted).

standard may be met by looking to the nature of the undisclosed facts and determining whether those facts could create the reasonable impression of partiality, regardless of whether there is evidence of actual bias. In adopting this standard, the Ninth Circuit explained in *Schmitz v. Zilveti* its view that *Commonwealth Coatings* was "not a plurality opinion."[51] Instead, the Ninth Circuit read Justice White's concurrence in *Commonwealth Coatings* as accepting the "appearance of bias" language in Justice Black's opinion while merely recognizing that arbitrators and judges face different standards inherent to their positions.[52] Therefore, the Ninth Circuit viewed its "reasonable impression of partiality" standard as "the best expression of the *Commonwealth Coatings* court's holding."[53]

In contrast, the First, Second, Third, Fourth, Fifth, and Sixth Circuits have adopted a relatively stricter evidentiary standard, requiring that a party must show that, because of the nature of the undisclosed relationship, "a reasonable person would have to conclude that an arbitrator was partial to one party to the arbitration," though there is no requirement for a party to demonstrate proof of "actual bias."[54]

The Second Circuit first articulated this standard in *Morelite Construction Corp. v. N.Y.C. District Council Carpenters Benefit Funds*.[55] In analyzing *Commonwealth Coatings*, the Court found differences between Justice Black's and Justice White's opinions that it interpreted to be irreconcilable, meaning that much of Justice Black's opinion "must be read as dicta" and that the Court

51 *Schmitz v. Zilveti*, 20 F.3d 1043, 1045 (9th Cir. 1994).

52 *Id.* at 1046–47.

53 *Id.* at 1047. The Eleventh Circuit's standard, though using the same language, is arguably higher than the Ninth Circuit's standard, as the Eleventh Circuit has stated that more than an "appearance of bias" is needed to satisfy evident partiality, though it later held that evidence of a "potential conflict" is enough. *Compare Lifecare Int'l, Inc. v. CD Med., Inc.*, 68 F.3d 429, 433 (11th Cir. 1995), *opinion modified and supplemented*, 85 F.3d 519 (11th Cir. 1996) ("the mere appearance of bias or partiality is not enough to set aside an arbitration award"), *with Univ. Commons-Urbana, Ltd. v. Universal Constructors Inc.*, 304 F.3d 1331, 1339 (11th Cir. 2002) ("an arbitration award may be vacated due to the 'evident partiality' of an arbitrator only when either (1) an actual conflict exists, or (2) the arbitrator knows of, but fails to disclose, information which would lead a reasonable person to believe that a potential conflict exists.") (internal citations omitted).

54 *Morelite Construction Corp. v. N.Y.C. District Council Carpenters Benefit Funds*, 748 F.2d 79, 84 (2d Cir. 1984); *see also JCI Commc'ns, Inc. v. Int'l Bhd. of Elec. Workers, Local 103*, 324 F.3d 42, 51 (1st Cir. 2003); *Freeman v. Pittsburgh Glass Works, LLC*, 709 F.3d 240, 252–53 (3d Cir. 2013); *Three S Del., Inc. v. DataQuick Data Sys.*, 492 F.3d 520, 530 (4th Cir. 2007); *Cooper v. WestEnd Capital Mgmt., LLC*, 832 F.3d 534, 545 (5th Cir. 2016); *Nationwide Mut. Ins. v. Home Ins.*, 429 F.3d 640, 644–45 (6th Cir. 2005).

55 748 F.2d 79 (2d Cir. 1984).

was "left in the dark as to whether an 'appearance of bias' will suffice to meet the seemingly more stringent 'evident partiality' standard" of the FAA.[56]

The Second Circuit viewed its articulation of the standard as one which addressed the "competing interests inherent in the use of arbitration," which it went on to describe.[57] The first interest is parties' desire for arbitrators with relevant experience, which leads to the selection of arbitrators from narrow fields of closely-knit communities of experts. The Court found that this desire implied the need for a higher evidentiary standard than the "appearance of bias" standard applied to judges so as not to "render this efficient means of dispute resolution ineffective in many commercial settings."[58] On the other hand, the Court rejected a standard requiring proof of actual bias, recognizing the importance of ensuring fair proceedings and that "[b]ias is always difficult, and indeed often impossible, to 'prove.'"[59] The Court explained that its standard would create the proper balance between these competing interests. Other circuits implementing the standard articulated by the Second Circuit have also explained that the inclusion of the word "evident" in the FAA "suggests that the statute requires more than a vague appearance of bias" in contrast to the less demanding evidentiary standard for demonstrating the more stringent standard for impartiality in judges articulated by Justice Black.[60]

The Supreme Court has been asked to resolve the circuit split multiple times. As one recent example, the Court was presented with the question in 2020 following the Ninth Circuit's decision in *Monster Energy Co. v. City Beverages LLC*. In that case, the Ninth Circuit vacated a JAMS arbitration award based on an arbitrator's failure to fully disclose his financial interest in JAMS as an owner-shareholder as well as the substantial business relationship between JAMS and one of the parties.[61] While the arbitrator disclosed at the commencement of the arbitration that "[e]ach JAMS neutral, including me, has an economic

56 *Id.* at 83.

57 *Id.*

58 *Id.* at 84.

59 *Id.*

60 *See Freeman v. Pittsburgh Glass Works, LLC*, 709 F.3d 240, 253 (3d Cir. 2013) ("The Federal Arbitration Act requires a party to show 'evident partiality.' 9 U.S.C. § 10(a)(2). The word 'evident' suggests that the statute requires more than a vague appearance of bias. Rather, the arbitrator's bias must be sufficiently obvious that a reasonable person would easily recognize it. By contrast, the judicial standard requires recusal if a judge's 'impartiality might reasonably be questioned.' 28 U.S.C. § 455(a). This language suggests that the judicial inquiry focuses on appearances—'not on whether the judge actually harbored subjective bias.'").

61 *See Monster Energy Co. v. City Beverages LLC*, 940 F.3d 1130 (9th Cir. 2019), *cert. denied*, No. 19-1333 (U.S. June 29, 2020).

interest in the overall financial success of JAMS," he did not disclose that he was a co-owner of JAMS or that JAMS administered a large number of cases for one of the parties.[62] The Ninth Circuit held that this ownership interest "greatly exceeds the general economic interest that all JAMS neutrals naturally have in the organization" and was therefore "substantial."[63] The Court additionally held that because JAMS administered arbitrations for the other party at "an average rate of more than one arbitration a month," the business relationship between the arbitrator and the other party was more than "trivial," thus creating a "reasonable impression of bias."[64]

Following the appeal to the Supreme Court, JAMS itself, in an unprecedented move, filed an amicus brief in the case, urging the Court to overrule the Ninth Circuit's decision and provide much needed clarity on the "evident partiality" standard and its implications for disclosure obligations.[65] The Supreme Court declined to take up the case.[66] To this day *Commonwealth Coatings* thus remains the Supreme Court's only guidance on the meaning of "evident partiality." Furthermore, because *Commonwealth Coatings* assessed the "evident partiality" standard only in a non-disclosure context, the Supreme Court has left lower courts without guidance as to how to apply the standard to "actual bias" cases—for example, where an arbitrator fails to step down following a party's challenge to their impartiality.

As a result, parties face different standards for vacatur on grounds of "evident partiality" depending on the circuit in which set aside proceedings are pursued, and similar allegations of impropriety can lead to different outcomes. As just one example, in the same month that the Supreme Court declined to take up *Monster Energy*, a U.S. District Court in the Third Circuit held that an arbitrator's failure to disclose her status as an owner-shareholder in JAMS, while showing "clear appearances of impropriety," did not warrant vacatur under the Third Circuit's standard requiring "proof *so powerfully suggestive of bias* that a reasonable person would *have* to believe" the arbitrator was impartial in order to find "evident partiality."[67] In explaining its departure from the decision in *Monster Energy*, the U.S. District Court contrasted the Third Circuit's standard

62 *Id.* at 1133.

63 *Id.* at 1136.

64 *Id.* at 1136, 1138.

65 *See* Brief of JAMS, Inc. as Amicus Curiae in Support of Petitioner, *Monster Energy*, 940 F.3d 1130 (No. 19-1333).

66 The Supreme Court again declined to take up the question in March 2024. *See Grupo Unidos por el Canal, S.A. v. Autoridad del Canal de Panama*, 144 S. Ct. 1096 (2024).

67 *See Martin v. NTT Data, Inc.*, No. 20-CV-0686, 2020 WL 3429423, at *8–9 (E.D. Pa. June 23, 2020) (emphasis in original).

with that of the Ninth Circuit, "which evidently adheres to the viewpoint that failure to disclose is by itself a sufficient basis upon which to vacate an arbitration award."[68]

### 3.2 *Implications for Practice*

*Commonwealth Coatings* and its interpretations by lower courts have at least two important implications for parties, arbitration practitioners, and arbitrators. The first and perhaps foremost implication is the central importance of disclosure by arbitrators. The easiest way for an arbitrator to avoid a later accusation of evident partiality is to ensure that all potential conflicts are disclosed, in full, and at the outset of the arbitration. In Justice White's words, disclosure is the best means of "establishing an atmosphere of frankness at the outset" of an arbitration and ensuring protection from "a suspicious or disgruntled party" seeking to seize on a failed disclosure "as a pretext for invalidating the award."[69] In an era where parties have unprecedented access to information on the professional and personal associations of arbitrators, the risk accompanying non-disclosure arguably has never been greater.

By disclosing any non-trivial relationship, arbitrators give parties the opportunity to object to their appointment. If parties do not object, they risk waiving an impartiality objection to an eventual award, even in circuits with lower thresholds for finding "evident partiality" like the Ninth Circuit.[70] In light of the demanding disclosure requirements applied in some circuits, arbitrators sitting in cases which may culminate in set-aside proceedings in those circuits (because the seat of arbitration is located in one of those circuits) should also consider conducting a reasonable investigation at the outset of a case so that they can discover and disclose potential conflicts of which they may not be fully aware but which they could discover through reasonable investigation. The Ninth Circuit, for example, has held that arbitrators have a duty to investigate conflicts, such as relationships between the parties and the arbitrator, in addition to the duty to disclose them.[71]

---

68 *Id.*

69 *Commonwealth Coatings Corp. v. Continental Cas. Co.*, 393 U.S. 145, 151 (1968) (White, J., concurring).

70 *See, e.g., Haddad v. Jackson*, No. 1:07CV016760WWTAG, 2010 WL 2816320, at *5 (E.D. Cal. July 16, 2010) ("Assuming *arguendo* that the record could support a finding of evident partiality, Plaintiff waived his claim by failing to lodge any objection until after the entry of the arbitration award. It is settled that claims alleging bias on behalf of an arbitrator pursuant to section 10(a)(2) of the FAA are subject to waiver.").

71 *Schmitz v. Zilveti*, 20 F.3d 1043, 1048 (9th Cir. 1994) ("[A]n arbitrator may have a duty to investigate independent of its *Commonwealth Coatings* duty to disclose. A violation of

This emphasis on disclosure comports with international principles of arbitrator impartiality. For example, the IBA Guidelines on Conflicts of Interest in International Arbitration includes among its General Standards that:

> If facts or circumstances exist that may, in the eyes of the parties, give rise to doubts as to the arbitrator's impartiality or independence, the arbitrator shall disclose such facts or circumstances to the parties, the arbitration institution or other appointing authority (if any, and if so required by the applicable institutional rules) and the co-arbitrators, if any, prior to accepting his or her appointment or, if thereafter, as soon as he or she learns of them ... Any doubt as to whether an arbitrator should disclose certain facts or circumstances should be resolved in favour of disclosure.[72]

Similar language can be found in UNCITRAL's code of conduct for arbitrators in international investment dispute resolution:

> A Candidate and an Arbitrator shall disclose any circumstances likely to give rise to justifiable doubts as to his or her independence or impartiality ... A Candidate and an Arbitrator shall err in favour of disclosure if he or she has any doubt as to whether a disclosure shall be made.[73]

Duties of disclosure are also required by institutional arbitration rules. For example, both the International Chamber of Commerce ("ICC") Arbitration Rules and the American Arbitration Association ("AAA") Commercial Arbitration Rules require that arbitrators disclose any facts or circumstances which would likely create reasonable doubts as to the arbitrator's impartiality.[74] Arbitrators,

---

this independent duty to investigate may result in a failure to disclose that creates a reasonable impression of partiality *under Commonwealth Coatings*.").

72 IBA Guidelines on Conflicts of Interest in International Arbitration, General Standard 3 (2014).

73 *See* UNCITRAL code of conduct for arbitrators in international investment dispute resolution and commentary, Article 11 (February 2024).

74 *See* 2021 ICC Arbitration Rules, Article 11(2) ("Before appointment or confirmation, a prospective arbitrator shall sign a statement of acceptance, availability, impartiality and independence. The prospective arbitrator shall disclose in writing to the Secretariat any facts or circumstances which might be of such a nature as to call into question the arbitrator's independence in the eyes of the parties, as well as any circumstances that could give rise to reasonable doubts as to the arbitrator's impartiality."); 2022 AAA Commercial Arbitration Rules, R-18 ("Any person appointed or to be appointed as an arbitrator, as well as the parties and their representatives, shall disclose to the AAA any circumstance likely to give rise to justifiable doubt as to the arbitrator's impartiality or independence,

practitioners and parties should be aware, however, that these institutional standards do not displace the FAA standard in any vacatur action. Multiple U.S. circuit courts have found that whether an arbitrator violates applicable institutional disclosure rules does not, by itself, determine whether that arbitrator has shown "evident partiality" for the purposes of the FAA.[75]

Despite these international standards for disclosure, arbitrators apply them differently in practice, in line with expectations generated by their own legal traditions. U.S. arbitrators, for example, frequently make much broader disclosures than their European counterparts. This can be a barrier to appointment for some U.S. arbitrators, as such disclosures may prevent them from accepting an appointment from a party seeking (in an abundance of caution) to avoid an arbitrator challenge, cause an institution to remove them from consideration for appointment as presiding arbitrators, or provide additional possible grounds for an arbitrator challenge.

A second important implication is the choice of seat of arbitration, as the proper venue for vacating an arbitral award governed by the FAA in the United States is the U.S. district court where the award was rendered absent an agreement otherwise between the parties.[76] Parties should be cautious in choosing a seat of arbitration which may implicate circuits with lower evidentiary

---

including any bias or any financial or personal interest in the result of the arbitration or any past or present relationship with the parties or their representatives.").

75 *See, e.g., Merit Ins. Co. v. Leatherby Ins. Co.*, 714 F.2d 673, 680 (7th Cir. 1983) ("[E]ven if the failure to disclose was a material violation of the ethical standards applicable to arbitration proceedings, it does not follow that the arbitration award may be nullified judicially. Although we have great respect for the Commercial Arbitration Rules and the Code of Ethics for Arbitrators, they are not the proper starting point for an inquiry into an award's validity under section 10 of the United States Arbitration Act"); *Scandinavian Reinsurance Co. v. Saint Paul Fire & Marine Ins. Co.*, 668 F.3d 60, 77 n.22 (2d Cir. 2012) ("Even where an arbitrator fails to abide by arbitral or ethical rules concerning disclosure, such a failure does not, in itself, entitle a losing party to vacatur."); *Positive Software Sols., Inc. v. New Century Mortg. Corp.*, 476 F.3d 278, 285 n.5 (5th Cir. 2007) ("The American Arbitration Association ('AAA'), whose rules governed this proceeding, requires broad prophylactic disclosure of 'any circumstance likely to affect impartiality or create an appearance of partiality,' so that parties may rely on the integrity of the selection process for arbitrators. Whether Shurn's nondisclosure ran afoul of the AAA rules, however, is not before us and plays no role in applying the federal standard embodied in the FAA.").

76 *See* 9 U.S.C. § 9 (stating that for petitions to confirm an award, "[i]f no court is specified in the agreement of the parties, then such application may be made to the United States court in and for the district within which such award was made."); 9 U.S.C. § 10(a) ("In any of the following cases the United States court in and for the district wherein the award was made may make an order vacating the award upon the application of any party to the arbitration.")

thresholds for finding "evident partiality" like the Ninth and Eleventh Circuits. By choosing a seat in one of those circuits, parties take on relatively more risk that any award rendered will be vacated if a party unhappy with the outcome is able to uncover a deficiency in an arbitrator's disclosures. Arbitrators themselves should also keep the seat of the arbitration in mind and ensure that their disclosures are comprehensive enough to mitigate any risk of set aside. This consideration applies to international arbitrations seated in the United States[77] and domestic arbitrations other than those which do not involve interstate commerce, which are all governed by the FAA.

## 4 Conclusion

Parties choose arbitration in part because it offers an impartial forum for achieving a final and binding award. The risk of an award being set aside due to the apparent partiality of an arbitrator undermines that goal. While *Commonwealth Coatings* is clear on the importance of disclosure in arbitration to mitigate the risk of perceived arbitrator partiality, the lack of clarity on how judges should assess a failure by an arbitrator to disclose a potential conflict of interest has left a gap in U.S. arbitration law that the Supreme Court will eventually need to address. Until that time, parties and arbitrators should consider taking proactive steps during the appointment process to seek and provide comprehensive disclosures to safeguard the appearance of impartiality in arbitrations and minimize the risk of an opportunistic challenge to an award based on an arbitrator's failure to disclose.

---

77 *See* 9 U.S.C. § 204 ("An action or proceeding over which the district courts have jurisdiction pursuant to section 203 of this title may be brought in any such court in which save for the arbitration agreement an action or proceeding with respect to the controversy between the parties could be brought, or in such court for the district and division which embraces the place designated in the agreement as the place of arbitration if such place is within the United States.").

CHAPTER 6

# *Scherk v. Alberto-Culver Co.* (1974)

*Michael B. Carlinsky and Andre Luis Monteiro*

## 1 Introduction[1,2]

This chapter analyses the U.S. Supreme Court's (the "Supreme Court" or the "Court") landmark decision in *Scherk v. Alberto-Culver Co* ("*Scherk v. Alberto-Culver*"),[3] in which the Court held for the first time (and by a 5–4 majority) that securities claims were arbitrable under U.S. law, at least when arising out of an international transaction.

The decision also established, although implicitly, that the possibility of a specific subject matter being submitted to arbitration is governed by the *lex fori*, and not the law of the seat of the arbitration or any potential international standard.[4] As detailed below, the Convention on the Recognition and Enforcement of Foreign Arbitral Awards of 1958 (the "New York Convention") played an important role in the case.

The chapter is structured as follows. First, we present a brief overview of the case (Section 2.1), and discuss the issues at stake and the parties' arguments (Section 2.2). We then analyze the Supreme Court's judgment in detail, including the majority and dissenting opinions (Section 2.3). This is followed by a discussion of the key takeaways from the decision (Section 2.4) and our critical analysis of the Court's reasoning (Section 3). Finally, we set out a number of conclusions to be drawn from the case (Section 4).

---

1 This essay represents the authors' views about the case, which does not necessarily represent those of their law firm and/or of their clients.

2 The authors want to express their gratitude to Myron Phua, a former associate at Quinn Emanuel Urquhart & Sullivan and current Barrister at Blackstone Chambers, for his research assistance on the case law and academic commentaries.

3 *Scherk v Alberto-Culver Co* 417 U.S. 506 (1974).

4 Justice Stewart delivered the majority opinion, which was joined by Chief Justice Burger and Justices Blackmun, Powell, and Rehnquist. The dissenting opinion was rendered by Justice Douglas and joined by Justices Brennan, White, and Marshall.

 | DOI:10.1163/9789004715820_007

## 2 The Case

### 2.1 *Background of the Case*

Founded in 1955, Alberto-Culver Co. ("Alberto-Culver" or the "Plaintiff"[5]) was an American manufacturer incorporated in Delaware and with its main offices in Illinois. The company produced, distributed, and exported hair and skin beauty care products in the United States and abroad.[6] Alberto-Culver had its stock listed on the New York Stock Exchange.

Fritz Scherk ("Mr. Scherk" or the "Defendant"[7]) was a German citizen residing in Switzerland, and the owner of a group of companies organized under the laws of Germany and Liechtenstein. His companies also manufactured toiletries and held the corresponding trademark licenses.

Alberto-Culver wanted to expand its business overseas and, at the start of 1967, contacted Mr. Scherk with a proposal to purchase his corporate enterprises. After a couple of years negotiating, with the help of lawyers and experts from multiple jurisdictions, the parties entered into a business purchase agreement in Vienna, Austria, in February, 1969 (the "Business Purchase Agreement" or the "Agreement"). As agreed by the parties, the Defendant transferred the ownership of his companies to the Plaintiff, alongside all trademark rights to their cosmetic products. The transaction could be described as the acquisition of a going concern. The closing of the transaction took place in Geneva, Switzerland, in June 1969.

The Business Purchase Agreement contained express warranties to the effect that all trademarks were unencumbered. The Agreement also contained an arbitration clause, under which "any controversy or claim shall arise out of this agreement or the breach thereof (...) shall be settled exclusively by arbitration" under the ICC Arbitration Rules, seated in Paris, France, and a choice of law provision stating that the agreement was governed by the "*laws of the State of Illinois, U.S.A.*"[8]

---

5 The Plaintiff, Alberto-Culver, is referred to in the Supreme Court proceedings as the "*Respondent*". In order to avoid the use of multiple names and any potential confusion (in particular for those not familiar with U.S. litigation), we prefer not to use the term "*Respondent*" in this essay.

6 The company was purchased by Unilever in 2010.

7 The Defendant, Fritz Scherk, is referred in the Supreme Court proceedings as the "*Petitioner*". In order to avoid the use of multiple names and any potential confusion (in particular for those not familiar with U.S. litigation), we prefer not to use the term "*Petitioner*" in this essay.

8 The arbitration clause read as follows: "The parties agree that, if any controversy or claim shall arise out of this agreement or the breach thereof and either party shall request that the matter shall be settled by arbitration, the matter shall be settled exclusively by arbitration in accordance with the rules then obtaining of the International Chamber of Commerce, Paris, France, by a single arbitrator, if the parties shall agree upon one, or

Almost a year later, the Plaintiff discovered that the trademarks were actually subject to substantial encumbrances. These encumbrances potentially gave others superior rights to the trademarks and restricted or precluded Alberto-Culver's use of them. The Plaintiff attempted to rescind the Agreement, but the Defendant objected, forcing the Plaintiff to bring claims for fraudulent misrepresentation under Section 10(b) of the Securities Exchange Act of 1934 and Rule 10b-5 promulgated thereunder. The allegation was that Alberto-Culver had been defrauded by the issuance of securities (*i.e.*, promissory notes) for assets which were worthless or of a much lower value than represented.

Despite the arbitration clause in the Business Purchase Agreement, the Plaintiff decided to file court proceedings against the Defendant before the Federal District Court in Illinois (the "Illinois Court"). In response, the Defendant filed a motion to dismiss the action on the basis of *lack of jurisdiction* and *forum non conveniens, or, alternatively, to stay the court proceedings* pending arbitration. The Plaintiff opposed to the motion and sought an injunction to restrain the Defendant from commencing arbitration proceedings in Paris.

In December 1971, relying entirely on *Wilko v. Swan*,[9] the Illinois Court denied the motion to dismiss, held the arbitration clause unenforceable and enjoined the Defendant against proceeding with arbitration (which Mr. Scherk had already commenced in Paris in November 1971). The Court of Appeals for the Seventh Circuit affirmed the first-instance decision by a majority, again applying *Wilko v. Swan*, essentially reasoning that U.S. federal securities legislation made arbitration clauses relating to securities transactions null and void.[10]

---

by one arbitrator appointed by each party and a third arbitrator appointed by the other arbitrators. In case of any failure of a party to make an appointment referred to above within four weeks after notice of the controversy, such appointment shall be made by said Chamber. All arbitration proceedings shall be held in Paris, France, and each party agrees to comply in all respects with any award made in any such proceeding and to the entry of a judgment in any jurisdiction upon any award rendered in such proceeding. The laws of the State of Illinois, U.S.A. shall apply to and govern this agreement, its interpretation and performance."

9 *Wilko v Swan* 346 U.S. 427 (1953).

10 Section 14 of the Securities Act of 1933 (Pub L 73–291, 15 USC §78a et seq) (hereafter the "Securities Act of 1933") reads as follows: "Any condition, stipulation, or provision binding any person acquiring any security to waive compliance with any provision of this subchapter or of the rules and regulations of the Commission shall be void." Similarly, Section 29(a) of the Securities Exchange Act of 1934 reads as follows: "Any condition, stipulation, or provision binding any person to waive compliance with any provision of this chapter or of any rule or regulation thereunder, or of any rule of an exchange required thereby shall be void."

The U.S. Supreme Court granted the Defendant's petition for a writ of certiorari, and subsequently decided the case on June 17, 1974, favoring the Defendant's position and declaring enforceable the arbitration clause in the Business Purchase Agreement. As described below, *Scherk v. Alberto-Culver* is a landmark decision by the Supreme Court, which set the scene for a series of liberal decisions toward arbitration in the United States.

## 2.2 *Issue and Parties' Arguments*

### 2.2.1 The Main Challenge

The main challenge for the Defendant in the case was to convince the Supreme Court to distance itself from its seminal decision in *Wilko v. Swan*, decided in 1953, either by distinguishing it on its facts or by overruling its previous precedent altogether. Conversely, the Plaintiff had to persuade the Court that *Wilko v. Swan* perfectly fit the facts and could not be distinguished.

In *Wilko v. Swan*, the Court found that "[t]wo policies, not easily reconcilable" were engaged in that case, and were potentially at odds with each other.[11] The first was that Congress had enacted the Securities Act of 1933 "to protect the rights of investors" and, therefore, forbade "a waiver of any of those rights".[12] The second policy was that Congress had passed the Federal Arbitration Act of 1925 ("FAA") to secure "the desirability of arbitration as an alternative to the complications of litigation" as well as to avoid "the delay and expense of litigation".[13] The question that best summarized this potential clash of policies was: does arbitration undermine investors' rights under securities law?

In deciding *Wilko v. Swan*, the Supreme Court chose to prioritize the first policy over the second one, observing that "the intention of Congress concerning the sale of securities is better carried out by holding invalid such an agreement for arbitration of issues arising under the Act".[14] This was reflected in the Court's interpretation of Section 14 of the Securities Act of 1933, which stated that "any condition, stipulation, or provision binding any person acquiring any security to waive compliance with any provision of this title or of the rules and regulations of the Commission shall be void".

The Court reasoned that arbitration clauses relating to securities transactions were null and void because they were binding stipulations under which purchasers waived the legal protections of the Securities Act of 1933, specifically the investor's right to access the U.S. courts. The Court expressly said that

---

11 *Wilko* (n 11) 438.
12 Ibid 438.
13 Ibid 431–432.
14 Ibid 438.

"the right to select the judicial forum is the kind of 'provision' that cannot be waived under §14 of the Securities Act".[15] Since 1953, that had been the law in the United States, and *Scherk v. Alberto-Culver* was an opportunity for the Court, after approximately 25 years, to reaffirm its previous understanding or to depart from it and broaden the scope of arbitrable disputes in the U.S.

### 2.2.2 Defendant's Oral Arguments

During the oral argument session,[16] held by the Court on April 29, 1974, the Defendant (represented by Robert F. Hanley) attempted to persuade the Court to distinguish *Wilko v. Swan* by advancing four main arguments.

First, the Defendant argued that, in *Wilko v. Swan*, the Court dealt with alleged violations of the Securities Act of 1933, whereas in the case at hand the relevant statute was the Securities Exchange Act of 1934. The Defendant took the position that the language used by the latter Act was narrower than that under the former Act, which meant that the latter Act allowed parties to submit securities claims to arbitration.

The Defendant's argument was based on the premise that, while Section 12(2) of the Securities Act of 1933 provided for investors' private rights and remedies to be pursued and vindicated before the federal courts,[17] Section 10(b) (and Rule 10b-5) of the Securities Exchange Act of 1934 were silent on this point.[18] This was effectively an argument that the scope of the protections

---

15 Ibid 435.

16 We cite passages of the oral arguments in many occasions in this essay. The audio recording and transcript can be found at https://www.oyez.org/cases/1973/73-781.

17 Section 12(2) of the Securities Act of 1933 reads as follows: "Any person who (…) offers or sells a security (whether or not exempted by the provisions of section 3, other than paragraphs (2) and (14) of subsection (a) thereof), by the use of any means or instruments of transportation or communication in interstate commerce or of the mails, by means of a prospectus or oral communication, which includes an untrue statement of a material fact or omits to state a material fact necessary in order to make the statements, in the light of the circumstances under which they were made, not misleading (the purchaser not knowing of such untruth or omission), and who shall not sustain the burden of proof that he did not know, and in the exercise of reasonable care could not have known, of such untruth or omission shall be liable, subject to subsection (b), to the person purchasing such security from him, who may sue either at law or in equity in any court of competent jurisdiction, to recover the consideration paid for such security with interest thereon, less the amount of any income received thereon, upon the tender of such security, or for damages if he no longer owns the security."

18 Section 10(b) of the Securities Exchange Act of 1934 reads as follows: "It shall be unlawful for any person, directly or indirectly, by the use of any means or instrumentality of interstate commerce or of the mails, or of any facility of any national securities exchange (…) (b) To use or employ, in connection with the purchase or sale of any security registered on a national securities exchange or any security not so registered, or any securities-based

conferred by both statutes differed. Unlike Section 12(2) of the Securities Act of 1933, the anti-fraud provisions of the Securities Exchange Act of 1934, including Section 10(b), did not expressly grant investors such a private remedy and, therefore, did not establish any special right to access the U.S. courts.[19]

Second, the Defendant entreated the Court not to apply its previous precedent "mechanically" where "security violations are alleged in this international context". According to the Defendant, *Wilko v. Swan* was a domestic case in which a customer of a brokerage house signed a 17-page form agreement containing an arbitration clause along with provisions which purported to waive its protective rights under U.S. federal securities law. The Defendant further argued that the contract in question in *Wilko v. Swan* was a contract of adhesion, and there was "tremendous disparity" in the parties' respective bargaining power.

By contrast, in *Scherk v. Alberto-Culver*, the parties were sophisticated businesspeople, who entered into an arm's length transaction in respect of assets located in different countries, well-advised by "an array of European-American lawyers, trademark experts, business consultants," through a two-year negotiating process. In the course of oral argument, however, Justices Douglas and Rehnquist pointed out that the Securities Exchange Act of 1934 did not create any distinction between sophisticated and non-sophisticated parties.[20,21]

In the Defendant's view, "the international aspects to this case [were] compelling enough not to extend the Wilko rule in this case." This was because, in the Defendant's words, "it's essential for the foreign businessmen to know in advance where and how they're going to resolve their conflicts." The Defendant specifically argued that in international transactions an arbitration clause may be "the sine qua non," *i.e.*, a deal breaker clause. Business people needed "certainty in international transaction[s]." The argument was that, in domestic

---

swap agreement any manipulative or deceptive device or contrivance in contravention of such rules and regulations as the Commission may prescribe as necessary or appropriate in the public interest or for the protection of investors."

19 It should be noted that, in 1971, the U.S. Supreme Court implicitly accepted (although in a footnote) that the Act conferred such a remedy in *Superintendent of Ins. v Bankers Life & Cas. Co* 404 U.S. 6 (1971) and then expressly reaffirmed this understanding, in 1975, in *Blue Chip Stamps v Manor Drug Stores* 421 U.S. 723 (1975), and therefore after *Scherk* (n 5).

20 Justice Douglas's comment on this point was: "As you see this definition of security doesn't—in 34, it doesn't turn upon how strong one party is and how weak the other party is".

21 Justice Rehnquist's comment on this point was: "It seems to me it is not entirely satisfactory to say this was a wealthy man and he had three lawyers and the guy Wilko against Swan did not have any lawyer?"

transactions, questions about the applicable law and the competent forum to hear potential disputes were unlikely. The parties would know the law and the forum from the outset. By contrast, in international transactions, there may be numerous disputes about the applicable law and the competent forum, including potential parallel proceedings in different places.

Third, the Defendant also argued that the parties agreed to arbitrate their disputes freely and in good faith, and it be unfair if the Court permitted the Plaintiff "to refuse to honor its promise to arbitrate." This argument highlighted the fact that well-advised parties had freely chosen arbitration as the appropriate method of resolution for their potential conflicts, and only strong policy reasons could override party autonomy and choice. There was no allegation of coercion, misrepresentation, fraud, bad faith, or anything specifically related to the arbitration clause, that could justify not giving effect to that choice.

Fourth, the Defendant also submitted to the Court that it "does not comport with reality" for the U.S. courts to have exclusive jurisdiction to hear securities claims (as was decided in *Wilko v. Swan*), as many arbitrations relating to securities were conducted from day to day in the United States. The Defendant gave as examples arbitrations between "members of exchanges," "non-members and members of exchange" and brokers and customers. Referring to Chapter 2 of the FAA and the New York Convention, the Defendant explained that, after *Wilko v. Swan*, the country has "articulated a strong national policy in favor of arbitration of international transactions."

This argument emphasized the important role played by the New York Convention and its significance for the correct determination of the case. *Wilko v. Swan* was decided in 1953, while the Convention had since entered into force in the United States in 1970. The fact that the United States had now ratified the Convention afforded the Defendant the argument that legal attitudes and policy considerations in respect of arbitration in 1974 (when the Court heard *Scherk v. Alberto-Culver*) differed from what they were in 1953 (when the Court decided *Wilko v. Swan*).

### 2.2.3 The American Arbitration Association's Oral Arguments

The American Arbitration Association (the "AAA", represented by Gerald Aksen) participated in the case as *amicus curiae*. The arbitration clause in the Business Purchase Agreement provided for an ICC Arbitration, not an AAA Arbitration. Nevertheless, the AAA decided to file an *amicus curiae* brief as the arbitral institution was "terribly concerned" about the impact of the case on "international business contract drafting." The brief filed by the AAA and its participation in the oral argument session were particularly relevant for how the case was presented before the Court.

The main line of argument employed by the AAA was the impact of the New York Convention on U.S. law. In that regard, the AAA highlighted to the Supreme Court four "major developments" which had occurred in the United States after it ratified the New York Convention on September 30, 1970.

First, the "Congress amended Chapter 2 of the Federal Arbitration Act", thereby incorporating the New York Convention into U.S. law. As the Convention's ratification occurred in 1970, almost 20 years after the decision in *Wilko v. Swan*, there was an argument that the correct legal position had changed.

Second, in *Wilko v. Swan*, the Court was only addressing Chapter 1 of the FAA. The AAA stressed that "Congress not only added a new chapter to that Act, but the Senate advised and consented on this International Treaty." This point was intended to make clear the full support to arbitration given by the U.S. Congress in recent years.

Third, the AAA pointed out that, only two years prior, the United States had entered into joint agreements[22] with Russia, Poland, and other countries providing for arbitration as a dispute resolution method for all commercial matters. The AAA wanted to demonstrate that any decision taken by the Supreme Court against the enforceability of the arbitration clause would be contrary to the international agreements which the United States had been entering with other countries, under which arbitration had been the country's own preference.

Fourth, the AAA pointed out to the Court that the American Bar Association had written a letter to "all of the other countries in the world" recommending them to ratify the New York Convention.

In another passage relating to these last two arguments, the AAA emphasized that if the Supreme Court allowed the Plaintiff not to honor the arbitration clause, the Court would "drive a caravan though this convention [i.e., the New York Convention]", meaning that a decision holding the arbitration clause unenforceable would completely undermine the applicability of the New York Convention. The AAA also left a subtle message that, if the Supreme Court applied *Wilko v. Swan* to the case, that could constitute a breach of the New York Convention by the United States.

During the course of oral argument,[23] Chief Justice Burger raised an extreme relevant point, by questioning the AAA about the potential relevance

22 The AAA did not name the joint agreements.

23 Also, during the oral argument session, Justice Blackmun raised concerns about public policy. The AAA explained that, in the section dedicated to the recognition and enforcement of foreign arbitral awards (Article V), the New York Convention provides that the host country may refuse to enforce an arbitral award if it offends its public policy. In the

of the Court's[24] previous decision in *The Bremen* to the case.[25] Any discussion of the continued applicability of *Wilko v. Swan* would be wholly inaccurate and incomplete without taking seriously the Supreme Court's seminal analysis in *The Bremen*.[26] In that case, the Supreme Court upheld a choice-of-forum clause selecting the English courts in London to adjudicate any disputes arising from an international contract signed between an American company and a German company. In response to the point raised by Justice Burger, the AAA explained that *Scherk v. Alberto-Culver* was very similar to *The Bremen*, but instead of a choice-of-forum clause, the case dealt with an arbitration clause. In both cases, the parties to an international contract had contracted to resolve potential disputes abroad, *i.e.*, outside the realm of the American courts.

Finally, the AAA also made clear to the Court that "all of the businessmen in the world would welcome the free use of arbitration", including the American businesspeople, given the global and transnational character of the country's economy.

### 2.2.4 Plaintiff's Oral Arguments

The Plaintiff, Alberto-Culver (represented by Francis J. Higgins), contended that the arbitration clause in the Business Purchase Agreement was unenforceable since, under U.S. law, parties cannot arbitrate disputes arising under securities transactions.

After highlighting that the Defendant had conceded that the U.S. courts had personal and subject matter jurisdiction over the case, the Plaintiff stressed that what the Defendant was essentially seeking was for the Court to overrule *Wilko v. Swan*. In order to rebut the Defendant's pleaded case, the Plaintiff advanced five main arguments.

---

section on enforcement of arbitration agreements (Article II), however, the Convention does not mention public policy as a legal ground to refuse arbitration agreements. This argument did not gain much traction. As Article II(3) of the Convention allows the courts not to refer the parties to arbitration when it finds the arbitration agreement "null and void, inoperative or incapable of being performed", it is not straightforward to argue that this expression would not encompass public policy.

24 Chief Justice Burger's comment on this point was: "Did we not have something to say in the Zapata case of the impact on international trade and commerce if arm's length transactions by American companies and foreign companies could not freely commit themselves to arbitration. Wasn't there some discussions of that?"

25 *The Bremen v Zapata Off-Shore Co* (1972) 407 U.S. 1.

26 Pedro J Martinez-Fraga, *The American Influence on International Commercial Arbitration* (CUP 2009) 21.

First, the Plaintiff argued that the Defendant overlooked the fact that securities fraud had been committed within the territorial boundaries of the United States. Moreover, a fraud was committed against an American citizen. This was, in the Plaintiff's view, enough to justify the U.S. courts having jurisdiction to hear the case. Indeed, the alleged fraud took place in the United States by a German party which harmed an American party. The Plaintiff's contention also highlighted the connections of the case to the United States.

Second, the Plaintiff disagreed with the Defendant's interpretation of Section 14 of the Securities Act of 1933 and Section 29(a) of the Securities Exchange Act of 1934. The Plaintiff claimed that the language of those legal provisions was "the same" and, therefore, they could not be interpreted and/or applied differently by the Court.[27]

Third, based on the textual similarity of the two legal provisions, the Plaintiff supported the position that the New York Convention "ma[de] no change in this law" and, actually, "it expressly accommodate[d] Wilko and [Section] 29(a) [of the Securities Exchange Act of 1934] in international transactions". This, argued the Plaintiff, was because the New York Convention expressly authorized a court not to refer the parties to arbitration if "it finds that the said agreement is null and void, inoperative or incapable of being performed", as per Article II(3). If, as advocated by the Plaintiff, the U.S. securities law prohibited arbitration involving securities transactions, the court would be allowed to declare the arbitration clause "null and void, inoperative or incapable of being performed". Hence, the crucial question was whether the securities legislation had prohibited securities claims from being submitted to arbitration in the U.S.

Fourth, the Plaintiff argued that, if the Supreme Court were to decide that an arbitration clause was enforceable in this case by virtue of it involving an international transaction, the decision would allow "a foreigner [who] has come into this country to [de]fraud an American citizen" to "escape [from the jurisdiction of the U.S. courts] because he is a foreigner." The Plaintiff attempted a nationalistic angle, arguing that the Court would be leaving American citizens without any protection in their own country against frauds committed by foreigners on U.S. territory if it agreed with the Defendant.

---

27 Section 14 of the Securities Act of 1933 states as follows: "Any condition, stipulation, or provision binding any person acquiring any security to waive compliance with any provision of this subchapter or of the rules and regulations of the Commission shall be void." Similarly, Section 29(a) of the Securities Exchange Act of 1934 reads as follows: "Any condition, stipulation, or provision binding any person to waive compliance with any provision of this chapter or of any rule or regulation thereunder, or of any rule of an exchange required thereby shall be void."

Interestingly, Chief Justice Burger interrupted the Plaintiff to point out that the hypothesized party would be "[escaping the U.S. courts' jurisdiction] not just because he is a foreigner but because he made an agreement and he is also a foreigner," highlighting that, at the end of the day, there was no question that the Plaintiff freely agreed to sign the arbitration clause and, therefore, to submit any potential dispute between the parties to arbitration.

In response, the Plaintiff said that the arbitration clause was a "stipulation," as provided for Section 29(a) of the Securities Exchange Act of 1934, and therefore U.S. courts had exclusive jurisdiction under Section 27 of the same Act. In addition, the Plaintiff relied on *Leasco v. Maxwell*[28] and *Travis v. Anthes*[29] for the proposition that the U.S. courts already applied the same reasoning as that advocated for by the Plaintiff in an international context, being that foreign companies had come to the United States to defraud American citizens. Justice Stewart, however, pointed out that those cases did not involve arbitration.

After the Plaintiff argued that the transaction was international, but the fraud was domestic, which would give the Plaintiff "the right to access [...] the United States courts", Justice Powell asked the Plaintiff why it had insisted during the negotiations that one of the enterprises should be converted into a Liechtenstein Stock Corporation. The Plaintiff replied explaining that "there were certain tax considerations which Alberto-Culver deserved." It is unclear what point Justice Powell wanted to make with his question. Justice Powell might have just wanted to highlight how international the transaction was. Another interpretation is that his question raised an interesting situation: while the Plaintiff was claiming it should have access to the U.S. courts because it was an American company harmed in the U.S. by a foreign company, the Plaintiff wished to be removed from the reach of U.S. tax law in order to move its newly incorporated companies to a tax haven such as Liechtenstein, as to avoid paying tax in the U.S. One may say that this did not put the Plaintiff in a positive light.

Fifth, the Plaintiff also briefly addressed *The Bremen*. According to the Plaintiff, the Supreme Court made clear in that case that a choice-of-forum clause should be null and void if it contravened public policy (statutory or judicially-declared), as was decided in Boyd v. Grand Trunk Western Railroad.[30] Repeating some of the (controversial) assumptions which the Court made in *Wilko v. Swan*, the Plaintiff argued that referring the parties to arbitration

---

28 *Leasco Data Processing Equipment Corp. v Maxwell* 468 F2d 1326 (2d Cir 1972).

29 *Travis v Anthes Imperial Ltd* 473 F2d 515 (8th Cir 1973).

30 *Boyd v Grand Trunk Western R. Co.* 338 U.S. 263 (1949).

would not only be a procedural, but a substantive issue, as it "can affect and perhaps even destroy the plaintiff's right to recovery."

Essentially, the Plaintiff argued that the absence of appellate proceedings, the requirement of confidentiality, the "lack of discovery," the lack of a system of binding precedent, and "other infirmities of arbitration" would prejudice the Plaintiff's substantive rights. These differences between arbitration and court litigation underpinned the decision in *Wilko v Swan*, and the Plaintiff was trying to invoke the same rationale, basically contending that arbitration does not give the parties the same means to vindicate their rights in comparison to court litigation.

### 2.3 *The Court's Opinion*

#### 2.3.1 The Majority Opinion

As mentioned before, on June 17, 1974, the U.S. Supreme Court handed down its judgment in *Scherk v. Alberto-Culver* by a 5 to 4 majority. Justice Stewart delivered the majority opinion for the Court, joined by Chief Justice Burger and Justices Blackmun, Powell and Rehnquist. The dissenting opinion was rendered by Justice Douglas and joined by Justices Brennan, White and Marshall.

Justice Stewart began his judgment with a powerful observation: the FAA "revers[ed] centuries of judicial hostility to arbitration agreements".[31] Section 2 of the FAA established that an arbitration clause "shall be valid, irrevocable, and enforceable, save upon such grounds as exist at law or in equity for the revocation of any contract."[32] In addition, under Section 3 of the FAA, courts were required to stay proceedings brought in breach of arbitration clauses where satisfied that the dispute before it was covered by the clause.[33] Finally, Section 4 of the FAA directs the courts to order parties to proceed to arbitration

31 *Scherk* (n 5) 510.

32 Section 2 of the FAA reads as follows: "A written provision in any maritime transaction or a contract evidencing a transaction involving commerce to settle by arbitration a controversy thereafter arising out of such contract or transaction, or the refusal to perform the whole or any part thereof, or an agreement in writing to submit to arbitration an existing controversy arising out of such a contract, transaction, or refusal, shall be valid, irrevocable, and enforceable, save upon such grounds as exist at law or in equity for the revocation of any contract or as otherwise provided in Chapter 4."

33 Section 3 of the FAA reads as follows: "If any suit or proceeding be brought in any of the courts of the United States upon any issue referable to arbitration under an agreement in writing for such arbitration, the court in which such suit is pending, upon being satisfied that the issue involved in such suit or proceeding is referable to arbitration under such an agreement, shall on application of one of the parties stay the trial of the action until such arbitration has been had in accordance with the terms of the agreement, providing the applicant for the stay is not in default in proceeding with such arbitration."

if there has been a "failure, neglect, or refusal" of any party to honor an arbitration clause.[34]

Justice Stewart acknowledged that, in *Wilko v. Swan*, the Court recognized that the FAA reflected "a legislative recognition of the 'desirability of arbitration as an alternative to the complications of litigation," but also noted that "[the Supreme Court] declined to apply the Act's provisions."[35] Justice Stewart then proceeded to distinguish *Wilko* from the case before the court (instead of overruling it) based on four main points.

First, Justice Stewart explained that, in *Wilko v. Swan*, the action was brought under Section 12(2) of the Securities Act of 1933, which provides a defrauded purchaser with the "special right"[36] of a private remedy for civil

---

34 Section 4 of the FAA reads as follows: "A party aggrieved by the alleged failure, neglect, or refusal of another to arbitrate under a written agreement for arbitration may petition any United States district court which, save for such agreement, would have jurisdiction under title 28, in a civil action or in admiralty of the subject matter of a suit arising out of the controversy between the parties, for an order directing that such arbitration proceed in the manner provided for in such agreement. Five days' notice in writing of such application shall be served upon the party in default. Service thereof shall be made in the manner provided by the Federal Rules of Civil Procedure. The court shall hear the parties, and upon being satisfied that the making of the agreement for arbitration or the failure to comply therewith is not in issue, the court shall make an order directing the parties to proceed to arbitration in accordance with the terms of the agreement. The hearing and proceedings, under such agreement, shall be within the district in which the petition for an order directing such arbitration is filed. If the making of the arbitration agreement or the failure, neglect, or refusal to perform the same be in issue, the court shall proceed summarily to the trial thereof. If no jury trial be demanded by the party alleged to be in default, or if the matter in dispute is within admiralty jurisdiction, the court shall hear and determine such issue. Where such an issue is raised, the party alleged to be in default may, except in cases of admiralty, on or before the return day of the notice of application, demand a jury trial of such issue, and upon such demand the court shall make an order referring the issue or issues to a jury in the manner provided by the Federal Rules of Civil Procedure, or may specially call a jury for that purpose. If the jury find that no agreement in writing for arbitration was made or that there is no default in proceeding thereunder, the proceeding shall be dismissed. If the jury find that an agreement for arbitration was made in writing and that there is a default in proceeding thereunder, the court shall make an order summarily directing the parties to proceed with the arbitration in accordance with the terms thereof."

35 *Scherk* (n 5) 511.

36 In *Wilko* (n 11), the Court described this "special right" as follows: "To effectuate this policy, § 12(2) created a special right to recover for misrepresentation, which differs substantially from the common law action in that the seller is made to assume the burden of proving lack of scienter. The Act's special right is enforceable in any court of competent jurisdiction—federal or state—and removal from a state court is prohibited. If suit be brought in a federal court, the purchaser has a wide choice of venue, the privilege of

liability.[37] According to the Justice, there was no statutory counterpart to that provision in the Securities Exchange Act of 1934. In his words, "neither §10(b) of that Act [the Securities Exchange Act of 1934] nor Rule 10b-5 speaks of a private remedy to redress violations of the kind alleged here."[38]

Justice Stewart's judgment went on to reason that, while federal case law had established that Section 10(b) and Rule 10b-5 had created an implied private cause of action for investors,[39] the Securities Exchange Act of 1934 itself did not establish the "special right" that the Court considered as significant in *Wilko v. Swan.*[40]

Second, Justice Stewart explained that, while both the Securities Act of 1933 and the Securities Exchange Act of 1934 contained sections barring waiver of "any condition, stipulation, or provision" of the respective Acts, the jurisdictional provision in the latter Act (Section 27(a))[41] was narrower than in the

---

nationwide service of process, and the jurisdictional $3,000 requirement of diversity cases is inapplicable." (*Wilko* (*n 11*) 431).

37 *Scherk* (n 5) 513. Section 12(2) of the Securities Act of 1933 reads as follows: "Any person who (…) offers or sells a security (whether or not exempted by the provisions of section 3, other than paragraphs (2) and (14) of subsection (a) thereof), by the use of any means or instruments of transportation or communication in interstate commerce or of the mails, by means of a prospectus or oral communication, which includes an untrue statement of a material fact or omits to state a material fact necessary in order to make the statements, in the light of the circumstances under which they were made, not misleading (the purchaser not knowing of such untruth or omission), and who shall not sustain the burden of proof that he did not know, and in the exercise of reasonable care could not have known, of such untruth or omission shall be liable, subject to subsection (b), to the person purchasing such security from him, who may sue either at law or in equity in any court of competent jurisdiction, to recover the consideration paid for such security with interest thereon, less the amount of any income received thereon, upon the tender of such security, or for damages if he no longer owns the security."

38 *Scherk* (n 5) 513.

39 Unlike Section 12(2) of the Securities Act of 1933, the anti-fraud provisions of the Securities Exchange Act of 1934, including Section 10(b), do not expressly granted investors with a private remedy and, therefore, do not establish any special right to get access to courts. See also (n 21) above.

40 *Scherk* (n 5) 513–514.

41 Section 27(a) of the Securities Exchange Act of 1934 reads as follows: "The district courts of the United States and the United States courts of any Territory or other place subject to the jurisdiction of the United States shall have exclusive jurisdiction of violations of this title or the rules and regulations thereunder, and of all suits in equity and actions at law brought to enforce any liability or duty created by this title or the rules and regulations thereunder. Any criminal proceeding may be brought in the district wherein any act or transaction constituting the violation occurred. Any suit or action to enforce any liability or duty created by this title or rules and regulations thereunder, or to enjoin any violation of such title or rules and regulations, may be brought in any such district or in the district

former Act (Section 22(a)).[42,43] It is true that the Security Act of 1933 used the expression "shall have jurisdiction" while the Security Exchange Act of 1934 used the words "shall have exclusive jurisdiction," but it is not exactly easy to follow the distinction between these two legal provisions to the extent the Court did.

Third, the majority judgment reasoned that there were "crucial differences" in the factual matrices between the cases.[44] In the case before the Court, the arbitration clause was contained in a "truly international agreement," while in *Wilko v. Swan* the arbitration clause was associated with a purely domestic transaction.

---

wherein the defendant is found or is an inhabitant or transacts business, and process in such cases may be served in any other district of which the defendant is an inhabitant or wherever the defendant may be found. In any action or proceeding instituted by the Commission under this title in a United States district court for any judicial district, a subpoena issued to compel the attendance of a witness or the production of documents or tangible things (or both) at a hearing or trial may be served at any place within the United States. Rule 45(c)(3)(A)(ii) of the Federal Rules of Civil Procedure shall not apply to a subpoena issued under the preceding sentence. Judgments and decrees so rendered shall be subject to review as provided in sections 1254, 1291, 1292, and 1294 of title 28, United States Code. No costs shall be assessed for or against the Commission in any proceeding under this title brought by or against it in the Supreme Court or such other courts."

42 Section 22(a) of the Securities Act of 1933 reads as follows: "The district courts of the United States and United States courts of any Territory shall have jurisdiction of offenses and violations under this title and under the rules and regulations promulgated by the Commission in respect thereto, and, concurrent with State and Territorial courts, except as provided in section 16 with respect to covered class actions, of all suits in equity and actions at law brought to enforce any liability or duty created by this title. Any such suit or action may be brought in the district wherein the defendant is found or is an inhabitant or transacts business, or in the district where the offer or sale took place, if the defendant participated therein, and process in such cases may be served in any other district of which the defendant is an inhabitant or wherever the defendant may be found. In any action or proceeding instituted by the Commission under this title in a United States district court for any judicial district, a subpoena issued to compel the attendance of a witness or the production of documents or tangible things (or both) at a hearing or trial may be served at any place within the United States. Rule 45(c)(3)(A)(ii) of the Federal Rules of Civil Procedure shall not apply to a subpoena issued under the preceding sentence. Judgments and decrees so rendered shall be subject to review as provided in sections 1254, 1291, 1292, and 1294 of title 28, United States Code. Except as provided in section 16(c), no case arising under this title and brought in any State court of competent jurisdiction shall be removed to any court of the United States. No costs shall be assessed for or against the Commission in any proceeding under this title brought by or against it in the Supreme Court or such other courts."

43 *Scherk* (n 5) 514.

44 Ibid 515.

In order to substantiate that point, Justice Stewart relied on a number of relevant facts. In *Scherk v. Alberto-Culver*, he said, (i) the parties were from different countries; (ii) the negotiations and closing of the transaction took place in several countries; (iii) lawyers and experts from different countries advised the parties in the deal; and, "most significantly," (iv) the companies involved in the transactions were all incorporated in Europe.[45] By contrast, in *Wilko v. Swan*, (i) the parties were both American; (ii) the negotiations took place only in the U.S.; (iii) the subject matter of the transaction was exclusively related to the U.S.; and (iv) all the applicable laws were U.S. laws (hence, no conflict of laws problems could arise).[46]

Justice Stewart said that, absent the arbitration clause, "considerable uncertainty existed at the time of the agreement, and still exists, concerning the law applicable to the resolution of disputes arising out of the contract."[47] The Justice explained that, in an international context, conflict of laws problems certainly were prone to arise,[48] and a contractual provision, such as an arbitration clause, specifying in advance the forum in which disputes should be resolved and the law applicable to the parties' relationship is "an almost indispensable precondition to achievement of the orderliness and predictability essential to any international business transaction".[49] The majority opinion went on and stated affirmatively that such contractual provisions "obviate the danger that a dispute under the agreement might be submitted to a forum hostile to the interests of one of the parties or unfamiliar with the problem area involved."[50]

The majority judgment specifically mentioned that a refusal by the courts of a State to enforce an arbitration clause in an international context would be "parochial" and, also, would "invite unseemly and mutually destructive jockeying by the parties to secure tactical litigation advantages."[51] According to the Court, if the Defendant anticipated that the Plaintiff would file court proceedings in the United States, it might have sought anti-suit injunctions or similar

45 *Scherk* (n 5) 515.

46 *Scherk* (n 5) 515–516.

47 *Scherk* (n 5) 516.

48 At Ibid fn 10, Justice Stewart specifically mentions that "while the arbitration agreement involved here provided that the controversies arising out of the agreement be resolved under '[t]he laws of the State of Illinois,' supra, n. 1, a determination of the existence and extent of fraud concerning the trademarks would necessarily involve an understanding of foreign law on that subject."

49 Ibid 516.

50 Ibid 516.

51 Ibid 516–517.

remedies in other jurisdictions, in particular in France (the seat of the arbitration), or directly with the arbitral tribunal. Regardless of the outcome of these potential parallel proceedings, the reality is that it would "surely damage the fabric of international commerce and trade", as stressed by the Court.[52]

Fourth, and closely related to the third point, the Supreme Court made a fruitful comparison between arbitration clauses and choice-of-forum clauses, which rendered the reasoning of *The Bremen* applicable.[53] As explained above, in that case, the Supreme Court upheld a choice-of-forum clause in an international contract favoring London courts, stating that "a [choice-of-] forum clause should control absent a strong showing that it should be set aside"[54] because, among other reasons, these clauses eliminate "much uncertainty and possibly great inconvenience" and such elimination is "an indispensable element in international trade, commerce, and contracting."[55]

Relying entirely on *The Bremen*, Justice Stewart explained that "an agreement to arbitrate before a specified tribunal is, in effect, a specialized kind of forum selection clause" and the invalidation of the arbitration clause "would not only allow the respondent to repudiate its solemn promise, but would, as well, reflect a parochial concept that all disputes must be resolved under our laws and in our courts."[56] Citing *The Bremen*, the Court stated that "we cannot have trade and commerce in world markets and international waters exclusively on our terms, governed by our laws, and resolved in our courts."[57]

52 Ibid 517.

53 *The Bremen* (n 27).

54 Ibid 15. In *Scherk* (n 5), an example given of a situation where a choice-of-forum clause (and an arbitration agreement) should not be enforced was where it was induced by fraud. At footnote 14 of *Scherk* (n 5), Justice Stewart explained that "this qualification [unless obtained by fraud] does not mean that, any time a dispute arising out of a transaction is based upon an allegation of fraud, as in this case, the clause is unenforceable." Rather, continued the Justice, "it means that an arbitration or forum selection clause in a contract is not enforceable if the inclusion of that clause in the contract was the product of fraud or coercion. Although we do not decide the question, presumably the type of fraud alleged here could be raised, under Art. V of the Convention on the Recognition and Enforcement of Foreign Arbitral Awards, see n. 15, infra, in challenging the enforcement of whatever arbitral award is produced through arbitration. Article V(2)(b) of the Convention provides that a country may refuse recognition and enforcement of an award if 'recognition or enforcement of the award would be contrary to the public policy of that country.'"

55 Ibid 13–14.

56 *Scherk* (n 5) 519.

57 Ibid 519, citing *The Bremen* (n 27) 9.

### 2.3.2 The Dissenting Opinion

Delivering the dissenting opinion, Justice Douglas presented six legal grounds in support of the dissenting justices' position that the arbitration clause should be held unenforceable.

First, Justice Douglas observed that the Securities Exchange Act of 1934 did not distinguish sophisticated and unsophisticated people dealing in securities. In his words, "the rules when the giants play are the same as when the pygmies enter the market."[58] Then, the Justice explained that, if there was a fraud, the victim was not Alberto-Culver, but the thousands of investors who were the securities holders in Alberto-Culver.[59]

Second, Justice Douglas argued that, if the dispute was limited to trademark rights, it could be submitted to arbitration, as the policy of Congress in implementing the New York Convention would prevail.[60] However, he added that Congress had specified a "precise way" whereby investors in American companies should be protected. This "precise way", i.e., the protective rules set forth in the securities legislation, was non-waivable.[61] Justice Douglas further pointed out that the New York Convention "does not substitute an arbiter for the settlement of disputes under the 1933 and 1934 Acts."[62] Relying on Articles II(3),[63] V(1)(a),[64] and V(2)(b)[65] of the Convention, Justice Douglas opined that

58 Ibid 526.

59 Ibid 526.

60 Ibid 526.

61 Ibid 527.

62 Ibid 526–527.

63 Article II(3) of the New York Convention reads as follows: "The court of a Contracting State, when seized of an action in a matter in respect of which the parties have made an agreement within the meaning of this article, shall, at the request of one of the parties, refer the parties to arbitration, unless it finds that the said agreement is null and void, inoperative or incapable of being performed."

64 Article V(1)(a) of the New York Convention reads as follows: "1. Recognition and enforcement of the award may be refused, at the request of the party against whom it is invoked, only if that party furnishes to the competent authority where the recognition and enforcement is sought, proof that: (a) The parties to the agreement referred to in article II were, under the law applicable to them, under some incapacity, or the said agreement is not valid under the law to which the parties have subjected it or, failing any indication thereon, under the law of the country where the award was made."

65 Article V(2)(b) of the New York Convention reads as follows: "2. Recognition and enforcement of an arbitral award may also be refused if the competent authority in the country where recognition and enforcement is sought finds that: (…) (b) The recognition or enforcement of the award would be contrary to the public policy of that country."

Section 29(a) of the Securities Exchange Act of 1934 made "agreements to arbitrate liabilities under §10 of the Act 'void' and 'inoperative'."[66]

According to the dissenting opinion, the reason behind such policy was to protect stockholders. Referring to the investors who purchased and held stock issued by Alberto-Culver, Justice Douglas argued that publicly-listed companies like the Plaintiff could not waive those statutory provisions because these companies were "guardians of a host of wards unable to care for themselves".[67] Complementing this point, the Justice reasoned that "it is important that American standards of fairness in security dealings govern the destinies of American investors until Congress changes these standards."[68]

Interestingly, at Footnote 2/6, the dissenting opinion listed substantive provisions of the federal securities laws in support of the contention that investors would lose the level of intended protection if securities claims were submitted to arbitrators instead of American courts.[69] The dissenting opinion, however, did not explain how investors would lose substantive provisions in arbitration, where arbitrators are bound to apply the substantive provisions in the same way as judge was. The dissenting opinion went on and stated that "not a word in the [New York] Convention governing awards adopts the standards which Congress has passed to protect the investors under the 1934 Act."[70] This argument seems to require that an international treaty to regulate the enforcement of arbitration clauses and foreign awards – such as the New York Convention – should provide for substantive legal provisions protecting securities holders, which would surely be very unusual.

Third, Justice Douglas addressed the 'international versus domestic context' issue. In his view, "the international contract talisman" did not make the securities legislation inapplicable to the case, as "§29 of the 1934 Act does not immunize such international transactions".[71] Justice Douglas also said that the New York Convention allowed a court to refuse to refer the parties to arbitration when the arbitration clause was void, inoperative or contrary to the

66 *Scherk* (n 5) 527. Section 29(a) of the Securities Exchange Act of 1934 reads as follows: "Any condition, stipulation, or provision binding any person to waive compliance with any provision of this title or of any rule or regulation thereunder, or of any rule of a self-regulatory organization, shall be void."

67 Ibid 527.

68 Ibid 528.

69 The dissenting opinion only mentioned the company's duty to disclose corporate action to security holders and the duty to fill with the SEC "*extensive annual reports*".

70 Ibid 526–527.

71 Ibid 530.

country's public policy.[72] In addition, the dissenting opinion explained that the uncertainty in international transactions, which was invoked by the majority opinion multiple times as a reason to enforce the arbitration clause in the case, "may persist for many contracts".[73]

Fourth, the dissenting opinion analyzed *The Bremen*. After saying that the majority opinion attempted to treat the case before the Court as "only a minor variation" of *The Bremen*, Justice Douglas stressed that the Supreme Court held in that case that "a contractual choice of forum clause should be held unenforceable if enforcement would contravene a strong public policy of the forum in which suit is brought, whether declared by statute or by judicial decision."[74]

Relying on this passage, Justice Douglas explained that nothing would justify the "abandonment of a national public policy that securities claims be heard by a judicial forum simply because some international elements are involved in a contract."[75] Based on this concept, Justice Douglas stated that, when a foreign corporation undertakes fraudulent actions under American securities laws, "nothing justifies the conclusion that only a diluted version of those laws protects American investors."[76] It appears that the Justice held that the enforcement of security legislation by an arbitral tribunal, instead of American courts, would represent the enforcement of a "diluted version" of the legislation.

Fifth, the dissenting opinion understood that Section 29(a) of the Securities Exchange Act of 1934 provided that a "stipulation" binding one to waive compliance with "any provision" of the act should be held void. In addition, according to the dissenting opinion, the Act expressly established the "exclusive jurisdiction" of federal district courts to hear lawsuits brought under Section 27(a) of the same Act.[77] The arbitration clause, therefore, should have been declared unenforceable because it was a stipulation binding a party to waive the provision that granted investors access to the U.S. courts.

Addressing some of the concerns articulated in *Wilko v. Swan* (in particular, no appellate proceedings and no extensive pre-trial discovery in arbitration[78]),

72 Ibid 530.

73 Ibid 530 fn 2/7.

74 Ibid 530, fn 2/10, citing *The Bremen* (n 27) 15.

75 Ibid 530, fn 2/10.

76 Ibid 530, fn 2/10.

77 Ibid 531.

78 Justice Douglas expressly said that "the arbitral court may improperly interpret the substantive protections of the Rule, and if it does, its error will not be reviewable, as would the error of a federal court" as well as "the ability of Alberto-Culver to prosecute its claim would be eviscerated by lack of discovery": Ibid 532, fn 2/11.

Justice Douglas pointed out that an arbitral award can be made "without explication of reasons," so that "the arbitrator's conception of our statutory requirement may be absolutely incorrect, yet functionally unreviewable, even when the arbitrator seeks to apply our law."[79] In his view, "the loss of the proper judicial forum carries with it the loss of substantial rights."[80] Justice Douglas went on and said that the securities legislation would be "a chimera" when foreign corporations forced defrauded American investors "to the uncertainty of arbitration on foreign soil" or when those investors could not "afford to arbitrate their claims in a far-off forum."[81]

Last but not least, the dissenting opinion relied on the doctrine of separation of powers as a sixth reason to declare the arbitration clause unenforceable. Justice Douglas explained that multinational corporations were a reality and they existed in many parts of the world. Such corporations attracted investment from many American investors and it has been assumed by reason of *Wilko v. Swan* that these investors were all protected by U.S. securities legislation. Justice Douglas asserted that "if these guarantees are to be removed, it should take a legislative enactment".[82] In other words, given what had been established by the previous precedent, the dissenting opinion considered that it was not within the role of the Supreme Court to remove the investors' protective rights provided by the Securities Exchange Act of 1934.

### 2.4 *Key Takeaways*

There are a few takeaways from the decision in *Scherk v. Alberto-Culver*. These takeaways are exclusively based on the reasoning given by the Court at the time of the decision, without reference to subsequent developments in the U.S. arbitration law and practice.

First, unless otherwise expressly provided by statutory provisions, the Supreme Court may be disposed to treat international and domestic cases differently, even where the applicable legal provisions look exactly the same. The Court clearly adopted a more liberal approach when it realized the case involved a cross-border deal.

Second, the Court may have been influenced by the economic environment and further non-legal aspects of the case. In *Scherk v. Alberto-Culver*, the economic globalization and the increase in international trade after World War II, in particular in the 1970s, influenced the interpretation adopted by the Court.

---

79 Ibid 532.
80 Ibid 532.
81 Ibid 533.
82 Ibid 533.

Third, the Court was extremely concerned about legal certainty in commercial matters, in particular in the international context. From a law and economics perspective, the Justices took into account the potential consequences of their decision for businesses between American companies and foreign companies.

Fourth, the United States' ratification of the New York Convention played an important role in the case, as was correctly argued by the AAA, allowing the Court (among other reasons) to depart from its previous decision in *Wilko v. Swan* and to take a more liberal interpretation of domestic legal concepts in an international context.

Fifth, as previously decided in *The Bremen*, the Court reinforced the importance of party autonomy and upheld the parties' choice of the forum in which they wished to solve their disputes. The Court treated choice-of-forum clauses and arbitration clauses as equivalent.

Sixth, any potential nationalist angle in the case – such as, for example, the alleged need to protect American investors against foreign entities – was decisively disregarded by the Court.

## 3 Critical Analysis of the Opinion and How It Impacted U.S. Arbitration Law and Practice

### 3.1 *General Comments*

As explained before, in *Scherk v. Alberto-Culver*, the U.S. Supreme Court reversed the decisions of the District Court and the Court of Appeals and referred the parties to arbitration. The decision was the first of a series of decisions that modernized U.S. arbitration law,[83] and clearly established a pro-arbitration attitude towards international arbitration.[84]

Although the Court did not explicitly overrule *Wilko v. Swan* (where negative assumptions were made about arbitration), *Scherk v. Alberto-Culver* in 1974 laid the groundwork for the mostly celebrated decision in *Mitsubishi v. Soler* in 1985 (where the Supreme Court recognized that "antitrust claims are arbitrable"[85]) and, thereafter, for the decisions in *Shearson/American Express v. McMahon* in 1987 (where the Court held that securities claims, even in a domestic context,

83 Martinez-Fraga (n 28) 21.

84 Julian D M Lew, 'Achieving the Dream: Autonomous Arbitration' (2006) 22(2) Arb Intl 196–197.

85 *Mitsubishi Motors Corp. v Soler Chrysler-Plymouth, Inc.* 473 U.S. 614 (1985).

were arbitrable[86]) and in *Rodriguez de Quijas v. Shearson/American Express* in 1989 (where the Court, finally, overruled *Wilko v. Swan*[87]). *Scherk v. Alberto-Culver* was definitely the turning point for the U.S. Supreme Court to abandon any remaining "parochial[ism]"[88] towards international arbitration.

The majority judgment was clearly influenced by the economic environment in the 1970s.[89] The end of the World War II in 1945 inaugurated a new wave of globalization, led by a new player, the United States. Less than 30 years later, the country was playing a major part in international trade, and many American companies became global conglomerates, spreading their goods, services and influence across different continents. At around 1974, when the Supreme Court decided *Scherk v. Alberto-Culver*, international trade was increasing world-wide. While in 1970, international trade represented 11% of the GDP of the United States and 25% of the world, in 1974 these percentages increased to 16% and 33%.[90] In 1970, the U.S. exports goods and services amounted to approximately USD $60 billion, while in 1975 this numbers surged to approximately USD $126 billion.[91] The amount doubled in only five years.

These economic considerations probably explain why Justice Stewart mentioned international business, commerce and trade so many times. Justice Stewart said that the arbitration clause was "an almost indispensable precondition to achievement of the orderliness and predictability essential to any international business transaction"[92] and that, if the lower courts decisions were upheld by the Supreme Court, it "would surely damage the fabric of international commerce and trade, and imperil the willingness and ability of businessmen to enter into international commercial agreements".[93] Importantly, the Court quoted its previous statement in *The Bremen* that "we cannot have trade and commerce in world markets and international waters exclusively on our terms, governed by our laws, and resolved in our courts."[94]

---

86 *Shearson/American Express v McMahon* 482 U.S. 220 (1987).

87 *Rodriguez de Quijas v Shearson/American Express, Inc.* 490 U.S. 477 (1989).

88 We should highlight that the word "*parochial*" was used by the own Supreme Court to describe the approach adopted in *Wilko* (n 11): see *Scherk* (n 5) 507, 516, 519 and 521.

89 Martinez-Fraga (n 28) 21.

90 Currently, international trade represents 25% of the GDP of the United States and 57% of the GDP of the world. The World Bank, 'Trade (% of GDP) – United States' <https://data.worldbank.org/indicator/NE.TRD.GNFS.ZS?end=2021&locations=US&start=1970&view=chart> accessed 31 August 2023.

91 Macrotrends, 'U.S. Exports 1970–2023' <https://www.macrotrends.net/countries/USA/united-states/exports> accessed 31 August 2023.

92 *Scherk* (n 5) 516.

93 Ibid 517.

94 Ibid 519, citing *The Bremen* (n 27) 9.

The decision also emphasized the importance of the United States' commitment to the New York Convention, and how the Convention's purposes had to be respected by enforcing international arbitration agreements. The decision did not analyze in detail the pertinent legal provisions of the New Convention to determine the case, but it was clearly influenced by the fact that the United States had ratified the Convention and incorporated its content into domestic law, *i.e.*, into Chapter 2 of the FAA. These steps were understood by the majority as a clear Congressional choice to favor international arbitration.

Justice Stewart expressly said, although in a footnote, that the principal purpose underlying the United States' adoption and implementation of the New York Convention "was to encourage the recognition and enforcement of commercial arbitration agreements in international contracts" and also "to unify the standards by which agreements to arbitrate are observed and arbitral awards are enforced in the signatory countries."[95] In the same footnote, the majority decision highlighted that "this country's adoption and ratification of the Convention and the passage of Chapter 2 of the United States Arbitration Act provide strongly persuasive evidence of congressional policy consistent with the decision we reach today."[96]

The distinction between international and domestic transactions permitted the Court to make a *volte-face* in its case law on whether securities claims could be submitted to arbitration,[97] which would lead the Court to extend its reasoning to domestic securities claims ten years later in *Shearson/American Express v. McMahon* and *Rodriguez de Quijas v. Shearson/American Express*. This change in approach also meant that the Supreme Court finally accepted that disputes concerning legal relationships subject to mandatory rules could be settled through arbitration.[98] Moreover, the Court's decision in *Scherk v. Alberto-Culver* anticipated what would be expressly stated in *Mitsubishi v. Soler*, *i.e.*, that the U.S. courts should subordinate domestic notions to the international policy favoring commercial arbitration.[99]

Also, with regard to the distinction between international and domestic transactions, *Scherk v. Alberto-Culver* further demonstrated that the Supreme

95 Ibid 520 fn 15.

96 Ibid 520 fn 15.

97 William W Park, 'The Lex Loci Arbitri and International Commercial Arbitration' (1983) 32 ICLQ 30.

98 Donald F Donovan and Alexander K A Greenawalt, 'Mitsubishi After Twenty Years: Mandatory Rules Before Courts and International Arbitrators' in Loukas A. Mistelis and Julian D M Lew (eds), *Pervasive Problems in International Arbitration* (Kluwer Law International 2006) para 1–14.

99 *Mitsubishi Motors Corp* (n 87) 639.

Court was particularly concerned about legal certainty. The Court wanted to ensure legal certainty in commercial relationships, and it assumed that, in international transactions, legal certainty was somehow more critical than in purely domestic transactions. Enforcing arbitration clauses was the best way, in the Court's view, to guarantee legal certainty in cross-border securities transactions. This construction was particularly well aligned with the expectations of businesspeople. An unexpected change in the dispute resolution regime selected by the parties would definitely undermine legal certainty in an international transaction. From an economic perspective, the unenforceability of a freely agreed arbitration clause changes the bargaining balance carefully designed by the parties. The arbitration clause is a relevant part of any international deal.

Another relevant aspect of the decision is that is it clearly reinforced party autonomy. Both parties were sophisticated companies, with operations spreading beyond their home countries. The negotiation took approximately two years and both parties were well-advised by lawyers and experts from different countries. They both knew exactly what they were doing when they agreed to submit any potential dispute to arbitration. The judgments did not explore in detail the language of the arbitration clause, but it is worth mentioning that the parties agreed that "any controversy or claim" arising out of the Business Purchase Agreement should be "settled exclusively by arbitration." The scope of the clause was broad, and the parties expressly used the word "exclusively," indicating their will to solve any conflicts through arbitration.

Given these clear words chosen by the parties, any decision taken by the Court to render the arbitration clause unenforceable would have been perceived as an inappropriate state interference in commercial relationships, which would weaken party autonomy: a cornerstone in arbitration and, in particular, in U.S. law. It is worth mentioning that the Court enforced the parties' agreement in a case where the Plaintiff was an American company allegedly defrauded by a foreign individual and the decision, in the end, found in favor of the foreign party and forced the American company to pursue its rights outside the United States. *Scherk v. Alberto-Culver* is a clear demonstration by the Supreme Court of judicial independence and neutrality, putting aside any nationalist considerations that could potentially have influenced its decision.

In distinguishing *Wilko v. Swan*, the Court also prevented itself from repeating prejudiced assumptions against arbitration which it made twenty years earlier. The Plaintiff, followed by the dissenting opinion on this point,[100] argued

100 *Scherk* (n 5) 532–533.

that the absence of a right of appeal in arbitration, the non-existence of a duty to give reasons in arbitral awards, the limited scope for discovery, and the lack of a system of binding precedent (*i.e.*, there is no *stare decisis* in arbitration) could "affect and perhaps even destroy the plaintiff's right to recovery."

There are obvious procedural differences between arbitration and court litigation. They do not, however, put any substantive rights of the parties at risk. These procedural differences only show that arbitration and court litigation have their own relative advantages and disadvantages. For example, while court litigation permits appeals, arbitration permits the parties to choose the arbitrators, who are normally specialists in the subject matter at stake. While court litigation allows broader discovery, arbitration gives the parties wider flexibility to establish a tailor-made procedure, including in the evidentiary stage. It is true that *stare decisis* applies in court litigation, which increases decisional predictability, but arbitrators are already obliged to apply the law chosen by the parties (which, in Common Law countries, encompasses judicial precedents). It is generally easier to enforce arbitral awards worldwide than court judgments, as the New York Convention basically applies to all relevant jurisdictions in the world and there is no similar convention for court judgments.[101]

In summary, arbitration and court litigation have their own advantages and disadvantages, which should be considered by the parties before signing any arbitration clause. Absent any consent issue specifically associated with the arbitration clause (incapacity, duress, fraud etc.), the parties should be free to choose which system they prefer to use to solve their potential disputes. In *Scherk v. Alberto-Culver*, the Supreme Court demonstrated that U.S. law upholds parties' choices and that the parties are absolutely free to resolve their disputes outside the jurisdiction of the U.S. without risking the loss of their substantive rights.

---

101 Currently, the New York Convention has been ratified by and is in force in 172 countries. See United Nations Commission On International Trade Law, 'Status: Convention on the Recognition and Enforcement of Foreign Arbitral Awards (New York, 1958)' <https://uncitral.un.org/en/texts/arbitration/conventions/foreign_arbitral_awards/status2> accessed 31 August 2023. It is worth mentioning that, in the court litigation field, the *Convention of 2 July 2019 on the Recognition and Enforcement of Foreign Judgments in Civil or Commercial Matters* (HCCH 2019 Judgments Convention) facilitates the effective international circulation of judgments in civil or commercial matters. Currently, the HCCH 2019 is in force in 28 countries. However, it is still not in force in, for example, U.S., China, Japan, India, United Kingdom, Russia, Canada, Brazil, Australia, South Korea, Mexico, Indonesia, Saudi Arabia, Turkey, Switzerland and Argentina, *i.e.*, in 17 of the 25 largest economies in the world.

Finally, the Court also put on an equal footing choice-of-forum clauses and arbitration clauses, citing, in particular, its decision in *The Bremen*. The Supreme Court, remarkably, said that "an agreement to arbitrate before a specified tribunal is, in effect, a specialized kind of forum selection clause that posits not only the situs of suit, but also the procedure to be used in resolving the dispute".[102] The decision not only equated choice-of-forum clauses and arbitration clauses but also foreign court proceedings and international arbitration. The same respect that courts around the world ought to demonstrate towards court proceedings in other countries (*i.e.*, international comity) may extend to international arbitration as well.

## 3.2 *Arbitrability of Securities Claims in* Scherk v. Alberto-Culver

### 3.2.1 Terminology

Despite all angles explored in the case, *Scherk v. Alberto-Culver* dealt with a very specific question: can securities claims be legally submitted to arbitration?

In the vast majority of countries (including England, France, Switzerland, Singapore, and Brazil), this type of issue is well understood as involving a question of "*arbitrability*."[103] The New York Convention does not mention "arbitrability" in its text, but addresses the same point by using the expression "subject matter capable of settlement by arbitration" (Article II(1)).[104] In this sense, arbitrability refers to whether certain types of disputes can (or cannot) be determined in arbitration.[105] Each State decides which matters can be submitted

102 *Scherk* (n 5) 517 and 519, citing *The Bremen* (n 27) 9.

103 The concept of arbitrability encompasses "*subjective arbitrability*" and "*objective arbitrability*". In this text, we only address "*objective arbitrability*." Bernard Hanotiau explains the concepts: "In its usual meaning, arbitrability can be challenged in two different ways: (a) by reason of the quality of one of the parties, when this party is a State, a public collectives or entity or public body. One refers in this case to subjective arbitrability or arbitrability ratione personae, which is directly related to the quality of the parties in dispute; and (b) by reason of the subject matter of the dispute which has been removed from the domain arbitration by the applicable national law. This is objective arbitrability or "arbitrability ratione materiae"": Bernard Hanotiau, 'The Law Applicable to Arbitrability', in Albert Jan van den Berg (ed), *Improving the Efficiency of Arbitration Agreements and Awards: 40 Years of Application of the New York Convention* (Kluwer Law International 1999) 147. Piero Bernardini, 'The Problem of Arbitrability in General' in Emmanuel Gaillard and Domenico Di Pietro (eds), *Enforcement of Arbitration Agreements and International Arbitral Awards: The New York Convention in Practice* (Cameron May 2008) 503.

104 United Nations Commission on International Trade Law, *UNCITRAL Secretariat Guide on the Convention on the Recognition and Enforcement of Foreign Arbitral Awards* (United Nations Publishing 2016) 49 ("UNCITRAL Secretariat Guide").

105 Discussing the doctrine of non-arbitrability, Gary Born explains that it "applies to categories of disputes or subject matters which are deemed by national law to be incapable

to arbitration ("arbitrable matters") and which matters belong exclusively to the domain of the courts ("non-arbitrable matters"). Classic examples of non-arbitrable matters include criminal offences, family disputes, administrative matters, employment claims, core insolvency issues etc.[106] In *Scherk v. Alberto-Culver*, the question was whether securities claims were arbitrable.

In the United States, however, courts have given the term "arbitrability" a far broader meaning than that discussed above.[107] As used by the U.S. courts, the term "arbitrability" also encompasses questions pertaining to the validity, enforceability and scope of the arbitration clause, compliance with pre-conditions to arbitration (for example, compliance with cooling-off periods or mediation in 'med-arb' clauses), the potential non-existence of the main contract, issues relating to non-signatories, potential waiver of the arbitration clause, statute of limitations, *res judicata*, etc.[108] In the United States, the term "arbitrability" refers to many more issues than merely whether a particular claim can (or cannot) be submitted to arbitration by virtue of its subject matter.

Moreover, in the United States, terms such as "threshold issues," "gateway issues" and "non-gateway issues" are commonly used by courts in the same context.[109] According to George Bermann, the term "gateway issues" is susceptible of two meanings. The first – and broader – meaning encompasses any legal issue that can potentially bar a particular claim against a particular party from proceeding in arbitration (also referred to as "threshold issues" or "arbitrability," as explained in the previous paragraph).[110] The second – and

---

of resolution by arbitration, even if the parties have otherwise validly agreed to arbitrate such matters": Gary B Born, *International Commercial Arbitration* (Online updated edn, Kluwer Law International 2022) §6.01.

106 International Council for Commercial Arbitration, *ICCA's Guide to the Interpretation of the 1958 New York Convention: A Handbook for Judges* (ICCA 2011) <https://cdn.arbitration-icca.org/s3fs-public/document/media_document/judges_guide_nyc_english_2018_reprint.pdf> accessed 31 August 2023 ("ICCA Guide").

107 In this sense, Laurence Shore explains that "*arbitrability*' is a far broader concept in the United States than in other countries": Laurence Shore, 'The United States' Perspective on "Arbitrability"' in Loukas A. Mistelis and Stavros Brekoulakis (eds), *International Arbitration Law Library*, Volume 19 (Kluwer Law International 2009) 69. Gary Born opines that "*this terminology is imprecise, even in the U.S. context, and should be avoided in international settings*": Born (n 107) §6.01.

108 George A Bermann, 'The "Gateway" Problem in International Commercial Arbitration' in Stefan M Kröll et al (eds), *International Arbitration and International Commercial Law: Synergy, Convergence and Evolution* (Kluwer Law International 2011) 60.

109 For example, the U.S. Supreme Court in *Howsam v Dean Witter Reynolds, Inc.* 537 U.S. 79 (2002).

110 This first meaning is sometimes also referred to as "*threshold issues*" and also as "*arbitrability*", as explained in Bermann (110) 60.

narrower – meaning signifies issues that, if raised before a court, it must resolve for itself rather than leave it to be decided by the arbitral tribunal.[111] In turn, "non-gateway issues" are those which are left initially to the arbitrators to decide, even if they are raised before the courts.[112,113]

For the purposes of this essay, the answer to the question of whether securities claims can be legally submitted to arbitration is, under the glossary commonly used by U.S. courts, one of many "gateway issues". This essay, however, uses the term "arbitrability" to refer to that question. That accords with international practice, international treaties, international academic papers and international decisions. It is also the preference of American arbitration commentators such as George Bermann.[114] In summary, the term "arbitrability" is used in this essay to refer to the particular "gateway issue" of whether claims under U.S. securities legislation can be legally submitted to arbitration

---

111 Ibid 58.

112 George Bermann summarizes these terms, as they have been used by courts, as follows: "When reference is made to all preliminary issues – both those reserved for courts initially to decide ('gateway issues') and those reserved for the arbitrators initially to decide ('non-gateway issues) – the better term to use, and the one used in this article, is, as noted, simply 'threshold issues ... What distinguishes gateway issues is that they may and should instead be decided by a court if they first arise before it. Only 'non-gateway' issues are reserved initially for the tribunal, even if raised earlier before a court. In short, threshold issues do not fall into two mutually exclusive categories, the one to be decided exclusively by the court, the other exclusively by the arbitrators. Some threshold issues (viz., the gateway issues) will be addressed by the court or the tribunal, whichever is the first to be asked; others (viz., the non-gateway issues) are for the arbitrators to decide in the first instance, wherever the dispute over them happens to arise". Ibid 58–59.

113 George Bermann also highlights that "the fact that an issue is a gateway issue (hence for the court to decide when it is initially raised there) does not mean that arbitrators cannot decide that issue if it is raised initially before them". This is because arbitral tribunals are entitled to decide any threshold issues raised before them, as per the Kompetenz-Kompetenz rule. Therefore, "gateway issues" and "non-gateway issues" are not mutually exclusive categories, as arbitral tribunals can decide any of them. The author also explains that "gateway issues" will be addressed by the court or the arbitral tribunal, whichever is the first to be asked, but "non-gateway issues" are for the arbitrators to decide in the first instance, "wherever the dispute over them happens to arise". Ibid 58–59.

114 The author explains that "[t]he very last of these questions – namely, whether a dispute is one that may legally be submitted to arbitration – is a particularly important one in many jurisdictions. Legislatures do sometimes take the step of declaring a cause of action legally incapable of being arbitrated. That prospect is perhaps more alive than ever in the United States today. The term 'non-arbitrability' captures this particular notion very well, thus providing shorthand for the more cumbersome locution, 'not legally capable of arbitration.' I thus prefer to use the term arbitrability here in this narrow sense, signifying the legal capacity of a dispute to be subject to arbitration". Ibid 61.

notwithstanding their subject matter (as was addressed in *Scherk v. Alberto-Culver*), and not "arbitrability" in the broader sense adopted by the U.S. courts.

### 3.2.2 Arbitrability in *Scherk v. Alberto-Culver*

In *Scherk v. Alberto-Culver*, the question of whether claims under U.S. securities law could be legally submitted to arbitration was discussed by the Supreme Court by reference to two different legal doctrines: arbitrability (in the sense explained in the previous section), and public policy.[115]

The arbitrability point arose in the Court's discussion of whether the Securities Exchange Act of 1934 conferred upon investors special rights to access the U.S. courts which were non-waivable and, therefore, would render claims based on those rights non-arbitrable.[116] It was argued before the Court that the exclusive jurisdiction of the U.S. courts to hear securities claims could potentially make those claims non-arbitrable and the arbitration agreement unenforceable as far as they were concerned.

Arbitrability is a complex subject in international arbitration.[117] Courts have typically addressed it in two procedural contexts: (i) when a court needs to analyze an arbitration clause and decide whether the parties should be referred to arbitration (Article II of the New York Convention – "pre-enforcement stage"), and (ii) when a court needs to recognize an arbitral award and to decide whether it will allow enforcement in its territory (Article V of the New York Convention – "enforcement stage").

In *Scherk v. Alberto-Culver*, the Court dealt with a pre-enforcement stage. The New York Convention does not offer any guidance on what law governs arbitrability at the pre-enforcement stage,[118] which creates some challenges in practice.[119] In the United States, the FAA also does not address arbitrability, either directly or by implication.[120] In the case, the law governing the Business

115 Exploring the similarities and difference between arbitrability (actually, non-arbitrability) and public policy: see Born (107) §6.02[G].

116 *Scherk* (*n 5*) 513, 514, 525, 527, 527 (fn 2/5), 530 and 530 (fn 2/10).

117 As explained by Bernardini (n 105) 517, "under the majority of national laws, a dispute is capable of settlement by arbitration whenever the parties are free to dispose of the rights on which the claims before the arbitrator are based".

118 UNCITRAL Secretariat Guide (n 106) 49; International Council for Commercial Arbitration (n 108) 63–64, 65. See also Born (n 107) §4.05[A], which states, "[a]s discussed above, Article II of the New York Convention does not expressly address choice-of-law questions regarding non-arbitrability".

119 Bernard Hanotiau expressly says that "[a]rbitrability is indeed a condition of validity of the arbitration agreement and consequently, of the arbitrators' jurisdiction": Hanotiau (n 105) 153.

120 Born (n 107) §6.03[C][4].

Purchase Agreement was Illinois law, the seat of the arbitration was in France, the companies in which the relevant investment was made were incorporated in Germany and Liechtenstein, and the court proceedings were commenced in the United States. All these potential connections with different jurisdictions could engender conflict-of-laws problems in respect of the identification of the correct governing law for arbitrability.

Giving the lack of a specific legal provision on arbitrability during the pre-enforcement stage, courts around the world have assessed whether a dispute concerning a specific subject matter can be settled by arbitration by reference to (i) the applicable law to the arbitration clause, (ii) the law of the seat, or (iii) their own laws (*i.e.*, the *lex fori* or the domestic law of the forum where enforcement of the arbitration clause is sought).[121]

These possible solutions are based on the application, by analogy, of the choice-of-law provisions of the New York Convention at the enforcement stage. In Article V(1)(a), the Convention establishes that the enforcement of an arbitral award may de refused by the relevant court where the arbitration clause is "not valid under the law to which the parties have subjected it [the arbitration clause] or, failing any indication thereon, under the law of the country where the award was made." This interpretation assumes that arbitrability is one of the determinants of an arbitration clause's validity, which is a controversial matter between commentators.[122]

---

121 UNCITRAL Secretariat Guide (n 106) 49. Occasionally, it has been said that arbitrability issues at the pre-enforcement stage should be governed by "an international rule of substantive law" (Hanotiau (n 105) 165). References have also been made to the law of the forum in which the award will be enforced (which, however, is difficult to predict at an early stage of the arbitration, as quite often the claimant does not know where the respondent's assets are located) (ICCA Guide (n 108) 63–64).

122 Bernard Hanotiau expressly says that "Arbitrability is indeed a condition of validity of the arbitration agreement and consequently, of the arbitrators' jurisdiction": Hanotiau (n 105) 146. See also Bernardini (105) 503: "[a]rbitrability is, therefore, a condition of the validity of the arbitration agreement and, consequently, of the arbitrator's jurisdiction". By contrast, Gary Born expressly states that "a rule of non-arbitrability under the New York Convention (and parallel national arbitration legislation) is distinguishable in important ways from a rule of substantive invalidity of an arbitration agreement": Born (n 107) §6.02[E]. Loukas Mistelis also sees differences between arbitrability and validity of the arbitration clause, in particular regarding the applicable law: "[t]he New York Convention clearly and pertinently distinguishes between the law applicable to the issue of arbitrability and the law governing the validity of the arbitration agreement. While the latter is primarily submitted to the choice of the parties and in the absence of such a choice to the law of the place of arbitration, each national court determines the arbitrability of a dispute according to its own law": Loukas A Mistelis, 'Chapter 1 – Arbitrability – International and Comparative Perspectives' in Mistelis and Brekoulakis (109) 12–13.

Regardless of this discussion, some courts have applied the law chosen by the parties to govern the arbitration clause to determine arbitrability issues at the pre-enforcement stage (which, in reality, rarely happens) or, in its absence, the law of the seat of the arbitration ("law of the country where the award was made").[123] In *Scherk v. Alberto-Culver*, one could have argued that the question of whether securities claims could be legally submitted to arbitration should be governed by French law, as the seat of the arbitration was Paris, in France.[124]

Other courts have applied their own laws, *i.e.*, the *lex fori*. This is because the New York Convention, in Article V(2)(a), states that the enforcement of an arbitral award may de refused by the relevant court where the "the subject matter of the difference is not capable of settlement by arbitration under the law of that country."[125,126] If applied to the facts of *Scherk v. Alberto-Culver*, it would mean the application of federal U.S. law – or, more precisely, the FAA and the Securities Exchange Act of 1934, as both arbitration and securities are governed by federal law in the U.S.

The prevailing position is that arbitrability, at the pre-enforcement stage, should be determined by the courts under their own laws (*lex fori*).[127] In this sense, Stavros Brekoulakis explains that, "although different views have been

123 UNCITRAL Secretariat Guide (n 106) 49.

124 It is worth noting that the arbitration clause inserted in the Business Purchase Agreement specifically says that "the laws of the State of Illinois, U.S.A. shall apply to and govern this agreement, its interpretation and performance", which may mean the parties have chosen the applicable law to the arbitration clause. It is not clear, however, whether this choice-of-law sub-clause applies only to the Business Purchase Agreement (the word "agreement" is used to refer to the Business Purchase Agreement at the beginning of the clause), only to the arbitration clause, or to both.

125 UNCITRAL Secretariat Guide (n 106) 49. As mentioned before, by using the expression "*capable of settlement by arbitration*", the New York Convention is referring to arbitrability.

126 Bernard Hanotiau explains that "it is said that since Art. V refers to the law of the forum, the same approach should prevail when one applies Art. II(3)" and then manifests his disagreement by saying that "I do not think that this is the right approach" as "the enforcement of the award is another issue which should be dealt with separately on the basis of Art. V(2) of the New York Convention", and expressly says that "[a]rbitrability is indeed a condition of validity of the arbitration agreement and consequently, of the arbitrators' jurisdiction": Hanotiau (n 105) 163 and 164–165.

127 According to the ICCA Guide (n 108) 63–64, "in practice, the most suitable and least problematic solution is the application of the lex fori. It is the most suitable (as long as the court would have jurisdiction in the absence of an arbitration agreement) under the Convention since this approach accords with Article V(2)(a) which provides for the application of the standards of arbitrability of the lex fori in relation to the enforcement of awards" See also Mistelis (n 126) 12: "In the majority of cases, courts have determined the question of arbitrability at the pre-award stage according to their own national law".

argued here, the prevailing one seems to be that the national court reviewing an arbitration agreement should apply the lex fori to determine whether the pending dispute is arbitrable or not".[128] This is the solution provided by Article VI(2) of the European Convention on International Commercial Arbitration of 1961,[129] and it is arguably the most consistent approach in view of Article V(2)(a) of the New York Convention.[130,131]

Specifically in the United States, the Restatement of the U.S. Law of International Commercial and Investor-State Arbitration explains that "courts in the United States ordinarily look to federal law when a litigant resisting arbitration invokes a non-arbitrability defence to enforcement of an arbitration agreement".[132] Similarly, in the U.S., arbitrability at the pre-enforcement stage is assessed by courts in accordance with their own laws (*lex fori*).

In *Scherk v. Alberto-Culver*, the U.S. Supreme Court did not conduct a detailed analysis of the conflict-of-law issues regarding the law applicable to arbitrability. The Supreme Court simply applied U.S. law.[133] There are, however, some excerpts bearing on the discussion about the law applicable to arbitrability.

---

128 Stavros Brekoulakis, 'Chapter 6 – Law Applicable to Arbitrability: Revisiting the Revisited Lex Fori' in Mistelis and Brekoulakis (n 109) 103–104.

129 Article VI(2) of the European Convention reads as follows: "The courts may also refuse recognition of the arbitration agreement if under the law of their country the dispute is not capable of settlement by arbitration".

130 Born (n 107) §4.05[A][1]; ICCA Guide (n 108) 63–64.

131 It does not mean, however, that this solution can be applied mechanically to all cases. Imagine a case where parties from State A and State B agree to arbitrate a dispute in State C (seat of the arbitration). Apart from the seat, the case has no connection whatsoever with State C. In these circumstances, it is difficult to understand why the courts of State C, if required to enforce the arbitration clause, should apply their own laws to assess the subject matter arbitrability (in particular if the subject matter is arbitrable under the laws of States A and B). It may be reasonable to conduct such analysis at the enforcement stage, and this is what the New York Convention directs the courts to do (Article V(2)(a), as mentioned before). At the pre-enforcement stage, however, such analysis would be premature and there is no express legal provision in the New York Convention in this regard. See, in this regard, Born (n 107) §4.05[A][1]. Additionally, Brekoulakis (n 132) 103–104 considers that "the lex fori will be relevant only to the extent that the jurisdiction of the national courts before which the dispute is referred (the national courts of referral) will be relevant for the specific dispute at hand", as well as "the lex fori will apply only when there is a jurisdictional conflict between an arbitral tribunal and the national courts of referral", meaning that "the legislative purpose of a state provision on arbitrability is to apply when there is a jurisdictional conflict between an arbitral tribunal and the courts of that state and allocate exclusive jurisdiction to the latter with regard to specific disputes".

132 American Law Institute, *Restatement of the U.S. Law of International Commercial and Investor-State Arbitration* (American Law Institute 2023) 292 §2.16.

133 Born (n 107) §4.05[B].

Referring to Article II(1) of the New York Convention, which imposes on Contracting States the duty to give legal effect to arbitration clauses "concerning a subject matter capable of settlement by arbitration",[134] Justice Stewart explained that, as revealed by the *travaux préparatoires*, there was a concern frequently raised that courts could "decline enforcement of such agreements on the basis of parochial views of their desirability or in a manner that would diminish the mutually binding nature of the agreements."[135] This passage gives the impression that the Supreme Court, in its desire to avoid taking a "parochial view," would possibly apply an international rule of substantive law towards arbitrability.

The dissenting opinion also mentioned the *travaux préparatoires*, but in order to interpret Article II(3) and, in particular, in respect of the issue of whether courts could apply their own laws to refuse to give legal effect to arbitration clauses. Citing G. W. Haight's analysis of the record of the United Nations Conference of May/June 1859,[136] Justice Douglas explained that "as the applicable law is not indicated, courts may under this wording be allowed some latitude; they may find an agreement incapable of performance if it offends the law or the public policy of the forum".[137] The dissenting Justice then stated that the delegates "contemplated that a court may decline to enforce an agreement which offends its law or public policy."[138] As mentioned above, the prevailing opinion is, indeed, that courts should determine a dispute's arbitrability under their own laws (*lex fori*).

In doing so, however, the dissenting opinion held that "§29(a) of the 1934 Act [Securities Exchange Act of 1934] makes agreements to arbitrate liabilities under §10 of the Act 'void' and 'inoperative'."[139] It is clear from this passage – and by the majority's detailed analysis of the relevant sections of the Securities Exchange Act of 1934 – that the Supreme Court was considering the arbitrability of the dispute under its own law. The disagreement between

---

134 Article II(1) of the New York Convention reads as follows: "Each Contracting State shall recognize an agreement in writing under which the parties undertake to submit to arbitration all or any differences which have arisen or which may arise between them in respect of a defined legal relationship, whether contractual or not, concerning a subject matter capable of settlement by arbitration."

135 Scherk (n 5) 520 fn 1.

136 G W Haight, *Convention on the Recognition and Enforcement of Foreign Arbitral Awards: Summary Analysis of Record of United Nations Conference May/June 1958* (UN Press 1958).

137 *Scherk* (n 5) 530 fn 2/10.

138 Ibid 530 fn 2/10.

139 Ibid 527 and 530.

the majority and dissenting opinion did not relate to the law applicable to arbitrability (they agreed it should be subject to U.S. law), but whether U.S. law made securities claims non-arbitrable.

### 3.2.3 Public Policy in *Scherk v. Alberto-Culver*

The public policy argument was discussed when the Court analyzed whether a decision declaring an arbitration clause unenforceable would lead to legal uncertainty for international business transactions (majority opinion), and whether enforcing the arbitration clause would be inconsistent with Congress' object of protecting American investors from frauds perpetrated by non-U.S. entities, leaving them without access to the U.S. courts.[140]

The public policy defense relates to the possibility that the recognition of certain arbitration clauses and arbitral awards violates basic mandatory laws or public policies of the host country.[141] Article V(2)(b) of the New York Convention expressly states that the host country may refuse the recognition or enforcement of an arbitral award whether it "would be contrary to the public policy of that country." It expressly provides for public policy as a legal ground for non-enforcement of arbitral awards.

At the pre-enforcement stage, however, Article II(3) of the Convention only states that a court may not refer the parties to arbitration where the arbitral clause is "null and void, inoperative or incapable of being performed". In other words, unlike Article V(2)(b) at the enforcement stage, Article II(3) is silent as regards whether public policy can be a defense at the pre-enforcement stage.

There is a lively debate about whether the New York Convention implicitly allows a court to refuse to enforce an arbitration clause based on public policy considerations. Gary Born, for example, explains that "public policy does not provide a proper basis for resisting recognition or enforcement of arbitration agreements under the Convention or most national arbitration legislation."[142] This is because, in general, public policy considerations are best considered in respect of the enforcement of actual arbitral awards, without speculating about what the arbitral award may be in the future.[143] According to Gary Born, what normally occasions a potential violation of public policy is the content of the arbitral award, not the possibility of referring the case to arbitration.

Taking the contrary view, Albert Jan van den Berg argues that the distinction between arbitrability and public policy "is an historical one and could

140 Ibid 515, 517–518, 527 fn 2/5, and 533.
141 Born (n 107) §5.06[D][12](a).
142 Ibid §5.06[D][12].
143 Ibid §5.06[D][12](d).

have been dealt with in one ground for refusal of enforcement [of arbitration clauses] being public policy only".[144] The author continues by saying that, alternatively, "public policy can be regarded as falling under the words 'null and void' appearing in the terminal part of Art. II(3)."[145] This interpretation basically extends the public policy defense at the enforcement stage to the pre-enforcement stage, seeking a more consistent approach between Articles II(3) and V(2)(b) of the New York Convention.

The Restatement of the U.S. Law of International Commercial and Investor-State Arbitration describes the position under U.S federal law to be that "a court decides whether enforcement of an arbitration agreement would be repugnant to the public policy of the United States, and, to the extent it so finds, decline to enforce the arbitration agreement".[146] In other words, according to the Restatement, the public policy defense is available at the pre-enforcement stage in the United States.

In *Scherk v. Alberto-Culver*, the Supreme Court took into account public policy arguments to determine the enforceability of the arbitration clause. Justice Stewart's judgment focused on the arbitrability issue, but, at some point, he explained that "the country's adoption and ratification of the Convention and the passage of Chapter 2 of the United States Arbitration Act provide strongly persuasive evidence of congressional policy" militated in favor of the enforcement of arbitration clauses, which was consistent with the majority's conclusion that the arbitration agreement ought to be enforced.[147]

In comparison, the dissenting opinion placed more emphasis on public policy in a number of ways. First, Justice Douglas said that Section 29 of the Securities Exchange Act of 1934 made arbitration clauses "void and inoperative" even in the international context and the New York Convention "makes provision for such national public policy in Art. II(3)".[148] Second, the dissenting opinion, relying on the *travaux préparatoires*, reasoned that courts were allowed to refuse to enforce arbitration clauses if they offended "the public policy of the forum".[149] Third, citing *The Bremen*, Justice Douglas explained that a choice-of-forum clause (and an arbitration clause) should be held

144 Albert Jan van den Berg, 'Arbitrability' in Albert Jan van den Berg (ed), *ICCA Yearbook of Commercial Arbitration* (2003) Vol XXVIII 562, 629.

145 Ibid 629. See also Carolyn B Lamm and Jeremy Sharpe, 'Inoperative Arbitration Agreements Under the New York Convention' in Emmanuel Galliard and Domenico Di Pietro (eds), *Enforcement of Arbitration Agreements* (Cameron May 2008) 307 fn 57.

146 American Law Institute (n 136) 300 §2.17.

147 *Scherk* (n 5) 520 fn 15.

148 Ibid 534.

149 Ibid 530, ft 2/10.

unenforceable if it contravened "a strong public policy of the forum."[150] Finally, the dissenting opinion conceived that neither the Securities Exchange Act of 1934, the New York Convention, nor the Court's prior decision in *The Bremen* permitted the "abandonment of a national public policy that securities claims be heard by a judicial forum simply because some international elements are involved in a contract."[151]

In the end, the Supreme Court rejected the allegation that the submission of securities claims to arbitration would violate public policy. At the same time, however, the Court implicitly admitted that the public policy defence is available for a party who wants to resist the enforcement of an arbitration clause before the U.S. courts.

## 4 Conclusions

*Scherk v. Alberto-Culver* brought about a remarkable change to the law on the arbitrability of securities claims under federal U.S. law. Whilst the decision was itself limited to transactions in an international context, it opened the door to a series of Supreme Court decisions which extended the rule further and heralded a new pro-arbitration approach in the Court's jurisprudence. Additionally, the Court determined the arbitrability issue by reference to U.S. law (*i.e.*, the law of the enforcement forum), rather than the law of the arbitral seat or by applying international standards, which reflects the prevailing conflict of laws approach now adopted in many jurisdictions. The decision also placed choice-of-forum clauses and arbitration clauses on an equal footing, decisively upholding party autonomy by respecting the parties' choice of the forum for settling their disputes. Finally, the Supreme Court admitted – although implicitly – that a party who wants to resist the enforcement of an arbitration clause before the U.S. court may use the public policy defense, which is still the prevailing position under U.S. law.

---

150 Ibid 530, ft 2/10.

151 Ibid 530, ft 2/10.

CHAPTER 7

# *Mitsubishi Motors Corp. v. Soler Chrysler-Plymouth, Inc. et al.*, 473 U.S. 614 (1985)

*Sherman Kahn*

## 1 Introduction

In *Mitsubishi Motors Corp. v. Soler Chrysler-Plymouth, Inc. et al,* 473 U.S. 614 (1985), the U.S. Supreme Court addressed the issue of arbitrability of statutory antitrust claims in international agreements and concluded that such claims are arbitrable, at least in the international context. *Mitsubishi* is also important as one of the earliest in a line of cases in which the Supreme Court emphasized the liberal federal policy favoring arbitration agreements and the need to U.S. courts to put aside resistance to the arbitration of international disputes. The Court also suggested that arbitral tribunals with jurisdiction over U.S. statutory claims should be bound to apply U.S. mandatory law even if the substantive law chosen in the arbitration is the law of another jurisdiction.

## 2 The Case

In *Mitsubishi Motors Corp. v. Soler Chrysler-Plymouth, Inc. et al,* 473 U.S. 614 (1985), the Court held that antitrust claims were arbitrable in international agreements and issued important guidance about the application of mandatory law in arbitration. *Mitsubishi* is often cited for its broad language in support of arbitration as a fundamental part of the federal policy, bolstered by the United States' accession to the New York Contention, in favor of arbitral resolution of international commercial disputes.

### 2.1 *Background of the Case*

*Mitsubishi* arose out of a dispute between an automobile dealer in Puerto Rico and its suppliers. The Claimant in the arbitration was Mitsubishi Motors Corporation ("Mitsubishi"), a Japanese Corporation based in Tokyo, Japan which was the product of a joint venture between Chrysler International, S.A. ("CISA"), a Swiss Corporation owned by the Chrysler Corporation and Mitsubishi Heavy Industries, Inc., a Japanese Corporation. The Respondent at

 | DOI:10.1163/9789004715820_008

the Supreme court was the auto dealer, Soler Chrysler-Plymouth, Inc. ("Soler"), and was a Puerto Rico Corporation based in San Juan, Puerto Rico.

The joint venture between Mitsubishi and Chrysler was for the purpose of United States distribution of vehicles manufactured in Japan by Mitsubishi and bearing Mitsubishi and Chrysler trademarks. On October 31, 1979, Soler simultaneously entered (a) a Distributor Agreement with CISA which provided for the sale of Mitsubishi-manufactured vehicles in a defined territory which included San Juan, Puerto Rico; and (b) a Sales Procedure Agreement ("Sales Agreement") with Mitsubishi which provided for the direct sale by Mitsubishi of products to Soler. The Sales Agreement with Mitsubishi (but not the agreement with CISA) included an arbitration clause as follows:

> All disputes, controversies or differences which may arise between [Mitsubishi] and [Soler] out of or in relation to Articles I-B through V of this Agreement or for the breach thereof, shall be finally settled by arbitration in Japan in accordance with the rules and regulations of the Japan Commercial Arbitration Association. *Mitsubishi*, 473 U.S. at 617.

After entering the agreements, Soler was unable to meet the sales volume expected under the agreements and requested that Mitsubishi delay or cancel shipments and also requested the ability to transship vehicles outside of his territory into the continental United States and Latin America. Mitsubishi and CISA refused the request for transshipment and Mitsubishi brought an action against Soler in the U.S. District Court for the District of Puerto Rico under the Federal Arbitration Act and the New York Convention to compel arbitration under the Sales Agreement. Mitsubishi also filed a request for arbitration with the Japan Commercial Arbitration Association ("JCAA").

Soler denied the allegations and brought a variety of counterclaims in the district court against Mitsubishi and cross-claims against CISA. Against Mitsubishi, Soler alleged a variety of breaches of the Sales Agreement, defamation claims and statutory claims under the Sherman Act, the federal Automobile Dealers' Day-in-Court Act, and certain Puerto Rican statues. The Sherman Act claim alleged that Mitsubishi and CISA had conspired to divide markets in restraint of trade including by refusing to allow Soler to transship vehicles into other markets and by coercively attempting to replace Soler and other dealers with a wholly owned subsidiary to serve as the exclusive Mitsubishi distributor in Puerto Rico.

The district court ordered Mitsubishi and Soler to arbitrate all of the issues in the complaint and counterclaims except for the defamation counterclaims and certain parts of other claims. The district court also excluded all claims against CISA from arbitration. Those claims were retained in the district court and were not at issue before the Supreme Court. In sending the antitrust claims to arbitration, the district court acknowledged a line of cases following the Second Circuit's opinion in *American Safety Equipment Corp. v. J.P. Maguire & Co.*, 391 F.2d 821 (2d Cir. 1968) in which the courts of appeals up to that time had uniformly held that rights conferred by the antitrust laws were of a character inappropriate for arbitration, but held that the international character of the relationship between Mitsubishi and Soler required enforcement of the agreement to arbitrate even as to the antitrust claims.

The First Circuit reversed as to the antitrust issues, concluding that the *American Safety* line of cases should not be disregarded in the case of an international transaction.

### 2.2 *Issue and the Parties' Allegations*

The Supreme Court granted certiorari primarily to consider whether an American court should enforce an agreement to resolve antitrust claims through arbitration when the agreement arises from an international transaction.

### 2.3 *The Court's Opinion*

#### 2.3.1 Arbitrability of International Antitrust Claims

The Supreme court analyzed the arbitrability question in two parts, first looking at whether the parties actually chose arbitration of statutory claims in their arbitration agreement, and then if it found the first question in the affirmative, turning to whether the claims at issue were properly arbitrable.

As to the first question, Soler argued that, regardless of their ordinary meaning, as a matter of law arbitration clauses should be interpreted to exclude claims arising out of statutes intended to protect a class of whom the contracting party is a member unless that party has expressly agreed to arbitrate that claim. Based upon that reasoning, Soler argued that because the arbitration clause did not mention the antitrust and dealer protection statutes at issue in the case, it could not be read to contemplate arbitration of those statutory claims.

The Supreme Court rejected Soler's argument, stating "we find no warrant in the Arbitration Act for implying in every contract within its ken a presumption against arbitration of statutory claims." *Mitsubishi*, 473 U.S. at 625. The court identified as the centerpiece provision of the FAA the provision that makes a written agreement to arbitrate "in any maritime transaction or a contract evidencing a transaction involving commerce ... valid, irrevocable and enforceable, save upon grounds as exist in law or in equity for the revocation of any contract." *Id., quoting* 9 U.S.C. § 2. The court continued that the liberal policy favoring arbitration agreements manifested by this provision and the Act as a whole is at bottom a policy guaranteeing the enforcement of private contractual arrangements. *Id.* The Court further stated that the "preeminent concern of Congress" in the FAA to enforce private arbitration agreements required the Court to rigorously enforce agreements to arbitrate.

As a result, the Supreme Court found that the first task of a court asked to compel arbitration is to determine whether the parties agreed to arbitrate that dispute by applying the federal substantive law of arbitrability, which counsels that "arbitrability must be addressed with a healthy regard for the federal policy favoring arbitration" and that the FAA "establishes as a matter of federal law, any doubts concerning the scope of arbitrable issues should be resolved in favor of arbitration." *Mitsubishi,* 473 U.S. at 626.

The Court found that there was no reason to depart from the guidelines established by the FAA where a party bound by an arbitration agreement raises statutory claims. With reference to its prior decision in *Wilko v. Swan,* 346 U.S. 427 (1953) *overruled,* 490 U.S. 477, 484 (1989), the Court expressed the hope for the FAA's usefulness in controversies based on statutes and held that non-arbitrability of a statutory claim must be derived from specific Congressional direction with respect to a particular statutory claim rather than a presumption against arbitrability of such claims.[1] The *Mitsubishi* Court concluded on this issue "[h]aving made the bargain to arbitrate, the party should be held to it unless Congress itself has evinced an intention to preclude a waiver of judicial remedies for the statutory rights at issue." *Mitsubishi,* 473 U.S. at 628.

Having decided that the statutory claims at issue fell within the scope of the parties' arbitration clause,[2] the Supreme Court turned to the issue of whether the Sherman Act claim was non-arbitrable even though the parties agreed to arbitrate it. The Supreme Court declined to overrule the Second Circuit's decision in *American Safety* holding that the pervasive public interest in antitrust claims and the nature of the claims that arise in such cases make antitrust

1 It is worth noting in this regard that only four years after deciding *Mitsubishi,* the Supreme Court overruled its holding in *Wilko* that claims under Section 12(2) of the Securities act were non-arbitrable. *Rodriguez de Quijas v. Shearson/American Express, Inc.,* 490 U.S. 477, 484 (1989).

2 The Supreme Court addressed in a footnote Soler's argument that the clause at issue was limited only to certain sections of the Sales Agreement, pointing to broad arbitration language in the clause providing that with respect to those sections "[a]ll disputes, controversies or differences which may arise between [Mitsubishi] and [Soler] out of or in relation to [the specified provisions] or for the breach thereof." *Mitsubishi,* 473 U.S. at 624, n. 13.

claims inappropriate for arbitration. However, the Court limited *American Safety* to the domestic context, concluding that respect for international comity, respect for the capacity of foreign and transnational tribunals, and sensitivity to the need of the international commercial system for predictability in the resolution of disputes required enforcement of the parties' arbitration agreement as to antitrust claims even if the result would be different in a domestic context.

The Supreme Court relied on its prior opinion in *Scherk v. Alberto -Culver Co.*, 417 U.S. 506, 519 (1974) which had held that a claim under the Securities Exchange Act of 1934 was arbitrable in the context of an international agreement and had characterized an agreement to arbitrate as in effect a specialized kind of forum selection clause that posits not only the situs of the suit but also the procedure to be used in resolving the dispute.

While the *Mitsubishi* court declined to specifically overrule the Second Circuit's decision in *American Safety,* it nonetheless criticized the reasoning for that decision at length. The Supreme Court identified four factors underlying the *American Safety* doctrine: (1) the importance of the private enforcement of the antitrust laws through treble damages as a matter of policy; (2) the likelihood that contracts violating antitrust laws will be contracts of adhesion; (3) that antitrust suits are complicated and thus ill-suited to the arbitral process; and (4) that antitrust regulation of business is arguably too important to be decided by arbitrators from the business community.

The Court quickly rejected factors (2) through (4). Supreme Court rejected the second factor on the ground that absent a showing of fraud or undue influence there is no basis to show that arbitration would be inadequate. It rejected the third factor on the ground that arbitration allows for the appointment of arbitrators with appropriate expertise. It rejected the fourth factor as well stating "[w]e decline to indulge the presumption that the parties and arbitral body conducting a proceeding will be unable or unwilling to retain competent, conscientious and impartial arbitrators." *Mitsubishi*, 473 U.S. at 634.

The Supreme Court then analyzed, the first *American Safety* factor, which it called the core of the *American Safety* doctrine – "the fundamental importance to American democratic capitalism of the regime of the antitrust laws." *Mitsubishi*, 473 U.S. at 627. The Court recognized that the treble damages remedy plays a central role in enforcing that regime, but held that the importance of the private damages remedy does not compel the conclusion that it may not be sought outside of an American court. The Court concluded that as the antitrust claim remains under the control of the individual litigant, at least in the international context, that litigant is free to choose arbitration as the procedure for seeking antitrust recovery.

In light of this analysis, the court held that it was necessary for courts to subordinate domestic notions of arbitrability to the international policy favoring commercial arbitration and that the antitrust claims at issue in the international commercial relationship the court was examining were arbitrable.

### 2.3.2 Application of Mandatory Law by Arbitrators

The Supreme Court commented that, while an international arbitral tribunal owes no allegiance to the laws of particular states, it is bound to effectuate the intentions of the parties. The court therefore held that "[w]here the parties have agreed that the arbitral body is to decide a defined set of claims which includes … those arising from the application of American antitrust law, the tribunal therefore should be bound to decide that dispute in accord with the national law giving rise to the claim." *Mitsubishi*, 473 U.S. at 636–37.

The *Mitsubishi* opinion is supported by an extensive set of footnotes. In footnote 19 of the decision, the Court addresses arguments that the agreement at issue provides for resolution in Japan before the JCAA and that the choice of law clause in the relevant agreement provides for the application of Swiss law. Amici had argued that this combination of factors might lead to a possibility that the arbitral tribunal would decide the U.S. antitrust claim under Swiss law and not the U.S. Sherman Act. The Supreme Court commented that it need not decide the issue because counsel for *Mitsubishi* had conceded at oral argument that U.S. law applied and that it had submitted the claims to the JCAA tribunal on that basis. The Court nonetheless went on to opine that "in the event the choice-of-forum and choice-of-law clauses operated in tandem as a prospective waiver of a party's right to pursue statutory remedies for antitrust violations, we would have little hesitation in condemning the agreement as against public policy." *Mitsubishi*, 473 U.S. at 637, n. 19.

The court also stated that, having permitted the arbitration to go forward, U.S. courts will have the opportunity at the award-enforcement stage to ensure that the legitimate interest in the antitrust laws have been addressed through the right under the New York convention to refuse enforcement of awards that are contrary to public policy. The Court stated "[w]hile the efficacy of the arbitral process requires that the substantive review at the award-enforcement stage remain minimal, it would not require intrusive inquiry to ascertain that the tribunal took cognizance of the antitrust claims and actually decided them." *Mitsubishi*, 473 U.S. at 638.[3]

---

3 The Seventh Circuit has opined that any such review to determine whether the arbitrators applied the antitrust law should indeed remain minimal. *Baxter Int'l, Inc. v. Abbott Laboratories, Inc.*, 315 F.3d 829, 832–33 (7th Cir. 2003).

### 2.4 *Key Takeaways*

*Mitsubishi* was at the forefront of a line of cases in which the Supreme Court emphasized the United States courts should give full effect to the scope of parties' international arbitration agreements. The emphasis in *Mitsubishi* on the importance of international commercial dispute resolution is striking.

*Mitsubishi* is also important for its suggestion that international arbitrators adjudicating U.S. statutory claims are bound to follow U.S. mandatory law even if the parties have chosen the law of another jurisdiction as the substantive law governing their agreement.

## 3 *Mitsubishi*'s Impact on U.S. Arbitration Law

*Mitsubishi* firmly established that in international disputes antitrust laws and other laws bearing on United States public policy are presumptively arbitrable unless Congress has clearly expressed an intent to the contrary. While its rationale in many respects should be equally applicable to domestic arbitration, *Mitsubishi* declined to expressly apply its holding in the domestic context. Even today, the Supreme Court has not expressly overruled the Second Circuit's decision in *American Safety*. The closest the Court has come is dictum in a domestic case stating that "[t]he Sherman Act, the Securities Exchange Act of 1934, RICO, and the Securities Act of 1933 all are designed to advance important public policies, but, as noted above, claims under those statutes are appropriate for arbitration." *Gilmer v. Interstate/Johnson Lane Corp.*, 500 U.S. 20, 28 (1991).

Several circuit courts have decided based on *Mitsubishi* and the Supreme Court's later overruling of *Wilko v. Swan,* that domestic antitrust suits should be arbitrable. *See e.g., Seacoast Motors of Salisbury, Inc. v. DaimlerChrysler Motors Corp.,* 271 F.3d 6, 11 (1st Cir. 2001); *Kotam Electronics, Inc. v. JBL Consumer Products, Inc.,* 93 F.3d 724, 728 (11th Cir. 1996); *Nghiem v. NEC Electronic, Inc.,* 25 F.3d 1437 (9th Cir. 1994). Even the Second Circuit, which decided *American Safety,* has affirmed without opinion a district court decision finding that "the reasoning of *Mitsubishi* should apply with equal force to domestic claims" and that "none of the justifications for the *American Safety* doctrine retain their vigor.'" *Hough v. Merrill Lynch,* 757 F.Supp. 283, 286 (S.D.N.Y.), *aff'd without op.,* 946 F.2d 883 (2d Cir.1991). It nonetheless remains the case that the Supreme Court has not directly decided that domestic antitrust claims are arbitrable.

## 4 Conclusions

*Mitsubishi* remains a key decision of the Supreme Court with respect to the arbitrability of statutory claims and the application of United States mandatory law to such claims as decided by arbitrators.

CHAPTER 8

# *Shearson/Am. Exp., Inc v. McMahon* (1987)

*Steven Skulnik*

## 1 Introduction

Beginning with *Scherk v. Alberto-Culver Co.*, 417 U.S. 506 (1974), a case involving claims of securities fraud in an international transaction, the U.S. Supreme Court began referring disputes to arbitration that had previously been considered to be inarbitrable.[1] In *Mitsubishi Motors Corp. v. Soler Chrysler–Plymouth, Inc.*, 473 U.S. 614, 631 (1985), the Court declared that there is an "emphatic federal policy in favor of arbitral dispute resolution," which "applies with special force in the field of international commerce." The Supreme Court in those cases held that the international character of the parties' relationship required enforcement of the agreement to arbitrate even as to statutory securities fraud and antitrust claims. Those decisions left open the question of whether purely domestic federal statutory claims would likewise be found to be arbitrable.

## 2 The Case

In *Shearson/Am. Exp., Inc. v. McMahon*, 482 U.S. 220 (1987) the Court was faced with the issue of whether claims by U.S. citizens against a U.S. brokerage firm brought under section 10(b) of the Securities Exchange Act ("Exchange Act") and the Racketeer Influenced and Corrupt Organizations Act ("RICO") were arbitrable. The Court held that section 2 of the Federal Arbitration Act ("FAA") makes arbitration agreements enforceable absent a showing that Congress intended in a separate statute to preclude a waiver of a judicial forum, or that a waiver of a judicial forum inherently conflicts with the underlying purposes of that statute. The Court held that nothing in the text or history of the Exchange

1 There is confusion in U.S. caselaw as the term "arbitrability" often refers to the existence, validity, or scope of an alleged agreement to arbitrate. The discussion in this chapter concerns the concept of arbitrability as understood in the international context, *viz.*, whether the issues sought to be arbitrated may be decided by private arbitrators, or, as a matter of public policy, must be decided by courts. This is sometimes referred to as "subject matter arbitrability." *See* Restatement (Third) U.S. Law of Int'l Comm. Arb. § 4.15, cmt. a.

 | DOI:10.1163/9789004715820_009

Act nor the RICO statute suggests that such claims may only be decided by courts.

## 2.1 *Background of the Case*

The case involved a claim by Mr. and Mrs. McMahon, who were customers of Shearson/American Express Inc. ("Shearson"), a brokerage firm registered with the Securities and Exchange Commission ("SEC"). The agreement signed by both sides provided for arbitration of any controversy relating to the accounts the McMahons maintained with Shearson. The arbitration provision provided in relevant part as follows:

> Unless unenforceable due to federal or state law, any controversy arising out of or relating to my accounts, to transactions with you for me or to this agreement or the breach thereof, shall be settled by arbitration in accordance with the rules, then in effect, of the National Association of Securities Dealers, Inc. or the Boards of Directors of the New York Stock Exchange, Inc. and/or the American Stock Exchange, Inc. as I may elect.

The McMahons filed a federal lawsuit against Shearson and the representative who managed their accounts alleging that the defendants violated the section 10(b) of the Exchange Act and SEC Rule 10b-5 by engaging in fraudulent conduct by making false statements and omitting material facts from the advice given to them.[2] The McMahons also alleged a RICO claim[3] and state law claims for fraud and breach of fiduciary duties.

Relying on the arbitration agreement, the defendants moved to compel arbitration of all claims. The district court, citing the federal policy in favor of arbitration, compelled arbitration of the Exchange Act and state law claims but held that the RICO claim was not arbitrable "because of the important federal policies inherent in the enforcement of RICO by the federal courts." 482 U.S. at 224.

2 Rule 10b-5, created under the authority given to the SEC in Section 10(b) of the Exchange Act, prohibits conduct, in connection with the purchase or sale of securities, that (a) employs any scheme to defraud investors, (b) makes untrue statements of material facts or omits material facts that would be necessary to prevent other statements made from being misleading, or (c) engages in practices that operate as a fraud or deceit upon others. 17 C.F.R. § 240.10b-5.

3 RICO provides for both criminal and civil penalties for acts performed as part of an ongoing criminal scheme. 18 U.S.C. §§ 1961–1968. The statute's civil provisions grant substantial remedies, including treble damages, costs, and reasonable counsel fees. 18 U.S.C. § 1964(c).

The Second Circuit affirmed on the RICO and state law claims but reversed on the Exchange Act claims, holding that *Wilko v. Swan*, 346 U.S. 427 (1953), which held that claims arising under the Securities Act of 1933[4] were inarbitrable, compelled that result.[5] The Court of Appeals distinguished the *Scherk* and *Mitsubishi* holdings because those cases involved international business transactions.

### 2.2 *Issue and the Parties' Allegations*

The Supreme Court noted a conflict among the Courts of Appeals regarding the arbitrability of Exchange Act and RICO claims, outside the international arena, and granted *certiorari* to resolve that conflict.

### 2.3 *The Court's Opinion*

The Supreme Court first noted, quoting from *Mitsubishi*, that the FAA "provides no basis for disfavoring agreements to arbitrate statutory claims." 482 U.S. at 226. To avoid arbitration, the McMahons would have to demonstrate that Congress intended to make an exception to the FAA for Exchange Act or RICO claims. *Id.* at 227.

#### 2.3.1 The Exchange Act

The McMahons argued that section 27 of the Exchange Act (15 U.S.C. § 78aa) granted federal district courts exclusive jurisdiction over violations of the Exchange Act or rules thereunder and section 29(a) (15 U.S.C. § 78aa) makes void "[a]ny condition, stipulation, or provision binding any person to waive compliance with any provision of [the Exchange Act or any rule thereunder]." According to the McMahons, the arbitration agreement here waives their right to proceed in federal court, as provided in the Exchange Act, and any waiver of that right must be void.

The Court rejected this argument, noting that section 29(a) only prohibits waiver of the Exchange Act's compliance duties. The grant of jurisdiction in section 27 does not concern any compliance duty.

---

4 The Securities Act applies to initial public offerings, while the Exchange Act applies to sales of securities in the secondary market.

5 The *Wilko* Court's holding was motivated, in part, by the lack of judicial review of legal conclusions made be arbitrators. In a famous piece of *dictum*, the Court stated that "[i]n unrestricted submission, such as the present margin agreements envisage, the interpretations of the law by the arbitrators *in contrast to manifest disregard* are not subject, in the federal courts, to judicial review for error in interpretation." 346 U.S. at 436–37 (emphasis added). This *dictum* has caused a Circuit split that lasts to this day on the issue of whether an arbitral award may be set aside for "manifest disregard of the law."

Next, the Court distinguished the McMahons' claims from those by the plaintiff in *Wilko*.[6] The Court stated that the arbitration agreement in that case was unenforceable only because the Court in that case decided that arbitration is inadequate to enforce the statutory rights created by section 12(2) of the Securities Act of 1933. *Id.* at 229. To the extent there is inconsistency between the rationale in *Wilko* and that in *Scherk*, the Court found decision in *Scherk* was more persuasive.[7] Although *Scherk* concerned an international transaction, the Court found no reason not to extend its holding to domestic cases noting that "the competence of arbitral tribunals to resolve § 10(b) claims is the same in both settings." *Id.* at 232.

The Court also noted that the regulatory setting has changed since *Wilko*. At the time of the *Shearson* decision, the SEC, by regulation, had endorsed arbitration before the National Association of Securities Dealers, Inc., the New York Stock Exchange, Inc., and the American Stock Exchange, which are the providers specified in the McMahons' arbitration agreement. Therefore, the Court found no basis in the Exchange Act nor in the SEC rules to prohibit arbitration of the section 10(b) claims in this case.[8]

### 2.3.2 RICO

The Court began its analysis of the RICO claim by noting that there is nothing in RICO's text or legislative history that shows any intent to prohibit arbitration. *Id.* at 239. Therefore, to hold RICO claims inarbitrable, the McMahons must show an "irreconcilable conflict between arbitration and RICO's underlying purposes." *Id.* The McMahons made three arguments in this regard: (a) RICO claims are complicated, (b) there are both civil and criminal components to the RICO statute, and (c) there is a public interest in RICO enforcement. The Court held all three arguments are foreclosed by the reasoning in *Mitsubishi*. RICO is no more complicated than the antitrust laws; the Sherman Act, while not imposing criminal liability, does contain a punitive treble damages

6 A couple of years later, the Court overruled *Wilko*. *Rodriguez de Quijas v. Shearson/Am. Exp., Inc.*, 490 U.S. 477 (1989).

7 The Court also noted in footnote 1 of the opinion that a cause of action under section 10(b) is implied, not expressed. The phrase "waive compliance with any provision of this chapter," 15 U.S.C. § 78cc(a), would appear to be inapplicable. *See also Dean Witter Reynolds, Inc. v. Byrd*, 470 U.S. 213, 225 (1985) (White, J. concurring).

8 The McMahons' final argument was that Congress made extensive revisions to the Exchange Act in 1975 but those revisions did not overrule *Wilko*. The Court rejected this argument, noting that Congressional silence meant that "the *Wilko* issue was left to the courts." 482 U.S. at 238.

provision; and, as in *Mitsubishi*, as long as plaintiffs can effectively vindicate their statutory claims in arbitration, the public interest is satisfied.

In sum, the Court found the McMahons arguments even less compelling than those of the plaintiff in *Mitsubishi*. The Court reasoned that "[t]he private attorney general role for the typical RICO plaintiff is simply less plausible than it is for the typical antitrust plaintiff and does not support a finding that there is an irreconcilable conflict between arbitration and enforcement of the RICO statute." *Id.* at 242.

### 2.4 *Key Takeaways*

*Shearson* expanded a line of cases in which the Supreme Court held that the U.S. courts should give full effect to parties' arbitration agreements. The emphasis in prior decisions that relied on the importance of *international* commercial dispute resolution no longer carried the day. Arbitration of statutory claims will be compelled, absent a limitation imposed by Congress.[9] Indeed, *Shearson* paved the way for the later Supreme Court decisions compelling arbitration of claims brought by employees[10] and consumers.[11]

## 3 The Case's Impact on U.S. Arbitration Law

*Shearson* firmly established that customers of banks and brokerage firms that have agreed to broad arbitration clauses must arbitrate their statutory claims. In 2007, the Financial Industry Regulatory Authority ("FINRA") was created to

9 As noted, the FAA expressly carves out claims brought by transportation workers. 9 U.S.C. § 1. Congress has also prohibited, for example, enforcement of pre-dispute arbitration agreements regarding motor-vehicle-franchise contracts (*see* Motor Vehicle Franchise Contract Arbitration Fairness Act, 15 U.S.C. § 1226(a)(2)) and pre-dispute arbitration agreements for cases relating to sexual assault or sexual harassment (*see* Ending Forced Arbitration of Sexual Assault and Sexual Harassment Act, 9 U.S.C. § 402(a)).

10 *See Circuit City Stores, Inc. v. Adams*, 532 U.S. 105, 119 (2001) (compelling arbitration of California state law discrimination claims and holding that the FAA applies to all employment contracts, except for those regarding transportation workers). The federal circuit courts of appeal have consistently found that claims under Title VII of the Civil Rights Act of 1964 are arbitrable. *See, e.g., E.E.O.C. v. Luce, Forward, Hamilton & Scripps*, 345 F.3d 742, 748–49 (9th Cir. 2003) (joining all other circuits in holding that Title VII claims were arbitrable).

11 In *AT&T Mobility LLC v. Concepcion*, 563 U.S. 333, 337 (2011), consumers sued AT&T in federal court, when they entered into contracts which advertised as including free cellular phones but were charged $30.22 in sales tax based on the phones' retail value. The Supreme Court compelled arbitration of those claims. *Id.* at 346–47.

consolidate customer arbitrations that were once administered by the organizations specified in the Shearson/McMahon arbitration agreement. Indeed, customers have a right to FINRA arbitration of a dispute with a FINRA member firms whether or not the parties have a written arbitration agreement.[12] Therefore, *Shearson* paved the way for most customer/broker disputes to be resolved in arbitration.

## 4 Conclusions

*Shearson* remains a major decision of the Supreme Court with respect to the arbitrability of statutory claims. It is now clear that absent evidence of contrary Congressional intent, claims arising under federal statutes must be arbitrated where the parties' arbitration agreement is broad enough in scope to encompass those claims.

12 *See Goldman, Sachs & Co. v. Golden Empire Sch. Fin. Auth.*, 764 F.3d 210, 214 (2d Cir. 2014).

CHAPTER 9

# *Volt Information Sciences, Inc. v. Board of Trustees of the Leland Stanford Junior University* (1989)

*Peter Fox*

## 1 Introduction

Going into oral argument at the Supreme Court on November 30, 1988, the lawyers for Volt Information Sciences must have believed that luck was on their side. As a defendant in a lawsuit arising out of a contract with an indisputably applicable arbitration clause, Volt's efforts to compel arbitration were without success until – having lost in the trial court, lost on appeal as of right in the California Court of Appeal, and having had its petition for discretionary review by the California Supreme Court denied – the Supreme Court stepped in. To say this was unusual would be an understatement. The Supreme Court is reported to grant only around 1% of petitions for certiorari, and grants of petitions from intermediate state courts of appeal, where the *state* supreme court has already declined to exercise appellate jurisdiction, are rarer still.

Unfortunately for Volt's lawyers, their confidence was misplaced. Although the California courts had denied Volt's motion to compel arbitration under a state statute that seemed clearly in conflict with (and thus preempted by) the Federal Arbitration Act (the "FAA"), and although all parties recognized that the FAA applied to the arbitration clause, the Court nevertheless affirmed the California courts' decision by a vote of 6-2. It did so on the basis of the California Court of Appeal's tortured interpretation of the contract's choice of law clause as incorporating, not only the substantive law of California, but also its rules of arbitration – even those rules that are arguably at odds with the FAA.

It is unlikely that any member of the Court believed that the parties actually intended for California procedural law to apply to the exclusion of the FAA when they signed a form contract designating – in a clause separate from the arbitration clause – that "[t]he Contract shall be governed by law of the place where the Project is located," but majority used the case to emphasize that "interpretation of private contracts is ordinarily a question of state law, which this Court does not sit to review."

 | DOI:10.1163/9789004715820_010

Whether such federalism concerns were the primary reason for the Court's decision to take the case,[1] is a question for Supreme Court insiders to answer. But the Court's reinforcement of *Erie* principle[2] – even in the context of a federal interest – is one legacy of *Volt*. The other legacy of the case is what the Court said *about* that federal interest, which is the policies reflected by the FAA. For the Court in Volt, the FAA is not "pro-arbitration" in the sense that arbitration is to be always favored over litigation, rather the FAA is pro-*agreement* to arbitrate in so far as the parties are given the freedom to expand or circumscribe their arbitral rights as they see fit.

## 2 The Case

### 2.1 *Background*

The background of Volt is fairly straightforward. Volt Information Sciences entered into a construction contract with Stanford University to install electrical conduits on Stanford's campus in Palo Alto, California.[3] The contract was a standard form contract prepared by the American Institute of Architects, and contained and arbitration provision and a choice of law clause.[4] The choice of law clause stated, "[t]he Contract shall be governed by the law of the place where the Project is located."[5]

During the course of the project a dispute arose over payment.[6] The dispute was clearly covered by the arbitration clause and Volt served Stanford a demand for arbitration.[7] Stanford filed an action in California Superior Court against Volt over the same dispute and also sued for indemnification two other companies involved in the construction project with whom Stanford was not bound to arbitrate.[8]

When Volt filed a motion to compel arbitration, Stanford responded with a motion to stay the arbitration under Section 1281.2(c) of the California Code of

1 Under Supreme Court rules grants of petitions for certiorari require four votes, and so at least two justices from the majority must have agreed to take the case.

2 See Erie Railroad Co. v. Tompkins, 304 U.S. 64, 78 (1938) ("There is no federal general common law").

3 489 U.S. 468, 470 (1989).

4 Id. at 479–480 (Brennan, J. dissenting).

5 Id. at 470.

6 Id.

7 Id.

8 Id. at 471.

Civil Procedure.[9] Section 1281.2(c) allows a court to stay an arbitration pending the resolution of a related litigation between a party to the arbitration agreement and third-parties not bound by the arbitration agreement – in this case, the litigation between Stanford and two companies it sued for indemnification.[10] The FAA has no comparable provision.

The Court granted Stanford's motion to stay the arbitration and denied Volt's motion to compel arbitration. Volt appealed to the California Court of Appeal, which affirmed the trial court's ruling.[11] The Court of Appeal determined that the FAA applied to the arbitration clause, but nevertheless held that the parties had agreed to incorporate California's procedural rules concerning arbitration through the choice of law clause, even if such rules contained bases for arbitral stays not found in the FAA.[12] Volt appealed again, but the California Supreme Court refused to hear the case.[13] Volt then filed a petition for certiorari, which – as described above – the Supreme Court surprisingly granted.

### 2.2 *Arguments*

Volt's primary concern at the Supreme Court was to reverse the California Court of Appeals highly dubious interpretation of the choice of law clause. It first argued that a federal court could upset the state court's holding of state law because the state court had found a waiver of federal rights – namely the right under the FAA to compel arbitration of a clearly arbitral dispute.[14] As an alternative, Volt relied on the Court's decision *Moses H. Cone Memorial Hospital v. Mercury Construction* to argue the federal arbitration policy must factor into the interpretation of otherwise state-law controlled contract interpretation, and, on these facts, compel a different interpretation of the choice of law provision.[15]

Stanford, of course, argued the opposite. In addition to contesting that Volt had any federal right that the California courts could have found waived and that the California Court of Appeals decision was inconsistent with federal arbitral policy, Stanford argued that Sections 3 and 4 of the FAA – which Volt claimed ought to control its motion to compel arbitration in the case – did not even apply in California state courts.[16]

9 Id.
10 Id.
11 Id. at 472.
12 Id. at 472.
13 Id. at 472–73.
14 Id. at 474.
15 Id. at 475–76.
16 Id. at 476–77.

### 2.3 *The Opinion*

Writing for the Court, Justice Renquist rejected Volt's attempts to secure review of the California Court of Appeal's interpretation of the choice of law clause. The Court ruled that the California court's holding could not be construed as finding a waiver of a federal right to compel arbitration because Volt never had an absolute right to do so. Specifically, the Court held that Section 4 of the FAA "does not confer a right to compel arbitration of any dispute at any time; it confers only the right to proceed *in the manner provided for in the parties agreement.*"[17] This statement followed a robust argument that the purpose of the FAA is to place agreements to arbitrate "upon the same footing as other contacts."[18] In other words, the Court held that the FAA protects the parties' right to contract away other rights under the FAA.

The Court likewise refused to review the state court interpretation of the choice of law clause under *Moses H. Cone* because – while the Court conceded that federal law does constrain anti-arbitration state law readings of contracts – the California Court of Appeal's interpretation was consistent with the FAA.[19] "There is no federal policy favoring arbitration under a certain set of procedural rules" the Court wrote.

Finally, the Court declined to rule on whether Sections 3 and 4 of the FAA apply in state court, but held that, if they did so apply, they would not preempt Section 1281.2 where the parties themselves had elected to abide by the state rule.[20] Since the Court refused to disturb the California Court Appeal's determination that the parties had indeed so elected, their agreement would be enforced. The Court wrote, "it does not follow that the FAA prevents the enforcement of agreements to arbitrate under different rules than those set forth in the Act itself."[21]

### 2.4 *The Dissent*

Justices Brennan and Marshall, clearly thinking about other instances where state court interpretations of private contacts could disturb federal rights, argued that the California Court of Appeal's interpretation of the choice of law clause should have been subject to federal review.

First, they invoked the doctrine of "adequacy" – which essentially allows the federal courts to review state court construction of contacts where such

17 Id. at 474–75 (emphasis in the original).

18 Id. at 474 (quoting Scherk v. Alberto-Culver Co., 417 U.S. 506 (1974)).

19 Id. at 476.

20 Id. at 477–78.

21 Id. at 479.

construction appears motivated by a desire to circumvent federal law.[22] Summing up the doctrine by quoting Herbert Wechsler, the Dissenters wrote, "[w]here the existence or application of a federal right turns on a logically antecedent finding on a matter of state law, it is essential to the Court's performance of its function that it exercise an ancillary jurisdiction to consider the state question. Federal rights could otherwise be nullified by the manipulation of state law."[23]

The Dissenters next disagreed with the Court's position on *Moses H. Cone*, which they believed provided sufficient authority to revisit the state court's ruling.[24] According to them, "interpreting the parties' agreement to say that the California procedural rules apply rather than the FAA, where the parties arguably had no such intent, implicates the *Moses H. Cone* principle no less than would an interpretation of the parties' contract that erroneously denied the existence of an agreement to arbitrate."[25]

The Dissenters concluded by arguing (persuasively) that it was very unlikely that the parties had intended to displace the procedural rules of the FAA with the California rules simply by signing a form contract with a generic choice of law clause.[26] As the dissent pointed out, "the normal purpose of such choice-of-law clauses is to determine that the law of one State rather than that of another state will be applicable; they simply do not speak to any interaction between state and federal law."[27]

## 3 Key Takeaways

The decision in *Volt* shows: (i) A strong reluctance on the part of the Court to review state court constructions of arbitration agreements, even when they implicate the procedural rules of the FAA; and (ii) a parallel conception of the FAA as a guarantee of freedom to contract, rather than of any specific procedural rights.

22 Id. at 481–84.

23 Id at 484 (quoting Wechsler, The Appellate Jurisdiction of the Supreme Court: Reflections on the Law and Logistics of Direct Review, 34 Wash. & Lee L. Rev. 1043, 1052 (1977)).

24 Id. at 487.

25 Id.

26 Id. at 488.

27 Id.

## 4 Analysis/Conclusion

In practice, *Volt* is probably an outlier. Outside of California – where the Court of Appeal decision may have become precedent – it is very unlikely that a state court would interpret a garden-variety choice of law clause to work a wholesale displacement of the FAA's procedural rules. But the case is important for what it says about the parties' freedom to contract under the FAA and the role of state law as the nearly exclusive recourse for disputes over the meaning of such contracts.

*Volt* reflects a minimalist approach to federal arbitral policy. While the FAA sets out basic procedural rules, the parties are free to contract around them, and the federal courts are likely to defer entirely to state court constructions of those agreements.

CHAPTER 10

# *First Options of Chicago, Inc v. Kaplan*, 514 U.S. 938 (1995): To Delegate or Not to Delegate, Forty Years On

*Kabir Duggal, Yasmine Lahlou, Carlos Alberto Carmona and Gustavo Favero Vaughn*

## 1 Introduction

Though one of its shortest rulings on arbitration, the United States Supreme Court's decision in *First Options of Chicago v. Manual Kaplan, et ux. and MK Investments, Inc.*, 514 U.S. 938 (1995) ("*First Options*"), is also one of its most consequential decisions.[1] In this case, the Supreme Court determined who, between the courts and the arbitrators, must decide the so-called issue "arbitrability," which, unlike how the term is understood in the rest of the world, refers to whether a party is bound to arbitrate a particular dispute in the United States.[2] In doing so, the U.S. Supreme Court (the "Court") also clarified

1 George A. Bermann, The "Gateway" Problem in International Commercial Arbitration, 37 YALE J. INT'L L. 1, 5 (2012) (confirming the importance of the issue addressed in *First Options*: "[b]ut it is at the outset of arbitration that the tradeoff between efficacy and legitimacy interests in arbitration assumes its purest form. The question occupying center stage at this moment is whether a party unwilling to arbitrate is obligated, on the basis of a prior undertaking, to do so.[8] If a court compels a party to arbitrate despite its not having consented to arbitration,[9] the legitimacy of both the arbitration and any resulting award is compromised.[10] This follows from the fundamental principle that commercial arbitration is consent-based, and that a party cannot be bound by an agreement to arbitrate or by the resulting award unless it consented to be so bound.[11] On the other hand, arbitration becomes a less effective means of dispute resolution to the extent that, prior to arbitration, parties may have recourse to courts to advance reasons why arbitration should not go forward, with the attendant costs and delays. The objectives associated with arbitration thereby stand to be thwarted.")

2 Joseph R. Profaizer & Dominique Borde, Professor Bermann's "Who Decides" Bombshell: Bold, Brave, and Beautiful, *in* REFLECTIONS ON INTERNATIONAL ARBITRATION: ESSAYS IN HONOUR OF PROFESSOR GEORGE BERMANN (eds. Julie Bédard & Patrick W. Pearsall, 2022), 28 (this issue is popularly known in the U.S. arbitration landscape as the "who decides" controversy, which "arises out of the friction in the fault line between courts and arbitral tribunals, and more specifically, the allocation of power between them to decide questions of arbitrability.")

 | DOI:10.1163/9789004715820_011

the standard of review by the courts of the arbitrators' determination on their own jurisdiction. Indeed, as Professor William W. Park puts it, *First Options* "serves as a springboard for discussion of the allocation of power between judge and arbitrator."[3]

Under the Federal Arbitration Act ("FAA"), courts give a large degree of deference to the arbitrators' decisions on the merits of a dispute, setting aside his or her decision only in narrow circumstances. *See e.g.*, 9 U.S.C. § 10. By contrast, for the arbitrators' jurisdictional determinations, the Court in *First Options* held that it is presumptively for the courts – not arbitrators – to decide questions of arbitrability unless there is "clear and unmistakable evidence" of the parties' intent to submit questions of arbitrability to the arbitrators. What this means in practice is that, unless that presumption is reversed and the parties are found to have intended to delegate arbitrability to the arbitrators, courts review the arbitrators' decision on jurisdiction *de novo*. If the presumption is reversed, however, courts will give the same deference to arbitrators' decisions on jurisdiction as they do on their rulings on the merits.

In a lesser-known aspect of that decision, addressing the standard of review of district court rulings, the Court mandates courts of appeal to "apply ordinary standards when reviewing district court decision upholding arbitration awards."

In this note, after summarizing the case's background and examining the Court's ruling and its key takeaways, we examine how lower courts have grappled with the Court's categorical mandate to best honor the parties' agreement.

## 2 The Case

### 2.1 *Factual Background and the Arbitration*

The dispute has its origins in the October 1987 stock market crash. First Options of Chicago, Inc. ("First Options"), a clearinghouse on the Philadelphia Stock Exchange, was acting as the clearing firm for Pennsylvania-based corporation MK Investments, Inc. ("MKI"). MKI was an options market-maker who entered into a Market Maker's Agreement with First Options on November 15, 1984. This Agreement provided that any dispute arising therefrom would be submitted to arbitration. Manuel Kaplan had been the president, director and sole shareholder of MKI. On October 19, 1987, stocks on the New York and several

3 William W. Park, The Arbitrability Dicta in *First Options* v. *Kaplan*: What Sort of Kompetenz-Kompetenz Has Crossed the Atlantic? 12 ARB. INT'L. 138, 140 (1996).

other exchanges in the U.S., including in Philadelphia, suffered an unprecedented drop in value. MKI's trading account balance of $10.5 million just five days before the crash turned into a deficit of $2.1 million by the end of that day.

As MKI's clearing firm, First Options had guaranteed to the exchange and MKI's counterparties that it would cover MKI's positions, as a result it was exposed on MKI's account deficit. As it was entitled to under its Market Maker's agreement with MKI, First Options liquidated MKI's position, which resulted in an increased deficit of $5.1 million. Thereafter, MKI and First Options entered into settlement negotiations. During those negotiations, Mr. Kaplan rejected First Options' demand that he assumes personal liability for MKI's obligations. Instead, he and MKI faulted First Options' mishandling of the liquidation as the primary cause of the deficit.

As the negotiations continued, on March 24, 1988, the Kaplans, MKI, and First Options separately executed four separate documents to resolve their dispute and MKI's October 19, 1987 deficit. Those were: (1) a Letter Agreement executed by First Options, MKI, Mr. Kaplan, Mrs. Kaplan, and certain other entities and individuals;[4] (2) a Guaranty executed only by MKI; (3) a Subordinated Loan Agreement executed by First Options, MKI, and a separate entity; and (4) a Subordinated Promissory Note executed by MKI (altogether the "Workout Agreements"). Only one of these four documents, the Subordinated Loan Agreement, contained an arbitration clause, and only First Options and MKI signed that document. Individually, Mr. Kaplan and his wife Carol Kaplan signed only the Letter Agreement, which did not contain an arbitration clause.

After MKI resumed trading in 1988 but before the parties had carried out all the terms of the March 1988 workout, MKI suffered another significant loss, which caused First Options' taking control of, and liquidating, MKI's position. After MKI and the Kaplans defaulted under the Workout Agreements, and rejected various of First Options' demands, First Options declared all sums due under the workout accelerated and demanded immediate payment of the accelerated debt. Ultimately, First Options initiated arbitration before a panel of the Philadelphia Stock Exchange seeking to hold MKI as well as the Kaplans liable for the outstanding debt.

While MKI, who had signed one of the Workout Agreements, consented to arbitrate, the Kaplans denied they were bound to arbitrate their dispute under the Workout Agreements, which they had not signed, and filed written

4 Although there is no indication that Mrs. Kaplan was involved in MKI's management, she signed one of the agreements between the parties' settlement. It contemplated that the Kaplans would relinquish to MKI a tax refund, which both Kaplans were entitled to receive from the IRS.

objections to the jurisdiction of the arbitration panel. The Kaplans and MKI filed responses denying liability, and Mr. Kaplan and MKI filed counterclaims against First Options. The Kaplans also submitted written objections to the arbitrators' jurisdiction under the Exchange's arbitration rules. In them, the Kaplans stated, "The Philadelphia Stock Exchange ... and the Arbitration Committee ... lack jurisdiction over this matter and the purported claim should be dismissed."

Two years into the arbitration, on February 26, 1990, there was a pre-hearing discovery conference. The Kaplans' former counsel participated in it without renewing the objections to the arbitrators' jurisdiction. For the next twenty-two months, no discovery took place, and no motions were filed; nor did the arbitration panel conduct any proceedings or issue any rulings. In December 1991, the Kaplans retained new counsel. On January 6, 1992, they filed a motion to dismiss for lack of jurisdiction. The Exchange denied the Kaplans' motion to dismiss for lack of jurisdiction without comment.

Sometime in May 1992, the matter finally proceeded to arbitration and, after eight days of hearings, the seven-member arbitration panel voted five to two to pierce the corporate veil and, on June 5, 1992, entered an award for $5,662,188 plus interest in favor of First Options and against Mr. Kaplan and MKI, jointly and severally. The panel also ordered the Kaplans, jointly and severally, to remit their 1987 tax refund, $346,342.00, plus interest. Finally, it found for First Options on Mr. Kaplan's and MKI's counterclaims.

## 2.2 *The Lower Courts' Rulings*

The Kaplans and MKI filed a petition to vacate the award under Section 10 of the FAA before the U.S. District Court for the Eastern District of Pennsylvania and First Options filed a cross petition for its confirmation under Section 9. On September 25, 1992, the District Court confirmed the award. It held that Mr. and Mrs. Kaplan had consented to arbitration under the arbitration clause in the Subordinated Loan Agreement even though neither had ever signed that particular document. Alternately, the Court held that the Kaplans' former counsel's participation in the 1990 discovery conference had waived their jurisdictional objections. The District Court then went on to affirm the arbitrators' decision to pierce the corporate veil on the merits.

On March 31, 1994, the Court of Appeals for the Third Circuit agreed with the Kaplans that the arbitration tribunal did not have jurisdiction over their dispute with First Options and reversed the District Court's decision.[5] In doing

5 *Manuel Kaplan; Carol Kaplan; MK Investments, Inc. v. First Options of Chicago*, 19 F.3d 1503 (3d Cri. 1994).

so, the Court of Appeals relied on its prior holdings and ruled that it would review the District Court's denial of a motion to vacate a commercial arbitration award *de novo*, rejecting First Options' request that the court review the District Court's decision denying the petition to vacate for abuse of discretion.[6] It also held that district courts should independently decide whether an arbitration panel has jurisdiction over the merits of any particular dispute. It then proceeded to find that the Kaplans had never consented to arbitrate any portion of their dispute with First Options nor had they waived their objection to the arbitrators' jurisdiction when their counsel appeared at a conference without raising the jurisdiction objection, having raised it at the outset of the proceedings.[7] Further, a party does not have to try to enjoin or stay an arbitration proceeding in order to preserve its objection to jurisdiction, and requiring parties to refuse to participate in an arbitration to preserve their challenge to arbitral jurisdiction was unwise policy. Moreover, a jurisdictional objection, once stated, remains preserved for judicial review absent a clear and unequivocal waiver.[8]

First Options appealed this decision and the Supreme Court granted *certiorari*.

### 2.3 *Issues and the Petitioner's Allegations*

Two issues were before the Court in *First Options*. *First*, what standard a district court should apply when reviewing an arbitrator's decision that the parties agreed to arbitrate the dispute. *Second*, how a court of appeals should review a district court's decision confirming or refusing to vacate an arbitral award.

On the first issue, First Options argued that a party resisting arbitration may obtain an advance judicial determination of whether a dispute is arbitrable or it may instead take advantage of the relative simplicity, efficiency and finality of arbitration by submitting the arbitrability question to the arbitrator. But once a party decided to submit the issue of arbitrability to the arbitrator in the first instance, the arbitrator's determination is entitled to deference. The Kaplans having submitted their objection to the arbitrators, the courts should defer to the arbitrators' decision on arbitrability just as they defer to their decision on the merits.

On the second one, First Options argued that the Court of Appeals should not have applied a *de novo* standard of review but should instead have used the more lenient "abuse of discretion" standard, applied by the Eleventh Circuit.

6 *Id.* at 1509.

7 *Id.* at 1512–23.

8 *Id.* at 1510.

### 2.4 *The Court's Opinion*

Justice Breyer, a prolific author of Supreme Court opinions on arbitration until he retired in 2022, delivered the unanimous opinion of the Court.

For the Court, the standard of review of an arbitrator's decision about arbitrability hinges on the simple question of who has the primary power to decide arbitrability: "[d]oes that power belong primarily to the arbitrators (because the court reviews their arbitrability decision deferentially) or to the court (because the court makes up its mind about arbitrability independently)?"[9] The answer to that question was "fairly simple": "[j]ust as the arbitrability of the merits of the dispute depends upon whether the parties agreed to arbitrate that dispute,"[10] "so the question 'who has the primary power to decide arbitrability' turns upon what the parties agreed about that matter."[11]

Thus, the Court agreed with First Options that if the parties agreed to submit arbitrability to the arbitrators, the courts should give considerable leeway to the arbitrators, setting aside their decision only in certain narrow circumstances.[12] Conversely, if the parties did not agree to submit the question of arbitrability to the arbitrators, then courts should decide that question independently.[13]

Unfortunately for First Options, that was not the end of the inquiry and the Court's response to the question on "how a court should decide whether the parties have agreed to submit the arbitrability issue to arbitration" was as critical.[14] And looking at the record before it, the Court rejected First Options' claim that the Kaplans had agreed to submit the arbitrability question to the arbitrators. While the answer to that question lied in ordinary contract law principles, Justice Breyer imposed an important qualification, namely that "[c]ourts should not assume that the parties agreed to arbitrate arbitrability unless there is 'clear and unmistakable' evidence that they did so."[15]

In other words, the Court was reversing the relevant presumption and requiring courts to treat silence or ambiguity about the question *who* has the power to decide arbitrability differently from the way they treat silence or ambiguity about the question *whether* a particular merits-related dispute is arbitrable

---

9 *First Options of Chicago v. Manual Kaplan, et ux. and MK Investments, Inc.*, 514 U.S. 938, 942 (1995).

10 *Id.* at 943 citing *Mastrobuono v. Shearson Lehman Hutton, Inc.*, 514 U.S. 52, 57 (1995).

11 *Id.* citing *AT&T Technologies Inc. v. Communications Workers*, 475 U.S. 643, 649 (1986).

12 *Id.*

13 *Id.*

14 *Id.* at 944.

15 *Id.* citing *AT&T Technologies* at 649.

because this latter question assumes the existence of a valid arbitration agreement. According to the Court, such different treatment is reasonable because if the parties have a contract that provides for arbitration of some issues, the parties have presumably given some thought to the scope of arbitration. On the other hand, parties are unlikely to have focused on the more arcane question of who should decide arbitrability. Therefore, as a party can be forced to submit to arbitration only those issues it specifically agreed to arbitrate, courts should be hesitant to interpret silence or ambiguity on the who should decide arbitrability as giving that power to the arbitrators because "doing so might too often force unwilling parties to arbitrate a matter they reasonably would have thought a judge, not an arbitrator, would decide."[16]

Turning to the case, for the Court, the fact that the Kaplans had argued the arbitrability issue before the arbitrators alone "[did] not indicate a clear willingness to arbitrate that issue, i.e., a willingness to be effectively bound by the arbitrator's decision on that point."[17] This was all the more so that under the law of the Third Circuit, parties can argue an issue before the arbitrators without losing their right to submitting that issue to a court's independent review.

The Court then quickly disposed of First Options' other arguments: while it agreed that the Kaplans had ways to get an independent court decision on arbitrability other than raising it at the award vacatur stage, the Court found that was irrelevant to the issue of whether the Kaplans had agreed to arbitrate arbitrability. The Court was also not persuaded by First Options' argument that allowing litigants to argue arbitrability before the arbitrators would cause delay and waste resources. The Court found the evidence inconclusive in that respect.

The Court finally forcefully rejected the argument that there was any "strong arbitration-related policy" supporting First Options because "the basic objective in this area is not to resolve disputes in the quickest manner possible … but to ensure that commercial arbitration agreements, like other contracts 'are enforced according to their terms' [] and according to the intentions of the parties."[18] As the Kaplans had not clearly agreed to submit arbitrability to the arbitrators, the Supreme Court upheld the Court of Appeals' determination that the arbitrability of the First Options / Kaplans dispute was subject to an independent review by the courts.[19]

16 *Id.* at 945.
17 *Id.* at 946.
18 *Id.* at 947.
19 *Id.*

Turning to the second question, the Supreme Court sided with the Third Circuit and the majority of the other Court of Appeals at the time that they "should apply ordinary, not special, standards when reviewing district court decisions upholding arbitration awards[,]" and they should accept findings of fact that are not clearly erroneous but decide questions of law de novo.[20]

## 2.5 *Key Takeaways*

In *First Options*, Justice Breyer was quick to acknowledge that though the Court was resolving a narrow issue, that issue had a significant practical importance: A party who did not agree to arbitrate arbitrability will be allowed to have the merits of that issue decided *de novo* by a court. As Professor George Bermann noted, this issue "so seriously implicate[s] the consent of the parties to arbitrate their disputes that a party contesting the enforceability of an arbitration agreement on those grounds is entitled to a judicial determination of the matter[.]"[21]

What the Court said happens when the parties did agree to arbitrate arbitrability, then the courts should give the same leeway to the arbitrators' determination of that issue as any other matter that was agreed to be subject to arbitration, would to most foreign practitioners seem the most radical aspect of its ruling. Indeed, one of the cornerstones of international arbitration is the principle of *Kompetenz-Kompetenz*, or competence-competence, which has both a positive and a negative implication. On the positive side, an arbitral tribunal has jurisdiction to consider and decide any disputes regarding its own jurisdiction, subject to subsequent judicial review.[22] The negative corollary of that principle is that during the pendency of an arbitration, national courts do not have jurisdiction over disputes relating to the jurisdiction of an arbitral tribunal, unless the underlying arbitration agreement is *prima facie* null and void.[23]

---

20 *Id.* at 947–948.

21 George A. Bermann, After First Options: Delegation Run Amok, 32 AM. REV. INT'L ARB. 15, 15 (2021).

22 George A. Bermann & Gustavo Favero Vaughn, The Nuts and Bolts of Competence-Competence: American and Brazilian Perspectives, *in* ARBITRAGEM E PODER JUDICIÁRIO (eds. Gilberto Giusti et al., 2023), 1174 (explaining that the "U.S. legal system recognizes only the positive dimension of competence-competence," meaning that the fact that "tribunals have competence to determine their own authority does not in itself mean that courts lack that authority.")

23 This principle is embodied in Article II(3) of the New York Convention, which requires that the courts of the Contracting State when requested to rule upon a dispute subject to an arbitration agreement "refer the parties to arbitration, unless [they] find[] that the said agreement is null and void, inoperative or incapable of being performed." Article 16(1) of

While First Options may seem on a first read to give courts a larger role during the pendency of an arbitration than under *Kompetenz-Kompetenz*, this is only true provided the parties have not delegated the arbitrability issue to the arbitrators.[24] And as we will see below, lower courts have interpreted the arbitration agreements most commonly found in international arbitration as precisely evidence of the parties' intent to delegate the question of arbitrability to arbitrators. In that latter case however, the level of deference that U.S. courts must give to the arbitrators' decision on arbitrability in their award is unmatched under the law on international arbitration elsewhere governing the standard of the courts' review of the arbitrators' ruling on jurisdiction.

## 3 The Case's Impact on U.S. Arbitration Law

### 3.1 *The Courts' Quest for the Clear and Unmistakable Intent to Delegate Arbitrability to Arbitrators*

While the Court's ruling in *First Options* would suggest that delegating the arbitrability issue to the arbitrators is the exception, not the norm, the reality has proved far more nuanced. Most circuit courts in the U.S. have since *First Options* recognized that the parties' "clear and unmistakable intent" to submit arbitrability issues to the arbitrators need not be express, such as when the parties expressly state in their arbitration agreement that the arbitrators have the authority to decide arbitrability/jurisdictional questions, but also may be implied.[25] Thus, the Court of Appeals for the Second Circuit, which has

---

the UNCITRAL Model Law provides: "The arbitral tribunal may rule on its own jurisdiction, including any objections with respect to the existence or validity of the arbitration agreement." The Model Law goes even further as Article 8(2) provides that "where an action [has been brought before a court in a matter which is the subject of an arbitration agreement], arbitral proceedings may nevertheless be commenced or continued, and an award may be made, while the issue is pending before the court."

24 William W. Park, Determining an Arbitrator's Jurisdiction: Timing and Finality in American Law, 8 NEV. L. J. 135, 137 (emphasizing that "[c]ourts in the United States will generally accept the litigants' agreement to have arbitral authority determined by the arbitrators themselves. Judges must still ask whether (and to what extent) the parties did indeed give such a role to the arbitrators. However, if courts ascertain that the contract confers on arbitrators the role of jurisdictional decision-makers, the matter is settled.")

25 Georgina Fabian, The Resolution of Arbitrability Disputes in the United States, *in* INTERNATIONAL ARBITRATION IN THE UNITED STATES (eds. Laurence Shore et al., 2017) ("Applying First Options, courts have ruled that the standard of clear and unmistakable evidence of intent to submit the substantive arbitrability issue to an arbitral tribunal is met when the parties agree that the arbitration will be governed by institutional

jurisdiction over arbitrations seated in New York, has on numerous occasions found such implied intent in the parties' agreement to have their disputes arbitrated under rules that vest the arbitrators with the authority to decide on their own jurisdiction.[26] All of the other circuits in the U.S. except the Seventh Circuit agree.[27]

Although the FAA does not directly address the issue of competence-competence, the reality is that in practice all international arbitrations are based on agreements that designate a set of institutional or *ad hoc* rules that incorporate that principle, and give the arbitrators the power to rule on their own jurisdiction.[28] Therefore, the Supreme Court's decision to honor such agreements and construe them as giving arbitrators the authority to rule on their own jurisdiction in the first place means that jurisdiction in international arbitration will be decided by arbitrators in the first instance.

Sticking to its commitment to honoring the parties' agreement, the Court ruled in *Henry Schein, Inc. v. Archer & White Sales, Inc.*[29] that, once a delegation

---

rules explicitly providing that questions of arbitrability will be decided by the arbitral tribunal.")

26 *Contec Corp. v. Remote Sol., Co.*, 398 F.3d 205, 208 (2d Cir. 2005) (In a case where parties had agreed to arbitrate their dispute under the AAA rules, a court held that where "parties explicitly incorporate rules that empower an arbitrator to decide issues of arbitrability, the incorporation serves as clear and unmistakable evidence of the parties' intent to delegate such issues to an arbitrator."); *Schneider v. Kingdom of Thailand*, 688 F.3d 68, 72 (2d Cir. 2012) (same for UNCITRAL Rules); *Republic of Ecuador v. Chevron Corp.*, 638 F.3d 384, 394 (2d Cir. 2011) (same for bilateral investment treaty incorporating the UNCITRAL rules).

27 *See e.g., See Chevron Corp. v. Ecuador*, 795 F.3d 200, 207–08 (D.C. Cir. 2015); *Oracle Am., Inc. v. Myriad Group A.G.*, 724 F.3d 1069, 1073 (9th Cir. 2013); *Brittania-U Nigeria, Ltd. v. Chevron USA, Inc.*, 866 F.3d 709, 714 (5th Cir. 2017); *Blanton v. Domino's Pizza Franchising LLC*, 962 F.3d 842, 845 (6th Cir. 2020). And even the Seventh Circuit's precedent suggests that it may join this consensus. *See Commonwealth Edison Co. v. Gulf Oil Corp.*, 541 F.2d 1263, 1272–73 (7th Cir. 1976) (relying on the incorporation of the AAA Rules to find that the parties had agreed to binding arbitration).

28 *See, e.g.* Article 23.1 of the 2021 UNCITRAL Arbitration Rules ("*Article 23 1. The arbitral tribunal shall have the power to rule on its own jurisdiction, including any objections with respect to the existence or validity of the arbitration agreement.*"); Article 6.5 of the 2021 ICC Rules ("[A]ny decision as to the jurisdiction of the arbitral tribunal, except as to parties or claims with respect to which the Court decides that the arbitration cannot proceed, shall then be taken by the arbitral tribunal itself."); Article 21 of the 2021 ICDR Rules ("The arbitral tribunal shall have the power to rule on its own jurisdiction, including any objections with respect to arbitrability, to the existence, scope, or validity of the arbitration agreement(s), or with respect to whether all of the claims, counterclaims, and setoffs made in the arbitration may be determined in a single arbitration, without any need to refer such matters first to a court.").

29 586 U.S. 63 (2019).

is made, a court must respect it even if it considers the challenge to enforceability of an arbitration agreement to be *"wholly groundless."* And in *Rent-A-Center, West, Inc. v. Jackson*,[30] the Court assumed that the parties had in fact made a delegation when their agreement to arbitrate stated that "[t]he Arbitrator, and not any federal, state, or local court or agency, shall have exclusive authority to resolve any dispute relating to the interpretation, applicability, enforceability or formation of this Agreement including, but not limited to any claim that all or any part of this Agreement is void or voidable."

Heeding however to Justice Breyer's caution against mistaken assumptions that would run roughshod against the parties' intent, courts are much more circumspect when dealing with delegation clauses in the context of non-signatory disputes. In a case where arbitration clause delegating the arbitrability disputes to the arbitrators, but that provided that disputes "shall be referred by either Party to arbitration" and only to the two parties to the relevant agreement, the Second Circuit Court of Appeals ruled that "[t]hese observations are sufficient to preclude a finding that [the parties] 'clearly and unmistakably' intended to afford anyone other than themselves the right to arbitrate arbitrability." Therefore, "[t]here is simply no 'clear and unmistakable evidence' from the arbitration agreement that the Republic [non-signatory] and BNP agreed to arbitrate the issue of whether their dispute is arbitrable for the simple reason that there is no contract between them."[31]

### 3.2 *The Limits to Delegation*

The outcome is less clear when dealing with arbitration provisions carving out certain claims. In *Schein*, on remand, a case in which the parties had agreed that "[a]ny dispute arising under or related to this Agreement (except for actions seeking injunctive relief ...), shall be resolved by binding arbitration in accordance with the arbitration rules of the American Arbitration Association [AAA][,]" the Court of Appeals for the Fifth Circuit held that the incorporation of institutional rules was insufficient to delegate arbitrability to the arbitrators where clause clearly carves-out claims for injunctive relief. Specifically, the court held that the "plain language incorporates the AAA rules—and therefore delegates arbitrability—for all disputes except those under the carve-out."[32] Thus, the parties did not clearly and unmistakably delegate all questions of jurisdiction to the arbitrators, and whether plaintiff's claims fell within the

30 561 U.S. 63 (2010).

31 *Republic of Iraq v. ABB AG*, 769 F. Supp. 2d 605, 610 (S.D.N.Y. 2011), aff'd sub nom. *The Republic of Iraq v. BNP Paribas USA*, 472 F. App'x 11 (2d Cir. 2012).

32 *Archer & White Sales, Inc. v. Henry Schein, Inc.*, 935 F.3d 274 (5th Cir. 2019).

carve-out, and therefore outside the scope of the agreement to arbitrate, was a question for the court in the first instance.[33] Similarly, the Second Circuit held that the incorporation of the ICC Rules is not always clear and unmistakable agreement to delegate arbitrability determinations to the arbitrators. It held instead that where contract carved out certain disputes from arbitration clause, whether claims at issue fell within the carve-out was a question for the court.[34]

Finally, in *Suski v. Coinbase*, the Court addressed who should decide the impact of a superseding agreement on a valid delegation clause. Users of a crypto-currency exchange were required to enter into an agreement with the exchange (the "User Agreement"). This User Agreement contained a broad arbitration agreement and incorporated the AAA Rules providing that the arbitrator had the power to rule on the existence, scope, or validity of the arbitration agreement. After entering into this User Agreement, some users participated in a sweepstakes run by Coinbase and another company which offered contestants the chance to win prizes of over $1 million of a digital currency. The sweepstakes contained official rules which contained a forum selection clause providing that any dispute would be decided solely by California state and federal courts.

Certain users sued in federal court asserting that Coinbase's promotion of the sweepstakes violated California law. Coinbase moved to compel arbitration relying on the terms of the User Agreement. The Court upheld the decision by the Court of Appeals for the Ninth Circuit, finding that a court rather than an arbitrator must decide whether this subsequent contract had narrowed the arbitration agreement.[35]

## 4 Conclusion

A testament to the place of that ruling in arbitration law, a lot has been written on *First Options* both approvingly and disapprovingly. Though many feared

---

33 *Archer & White Sales, Inc. v. Henry Schein, Inc.*, 935 F.3d 274 (5th Cir. 2019).

34 *Lavvan, Inc. v. Amyris, Inc.*, No. 21–1819 (2d Cir. Sept. 15, 2022); *see Continental Materials, Inc. v. Veer Plasticas Private Limited*, No. 22-cv-3685-MRP (E.D. Pa. April 4, 2023) (finding that an agreement to arbitrate under ICC rules was not clear and unmistakable evidence that the parties agreed to arbitrate arbitrability where dispute arguably fell within arbitration agreement's carveout for equitable claims).

35 *Coinbase Inc. v. Suski et al*, 602 U.S. ___ (2024), Opinion of the Court, p. 6–7 affirming *Suski v. Coinbase*, 55 F.4th 1227 (9th Cir. 2022).

an unwanted encroachment by the courts on the arbitrators' authority during the arbitration and the sacrosanct *Kompetenz-Kompetenz* principle, the reality is that courts were quick to reconcile *First Options* with the parties' practice of choosing arbitration rules that delegated arbitrability to the arbitrators. Still, others complain probably unfairly that *First Options*' division of labor between the courts and arbitrators could overcomplicate the law, where *First Options* and its progeny merely seek to give effect to the parties' agreement. It is only when parties are too creative that they trip up. The fact remains that *First Options* remains one of the most seminal cases on arbitration law in the United States.

CHAPTER 11

# *Vimar Seguros y Reaseguros*, S.A. *v.* M/V *Sky Reefer et al.* (1995)

*Rodrigo Tannuri, Matheus Soubhia Sanches, Felipe Conrado and Rekha Rangachari*

## 1 Introduction

For nearly three decades beginning in the mid-1960's, the U.S. Court of Appeals held foreign forum selection clauses, extended to foreign arbitration clauses, can be invalid in bills of lading. In 1995, the Supreme Court in *Vimar Seguros y Reaseguros*, S.A. *v.* M/V *Sky Reefer et al*[1] directly tackled the issue of enforceability of an international arbitration agreement included in a bill of lading.

The Supreme Court in *Vimar Seguros* addressed Petitioner's argument that the inclusion of an international arbitration agreement in a bill of lading lessens the shipper's liability in contravention of the Carriage of Goods by Sea Act ("COGSA") Section 3(8) by analyzing the explicit standards provided therein on carrier liability arising from negligence, fault or failure in duties and obligations. Additionally, the Court addressed provisions of the Federal Arbitration Act ("FAA") to minimize future conflicting interpretations and applications.

Cases prior to *Vimar Seguros* held that the choice of a foreign jurisdiction can lessen the shipper's liability, thereby running afoul to COGSA Section 3(8). However, in cases where the COGSA was inapplicable, the Court accepted and applied forum selection clauses on a *prima facie* basis. While the discussion on foreign forum selection clauses resembles international arbitration agreements, the ruling in *Vimar Seguros* reaffirmed the validity of arbitration clauses within international maritime shipping contracts and, by extension, that international forum selection clauses are generally permissible.

The Supreme Court ultimately held that party choice selecting international arbitration as a dispute resolution forum was valid under COGSA, in spite of prior considerations regarding the additional hurdles for parties seeking jurisdiction in foreign venues. Moreover, the Court in upholding the spirit of international commerce determined that a foreign forum selection clause does not

1 *Vimar Seguros y Reaseguros* SA *v.* M/V *Sky Reefer*, 515 U.S. 528 (1995).

 | DOI:10.1163/9789004715820_012

"lessen" liability for the parties and is a valid contractual consideration when conducting cross-border business.

## 2 The Case

### 2.1 *Case Background*

Although the validity of international forum selection clauses had been addressed prior to *Vimar Seguros*, the Court granted certiorari on the admissibility of an international arbitration agreement under COGSA.

Early decisions on forum selection clauses include *Knott v. Botany Mills*,[2] where the Supreme Court nullified a foreign forum selection clause under the Harter Act, a precursor to COGSA, upholding liability for negligence of a foreign vessel in spite of liability exemptions in the bill of lading. The U.S. enacted COGSA in 1936 based on the Hague-Visby Rules of 1924. Thereafter, the Second Circuit Court of Appeals offered the leading case for invalidation of a forum selection clause in *Indussa Corp. v. S. S. Ranborg* (1967).[3] The court in *Indussa Corp.*, reviewing a bill of lading containing a provision requiring disputes to be resolve in Norway under Norwegian law, held that Congressional intent behind Section 3(8) of COGSA was to invalidate any provision in a bill of lading that could prevent a party from obtaining jurisdiction over a carrier in a U.S. court, if said party would be able to do so under general procedural rules.

According to the ruling in *Indussa Corp.*, "[f]rom a practical standpoint, to require an American plaintiff to assert his claim only in a distant court lessens the liability of the carrier quite substantially, particularly when the claim is small."[4] The invalidity of foreign forum selection clauses under COGSA became established legal doctrine.[5]

---

2 *Knott v. Botany Mills*, 179. U.S. 69 (1900).

3 *Indussa Corporation v. s.s. Ranborg*, 377 F.2d 200 (2d Cir. 1967) (en banc).

4 *Vimar Seguros*, 515 U.S. at 546.

5 *See Carbon Black Export, Inc. v. The SS Monrosa, 254 F.2d 297, 300–01 (5th Cir. 1958)* ("It is a 'universally accepted rule that agreements in advance of controversy whose object is to oust the jurisdiction of the courts are contrary to public policy and will not be enforced"), *cert. dismissed, 359 U.S. 180 (1959); Wood & Selick, inc. v. Compagnie Generali Transatlantique, 43 F.2d 941, 942 (2d Cir. 1930)* ("We may at the start lay aside the clauses in the bills of lading, which apparently were intended to confine any litigation over the contracts to a French court ... [I]t is of course well settled that they would not [be valid]." (citations omitted))*; The Ciano, 58 F. Supp. 65 (E.D. Pa. 1944); Kuhnhold v. Compagnie Generali Transatlantique, 251 F. 387 (S.D.N.Y. 1918). But see William H. Muller & Co. v. Swedish American Line Ltd., 224 G.2d 806, 808 (2d Cir.)* (stating that "enforceability of such an agreement depends upon its reasonableness"), *cert. denied, 350 U.S. 903 (1955),* and overruled in part by *Indussa Corp. v. s.s. Ranborg, 377*

The holding in *Indussa Corp.* remained unchallenged until 1972, when the Supreme Court decided *The Bremen v. Zapata Off-Shore Co.*[6] Considering commercial globalization, the Court ruled that forum selection clauses were, in general, enforceable. The Court concluded that the choice of forum should be considered *prima facie* valid and would only be unenforceable if a party demonstrated that: "(1) the contract was induced by misrepresentation or overwhelming bargaining power; (2) enforcement did not meet a 'reasonableness' test which it set forth; or (3) enforcement would contravene a strong public policy of the United States."[7]

The Supreme Court extended the reasonableness test established in *Bremen* to *Carnival Cruise Lines, Inc. v. Shute.*[8] The Court considered a forum selection clause inserted on the back of passengers' cruise tickets – an adhesion contract, where Washington resident passengers argued that a Florida forum selection clause should not be enforced due to hardship bearing on expense and inconvenience of Florida litigation. The Court enforced the agreement, ruling that the clause did not limit liability and the lack of bargaining power was not alone sufficient to invalidate the forum selection provision where the *Bremen* criteria were also not met.

It is important to note that neither *Bremen*, nor *Carnival Cruise Lines*, dealt directly with COGSA. Both cases addressed consumer contracts, which fall outside the scope of COGSA. Notwithstanding, these cases serve as benchmarks on the enforceability of foreign forum selection clauses. The Supreme Court in *Vimar Seguros* clarified the Second Circuit's decision in *Indussa Corp*, reviewing in turn the legislative history of the Hague Rules. Sixty-six countries at that time were parties to the Convention and none had interpreted COGSA Section 3(8) as a prohibition on foreign forum selection clauses nor a lessening of carrier liability.

---

*F.2d 200 (2d Cir. 1967)*. Muller represents a second, less widely followed approach to foreign forum selection clauses in bills of lading. *See* C. Andrew Waters, *The Enforceability of Forum Selection Clauses in Maritime Bills of Lading: An Update,* 15 Tul. Mar. L.J. 29, 31 (1990). *See id. at. 30–31 for a fuller discussion of the pre-Bremen cases* (Elizabeth A. Clark, Foreign Arbitration Clauses and Foreign Forum Selection Clauses in Bills of Lading Governed by COGSA: *Vimar Seguros y Reaseguros, SA. v. MIV Sky Reefer*, 1996 BYU L. Rev. 483 (1996), p. 486).

6 *The Bremen* v. *Zapata Off-Shore Co.*, 407 U.S. 1 (1972).

7 Fahrenback, C. Christine, *Vimar Seguros Reaseguros v. M/V Sky Reefer: A Change in Course: COGSA Does Not Invalidate Foreign Arbitration Clauses in Maritime*, Akron Law Review: Voll. 29: Iss 2, Article 8, p. 4.

8 *Carnival Cruise Lines, Inc v. Shute*, 499 U.S. 585 (1991).

### 2.2 *Issues and Parties' Allegations*

Bacchus Associates ("Bacchus"), a New York wholesale fruit importer and distributor, contracted with Galaxie Negoce SA ("Galaxie"), a Moroccan fruit supplier, for the purchase of a shipload of Moroccan oranges and lemons. Bacchus then chartered a refrigerated cargo ship, the *M/V Sky Reefer*, owned by Panamanian company MH Maritima SA, time chartered to Japanese company Nichiro Gyogyo Kaisha Ltd. ("Nichiro") as ultimate carrier. Nichiro issued the bill of lading to Galaxie, tendered to Bacchus, and Bacchus extended a letter of credit to Galaxie, while Bacchus in parallel obtained marine cargo insurance through Vimar Seguros y Reasurgos ("Vimar Seguros").

During transit from Morocco to Massachusetts, several thousand fruit boxes were ruined. Insurer Vimar Seguros settled Bacchus' claim. Subsequently, Petitioner Vimar Seguros initiated legal proceedings against the Respondents in charge of the carrier ship, citing violations of the standard form bill of lading provided to Bacchus by Galaxie. The Respondents moved to stay the action and compel arbitration in Tokyo pursuant to the bill of lading's foreign arbitration clause and the FAA.[9]

The Supreme Court accepted the case to determine the validity and enforceability of the arbitration agreement inserted into the bill of lading. The parties' arbitration clause provided for arbitration in Japan administered by the Tokyo Maritime Arbitration Commission ("TOMAC") of the Japan Shipping Exchange, Inc., with the arbitral award final and binding on both parties.[10]

Petitioner Vimar Seguros argued that the arbitration agreement was unenforceable pursuant to Section 3(8) of COGSA, which provides:

> Any clause, covenant, or agreement in a contract of carriage relieving the carrier or the ship from liability for loss or damage to or in connection with the goods, arising from negligence, fault, or failure in the duties and obligations provided in this section, or lessening such liability otherwise than as provided in this chapter, shall be null and void and of no effect.

9 *Vimar Seguros* 515 U.S. at 528.

10 *Id.* at 531. The arbitration clause provides: (1) The contract evidenced by or contained in the Bill of Lading shall be governed by the Japanese Law. (2) Any dispute arising from this Bill of Lading shall be referred to arbitration in Tokyo by the Tokyo Maritime Arbitration Commission (TOMAC) of The Japan Shipping Exchange, Inc., in accordance with the rules of TOMAC and any amendment thereto, and the award given by the arbitrators shall be final and binding on both parties.

According to the Petitioner, the inconvenience and cost of arbitrating in Japan would "lessen liability" prohibited by COGSA by increasing the transaction cost of obtaining relief. Petitioner also argued that there was lack of clarity on COGSA's application, where the Japanese version adopting the Hague Rules differed from the United States version. With arbitration seated in Japan, Petitioner argued, "the arbitrators will follow the Japanese Hague Rules, which significantly lessen respondents' liability by providing carriers with a defense based on the acts or omissions of the stevedores hired by the shipper, rather than COGSA, which makes nondelegable the carrier's obligation to properly and carefully stow the goods."[11]

Respondents argued that Section 3(8) of COGSA did not address issues of choice of forum, and thus could not be used to invalidate an arbitration agreement inserted in a bill of lading. Respondents also argued that the choice to resolve disputes by arbitration did not lessen the shipper's liability, and Petitioner's reading of Section 3(8) of COGSA contravened provisions of the FAA which post-dated COGSA and should prevail in cases of inconsistency.

### 2.3 *The Court's Opinions*

By seven votes to one, the Supreme Court held "COGSA does not nullify foreign arbitration clauses contained in maritime bills of lading."[12]

The majority opinion delivered by Justice Kennedy determined, "§3(8) does not support petitioner's argument that a foreign arbitration clause lessens COGSA liability by increasing the transaction costs of obtaining relief."[13] Rather, "§3(8) is concerned with the liability imposed elsewhere in §3, which defines that liability by explicit obligations and procedures designed to correct certain abuses by carriers, but *does not* address the separate question of the particular forum or other procedural enforcement mechanisms"[14] (emphasis added).

The Court considered the international impact of its ruling, noting, "for the United States to be able to gain the benefits of international accords, its courts must not construe COGSA to nullify foreign arbitration clauses because of inconvenience to the plaintiff or insular distrust of the ability of foreign arbitrators to apply the law."[15]

The Court also dismissed Petitioner's argument that enforcement should not be granted since there would be no guarantee that foreign arbitrators

11 *Id.* at 529.
12 *Id.* at 528.
13 *Id.*
14 *Id.*
15 *Id.* at 529.

would apply COGSA. The Court concluded that "whatever the merits of this comparative reading, petitioner's claim is premature because, at this interlocutory stage, it is not established what law the arbitrators will apply or that petitioner will receive diminished protection as a result."[16] The Court held the issue of applicable law can and should only be addressed, as necessary, at the award enforcement stage.

The Supreme Court also held that "the relevant provisions of COGSA and the FAA are in accord, and both Acts may be given full effect,"[17] precluding any discussion of whether the FAA overrides COGSA.

### 2.4 *Key Takeaways*

The Supreme Court's decision relied on a historical interpretation of COGSA, highlighting congressional intent behind Section 3(8). Justice Kennedy for the majority noted, "in the 19th century it was a prevalent practice for common carriers to insert clauses in bills of lading exempting themselves from liability for damage or loss, limiting the period in which plaintiffs had to present their notice of claim or bring suit, and capping any damages awards per package."[18]

For this reason, COGSA enumerated substantial obligations and imposed liability on carriers defined by explicit standards of conduct to correct specific abuses by carriers. Section 3(8) prohibits the alteration of said obligations and proceedings.[19] As noted by Justice Kennedy, "nothing in this section, however, suggests that the statute prevents the parties from agreeing to enforce these obligations in a particular forum. By its terms, it establishes certain duties and obligations, separate and apart from the mechanisms for their enforcement."[20]

The Court held that Petitioner's reading of COGSA Section 3(8) undermined the ruling in *Carnival Cruise Lines*.[21] Justice Kennedy emphasized, "if the

16 *Id.*

17 *Id.*

18 *Id.* at 534–35.

19 *Id.* at 528. The Court stated: Thus, §3, entitled 'Responsibilities and liabilities of carrier and ship' requires that the carrier 'exercise due diligence to … [m]ake the ship seaworthy' and '[p]roperly man, equip, and supply the ship' before and at the beginning of the voyage, §3(1), 'properly and carefully load, handle, stow, carry, keep, care for, and discharge the goods carried', §3(2), and issue a bill of lading with specified contents, §3(3). 46. U.S.C. App. §§1303(1), (2) and (3). Section 3(6) allows the cargo owner to provide notice of loss or damage within three days and to bring suit within one year. These are substantive obligations and particular procedures that §3(8) prohibits a carrier from altering to its advantage in a bill of lading.

20 *Id.* at 535.

21 *Id.* at 535–36. The Court stated: Petitioner's contrary reading of §3(8) is undermined by the Court's construction of a similar statutory provision in *Carnival Cruise Lines, Inc.*

question whether a provision lessens liability were answered by reference to the costs and inconvenience to the cargo owner, there would be no principled basis for distinguishing national from foreign arbitration clauses."[22] Justice Kennedy affirmed that even national forum selection clauses would impose different costs and expenses, depending on which state was elected by the parties.[23]

Justice Kennedy also noted that no other country, when interpreting the Hague Rules, which served as the basis for COGSA, concluded that Section 3(8) prohibited the enforceability of international arbitration clauses. He stressed that:

> "in light of the fact that COGSA is the culmination of a multilateral effort 'to establish uniform ocean bills of lading to govern the rights and liabilities of carriers and shippers inter se in international trade', *Robert C. Herd & Co. v. Krawill Machinery Corp.*, 359 U.S. 297, 301 (1959), we decline to interpret our version of the Hague Rules in a manner contrary to every other nation to have addressed this issue."[24] He continued, "if the United States is to be able to gain the benefits of international accords and have a role as a trusted partner in multilateral endeavors, its courts should be most cautious before interpreting its domestic legislation in such manner as to violate international agreements"[25]

Lastly, regarding the possibility of COGSA applied inconsistently by arbitrators in Japan, Justice Kennedy concluded that the claim was premature, to be addressed as necessary during award enforcement.[26]

---

*v. Shute*, 499 U.S. 585 (1991) … We observed that the clause 'does not purport to limit petitioner`s liability for negligence', 499 U.S., at 596–597, and enforced the agreement over the dissent's argument, based in part on the *Indussa* line of cases, that the cost and inconvenience of traveling thousands of miles 'lessens or weakens [plaintiffs'] ability to recover', 499 U.S., at 603 (Stevens, J., dissenting).

22 *Id.* at 536.

23 *Id.* The Court stated: Even if it were reasonable to read §3(8) to make a distinction between domestic and foreign forums. Requiring a Seattle cargo owner to arbitrate in New York likely imposes more costs and burdens than a foreign arbitration clause requiring it to arbitrate in Vancouver. It would be unwieldy and unsupported by the terms or policy of the statute to require courts to proceed case by case to tally the costs and burdens to particular plaintiffs in light of their means, the size of their claims, and the relative burden on the carrier.

24 *Id.* at 537.

25 *Id.* at 539.

26 *Id.* at 540. The Court stated: Whatever the merits of petitioner`s comparative reading of COGSA and its Japanese counterpart, its claim is premature. At this interlocutory stage it

Justice O'Connor concurred in the judgment. Ever cautious not to disrupt existing authority, she added that foreign arbitration clauses as presented in the instant case do not divest domestic courts of jurisdiction, in contrast to *Indussa Corp.* and its clear foreign selection clause.

Justice Stevens dissented, finding that COGSA Section 3(8) could not be interpreted simply in a formalistic fashion to limit applicability. He noted, "this section responds to the inequality of bargaining power inherent in bills of lading and to carriers` historic tendency to exploit that inequality for their own fault."[27]

Justice Stevens explained, "the foreign-arbitration clause imposes potentially prohibitive costs on the shipper, who must travel – and bring his lawyer, witnesses, and exhibits – to a distant country in order to seek redress. The shipper will therefore be inclined to settle the claim at a discount or to forgo bringing the claim at all."[28] Considering the rationale behind Section 3(8), Justice Stevens observed that a foreign arbitration agreement would, in practice, lessen the carrier's liability by creating an incentive for the shipper to settle or, at least, minimize net recovery.[29] Justice Stevens determined, pursuant to Section 3(8), the foreign arbitration clause could not be enforced, particularly where international obligations do not require the U.S. to enforce a contractual term that was not freely negotiated.[30]

---

is not established what law the arbitrators will apply to petitioner`s claims or that petitioner will receive diminished protection as a result. The arbitrators may conclude that COGSA applies of its own force or that Japanese law does not apply so that, under another clause of the bill of lading, COGSA controls. (…) As the District Court has retained jurisdiction, mere speculation that the foreign arbitrators might apply Japanese law which, depending on the proper construction of COGSA, might reduce respondents 'legal obligations, does not in and of itself lessen liability under COGSA §3(8).

27 *Id.* at 550.

28 *Id.* at 548.

29 *Id.* at 551. The Court stated: Even if the value of the shipper`s claim is large enough to justify litigation in Asia, contractual provisions that impose unnecessary and unreasonable costs on the consignee will inevitably lessen net recovery. If, as under the Court`s reasoning, such provisions do not affect the carrier`s legal liability, it would appear to be permissible to require the consignee to pay the costs of the arbitration, or perhaps the travel expenses and fees of the expert witnesses, interpreter, and lawyers employed by both parties. Judge Friendly and the many other wise judges who shared his opinion were surely correct in concluding that Congress could not have intended such a perverse reading of the statutory text.

30 *Id.* at 553. The Court determined: "Our international obligations do not require us to enforce a contractual term that was not freely negotiated by the parties. Much less do they require us to ignore the clear meaning of COGSA – itself the product of international negotiations – which forbids enforcement of clauses lessening the carriers liability."

## 3 Analysis of the Court's Opinions

The ruling in *Vimar Seguros* reaffirmed access to arbitration and party autonomy in drafting contracts with specialized international arbitration clauses.

While the inconvenience and costs associated with arbitrating in a foreign country may present difficulties for a party, this issue is not unique to arbitration, and exists in cross-border disputes in state and federal court. Justice Kennedy discussed party difficulty regarding forum selection clauses in distant U.S. courts. Moreover, prohibition of a forum selection clause simply because it selects a foreign court lacks objective criteria.

Although Justice Stevens argued that by having to arbitrate in a foreign country, a party would have an incentive to settle or minimize its net recovery due to increased transactional costs and expenses, this does not qualify as "lessening the carrier's liability" as prohibited by Section 3(8).

There are several things a party can do to initiate an arbitral proceeding even if it does not have resources at its disposal. For example, there is the possibility of finding a third-party funder or advancing filing fees in installments. Additionally, in some arbitral proceedings the prevailing party clause may allow the winning party to have all or some of its costs and expenses reimbursed by the losing party, i.e., if the cargo owner wins the arbitration, its net recovery will not be diminished by the additional costs of arbitrating in another jurisdiction.

In the modern era of dispute resolution and litigation, particularly in a post-pandemic world, parties have availed themselves of electronic submissions and video-conference pre-hearing and hearing sessions to defray costs and increase efficiency.

The Petitioner's risk argument, that a foreign-seated tribunal would not properly interpret U.S. law and conventions, is controlled by access to judicial oversight. According to the Convention on the Recognition and Enforcement of Foreign Arbitral Awards ("New York Convention"), the enforcement of an arbitral award shall be refused if "the competent authority in the country where recognition and enforcement is sought finds that: (…) (b) the recognition or enforcement of the award would be contrary to the public policy of that country."[31]

Arbitration is one of many dispute resolution options for contracting parties. An automatic prohibition to arbitration would be antithetical to the spirit

31 United Nations Convention on the Recognition and Enforcement of Foreign Arbitral Awards, Article V, 2, (b) (1958).

of the COGSA, in kind censoring international forums for dispute resolution. Arbitration may be the best option for parties offering benefits including confidentiality and the ability to select arbitrators with specialized expertise.

Ultimately, the Supreme Court in *Vimar Seguros* correctly enforces arbitration and forum selection clauses in bills of lading. The parties' choice of arbitration is *prima facie* valid, while subject to the reasonableness test established in *Breman*.

## 4 Conclusion

*Vimar Seguros* demonstrates U.S. respect for the choices of international contracting parties, underscoring *pacta sunt servanda* and arbitration as a preferred dispute resolution mechanism, in addition to demonstrating that the choice of arbitration alone does not lessen the liability of a party.

There is no doubt that arbitration may present different costs and expenses for each party. However, this does not mean it is less difficult to seek jurisdiction before state courts rather than before an arbitral tribunal. As a private form of dispute resolution, arbitration offers creative and alternative approaches through mutual selection by the parties, dissimilar to the procedural constructs of litigation.

The Supreme Court in *Vimar Seguros* adds clarity to the juridical and jurisdictional landscape regarding international maritime shipping contracts, bills of lading, forum selection clauses including arbitration clauses, and the application of COGSA. Parties that specifically contract for international arbitration seated in a foreign jurisdiction may do so for any number of reasons – including choice of a neutral forum, ease of the key players, and trust in the process.

*Vimar Seguros* reaffirms arbitration and party autonomy in parallel with international comity and commercial practice. The central guarantee of COGSA Section 3(8), upheld by the Supreme Court, is that the terms of a bill of landing may not relieve the carrier of obligations or diminish legal duties. Mere speculation about the transactional costs of arbitration or the substantive law to be applied by the arbitral tribunal are not alone sufficient to dislodge the parties' right and access to international arbitration and a foreign forum selection clause.

CHAPTER 12

# *Mastrobuono v. Shearson Lehman Hutton, Inc.*, 514 U.S. 52 (1995)

*Caline Mouawad and Alex Lupsaiu*

## 1 Introduction

An often-repeated maxim of arbitration law is that arbitration is a creature of contract. Consequently, the rights, duties, and remedies available to parties in arbitration depend on how the parties agreed to be bound in their underlying agreement. In *Mastrobuono v. Shearson Lehman Hutton, Inc.*, the Supreme Court applied ordinary contract construction principles to conclude that the parties did not intend to limit the arbitrators' power to award punitive damages, notwithstanding the applicable New York law to that effect. On closer examination, however, the Court's holding that punitive damages were available in the underlying arbitration showcases the Court's eagerness to promote arbitration as a dispute resolution forum on equal footing as domestic courts. *Mastrobuono* should be read as part of a line of Supreme Court cases protecting the arbitral forum from discriminatory state laws, in support of a national policy favoring arbitration.

## 2 The Case

### 2.1 *Background*

The dispute in *Mastrobuono* arose when two clients of a securities brokerage firm, Mr. and Mrs. Mastrobuono, alleged that their brokerage firm, Shearson Lehman Hutton, Inc. ("Shearson"), mishandled their investment account. The Mastrobuonos filed suit in the United States District Court for the Northern District of Illinois and claimed relief, including punitive damages, under various state and federal law theories. However, the parties' standard-form contract under which the brokerage account was opened contained both a choice-of-law provision and an arbitration provision. The choice-of-law provision stated that the entire agreement "shall be governed by the laws of the

 | DOI:10.1163/9789004715820_013

State of New York."[1] The arbitration provision required that "any controversy" arising from the parties' transaction "shall be settled by arbitration" under the rules of the National Association of Securities Dealers ("NASD"), or the Boards of Directors of the New York Stock Exchange or American Stock Exchange.[2] Accordingly, Shearson moved to stay the litigation and to compel arbitration of the parties' dispute pursuant to the contract and the Federal Arbitration Act ("FAA") §§ 3 and 4.[3] The District Court granted the motion, and a three-member arbitral tribunal was convened.

During the arbitration, Shearson argued that the arbitral tribunal lacked authority to award punitive damages given the New York Court of Appeals' previous ruling in *Garrity v. Lyle Stewart, Inc.*[4] that, under New York law, the power to award such damages belonged exclusively to judicial tribunals. The tribunal nonetheless awarded the Mastrobuonos both compensatory and punitive damages. Shearson then moved to vacate the punitive damages award in the District Court, which granted the motion, and the United States Court of Appeals for the Seventh Circuit affirmed. Both courts found that *Garrity* applied under the choice-of-law provision and dispositively deprived the tribunal of the power to award punitive damages. The Mastrobuonos subsequently petitioned for and were granted certiorari by the Supreme Court of the United States.

### 2.2 *Issue before the Supreme Court*

The sole issue before the Supreme Court was whether the contractual choice-of-law provision precluded an otherwise proper award of punitive damages. The Mastrobuonos argued that *Garrity* did not control because its restriction on arbitral tribunals was merely a "vestige of the ancient judicial hostility to arbitration" and was preempted by the FAA, which "declared a national policy favoring arbitration."[5] Under the FAA, the parties' intent—not state law—should determine which remedies the tribunal was empowered to grant. Because the parties' contract did not preclude punitive damages, the tribunal thus was free to award them. Shearson, on the other hand, contended that the choice-of-law provision was precisely evidence of the parties' intent to exclude punitive damages:[6] by choosing New York law to govern the entire agreement,

1 *Mastrobuono v. Shearson Lehman Hutton, Inc.*, 514 U.S. 52, 54–55 (1995).
2 *Id.* at 58–59.
3 *Id.* at 54; 9 U.S.C. §§ 3, 4.
4 40 N.Y.2d 354, 386 (N.Y. 1976).
5 *Mastrobuono*, 514 U.S. at 56 (internal quotations omitted).
6 *See id.* at 56–57.

the parties intended to apply New York's law governing arbitration, which included *Garrity*. Irrespective of whether *Garrity* is preempted, the parties' decision to be bound by New York law—including *Garrity*—must be respected.

### 2.3 *The Supreme Court's Opinion*

The Supreme Court sided with the Mastrobuonos and reversed the Seventh Circuit's decision. The Supreme Court first observed that *Garrity*'s discriminatory holding that allowed judicial but not arbitral tribunals to award punitive damages was indeed preempted by the FAA, leaving the determination of which remedies are available to the contracting parties instead of state law.[7] The issue before the Court thus was, at its core, a contract interpretation question: did the parties' contract include or exclude claims for punitive damages from the issues to be arbitrated?

After acknowledging that the contract contained "no express reference to claims for punitive damages,"[8] the Court turned to the two relevant provisions at issue: the choice-of-law provision designating New York law as the governing law, and the arbitration agreement submitting "any controversy" to arbitration. The Court first construed these two provisions separately. Viewed in isolation, the Court found the choice-of-law provision might be "merely a substitute for the conflict-of-laws analysis that otherwise would determine what law to apply to disputes arising out of the contractual relationship," and not "evidence of an intent to exclude punitive damages claims."[9] That is, the Court found the choice-of-law provision ambiguous: it could "include only New York's substantive rights and obligations," or it also could include "the State's allocation of power between alternative tribunals."[10] In any event, the choice-of-law provision was "not, in itself, an unequivocal exclusion of punitive damages claims."[11] In contrast, the arbitration provision supported the availability of punitive damages by explicitly incorporating the NASD arbitration rules. The NASD Code of Arbitration authorized awards for "damages and other relief," which the Court found sufficiently broad to authorize punitive damages.[12] Moreover, a manual providing guidance to NASD arbitrators on conducting arbitral proceedings specified that "arbitrators can consider punitive damages as a remedy."[13]

---

7 *See id.* at 59.
8 *Id.*
9 *Id.*
10 *Id.* at 60.
11 *Id.*
12 *Id.* at 61.
13 *Id.*

The Court then construed the two provisions together and found that the choice-of law provision "introduce[d] ambiguity into an arbitration agreement that would otherwise allow punitive damages awards" given the incorporation of the NASD rules.[14] Resolving this ambiguity required appeal to two key interpretive maxims. First, any "ambiguities as to the scope of [an] arbitration clause" should be "resolved in favor of arbitration."[15] Second, and more generally, a contract must be construed to "give effect to all its provisions and to render them consistent with one another."[16] The best way to "harmonize the choice-of-law provision with the arbitration provision" in a manner that favored arbitration, the Court observed, was to read the choice-of-law provision "to encompass substantive principles that New York courts would apply, but not to include special rules liming the authority of arbitrators."[17] As a result, the "choice of law provision cover[ed] the rights and duties of the parties, while the arbitration clause cover[ed] arbitration; neither sentence intrude[d] upon the other."[18]

Justice Thomas authored a sole dissent arguing that (i) the Majority cannot reconcile its holding in *Mastrobuono* with its prior decision in *Volt Information Science, Inc. v. Board of Trustees of Leland Stanford Junior Univ.*[19]; and (ii) the Majority misread the applicable institutional arbitration rules and consequently incorrectly determined the parties' intent as allowing for punitive damages.[20] The Dissent first observed that, in *Volt,* the Court considered a dispute arising from an underlying contract that, as in *Mastrobuono*, contained both an arbitration provision and a choice of law provision identifying California law as applicable.[21] In that case, Volt initiated arbitration, and Stanford responded by moving in California state court to stay arbitration under a California statute.[22] Although the Court found that the FAA preempted the California statutory

14 *Id.* at 62.

15 *Id.*

16 *Id.* at 63. The Court dismissed Shearson's position as "untenable" because it "set up the two clauses in conflict with one another: one foreclosing punitive damages, the other allowing them." *Id.* at 64.

17 *Id.* at 64. The Court further observed that, "[a]s a practical matter, it seems unlikely that [the Mastrobuonos] were actually aware of New York's bifurcated approach to punitive damages, or that they had any idea that by signing a standard-form agreement to arbitrate disputes they might be giving up an important substantive right. In the fact of such doubt, we are unwilling to impute this intent to [the Mastrobuonos]." *Id.* at 63.

18 *Id.* at 64.

19 489 U.S. 468 (1989).

20 *See Mastrobuono*, 514 U.S. at 65–69.

21 *See id.* at 65.

22 *See id.*

provision authorizing the stay, it nevertheless held that the parties' choice of California law evidenced the intent to be bound by the preempted provision, and accordingly enforced the stay of arbitration.[23] Justice Thomas argued that *Volt* was directly on point and demanded the same result in *Mastrobuono*.

Indeed, Justice Thomas noted that the only distinguishing feature in *Mastrobuono* was the purported express allowance for punitive damages in the NASD arbitration rules. However, the NASD rules themselves were silent with respect to punitive damages. Instead, the Majority located a provision stating that "arbitrators can consider punitive damages" in a manual provided to NASD arbitrators, which the Dissent described as a "how to" guide for NASD arbitrators.[24] Moreover, the manual providing such guidance was not part of the institutional rules, but separately promulgated by a securities arbitration advisory committee.[25] Consequently, per the Dissent, the manual should not have informed the interpretation of the NASD rules,[26] which are silent with respect to punitive damages.[27] Read together with the parties' choice that New York law governs their entire agreement without limitation, including *Garrity*[28]—and thus that New York law bars punitive damages in arbitration—the natural way to harmonize the two provisions was to exclude punitive damages as an available remedy.[29]

### 2.4 *Key Observations*

The critical upshot for applying *Mastrobuono* is undoubtedly that, in light of the FAA's national policy of favoring arbitration, a choice-of-law provision in a contract with an arbitration clause will not—in itself—be read as importing aspects of the chosen state law that limit the authority of arbitrators. Rather, choice-of-law provisions will be interpreted only as containing substantive state-law rights and duty. Any waiver of a right in arbitration to which the parties otherwise would be entitled in a judicial forum may likely require "unequivocal exclusion" in the contract.

*Mastrobuono* also provides a good example of the Supreme Court's readiness to protect arbitration as a forum for dispute resolution on equal footing to domestic courts. As the Dissent observed, the Court's contractual

23 *See id.* at 65–66.
24 *See id.* at 69.
25 *See id.*
26 *See id.*
27 *See id.* at 70–71.
28 *See id.*
29 *See id.* at 72.

interpretation found ambiguity in a choice of law provision plainly stating that New York law governed any contractual dispute and imported language from a separately promulgated user manual into institutional arbitration rules to find affirmative evidence of the parties' intent to allow for punitive damages. This interpretive approach is best viewed through the prism of the Court's efforts to ensure that state law does not privilege its own courts by limiting or burdening the arbitral forum. As the Court observed, New York law allows its courts to award punitive damages and stripped only arbitrators of that ability. It appears likely that the Court did not want to allow this "vestige of the ancient judicial hostility" to survive through the back door, by including anti-arbitration laws in contractual provisions. At the very least, the bar for incorporating such anti-arbitration elements is higher than simply choosing a particular state law as governing law; it would require an explicit reference to such anti-arbitration elements.

## 3 Impact on U.S. Arbitration Practice

*Mastrobuono* is part of a collection of Supreme Court decisions striking down restrictions on arbitration under various state laws, thereby attempting to curb state judicial hostility to arbitration and to give effect to the FAA's national policy favoring arbitration.[30] Specifically, *Mastrobuono* established the cornerstone principle that choice-of-law provisions in contracts containing arbitration provisions refer only to substantive principles of state law, and therefore do not import limitations to the arbitrators' powers in the applicable state laws. Various U.S. Courts of Appeals have built on this key holding and have extended it to find that choice-of-law provisions in contracts with arbitration provisions also will not be construed as including state-law limitations on which *issues* may be arbitrated (in addition to state-law limitations on the authority of arbitrators).[31]

30 For instance, prior to *Mastrobuono*, the Court in *Southland Corp., et al. v. Keating* overturned a judgment of the California Supreme Court that claims asserted under the state's franchise investment laws were not arbitrable. 461 U.S. 1, 2–3 (1984). A few years later, the Court ruled in *Perry v. Thomas* that the FAA preempted a California labor law that wage collection claims were not arbitrable. 482 U.S. 483, 483–484 (1987). Additionally, immediately prior to *Mastrobuono*, the Court in *Allied-Bruce Terminix Cos. v. Dobson* upheld the enforceability of an arbitration agreement governed by Alabama law despite an Alabama statute specifying that arbitration agreements were unenforceable. 513 U.S. 265 (1995).

31 *See, e.g., PaineWebber Inc. v. Bybyk*, 81 F.3d 1193, 1200 (2d Cir. 1996) (finding *Mastrobuono* "squarely on point" for the proposition that a choice-of-law provision did not prevent

## 4 Conclusion

*Mastrobuono* provides an example of the Supreme Court using canons of contractual interpretation to resolve an ambiguity in a contract containing both an arbitration provision and a choice-of-law provision. However, the manner in which the Court used these canons, beginning with the Court's willingness to find a contractual ambiguity in the first instance, illustrates its willingness to use malleable interpretive methods to achieve a pro-arbitration result.

---

arbitration of issues of timeliness and attorneys' fees because the provision applied only to "substantive principles" of law, not to special rules regarding arbitration); *Nat'l Union Fire Insurance Co. v. Belco*, 88 F.3d 129 (2d Cir. 1996) (finding that a choice-of-law provision did not incorporate the New York "rule that requires the preclusive effect of a prior arbitration to be decided by the court" because the choice-of-law provision only included "substantive principles that New York courts would apply").

CHAPTER 13

# *Howsam v. Dean Witter Reynolds, Inc.* (2002)

*Gary L. Benton*

## 1 Introduction

Howsam v. Dean Witter Reynolds, Inc., 537 U.S. 79 (2002) is one of the long line of U.S. Supreme Court decisions, beginning most notably with Moses H. Cone Memorial Hospital v. Mercury Const. Corp., 460 U.S. 1 (1983), that provide a strong federal policy favoring arbitration. That policy is limited by the Supreme Court in its reservation of questions of arbitral jurisdiction to the courts, as articulated in First Options of Chicago, Inc. v. Kaplan, 514 U.S. 938 (1995). This U.S. approach represents a limitation on the internationally recognized competence-competence principle authorizing arbitrators to decide their own jurisdiction in the first instance.

The Howsam opinion addresses the particular question of what constitutes a gateway question of arbitrability and, in so doing, distinguishes a "question of arbitrability," which is to be decided by a court, from a procedural question, which is to be decided by an arbitrator.[1]

At its core, Howsam is a dispute between an investor and an investment firm over access to arbitration. In leaving certain gateway questions for the arbitrators, Howsam has advanced access to arbitration.

## 2 Preliminary Considerations

Howsam defines the "what" in the question of "who decides" jurisdictional disputes. In considering what gateway issues are properly matters for the Court, Howsam establishes a framework that leaves gateway procedural questions to the arbitrator.

1 Of note from an international arbitration standpoint, Howsam, like other U.S. opinions, refers to "arbitrability" broadly to mean arbitral jurisdiction, i.e., whether a dispute should properly proceed to arbitration, rather than the narrower reference more commonly used outside the U.S. as to whether the subject matter of the dispute is proper for determination by arbitration.

 | DOI:10.1163/9789004715820_014

Howsam focuses on an arbitration rule of the National Association of Securities Dealers (NASD).[2] The rule states that no dispute "shall be eligible for submission to arbitration ... where six (6) years have elapsed from the occurrence or event giving rise to the ... dispute." Howsam, 537 U.S. at 81; NASD Code of Arbitration Procedure § 10304 (1984) ("NASD Code"). At issue in Howsam was whether a court or an NASD arbitrator should apply the rule to the underlying controversy. The Court determined this was not a question of arbitrability but instead a procedural question to be decided by an NASD arbitrator.

Howsam's key contribution is the distinction it makes between what may be called substantive arbitrability and procedural arbitrability, a distinction that has been applied beyond the narrow confines of the NASD time-limitation rule at issue. As discussed herein, this distinction has led to additional questions in application.

Nevertheless, the Howsam opinion is an important step forward in the long line of Supreme Court cases favoring arbitration and providing a liberal view of arbitration agreements.

## 3 The Case

### 3.1 *Background of the Case*

The underlying controversy in Howsam arises out of investment advice that brokerage firm Dean Witter Reynolds, Inc. ("Dean Witter") provided its client Karen Howsam when, sometime between 1986 and 1994, it recommended that she buy and hold interests in four limited partnerships. In bringing her claim, Howsam contended that Dean Witter misrepresented the virtues of the investment. 537 U.S. at 81. The dispute fell within Dean Witter's standard Client Services Agreement providing for arbitration before "any self-regulatory organization or exchange of which Dean Witter is a member" and that the client can select the arbitration forum. Id at 80–81. Howsam chose arbitration before the NASD. Id at 81.

2 The National Association of Securities Dealers (NASD) was a self-regulatory organization of the securities industry and a predecessor of the Financial Industry Regulatory Authority (FINRA). Founded in 1939 under the provisions of the 1938 Maloney Act amendments to the Securities Exchange Act of 1934, NASD was the leading founder of the NASD stock market in 1971 and was responsible for the operation and regulation of the NASDAQ and over-the-counter markets. In 2007, NASD merged with the regulation, enforcement and arbitration arm of the New York Stock Exchange to form FINRA. *National Association of Securities Dealers (NASD) Definition*, Investopedia, https://www.investopedia.com/terms/n/nasd.asp (as of October 10, 2023).

To obtain NASD arbitration, Howsam signed the NASD Uniform Submission Agreement that specified that the "present matter in controversy" was submitted for arbitration "in accordance with the NASD Code of Arbitration Procedure." That Code contained the six-year limitation provision at issue. Id at 82.

After the Uniform Submission Agreement was executed, Dean Witter filed an action in the United States District Court for the District of Colorado for a declaration that the dispute was "ineligible for arbitration" because it was more than six years old. It also sought an injunction to prohibit Howsam from proceeding with the arbitration. Id.

The District Court dismissed the action on the ground that the NASD arbitrator, not the court, should interpret and apply the NASD Rule. The Court of Appeals for the Tenth Circuit reversed. 261 F. 3d 956 (2001). In its view, application of the NASD rule presented a question of the underlying dispute's "arbitrability" and, relying on First Options of Chicago, Inc. v. Kaplan, 514 U.S. 938 (1995) and precedent in the Circuit, the Tenth Circuit held that the presumption is that a court, not an arbitrator, will ordinarily decide "arbitrability" questions. Id.

The Supreme Court noted a Circuit split as to whether a court or an arbitrator primarily should interpret and apply this particular NASD rule. The Tenth Circuit followed the Third, Sixth, Seventh, Tenth and Eleventh Circuits in holding that the question is for the courts and the First, Second, Fifth, Eight and Ninth Circuits all held the question was for an arbitrator. The Supreme Court granted certiorari to resolve the disagreement. Howsam, 537 U.S. at 83; Howsam, 261 F. 3d. at 970.

Briefs of *amici curiae* urging affirmance were filed for the Competitive Enterprise Institute, the Securities Industry Association. An additional *amici curiae* brief was filed for the Trial Lawyers for Public Justice et al.

### 3.2 *Issue and Parties' Allegations*

Narrowly focused, the issue in Howsam was whether the six-year limitations provision in NASD Code of Arbitration Procedure § 10304 is a question for the courts or the NASD arbitrator. More broadly, the issue reached to whether contractual limitation periods and similar provisions incorporated into arbitration agreements are gateway questions of jurisdiction for the courts or are procedural questions for determination by an arbitrators.

Howsam, argued the limitation rule was a matter for the arbitrator. Dean Witter, supported by industry amici curiae, argued the limitation rule was a gateway matter for determination by a court.

### 3.3 *Holding*

The Supreme Court reversed, holding that consideration of a time-limit provision in the arbitration rules was for the arbitrator. Id. The Court held that the provision did not give rise to a gateway "question of arbitrability" for a court and, instead, was a procedural question for the arbitrator. In reaching this conclusion, the Court held that the phrase "question of arbitrability" has a narrow scope based on the expectations of the parties as to whether the court or an arbitrator would decide the issues and procedural questions for the arbitrator are those which grown out of the dispute and bear on its final disposition.

Justice Breyer was joined in the opinion by Chief Justice Rehnquist and Justices Stevens, Scalia, Kennedy, Souter and Ginsburg. Justice Thomas filed a concurring opinion. Justice O'Connor did not participate in the case.

### 3.4 *The Court's Opinion*

The Court's analysis begins with the recognition that "arbitration is a matter of contract, and a party cannot be required to submit to arbitration [of] any dispute which he has not agreed so to submit," citing to Steelworkers v Warrior & Gulf Nav. Co, 363 U.S. 574, 582 (1960) and First Options at 943–943. The Court recognized case-law provides a presumption, as followed by the Tenth Circuit, that a court, not an arbitrator, will ordinarily decide an "arbitrability" question. As stated by the Court, "(A)lthough the Court has also recognized and enforced a 'liberal federal policy favoring arbitration agreements,' Moses H. Cone Memorial Hospital v. Mercury Const. Corp, 460 U.S. 1, 24–25 (1983), it has made clear there is an exception to this policy: The question whether the parties have submitted a particular dispute to arbitration ... is 'an issue for judicial determination [u]nless the parties clearly and unmistakably provide otherwise.'" AT&T Technologies, Inc. v. Communications Workers, 475 U.S. 643, 649 (1975); First Options ... at 944.

The Court framed the issue as a decision whether application of the NASD time limit provision falls within the scope of this interpretative rule. The Court acknowledged that, linguistically speaking, any potentially dispositive gateway question could be such a "question of arbitrability" because the answer will determine whether the underlying controversy will proceed to arbitration on the merits. Looking to First Options at 942, the Court stated that its case law makes clear that "for purposes of applying the interpretative rule, the phrase 'question of arbitrability' has a far more limited scope" and "(t)he phrase is applicable in the kind of narrow circumstance where the contracting parties would likely have expected a court to have decided the gateway matter, where they are not likely to have though that they had agreed that an arbitrator would do so, and, consequently, where reference of the gateway dispute to the court avoids the risk of forcing parties to arbitrate a matter they may well not have agreed to arbitrate." Howsam at 83–84.

Accordingly, the Court held that a gateway dispute about whether the parties are bound by a given arbitration clause raises a "question of arbitrability" for the court to decide. As examples of this proposition, the Court cited John Wiley & Sons, Inc. v. Livingston, 376 U.S 543, 546–547 (1964) (holding that court should decide whether an arbitration agreement survived a corporate merger) and two decisions addressing whether an arbitration contract in a concededly binding contract applies to a particular controversy: AT&T Technologies at 651–652 (holding that a court should decide whether a labor management layoff controversy falls within a collective bargaining agreement) and Atkinson v. Sinclair Refining Co., 370 U.S. 238, 241–243 (1962) (holding that a court should decide whether clause providing for arbitration of various "grievances" covers claims for damages of a no-strike agreement). Howsam at 84.

The Court stated that, at the same time, it has found the phrase "question of arbitrability" not applicable in other kinds of general circumstances where the parties would likely expect the arbitrator would decide the gateway matter. As examples, the Court referenced "procedural questions which grow out of the dispute and bear on its final disposition," citing to John Wiley at 557 (holding an arbitrator should decide whether grievance procedure steps prerequisite to an arbitration), and "allegation[s] of waiver, delay, or a like defense to arbitrability," citing to Moses H. Cone Memorial Hospital at 24–25.

The Court observed that the Revised Uniform Arbitration Act of 2000 ("RUAA"), which seeks to incorporate the holdings of the majority of state courts and the law developed under the FAA states that "an arbitrator shall decide whether a condition precedent to arbitration has been fulfilled," RUAA § 6(c) comment 2, 7 U.L.A. at 13. It notes that the comments add that issues of substantive arbitrability are for a court to decide and issues of procedural arbitrability, i.e., time limits, notice, laches, estoppel, and other conditions precedent to an obligation to arbitrate are for the arbitrators to decide. Id. at 85.

Following this precedent, the Court found that the applicability of the NASD time limit rule is a matter presumptively for the arbitrator not a court as it resembles gateway questions that the Court has found not to be "questions of arbitrability." Id.

The Court stated that, moreover, NASD arbitrators, comparatively more expert about the meaning of their own rule, are comparatively better able to interpret and apply it. The Court added that "for the law to assume an expectation that aligns (1) decisionmaker with (2) comparative expertise will help better to secure a fair and expeditious resolution of the underlying controversy – a goal of arbitration and judicial systems alike." Id.

Accordingly, the Court held that the NASD time limit rule is not a "question of arbitrability" and the "strong pro-court presumption as to the parties' likely intent" does not apply. Id. at 85–86.

Finally, the Court addressed Dean Witter's argument that, in any event, i.e., even without an antiarbitration presumption, the Court should interpret the contract between the parties calling for judicial determining. The Court rejected Dean Witter's view that the Code's time limit rule uses of the word "eligible" indicates the parties' intent for the time limit rule to be resolved by the court prior to arbitration. The Court held that, for the reasons stated earlier, parties to an arbitration contract would normally expect a forum-based decisionmaker to decide forum-specific procedural gateway matters and temptation to place special antiarbitration weight on the word "eligible" is counterbalance by the NASD Code § 10324 which empowers the arbitrators to interpret and determine the applicability of all provisions of the Code. Id at 86.

In concluding, the Court stated that without the help of a special arbitration-disfavoring presumption, it cannot conclude that the parties intended to have a court, rather than the arbitrator, interpret and apply the NASD time limit rule and, here, the presumption does not apply. Accordingly, for the reasons given, the Court reversed the judgment of the Tenth Circuit. Id.

In a one-page concurrence, Justice Thomas stated that a straight-forward application of the principles that arbitration is a matter of contract and courts must enforce private arbitration agreements to arbitrate just as they would ordinary contracts in accordance with their terms easily resolves the question presented, citing to Volt Information Sciences, Inc. v. Board of Trustees of Leland Stanford Junior Univ., 489 U.S. 468 (1989) and Mastrobuono v. Shearson Lehman Hutton, Inc. 514 U.S. 52 (1995). Justice Thomas found that in interpreting two agreements containing provisions virtually identical to the ones in dispute here, all of which are to be construed under New York law, the New York Court of Appeals held that issues implicating the section are for arbitrators to decide, citing to Smith Barney Shearson Inc. v. Sacharow, 91 N.Y. 2d 39, 689 N.E. 2d 884 (1997). Accordingly, because the parties here agreed to be bound by New York law and because Volt requires enforcement of the agreement, Justice Thomas stated that he would permit arbitrators to resolve the time limit issue just as New York case law provides. He stated the majority follows a different route to reach the same conclusion and, accordingly, he concurred only in the judgment.

### 3.5 *Key Takeaways*

In answering the "who decides" gateway questions of arbitrability, Howsam relies on the framework of party expectations. Howsam distinguishes questions going to the existence and validity of an arbitration agreement, which are questions the parties would expect to be decided by a court, from questions pertaining to the procedure and outcome of the arbitration, which are questions the parties would expect to be decided by an arbitrator. The Court held that, absent an agreement to the contrary, "questions of arbitrability," which are limited to questions that go to the existence and validity of an arbitration agreement, are to be decided by the court, whereas procedural questions are for arbitrators to decide.

The Court found that the NASD time-limit provision was a matter for the arbitrator as it was a question of procedure not a "question of arbitrability."

Howsam has been read broadly for the general proposition that, absent delegation otherwise, "questions of arbitrability" are for the courts but procedural questions such as time limits, laches, notice and other conditions precedent are for the arbitrators.

By this outcome, Howsam expands the opportunity for arbitration for all claimants.

## 4 Critical Analysis of the Howsam Opinion and How It Impacted the U.S. Arbitration Law and Practice

In holding that consideration of the NASD time-limit provision is a procedural question for an arbitrator and not the courts, and resolving a Circuit split on the issue, Howsam is consistent with the strong line of Supreme Court authority favoring arbitration as a means of dispute arbitration. The exception to this approach is with respect to what the courts refer to as gateway jurisdictional issues, which Howsam calls "questions of arbitrability" that are to be decided by the courts.

Howsam asks the "who decides" question in the context of a time limitation provision in the arbitration rules. In determining that the time limitation provision was a matter for the arbitrator, the Court explained that not all gateway questions are "questions of arbitrability" for a court to decide. Rather, the framework implemented by the court is whether the gateway issue is one the parties would expect a court to decide or whether it is a question of procedural arbitrability, that the parties would expect the arbitrator to decide. Relying on precedent, the Court found that questions which grow out of the dispute and bear on its final disposition as well as questions such as delay, waiver and like defenses are questions the courts have left for the arbitrator to decide. In support of this conclusion, the Court concluded this was an appropriate outcome because an arbitrator would have comparatively more experience interpreting the arbitration rules and this would help secure the goal of fair and expeditious resolution. This conclusion comports with the well-established understanding that agreements are to be interpreted, where possible, to reflect the intent of the parties.

Howsam is widely relied on for the proposition that "questions of arbitrability" are for the courts but procedural questions are for the arbitrators.

Howsam is a relatively straightforward case that narrows court consideration of gateway issues, but it has led to confusion in some areas. Although Howsam addressed a time limitation in the applicable rules, its citation to Moses at 25, makes broad reference to other procedural defenses, particularly waiver, has been subject to debate. Courts have distinguished waiver from prelitigation conduct from waiver in the course of litigation and, in turn, have distinguished Howsam by holding that waiver in the course of litigation remains a matter for the courts.[3]

As well, Howsam was not directed to the delegation of jurisdictional questions to arbitrators, which is now a typical provision in the rules of most arbitration providers. Accordingly, Howsam should not be relied on for the proposition that "questions of arbitrability" are always for the courts. To the contrary, as demonstrated by First Options and Rent-A-Center v. Jackson, 561 U.S. 63 (2010), jurisdictional matters as to the existence and validity on arbitration agreement, the arbitrability of claims and the scope of the arbitration clause can be delegated by the parties to the arbitrator. In court, such delegation will be honored upon the court's preliminary determination as to the existence of a valid arbitration agreement and delegation clause. Rent-A-Center, 561 U.S. at 70. Likewise, where a matter is initiated in arbitration, the delegation, generally avoids any requirement to refer "questions of arbitrability" to the court. Any confusion over Howsam with respect to delegation is attributable to failing to put Howsam in context, not a lack of clarity in the opinion.

On whole, in drawing the distinction between substantive questions and procedural questions, Howsam represents an important step forward in clarifying the scope of the gateway inquiry for the courts. Although Howsam was a victory for the Claimant and similarly situated investors, it cleared a hurdle providing all claimants increased access to arbitration.

---

3 See Scharpf, *Court vs. Arbitrator: Who Should Decide Whether Prelitigation Conduct Waives the Right to Compel an Arbitration Agreement*, St. Johns Law Review, vol. 84, Winter 2020, No. 1, Art. 9, p. 363.

## 5 Conclusion

Howsam fits firmly in the line of U.S. Supreme Court opinions preceding and following it that represent an ongoing trend in favor of the arbitration process. It was a victory for many claimants seeking ready access to arbitration. In addressing the uniquely U.S. question of reservation of gateway issues to the courts, Howsam moved the trend line forward by drawing a distinction between substantive questions of arbitrability that the courts will consider and procedural questions, such as the time limit rule at issue in Howsam, that the courts will leave for arbitration. The widespread reliance on delegation provisions today takes the decision-making grant provided to arbitrators in Howsam even further.

CHAPTER 14

# *PacifiCare Health Systems, Inc. v. Book* (2003)

*Samaa Haridi and Jessica Beess und Chrostin*

## 1 Introduction

In the context of international arbitration, many jurisdictions around the world recognize the principle of Compétence-Compétence, which empowers an arbitral tribunal in the first instance to consider and decide any dispute regarding its own jurisdiction. In the United States, however, there is no default rule granting arbitrators authority to decide their own jurisdiction. Rather, the general rule is that arbitrability[1] is decided by the national court unless there is clear and unmistakable evidence that the parties agreed to empower the arbitrator to make that decision.[2] This rule has given rise to numerous litigations concerning complex questions of arbitrability, some of which have reached the United States Supreme Court, including *PacifiCare Health Systems, Inc. v. Book*,[3] which is the subject of this Chapter.

In its October 2002 term, the Supreme Court decided a trio of arbitration-related cases: *PacifiCare*; *Howsam v. Dean Witter Reynolds, Inc.*;[4] and *Green Tree Financial Corp. v. Bazzle*.[5] All three involved arbitration clauses that could be construed to deprive a party of its statutory rights, *i.e.* rights derived from state

1 As the Supreme Court explained in *Rent-A-Ctr., W., Inc. v. Jackson*, 561 U.S. 63, 68–69 (2010) and *BG Grp. PLC v. Republic of Argentina*, 572 U.S. 25, 34 (2014), arbitrability disputes include, for example, "questions such as 'whether the parties are bound by a given arbitration clause,' or 'whether an arbitration clause in a concededly binding contract applies to a particular type of controversy'" (quoting *Howsam v. Dean Witter Reynolds, Inc.*, 537 U.S. 79, 84 (2002); *Green Tree Fin. Corp. v. Bazzle*, 539 U.S. 444, 452 (2003); *Schneider v. Kingdom of Thailand*, 688 F.3d 68, 71 (2d Cir. 2012)).

2 See e.g., *Henry Schein, Inc v Archer & White Sales, Inc*, 139 S Ct 524 (2019).

3 *PacifiCare* was part of a trio of arbitration-related cases that the Supreme Court decided in the October 2002 term. All three – *PacifiCare Health Systems, Inc. v. Book*, *Howsam v. Dean Witter Reynolds, Inc.*, 537 U.S. 79 (2002), and *Green Tree Financial Corp. v. Bazzle*, 539 U.S. 444 (2003) – involved arbitration clauses that could be construed to limit statutory rights. David S. Schwartz, "Understanding Remedy-Stripping Arbitration Clauses: Validity, Arbitrability, and Preclusion Principles," 38 *University of San Francisco Law Review* 49, 2003, at 51.

4 *Howsam v. Dean Witter Reynolds, Inc.*, 537 U.S. 79 (2002).

5 *Green Tree Financial Corp. v. Bazzle*, 539 U.S. 444 (2003).

 | DOI:10.1163/9789004715820_015

or federal law.[6] In *PacifiCare*, a group of physicians filed a class action against certain managed care organizations ("MCOs") for failure to reimburse them for patient services provided by the physicians. They alleged, among other things, that the MCOs violated the Racketeer Influenced and Corrupt Organizations Act (RICO), the Employee Retirement Income Security Act of 1974 (ERISA), and federal and state prompt-pay statutes, as well as claims for breach of contract, unjust enrichment, and *in quantum meruit*.[7] The MCOs moved to compel arbitration based on various arbitration agreements with the physicians, who opposed the motion to compel. The physicians argued, in relevant part, that the arbitration clauses in issue did not permit arbitrators to award punitive damages, thus preventing the vindication of the statutory right to treble damages under RICO and undermining the policy underlying RICO's remedial provisions. This being a question of arbitrability because it concerned whether the physicians' claims were arbitrable in light of the limitation on punitive damages in the arbitration clauses, it was for the courts to decide.

## 2 The Case

### 2.1 *Background*

In August 2000, over 600,000 physicians filed a class action against 10 MCOs for failing to reimburse them for patient services provided by the physicians. Among their claims, the physicians accused the MCOs of violating RICO by acting as part of a conspiracy with other defendant MCOs to deny the physicians payment for their services.

The MCOs, including PacifiCare, moved before the United States District Court for the Southern District of Florida to compel arbitration on the basis that the various contracts between the MCOs and the physicians contained arbitration clauses.[8] The physicians opposed this motion. They pointed out that the arbitration clauses expressly prohibited arbitrators from awarding punitive damages and argued that, as such, arbitration would prevent the physicians from obtaining meaningful relief under RICO, which allows for treble

6 David S. Schwartz, "Understanding Remedy-Stripping Arbitration Clauses: Validity, Arbitrability, and Preclusion Principles," 38 *University of San Francisco Law Review* 49, 2003, at 51.

7 *PacifiCare*, 538 U.S. 402–3.

8 In *Shearson/American Express, Inc. v. McMahon*, 482 U.S. 220 (1987), the U.S. Supreme Court held that courts could compel arbitration of claims based on alleged RICO violations.

damages.[9] According to the physicians, treble damages would be considered punitive and therefore compelling arbitration would prevent the physicians from vindicating a statutory right under RICO and thus undermine the policy underlying the RICO statute's remedial provisions.

The District Court declined to compel arbitration of the RICO claims reasoning that the arbitration clauses prohibiting the award of punitive damages prevented arbitrator(s) from awarding treble damages under RICO. Put differently, the District Court denied the motion to compel arbitration because the underlying arbitration clause effectively deprived a party of its statutory rights. In so holding, the District Court relied on *Paladino v. Avnet Computer Technologies, Inc.*, which held that where an arbitration agreement prevents a party from obtaining "meaningful relief" for a statutory claim, the court cannot compel arbitration with respect to that claim.[10]

On appeal by the MCOs, the Eleventh Circuit Court of Appeals affirmed the District Court's holding.

### 2.2 *Issue Presented and the Parties' Allegations*

The key issue in *PacifiCare* was whether to compel the physicians to arbitrate their RICO claims under arbitration agreements that could be construed to limit the arbitrators' ability to award the statutory remedy of treble damages for a RICO breach.

The physicians argued that this issue was a gateway question of arbitrability, meaning that it was a question of whether their RICO claims could be arbitrated in the first place. Thus, they argued it should be decided by the court in the first instance unless the parties to the arbitration agreement in issue clearly intended to delegate the issue of arbitrability to the arbitrator(s).

They further argued that denying judicial review until after the conclusion of the arbitration[11] would be inefficient and prejudicial, and would deny

9 RICO was enacted by Congress in October 1970 for "the elimination of the infiltration of organized crime and racketeering into legitimate organizations operating in interstate commerce." S.Rep. No. 617, 91st Cong., 1st Sess. 76 (1969). A private party can bring a civil RICO claim and seek recovery in the form of treble damages, costs, and attorney fees.

10 *Paladino v. Avnet Computer Technologies, Inc.*, 134 F.3d 1054 (11th Cir. 1998).

11 Courts generally have very limited review powers over arbitration awards, and do not have authority to reconsider the merits of a party's claims. However, one of the limited grounds recognized for the judicial set aside of arbitration awards is the arbitrator's excess of power. *See* United Nations Convention on the Recognition and Enforcement of Arbitral Awards 1958 ("New York Convention"), Article V(1)(c) (allowing set aside of an arbitral award upon proof that "the award deals with a difference not contemplated by or not falling within the terms of the submission to arbitration, or it contains decisions on matters beyond the scope of the submission to arbitration, provided that, if the decisions

the physicians their substantive rights to meaningful relief if they could not receive punitive treble damages under RICO. Thus, according to the physicians, the restriction on punitive damage in the arbitration agreements made them unenforceable.

The MCOs argued that this was not a gateway question concerning arbitrability, but rather a limited question of the validity of the damage limitations agreed by sophisticated parties who had the opportunity to negotiate their arbitration agreements. Since the question pertained to remedies rather than arbitrability of the claims themselves, the MCOs argued that it should be decided by arbitrators in the first instance and not the court. The MCOs submitted that allowing judicial review of agreed upon restrictions on statutory remedies would run afoul of the well-recognized presumption in favor of arbitration under the Federal Arbitration Act.

Finally, the MCOs submitted that even if the court found that the damage limitation could not be enforced because it violated public policy, the court could rely on the doctrine of severability to sever the offending damages limitation while leaving the remainder of the arbitration agreements intact. Thus, whether the limitations were valid did not affect the arbitrability of this case.

### 2.3 *The Supreme Court's Opinion*

Justice Scalia delivered the unanimous opinion of the Supreme Court[12] overturning the Eleventh Circuit's decision.

The Court held that it would be premature for the Court to decide whether the physicians' RICO claims were arbitrable or whether the limitation on punitive damages should be severed from the otherwise valid arbitration agreements because it was unclear whether the agreements actually prevented an arbitrator from awarding treble damages under RICO. The Court recalled that it had repeatedly found that RICO's treble damages provision is remedial in nature, and "it was not clear that the parties intended the term 'punitive' to encompass claims for treble damages under RICO."[13] The Court cited, *Agency Holding Corp. v. Malley-Duff & Associates, Inc.*, among other cases, in which it stated that "[b]oth RICO and the Clayton Act are designed to remedy economic

on matters submitted to arbitration can be separated from those not so submitted, that part of the award which contains decisions on matters submitted to arbitration may be recognized and enforced[.]").

12 Justice Thomas took no part in the consideration or decision of the case. *PacifiCare*.

13 *PacifiCare*, 538 U.S. 401.

injury by providing for the recovery of treble damages, costs, and attorney's fees."[14]

Consistent with its decision in *Vimar*, the Supreme Court reiterated that a court "should not, on the basis of 'mere speculation' that an arbitrator might interpret these ambiguous agreements in a manner that casts their enforceability into doubt, take upon ourselves the authority to decide the antecedent question of how the ambiguity is to be resolved."[15] Because the Court could not predict how an arbitrator would rule on whether RICO's treble damages fall within the scope of punitive damages in the arbitration agreements, it was premature to decide whether this limitation on damages rendered the parties' agreements unenforceable.

On this basis, the Supreme Court reversed the judgment of the Court of Appeals.

## 3 Analysis of the Opinion and How It Impacted U.S. Arbitration Law and Practice

As noted above, the Court's decision in *PacifiCare* was one of a trio of decisions rendered around the same time on the issue of arbitrability. In *Howsam*, the Court limited the scope of "arbitrability" by holding that a statute of limitations question was for the arbitrator, rather than the court, to decide. In *PacifiCare* and *Bazzle*, the Court avoided deciding the arbitrability of remedy-stripping provisions that limit punitive damages in the former and class actions in the latter. Instead, the Court deferred the interpretation and application of these provisions to arbitrators.

Both *PacifiCare* and *Bazzle* concerned arbitration agreements that contained remedial provisions, the application of which *might* violate a statute. In each case, the Court found that it was too "speculative" to assume that the application of these provisions would necessarily violate a statute, and it gave arbitrators the authority to decide whether and if so, how to sever the provisions and grant remedies without violating the relevant statutes.

Without overturning the general rule that arbitrability in the United States is decided in the first instance by courts, all three of these cases effectively limited the scope of "arbitrability" by referring certain issues to arbitrators rather than courts. Thus, the Court held in these cases that arbitrators, rather

14 *PacifiCare*, 538 U.S. 406 (citing *Agency Holding Corp. v. Malley-Duff & Associates, Inc.*, 483 U.S. 143, 151 (1987) (emphasis omitted)).

15 *PacifiCare*, 538 U.S. 406.

than courts, should decide in the first instance (1) the import of statutes of limitations (*Howsam*), (2) whether a limitation on punitive damages deprived a party of the ability to vindicate its statutory rights (*PacifiCare*), and (3) whether a limitation on class actions was enforceable (or severable). All three decisions can be seen as manifestations of the federal public policy in favor of enforcement of arbitration agreements.

*PacifiCare,* along with *Howsam* and *Bazzle*, however, did not entirely resolve the Circuit split over remedy-stripping provisions in arbitration agreements.[16] The First, Third, Seventh, and Eight Circuits have ruled that the validity of damages limitations should be addressed by the arbitrator in the first instance.[17] By contrast, the Second, Fifth, Sixth, Ninth, and Eleventh Circuits have held that the validity of damages limitations should be addressed by courts in the first instance.[18] Who decides the validity of damages limitations in arbitration clauses implicating statutory rights remains regrettably unclear.

Similarly, it is now well-established in the United States that agreements to arbitrate disputes involving statutory claims are enforceable under the Federal Arbitration Act. However, a party may still be able to invalidate an arbitration clause if its enforcement would prevent the vindication of a statutory right in arbitration. But who should decide an effective vindication challenge? In *PacifiCare,* the Supreme Court had the opportunity to address this issue (even if in *dictum*) but the Court sidestepped it entirely.[19] As a result, lower federal courts continue to lack guidance regarding whether the court or an arbitrator should determine effective vindication challenges.

---

16 *See* Jay E. Grenig, "When Would It Violate Public Policy to Require a Party to Arbitrate a RICO Claim?" *2002–03 Term Preview U.S. Sup. Ct. Cas.* 266 (2003).

17 See, e.g., *Thompson v. Irwin Home Equity Corp.*, 300 F.3d 88 (1st Cir. 2002); *Great Western Mortgage Corp. v. Peacock*, 110 F.3d 222 (3d Cir. 1997); *Boomer v. T&T Corp.*, 309 F.3d 404, 419 (7th Cir. 2002); *Arkcom Digital Corp. v. Xerox Corp.*, 289 F.3d 536, 539 (8th Cir. 2002).

18 *See, e.g., Brooks v. Travelers Ins. Co.*, 297 F.3d 167 (2d Cir. 2002); *Investment Partners, LLP v. Glamour Shots Licensing, Inc.*, 298 F.3d 314 (5th Cir. 2002); Morrison v. Circuit City Stores, Inc., 317 F.3d 646 (6th Cir. 2003); *Graham Oil Co. v. ARCO Prods. Co.*, 43 F.3d 1244 (9th Cir. 1995); *Paladino v. Avnet Computer Technologies, Inc.*, 134 F.3d 1054 (11th Cir. 1998).

19 While *PacifiCare* arguably resolved the split in cases where there is *ambiguity* as to whether an arbitration clause restricts a statutory right, a circuit division remains in cases where there is no ambiguity. *See* Howard S. Suskin and Marek H. Badyna, "Enforceability of Arbitration Agreements that Restrict Statutorily-Mandated Rights: the Sharpening Split Among the Circuits," 2008, at 1.

CHAPTER 15

# *Green Tree Financial Corp. v. Bazzle* (2003): The Supreme Court's First Look at Class Action Arbitrability

*Andrew Behrman, Yining Bei and Zeinab Bailoun*

## 1 Introduction

Prior to the U.S. Supreme Court's 2003 decision in *Green Tree Financial Corp. v. Bazzle*,[1] arbitration was routinely viewed as a long-standing, effective shield against class action proceedings.[2] A prevailing majority of federal appellate courts had held that arbitrators and courts lacked the authority to allow or compel class arbitrations unless the arbitration clauses in the contracts at issue explicitly provided for such proceedings.[3] Those court rulings fostered the perception that arbitration served to mitigate the risks faced by respondents, who might otherwise have had to contend with potential class members disinclined to pursue their individual claims in separate arbitration processes.[4]

To some extent, *Bazzle* changed that understanding. Although *Bazzle* was splintered into four opinions and left many open-ended questions unanswered, the Supreme Court's first foray into the availability of class arbitration, while limited in the scope of its reach, did cast doubt on the perception that arbitration was an effective tool to deter class actions.

*Bazzle* was a case initiated by Lynn and Burt Bazzle, in state court in South Carolina. The Bazzles had entered into a loan contract with the lender, Green Tree Financial Corporation. The loan contract included an arbitration clause

1 539 U.S. 444 (2003).

2 Edward Wood Dunham, *The Arbitration Clause as Class Action Shield*, 16 Franchise L.J. 141, 142 (1997).

3 *See* Champ v. Siegel Trading Co., Inc., 55 F.3d 269 (7th Cir. 1995) (ruling that class certification in arbitration proceeding could not be ordered, as there was no provision for such certification in the arbitration agreement); Am. Centennial Ins. Co. v. Nat'l Cas. Co., 951 F.2d 107 (6th Cir. 1991) (holding that courts lacked the power to consolidate arbitration proceedings when the agreement was silent regarding consolidation); *see also* Application of Deiulemar Compagnia Di Navigazione S.p.A. v. M/V Allegra, 198 F.3d 473, 482 (4th Cir. 1999); Gov't of United Kingdom v. Boeing Co., 998 F. 2d 68, 74 (2d Cir. 1993).

4 Dunham, *supra* note 2, at 142.

 | DOI:10.1163/9789004715820_016

that did not explicitly provide for class arbitration. Nonetheless, the state's trial court certified a class of plaintiffs and subsequently ordered arbitration. The arbitrator eventually granted the class of plaintiffs an award of more than 10 million dollars, which the trial court subsequently confirmed. Green Tree appealed, contending that the contract did not allow for class arbitration. After consolidating the Bazzles' proceeding with another similar proceeding, the South Carolina Supreme Court held that although the relevant contracts were silent on class arbitration, class arbitration was permissible in both cases. The U.S. Supreme Court granted certiorari to determine the compatibility of this ruling with the Federal Arbitration Act (FAA).

To effectively evaluate the ruling of South Carolina's highest court, the Supreme Court considered three questions: first, which decision-maker—court or arbitrator—should decide whether the contracts in question were "silent" on the issue of class arbitration? Second, what standard should the appropriate decision-maker apply in determining whether a contract allows class arbitration—*i.e.*, the FAA or state law? Third, under whatever standard was appropriate, was class arbitration properly ordered in the cases at hand?[5]

In the Court's analysis of the three questions, the Justices found no single rationale that commanded a majority. The plurality opinion, authored by Justice Breyer, decided only the first question, concluding that the arbitrator and not a court should decide whether the contracts were indeed "silent" on the issue of class arbitration. The plurality did note that in certain limited circumstances involving gateway matters, it is assumed that the parties intended courts, not arbitrators, to make a decision, but opined that the question of whether a contract with an arbitration clause forbids class arbitration does not fall into this narrow exception. But because Justice Stevens' concurrence in the judgment did not take a definitive position on this first question, the issue remained open.[6]

Justice Stevens' opinion, on the other hand, bypassed the first question and rested instead on his resolution of the second and third questions.[7] For Justice Stevens, the parties' agreement that South Carolina law would govern their arbitration contract, together with the fact that nothing in the FAA precluded the South Carolina Supreme Court's determinations as a matter of state law concerning the permissibility of class action arbitration and whether the agreement was silent on the issue, meant that the decision to conduct a class

5 Stolt-Nielsen S.A. v. AnimalFeeds International Corp., 559 U.S. 662, 678 (2010).
6 *Id.* at 679.
7 *Id.*

action arbitration was correct as a matter of law.[8] But to avoid the outcome of no controlling judgment of the Court, and because Justice Breyer's opinion expressed a view of the case close to his own, Justice Stevens concurred with the judgment.[9]

As explained in more detail below, in the aftermath of the decision, the *Bazzle* ruling was taken to implicitly condone class arbitration where the relevant arbitration agreement was silent as to that issue. Contractual parties therefore scrambled to make sure that their arbitration agreements expressly prohibited class arbitration (if that was the outcome they wanted), so as to avoid any possibility that a court applying *Bazzle* would impose class arbitration over the wishes of the parties.

However, more recent Supreme Court decisions have shown that interpretation of the *Bazzle* case to potentially be overblown. For example, the Court recently cited *Bazzle* in support of the principle that the Court "refus[es] to infer consent when it comes to [] fundamental arbitration questions."[10] As the Court construed it, neither silence nor ambiguity "provides a sufficient basis for concluding that parties to an arbitration agreement agreed to undermine the central benefits of arbitration itself."[11] Instead, the Supreme Court has reminded us that the ultimate question in cases relating to arbitration is: What did the parties agree to and intend?

## 2 The Case

### 2.1 *Background of the Case*

#### 2.1.1 The Bazzle Proceedings

In 1995, South Carolina residents Lynn and Burt Bazzle were approached by home improvement contractor Patton General Contracting, a non-exclusive dealer for Green Tree Financial Corporation, with an offer to perform home improvements financed through Green Tree.[12] The Bazzles filled out the Green Tree financing application—which contained no attorney or insurance agent preference notice, though such notice was required by the South Carolina Consumer Protection Code—and soon after, on May 20, 1995, the

8 Green Tree Fin. Corp. v. Bazzle, 539 U.S. 444, 455 (2003) (Stevens, J., concurring in the judgment and dissenting in part).

9 *Id.*

10 Lamps Plus, Inc. v. Varela, 139 S. Ct. 1407, 1416 (2019).

11 *Id.* at 1417.

12 Bazzle v. Green Tree Fin. Corp., 351 S.C. 244, 249 (S.C. 2002), *vacated*, 539 U.S. 444 (2003).

couple executed a Retail Installment Contract and Security Agreement for $15,000, along with a number of other documents identifying Green Tree as the lender.[13] The agreement entered into by the Bazzles contained an arbitration clause that provided, in pertinent part:

> ARBITRATION—All disputes, claims, or controversies arising from or relating to this contract or the relationships which result from this contract, or the validity of this arbitration clause or the entire contract, shall be resolved by binding arbitration by one arbitrator selected by us with consent of you. This arbitration contract is made pursuant to a transaction in interstate commerce, and shall be governed by the Federal Arbitration Act at 9 U.S.C. section 1. Judgment upon the award rendered may be entered in any court having jurisdiction. The parties agree and understand that they choose arbitration instead of litigation to resolve disputes. The parties agree and understand that they have a right or opportunity to litigate disputes through a court, but that they prefer to resolve their disputes through arbitration.[14]

On March 25, 1997, the Bazzles filed suit against Green Tree for violating the South Carolina Consumer Protection Code. The Bazzles were apparently not alone in obtaining home improvement loans from Green Tree without the required notice of their attorney and insurance agent rights. Green Tree evidently engaged in "at least 3,600 similar type transactions."[15]

Less than a month after filing their initial complaint, on April 21, 1997, the Bazzles sought class certification. In response, Green Tree moved to stay the case and to compel arbitration. The trial court granted both motions, issuing an order granting class certification and a separate order compelling arbitration.[16]

Green Tree moved for reconsideration of the order granting class certification, which was denied; filed an appeal with the Court of Appeals, which was also denied; and then filed a petition for rehearing, which was likewise denied. Green Tree next filed a petition for certiorari with the Supreme Court of South Carolina, which summarily denied the petition and remitted the case to the trial court.[17]

---

13 *Id.* at 249–250.

14 Petition for Writ of Certiorari, Green Tree Financial Corp. v. Bazzle, 539 U.S. 444 (2003) (No. 02–634), 2002 WL 32101094, at *6.

15 Brief for Respondents, Green Tree Financial Corp. v. Bazzle, 539 U.S. 444 (2003) (No. 02–634), 2003 WL 1701523, at *11.

16 *Bazzle*, 351 S.C. at 250.

17 *Id.* at 250–51.

On February 24, 1999, the Bazzles filed a motion to compel the appointment of an arbitrator.[18] The trial court appointed the Honorable Thomas J. Ervin, a retired state circuit court judge,[19] as arbitrator, and after that, all class action proceedings were administered by the arbitrator, without further involvement of the trial court.[20]

On July 24, 2000, the arbitrator issued a final award, finding Green Tree liable for violating the Code and awarding relief to the class of 1,899 individuals in the amount of $10.9 million, plus $3.6 million in attorney's fees and costs. The next day, the Bazzles filed a motion to confirm the award in the trial court. Less than a month later, Green Tree filed a motion to remand the award, an objection to the motion to confirm, and a motion to vacate the award. The trial court confirmed the award and denied Green Tree's various motions; Green Tree appealed, and the South Carolina Supreme Court consolidated the appeal with that in a parallel case, the Lackey Proceedings.[21]

### 2.1.2 The Lackey Proceedings

While the Bazzles and others were entering into financing agreements for home renovations, other South Carolina residents—including an individual named Daniel Lackey—were entering into preprinted consumer installment contracts and security agreements with Green Tree for the purchase of mobile homes. These transactions were secured by real property and were likewise subject to the South Carolina Consumer Protection Code, which required a Preference Statute disclosure advising each consumer of her right to retain an attorney and insurance agent to provide professional services at the closing of real estate transactions.[22]

In a typical mobile home purchase transaction, the purchaser entered into a preprinted consumer installment contract and security agreement with Green Tree to buy a mobile home. The Green Tree dealer had the purchaser fill out a Green Tree credit application. Upon receipt and review of the purchaser's credit application, if Green Tree elected to extend credit, it set the terms of the credit, prepared all necessary documents for closing, and transmitted the documents to its dealer. The documents included a mortgage prepared by Green Tree.[23]

---

18 *Id.*

19 Brief for Respondents, *supra* note 15, at *8.

20 *Bazzle*, 351 S.C. at 251.

21 *Id.*

22 *Id.*

23 Brief for Respondents, *supra* note 15, at *5.

The mobile home purchase transaction documents were standard preprinted form contracts of adhesion prepared by Green Tree, without involvement of the customer. Many purchasers did not understand that they were securing the credit transaction with a mortgage on their home and would only discover Green Tree's mortgage when they attempted to sell or refinance their homes.[24]

On May 28, 1996, Daniel Lackey—together with George and Florine Buggs[25]—filed a class action complaint in South Carolina state court, alleging that Green Tree systematically violated the Preference Statute in manufactured housing and home improvement transactions secured by South Carolina real estate. The Lackey plaintiffs then moved for class certification, and Green Tree moved to stay the matter and to compel arbitration. The trial court denied the motion to compel arbitration, finding that Green Tree's contract was an adhesion contract with an unconscionable and unenforceable arbitration clause. Green Tree appealed and the Court of Appeals reversed, finding that though the contracts were ones of adhesion, the arbitration clause within them was not itself unconscionable.[26]

Following remand to the trial court, the parties entered into a consent order appointing the same arbitrator who was hearing the *Bazzle* arbitration. The arbitrator, after holding a hearing to determine whether a class action could proceed under the applicable arbitration clause, issued an order permitting class action arbitration and scheduling a class certification hearing. In November 1998, upon holding that hearing—which Green Tree's counsel attended but in which it refused to participate, perhaps due to the declaratory action it had initiated in federal district court in parallel, seeking to enjoin the arbitrator from certifying the class—the arbitrator found the class certification requirements were met. Separately, the trial court denied Green Tree's motion to stay the arbitration proceedings on the ground that it lacked jurisdiction to interfere with the arbitration.[27]

On January 28, 2000, the arbitrator held a pre-hearing conference.[28] At the conference, the parties entered into a consent agreement redefining the Lackey plaintiff class to include all mobile home transactions and placing all home improvement class members in the Bazzle class.[29]

---

24 *Id.* at *5, 7–8.

25 *Bazzle*, 351 S.C. at 252.

26 *Id.*

27 *Id.*

28 *Id.*

29 *Id.* at 254.

On March 8, 2000, the arbitrator concluded the hearing on the Lackey claims and ruled that Green Tree had violated the attorney and insurance agent preference requirements of the Consumer Protection Code. He awarded $9.2 million in damages for violation of the statute and $3 million in attorney's fees costs. On July 24, 2001, the Lackey plaintiffs moved to confirm the award in trial court. After the trial court confirmed the award, Green Tree appealed. The South Carolina Supreme Court subsequently withdrew the appeal from the Court of Appeals and assumed jurisdiction to hear the consolidated *Bazzle* and *Lackey* appeals.[30]

### 2.1.3 The Consolidated Appeals in South Carolina Supreme Court

While the *Bazzle* and *Lackey* cases involved financing for different purposes—home improvement for the *Bazzle* set of consumers, and mobile home purchases for the *Lackey* group—Green Tree structured and conducted the transactions in the same manner, binding the consumers in both classes to arbitration by the same clause in their Retail Sales Agreements.[31]

Procedurally, however, class certification was granted differently in each case. In *Bazzle*, the trial court certified the class and granted Green Tree's motion to compel arbitration. Meanwhile, in *Lackey*, it was the arbitrator who authorized class certification, as the trial court compelled arbitration before it considered the motion to certify the class.[32]

Facing now the common question of class action arbitrability in both cases, the South Carolina Supreme Court unanimously affirmed the two trial courts' decisions—that of the *Bazzle* trial court, which granted class certification, granted Green Tree's motion to compel arbitration, and confirmed the class action arbitration award; and that of the *Lackey* trial court, which compelled arbitration and confirmed the class action arbitration award. The South Carolina Supreme Court stressed that South Carolina law "favors arbitration of disputes,"[33] that the state courts accordingly "resolve any doubts concerning the scope of arbitrable issues in favor of arbitration,"[34] and that Green Tree's contract language "does not limit the arbitration to non-class arbitration."[35]

Noting that the parties did not dispute the applicability of the Federal Arbitration Act to the arbitration agreements in both cases, the South Carolina

30 *Id.*

31 *Id.*

32 *Id.*

33 *Id.* at 262.

34 *Id.*

35 *Id.* at 264.

Supreme Court framed the issue before it as how the FAA impacts the class-wide arbitration question when the arbitration agreement is silent on that issue.[36] The court recognized that other courts had reached two different answers: several federal circuits had precluded class-wide arbitration when the arbitration agreement was silent, based on their interpretation of section 4 of the FAA. But California courts had, to the contrary, permitted class-wide arbitration on a case-by-case basis when the arbitration agreement is silent.[37]

The South Carolina Supreme Court found as a preliminary matter that Green Tree's arbitration clause was silent regarding class-wide arbitration—indeed, that *at best* the portion of the clause providing for "arbitration of 'disputes, claims, or controversies arising from or relating to *this contract*, or the relationships which result from *this contract*[...]' creates an ambiguity, and should, therefore, be construed against the drafting party, Green Tree."[38]

The court then adopted the approach taken by the California courts, holding that "class-wide arbitration may be ordered when the arbitration agreement is silent if it would serve efficiency and equity, and would not result in prejudice."[39] Since the contracts were silent with respect to class arbitration, the court held that they consequently authorized class arbitration, and that arbitration had properly taken that form.[40]

## 3 Issue and Parties' Arguments

### 3.1 *Green Tree's Petition for a Writ of Certiorari*

On October 23, 2002, Green Tree petitioned the U.S. Supreme Court for a writ of certiorari to the Supreme Court of South Carolina, to address the question whether the FAA prohibits class action procedures from being imposed when the relevant arbitration agreement does not expressly provide for class action arbitration.[41] As Green Tree described it, the South Carolina Supreme Court's decision only deepened an "already mature judicial conflict" on that question. On the one hand, a majority of federal courts of appeals had held that class wide arbitration proceedings cannot be imposed on an arbitration agreement that is "silent" as to the availability of class action arbitration. On the other side

36 *Id.* at 257.
37 *Id.*
38 *Id.* at 263–64 (emphases in original).
39 *Id.* at 266.
40 Green Tree Fin. Corp. v. Bazzle, 539 U.S. 444, 450 (2003).
41 Petition for Writ of Certiorari, *supra* note 14, at *12.

of the conflict, the California courts had ruled that class action procedures *can* be imposed on arbitration agreements that are silent regarding that issue.[42]

Green Tree based its theory on the principles underlying the FAA, arguing that Congress's goal in enacting the FAA was to overcome deep-seated judicial hostility to arbitration and thereby allow private parties to choose to resolve their disputes through arbitration rather than litigation.[43] Essential to this goal, according to Green Tree, was the principle that arbitration agreements may not be rewritten by the courts—rather, state and federal courts must "'rigorously enforce' such agreements according to their terms."[44]

To Green Tree, the South Carolina Supreme Court's embrace of the view that the FAA does not prohibit a court from imposing class action procedures onto an arbitration agreement—if the procedures further the court's notions of judicial efficiency and equity—permitted courts to frustrate private agreements to arbitrate by allowing those agreements to be modified whenever they do not unambiguously preclude a particular procedure or result.[45] The implication was that this frustration of private arbitration agreements was in direct contravention of Congress's goal in enacting the FAA.

### 3.2 *Respondents' Arguments*

The Bazzle and Lackey plaintiffs—now Respondents before the U.S. Supreme Court—framed the question presented to the Court as whether the FAA divests a state court of authority to allow an arbitrator to decide state-law claims on a class-wide basis in accordance with the arbitration agreement and state law.[46] In other words, Respondents contended that the question at the heart of the case was "whether the Federal Arbitration Act [] requires that an arbitration clause, governed by state law and interpreted by the state's highest court to allow class arbitration, be reinterpreted under a new federal standard of FAA contract interpretation to foreclose class arbitration."[47]

Respondents noted at the outset that when they initially sought redress for Green Tree's predatory lending practices, they were bound by contract to arbitrate before an arbitrator chosen by Green Tree.[48] Further, they emphasized

42 *Id.* at *3.

43 *Id.* at *4 (citing Volt Info. Scis, Inc. v. Board of Trs. of Leland Stanford Junior Univ., 489 U.S. 468, 478 (1989); Dean Witter Reynolds, Inc. v. Byrd, 470 U.S. 213, 219–20 (1985)).

44 *Id.* at *5.

45 *Id.* at *13.

46 Brief for Respondents, *supra* note 15, at *i.

47 *Id.* at *1.

48 *Id.* at *2.

that every legal decision-maker to have considered the question, including the arbitrator himself and the state courts, had uniformly concluded that the underlying agreement permitted class arbitration.[49] Green Tree's position, according to Respondents, would result in a dramatic expansion of the reach of the FAA into routine matters of state law, an expansion never intended by Congress and that could not be squared with the Court's precedent.[50]

For Respondents, the fact that the parties' agreement placed no limits on an arbitrator's ability to conduct class arbitration meant that the agreement had left matters of arbitration procedure to the arbitrator's discretion, within the parameters set by state law and the FAA.[51] Respondents argued that the FAA said nothing about the procedures to arbitrate state-law claims and did not speak to whether an arbitrator may permit plaintiffs to proceed on a class wide basis, concluding that selection of arbitration procedures not specified by an arbitration agreement or mandated by state law rests within the arbitrator's discretion.[52]

## 3.3 *The Court's Opinion*

### 3.3.1 Justice Breyer's Plurality Opinion

When the U.S. Supreme Court heard oral argument in *Bazzle* on April 22, 2003, before it were two questions that the plurality eventually directly addressed: First, which decision-maker—court or arbitrator—should decide whether the contracts at issue were silent on, or prohibited, class arbitration? And second, had the class arbitrations been properly ordered in these cases?

The Court's plurality opinion answered only the first question, resolving it in favor of the arbitrator being the correct decision-maker. The Court's analysis began with the presumption that whether the contracts were silent as to class arbitration was not a resolved issue—indeed, it presented a disputed issue of contract interpretation.[53] And, as the Court noted, the parties had agreed to submit to the arbitrator "[*a*]*ll* disputes, claims, or controversies arising from or relating to this contract or the relationships which result from this

---

49 *Id.*

50 *Id.*

51 *Id.* at *21.

52 *Id.*

53 Justice Breyer announced the judgment of the Court and delivered the plurality opinion, in which Justices Scalia, Souter, and Ginsburg joined. Justice Stevens concurred in the judgment and dissented in part. Chief Justice Rehnquist issued a dissenting opinion, in which Justices O'Connor and Kennedy joined, and Justice Thomas wrote a separate dissenting opinion.

contract[,]"[54] evidencing an agreement that an arbitrator, not a judge, would answer the relevant question.[55]

The Court observed that there are certain limited circumstances in which courts assume that the parties intended courts, not arbitrators, to decide a particular arbitration-related matter (in the absence of clear and unmistakable evidence to the contrary).[56] These included certain "gateway" matters, such as whether the parties have a valid arbitration agreement at all or whether a concededly binding arbitration clause applies to a certain type of controversy.[57]

But to the Court, the question here—whether the contracts prohibited class arbitration—did not fall into that narrow "gateway" exception for so-called questions of arbitrability.[58] The question concerned neither the validity of the arbitration clause nor its applicability to the underlying dispute between the parties, and instead merely concerned contract interpretation and arbitration procedures—making the question one that arbitrators are well situated to address.[59]

The Court then observed that there was at least a strong likelihood that in both proceedings the arbitrator's decision on class certification was influenced by a court's interpretation of the contracts rather than being an independent decision of the arbitrator.[60] In the *Bazzle* case, the trial court granted class certification, after which the arbitrator administered class arbitration proceedings; and in the *Lackey* case, though the arbitrator did certify the class, this was after the trial court in *Bazzle* had determined that the identical contract authorized class arbitration procedures—and, given that the arbitrator was the same in both proceedings, he would of course have been aware of that trial court decision, which could therefore have improperly influenced his decision to certify the class.[61] Accordingly, the plurality remanded the case back to the arbitrator to ensure that he would independently interpret the contracts without influence from the courts.

---

54 Green Tree Fin. Corp. v. Bazzle, 539 U.S. 444, 445 (2003) (emphasis in original).

55 *Id.*

56 *Id.* at 452 (citing AT&T Technologies, Inc. v. Communications Workers, 475 U.S. 643, 649 (1986)).

57 *Id.*

58 *Id.*

59 *Id.* at 452–53.

60 *Id.* at 446.

61 *Id.* at 445.

### 3.3.2 Justice Stevens' Concurrence in the Judgment and Dissent in Part

Justice Stevens wrote separately to note that while arguably the interpretation of the parties' agreement should have been made in the first instance by the arbitrator, rather than the court, and there was a possibility that the decision to conduct a class action arbitration was made by the wrong decision-maker, the fact that the decision was correct *as a matter of law* and also that petitioner had merely challenged the *merits* of that decision meant there was no need to remand the case to correct that possible error.[62] In other words, Justice Stevens did not give a definitive answer to the first question, but rather expressed his conclusive view on the second question. His view was that the FAA did not preclude the state law determination made by the Supreme Court of South Carolina that class-action arbitrations were permissible if not expressly prohibited by the applicable arbitration agreement. Accordingly, Justice Stevens would have simply affirmed the judgment of the Supreme Court of South Carolina.[63]

### 3.3.3 Chief Justice Rehnquist's Dissent

Joined by Justices O'Connor and Kennedy, Chief Justice Rehnquist dissented. He determined that the contracts did not by their terms permit class action arbitration. Accordingly, the South Carolina Supreme Court's decision should be reversed because it contravened the terms of the contracts and was therefore prohibited by the FAA.[64] Though Chief Justice Rehnquist recognized that the decision of the arbitrator on matters agreed to be submitted to him is given considerable deference by the courts, he noted that the decision of *what* to submit to the arbitrator is a matter of contractual agreement by the parties, and the interpretation of that contract is for the court, not for the arbitrator.[65]

### 3.3.4 Justice Thomas's Dissent

Justice Thomas wrote only to observe that he continued to believe that the FAA does not apply to proceedings in state courts.[66] For that reason, in Justice Thomas's view, the FAA cannot be a ground for preempting a state court's interpretation of a private arbitration agreement, and accordingly he would have left undisturbed the judgment of the South Carolina Supreme Court.[67]

---

62 *Id.* at 455 (Stevens, J., concurring in the judgment and dissenting in part).

63 *Id.*

64 *Id.* at 455 (Rehnquist, CJ., dissenting).

65 *Id.*

66 *Id.* at 460 (Thomas, J., dissenting).

67 *Id.*

## 4 Analysis of the Opinion and How It Impacted U.S. Arbitration Law and Practice

The plurality opinion avoided reaching a conclusion on the merits of the core issue in dispute—whether the class arbitration orders in this case were proper and consistent with the FAA. Instead, it focused on the threshold question that neither party contemplated in their briefs to the court: who the right decision-maker was to determine whether the contracts were silent on or prohibited class arbitration. Justices Breyer, Scalia, Souter, and Ginsburg had the opportunity to affirmatively decide on whether class arbitration was or was not allowed absent an express agreement of the parties. However, they chose not to take that opportunity. They did not overturn the Supreme Court of South Carolina's decision based on their interpretation of the FAA, nor did they affirm its decision to approve class arbitration based on the state's own contract law interpretations. Instead, they ended their analysis after determining that the arbitrator had the responsibility to determine whether the contracts forbade class arbitration. They did not clarify what might happen in the event that the arbitrator determined that the contracts were indeed silent on the issue of class arbitration—which decision-maker then should be tasked with determining whether the silent contracts permitted class arbitration? Furthermore, to what standard should that decision-maker look in their analysis, the FAA or the South Carolina's contract law? In other words, does the FAA permit class arbitration when contracts do not expressly provide so? Is this question entirely left to state law?

For the parties in *Bazzle*, this was certainly a curious result given that they were not in disagreement about the authority of the courts to make a merit-based decision. Perhaps it was even more peculiar for the arbitrator, who was tasked on remand with determining whether the contract prohibited him from trying the very two class arbitration cases over which he had just presided. For the broader legal community and beyond, those lingering questions that the plurality opinion refused to answer created much uncertainty.

Since *Bazzle* did not provide explicit guidance over either how silence on class arbitration in agreements should be treated or how the Court would address the compatibility between the FAA and the state contract law, observers were left to guess.

One could argue that the *Bazzle* Court would rule in favor of class arbitration if the arbitrator determined that the contracts at issue in that case were silent. That is because, presumably, the Court's reluctance to rule on the merits of the case and its decision to remand meant that a silent clause did not have the same consequence as a clause that prohibited arbitration.[68] If a silent clause necessarily had the same consequence as one that prohibited arbitration, there would not have been the need to remand to the arbitrator in the first place.[69] The Court could have simply ruled in favor of Green Tree, stating that only an express agreement to class arbitration entitled such a proceeding; that the threshold issue of who should decide whether the contracts were silent on class arbitration did not matter; and that the failure to expressly authorize class arbitration was an absolute bar.

With respect to whether the state law interpretation was consistent with the FAA, one could argue that the *Bazzle* plurality implied that it was. Unlike the dissent, nothing in the plurality opinion suggested that the four Justices disagreed with the analysis of the South Carolina Supreme Court. Justice Stevens, who wrote that the South Carolina Supreme Court's decision was correct as a matter of law, concurred with the plurality precisely because he understood the plurality opinion to express a view close to his own, and his view was that the FAA did not preclude a determination by the state law.

Therefore, while the Court did not explicitly decide that class arbitration was permitted when the contract was silent, some courts viewed *Bazzle* as an implicit endorsement of such an outcome.[70] Some lower courts concluded that the Court's judgment in *Bazzle* implicitly supported the permissibility of class arbitrations in contracts silent on the issue as long as the arbitration agreements did not expressly prohibit them.[71]

The American Arbitration Association (the "AAA") also seemed to agree that the Court took a rather permissive approach towards the propriety of class arbitration in the event that the agreement between parties was silent on the issue. Anticipating growing demands for class arbitration, the AAA developed a set of procedures, entitled Supplementary Rules for Class Arbitrations, which became effective on October 8, 2003.[72] Importantly, the AAA policy stated that it would administer demands for class arbitration if "(1) the underlying agreement specifie[d] that disputes arising out of the parties' agreement shall be resolved by arbitration in accordance with any of the Association's rules,

68 Brief for Respondent, Stolt-Nielsen S.A. v. AnimalFeeds International Corp., 559 U.S. 662, 678 (2010) (No. 08–1198), 2009 WL 3404244, at *37.

69 *Id.*

70 *See e.g.*, *Shroyer v. New Cingular Wireless Servs., Inc.*, 498 F.3d 976, 992 (9th Cir. 2007).

71 *See e.g.*, *Kinkel v. Cingular Wireless LLC*, 223 Ill. 2d 1, 19, 857 N.E.2d 250, 262 (Ill. 2006).

72 Brief of American Arbitration Association as Amicus Curiae in Support of Neither Party, Stolt-Nielsen S.A. v. AnimalFeeds International Corp., 559 U.S. 662, 678 (2010) (No. 08–1198), 2009 WL 2896309, at *12.

and (2) the agreement [was] silent with respect to class claims, consolidation or joinder of claims."[73] AAA interpreted *Bazzle* to imply that an arbitrator's role extended beyond merely determining if a contract was silent; it instead included deciding whether a contract allowed class arbitration. The AAA also assumed that mere silence in the arbitration agreement was sufficient to permit the initiation of class arbitration. Such an assumption was later refuted by the Supreme Court in its 2010 decision, *Stolt-Nielsen S.A. v. AnimalFeeds International Corp.*[74]

After *Bazzle*, the number of class arbitrations administered by the AAA grew dramatically. Prior to *Bazzle*, the AAA had administered only a small number of class arbitrations, and typically did so only when a class action was referred by a court to arbitration.[75] Between 2003 and 2009, the AAA administered 283 class arbitrations.[76] Statistically speaking, among the 135 that reached the Clause Construction Award phase,[77] arbitrators had a tendency to recognize the propriety of class arbitrations. Only in 7 out of the 135 cases did the arbitrator hold that the arbitration clause did not permit class arbitration. In the vast majority of the cases, either the parties stipulated that their contract authorized it (33 of 135, or 24%), or the arbitrators interpreted the clause as permitting class arbitration (95 of 135, or 70%).[78]

Beyond the legal landscape, in light of the uncertainty created by *Bazzle*, the business community could no longer rely on older cases in lower courts that ruled against class arbitration when contracts were silent. This had notable consequences, especially for contracts before *Bazzle*. For example, one survey estimated that only 53 percent of the arbitration clauses in franchise agreements executed in 1999 among the country's seventy-five largest franchise systems expressly precluded class claims. Most of the remaining clauses

---

73 The AAA's policy, while not available on its website, was quoted in various cases including *Kinkel*, 223 Ill. 2d at 20.

74 559 U.S. 662, 678 (2010).

75 Brief of American Arbitration Association, *supra* note 72, at *10.

76 *Id.* at *22.

77 "Clause Construction Award" phase refers to the first phase under the AAA Supplementary Rules for Class Arbitrations. It was designed to permit the arbitrator to fulfill the Court's directive by determining, "in a reasoned, partial final award on the construction of the arbitration clause, whether the applicable arbitration clause permits the arbitration award to proceed on behalf of or against a class." After the Clause Construction Award is rendered, the Rules require the arbitrator to stay proceedings for a period of at least thirty days to "permit any party to move a court of competent jurisdiction to confirm or to vacate the Clause Construction Award." Rule 3 of AAA Supplementary Rules for Class Arbitrations.

78 Brief of American Arbitration Association, *supra* note 72, at *22.

were silent on the issue.[79] Seeking to avoid class arbitration and finding themselves no longer capable of getting by without explicit language after *Bazzle*, businesses increasingly included express class arbitration waivers in their contracts.[80]

In other words, despite *Bazzle*'s potential ambiguity, both the legal and the business communities expected that, in a subsequent case, the Supreme Court would definitively rule in favor of the compatibility of state contract law with the FAA and the validity of class arbitration in cases of contractual silence.

However, the Supreme Court's 2010 decision in *Stolt-Nielsen* defied such expectations. In *Stolt-Nielsen*, the parties had a dispute arising under an agreement with an arbitration clause. AnimalFeeds served a demand for arbitration on Stolt-Nielsen, after which both parties "entered into a supplemental agreement providing for the question of class arbitration to be submitted to a panel of three arbitrators."[81] The parties also stipulated that "the arbitration clause was 'silent' with respect to class arbitration."[82] The arbitrators concluded that the contract permitted class arbitration and stayed the proceeding so the parties could pursue judicial review of that decision.[83]

After the *Stolt-Nielsen* case reached the Supreme Court, the question before it was the same as the one originally before the *Bazzle* Court: whether imposing class arbitration on parties whose arbitration clauses were silent on that issue was consistent with the FAA. Unlike the *Bazzle* Court, the *Stolt-Nielsen* Court did not need to address the preliminary questions of whether the contract was indeed silent and which decision-maker had the authority to decide whether the contract permitted class arbitration, as the parties had explicitly agreed on both issues already. Before it delved into the merits of the core issue of dispute, the Court did note, however, that *Bazzle* in its judgment never decided on the right decision-maker to determine whether a contract permitted class arbitration; instead, only a plurality of justices addressed the issue.[84] That issue remained open. As to whether silence justified class arbitration, the Supreme Court answered with a resounding no. The Supreme Court held that a contract that is silent on the issue of class arbitration is not sufficient evidence

79 Kevin M. Kennedy & Bethany Appleby, *Green Tree Financial Corp. v. Bazzle: A New Day for Class Arbitrations?*, 23 Franchise L.J. 84, 86 (2003).

80 Peter B. Rutledge & Christopher R. Drahozal, *"Sticky" Arbitration Clauses? The Use of Arbitration Clauses After Concepcion and Amex*, 67 Vand. L. Rev. 955, 968 (2014).

81 Stolt-Nielsen S.A. v. AnimalFeeds International Corp., 559 U.S. 662, 668 (2010).

82 *Id.*

83 *Id.*

84 *Id.*

that the parties agreed to submit to class arbitration, because the differences between simple bilateral and complex class action arbitration are too great for such a presumption; and a party may not be compelled under the FAA to submit to class arbitration unless there is a contractual basis for concluding that the parties agreed to do so.[85]

In 2019, in *Lamps Plus, Inc. v. Varela*,[86] the Supreme Court again made it clear that "the Court has not decided whether the availability of class arbitration is a so-called 'question of arbitrability' which includes ... gateway matters." Further, it sealed the deal on any remaining confusion around whether a contract that does not explicitly provide for class arbitration allows such a proceeding. The answer was that even if a contract is technically not silent about class arbitration but is ambiguous on the matter, still the FAA bars an order requiring class arbitration, regardless of what state contract law might suggest.

Perhaps unsurprisingly in light of the lack of a clear majority opinion, the *Bazzle* decision, in hindsight, did not actually decide that much at all. At most, a plurality of the Supreme Court held that it was for the arbitrator, and not a court, to determine whether an arbitration agreement was silent as to class certification. However, the question of whether the propriety of class arbitration is a threshold arbitrability matter for the court to decide or a matter of contractual interpretation for the arbitrator to decide ultimately remained unresolved after *Bazzle*. Maybe *Bazzle*'s strongest impact was to underscore the importance of precise language in arbitration clauses. Both businesses and consumers became more vigilant about explicitly addressing the issue of class arbitration in their arbitration agreements to avoid confusion as to who should decide on such issue and how that decision-maker should make its ruling.

---

85 *Id.*

86 139 S. Ct. 1407, 1416 (2019).

CHAPTER 16

# *Intel Corp. v. Advanced Micro Devices, Inc.* (2004)

*Preeti Bhagnani and Stephen Hogan-Mitchell*

## 1 Introduction

Section 1782 of Title 28 of the United States Code has been described as a powerful tool for persons involved in, or with an interest in, contentious proceedings in a foreign forum. This federal statute grants U.S. federal courts the power to order discovery in the United States, under broad U.S. discovery rules, "for use in a proceeding in a foreign or international tribunal."[1]

In the decades after the statute was enacted, U.S. courts diverged as to whether the statute allowed courts to order discovery for use in an international arbitration proceeding, reaching different conclusions as to whether an international arbitral tribunal, *i.e.*, an arbitral tribunal seated in a foreign jurisdiction, qualified as a "foreign or international tribunal" within the meaning of the statute. U.S. courts also debated who may seek judicial assistance under Section 1782. In a 2004 decision, *Intel Corp. v. Advanced Micro Devices, Inc.*,[2] the U.S. Supreme Court provided guidance on both these issues, as well as the factors that courts should consider in exercising their discretionary authority under Section 1782. Although the decision related to an investigation by the Directorate-General for Competition ("DG-Competition") of the Commission of the European Communities ("European Commission" or "Commission"), rather than an international arbitration proceeding, it opened the door to U.S. courts entertaining requests for discovery for use in proceedings before international arbitral tribunals. This chapter provides an overview of Section 1782 (Section 2) and the *Intel* decision (Section 3), and explores the decision's impact on U.S. arbitration law and practice (Section 4).

## 2 Overview of Section 1782

The text of Section 1782(a) states as follows:

1 28 U.S.C. § 1782(a).

2 542 U.S. 241 (2004).

 | DOI:10.1163/9789004715820_017

> The district court of the district in which a person resides or is found may order him to give his testimony or statement or to produce a document or other thing for use in a proceeding in a foreign or international tribunal, including criminal investigations conducted before formal accusation. The order may be made pursuant to a letter rogatory issued, or request made, by a foreign or international tribunal or upon the application of any interested person and may direct that the testimony or statement be given, or the document or other thing be produced, before a person appointed by the court. By virtue of his appointment, the person appointed has power to administer any necessary oath and take the testimony or statement. The order may prescribe the practice and procedure, which may be in whole or part the practice and procedure of the foreign country or the international tribunal, for taking the testimony or statement or producing the document or other thing. To the extent that the order does not prescribe otherwise, the testimony or statement shall be taken, and the document or other thing produced, in accordance with the Federal Rules of Civil Procedure.
>
> A person may not be compelled to give his testimony or statement or to produce a document or other thing in violation of any legally applicable privilege.[3]

In essence, an applicant seeking discovery under Section 1782(a) must show that:

(1) the applicant is an "interested person,"
(2) the proceeding for which the applicant seeks discovery is in a "foreign or international tribunal," and
(3) the person from whom evidence is sought resides or is found in the district of the court in which the application is filed.

Upon such showing, the Court has discretion whether to grant the discovery requested. The evidence that may be obtained under Section 1782 includes both testimony and documents.

Section 1782 is the product of a long legislative tradition of enabling U.S. courts to assist foreign courts in collecting evidence within the U.S. This tradition, grounded in principles of comity, dates back to 1855, when the U.S. passed the first federal law permitting U.S. courts to execute letters

3 28 U.S.C. § 1782(a).

rogatory, which were the customary means of obtaining judicial assistance from overseas in the absence of a treaty or other agreement.[4]

Section 1782, enacted in 1948,[5] represented a liberalization of these earlier statutes. Unlike prior statutes, it did not include a requirement that a foreign government be a party to, or have an interest in, the foreign or international proceeding.[6] Subsequent revisions expanded Section 1782's scope to allow U.S. courts to order discovery for use in a proceeding in a "foreign or international tribunal" rather than merely a foreign "court."[7]

In the decades following the enactment of Section 1782, courts differed in their interpretations of what constituted a "foreign or international tribunal," who qualified as an "interested person," and the circumstances in which Section 1782 discovery would be available. Some lower courts found that for Section 1782 to apply, the foreign proceeding must be "imminent," while others concluded that the proceeding need only be within "reasonable contemplation."[8] Some courts determined that Section 1782 discovery would be available only if the information requested would be discoverable were the application made under the law of the foreign jurisdiction.[9] As regards the availability of Section 1782 discovery for use in an international arbitration, both the Second and Fifth Circuits found that arbitral tribunals did not qualify as "foreign or international tribunals" under the statute and that the statute therefore did not extend to private international arbitration.[10] It was against this backdrop that the Supreme Court in 2004 for the first time analyzed Section 1782 in *Intel v. Advanced Micro Devices.*

---

4 Letters rogatory are requests from courts in one country to the courts of another country requesting judicial assistance, such as the taking of evidence or the serving of a summons, subpoena, or other legal notice. *See An Act to Prevent Mis-trials in the District and Circuit Courts of the United States, in Certain Cases*, 33 Cong. Ch. 140; 10 Stat. 630 (1855).

5 *See Act of June 25, 1948*, Pub. L. No. 80–773, § 1782, 62 Stat. 869, 949.

6 *See Act of Mar. 3, 1863*, ch. 95, § 4, 12 Stat. 769.

7 *Compare Act of June 25, 1948*, Pub. L. No. 80–773, § 1782, 62 Stat. 869, 949, *with Act of Oct. 3, 1964*, Pub. L. No. 88–619, § 9, 78 Stat. 997.

8 *Compare In re Ishihara Chem. Co.*, 251 F.3d 120, 125 (2d Cir. 2001) ("[T]his Court has held that 'a proceeding need not actually be pending, but rather … a proceeding must be imminent—very likely to occur and very soon to occur.'") (internal citations omitted), *with In re Letter of Request from Crown Prosecution Serv. Of United Kingdom*, 870 F.2d 686, 687 (D.C. Cir. 1989) ("The judicial proceeding for which assistance is sought, we further hold, need not be pending at the time of the request for assistance; it suffices that the proceeding in the foreign tribunal and its contours be in reasonable contemplation when the request is made.").

9 *Application of Asta Medica, S.A.*, 981 F.2d 1, 7 (1st Cir. 1992).

10 *See, e.g., Kazakhstan v. Biedermann Int'l*, 168 F.3d 880, 883 (5th Cir. 1999); *Nat'l Broadcasting Co. v. Bear Stearns & Co.*, 165 F.3d 184, 191 (2d Cir. 1999).

## 3 The *Intel* Case

### 3.1 *Background*

The *Intel* case arose from an antitrust complaint that Advanced Micro Devices, Inc. ("AMD") filed against Intel Corporation ("Intel") with the DG-Competition of the European Commission, alleging that Intel had violated European competition law.[11] AMD petitioned the District Court for the Northern District of California under Section 1782 for an order directing Intel to produce documents that Intel had produced in a private antitrust suit in an Alabama federal court which AMD considered relevant to the Commission's investigation.[12]

In the District Court proceedings, AMD argued that the European Commission qualified as a "foreign or international tribunal" for purposes of Section 1782, because it exercised "quasi-judicial powers."[13] AMD drew parallels between the Commission's powers and the those of the U.S. Federal Trade Commission ("FTC") and noted that the Supreme Court in an unrelated decision had described the FTC as acting in part "quasi-judicially."[14] AMD also cited the opinion of Professor Hans Smit, one of Section 1782's draftsmen, that the Commission exercised quasi-judicial powers that made 1782 applicable to proceedings before it.[15]

The District Court disagreed, pointing out that the Commission had in a policy document described its procedures as "administrative and not judicial," which contradicted AMD's argument.[16] The Court found that "[a] 'proceeding' within the meaning of § 1782 means one in which an 'adjudicative function is exercised.'"[17] Finding that the European Commission lacked the adjudicatory functions of the FTC, the District Court concluded that it was not a "foreign or international tribunal" within the meaning of Section 1782, and denied AMD's request.[18]

---

11 *Intel Corp. v. Advanced Micro Devices, Inc.*, 542 U.S. 241, 250 (2004).

12 *Id.* at 251.

13 *Advanced Micro Devices, Inc. v. Intel Corp.*, No. C-01–7033 MISC WAI, 2002 WL 1339088, at *1 (N.D. Cal. Jan. 7, 2002), *rev'd and remanded*, 292 F.3d 664 (9th Cir. 2002), *aff'd*, 542 U.S. 241 (2004).

14 *See Humphrey's Ex'r v. United States*, 295 U.S. 602, 628 (1935).

15 *Advanced Micro Devices, Inc. v. Intel Corp.*, No. C-01-7033 MISC WAI, 2002 WL 1339088, at *1 (N.D. Cal. Jan. 7, 2002), *rev'd and remanded*, 292 F.3d 664 (9th Cir. 2002), *aff'd*, 542 U.S. 241 (2004), (citing Hans Smit, *International Litigation Under the United States Code*, 65 COLUM. L. REV., 1015, 1026 n.71, 1027 n.3 (1965)).

16 *Id.*

17 *Id.*

18 *Id.* (internal citations omitted).

On appeal by AMD, the Court of Appeals for the Ninth Circuit reversed the District Court's decision.[19] In reaching its decision, the Ninth Circuit considered two main questions: (i) whether the Commission's investigation qualified as a proceeding in a "foreign or international tribunal," and (ii) whether, as Intel argued, Section 1782 also required "a showing that the information sought would be discoverable or admissible" in the proceedings before the European Commission.[20]

On the first question, the Ninth Circuit stated that Section 1782's language and legislative history indicated that the statute extended to "'bodies of a quasi-judicial or administrative nature' as well as preliminary investigations leading to judicial proceedings," and did not require that those proceedings be "pending."[21] The Court concluded that because the DG-Competition reported to the European Commission, an entity that made binding decisions that were appealable to European courts, a judicial proceeding was a likely sequel to the investigation before the Commission. The investigation by the DG-Competition was thus "related to a quasi-judicial or judicial proceeding," which satisfied the "foreign or international tribunal" requirement for purposes of Section 1782.[22]

On the second question, the Ninth Circuit rejected Intel's argument that Section 1782 required a showing that the documents AMD sought, if located in the European Union, would have been discoverable in the European Commission investigation.[23] The Court found that "nothing in the plain language or legislative history of Section 1782" imposed a "foreign-discoverability" rule of that sort.[24] The Court further opined that "liberal discovery" was consistent with the "twin aims of Section 1782: providing efficient assistance to participants in international litigation and encouraging foreign countries by example to provide similar assistance to our courts."[25]

### 3.2 *Arguments before the Supreme Court*

Intel appealed the Ninth Circuit's ruling to the Supreme Court, advancing three primary arguments. First, Intel argued that Section 1782 did not authorize discovery that would be unavailable to the requesting party under applicable

19 *Advanced Micro Devices, Inc. v. Intel Corp.*, 292 F.3d 664, 665 (9th Cir. 2002), *aff'd*, 542 U.S. 241 (2004).

20 *Id.*

21 *Id.* at 667 (internal citations omitted).

22 *Id.* at 667–68.

23 *Id.*

24 *Id.* at 669.

25 *Id.*

U.S. law as well as foreign law (the so-called "foreign discoverability" requirement). According to Intel, the discovery that AMD requested was unavailable under both U.S. law and the relevant foreign law because AMD was not an "interested person" as it was not a "litigant"—the word used in the title of Section 1782—but was rather a "mere complainant" with limited rights in the Commission's proceedings.[26] Second, Intel argued that 1782 discovery would be inappropriate because the investigation by the DG-Competition was not a "proceeding in a foreign or international tribunal" because of its preliminary, non-adjudicative nature and because no adjudicative proceeding was pending or imminent.[27] Finally, Intel contended that even if the Supreme Court disagreed with Intel's interpretation of Section 1782, the Court should exercise its authority to adopt rules of practice limiting 1782 discovery "(i) where such discovery would be unavailable in the foreign jurisdiction if the documents were located there or (ii) where there is no live foreign 'proceeding.'"[28] On Intel's view, such a result would better respect the principles of comity that underpinned Section 1782.[29]

AMD advanced the following primary arguments in response. AMD argued that the fact that the Commission would not allow the requested discovery under its own rules did not necessarily imply that evidence obtained under Section 1782 would not be welcomed or used by the Commission.[30] AMD argued that there was no evidence in the statute or its legislative history supporting the existence of a "foreign discoverability" requirement, as proposed by Intel.[31] AMD argued that the investigation was a "proceeding" for purposes of the statute because the Commission exerted "quasi-judicial" power, and that Section 1782 did not require that a proceeding be "pending" or that the party bringing the application be a "litigant." AMD pointed out that Congress had removed the word "pending" from the earlier version of the statute and used the word "litigant" only in the statute's title and not its primary text.[32] Finally, AMD rejected Intel's argument that the Supreme Court should adopt Intel's proposed rules of practice, arguing that such a ruling would run counter to the language and purpose of Section 1782 and that the supposed comity concerns

26 *See* Brief for Petitioner, *Intel Corp. v. Advanced Micro Devices, Inc.*, 542 U.S. 241, 2003 WL 23138394, at *19–27.

27 *Id.* at *27–33.

28 *Id.* at *18, 34–38.

29 *Id.* at *38.

30 *See* Brief for Respondent, *Intel Corp. v. Advanced Micro Devices, Inc.*, 542 U.S. 241, 2004 WL 297864, at *24–25.

31 *Id.* at *26–34.

32 *Id.* at *34–47.

raised by Intel were overstated, given that the Commission had not said that it would object to the submission of any documents that AMD may obtain under Section 1782.[33]

During the oral arguments, the Supreme Court gave special leave for counsel for the European Commission to present its position on the case. The Commission argued that it was not a "tribunal" under Section 1782 because its actions were purely investigatory and not adjudicatory.[34] The Commission contended that permitting AMD to seek assistance from the U.S. courts would interfere with the Commission's "orderly process" for gathering evidence and permit "a private entity to run to a United States court and use essentially the [C]ommission as a pawn in an effort to obtain pre-complaint discovery."[35] The Commission viewed such behavior as "direct interference" in its operations that would also unnecessarily increase its workload.[36]

### 3.3 *The Supreme Court's Opinion*

The Supreme Court in a 7–1 decision[37] affirmed the Ninth Circuit's decision and remanded the case to the District Court.[38] Justice Ruth Bader Ginsburg, writing for the majority, rejected Intel's argument that AMD was not an "interested person" under Section 1782 because it was not a "litigant" (the word used in the caption of Section 1782).[39] The majority observed that a complainant who triggered a European Commission investigation had significant participation rights—including the ability to prompt an investigation, the right to submit information for the DG-Competition's consideration, and the right to proceed to court if the Commission discontinued the investigation or dismissed the complaint—and therefore qualified as an "interested person" within any fair construction of that term.[40]

The majority also found that the requirement that the documents requested be "for use in a foreign or international tribunal" was satisfied. The majority observed that Section 1782 had previously referred to "any judicial proceeding," but Congress had replaced that term with "a proceeding in a foreign or

33 *Id.* at *47–50.
34 *See* Transcript of Oral Argument at 19–20, *Intel Corp. v. Advanced Micro Devices, Inc.*, 542 U.S. 241 (2004) (No. 02–572).
35 *Id.* at 18.
36 *Id.* at 22.
37 Justice Sandra Day O'Connor did not participate in the decision.
38 *Intel Corp. v. Advanced Micro Devices, Inc.*, 542 U.S. 241, 246–47 (2004).
39 *Id.* at 256.
40 *Id.*

international tribunal."[41] For the majority, Congress understood this change as providing for "the possibility of U.S. judicial assistance in connection with administrative and quasi-judicial proceedings abroad."[42] The majority quoted Professor Smit's opinion that Section 1782 encompassed investigating magistrates, administrative and arbitral tribunals, and quasi-judicial agencies, as well as conventional civil, commercial, criminal, and administrative courts, and proceedings by the Commission in which it exercised "quasi-judicial powers."[43] Relying on the European Commission's submission that "[w]hen the Commission acts on DG Competition's final recommendation ... the investigative function blur[s] into decision making," the majority concluded that the European Commission fell within Section 1782's ambit to the extent that it acted as a first-instance decisionmaker.[44]

The majority also rejected Intel's argument that Section 1782 discovery was unavailable because the proceeding before the Commission was at an investigative stage.[45] The majority pointed out that Congress had deleted the requirement that a proceeding be "pending" when it amended the statute, and further observed that the legislative history of the statute reflected that judicial assistance would be available to a foreign or international "proceeding or *investigation*."[46] Accordingly, the majority concluded that Section 1782 required only that a dispositive ruling by the European Commission, reviewable by the European courts, be "within *reasonable contemplation*."[47]

The majority also declined to introduce a "foreign discoverability" rule for 1782 applications. The majority noted that besides protecting privileged material, "nothing in the text of § 1782 limits a district court's production-order authority to materials that could be discovered in the foreign jurisdiction if the materials were located there."[48] The legislative history likewise contained

---

41 *Id.* at 258.

42 *Id.* (internal citations omitted).

43 *Id.* (citing Hans Smit, *International Litigation Under the United States Code*, 65 COLUM. L. REV. 1015, 1026 n.71, 1027 n.3 (1965)) ("'[t]he term 'tribunal' ... includes investigating magistrates, administrative and arbitral tribunals, and quasi-judicial agencies, as well as conventional civil, commercial, criminal, and administrative courts'; in addition to affording assistance in cases before the European Court of Justice, § 1782, as revised in 1964, 'permits the rendition of proper aid in proceedings before the [European] Commission in which the Commission exercises quasi-judicial powers'").

44 *Id.*

45 *Id.*

46 *Id.* at 258–59 (emphasis in original).

47 *Id.* at 259 (emphasis added).

48 542 U.S. at 260.

no such restriction.[49] The majority was skeptical of the policy concerns that Intel advanced, namely, "avoiding offense to foreign governments and maintaining parity between litigants,"[50] and questioned whether foreign governments would in fact be offended by a domestic statute permitting, but not requiring, judicial assistance.[51] The Court similarly rejected the suggestion that concerns about maintaining parity among adversaries warranted the "foreign-discoverability rule," emphasizing that a district court could condition relief upon the parties' reciprocal exchange of information or the foreign tribunal could place conditions on its acceptance of information to maintain parity between litigants.[52]

Finally, the majority stressed that while district courts were permitted to grant discovery requests under Section 1782, they were not *required* to do so.[53] The majority enumerated several factors that should be considered when ruling on a Section 1782 request (the so-called "*Intel*" factors). These factors included whether the party from whom discovery is sought was a participant in the foreign proceeding—as the need for discovery is reduced when the foreign tribunal has jurisdiction over that party and may itself order it to produce evidence—as well as "the nature of the foreign tribunal, the character of the proceedings underway abroad, and the receptivity of the foreign government or the court or agency abroad to U.S. federal-court judicial assistance."[54] Additional factors included whether the request "conceals an attempt to circumvent foreign proof-gathering restrictions or other policies of a foreign country or the United States" or if the request was "unduly intrusive or burdensome" on the requested party.[55] The majority remanded the case to the District Court to address the merits of the application taking into account these factors.[56]

Justice Stephen Breyer dissented, arguing that the majority's interpretation of Section 1782 went beyond what Congress might reasonably have intended, and encompassed a broad range of proceedings before foreign governmental authorities who may not be receptive to assistance from U.S. courts.[57]

49 *Id.*

50 *Id.* at 261.

51 *Id.* at 261–62.

52 *Id.* at 262.

53 542 U.S. at 264.

54 *Id.*

55 *Id.* at 265.

56 Justice Scalia in a concurring judgment disagreed with the majority's reliance on the legislative history of Section 1782 in reaching its conclusion. *Intel Corp. v. Advanced Micro Devices, Inc.*, 542 U.S. 241, 267 (2004) (Scalia, J., concurring).

57 542 U.S. 241, 267–69 (2004) (Breyer, J., dissenting).

For Justice Breyer, the majority's decision would lead to expensive, time-consuming discovery battles that would distract and burden both foreign and domestic adjudicatory bodies.[58]

Justice Breyer argued for two categorical limits on the district courts' authority to order discovery under Section 1782. First, he proposed that where a foreign entity "possesses few tribunal-like characteristics," that foreign entity's own view of whether it constituted a tribunal should be afforded deference.[59] For Justice Breyer, the European Commission fell within this category.[60] In his view, such a limitation would better achieve "Congress' basic cooperative objectives in enacting the statute."[61] Second, Justice Breyer favored precluding Section 1782 discovery where the discovery sought would not otherwise be available under both foreign law *and* under "domestic law in analogous circumstances."[62] Justice Breyer contended that application of either of these limiting principles would bar Section 1782 discovery in the *Intel* case.[63]

On remand, the District Court applied the factors articulated by the Supreme Court and concluded that AMD's request should be denied. The District Court pointed out that (i) Intel was a participant in the Commission proceedings and thus subject to the jurisdiction of the Commission, who could order it to produce evidence if it found necessary, (ii) the Commission was not receptive to the discovery requested, and (iii) the application appeared to be a way for AMD to circumvent the Commission's decision not to pursue the discovery.[64]

## 4 Key Takeaways

The majority's decision in *Intel* adopted an expansive interpretation of Section 1782, both as to *who* may make a Section 1782 application for discovery and as to the types of proceedings for which such discovery would be available. It clarified that an "interested person" with standing to request Section 1782 discovery was not limited to a litigant, a foreign sovereign, or a sovereign's designated agents (as Intel argued). It established that "foreign or international

58 *Id.* at 268–69.

59 *Id.* at 269.

60 *Id.* at 271.

61 *Id.*

62 *Id.* at 270.

63 *Id.* at 270, 273.

64 *Advanced Micro Devices v. Intel Corp.*, No. C 01–7033, 2004 WL 2282320, at *2–3 (N.D. Cal. Oct. 4, 2004).

tribunals" included *quasi*-judicial bodies, which extended to the European Commission when acting as a "first-instance decisionmaker."[65] It also established that the foreign or international proceeding need not be "pending" but need only be within "reasonable contemplation."[66] The majority also rejected a "foreign discoverability" rule as a threshold requirement for seeking Section 1782 discovery. U.S. discovery rules tend to be far more liberal than the rules in many other countries, and generally permit discovery of non-privileged material that is relevant to any claim or defense and is proportional to the needs of the case, including through the use of depositions.[67] The Court's rejection of the "foreign discoverability" rule thus meant that applicants could in principle obtain discovery that they could not have obtained if they had followed the discovery procedures of the foreign forum.

The *Intel* factors guided courts in exercising their discretion under the statute in a manner that balances comity and access to relevant information. The first enumerated factor—whether the party from whom discovery is sought was a participant in the foreign proceeding—helps to prevent U.S. courts from getting involved where the foreign tribunal is capable of ordering production of the requested discovery if it deems it appropriate. The second factor, *i.e.*, "the nature of the foreign tribunal, the character of the proceedings underway abroad, and the receptivity of the foreign government or the court or agency abroad to U.S. federal-court judicial assistance," similarly ensures that U.S. courts are truly assisting—not interfering—with the foreign proceedings.[68] The third factor—whether the request "conceals an attempt to circumvent foreign proof-gathering restrictions or other policies of a foreign country or the United States"—likewise encourages respect for comity and guards against abuse of Section 1782 applications. The final factor–whether the request is "unduly intrusive or burdensome" on the requested party—ensures that discovery is guided by considerations of burden and proportionality.[69]

65 *Intel Corp. v. Advanced Micro Devices, Inc.*, 542 U.S. 241, 258 (2004).

66 *Id.* at 259.

67 In simple terms, depositions are proceedings conducted outside the court but subject to the court's supervision, in which a witness is asked questions and provides sworn answers that are transcribed by a court reporter.

68 *Id.* at 265.

69 *Id.*

## 4 *Intel's* Impact on U.S. Arbitration Law and Practice

Section 1782 applications proliferated after the *Intel* decision, with the number of requests related to civil proceedings increasing more than fourfold between 2005 and 2017.[70] Courts liberally granted requests, allowing nearly 92% of Section 1782 applications submitted between 2005 and 2017.[71]

*Intel* left open the question whether the phrase "foreign or international tribunal" extended to international arbitral tribunals. Some lower courts, relying on *Intel*, concluded that Section 1782 extended to requests for discovery in aid of foreign-seated commercial arbitrations[72] and investment arbitrations.[73] The availability of Section 1782 discovery has had tangible impact on arbitrations by revealing evidence that would otherwise never have been disclosed, with direct and significant consequences for litigants. A prominent example involves the disputes between Ecuador and Chevron Corporation in which Chevron successfully used Section 1782 to obtain a treasure trove of video footage that allowed Chevron to expose the plaintiffs' fraud.[74]

In the wake of the Chevron-Ecuador saga, commentators and courts expressed concerns about Section 1782's potential to produce costly satellite litigations that undercut the benefits of international arbitration.[75] As one court stated, "empowering parties in international arbitrations to seek ancillary discovery through federal courts could destroy arbitration's principal advantage as 'a speedy, economical, and effective means of dispute resolution' if the parties 'succumb to fighting over burdensome discovery requests far from the place of arbitration.'"[76] Courts also cautioned against allowing Section 1782 to

70 Yanbai Andrea Wang, *Exporting American Discovery*, 87 U. CHI. L. REV. 2089, 2111 (2020).

71 *Id.* at 2121.

72 *See, e.g., Servotronics, Inc. v. Boeing Co.*, 954 F.3d 209 (4th Cir. 2020); *Abdul Latif Jameel Transp. Co. Ltd v. FedEx Corp.*, 939 F.3d 710 (6th Cir. 2019).

73 *See, e.g., In re Application of Chevron Corp. for An Order Pursuant to 28 U.S.C. §1782 to Conduct Discovery for Use in Foreign Proceedings: Uhl, Baron, Rana & Assocs., Inc.*, 633 F.3d 153, 161 (3d Cir. 2011) (finding that a tribunal constituted under bilateral investment treaty ("BIT") was an international tribunal within the meaning of Section 1782); *Pakistan v. Arnold & Porter Kaye Scholer LLP*, No. 18–103 (RMC), 2019 WL 1559433, at *7 (Apr. 10, 2019 D.D.C.) (same).

74 *See* Roger Parloff, *Evidence of fraud mounts in Ecuadorian suit against Chevron*, CNN Money (Sept. 13, 2010), available at https://money.cnn.com/2010/09/13/news/international/chevron_ecuador_litigation.fortune/ (last visited Aug. 30, 2023).

75 *See, e.g*, GARY BORN, INTERNATIONAL COMMERCIAL ARBITRATION (THIRD EDITION) (2022), § 16.03(A)(4)(b).

76 *El Paso Corp. v. La Comisión Ejecutiva Hidroeléctrica del Rio Lempa*, 341 F. App'x 31, 34 (5th Cir. 2009) (internal citations omitted).

be used to circumvent the decisions of the arbitral tribunal related to the production of evidence.[77] Many lower courts that granted Section 1782 requests for use in international arbitration did so only upon evidence the tribunal welcomed (or at least did not reject) judicial assistance, which is among the *Intel* factors.[78] Numerous courts denied the Section 1782 application where there was evidence that the tribunal did not support the application.[79]

More than a decade after *Intel*, a circuit split emerged on the question whether the statute extended to private international commercial arbitration, with the Second and Seventh Circuits holding that Section 1782 did not extend to private international arbitration,[80] and the Fourth and Sixth Circuits holding that it did.[81] The Supreme Court would eventually address the Circuit split in its 2022 decision in *ZF Auto. U.S., Inc. v. Luxshare, Ltd.*, where it determined that only a "governmental or intergovernmental adjudicative body" qualifies as a "foreign or international tribunal" under Section 1782, thus closing the door to Section 1782 discovery for use in private international arbitration while arguably leaving open its use for investor-state arbitrations.[82]

## 5 Conclusion

The *Intel* decision initiated an era in which parties involved in a range of proceedings outside the U.S. had the option to access evidence in the U.S. that would not otherwise have been available to them. While the *Intel* decision did not directly relate to international arbitration, the Supreme Court's finding that "foreign or international tribunal" included quasi-judicial bodies established the foundation for decisions that this phrase encompassed foreign-seated private commercial arbitral tribunals as well as investor-state tribunals. Courts

77 *See, e.g., In re Application of Caratube Int'l Oil Co.,* LLP, 730 F. Supp. 2d 101, 106–07 (D.D.C. 2010).

78 *See, e.g., In re* CMPC *Celulose Riograndense Ltda*, No. 19-MC-00005 WES, 2019 WL 2995950, at *3 (D.R.I. July 9, 2019); *In re MoneyOnMobile, Inc.*, No.19-mc-80128-VKD, 2019 WL 2515612, at *3 (N.D. Cal. June 18, 2019).

79 *See, e.g., Interglobe Enters. Pvt Ltd v. Gangwal*, No. 19-24257-MC-Gayles/Otazo-Reyes, at 4 (S.D. Fla. Apr. 30, 2020).

80 *See In re Guo*, 965 F.3d 96, 108 (2d Cir. 2020); *Servotronics, Inc. v. Rolls-Royce* PLC, 975 F.3d 689, 696 (7th Cir. 2020). The Fifth Circuit also had held prior to the *Intel* decision that 1782 did not apply to private arbitration. *See Kazakhstan v. Biedermann Int'l*, 168 F.3d 880, 883 (5th Cir. 1999).

81 *Servotronics, Inc. v. Boeing Co.*, 954 F.3d 209, 213 (4th Cir. 2020); *Abdul Latif Jameel Transp. Co. Ltd v. FedEx Corp.*, 939 F.3d 710, 723 (6th Cir. 2019).

82 *ZF Auto. U.S., Inc. v. Luxshare, Ltd.*, 142 S. Ct. 2078, 2089 (2022).

have generally faithfully applied the *Intel* factors, which commentators have praised as establishing a solid foundation to decide 1782 applications in a way that supports that arbitral process without undue cost, delay, or interference.[83]

---

83 *See, e.g,* GARY BORN, INTERNATIONAL COMMERCIAL ARBITRATION (THIRD EDITION) (2022), § 16.03(A)(4)(b)(iii).

CHAPTER 17

# *Buckeye Check Cashing, Inc., v. Cardegna* (2006)

*Lea Haber Kuck*

## 1 Introduction

In *Buckeye Check Cashing, Inc., v. Cardegna*,[1] the Supreme Court considered the issue of whether, where a contract containing an arbitration clause is alleged to be illegal and void as a matter of state law, the illegality issue should be considered in the first instance by the state court or by the arbitrator. It held that the rule of severability requires a court to send such a case to arbitration for the arbitrator to decide the issue of the contract's validity.[2]

The severability rule, recognized by the Supreme Court 40 years earlier in *Prima Paint Corp. v. Flood & Conklin Manufacturing Co.*,[3] created the legal fiction that an arbitration provision is "severable" or "separable" from the rest of the contract.[4] Applying this principle in *Buckeye*, the Court held that where a contract contains an arbitration clause, any challenge to the validity of the contract as a whole (sometimes referred to as the "container contract"), rather than to the arbitration clause specifically, must be decided in the first instance by the arbitrator rather than the court.[5] As the Court explained in *Buckeye*:

> It is true … that the *Prima Paint* rule permits a court to enforce an arbitration agreement in a contract that the arbitrator later finds to be void. But it is equally true that [the opposite] approach permits a court to deny effect to an arbitration provision in a contract that the court later

1 546 U.S. 440 (2006).

2 *Id.* at 449.

3 388 U.S. 395 (1967).

4 In this context, the terms "separability" and "severability" are generally used interchangeably. The Supreme Court explained in *Prima Paint* that, at that time, some courts considered that arbitration agreements, as a matter of federal law, were "separable" from the contracts in which they were embedded; other courts viewed the issue as one of "severability" under state law and held that "where a State regards such a clause as inseparable," a challenge to the contract as a whole was to be decided by the court. 388 U.S. at 402–03. In *Prima Paint* and *Buckeye*, the former view prevailed, although the Court used the term "severability." In the context of international arbitration, the term "separability" is generally used.

5 546 U.S. at 449.

 | DOI:10.1163/9789004715820_018

> finds to be perfectly enforceable. *Prima Paint* resolved this conundrum – and resolved it in favor of the separate enforceability of arbitration provisions.[6]

In addition, the Court in *Buckeye* not only delineated the division of authority between the court and the arbitrator by applying the severability rule, but it also made clear the relationship between state and federal law. It held, consistent with its decision in *Southland Corp. v. Keating*,[7] that the severability rule, grounded in the Federal Arbitration Act ("FAA"), applies as a matter of substantive federal law in actions pending in state court and is not merely a federal procedural rule.[8]

## 2 The Case

### 2.1 *Background of the Case*

John Cardegna and Donna Rueter ("Plaintiffs") brought a putative class action in Florida state court alleging that Buckeye Check Cashing, Inc. ("Buckeye") made usurious loans disguised as check cashing transactions in violation of various Florida laws.[9] Plaintiffs had entered into various transactions with Buckeye where they "received cash in exchange for a personal check in the amount of the cash plus a finance charge."[10] They alleged that the agreement pursuant to which these transactions were made was void as a matter of illegality and public policy.[11]

The arbitration clause in the agreement they entered into for each transaction provided:

> Any claim, dispute or controversy ... arising from or relating to this Agreement ... or the validity, enforceability, or scope of this Arbitration Provision or the entire Agreement ... shall be resolved, upon the election of you or us ... by binding arbitration pursuant to this Arbitration Provision. ... This arbitration Agreement is made pursuant to a transaction

---

6 *Id.* at 448–49.
7 465 U.S. 1 (1984).
8 546 U.S. at 447.
9 *Id.* at 442.
10 *Id.*
11 *Id.*

involving interstate commerce, and shall be governed by the Federal Arbitration Act.[12]

Although the parties did not dispute that they had agreed to arbitrate disputes between them, or that the dispute was within the scope of the arbitration agreement, Plaintiffs asserted that the entire agreement containing the arbitration clause was void as a matter of public policy.[13]

Buckeye first removed the case to federal court on diversity grounds and moved to compel arbitration and to stay the proceedings.[14] The federal court remanded the case to state court on the grounds that Buckeye had failed to establish that the amount in controversy exceeded the jurisdictional threshold.[15] The state trial court denied the motion to compel arbitration, but the Florida Fourth District Court of Appeal reversed.[16] The Florida Supreme Court then reversed the Fourth District Court, holding that arbitration could not be compelled under a contract that could be void under Florida law, and that the issue of the legality of the contract was for determination by the Florida courts.[17]

The Florida Supreme Court acknowledged that in *Prima Paint*, the Court had held that the FAA "required a federal court to order arbitration to proceed if it is determined that the making of the arbitration agreement itself or failure to comply with the arbitration agreement was not in issue."[18] Nevertheless, it ruled that *Prima Paint* should not be "extended" to the facts of the *Buckeye* case.[19]

The Florida Supreme Court's decision rested on its distinction between "void" contracts and "voidable" contracts.[20] *Prima Paint* involved a contract that was allegedly voidable on the grounds fraud in the inducement, not a contract alleged to have been void from the inception as against state law public policy. The Florida Supreme Court held "that Florida public policy and contract law prohibit breathing life into a potentially illegal contract by enforcing the included arbitration clause of a void contact."[21] It concluded "[w]e do not

12 *Id.* at 442–43.
13 *Id.* at 443.
14 *See* Pet. Br. 7.
15 *Id.*
16 *See Buckeye Check Cashing, Inc. v. Cardegna*, 824 So.2d 228 (Fla. 4th DCA 2022).
17 *Cardegna v. Buckeye Check Cashing, Inc.*, 894 So. 2d 860 (Fla. 2005).
18 894 So.2d at 863 (citing *Prima Paint*, 388 U.S. at 402).
19 *Id.*
20 *Id.*
21 *Id.* at 864.

believe federal arbitration law was ever intended to be used as a means of overruling state substantive law on the legality of contracts."[22]

The United States Supreme Court granted Buckeye's petition for certiorari on the question of:

> Whether the Florida Supreme Court erred by holding, consistent with the Alabama Supreme Court but in direct conflict with six federal courts of appeals, that the Federal Arbitration Act allows a party to avoid arbitration by claiming that the underlying contract containing an arbitration clause (but not the arbitration clause itself) is void for illegality.[23]

### 2.2 *Issue and the Parties' Allegations*

In its opening brief, Buckeye asserted that the Florida Supreme Court decision should be reversed on the grounds that it was contrary to *Prima Paint*. Buckeye argued that whether the contract was void or voidable under state law was irrelevant because, under *Prima Paint*, the severability issue was a matter of federal law governed by the FAA and a party could not avoid arbitration simply by challenging the underlying contract as illegal.[24] Because Plaintiffs' challenge related to the contract as a whole and was not specific to the arbitration provision, and the parties did not dispute that they had agreed to arbitrate, Buckeye asserted that the question of illegality was for determination by the arbitrators.[25]

Buckeye stressed that any "preemption" issue was limited to state law rules concerning severability; the arbitrator would ultimately apply state law to decide the challenge and the arbitrator's decision would be reviewable by a court, albeit on limited grounds.[26] It noted that federal law favoring arbitration recognized that an arbitrator was just as competent decide the legal issue as a judge.[27]

Buckeye concluded by arguing that, as a practical matter, affirming the approach of the Florida Supreme Court would "effectively emasculate arbitration agreements by allowing plaintiffs to avoid such agreements at will by challenging the underlying contract as illegal on any ground."[28]

---

22 *Id.* at 864–65.
23 *See Buckeye Check Cashing v. Cardenga*, No. 04–1264 (June 20, 2005).
24 Pet. Br. 10–16.
25 *Id.* at 9–10.
26 *Id.* at 17–19.
27 *Id.* at 17–18.
28 *Id.* at 20.

In response, Plaintiffs argued that *Prima Paint* did not govern the case because the case was filed in state court and involved an agreement that was allegedly void ab initio as a matter of state public policy.[29]

Plaintiffs framed the issue as a matter of federal preemption of state law.[30] They asserted that Buckeye's position would require the Florida state courts to enforce arbitration clauses in agreements before, and without determining, whether these agreements were criminal and void under state law. If adopted, they argued, it would "essentially … require[] state courts to recognize an exception to the normal principles of contract law governing illegal agreements,"[31] creating a "rule of law that makes arbitration clauses more enforceable than all other types of contracts."[32] They further argued that Buckeye's position would impose a new federal rule governing procedure in state courts, *i.e.,* that a state court must send the dispute to arbitration before deciding threshold issue of whether a contract exists.[33]

Plaintiffs also advanced a statutory interpretation of the FAA in support of their position that *Prima Paint* did not apply. They noted that *Prima Paint* involved a case in federal court on diversity grounds decided under FAA §§ 3 and 4.[34] They asserted that the severability rule was grounded in FAA § 4 and directs federal district courts to compel arbitration where "the making of the agreement for arbitration … is not in issue."[35] Plaintiffs thus asserted that the severability rule was not a matter of federal substantive law, but rather a matter of federal procedure that only applies in federal court.[36] They argued that the result sought by Buckeye would represent an extension of *Prima Paint* requiring state courts to enforce contracts potentially void under state law.[37]

Plaintiffs focused on the language of FAA § 2,[38] which they contended was the only FAA provision held by the Court to have any preemptive effect on the

29 Respondents' Br. 2.
30 *Id.* at 6–7, 9–13.
31 *Id.* at 9.
32 *Id.* at 42.
33 *Id.* at 11.
34 *Id.* at 13–19.
35 *Id.* at 14–15 (quoting *Prima Paint*, 388 U.S. at 403).
36 *Id.* at 16–18.
37 *Id.* at 7, 18.
38 At the time, FAA §2 provided:

> A written provision in … a contract evidencing a transaction involving commerce to settle by arbitration a controversy thereafter arising out of such contract or transaction, or the refusal to perform the whole or any part thereof, or an agreement in writing to submit to arbitration an existing controversy arising out of such a contract, transaction,

states.[39] They asserted that FAA § 2 does not apply until it is shown that the arbitration provision resides "in" a "contract" involving commerce; therefore, in order to determine if FAA applies, the state court would need first to determine the existence of a contract in which the arbitration agreement could sit.[40]

Buckeye replied that Plaintiffs were effectively asking the Court to overrule both *Prima Paint* and *Southland*, which held that federal substantive law governing arbitrability applies in state courts where matters of commerce are implicated.[41] It contended that Plaintiffs' arguments were in fact "essentially indistinguishable from Justice Black's dissent in *Prima Paint*"[42] and that Plaintiffs' complaints were more properly addressed to Congress, rather than the Court.[43]

Buckeye further asserted that Plaintiffs had waived the argument that *Prima Paint* does not apply in state court by failing to raise it below,[44] but in all events, argued that under *Southland*, *Prima Paint* applied as a matter of substantive federal law; *Prima Paint* did not create a rule of federal procedure.[45] It noted that in *Southland*, the Court examined FAA § 2 and concluded that because it includes the commerce requirement, Congress was creating substantive federal law under the Commerce Clause that applied in both state and federal courts.[46]

Buckeye also argued that Plaintiffs' interpretation would create a system where one law applied to an arbitration agreement considered by a federal court in a diversity case, while a different law could apply to the same case if the case proceeded in state court, thereby encouraging forum shopping.[47]

On the statutory interpretation issue, Buckeye argued that FAA §§ 2 and 4 must be read together.[48] It asserted that the language in FAA § 2 referring to a "ground ... for the revocation of any contract" was limited to grounds specific or related to the arbitration agreement itself, not the container contract.[49]

---

or refusal, shall be valid, irrevocable, and enforceable, save upon such grounds as exist at law or in equity for the revocation of any contract.

9 U.S.C. § 2. In 2022, Congress amended the statute to add the words "or as otherwise provided in Chapter 4" to the end of the provision.

39 *Id.* at 17, 19–27.

40 *Id.* at 21–25.

41 Petitioner Reply Br. 1, 4–10.

42 *Id.* at 12.

43 *Id.* at 2.

44 *Id.* at 3–4.

45 *Id.* at 4–8.

46 *Id.* at 5.

47 *Id.* at 7–8.

48 *Id.* at 6.

49 *Id.* at 6–7, 15.

A total of eleven amicus briefs were also submitted to court by amici ranging from business groups and financial services associations to consumer rights organizations, as well as by the State of Florida.

### 2.3 *The Court's Opinion*

Justice Scalia authored the Court's 7–1 opinion reversing the Florida Supreme Court. By the time of the decision, Justice O'Connor, who had dissented in *Southland*, had left the Court and her successor, Justice Alito, took no part in the decision.

The Court began its analysis by quoting FAA § 2 which it stated was passed by Congress "[t]o overcome judicial resistance to arbitration" and "embodies the national policy favoring arbitration and places arbitration agreements on equal footing with all other contracts."[50] It then reasoned that challenges to the validity of arbitration agreements can be divided into two types, those that specifically challenge the validity of the arbitration agreement itself and those that the challenge the contract as a whole.[51] The Buckeye case involved the second type because "[t]he crux of the complaint is that the contract as a whole (including its arbitration provision) is rendered invalid by the usurious finance charge."[52] In other words, the challenge to the contract went to the merits of the dispute itself which the parties had agreed to arbitrate.

The Court next turned to *Prima Paint* and *Southland*. It held that these cases established three propositions which answered the question before it: (1) "as a matter of substantive federal arbitration law, the arbitration provision is severable from the remainder of the contract;" (2) the issue of the validity of the contract is determined by the arbitrator in the first instance unless the challenge is to the arbitration clause itself as opposed to the contract as a whole; and (3) "this arbitration law applies in state as well as federal counts."[53] The Court concluded that application of these principles required that Plaintiffs' challenge to the contract as a whole must be considered in the first instance by the arbitrator.[54]

The Court rejected the void/voidable distinction relied on by the Florida Supreme Court, holding that there was no basis in *Southland* or *Prima Paint* for such a distinction, and it rejected any application of state law rules concerning the severability of the arbitration clause.[55]

---

50 546 U.S. at 443.
51 *Id.* at 444.
52 *Id.*
53 *Id.* at 445–46.
54 *Id.* at 446.
55 *Id.*

Finally, the Court rejected Plaintiff's argument that *Prima Paint*'s rule of severability did not apply in state court.[56] It held that although *Prima Paint* focused on FAA § 4, the severability rule in fact arose out of FAA § 2 which applies to the states.[57] It ruled that the idea that severability was a procedural rule that only applied to the federal courts was contrary to *Southland*. It confirmed that the FAA fashioned substantive rules under the Commerce Clause, noting that "*Southland* itself refused to 'believe Congress intended to limit the Arbitration Act to disputes only subject to *federal*-court jurisdiction.'"[58] It also rejected the argument that FAA § 2 was not implicated until a court made the preliminary ruling as to whether the container contract was valid.[59]

It concluded: "We reaffirm today that, regardless of whether the challenge is brought in federal or state court, a challenge to the validity of the contract as a whole, and not specifically to the arbitration clause, must go the arbitrator."[60]

Justice Thomas issued a short dissent in which he reiterated his position, expressed in several prior cases, that the FAA does not apply to proceedings in state courts and therefore could not displace state law prohibiting enforcement of an arbitration clause contained in a contract unenforceable under state law.[61]

### 2.4 *Key Takeaways*

In *Buckeye*, the Court affirmed the severability rule as a principle of federal substantive law, not federal procedural law, that applies in any case involving commerce, regardless of whether the case was filed in state or federal court. Accordingly, unless a challenge to the contract relates specifically to the agreement to arbitrate, a challenge to the validity of the contract at issue must be decided by the arbitrator in the first instance.

## 3 Critical Analysis of the Opinion and How It Impacted the U.S. Arbitration Law and Practice

While the *Buckeye* decision was a rather straightforward application of *Prima Paint* and *Southland*, it represented a victory for uniformity and consistency

56 *Id.* at 447.

57 *Id.*

58 *Id.* (quoting *Southland*, 465 U.S. at 15) (emphasis in original).

59 *Id.* at 447–48.

60 *Id.* at 449.

61 *Id.*

in arbitration practice, both across state and federal courts and among state courts. As between the state and federal courts, a different result would have meant that the federal courts would send challenges to the container contract to the arbitrator, while at the same time, the state courts might, depending on their own law on severability, decide the very same challenges themselves before sending the case to arbitration.

The void/voidable distinction relied on by the Florida Supreme Court could have also resulted in inconsistencies among the states. As Justice Ginsberg pointed out at oral argument, the classification of which contracts are void and which are voidable differs across the states.[62] Thus the rule advanced the Florida Supreme Court would mean that a particular challenge to a contract might be decided in some states by the court and in other states by the arbitrator.

*Buckeye* also advanced the Congressional purpose in enacting the FAA that arbitration procedure be speedy and efficient and not subject to delay and obstruction in the courts. In this regard, some of the justices were concerned that a contrary rule would allow parties to circumvent arbitration agreements by asserting that the contract was void on state law public policy grounds, an area that can be quite murky.[63] In fact, this may have been exactly what Plaintiffs in *Buckeye* were attempting to do.

Although the issue was not mentioned in the opinion or in the briefing, the origins of the *Buckeye* case can likely be traced to attempts to essentially extinguish consumer class actions through the use of arbitration clauses in consumer contracts. The struggle to address the intersection of class actions and arbitration, and the differing considerations involved in consumer disputes and commercial business disputes, has generated several Supreme Court cases over the last 20 years and has had a significant impact on the development of U.S. arbitration law more generally.[64]

Justice Breyer recognized this tension at oral argument, expressing concern that the principles being decided would apply not only to consumer contracts, where he indicated he felt "there were a lot of good arguments,"[65] but also to

---

62 Oral Argument ("OA") Tr. 13:8–13, 32:11–19.

63 *Id.* at 33–36, 39–40.

64 After *Buckeye*, the Supreme Court subsequently considered the intersection between arbitration and class actions in a string of cases that are addressed in other chapters. *See, e.g., American Express Co. v. Italian Colors Restaurant*, 570 U.S. 228 (2013); *Oxford Health Plans LLC v. Sutter*, 569 U.S. 564 (2013); *AT&T Mobility LLC v. Concepcion*, 563 U.S. 333 (2011); *Stolt-Nielson S.A. v. Animalfeeds Int'l Corp.*, 559 U.S. 662 (2010).

65 OA Tr. 29:14–16.

business contracts, where he stated that the "whole business community seems to have developed an arbitration system throughout the world" that relied on the severability rule. He expressed concern that deciding for Plaintiffs would "throw a large section of those contracts back into the laws of the 50 States and arbitration will be seriously injured as the commercial community has come to rely on it."[66]

Plaintiffs' counsel candidly admitted at oral argument what was at stake. When Justice Stevens asked whether, regardless of the Court's decision, the Florida Supreme Court would ultimately decide the question of illegality in the next few months in another case, Plaintiffs' counsel responded:

> I think that the question of whether or not this is illegal will be something that's decided by the Florida Supreme Court, but that question – first of all, if this case is sent back to arbitration, the arbitration clause, of course, is on an individual basis and this case could never be pursued on an individual basis. If it's not done as a class action, it would be the end of the case.[67]

In other words, the case was brought in court notwithstanding the arbitration clause because it could be filed in court as a class action; under the Plaintiffs' counsel's understanding of the law at that time, it could not have been filed as a class action in arbitration. Apparently, Plaintiffs hoped that they would be able to argue the underlying merits of their case to the state court in the context of arguing that the parties' agreement was void as a matter of public policy, and then if they prevailed, they could recover on a classwide basis. Based on counsel's statement, they had apparently determined that it would not be economically feasible for each class member to arbitrate their individual claims.

At the same time, it is important to recognize the parameters of the *Buckeye* decision. First, the criticism that *Buckeye* was a blow to federalism may be overstated. The Court did not attempt to impose a federal standard for determining which contracts are, and which are not, invalid as a matter of public policy. Rather, it determined *who* decides the challenge to the contract in the first instance. States still determine their public policy and rules of contract, including what contracts are void or voidable, and that state law will be brought before the arbitrators for consideration. The arbitrator's decision will

---

66 *Id.* at 29:17–25.

67 *Id.* at 51:16–23.

ultimately be subject to review by the courts, albeit on the very limited grounds set forth in the FAA, including that the arbitrators exceeded their authority or manifestly disregarded for the law.[68]

Second, while the severability rule addresses the issue of who should decide whether the container contract is valid and directs that issue to the arbitrator, issues dealing with the *formation* of the container contract, including the arbitration agreement contained therein, have been held to be issues for the courts.[69]

Plaintiffs in *Buckeye* unsuccessfully attempted to shoehorn their case into the formation category by arguing that a contract to commit an illegal act could never have been "formed" under Florida law.[70] However, their illegality argument related solely to the container contract and did not challenge the legality of the arbitration agreement. Because the parties did not dispute that they had agreed to arbitrate their disputes, the issue was plainly one of validity rather than formation. Indeed, the Supreme Court made a point of noting in dictum:

> The issue of the contract's validity is different from the issue whether any agreement between the alleged obligor and oblige was ever concluded. Our opinion today addresses only the former, and does not speak to the issue decided in the cases cited by [Plaintiffs] (and the Florida Supreme Court), which hold that it is for the courts to decide whether the alleged obligor ever signed the contract, … whether the signor lacked authority to commit the alleged principle …, and whether the signor lacked the mental capacity to assent.[71]

---

68 FAA § 10 provides that an arbitration award issued in the United States can be vacated on four grounds including fraud in procuring the award; evident partiality or corruption of an arbitrator; arbitrator procedural misconduct prejudicing the rights of a party; and arbitrators exceeding their powers. *See* 9 U.S.C. § 10. Manifest disregard of the law is not an enumerated ground, but rather is a phrase used by the Supreme Court in the vacatur context. In *Stolt-Nielsen*, the Court declined to resolve the issue of whether manifest disregard is an independent ground for review thath may no longer be valid under current Supreme Court jurisprudence or whether it serves as a "judicial gloss" on the enumerated grounds for vacatur in § 10 grounds. *See* 559 U.S. 662, n.3. In all events, challenges for manifest disregard of the law are rarely successful.

69 *See First Options of Chicago, Inc. v. Kaplan*, 514 U.S. 938 (1995).

70 *See* Respondents' Br. 6, 8, 18, 22, 24–27.

71 546 U.S. 440, n.1 (citations omitted).

The Supreme Court addressed the formation issue in the earlier case of *First Options of Chicago, Inc. v. Kaplan*,[72] which was not cited in *Buckeye* nor widely discussed in the papers or at argument. *First Options* did not mention the severability rule, but it too involved the allocation of authority between courts and arbitral tribunals over the enforceability of agreements to arbitrate. In *First Options*, the Court determined that issues concerning whether an agreement to arbitrate was validly formed fall within the category of "gateway issues," which are issues that "so seriously implicate the consent of the parties to arbitrate their disputes that a party contesting the enforceability of an arbitration agreement on those grounds is entitled to a judicial determination of the matter."[73] The Court in *First Options* thus held that issues of assent and authority, two of the formation issues mentioned by the Court in *Buckeye*, were issues for the court to determine.[74]

While the issues in *Buckeye* and *First Options* rather neatly fall into the categories of validity and formation respectively, other issues are not as clear.[75] For example, lower court decisions following *Prima Paint* have been divided on whether the issue of mental incapacity is a formation issue or a validity issue[76] and the issue of how to characterize duress has also been debated.[77]

Finally, the severability rule considered by the Court in *Buckeye* is distinct from the doctrine of "competence-competence" or "Kompetenz-Kompetenz." The latter doctrine refers to the right of the arbitral tribunal to rule on its own jurisdiction, including challenges to the validity of the arbitration agreement itself. Thus, where the doctrine applies, the arbitral tribunal may not

72 514 U.S. 938 (1995).

73 George A. Bermann, *After* First Options*: Delegation Run Amok*, 32 Am. Rev. Intern'l Arb. 15, 15 (2021). For a discussion of the relationship between *Buckeye* and *First Options*, *see* Stephen J. Ware, *Arbitration Law's Separability Doctrine After* Buckeye Check Cashing, Inc. v. Cardegna, 8 Nevada L.J. 107 (2007).

74 514 U.S. at 942–47.

75 For a discussion of the difficulties that arise from this distinction, *see* George A. Bermann, *The "Gateway" Problem in International Commercial Arbitration*, 37 Yale L.J. 1 (2012).

76 The Court's dicta in *Buckeye* suggests that mental capacity is a formation issue, although the lower federal courts had divided on this issue following *Prima Paint*. *See, e.g., Spahr v. Secco*, 330 F.3d 1266 (10th Cir. 2003) (no assent due to mental incapacity); *Primerica Life Ins. Co. v. Brown*, 304 F.3d 469 (5th Cir. 2002) (arbitrator to decide mental capacity defense not specific to arbitration agreement); *Amirmotazedi v. Viacom, Inc.*, 768 F. Supp. 2d 256 (D.D.C. 2011) (following dicta in *Buckeye*); *see also* Bermann, *supra* n.74 at 34–36.

77 *See* Ware, *supra* n.72, at 122; *see also* Bermann supra n.7 (opining that duress should be decided by arbitral tribunal). During the Buckeye oral argument, Chief Justice Roberts appeared to view duress as a formation issue stating that if "you put a gun to a person's head and say, sign this contract, and the person does. It contains an arbitration clause. They don't have to go to arbitration to challenge that." OA Tr. 4:18–21.

only decide issues relating to the validity of the container contract, but also issues concerning the validity of the separate arbitration agreement. Because the challenge in *Buckeye* related solely to the validity of the container contract, rather than the independent validity of the arbitration agreement, the doctrine was not directly implicated, nor does it appear that the parties considered it. Indeed, when Justice Breyer asked Plaintiffs' counsel about the implications of the doctrine at oral argument, counsel replied that he was not familiar with it.[78] However, because the scope of the *Buckeye* arbitration agreement included issues as to "the validity, enforceability, or scope of this Arbitration Provision *or* the entire Agreement,"[79] had there been a challenge to the arbitration agreement itself, it would have been appropriate to also send that issue to the arbitrators for resolution.

## 4 Conclusions

The Court's decision in *Buckeye* affirmed the *Prima Paint* severability rule as a matter of federal substantive law, making clear the division of authority between courts and arbitrators in disputes arising under any contracts involving commerce, regardless of whether the case was brought in state or federal court. By doing so, the Court prevented litigants from impeding the arbitration process by challenging the parties' contract as voidable or void as a matter of state public policy.

---

78 OA Tr. 40:6–12.

79 546 U.S. at 442 (emphasis added).

CHAPTER 18

# *Hall Street Associates,* LLC *v. Mattel, Inc.* (2008): The Scope and Limits of Party Autonomy: Judicial Review of Arbitral Awards

*Peter B. Rutledge*

The Federal Arbitration Act ("FAA" or the "Act"), enacted by Congress in 1925, governs the vacatur of arbitral awards in federal courts. Section 10 of the FAA lists four grounds for vacating an award:

> (1) where the award was procured by corruption, fraud, or undue means; (2) where there was evident partiality or corruption in the arbitrators, or either of them; (3) where the arbitrators were guilty of misconduct in refusing to postpone the hearing, upon sufficient cause shown, or in refusing to hear evidence pertinent and material to the controversy; or of any other misbehavior by which the rights of any party have been prejudiced; or (4) where the arbitrators exceeded their powers, or so imperfectly executed them that a mutual, final, and definite award upon the subject matter submitted was not made.[1]

The case of *Hall Street Associates,* LLC *v. Mattel, Inc.* concerns parties' ability to expand these grounds. *Hall Street* began when Mattel leased property from Hall Street Associates for use as a manufacturing site.[2] The lease provided that the tenant would indemnify the landlord for any costs related to disobeying environmental laws while using the premises.[3] In 2001, Mattel gave notice of intent to terminate the lease, but had not yet indemnified Hall Street for costs associated with high levels of pollutants in the property's well water.[4] Hall Street unsuccessfully sued Mattel, claiming the lease obliged Mattel to indemnify Hall Street for these cleaning costs.[5] Following the suit, the parties

1 9 U.S.C. § 10.
2 Hall St. Assocs., L.L.C. v. Mattel, Inc., 552 U.S. 576, 579 (2008).
3 *Id.*
4 *Id.*
5 *Id.*

 | DOI:10.1163/9789004715820_019

agreed to arbitration to resolve the indemnification claim. The parties wrote an arbitration agreement that said:

> [t]he United States District Court for the District of Oregon may enter judgment upon any award, either by confirming the award or by vacating, modifying or correcting the award. The Court shall vacate, modify or correct any award: (i) where the arbitrator's findings of facts are not supported by substantial evidence, or (ii) where the arbitrator's conclusions of law are erroneous.[6]

The arbitrator found for Mattel, holding that no indemnification was due, as the lease obligation did not require compliance with the Oregon Drinking Water Quality Act.[7] Hall Street then filed a motion to vacate or modify the award on the grounds that the arbitrator made a legal error.[8] The district court agreed and vacated the award, remanding the issue to the arbitrator.[9] In vacating the award, the district court cited *LaPine Technology Corp. v. Kyocera Corp.*[10] and invoked the standard of review chosen by the parties in the arbitration agreement: review for legal error.[11]

On remand, the arbitrator then found in favor of Hall Street.[12] Following this, both Hall Street and Mattel sought modification of the award, yet the district court applied the parties' standard of review for legal error, corrected the arbitrator's calculation of interest, and upheld the award in favor of Hall Street.[13] The individual parties then appealed to the Court of Appeals for the Ninth Circuit.[14]

Mattel argued that because the Ninth Circuit overruled its position in *LaPine* in *Kyocera Corp. v. Prudential-Bach Trade Servs. Inc.*, the provision calling for judicial review of legal error in the parties' arbitration agreement was actually unenforceable.[15]

---

6 *Id.*

7 *Id.* at 580.

8 *Hall St.*, 552 U.S. 576 at 580.

9 *Id.*

10 *Id.* (citing LaPine Tech. Corp. v. Kyocera Corp., 130 F.3d 884, 889 (9th Cir. 1997) (holding that the FAA authorizes parties to agree to a heightened judicial review of arbitration awards)).

11 *Id.* at 580.

12 *Id.*

13 *Id.*

14 *Hall St.*, 552 U.S. 576 at 580.

15 *Id.*

The Ninth Circuit agreed with Mattel's argument, reversed in favor of Mattel and remanded the case to the district court ordering confirmation of the original arbitration award, now subject only to vacatur under section 10 of the FAA, or modification or correction under the grounds of section 11.[16] The district court on remand again held for Hall Street, the Ninth Circuit then reversed yet again, and ultimately, the Supreme Court granted certiorari.[17]

The issue, at the heart of the matter, was whether statutory grounds for prompt vacatur and modification of arbitration awards can be supplemented by contract. The Supreme Court ultimately reasoned that they may not, because the statutory grounds for prompt vacatur and modification by judicial review are exclusive.[18]

Justice Souter, writing for the majority, began the analysis by assessing Hall Street's two main arguments in favor of expandable judicial review.[19]

First, Hall Street argued that the grounds set out in the FAA, for vacating or modifying an award, are not exclusive.[20] Hall Street attempted to support this by stating that expandable judicial review authority had been accepted since *Wilko v. Swan*.[21] In *Wilko*, the Court recognized the "manifest disregard" ground of review.[22] Hall Street argued that when the Court recognized the "manifest disregard" standard in *Wilko*, the Court accepted a new ground for vacatur.[23] However, the Court explained that this was not the correct interpretation of *Wilko*, and the position Hall Street is advocating for is at best arguably favored in the Court's discussion. The Court explained that Hall Street missed the mark in believing that "manifest disregard" established a new ground of vacatur – instead, "manifest disregard" more than likely referred to the section 10 grounds collectively, and therefore, it would not include general review for legal errors.[24]

Second, Hall Street argued that the agreement to review for legal error ought to prevail because "arbitration is a creature of contract, and the FAA is 'motivated, first and foremost by a congressional desire to enforce agreements into

16 *Id.* at 581.
17 *Id.*
18 *Id.* at 583.
19 *Id.* at 584.
20 *Hall St.*, 552 U.S. 576 at 584.
21 *Id.*
22 Wilko v. Swan, 346 U.S. 427 (1953).
23 *Hall St.*, 552 U.S. 576 at 584.
24 *Id.* at 585.

which parties ha[ve] entered.'"[25] However, the Court said this argument also "comes up short."[26]

The Court explained that the text of the FAA "compels a reading of the §§ 10 and 11 categories as *exclusive*."[27] The Court applied the rule of ejusdem generis: "when a statute sets out a series of specific items ending with a general term, that general term is confined to covering subjects comparable to the specifics it follows."[28] Invoking this rule, the Court reasoned that the terms listed in sections 10 and 11 of the Act are limited to departures related to "fraud," and therefore, mistake of law would not count.[29] The Court pointed to the language of section 9, in which the court "must grant" an order confirming the arbitration award "unless the award is vacated, modified, or corrected as prescribed in sections 10 and 11 of this title."[30] The usage of the terms "must" and "unless" signify mandatory direction to the courts. Justice Souter explained, "this does not sound remotely like a provision meant to tell a court what to do *just in case* the parties say nothing else."[31]

While the Court held that sections 10 and 11 provide exclusive regimes for statutory review of arbitration awards, the Court narrowed its holding to arbitration awards under the FAA and left open the doors for two alternative forms of review: judicial review based on state statutory or common law.[32]

Justice Souter suggested in his opinion that state law may provide an alternative avenue for expanded judicial review. In this suggestion, several state courts have indeed ruled that parties can contractually broaden the scope of judicial review of arbitration awards.[33] These states have held that the FAA is not controlling and does not preempt arbitration awards conducted in state court under the state's arbitration act. Texas is one such state that has come to this conclusion.

The Supreme Court of Texas in *Nafta Traders, Inc. v. Quinn* concluded that the Texas Arbitration Act ("TAA") did not preclude parties from agreeing to limit an arbitrator's authority.[34] The court held, "the TAA presents no impediment to an agreement that limits the authority of an arbitrator in deciding a matter and thus allows for judicial review of an arbitration award for reversible

25 *Id.*
26 *Id.* at 586.
27 *Id.* (emphasis added).
28 *Id.*
29 *Hall St.*, 552 U.S. 576 at 586.
30 *Id.* at 587.
31 *Id.* (emphasis added).
32 *Id.* at 590.
33 *See* cases cited *infra* notes 34, 37, and 44.
34 Nafta Traders, Inc. v. Quinn, 339 S.W.3d 84 (Tex. 2011).

error."[35] The court also held that the FAA did not preempt the TAA because the portion of the TAA was not in conflict with the FAA, because the arbitration agreement that the court was enforcing did not defeat the FAA's purposes and objectives.[36]

The Supreme Court of California came to a similar conclusion in *Cable Connection, Inc. v. DIRECTV, Inc.*[37] In *Cable Connection*, the arbitration clause provided that "[t]he arbitrators shall not have the power to commit errors of law or legal reasoning, and the award may be vacated ... for any such error."[38] The court concluded that this provision was enforceable, as the California Arbitration Act ("CAA") provided for vacatur where arbitrators "exceeded their powers," and concluded that legal errors are an excess of arbitral authority.[39] The court referenced the importance of the parties' intent and noted the consistent recognition by the California courts of an exception to the general rule of assigning "broad powers to the arbitrators."[40] The exception arises when "the parties have, in either the contract or an agreed submission to arbitration, explicitly and unambiguously limited those powers. ... 'The powers of an arbitrator derive from, and are limited by, *the agreement* to arbitrate.'"[41] Just as the Texas court in *Nafta Traders* held that the FAA did not preempt the TAA, the court here held the FAA did not preempt the CAA, because the CAA procedures did not conflict "with the FAA policy favoring the enforcement of arbitration agreements."[42] The court, in its holding, noted specifically that *Hall Street* left open the possibility that parties could contract under other avenues, such as state statute.[43]

In *Raymond James Financial Services, Inc. v. Honea*, the Alabama Supreme Court accepted as valid a provision in an arbitration agreement that authorized de novo review of an arbitration award.[44] The court held that even if the grounds for vacating the award fell outside the permissible bases under the FAA, the FAA did not preempt Alabama state law.[45]

35 *Id.* at 97.

36 *Id.* at 99–101 ("The only reasonable reading of the opinions in *Hall Street*, in our view, is that the FAA does not preempt state law that allows parties to agree to a greater review of arbitration awards.").

37 Cable Connection, Inc. v. DIRECTV, Inc., 190 P.3d 586 (Cal. 2008).

38 *Id.* at 589.

39 *Id.* at 600.

40 *Id.*

41 *Id.* (emphasis added).

42 *Id.* at 599.

43 *Cable Connection*, 190 P.3d at 596.

44 Raymond James Fin. Servs., Inc. v. Honea, 55 So. 3d 1161, 1170 (Ala. 2010).

45 *Id.*

While the courts mentioned above allowed expansion of judicial review under their states' arbitration acts, others have aligned their state statutes with the ruling in *Hall Street*.[46] In *Brookfield Country Club, Inc. v. St. James-Brookfield, LLC*, the Georgia Supreme Court concluded that the Court's rationale in *Hall Street* was consistent with the statutory law of Georgia, and therefore would be adopted.[47] The court said because arbitration is a creature of statute, it is the role of the legislature, and not the court, to address any "fundamental changes in the nature of the proceeding."[48]

Likewise, both the Maine Supreme Court and Tennessee Supreme Court adopted the logic followed in *Hall Street* to refuse expanded judicial review. In *Pugh's Lawn Landscape Co. v. Jaycon Development Corp.*, the Tennessee Supreme Court argued that because the Tennessee Uniform Arbitration Act ("TUAA") was substantially similar to the FAA, and to the point it differed, the TUAA was even more stringent, the TUAA could not provide for expanded review.[49] The Maine Supreme Court in *HL 1, LLC, v. Riverwalk, LLC* applied similar reasoning to the court in *Pugh's Lawn*, noting the textual similarities between the Maine Uniform Arbitration Act ("MUAA") and the FAA, to hold that the text of the MUAA only allows for the mechanisms for judicial review explicitly stated in the act.[50]

The other alternative mentioned by Justice Souter, enforcement under common law, has created a circuit split regarding how the "manifest disregard" doctrine has survived as a ground to vacate an arbitration award under the FAA. This split first began in the lower courts shortly after *Hall Street* was decided in March of 2008: that same month, the New York Supreme Court in *Chase Bank USA, N.A. v. Hale* held that because the Supreme Court in *Hall Street* did "nothing to jettison the 'manifest disregard' standard ... [T]his court will view 'manifest disregard of law' as judicial interpretation of the section 10 requirement."[51] Conversely, in May of 2008, the United States District Court for the District of Minnesota expressly stated that courts "can no longer vacate an arbitration award based on judicially-created grounds such as 'manifest disregard of the law.'"[52]

46 *See* cases cited *infra* notes 47, 49, and 50.

47 Brookfield Country Club, Inc. v. St. James-Brookfield, LLC, 696 S.E.2d 663, 666 (Ga. 2010).

48 *Id.*

49 Pugh's Lawn Landscape Co., Inc. v. Jaycon Dev. Corp., 320 S.W.3d 252 (Tenn. 2010).

50 HL 1, LLC v. Riverwalk, LLC, 15 A.3d 725, 736 (Me. 2011).

51 Chase Bank USA, N.A. v. Hale, 859 N.Y.S.2d 342, 349 (N.Y. Sup. Ct. 2008).

52 Prime Therapeutics LLC v. Omnicare, Inc., 555 F. Supp. 2d 993, 999 (D. Minn. 2008).

Since 2008, the Second, Fourth, and Ninth Circuits have all upheld manifest disregard challenges, while the Fifth, Seventh, Eighth, and Eleventh Circuits have held that manifest disregard is no longer a valid ground on which to vacate an arbitration award.[53] The Fifth Circuit, in *Citigroup Global Markets, Inc. v. Bacon*, rejected the doctrine as a ground for vacatur, stating:

> *Hall Street* unequivocally held that the statutory grounds are the exclusive means for vacatur under the FAA. Our case law defines manifest disregard of the law as a nonstatutory ground for vacatur … Thus, to the extent that manifest disregard of the law constitutes a nonstatutory ground for vacatur, it is no longer a basis for vacating awards under the FAA.[54]

By contrast, the Second Circuit recently reaffirmed the vitality of the manifest disregard ground. In *Weiss v. Sallie-Mae*, the court refused to vacate an award on the basis of manifest disregard, while upholding the doctrine itself.[55] The court, referencing the standard, claiming that "awards are vacated on grounds of manifest disregard only in those exceedingly rare instances where some egregious impropriety on the part of the arbitrator is apparent."[56]

While the circuits mentioned above have made express decisions regarding the manifest disregard standard, the remaining circuits have failed to formulate a view.[57] Their silence, or refusal to answer on the matter, has left a door open to the Supreme Court to make an ultimate decision. However, despite the silence, the Supreme Court has refrained from resolving the split.[58] The opportunity seemed to present itself in the case of *Stolt-Neilsen S.A. v. AnimalFeeds International Corp.*

In *Stolt-Nielsen*, the United States Court of Appeals for the Second Circuit had reversed the lower court's decision that an arbitrator acted in manifest

53 For the Second Circuit, *see* Weiss v. Sallie Mae, Inc., 939 F.3d 105, 109 (2d Cir. 2019); for the Fourth Circuit, *see* Dewan v. Walia, 544 F. App'x 240 (4th Cir. 2013); for the Ninth Circuit, *see* Comedy Club, Inc. v. Improv W. Assocs., 533 F.3d 1277 (9th Cir. 2009); for the Seventh Circuit, *see* Affymax, Inc. v. Ortho-McNeil-Janssen Pharms., Inc., 660 F.3d 281 (7th Cir. 2011); for the Eighth Circuit, *see* Med. Shoppe Int'l, Inc. v. Turner Invs., Inc., 614 F.3d 485 (8th Cir. 2010); for the Eleventh Circuit, *see* Frazier v. CitiFinancial Corp., LLC, 604 F.3d 1313 (11th Cir. 2010).

54 Citigroup Glob. Markets, Inc. v. Bacon, 562 F.3d 349, 355 (5th Cir. 2009).

55 Weiss v. Sallie Mae, Inc., 939 F.3d 105, 109 (2d Cir. 2019).

56 *Id.*

57 Stuart M. Boyarsky, *The Uncertain Status of the Manifest Disregard Standard One Decade After Hall Street*, 123 DICK. L. REV. 167, 197–201 (2018).

58 *Id.* at 209–10.

disregard of the law.[59] As a result of reversing the lower court's decision, the Second Circuit expressly validated the manifest disregard standard.[60] When the case went to the Supreme Court in 2010, it seemed like the perfect opportunity for the Court to finally resolve the circuit split and address the validity of the manifest disregard standard. However, the Court did not deem it necessary to decide the validity in order to decide the outcome of the case. Justice Alito wrote in a footnote, "[w]e do not decide whether 'manifest disregard' survives our decision in *Hall Street Associates, L.L.C. v. Mattel, Inc* … as an independent ground for review or as a judicial gloss on the enumerated grounds for vacatur set forth at 9 U.S.C. §10."[61]

In conclusion, *Hall Street* aimed to limit the ability for a party to contractually expand judicial review of arbitration awards. However, the resulting legal landscape undermines *Hall Street*'s holding. Parties have increasingly turned to contract under state law, or have found reprieve in circuits that have validated the "manifest disregard" standard as an additional ground to challenge awards. Despite the numerous avenues parties may navigate to thwart the limitations set forth by *Hall Street,* these paths are fraught with lingering questions and uncertainties as to the validity of the "manifest disregard" standard.

The absence of a definitive Supreme Court ruling on the validity of the "manifest disregard" standard leaves parties with unclear guidance and forum shopping opportunities. The doctrine's availability hinges on geographic happenstance rather than consistent legal principles. Additionally, parties seeking to contract under state law in some states find slightly broader horizons under state arbitration acts. But in states without a clear stance on this issue, the path to expanding judicial review under state law remains uncertain, complicating arbitration enforcement. As such, until the Supreme Court offers a decisive ruling, the arbitration landscape continues to be marked by ambiguity and regional variations.

---

59 Stolt-Nielsen S.A. v. AnimalFeeds Int'l Corp., 548 F.3d 85, 102 (2d Cir. 2008).

60 *Id.* at 101.

61 Stolt-Nielsen S.A. v. AnimalFeeds Int'l Corp., 559 U.S. 662, 672 n.3 (2010).

CHAPTER 19

# *Vaden v. Discover Bank*, 556 U.S. 49 (2009)

*Dana MacGrath*

## 1 Introduction

Section 4 of the Federal Arbitration Act ("FAA") authorizes a United States district court to entertain a petition to compel arbitration of a dispute if the federal court would have jurisdiction, "save for [the arbitration] agreement," over "a suit arising out of the controversy between the parties." 9 U.S.C. § 4. This means that Chapter 1 of the FAA requires an independent basis for subject matter jurisdiction over the parties' dispute to access a federal forum to compel arbitration. *See Hall Street Associates, L.L.C. v. Mattel, Inc.*, 552 U.S. 576, 582 (2008), citing *Moses H. Cone Memorial Hospital v. Mercury Constr. Corp.*, 460 U.S. 1, 25, n. 32 (1983).[1]

Under the well-pleaded complaint rule, a suit "arises under" federal law for 28 U.S.C. § 1331 purposes only when the plaintiff's statement of its own cause of action demonstrates that it is based upon federal law. *Louisville & Nashville R. Co. v. Mottley*, 211 U.S. 149, 152 (1908). Federal jurisdiction cannot be predicated on an actual or anticipated defense or rest upon an actual or anticipated counterclaim. *Holmes Group, Inc. v. Vornado Air Circulation Systems, Inc., Holmes Group*, 535 U.S. 826 (2002).

A complaint filed in court purporting to rely on state law can be recharacterized as one "arising under" federal law if the law governing the complaint is exclusively federal. *Beneficial Nat. Bank v. Anderson*, 539 U.S. 1, 8 (2003). However, a state law-based defense or counterclaim, even if similarly susceptible to recharacterization, does not supply federal district courts with subject matter jurisdiction.

The phrase "save for [the arbitration] agreement" in Section 4 of the FAA has been interpreted to mean that the district court should assume the absence of the arbitration agreement and determine whether it would have jurisdiction over "the controversy between the parties," which is the "underlying dispute" between the parties. *See Moses H. Cone*, 460 U.S. at 25 n.32.

1 In contrast, Chapter 2 of the FAA, applicable to international arbitration agreements, expressly grants U.S. district courts subject matter jurisdiction over disputes arising in those matters.

 | DOI:10.1163/9789004715820_020

The *Vaden* opinion considered two questions concerning a district court's subject matter jurisdiction over a Section 4 petition to compel arbitration, as discussed below.

## 2 The Case

The issue presented in *Vaden* was whether a district court, if asked to compel arbitration pursuant to Section 4 of the FAA, should "look through" the petition to compel arbitration and grant the requested relief if the federal court would have federal question jurisdiction over the underlying controversy in the absence of an arbitration agreement. *Vaden*, 556 U.S. at 53. If so, a secondary issue was whether a district court could exercise jurisdiction over a Section 4 petition to compel arbitration when the complaint is based on state law, but an actual or potential counterclaim is based on federal law. *Id.* at 53.

As discussed below, in *Vaden*, all nine justices of the Supreme Court agreed that that a federal court may "look through" a Section 4 petition and order arbitration if, "save for [the arbitration] agreement," the court would have jurisdiction over "the [substantive] controversy between the parties." 9 U.S.C. § 4. Regarding the second issue, the Supreme Court majority opinion applied the well-pleaded complaint rule and corollary rule that federal jurisdiction cannot be invoked on the basis of a defense or counterclaim. In other words, the basis for federal question jurisdiction for a Section 4 petition to compel arbitration must derive from the complaint itself, not any defense or counterclaim. Discover argued Section 4 permitted a petition to compel arbitration the petitioner's federal defenses and counterclaim despite the fact that the only pleading filed prior to the petition to compel arbitration was the petitioner's state court complaint asserting only state law claims.

### 2.1 *Background of the Case*

In *Vaden*, Discover Bank's servicing affiliate ("Discover") filed a complaint in Maryland state court presenting a claim arising solely under state law. Discover sought to recover past-due charges from Betty Vaden ("Vaden"), one of its credit cardholders. *Vaden*, 556 U.S. at 54. Vaden filed an answer and counterclaim, alleging that Discover's finance charges, interest, and late fees violated Maryland state law. *Id.*

Discover then invoked an arbitration clause in its cardholder agreement with Vaden by filing a Section 4 petition in the United States District Court for the District of Maryland to compel arbitration of Vaden's counterclaims. *Id.* (citing 9 U.S.C. § 4). Discover maintained that the district court had subject-matter jurisdiction over its petition because Vaden's state-law counterclaims were completely preempted by federal banking law, specifically Section 27(a) of the Federal Deposit Insurance Act (FDIA), 12 U.S.C. § 1831(a). *Id.* at 55.[2] Discover asserted that Vaden's counterclaim arose "under the exclusive governance of the FDIA" and therefore the district court had "authority to entertain the § 4 petition pursuant to 28 U.S.C. § 1331, which gives federal courts jurisdiction over cases 'arising under' federal law." *Id.* The district court agreed and compelled arbitration. *Id.* The district court also stayed Vaden's prosecution of her counterclaims in state court pending the outcome of the arbitration. *Id.*

Vaden appealed to the United States Court of Appeals for the Fourth Circuit. On Vaden's initial appeal, the Fourth Circuit examined whether the district court had federal question jurisdiction over Discover's Section 4 petition to compel arbitration. *Id.* The Fourth Circuit instructed that to make that determination, the district court should "look through" the Section 4 petition to the substantive controversy between the parties. *Id.* The Fourth Circuit then remanded the case for an express determination as to whether the controversy presented a properly invoked federal question. *Id.* On remand to the district court, Vaden conceded that the FDIA completely preempted any state claims against a federally insured bank. *Id.* Given this concession, the district court held that it had federal question jurisdiction over Discover's Section 4 petition and again ordered arbitration. *Id.* Vaden appealed again to the Fourth Circuit, which affirmed, in a split decision, the lower court decision. The Fourth Circuit majority performed its own analysis of FDIA Section 27(a) and concluded that the provision "completely preempted state law and therefore governed Vaden's counterclaims." *Id.* at 56. The Fourth Circuit majority found that the complete preemption doctrine was paramount, overriding the well-pleaded complaint rule. *Id.* Therefore, the Fourth Circuit majority concluded that a federal court has jurisdiction over a Section 4 petition if essentially any aspect of the parties' underlying dispute presents a federal question. *Id.*

The dissenting judge on the Fourth Circuit panel considered the well-pleaded complaint rule dispositive. Because the FDIA formed no part of Discover's complaint but arose only in response to Vaden's answer and counterclaims, there was no properly presented federal question in the underlying state-law based complaint. *Id.* at 56–57.

The Supreme Court granted certiorari to resolve the conflict among the federal circuits regarding whether district courts may "look through" a petition to

2 Discover apparently had no basis to assert diversity-of-citizenship jurisdiction. *Vaden*, 556 U.S. at 54, n.1.

compel arbitration pursuant to Section 4 of the FAA and examine the parties' underlying dispute to determine whether federal question jurisdiction exists. *Id.* at 56. *Compare Wisconsin v. Ho-Chunk Nation*, 463 F.3d 655, 659 (7th Cir. 2006) (the court may not "look through" the petition and focus on the underlying dispute to determine jurisdiction over a Section 4 petition); *Smith Barney, Inc. v. Sarver*, 108 F.3d 92, 94 (6th Cir. 1997) (same); *Westmoreland Capital Corp. v. Findlay*, 100 F.3d 263, 267–269 (2d Cir. 1996) (same); and *Prudential-Bache Securities, Inc. v. Fitch*, 966 F.2d 981, 986–989 (5th Cir. 1992) (same), *with Community State Bank v. Strong*, 485 F.3d 597, 605–606 (the court may "look through" the petition and examine the underlying dispute), *vacated, reh'g en banc granted*, 508 F.3d 576 (11th Cir. 2007); and 396 F.3d at 369–370 (case below) (same).

### 2.2 *Issue and the Parties' Allegations*

The central issue in *Vaden* was whether a federal court may "look through" the petition to compel arbitration pursuant to Section 4 of the FAA to determine whether the underlying claim as set out in the complaint provides a basis for federal subject matter jurisdiction. The secondary question was if a court may "look through" a petition at the underlying claim that initiated the litigation, what does it look at—the complaint filed by the party that commenced the action or the entire dispute between the parties, including the federal law issue raised by the counterclaim that Discover was looking to arbitrate.

Ms. Vaden alleged that her counterclaims arose solely under state law and that the dispute should be litigated in state court. Discover maintained that Vaden's answer and counterclaims were predicated on federal law (the Federal Deposit Insurance Act) and, therefore, Discover argued a federal court should "look through" the petition to compel arbitration pursuant to Section 4 of the FAA based on the federal nature of Vaden's defense and counterclaims, regardless of the fact that Discover's complaint arose under state law. The independent jurisdictional based upon which Discover relied was 28 U.S.C. § 1331, which vests federal courts with jurisdiction over civil law actions "arising under the Constitution, laws, or treaties of the United States." *Vaden*, 556 U.S. at 59–60.

### 2.3 *The Court's Opinion*

Justice Ginsburg delivered the opinion of the Court, in which Justices Scalia, Kennedy, Souter and Thomas joined.[3] The Supreme Court held that a federal

3 Chief Justice Roberts filed an opinion concurring in part and dissenting in part, in which Justices Stevens, Breyer and Alito joined, as discussed in Section 2.4 of this chapter.

court may "look through" a Section 4 petition to compel arbitration and order arbitration if, "save for [the arbitration] agreement," the court would have jurisdiction over "the [substantive] controversy between the parties." 9 U.S.C. § 4. *See Vaden*, 556 U.S. at 53. The Court explained that the text of Section 4 itself was the basis for the Court's conclusion that a federal court should determine its jurisdiction by "looking through" a Section 4 petition to the parties' underlying substantive controversy. Vaden, 556 U.S. at 62. The phrase "save for [the arbitration] agreement" was interpreted to indicate that the district court should assume the absence of the arbitration agreement and determine if it would "have jurisdiction under title 28" without it. *Id.*

The Court acknowledged that the majority of federal appellate courts that had addressed the issue had rejected the "look through" approach. *Vaden*, 556 U.S. at 63. However, the Court observed that when the parties' underlying dispute arises under federal law, the "look through" approach permits a Section 4 petitioner to seek an order compelling arbitration without first taking the formal step of initiating or removing a federal question lawsuit. In other words, the petitioner would not need to seek federal adjudication of the very questions it wants to arbitrate rather than litigate. *Id.* at 65.

After determining that a district court should "look through" a Section 4 petition to compel arbitration, the Court then considered the second issue, whether the federal court would have federal question jurisdiction over a suit arising out of the controversy between Discover and Vaden. *Id.* at 66. The Court acknowledged that Section 4 of the FAA "does not enlarge federal-court jurisdiction." *Id.* The Court concluded that the parties' controversy as reflected in Discover's state-law claim for the balance due on Vaden's account was not amenable to federal court adjudication. *Id.*

The Supreme Court further held that the Fourth Circuit "misidentified the dimensions of the controversy between the parties" by focusing on only a slice of the parties' entire dispute, namely Vaden's counterclaims. *Id.* at 53–54. The Fourth Circuit held the counterclaims to be completely preempted, and on that basis affirmed the District Court's order compelling arbitration. The Supreme Court concluded that the Fourth Circuit had lost sight of "the triggering plea—Discover's claim for the balance due on Vaden's account. Given that entirely state-based plea and the established rule that federal-court jurisdiction cannot be invoked on the basis of a defense or counterclaim, the whole 'controversy between the parties' does not qualify for federal court adjudication." *Id.* at 54. Accordingly, the Supreme Court reversed the decision of the Fourth Circuit.

The Supreme Court majority opinion summarized its reasoning as follows:

> In sum, § 4 of the FAA instructs district courts asked to compel arbitration to inquire whether the court would have jurisdiction, 'save for [the arbitration] agreement,' over 'a suit arising out of the controversy between the parties.' We read that prescription in light of the well-pleaded complaint rule and the corollary rule that federal jurisdiction cannot be invoked on the basis of a defense or counterclaim. Parties may not circumvent those rules by asking a federal court to order arbitration of the portion of a controversy that implicates federal law when the court would not have federal-question jurisdiction over the controversy as a whole. It does not suffice to show that a federal question lurks somewhere inside the parties' controversy, or that a defense or counterclaim would arise under federal law.

*Id.* at 70. The Supreme Court concluded that because the controversy between Discover and Vaden did not qualify for federal court jurisdiction, Section 4 of the FAA "does not empower a federal court to order arbitration of that controversy, in whole or in part." *Id.*

The majority opinion noted that this result did not leave Discover without recourse. Section 2 of the FAA, which is binding on state and federal courts, renders agreements to arbitrate "valid, irrevocable, and enforceable." *Id.* at 71. This provision requires state courts to recognize and enforce arbitration agreements in the same way federal courts are required by Sections 3 and 4 of the FAA. *Id.* Additionally, the Court observed that Maryland (like many other U.S. states), provides a statutory remedy nearly identical to Section 4, citing Md. Cts. & Jud. Proc. Code Ann. § 3–207 (2006) ("If a party to an arbitration agreement ... refuses to arbitrate, the other party may file a petition with a court to order arbitration. ... If the court determines that the agreement exists, it shall order arbitration. Otherwise, it shall deny the petition."). *Id.* Thus, Discover could have sought an order compelling arbitration in a Maryland state court of any agreement-related dispute between itself and Vaden before it filed its debt-recovery action. Federal court intervention was unnecessary to place the controversy between the parties before an arbitrator. *Id.* at 71–72.

The majority concluded that the district court lacked jurisdiction to entertain Discover's Section 4 petition to compel arbitration and therefore reversed the decision of the Fourth Circuit and remanded the case "for further proceedings consistent with this opinion." *Id.* at 72.

### 2.4 *The Dissenting Opinion*

Chief Justice Roberts wrote an opinion concurring in part and dissenting in part. His opinion agreed with the majority that a federal court asked to compel arbitration pursuant to Section 4 of the FAA should "look through" the dispute n determining whether it has jurisdiction to grant the requested relief. *Id.* at 71. However, the Chief Justice focused on the question of "look through to what?" *Id.* at 72. The dissent criticized the majority for focusing on the controversy underlying the complaint and its conclusion that because that litigation "was commenced as a state-law debt-collection claim, the majority concludes there is no § 4 jurisdiction." *Id.* at 74. The dissent found this approach contrary to the language of Section 4 and restricted the ability of federal courts to enforce agreements to arbitrate. *Id.* at 73. For the dissent, the "controversy" to which Section 4 refers is the dispute alleged to be subject to arbitration. *Id.* at 74. The petitioner must set forth the nature of that dispute in the Section 4 petition seeking an order to compel arbitration. Section 4 requires that the petitioner be "aggrieved" by the other party's "failure, neglect, or refusal ... to arbitrate under a written agreement for arbitration." 9 U.S.C. § 4. The dissent took the view that such statutory language guides the district court to the specific controversy that the other party is unwilling to arbitrate, including the alleged federal statutory preemption of Vaden's state law defense and counterclaims. *Vaden*, 556 U.S. at 73–74.

The dissent noted that Discover's petition to compel arbitration pursuant to Section 4 of the FAA did not seek to arbitrate its state law debt-collection claims, but rather Vaden's allegation that the fees Discover had been charging violated the FDIA. *Id.* at 74. The majority did not appear to dispute that a court would have federal jurisdiction over a suit arising out of a claim for a violation of the FDIA. By contrast, the majority found no jurisdiction here, however, because a federal court could not entertain Discover's state-law debt-collection claim and concluded there was no jurisdiction to compel arbitration of a plainly federal controversy—the FDIA dispute—because there was no jurisdiction to compel arbitration of the debt-collection dispute. *Id.* According to the dissent, it was a "mystery" as to why Discover should have to demonstrate federal jurisdiction over a state-court claim it does not seek to arbitrate, citing *Moses H. Cone*, 460 U.S. at 19–21 (affirming federal-court jurisdiction over a Section 4 petition seeking to arbitrate only one of two disputes pending in state-court litigation) and *Dean Witter Reynolds Inc. v. Byrd*, 470 U.S. 213, 218–221 (1985) (when litigation involves multiple claims, only some of which are covered by an arbitration agreement, a district court must compel arbitration of the entirety of the covered claims if so requested). *Vaden*, 556 U.S. at 75.

The dissent observed that if Ms. Vaden had filed her FDIA claim first, and Discover had answered with a state-law debt-collection counterclaim, that suit could be litigated in federal court. *Id.* at 76. Defining the controversy as the dispute that the Section 4 petitioner seeks to arbitrate would eliminate this problem by ensuring that the actual dispute subject to arbitration is federal. *Id.*

### 2.5 *Key Takeaways*

Following *Vaden*, a federal court may "look through" a petition to compel arbitration pursuant to Section 4 of the FAA to determine if there is federal subject matter jurisdiction based on the complaint or claim that commenced the action. However, in light of the well-pleaded complaint rule, a suit "arises under" federal law for 28 U.S.C. § 1331 purposes only when the plaintiff's statement of its own cause of action demonstrates that it is based upon federal law. A federal court does not have subject jurisdiction to compel arbitration of a counterclaim even when the counterclaim is arguably preempted by federal law.

## 3 The Case's Impact on U.S. Arbitration Law

The decision is significant in that Court ruled, for the first time, that a federal court may "look through" a Section 4 petition to determine if a federal court has federal subject matter jurisdiction based on the complaint or claim that is the basis of the dispute.

## 4 Conclusions

The Supreme Court's holding on the first issue, that a federal court may "look through" a Section 4 petition to determine if there is federal question jurisdiction, is based on a reading of unambiguous language in Section 4 of the FAA.

The Supreme Court's holding on the second question, that the "look through" does not extend to a counterclaim allegedly preempted by federal law, is based on the Supreme Court's attempt to harmonize Section 4 of the FAA with the "well pleaded" complaint rule. The latter question resulted in a divided Court and a spirited dissent.

CHAPTER 20

# *Rent-A-Center West, Inc. v. Jackson*, 561 U.S. 63 (2010)

*Zachary Kady and Rahim Moloo*

## Introduction and Background Considerations

In *Rent-A-Center West, Inc. v. Jackson* the Supreme Court held that, where an arbitration agreement includes a provision delegating questions of arbitrability to the arbitrator, parties must arbitrate the validity or scope of the arbitration agreement unless they specifically challenge the delegation provision itself. Thus, following *Rent-A-Center*, arbitration agreements that delegate arbitrability to the arbitrator are insulated from judicial review except in the rare circumstances where a party asserts a direct attack on the validity of the delegation provision.

*Rent-A-Center* is a critical stone in the Supreme Court's pro-arbitration jurisprudence. That pro-arbitration regime incorporates at least three key concepts that inform the importance and effect of *Rent-A-Center*.

First is the concept of arbitrability. A dispute is arbitrable (*i.e.*, must be arbitrated rather than litigated in court) only if it falls within the scope of a valid arbitration agreement. Thus, before a court can compel arbitration or before an arbitrator issues an award, the relevant decision-maker must first be satisfied that a dispute falls within the parties' agreement to arbitrate.[1]

In practice, parties often include in their arbitration agreements provisions delegating to an arbitrator the authority to decide arbitrability disputes. These provisions, commonly referred to as "delegation provisions," can also be incorporated by reference when included in rules promulgated by an arbitration institution that the parties agree will govern future disputes.[2]

1 *Howsam v. Dean Witter Reynolds, Inc.*, 537 U.S. 79, 84 (2002) ("[A] gateway dispute about whether the parties are bound by a given arbitration clause raises a question of arbitrability' for a court to decide. ... Similarly, a disagreement about whether an arbitration clause in a concededly binding contract applies to a particular type of controversy is for the court.") (internal quotations and citations omitted).

2 *See, e.g.*, *DDK Hotels, LLC v. Williams-Sonoma, Inc.*, 6 F.4th 308, 318 (2d Cir. 2021) ("Where the parties explicitly incorporate procedural rules that empower an arbitrator to decide issues of arbitrability, that incorporation may serve as clear and unmistakable evidence of the parties' intent to delegate arbitrability to an arbitrator.").

 | DOI:10.1163/9789004715820_021

Second is the Court's holdings in *First Options of Chicago v. Kaplan* ("First Options") and *AT&T Technologies., Inc. v. Communications Workers of America* ("AT&T"), which together established the presumption that disputes about arbitrability should presumptively be resolved by a court, not an arbitrator.[3] In *First Options*, the Court explained that this presumption "is understandable" because parties "often might not focus upon that question or upon the significance of having arbitrators decide the scope of their own powers."[4] Thus, absent a "clear and unmistakable" agreement to arbitrate questions of arbitrability, resolving such disputes in court is the only result consistent with the "the principle that a party can be forced to arbitrate only those issues it specifically has agreed to submit to arbitration."[5]

Third is the Court's severability jurisprudence, clarified in *Buckeye Check Cashing, Inc. v. Cardegna*, which establishes that arbitration agreements must be treated as distinct from the larger agreements to which they relate. Accordingly, "unless the challenge is to the arbitration clause itself, the issue of the contract's validity is considered by the arbitrator in the first instance."[6]

The dispute in *Rent-A-Center* arises from the application of these three principles in a single case. Specifically, the Court was asked to resolve what should happen when a party claims an arbitration agreement is generally unconscionable but does not specifically apply that claim to the delegation provision. Mr. Jackson, a former employee of Rent-A-Center alleging he was denied a promotion due to racial discrimination and later fired after complaining of discrimination, argued he could not be compelled to arbitrate until a court, not an arbitrator, ruled on his claim that the arbitration agreement signed in connection with his employment was unconscionable. The Supreme Court disagreed, holding that Mr. Jackson's unconscionability arguments were not directed at the delegation provision specifically, and therefore must be arbitrated.

---

3 *See AT&T Techs., Inc. v. Commc'ns Workers of Am.*, 475 U.S. 643 (1986); *First Options of Chicago, Inc. v. Kaplan*, 514 U.S. 938 (1995).

4 *Id.*

5 *Id.* at 945–46 (citing *AT & T*, 475 U.S. 643 at 649).

6 *Buckeye Check Cashing, Inc. v. Cardegna*, 546 U.S. 440, 445–46 (2006) (relying on earlier decisions in *Prima Paint Corp. v. Flood & Conklin Mfg. Co.*, 388 U.S. 395 (1967) and *Southland Corp. v. Keating*, 465 U.S. 1 (1984)).

## 1 Background

This case involved an employment dispute between Rent-A-Center ("RAC") and Antonio Jackson. Jackson, an African American man, alleged that after he was hired by RAC as an account manager, he repeatedly sought promotions but was turned down in favor of non-African American employees with less seniority. Eventually, Jackson was promoted but was terminated two months later. Jackson brought suit in the United States District Court for the District of Nevada alleging racial discrimination and retaliation in violation of 42 U.S.C. § 1981. Jackson alleged that he was initially not promoted due to his race and was then fired in retaliation for his earlier complaints about not being promoted.

RAC moved to dismiss or, in the alternative, stay the proceedings and compel arbitration pursuant to Jackson's employment with the company, which contained a Mutual Agreement to Arbitrate Claims (the "Agreement"). The arbitration Agreement was a standalone agreement, separate from Mr. Jackson's employment contract. It required arbitration of all "past, present or future" disputes arising out of Jackson's employment and, critically, contained a delegation provision mandating that "[t]he Arbitrator, and not any federal, state, or local court or agency, shall have exclusive authority to resolve any dispute relating to the interpretation, applicability, enforceability or formation of this Agreement including, but not limited to any claim that all or any part of this Agreement is void or voidable."

Jackson opposed arbitration of his discrimination and retaliation claims on the grounds that the arbitration Agreement was unconscionable. Under the applicable Nevada state law, an agreement must be both procedurally and substantively unconscionable to be unenforceable. Jackson argued that the Agreement was procedurally unconscionable because it was presented as a condition of his employment and there was unequal bargaining power between him and RAC. Jackson further alleged that the Agreement was substantively unconscionable because it was one-sided. In support of this substantive unconscionability argument, Jackson highlighted provisions in the Agreement requiring arbitration of claims he would likely raise (*e.g.*, tort claims) but allowing litigation of claims RAC would likely raise (*e.g.*, trade secret disclosures). In addition, Jackson pointed to provisions limiting the scope of discovery in arbitration and requiring the parties to split the fees associated with arbitration.

The District Court granted RAC's motion to dismiss Jackson's suit and compel arbitration. The court held that the delegation clause in the Agreement gave the arbitrator exclusive authority to decide issues of validity of the Agreement as a whole.

Jackson appealed the District Court's order to the Ninth Circuit, which reversed in part and affirmed in part. The Ninth Circuit agreed that the delegation clause clearly assigned the issue of arbitrability to the arbitrator. Nevertheless, the Ninth Circuit held that, when a party raises a challenge based on unconscionability of an arbitration provision, the question is one for the courts, not arbitrators, to decide. The Supreme Court granted RAC's request for a writ of certiorari on the following question:

> Is the district court required in all cases to determine claims that an arbitration agreement subject to the Federal Arbitration Act ("FAA") is unconscionable, even when the parties to the contract have clearly and unmistakably assigned this "gateway" issue to the arbitrator for decision?

## 2 Issue and Parties' Allegations

As framed by the Supreme Court, the issue to be decided was "whether, under the Federal Arbitration Act (FAA or Act), 9 U.S.C. §§ 1–16, a district court may decide a claim that an arbitration agreement is unconscionable, where the agreement explicitly assigns that decision to the arbitrator." *Rent-A-Ctr., W., Inc. v Jackson*, 561 U.S. 63, 65 (2010).

In its briefing and at oral argument, RAC emphasized the public policy concerns surrounding the enactment of the FAA that, it claimed, supported a decision compelling arbitration. In particular, RAC contended that the FAA was enacted to reverse a longstanding hostility toward arbitral agreements.

The Court's prior decisions in *First Options* and *AT&T* were also central to RAC's arguments. As discussed above, the Court in *AT&T* held that, "[u]nless the parties clearly and unmistakably provide otherwise, the question of whether the parties agreed to arbitrate is to be decided by the court, not the arbitrator."[7] In *First Options*, the Court held that courts "should not assume that the parties agreed to arbitrate arbitrability" but "should apply ordinary state-law principles that govern the formation of contracts" to determine if clear and unmistakable evidence exists to determine that they did so.[8] Therefore, RAC contended that the court's role is limited to determining whether the parties' contract expresses clear and unmistakable evidence that they delegated arbitrability issues to the arbitrator. Since both the District Court and the Ninth

---

7 *AT&T*, 475 U.S. at 649.

8 *First Options*, 514 U.S. at 944.

Circuit acknowledged that the language of the Agreement delegated issues of enforceability to the arbitrator, RAC argued the court should enforce the agreement as written, including the delegation provision.

At oral argument, the Court focused on comparisons of this case to prior decisions where parties sought to avoid arbitration because the underlying agreement was void due to fraud in the inducement. For example, in *Prima Paint Corp. v. Flood & Conklin Mfg. Co.*, the Supreme Court held that courts could not consider challenges to a contract as a whole unless the challenge relates specifically to the arbitration agreement contained in the agreement at issue.[9] Thus, if unconscionability would result in a ruling that no valid agreement to arbitrate ever came into existence, then the justices suggested the issue would be one for the court to decide. RAC argued that unconscionability, unlike fraudulent inducement, is an issue of fairness that does not rise to the same level as fraudulent inducement and does not go to issues of formation or mutual assent and is therefore not a "making" issue under *Prima Paint*.

The Court also considered at oral argument whether the delegation provision could be considered clear and unmistakable evidence of an agreement to arbitrate arbitrability in light of Jackson's allegation in briefing before the Supreme Court alleging the delegation provision is itself unconscionable. To this, RAC replied that Jackson had not attacked the delegation provision until he was before the Supreme Court. Instead, in the courts below, Jackson only raised issues regarding the alleged unconscionableness of discovery and fee provisions. Thus, the unconscionability argument at issue was general; it was not specific to the delegation provision. In addition, RAC contended that unconscionability is a post-formation attack not concerned with the making of an agreement.

Jackson argued that the issue of unconscionability was one for the courts to decide. In Jackson's view, Section 2 of the FAA requires *courts* to determine whether an arbitration agreement is unenforceable, including because it is unconscionable. Jackson set out three requirements that, he argued, must be determined by the court before enforcement can be allowed. First, there must be a written agreement. Second, the arbitration agreement must relate to a transaction involving interstate commerce. Third, the agreement must not be invalid under state contract law principles. Citing to *Doctor's Assocs., Inc. v. Casarotto*, Jackson contended that a "generally applicable contract defense, such as ... unconscionability" could render an agreement invalid.[10] Therefore,

---

9 *Prima Paint Corp. v. Flood & Conklin Mfg. Co.*, 388 U.S. 395, 403–404 (1967).

10 *Doctor's Assocs., Inc. v. Casarotto*, 517 U.S. 681, 687 (1996).

Jackson argued that RAC's approach would improperly require courts to enforce arbitration agreements before their validity has been confirmed. The Court pushed back at oral argument, noting that Section 2 of the FAA does not specify who decides the question of validity. Jackson conceded this point but argued that a logical reading of the FAA necessitates that these requirements must be met before an arbitrator has any authority to act.

Jackson further argued that his position was bolstered by Section 4 of the FAA, which states that, "if the making of the arbitration agreement or the failure, neglect or refusal to perform the same be in issue, the court shall proceed summarily to the trial thereof."[11] According to Jackson, contract defenses such as unconscionability were understood to be defenses to the "making" of the contract when the FAA was passed in 1925.

Turning to *Prima Paint*, Jackson argued the result is the same, regardless of whether a contract is challenged under theories of fraudulent inducement or unconscionability. Because both unconscionability and fraudulent inducement render a contract voidable, Johnson argued that both go to the "making" of the agreement and are therefore issues for the court to decide under Section 4 of the FAA.

With respect to *AT&T* and *First Options*, Jackson argued that those decisions concerned only the scope of a valid agreement. They did not involve disputes regarding the validity of the arbitration agreements in questions. Here, by contrast, Jackson highlighted that he disputed the validity of the arbitration agreement, not its scope. Validity, he argued, must be determined by a court. Jackson also noted that the Court had never applied the clear and unmistakable test to hold that parties may delegate the determination of validity issues. For example, in *Green Tree Fin. Corp.-Ala. v. Randolph*, the court ruled on an issue of validity despite language in the agreement delegating those issues to arbitrators.[12]

Finally, Jackson invoked public policy to argue that RAC's approach would result in essentially unreviewable decisions. Only Section 10(a)(4) of the FAA allows for substantive review of arbitration awards, and then only when an arbitrator exceeds their powers. If courts were to defer to arbitrators regarding the question of whether an arbitration agreement is valid, Johnson argued that litigants would have no way to challenge awards on the basis that the arbitrator exceeded their power to make that determination in the first place.[13] Thus,

---

11 9 U.S.C. § 4.

12 *Green Tree Fin. Corp.-Ala. v. Randolph*, 531 U.S. 79, 83 n.1 (2000).

13 Jackson overstates the severity of this concern. Cases preceding and post-dating *Rent-A-Center* confirm that Section 10(a)(4) of the FAA permits courts to vacate an arbitration award that "ignore[s] the plain language of the contract," *Pa. Power Co. v. Loc. Union*

decisions regarding arbitrability would be rendered essentially unreviewable. Jackson also argued that judicial review post-arbitration would be insufficient to guard against abuse by more powerful parties drafting unfair clauses, and that arbitrators cannot be relied upon to eliminate abuses of the arbitral system.

## 3 The Court's Opinion

The Court reversed the judgement of the Ninth Circuit and held that, because Jackson did not challenge the delegation provision specifically, that provision must be treated as valid under Section 2, and must be enforced under Sections 3 and 4 of the FAA.[14] Justice Scalia delivered the opinion of the court in which justices Roberts, Kennedy, Thomas, and Alito joined. Justice Stevens filed a dissent, in which justices Ginsburg, Breyer, and Sotomayor joined.

The court maintained that a delegation provision like the one in this case is an antecedent agreement the parties are asking the court to enforce. This agreement is subject to the FAA like any other agreement and is therefore valid under Section 2 "save upon such grounds as exist at law or in equity for the revocation of any contract."[15]

The Court explained that its reasoning stemmed from the line of severability cases following *Prima Paint*, which the court noted it was not asked to review by either party. Those precedents made clear that "a party's challenge to

---

*No. 272, Int'l Bhd. of Elec. Workers, AFL-CIO*, 276 F.3d 174, 178 (3d Cir. 2001), "manifestly disregards the [contract's] plain language," *Monongahela Valley Hosp. Inc. v. United Steel Paper & Forestry Rubber Mfg. Allied Indus. & Serv. Workers Int'l Union*, 946 F.3d 195, 200 (3d Cir. 2019), or "impose[s] a remedy which directly contradicts the express language of the" contract, *Leed Architectural Prods., Inc. v. United Steelworkers of Am., Local 6674*, 916 F.2d 63, 65 (2d Cir. 1990). In such cases the arbitrator has exceeded the scope of its powers and the resulting award will be vacated. *See, e.g.*, *See ExxonMobil Oil Corp. v. TIG Ins. Co.*, 44 F.4th 163, 179 (2d Cir. 2022) (when a "contract limit[s] the recovery available," it "thereby restrict[s] the arbitra[tor's] authority to grant any award beyond that amount"); *Williamson Farm v. Diversified Crop Ins. Servs.*, 917 F.3d 247, 257 (4th Cir. 2019) (affirming district court's vacatur of arbitral award of extra-contractual damages barred by the parties' agreement); *Mo. River Servs., Inc. v. Omaha Tribe of Neb.*, 267 F.3d 848, 855 (8th Cir. 2001) (arbitrator exceeded scope of authority by awarding profits of an Iowa casino despite contract's limitation of liability to earnings of a different casino in Nebraska); *S.D. Warren Co., Div. of Scott Paper Co. v. United Paperworkers' Int'l Union*, 845 F.2d 3, 8 (1st Cir. 1988) (holding that court could not enforce arbitrator's award determining remedies contrary to the "plain language of the contract").

14 *Rent-A-Ctr.*, 561 U.S. at 73.

15 *Rent-A-Ctr.*, 561 U.S. at 70.

another provision of the contract, or to the contract as a whole, does not prevent a court from enforcing a specific agreement to arbitrate."[16] However, "[i]f a party challenges the validity under § 2 of the precise agreement to arbitrate at issue, the federal court must consider the challenge before ordering compliance with that agreement under § 4."[17] Thus, a party must *specifically* challenge the arbitration clause in order for the *court* to review the challenge. Challenges to the contract as a *whole* or to non-arbitral provisions go to the arbitrator.

Here, Jackson challenged the validity of the arbitration Agreement as a whole, not the validity of the delegation provision specifically.[18] The court quickly dispensed with Jackson's argument that this case was distinguishable from *Prima Paint* because, unlike in that case, this dispute concerned a standalone contract that was solely concerned with arbitration. The Court explained that this distinction makes no difference because "[a]pplication of the severability rule does not depend on the substance of the remainder of the contract."[19] Instead, the Court reasoned, Section 2 is applied to whatever provision regarding arbitration the party is seeking to enforce, here, an arbitration agreement. Therefore, because Jackson did not specifically challenge the delegation provision, courts must treat that provision as valid and enforce it under the FAA.[20] Jackson's general unconscionability challenges would be left to be resolved by the arbitrator.[21]

Put simply, the court treated this arbitration Agreement as it would any other complete agreement, and treated the delegation provision as a mini-arbitration agreement within that contract. Thus, the Court held that, when a party challenges a delegation provision, courts may only review challenges if they are directed at the delegation provision itself, just as they would review only a specifically challenged arbitration clause contained within a larger contract.

Finally, the Court addressed the fact that, "[i]n his brief to this Court, Jackson made the contention, not mentioned below, that the delegation provision itself

---

16 *Id.*

17 *Id.*

18 *Id.* at 73.

19 *Id.*

20 Likely due to some confusion at oral argument regarding whether Jackson was challenging the delegation provision specifically, the arbitration agreement as a whole, or only specific provisions in the agreement (not including the delegation provision), the court quotes language in Jackson's various pleadings where he referred to the unconscionability of the agreement "as a whole" and argues that none of Jackson's arguments challenge the delegation provision specifically. *See id.*

21 *See id.*

is substantively unconscionable because the quid pro quo he was supposed to receive for it—that 'in exchange for initially allowing an arbitrator to decide certain gateway questions,' he would receive 'plenary post-arbitration [*sic*] judicial review'—was eliminated by the Court's subsequent holding in *Hall Street Associates,* L.L.C. *v. Mattel, Inc.*, 552 U.S. 576, 128 S.Ct. 1396, 170 L.Ed.2d 254 (2008), that the nonplenary [*sic*] grounds for judicial review in § 10 of the FAA are exclusive."[22] The Court held that Jackson brought this challenge to the delegation provision too late, and declined to consider it.[23]

The dissent strongly contested the logic and reasoning underlying the majority's holding. The opinion noted that, while *Prima Paint* allowed courts to sever a potentially valid arbitration agreement from a potentially invalid contract, "[t]oday the Court adds a new layer of severability—something akin to Russian nesting dolls—into the mix: Courts may now pluck from a potentially invalid arbitration agreement even narrower provisions that refer particular arbitrability disputes to an arbitrator." Thus, the dissent argued, "[i]t would seem the Court reads *Prima Paint* to require, as a matter of course, infinite layers of severability."[24]

## 4 Key Takeaways

Setting aside the merits of the Court's decision, the dissent is correct that *Rent-A-Center* adds "a new layer of severability—something akin to Russian nesting dolls—into the mix" of arbitration jurisprudence. Where an arbitration agreement includes a provision delegating arbitrability disputes to the arbitrator, *Rent-A-Center* makes clear that parties seeking to avoid arbitration must direct their arguments at the validity of the delegation provision itself. Challenges to the validity or enforceability of the overall contract, or even the arbitration agreement, are insufficiently specific to avoid arbitration of arbitrability disputes. In practice, it is difficult to imagine that many parties could formulate such a specific challenge to a delegation provision that does not apply to the arbitration agreement or contract as a whole. But that is the law.

22 Brief for Respondent 59–60.

23 *Id.* at 77.

24 *Id.* at 83, 87.

## 5 Analysis

*Rent-A-Center* is a logical extension of the Supreme Court's prior decisions regarding severability and the requirement that an agreement manifest clear and unmistakable intent to delegate questions of arbitrability to an arbitrator. If the federal presumption in favor of arbitration mandates insulation of arbitration agreements from attacks that seek to undermine the contract as a whole (as the Supreme Court held in *Prima Paint*, for example), then it is reasonable to treat delegation provisions as mini-arbitration agreements that are themselves severable from the larger arbitration clause. After all, an agreement to arbitrate arbitrability is an agreement to arbitrate a dispute that is separate from the merits of the case.

Other the other hand, the policy underlying the Court's severability jurisprudence does not require a further severance of delegation provisions from arbitration agreements generally. In *Prima Paint* and *Buckeye*, for example, it was alleged that the relevant contracts were unenforceable due to fraud in the inducement and illegality respectively. In those circumstances, there is "no gateway mater at all."[25] If a court decides that it cannot enforce the arbitration agreement because there was fraud in the inducement (or because the contract is illegal) then it has simultaneously decided the entire dispute that the parties agreed to submit to arbitration. *See id.* at 87–88.

The rule established in *Rent-A-Center* creates an extraordinary burden for litigants seeking to avoid arbitration. Applied consistently with prior precedent on severability, *Rent-A-Center* requires a party seeking to avoid arbitration to identify an infirmity that is "*particular and unique*" to the delegation provision but does not apply to the arbitration agreement as a whole.[26]

*Rent-A-Center* has unquestionably strengthened the position of any litigant seeking to compel arbitration not only of the merits, but also of disputes regarding arbitrability. This is not a trivial number of disputes. Many arbitration agreements contain explicit clauses delegating arbitrability disputes to the arbitrator. Sill more incorporate arbitral rules published by established institutions that delegate arbitrability disputes to arbitration. This is understandable, as the efficiency of arbitration can be lost if parties must first litigate for months (or more) in court just to obtain a ruling confirming they must resolve the remainder of their dispute through arbitration. On the other hand, it is nearly impossible to avoid arbitration of arbitrability disputes because

25 *Rent-A-Ctr.*, 561 U.S. at 86 (Stevens, J., dissenting).

26 *Rent-A-Ctr.*, 561 U.S. at 86 (Stevens, J., dissenting).

arguments that attack only the delegation provision, or which are so broad as to negate the delegation provision, will be available only in rare circumstances.[27] This burden is beneficial to compel parties to abide by their agreements to arbitrate. But for parties with good faith arguments that they did not agree to arbitration (or that the agreement should not be enforced), the burden can be difficult to justify, particularly in light of the fact that it is not necessary to protect the enforceability of arbitration provisions generally, as was true in the severability cases preceding *Rent-A-Center*.

Perhaps recognizing this potential for inequity, subsequent courts appear to have taken a lenient approach to the requirements in *Rent-A-Center*. Both the Third Circuit and Eleventh Circuit have since held that merely referencing the delegation provision is sufficient to state an argument that the delegation provision is invalid.[28]

If courts tasked with resolving challenges to delegation provisions follow the examples in *MacDonald* and *Parm*, the long-term effect of *Rent-A-Center* will be limited. Rather than compelling arbitration of arbitrability disputes in all but the rarest cases where a party asserts a challenge directly to the delegation provision, litigants would merely need to assert that their challenge to the arbitration provision includes a challenge to the delegation provision too.

## 6 Conclusions

In most cases, the rule established in *Rent-A-Center* is likely to lead to a just outcome that preserves the viability of arbitration and protects it from opportunistic litigants seeking to renege on their agreement to arbitrate. But the inflexibility of the rule, combined with the fact that it is neither intuitive nor easily satisfied, creates risks that parties will be wrongly compelled to arbitrate

27 *See, e.g.*, *Parm v. Nat'l Bank of California*, N.A., 835 F.3d 1331, 1338 (11th Cir. 2016) (resolving arbitrability dispute where chosen arbitral forum no longer available); *Kramer v. Toyota Motor Corp.*, 705 F.3d 1122, 1126 (9th Cir. 2013) (resolving arbitrability dispute because arbitration agreement was agreed between customer and car dealerships, but did not include car manufacture seeking to compel arbitration); *J.R. v. Elec. Arts Inc.*, 98 Cal. App. 5th 1107 (2024), *reh'g denied* (Jan. 30, 2024), *review filed* (Feb. 26, 2024) (resolving arbitrability dispute where minor had disaffirmed validity of all contracts under California law).

28 *See MacDonald v. CashCall, Inc*, 883 F.3d 220, 226 (3d Cir. 2018) (To contest "enforceability of a delegation clause" "the party must at least reference the provision in its opposition to a motion to compel arbitration."); *Parm v. Nat'l Bank of California*, N.A., 835 F.3d 1331, 1335 (11th Cir. 2016) (permitting judicial review where delegation provision was explicitly mentioned in challenge on unconscionability grounds).

disputes. That is neither just nor efficient, as a litigant who obtains an arbitral award confirming a dispute was not arbitrable would have wasted months or years in arbitration only to be left back at square one, commencing litigation all over again. In this regard, *Rent-A-Center* is best understood as a microcosm of the Court's pro-arbitration jurisprudence, pursuant to which parties can take comfort that their agreements to efficiently and (where necessary) confidentially resolve disputes will be strongly protected. But woe to the party seeking to avoid arbitration; *Rent-A-Center* is just one of many decisions stacking the odds against them.

CHAPTER 21

# *Stolt-Nielsen S. A. v. AnimalFeeds Int'l Corp.*, 559 U.S. 662 (2010): The Impact of the *Stolt-Nielsen* Decision on Class-Action Arbitration

*Andrew Finn and Pedro José Izquierdo*

## 1 Introduction[1]

Class actions—where one party seeks to pursue claims on behalf of a group of similarly situated individuals—for many years has been a common procedural feature of U.S. courts that is unique among court systems around the world.[2] While class actions can provide efficiencies in resolving certain types of disputes, they can also dramatically alter the stakes for defendants in a litigation and at times lead to abuse.[3] The use of the class action mechanism in the U.S. eventually led claimants subject to binding arbitration clauses to attempt to pursue claims on a class basis in arbitration, even when the arbitration clause did not specifically authorize such claims. Some arbitral institutions have developed rules tailored to address class arbitrations.

Against this backdrop of an increase in the use of class arbitration, the U.S. Supreme Court's decision in *Stolt-Nielsen* S.A. v. *AnimalFeeds International Corporation* in 2010 addressed a crucial threshold question: can a party be deemed to have consented to class arbitration when the arbitration agreement is silent on the matter? In a 5–3 decision, the Supreme Court held that imposing

---

1 The authors wish to thank Fernando Quiroz for his assistance in preparing this chapter.

2 *See* Robert H. Klonoff, *Why Most Nations Do Not Have U.S.-Style Class Actions*, BLOOMBERG LAW (May 11, 2015, 5:22 PM EDT), https://news.bloomberglaw.com/class-action/why-most-nations-do-not-have-us-style-class-actions (last visited Oct. 28, 2024) ("Large class action verdicts or settlements are rare outside the U.S.").

3 *See, e.g.*, *Merrill Lynch, Pierce, Fenner & Smith* v. *Dabit*, 547 U.S. 71, 81 (2006) (discussing the "ways in which the class-action device," particularly in the securities-litigation context, risked "abuses result[ing] in extortionate settlements"); *Blue Chip Stamps* v. *Manor Drug Stores*, 421 U.S. 723, 741–42 (1975) (discussing how securities class actions brought heightened "risk of strike suits" stemming from "possible abuse" of the discovery process to force "in terrorem" settlements); *In re Kingate Management Ltd. Litigation*, 784 F.3d 128, 138 & n.14 (2d Cir. 2015) (noting that Congress passed the Securities Litigation Uniform Standards Act to prevent attorneys from filing frivolous class action lawsuits in state court); *In re Herald*, 730 F.3d 112, 117–18 (2d Cir. 2013) (same); *Romano* v. *Kazacos*, 609 F.3d 512, 517-18 (2d Cir. 2010) (same).

 | DOI:10.1163/9789004715820_022

class arbitration in such circumstances would be inconsistent with the Federal Arbitration Act ("FAA") and the fundamental principle it enshrines that arbitration is a matter of consent. Instead, parties must be found to have *agreed* to class arbitration, and decision-makers cannot infer an implicit agreement to authorize class arbitration unless there is a contractual basis for doing so.

In the aftermath of *Stolt-Nielsen*, U.S. courts have been hesitant to extend its reasoning and, in many ways, have limited its application when it comes to related questions of arbitral jurisdiction in multi-party, multi-contract claims. As this chapter outlines, while *Stolt-Nelson*'s core holding remains unchallenged, it has uncertain application to arbitration agreements that are not entirely silent as to consent regarding procedural mechanisms (other than class arbitration) for grouping multiple claims.

## 2 Preliminary Considerations on Class Arbitration

In the late twentieth century, class arbitration emerged as a distinct form of alternative dispute resolution to address large-scale disputes involving numerous claimants with related claims, adopting a procedural mechanism that had largely been reserved to U.S. courts. With this mechanism, one or more claimants asserting claims with common issues of law or fact would pursue their claims collectively on behalf of a class of similarly situated individuals against a common respondent. Some arbitral institutions—like the American Arbitration Association ("AAA")—adopted special rules for administering class arbitrations.[4] However, because arbitration is inherently a creature of contract, questions arose as to when and whether a party subject to a bilateral arbitration clause between two parties consents to arbitrate class claims.

Courts applying the FAA in the U.S. have long held that only parties who consent to arbitrate a dispute as a matter of contract must do so. So, for an arbitration to proceed, both claimant and respondent must have consented to be governed by an arbitration agreement—a question that is generally resolved by applying the familiar principles of contractual consent.[5] Even in bilateral

4 *See* AM. ARB. ASS'N, SUPPLEMENTARY RULES FOR CLASS ARBITRATION (2003), https://www.adr.org/sites/default/files/document_repository/Supplementary%20Rules%20for%20Class%20Arbitrations.pdf (last visited Oct. 28, 2024).

5 *Stolt-Nielsen S.A.* v. *AnimalFeeds Int'l Corp.*, 559 U.S. 662, 682 (2010) ("[A]s with any other contract, the parties' 'intentions control'" when determining whether a party consented to arbitrate) (quoting *Mitsubishi Motors Corp.* v. *Soler Chrysler-Plymouth*, 473 U.S. 614, 626 (1985)).

arbitration, the issue of consent can be complicated and issues relating to arbitral jurisdiction over non-signatories frequently arise.[6]

In contrast to a bilateral arbitration between two parties, class arbitration can strain the principle of individualized consent to arbitrate. This is because in a class arbitration, one or more claimants pursue claims on behalf of a class of individuals, which can be numbered in the hundreds or thousands, against one respondent. An efficiency of the class action mechanism is that all members of the class do not need to be present in the proceeding, and yet can be bound by the result of the case. However, arbitration does not include all of the procedural protections for absent class members, or respondents, that U.S. courts provide. For example, arbitral awards are generally final and cannot be appealed on the merits. Nor can interim orders include, for example, certification and testing of whether the class mechanism is appropriate given the circumstances of the case.

Prior to *Stolt-Nielson*, U.S. courts adopted varying approaches to determining the consent necessary for a class arbitration to proceed. For example, some courts had interpreted arbitration agreements that were silent on the issue of consolidation as not necessarily prohibiting its use.[7] Other courts had refused to permit class arbitration when arbitration agreements did not expressly authorize the practice, thus requiring explicit consent.[8]

---

6 *See, e.g.*, *Bridas S.A.P.I.C.* v. *Gov't of Turkmenistan*, 345 F.3d 347, 366 (5th Cir. 2003) (reversing the district court's determinations as to whether a third party effectively bound the Government of Turkmenistan to an arbitration agreement on its behalf as its agent or alter ego, and whether the Government was nonetheless bound to the agreement by equitable estoppel or as a third-party beneficiary); *Grigson* v. *Creative Artists Agency L.L.C.*, 210 F.3d 524, 530–31 (5th Cir. 2000) (upholding the district court's determination that non-signatory third-party beneficiaries are bound by an arbitration, even against *another* non-signatory who had voluntarily sought arbitration under the agreement for an "intertwined" tortious interference claim).

7 *See, e.g.*, *Keating* v. *Superior Ct.*, 31 Cal. 3d 548, 613 (1982), *rev'd in part, appeal dismissed in part sub nom. Southland Corp.* v. *Keating*, 465 U.S. 1 (1984) (concluding that "a court is not without authority to" order "classwide arbitration in an appropriate case").

8 *See, e.g.*, *Glencore, Ltd.* v. *Schnitzer Steel Prod. Co.*, 189 F.3d 264, 268 (2d Cir. 1999) (holding that neither the FAA nor the Federal Rules of Civil Procedure "give the district court power to order either consolidation or joint hearing of two separate arbitrations where the arbitration provisions of the relevant agreements do not so provide"); *Champ* v. *Siegel Trading Co.*, 55 F.3d 269, 276–77 (7th Cir. 1995) (holding that a district court does not have the authority to order class arbitration "absent an express provision in the parties' arbitration agreement providing for class arbitration"); *U.K. Def. Procurement Off., Ministry of Def. ex rel. U.K.* v. *Boeing Co.*, 998 F.2d 68, 74 (2d Cir. 1993) (holding that "the district court cannot consolidate arbitration proceedings arising from separate agreements to arbitrate, absent the parties' agreement to allow such consolidation").

## 3 The Case

### 3.1 *Background of the Case*

In 2003, the U.S. Department of Justice alleged that a group of shipping companies that provided parcel tankers were engaged in an illegal price-fixing conspiracy.[9] AnimalFeeds International Corporation ("AnimalFeeds"), a shipping customer that supplied raw ingredients to animal-feed producers throughout the world, brought a putative class action in the U.S. District Court for the Eastern District of Pennsylvania against Stolt-Nielsen and other implicated shipping companies, asserting antitrust claims for supracompetitive prices.[10] Other charterers initiated similar suits against Stolt-Nielsen and a Judicial Panel on Multidistrict Litigation subsequently ordered the consolidation of various similar cases in the District Court of Connecticut.[11]

Under the agreement at issue, AnimalFeeds had chartered parcel tankers from shipping companies pursuant to a standard industry contract—the "Vegoilvoy charter party."[12] It contained an arbitration clause that did not specifically mention arbitration of class claims.[13] Rather, the charter party simply provided that in the case of arbitration, "[a]ny dispute arising from the making, performance or termination of [the] Charter Party shall be settled in New York, Owner and Charterer each appointing an arbitrator" and "[s]such arbitration shall be conducted in conformity with the provisions and procedure of the United States Arbitration Act [i.e., the FAA], and a judgment of the Court shall be entered upon any award made by said arbitrator."[14] Accordingly, in a separate line of litigation, the Court of Appeals for the Second Circuit held that antitrust claims against the shipping companies were subject to arbitration under the terms of the Vegoilvoy charter party's arbitration clause.[15] After the Second Circuit's decision, the parties agreed that given the judgements and orders, AnimalFeeds and Stolt-Nielsen had to arbitrate their antitrust dispute.[16]

In 2005, AnimalFeeds formally served Stolt-Nielsen with a demand for class arbitration.[17] The parties agreed in a supplemental agreement to submit to the arbitral tribunal the threshold question of whether the Vegoilvoy arbitration

---

9 *Stolt-Nielsen*, 559 U.S. at 667.

10 *Id.*

11 *Id.* at 667–68.

12 *Id.* at 666.

13 *Id.* at 667.

14 *Id.*

15 *See JLM Indus., Inc.* v. *Stolt–Nielsen S.A.*, 387 F.3d 163, 183 (2004).

16 *See Stolt-Nielson*, 559 U.S. at 668.

17 *Id.*

clause authorizes class arbitration, which they stipulated was "silent" on the issue.[18] AnimalFeeds argued that the arbitration clause should be construed to permit class arbitration for three reasons.[19] First, the arbitration clause was silent on the issue of class-action arbitration and, without express prohibition, class arbitration was permitted under the Supreme Court's prior opinion in *Green Tree Financial Corp.* v. *Bazzle*.[20] In *Bazzle*, the Supreme Court's plurality opinion determined that arbitrators, not courts, should be the ones to decide whether a contract is "silent" on the issue of class-action arbitration.[21] Second, AnimalFeeds argued that the arbitration clause should be construed to permit class arbitration as a matter of public policy.[22] And third, AnimalFeeds contended that the arbitration clause would be unconscionable and unenforceable if it forbade class arbitration.[23] For its part, Stolt-Nielsen argued that the parties did not expressly consent to class arbitration and presented expert evidence showing that it was "customary in the shipping business for parties to resolve their disputes through bilateral arbitration."[24] After hearing the parties' arguments and evidence, the arbitral tribunal issued a partial award concluding that the arbitration clause was broad and allowed for class arbitration because there was no evidence of the parties' intent to preclude class arbitration.[25] The arbitration was then paused to allow the parties to seek interlocutory judicial review of that decision.[26]

Stolt-Nielsen sought vacatur of the partial award before the District Court for the Southern District of New York. The district court vacated the arbitral award under § 10(a)(4) of the FAA (where arbitrators have exceeded their powers), finding that the tribunal had manifestly disregarded the law.[27] Specifically, the district court found that (1) "the arbitrators manifestly disregarded a well defined rule of governing maritime law that precluded class arbitration under the clauses here in issue" and (2) "even if the governing law here [was] New York law (as opposed to general maritime law), the result would still be that the Panel acted in manifest disregard of the applicable law, and, in so doing, impermissibly 'fashion[ed] a new contract under the guise of contract

---

18 *Id.* at 668–69.
19 *Id.* at 672.
20 *Id.*
21 *Green Tree Fin. Corp.* v. *Bazzle*, 539 U.S. 444, 447 (2003).
22 *Stolt-Nielson*, 559 U.S. at 672.
23 *Id.*
24 *Id.* at 674 n.6.
25 *Id.* at 669.
26 *Id.*
27 *Id.* at 669–70.

construction.'"[28] The Court of Appeals for the Second Circuit disagreed and held that because nothing in maritime law nor New York law banned class arbitration, the arbitrators had not manifestly disregarded the law, reversing the District Court's decision and reinstating the partial award.[29]

### 3.2 *The Supreme Court's Opinion*

The U.S Supreme Court granted certiorari to consider "whether imposing class arbitration on parties whose arbitration clauses are 'silent' on that issue is consistent with the Federal Arbitration Act[.]"[30] The Supreme Court began its analysis by acknowledging the high standard that must be met in order to vacate an arbitration award under the FAA—"[i]t is only when [an] arbitrator strays from interpretation and application of the agreement and effectively 'dispense[s] his own brand of industrial justice' that his decision may be unenforceable."[31] The Court found that "the arbitration panel imposed its own policy choice and thus exceeded its powers" when it permitted class-action arbitration, which satisfied this stringent standard.[32] Specifically, the Court determined that the arbitrators had improperly rested their decision on public policy considerations—namely the cost of litigating the claims absent class arbitration and the implication that if Stolt-Nielsen's anti-consolidation argument controlled, "there would appear to be no basis for a class action absent express agreement among all parties and the putative class members."[33] Because the parties had agreed that the arbitration clause was "silent" on the issue, the Court reasoned that "the arbitrators' proper task was to identify the rule of law that governs in that situation[,]" either in the FAA itself or in maritime or New York law.[34] Instead of seeking to identify that "default rule[,]" "the panel proceeded as if it had the authority of a common-law court to develop what it viewed as the best rule to be applied in such a situation."[35] In doing so, it "imposed its own policy choice and thus exceeded its powers."[36]

---

28 *Stolt-Nielsen S.A.* v. *AnimalFeeds Int'l Corp.*, 435 F. Supp. 2d 382, 386–87 (S.D.N.Y. 2006) *rev'd*, 548 F.3d 85 (2d Cir. 2008), *rev'd and remanded sub nom. Stolt-Nielsen S.A.* v. *AnimalFeeds Int'l Corp.*, 559 U.S. 662 (2010), and *aff'd sub nom. Stolt-Nielsen S.A.* v. *AnimalFeeds Int'l Corp.*, 624 F.3d 157 (2d Cir. 2010) (quoting *Slatt* v. *Slatt*, 64 N.Y.2d 966, 967 (1985)).

29 *Stolt-Nielson*, 559 U.S. at 670.

30 *Id.* at 666.

31 *Id.* at 671 (quoting *Major League Baseball Players Ass'n* v. *Garvey*, 532 U.S. 504, 509 (2001)).

32 *Id.* at 676–77.

33 *Id.* at 675 n.7.

34 *Id.* at 673.

35 *Id.* at 673–74.

36 *Id.* at 677.

The Court vacated the award and went further to determine the question that was originally referred to the arbitral tribunal: whether class claims were arbitrable.[37] The Court framed that question as whether an arbitration agreement that is "silent" on the issue of class arbitration permits class arbitration.[38] The Court emphasized that "[w]hile interpretation of an arbitration agreement is generally a matter of state law," the FAA does "impose certain rules of fundamental importance," among which is the "basic precept that arbitration 'is a matter of consent, not coercion[.]'"[39] Because of the contractual nature of arbitration, parties have the authority, in particular, to specify *with whom* to arbitrate their disputes.[40] Arbitrators and courts must give effect to these contractual terms and fulfill the parties' intent.[41] Therefore, the Court held that "a party may not be compelled under the FAA to submit to class arbitration unless there is a contractual basis for concluding that the party *agreed* to do so."[42]

As noted, the parties had stipulated that the arbitration agreement in the Vegoilvoy charter party was silent on that question, which in the Court's view invited the application of a default rule of law that might serve to supply the contractual rule on the issue in the absence of consent.[43] Because the arbitrators had not done this and instead had ruled on the basis of what the Court considered to be their own policy rationale, the Court concluded that the award's legal conclusion was "fundamentally at war with the foundational FAA principle that arbitration is a matter of consent."[44] While the Court acknowledged that arbitrators can generally infer an implicit agreement to authorize *procedures* that give effect to the parties' agreement to arbitrate,[45] it held that the differences between bilateral arbitration and class-action arbitration are so great that the parties' mere silence on class arbitration cannot reasonably be interpreted to accommodate an intent to allow the arbitrators to permit class arbitration as a matter of procedure.[46] The Court noted, for example, that class-action arbitration brings in multiple absent third parties to the dispute, creates confidentiality concerns, binds non-present parties to a decision, significantly

37 *See id.*

38 *Id.*

39 *Id.* at 681 (quoting *Volt Info. Scis., Inc.* v. *Bd. of Trs. of Leland Stanford Junior Univ.*, 489 U.S. 468, 479 (1989)).

40 *See id.* at 683.

41 *Id.*

42 *Id.* at 684 (emphasis in original).

43 *Id.*

44 *Id.*

45 *See id.* at 684–85.

46 *Id.* at 687.

raises the commercial stakes of a dispute, and complicates a process that is designed to be a simple, swift, and pragmatic alternative to lengthy litigation proceedings.[47] The Court concluded that these differences between bilateral arbitration and class arbitration are significant enough that allowing decision-makers to infer an agreement to class arbitration without a contractual basis to determine consent would run counter to the fundamental principle that arbitration is not a matter of "coercion[.]"[48]

In her dissent, Justice Ginsburg challenged the Court's characterization of the party's arbitration agreement as not addressing class-based arbitration. Pointing to the Vegoilvoy charter party's broad language referring to arbitration "*any* dispute arising from the making, performance or termination" of the agreement, as well as AnimalFeed's stated expectations regarding the clause, she concluded that the arbitral tribunal had adequate grounds to find that the clause applied to class-based arbitrations, too.[49] Justice Ginsburg further concluded that, in focusing on the clause's wording, the tribunal acted consistently within the relevant state and federal-maritime rules of contractual interpretation.[50] This, she stated, satisfied the only relevant question for which the FAA grants federal courts jurisdiction to vacate an arbitration tribunal's decision under §10(a)(4): whether the arbitrators had power, based on the arbitration agreement, to reach the issue in question.[51]

Justice Ginsburg went on to discuss what she considered to be two key limitations of the Court's decision. First, that the Court's opinion "does not insist on express consent to class arbitration[,]" only that there be *some* contractual basis for determining the parties agreed to such a method of dispute resolution.[52] Second, that the Court highlighted the sophisticated nature of the parties at issue, meaning that its holding does not extend to class-based arbitration concerning "contracts of adhesion presented on a take-it-or-leave-it basis."[53]

Justice Ginsburg also characterized the determination of whether the individual parties' claims could be adjudicated together in the arbitration as one regarding the "procedural mode" available for their presentation of the claims at issue.[54] To her, the question was merely whether the arbitrators had power to

47 *Id.* at 686–87.
48 *Id.* at 681.
49 *See id.* at 694–95 (Ginsburg, J., dissenting) (emphasis added).
50 *Id.* at 695.
51 *Id.* at 694.
52 *Id.* at 699.
53 *Id.*
54 *Id.* at 696.

hear all claims together or not, and did not concern the claimants' substantive legal rights.[55] The Court, however, held that this characterization "minimizes the[] crucial differences" between bilateral and class-based arbitration.[56]

Overall, *Stolt-Nielsen* delineated the limits of arbitral jurisdiction under the FAA to interpret contractual provisions and enforce those provisions according to the parties' intent. Arbitral tribunals lack the common-law authority to shape the rules of law that govern contract disputes or impose their policy preferences on the parties involved. Importantly, the majority was not persuaded by Justice Ginsburg's argument that the FAA did not permit the Court to vacate the award on the ground that "the parties' supplemental agreement, referring the class-arbitration issue to an arbitration panel, undoubtedly empowered the arbitrators to render their clause-construction decision."[57] Justice Alito, writing for the majority, explained that the Court was "obliged" to enforce the supplemental agreement "according to its terms[,]" which expressly provided that the supplemental agreement did not alter the scope of the arbitration clause in any of the charter party agreements.[58]

Further, Justice Alito found that "nothing in the supplemental agreement conferred authority on the arbitrators to exceed the terms of the charter party itself[,]" thus effectively limiting the scope of arbitral jurisdiction to the terms of the express parties' agreement.[59] But as Justice Ginsburg pointed out in her dissent, the Court stopped short of indicating what "contractual basis" could support a finding that parties agree to authorize class-action arbitration.[60]

55 *Id.*

56 *Id.* at 687 (majority opinion).

57 *Id.* at 694 (Ginsburg, J., dissenting).

58 *Id.* at 681 n.8 (majority opinion).

59 *Id.*

60 *Id.* at 699 (Ginsburg, J., dissenting); *see also Jock* v. *Sterling Jewelers Inc.*, 942 F.3d 617, 626 (2d Cir. 2019) (noting that *Stolt-Nielsen* affirmed the proposition that "an arbitration agreement may be interpreted to include implicit consent to class procedures"); *Fantastic Sams Franchise Corp.* v. *FSRO Ass'n Ltd.*, 683 F.3d 18, 22 (1st Cir. 2012) (rejecting the notion that *Stolt-Nielsen* requires "express contractual language evincing the parties' intent to permit class or collective arbitration"); *Sutter* v. *Oxford Health Plans LLC*, 675 F.3d 215, 222 (3d Cir. 2012) (finding that *Stolt-Nielsen* "did not establish a bright line rule that class arbitration is allowed only under an arbitration agreement that incants 'class arbitration' or otherwise expressly provides for aggregate procedures.").

## 4 The Impact of *Stolt-Nielsen* in U.S. Arbitral Law and Practice

Before the Supreme Court released its *Stolt-Nielsen* opinion, there was a lively debate over the significant impacts that the decision would have, particularly for consumer form contracts. On one side, some worried that if the Court allowed class arbitration to proceed in the absence of the parties' consent, respondents to arbitration claims would be forced into unfavorable settlement agreements.[61] The risk of a class arbitration could be enormous—businesses could be exposed to massive amounts of legal and financial liability if a single customer could purport to bring claims on behalf of hundreds or even thousands of others into a single arbitration.[62] Furthermore, arbitration lacks many of the procedural guardrails that protect defendants in regular litigation proceedings, including appeals as of right.[63] These factors combined would create an environment in which businesses are pressured to pay higher damages than they otherwise would to settle a consolidated claim.[64] This side of the debate also worried that allowing decision-makers to impose class arbitration without a contractual basis to infer the parties' consent would jeopardize the character of arbitration as a fair and efficient alternative to litigation.[65]

On the other side, there were those who predicted that requiring express consent to class arbitration would impose a huge economic burden on the parties seeking suit—namely, small businesses and individuals.[66] Without access to class-action arbitration, these parties would need to pay large sums of money to resolve similar or near-identical claims against the same respondent.[67] It was also argued that small businesses and individuals would not be able to afford competent counsel unless they were allowed to proceed as a class.[68] And as Justice Ginsburg observed in her dissent, "[w]hen adjudication

61 *See, e.g.*, Brief for DRI—the Voice of the Defense Bar as Amicus Curiae Supporting Petitioners, 2009 WL 2875371 at *17–20, *Stolt-Nielsen S.A. v. AnimalFeeds Int'l Corp.*, 559 U.S. 662 (2010).

62 *See* Brief for the Chamber of Commerce of the United States of America as Amicus Curiae Supporting Petitioners, 2009 WL 2875371 at *16–17, *Stolt-Nielsen*, 559 U.S. 662 (2010).

63 *See* Brief for DRI—the Voice of the Defense Bar as Amicus Curiae Supporting Petitioners, 2009 WL 2875371 at *16–22, *Stolt-Nielsen*, 559 U.S. 662 (2010).

64 *See* Brief for the Equal Employment Advisory Council as Amicus Curiae Supporting Petitioners, 2009 WL 2875372 at *19–20, *Stolt-Nielsen*, 559 U.S. 662 (2010).

65 *See* Brief for CTIA—The Wireless Association as Amicus Curiae Supporting Petitioners, 2009 WL 2875373 at *8, *Stolt-Nielsen*, 559 U.S. 662 (2010).

66 *See, e.g.*, Brief for the American Association for Justice and AARP as Amici Curiae Supporting Respondent, 2009 WL 3495338 at *9–12, *Stolt-Nielsen*, 559 U.S. 662 (2010).

67 *Id.* at 5–9.

68 *Id.* at 10–11.

is costly and individual claims are no more than modest in size, class proceedings may be 'the thing,' *i.e.*, without them, potential claimants will have little, if any, incentive to seek vindication of their rights."[69] To put a finer point on it, critics of what ultimately became the Supreme Court's holding worried that this outcome would risk depriving customers and employees of an opportunity to bring legal claims.[70]

Now that more than a decade has passed since this consequential decision came down, we can begin to assess its impact. The results have been mixed. Justice Ginsburg's dissent made the observation that the parties in the case were "sophisticated business entities" and the majority's holding did not seem to apply to "contracts of adhesion presented on a take-it-or-leave-it basis."[71] However, some courts have applied the *Stolt-Nielsen* holding to disputes involving form contracts.[72] The agreements at the center of these disputes are often "take-it-or-leave-it" contracts of adhesion in the employment and consumer agreements.

The Fifth Circuit's decision in *Reed* v. *Florida Metropolitan University, Inc.* is an illustrative example from the consumer realm.[73] This case involved a graduate of a Florida online university who was dissatisfied with his experience and filed a class arbitration against the university.[74] Although the agreement did not mention class arbitration, the arbitrator found an implicit agreement to the procedural mechanism and the district court confirmed the award.[75] The Fifth Circuit, however, reversed and vacated the award. It relied on *Stolt-Nielsen* to hold "that the arbitrator exceeded his authority by ordering the parties

69 *Stolt-Nielsen*, 559 U.S. at 699 (Ginsburg, J., dissenting) (citing *Amchem Pros., Inc.* v. *Windsor*, 521 U.S. 591, 617 (1997)); *see also* Brief for Lawyers' Committee for Civil Rights Under Law et al., as Amici Curiae Supporting Respondent, 2009 WL 3453652 at *17–19, *Stolt-Nielsen*, 559 U.S. 662 (2010) (arguing that the financial stakes for individual claimants are so small that the choice is not whether the claim will proceed as a bilateral arbitration or a class-action arbitration, but whether the claim will proceed as a class-action arbitration or not at all).

70 *See* Brief for Lawyers' Committee for Civil Rights Under Law et al., as Amici Curiae Supporting Respondent, 2009 WL 3453652 at 16–17, *Stolt-Nielsen*, 559 U.S. 662 (2010).

71 *Stolt-Nielsen*, 559 U.S. at 699 (Ginsburg, J., dissenting).

72 *See, e.g.*, *Tyskowski* v. *Int'l Bus. Machines Corp.*, 2023 WL 6394061, at *2 (S.D.N.Y. Sept. 30, 2023) (citing *Stolt-Nielsen* for the proposition that "to grant vacatur of an arbitrator's decision, the movant must meet a very high threshold" in the context of a dispute arising from an employment arbitration agreement).

73 *Reed* v. *Fla. Metro. Univ., Inc.*, 681 F.3d 630 (5th Cir. 2012), *abrogated by Oxford Health Plans LLC* v. *Sutter*, 569 U.S. 564 (2013).

74 *Id.* at 632.

75 *Id.* at 633.

into class arbitration without a sufficient basis for concluding that the parties agreed to resolve their dispute in this manner."[76] This decision, however, was subsequently abrogated by the Supreme Court's holding in *Oxford Health Plans LLC* v. *Sutter*.[77] There, the Supreme Court affirmed the holding in a Third Circuit case similar to *Reed*, which found that "[s]o long as an arbitrator 'makes a good faith attempt' to interpret a contract, 'even serious errors of law or fact will not subject his award to vacatur.'"[78] The Court's holding in *Oxford Health Plans* has therefore clarified that *Stolt-Nielsen* did not grant courts additional power to question the judgment of arbitrators when interpreting contractual ambiguity, even regarding consent to class arbitration. It simply affirmed that silence on an issue does not mean consent in the absence of an implicit indication to the contrary.

*NCR Corporation* v. *Jones*, a more recent case from the Western District of North Carolina, helps sharpen the distinction the Court made in *Oxford Health Plans*. In *Jones*, a former employee filed a class arbitration against his former employer for alleged violations of the Fair Credit Reporting Act.[79] The employer countersued, seeking declaratory judgment that the parties had not agreed to class arbitration.[80] The district court ruled in favor of the employer, finding that the employment contract did not "read to encompass class arbitration."[81] In reaching its decision, the court echoed the majority in *Stolt-Nielsen* in finding persuasive the "significant fact that the Agreement is silent on the issue of class arbitration" and "the significant differences between class and bilateral arbitration[.]"[82] And though it recognized that *Stolt-Nielsen* permitted an implicit agreement to class arbitration, it found no evidence of such an agreement within the relevant contract.[83]

---

76 *Id.* at 642.

77 *See Oxford Health Plans LLC* v. *Sutter*, 569 U.S. 564, 568 n.1 (2013).

78 *Id.* (quoting *Sutter*, 675 F.3d at 220).

79 *NCR Corp.* v. *Jones*, 157 F. Supp. 3d 460, 461–62 (W.D.N.C. 2016).

80 *Id.* Since the case was presented as a motion for declaratory judgment, there was not yet any arbitral determination regarding whether the employer consented to class arbitration under the relevant agreement. *See id.* at 462. The case therefore largely avoids the question of who decides—arbitrator or court—that was relevant in *Stolt-Nielsen* and *Oxford Health Plans*.

81 *Id.* at 471.

82 *Id.*

83 *Id.* at 467; *see also Anwar* v. *Fairfield Greenwich Ltd.*, 728 F. Supp. 2d 462, 467 (S.D.N.Y. 2011) (discussing how an agreement silent on class arbitration that provides for arbitration "in accordance with the rules of the AAA" is insufficient to consent to class arbitration, notwithstanding the AAA rules themselves providing for class arbitration).

Furthermore, following the *Stolt-Nielsen* decision, district courts have continued to largely defer to arbitrators' interpretation of an arbitration agreement as long as the arbitration delegates questions of arbitrability to the arbitrators to decide in the first instance, even when class arbitration is not explicitly mentioned in the text.[84] And the Second Circuit, in a decision that allowed class arbitration to proceed, has held that *Stolt-Nielsen* "did not create a bright-line rule" that class arbitration is allowed only under an arbitration agreement that expressly provides for it.[85]

Courts also have been reticent to extend *Stolt-Nielsen*'s reasoning to mass or consolidated arbitration. Judge Easterbrook explained why in his Seventh Circuit decision holding that *Stolt-Nielsen* did not apply outside the class-arbitration context.[86] Speaking for the court, he stressed that "class actions always have been treated as special[,]" given "one self-selected plaintiff represents others" and the "stringent requirements" on class certification.[87] Since neither of these are present in consolidated proceedings, they do not "change the fundamental nature of arbitration[,]" like class arbitration could.[88]

The aftermath of *Stolt-Nielsen* therefore shows that the Supreme Court's decision did not cut off the arbitrator's authority to decide whether a contract permits class arbitration, even in situations where the contract is silent on the issue, and courts have been cautious to extend its reasoning to related contexts like consolidation of multiple claims and multiple parties.

## 5 Conclusions

Though the Court's core holding in *Stolt-Nielsen* remains on firm ground, courts largely limited it to the class-arbitration context. And even within that context, they have been fairly cautious in using the case as an invitation to wade into related arbitrability questions of what constitutes consent to a class procedure for arbitration. Their reluctance has manifested in two key contexts. The first is when there is ambiguity regarding whether the parties consented to class

84 *See, e.g.*, *In re A2P SMS Antitrust Litig.*, 2014 WL 2445756, at *1 (S.D.N.Y. May 29, 2014) (concluding "that the issue of the availability of class arbitration ... is for the arbitrator to decide"); *Price* v. *NCR Corp.*, 908 F. Supp. 2d 935, 946 (N.D. Ill. 2012) (same).

85 *Jock* v. *Sterling Jewelers Inc.*, 646 F.3d 113, 124 (2d Cir. 2011).

86 *See Blue Cross Blue Shield of Mass.* v. *BCS Ins.*, 671 F.3d 635, 638–40 (7th Cir. 2011) (declining to apply *Stolt-Nielsen*'s holding to a consolidated arbitration).

87 *Id.* at 640.

88 *Id. Accord Anwar*, 728 F. Supp. 2d at 477–78 (same).

arbitration. Although *Stolt-Nielsen* states that neither courts nor arbitrators have the authority to impose class arbitration without both parties' affirmative consent, it only addressed contracts that are unquestionably "silent" on class arbitration. When there is ambiguity, courts still defer to the arbitrator's interpretation, who may find a contractual basis for permitting class arbitration to proceed. The second key context is when claimants use other procedural mechanisms for grouping multiple claims other than class arbitration, such as consolidation or mass arbitrations. In these scenarios, courts have been less willing to extend *Stolt-Nielsen*'s reasoning.

CHAPTER 22

# *Granite Rock Co. v. Int'l Bhd. of Teamsters* (2010)

*Steven Skulnik*

## 1 Introduction

In *First Options of Chicago, Inc. v. Kaplan*, 514 U.S. 938 (1995), the U.S. Supreme Court first addressed the issue of whether a U.S court or the arbitral tribunal has the primary authority to decide the tribunal's jurisdiction. Jurisdictional issues (often referred to as "arbitrability") concern the agreement's formation, validity, scope, or whether the agreement applies to non-signatories. Sections 3 and 4 of the Federal Arbitration Act (9 U.S.C. §§ 3 and 4) make clear that the court has the primary duty to decide jurisdictional issues. *First Options* recognized that primacy was only a legal presumption. To overcome this presumption, "the question 'who has the primary power to decide arbitrability' turns upon what the parties agreed about that matter." *Id.* at 943. Parties rebut that presumption if they clearly agree to arbitrate arbitrability. *Id.* at 946. The court noted, however, that where parties agree to arbitrate some matters but disagree on the scope of the arbitration clause, U.S. arbitration law requires that doubts concerning the scope of issues to be arbitrated should be resolved in favor of arbitration. *Id.* at 945.

Under the doctrine of separability, courts have traditionally held that, while courts have primary authority to decide challenges to the arbitration agreement, challenges to the contract as a whole are a matter for the arbitral tribunal to decide. *Prima Paint Corp. v. Flood & Conklin Mfg. Co.*, 388 U.S. 395, 403–404 (1967). In *Buckeye Check Cashing, Inc. v. Cardegna*, 546 U.S. 440, 444, n.1 (2006), the U.S. Supreme Court, in *dicta*, addressed whether the separability doctrine should apply where the party seeking to avoid arbitration challenges formation of the contract containing the arbitration clause.[1]

1 *Id.* ("The issue of the contract's validity is different from the issue whether any agreement between the alleged obligor and obligee was ever concluded. Our opinion today addresses only the former, and does not speak to the issue decided in the cases cited by respondents (and by the Florida Supreme Court), which hold that it is for courts to decide whether the alleged obligor ever signed the contract, *Chastain v. Robinson–Humphrey Co.*, 957 F.2d 851 (C.A.11 1992), whether the signor lacked authority to commit the alleged principal, *Sandvik AB v. Advent Int'l Corp.*, 220 F.3d 99 (C.A.3 2000); *Sphere Drake Ins. Ltd. v. All American Ins. Co.*, 256 F.3d 587 (C.A.7 2001), and whether the signor lacked the mental capacity to assent,

 | DOI:10.1163/9789004715820_023

## 2 The Case

In *Granite Rock Co. v. Int'l Bhd. of Teamsters*, 561 U.S. 287 (2010), the Court was faced with the issue of how to treat issue of who decides the issue of formation or existence of the main contract. The Court decided issues concerning formation of the main contract, as opposed to the contract's validity, are for the courts to determine. *Id.* at 296.

### 2.1 *Background of the Case*

The case involves a claim by an employer against a labor union[2] for damages arising out of a 2004 strike.[3] Granite Rock sought an injunction and damages, claiming the union violated a no strike clause in a collective bargaining agreement (CBA) reached in 2004. The answer to precisely when in 2004 the CBA was formed depended on when union members ratified it and the facts concerning that issue were disputed. Because the CBA contained an arbitration clause, the issue arose as to whether the parties' dispute over the CBA's ratification date was a matter for the court or an arbitrator to resolve.

Granite Rock Company is a concrete and building materials company. It had employees under different labor contracts with several unions, including the Teamsters. Granite Rock and the Teamsters were parties to a 1999 CBA that expired in April 2004. In June 2004, the workers went on strike. The strike continued until July 2, 2004, when the parties reached agreement on the terms of the CBA at issue. *Id.* at 292.

The parties also discussed a separate back-to-work agreement that would, among other things, hold the workers harmless for damages to Granite Rock caused by the strike but no such agreement was reached. Granite Rock informed the union that the company would view any continued strike activity as a violation of the new CBA's no-strike clause. The union responded on July 6, 2004, by announcing a company-wide strike. *Id.* at 293.

---

*Spahr v. Secco*, 330 F.3d 1266 (C.A.10 2003)"); *accord Rent-A-Ctr., W., Inc. v. Jackson*, 561 U.S. 63, 71, n.2 (2010) ("The issue of the agreement's "validity" is different from the issue whether any agreement between the parties "was ever concluded," and, as in [*Buckeye Check Cashing*], we address only the former").

2 The respondents were both the International Brotherhood of Teamsters and a local branch. As regards the arbitration issues in this case, there is no need to distinguish between the two entities.

3 The Court noted that precedents from commercial arbitration cases apply equally to labor disputes such as this one. Under each regime, "courts must typically decide any questions concerning the formation or scope of an arbitration agreement before ordering parties to comply with it." *Id.* at 299, n.6.

On July 9, 2004, Granite Rock sued the union in federal court, seeking an injunction against the ongoing strike and damages. The union opposed Granite Rock's request, asserting that because the CBA was not validly ratified at the time of the July strike, the CBA's no-strike clause did not apply. In response, Granite Rock offered testimony of a union member who claimed the union put the new CBA to a ratification vote on July 2, 2004, and that the voting members unanimously approved the agreement on that day. On August 22, 2004, the union conducted a successful ratification vote on the CBA, and on September 13, 2004, the union called off the strike. *Id.* at 295.

The union sought to compel arbitration over the parties' dispute over the CBA's effective date to arbitration. Granite Rock claimed the CBA was ratified on July 2 and the union claimed the date was August 22. The district court held that ratification date or was an issue for the court to decide and submitted the question to a jury.[4] The jury decided that the union members ratified the CBA on July 2, 2004, and the court then compelled arbitration. *Id.*

The Court of Appeals for the Ninth Circuit disagreed with the district court's decision that the date of the CBA's ratification was a matter for the court. The Ninth Circuit invoked the "national policy favoring arbitration" that requires that any ambiguity about the scope of the parties' arbitration clause be resolved in favor of arbitrability. Moreover, according to the Ninth Circuit, Granite Rock implicitly consented to arbitrate the ratification-date dispute by asserting claims under the 2004 CBA that provided for arbitration. *Id.* at 296. In effect, the Ninth Circuit held that Granite Rock cannot invoke one part of the 2004 CBA, the no-strike clause, but avoid another clause in the same agreement, the arbitration clause.

### 2.2 *Issue and the Parties' Allegations*

The issue presented was whether a court or an arbitrator should decide the ratification issue. The union contended that where, as here, parties concede that they have agreed to arbitrate some matters under an arbitration agreement, any doubts concerning the scope of the arbitration agreement should be resolved in favor of arbitration. Under the separability doctrine, moreover, according to

4 Section 4 of the Federal Arbitration Act (FAA) provides that "[i]f the making of the arbitration agreement or the failure, neglect, or refusal to perform the same be in issue, the court shall proceed summarily to the trial thereof. ... [w]here such an issue is raised, the party alleged to be in default may, ... demand a jury trial of such issue, and upon such demand the court shall make an order referring the issue or issues to a jury in the manner provided by the Federal Rules of Civil Procedure, or may specially call a jury for that purpose." 9 U.S.C. § 4.

the union, this presumption of arbitrability applies even to disputes about the enforceability of the contract containing the arbitration clause.

Granite Rock responded that this case did not present a dispute over the *scope* of an arbitration agreement but rather a question of formation of the agreement itself. When one party denies a contract exists, there cannot be a "clear and unmistakable" agreement to submit the formation issue to arbitration.[5] Under these circumstances, Granite Rock argued, the issue is for judicial determination.

### 2.3 *The Court's Opinion*

The Court reversed the Ninth Circuit's decision and held that the formation-date question must be decided by the district court. The Court noted that the CBA's arbitration clause applies only to disputes that "arise under" the CBA. Accordingly, to hold the parties' ratification-date dispute arbitrable, the district court had to decide whether that dispute could be characterized as arising under the CBA. According to the Court, the Ninth Circuit erred by conflating the arbitrability of the union's ratification-date defense with the arbitrability of the Granite Rock's claim of breach of the CBA's no strike provision. The Court noted that the CBA's arbitration clause "does not so obviously cover disputes about the CBA's own formation." *Id.* at 304–05.

The Court also concluded that, if the 2004 CBA was not ratified, and therefore not formed, until August 22, as the union asserts, there was no CBA for the July no-strike dispute to "arise under," and therefore no valid basis for the no basis to compel arbitration "along with, by extension, [the union's] formation-date defense to those claims." Therefore, the district court needed to determine the CBA's ratification date in order to decide whether the parties agreed to arbitrate Granite Rock's no-strike claim or the ratification-date dispute the union raised as a defense to that claim. *Id.* at 305.

Lastly, the Court rejected the argument that Granite Rock implicitly consented to arbitration when it sued to enforce the CBA's no-strike clause. The Court held that, by seeking an injunction against the strike, which it claims violated the 2004 CBA, Granite Rock did not exhibit consent to arbitrate the union's ratification defense. The Court acknowledged that, when Granite Rock sought that injunction, it viewed the CBA (and all of its provisions) as enforceable but the mere fact that the union raised the formation-date dispute as a defense to Granite Rock's suit does not make that dispute arbitrable.

5 The "clear and unmistakable" test was first announced in *AT&T Techs., Inc. v. Commc'ns Workers of Am.*, 475 U.S. 643, 649 (1986).

Accordingly, the Court held that the parties' dispute over the CBA's formation date was for the district court, not an arbitrator, to resolve. *Id.* at 308–09.[6]

Justice Sotomayor, joined by Justice Stevens, dissented with respect to the arbitrability issue. According to the dissent, the 2004 CBA, by its terms was made retroactive to May 2004, the day after the expiration of the 1999 CBA. Therefore, any claims relating to the continuation of the strike in July 2004 were covered by the CBA and its arbitration clause. Given the CBA's express retroactivity, treating the ratification-date defense as a formation dispute subject to judicial resolution is inconsistent with the terms of the contract. The dissent points out that the ratification defense is a merits defense in which the union argues that the no-strike clause should not apply to the July strike because the union had not ratified the CBA at that time. *Id.* at 317.

### 2.4 *Key Takeaways*

While the holding that courts have primary authority to decide issues of contract formation is welcome, its application to the facts here is questionable. The dissent fairly points out that whether Granite Rock had a valid claim for breach of the CBA and whether the union has a ratification defense are merits questions. Granite Rock had to prove that the union continued (and expanded) the strike after ratification as part of its *prima facie* case on the merits.

Challenges to the arbitrators' jurisdiction concern only the allocation of authority between arbitrators and the courts to decide a particular dispute. Challenges to the claimant's entitlement to relief are not jurisdictional objections. *See Benihana, Inc. v. Benihana of Tokyo, LLC*, 784 F.3d 887, 899 (2d Cir. 2015) (the objection "concerns what decision may be reached—that is, it concerns the proper interpretation of the Agreement—not who may reach it and is therefore a merits argument masked as a jurisdictional one").

## 3 The Case's Impact on U.S. Arbitration Law

The decision is groundbreaking in that Court, for the first time, held that its earlier pronouncements concerning the federal policy favoring arbitration and the maxim that doubts be resolved in favor of arbitration apply only to disputes over the scope of an arbitration clause and not its existence. This case makes clear that it is now well-established that, where a party denies that any

6 The case also presented certain labor law issues beyond the arbitrability dispute. Those issues are not discussed here.

contract was ever concluded, the challenge may be resolved initially by the court and not referred to arbitration. *See* G. Born, *International Commercial Arbitration* 1269–78.

The decision also announces an important exception to the separability principle, *viz.*, unlike challenges to the validity of the main contract, where the court will treat the arbitration agreement as a separate agreement from the main contract, when it comes to formation, the court may consider challenges to the main contract. The Restatement (Third) U.S. Law of International Commercial Arbitration recognizes that distinction: "[t]o the extent the court finds that the agreement or contract does not exist, it declines to enforce the arbitration agreement." Restatement (Third) U.S. Law of Int'l Comm. Arb. § 2.13 (2019).

Finally, this decision marks a turning point for the Court regarding the application of the policy favoring arbitration. While much of the Court's jurisprudence, beginning with *Mitsubishi Motors Corp. v. Soler Chrysler–Plymouth, Inc.*, 473 U.S. 614, 631 (1985), notes the "emphatic federal policy in favor of arbitral dispute resolution," the *Granite Rock* Court notes that the policy only comes into play after a court is persuaded that the parties validly formed their arbitration agreement. *Granite Rock*, 561 U.S. at 300.

Most recently in *Morgan v. Sundance, Inc.*, 142 S. Ct. 1708, 1709 (2022), the Court observed that "[t]he federal policy is about treating arbitration contracts like all others, not about fostering arbitration." This articulation of federal policy will not be applied to questions of allocation of authority as between courts and arbitral tribunals.

## 4 Conclusions

After previously noting only in dicta that questions about contract formation are for the courts, *Granite Rock's* holding in that regard is a welcome development. The application of that principle to what appears to be a merits defense is on less firm legal footing.

CHAPTER 23

# AT&T *Mobility* LLC *v. Concepcion*, 563 U.S. 333 (2011)

*Grant Hanessian*

## 1 Introduction

In AT&T *Mobility* LLC *v. Concepcion*, the United States Supreme Court, in a five-to-four decision, held that Section 2 of the Federal Arbitration Act ("FAA") preempted the application of state unconscionability law to invalidate a waiver of class-action proceedings in a consumer contract's arbitration agreement.[1]

## 2 Preliminary Considerations on the Validity of Arbitration Agreements

In 2005, the California Supreme Court held in *Discover Bank v. Superior Court*[2] that the waiver of class-arbitration in a consumer adhesion contract was unconscionable and therefore unenforceable. The California court held that the provision in Section 2 of the FAA[3] stating that an arbitration agreement "shall be valid, irrevocable, and enforceable, save upon such grounds as exist at law or in equity for the revocation of any contract." (the "savings clause") provided that arbitration agreements may be invalidated by "generally applicable contract defenses, such as fraud, duress, or unconscionability",[4] but not by defenses that apply only to arbitration or that derive their meaning from the fact that an agreement to arbitrate is at issue.[5]

1 563 U.S. at 344.

2 *Discover Bank v. Superior Court*, 36 Cal.4th 148, 30 Cal.Rptr.3d 76, 113 P.3d 1100 (2005).

3 Section 2 of the FAA provides in part: [a] written provision in any maritime transaction or a contract evidencing a transaction involving commerce to settle by arbitration a controversy thereafter arising out of such contract or transaction, or the refusal to perform the whole or any part thereof, or an agreement in writing to submit to arbitration an existing controversy arising out of such a contract, transaction, or refusal, shall be valid, irrevocable, and enforceable, save upon such grounds as exist at law or in equity for the revocation of any contract or as otherwise provided in Chapter 4.

4 *Discover Bank*, at 165, citing *Little v. Auto Stiegler, Inc.* (2003), 29 Cal. 4th at p. 1079, 130 Cal. Rptr. 2d 892, 63 P. 3d 979.

5 *Discover Bank*, at 165, citing the U.S. Supreme Court decision in *Perry v. Thomas* (1987), 482 U.S. 483, 105 S.Ct. 2520: [There is a] critical distinction made by the *Perry* court between a

 | DOI:10.1163/9789004715820_024

In *AT&T Mobility*, the U.S. Supreme Court majority ruled that the California court's application of the saving clause to invalidate a waiver of class arbitration as unconscionable under California law was inconsistent with, and pre-empted by, the FAA. The Supreme Court decided that the California rule adversely affected the efficacy of arbitration agreements by imposing a rule that class-arbitration proceedings (whether in arbitration or litigation) must always be available to consumers, a result incompatible with Congressional intent in adopting the FAA to promote arbitration as a streamlined and efficient dispute resolution mechanism.

## 3 The Case

### 3.1 *Background of the Case*

In February 2002, Vincent and Liza Concepcion and AT&T entered into a contract pursuant to which AT&T agreed to provide the Concepcions with cellular phone service (the "cell contract"). AT&T advertised that the cellular service purchased by the Concepcions included free cell phones. Although AT&T did not charge the couple for the phones, it did charge them sales tax in the amount of USD 30.22, based on the retail value of the phones.

In March 2006, the Concepcions filed a complaint against AT&T in the United States District Court for the Southern District of California, alleging that by advertising that the phones would be provided "free" and charging sales tax, AT&T engaged in false advertising and fraud. Their complaint was later consolidated into a class action against AT&T, on behalf of everyone who entered into such contracts with AT&T and were required to pay the tax.

In March 2008, AT&T moved to compel arbitration of the dispute, under the arbitration agreement in the parties' contract, which required arbitration of all disputes between the parties and that all claims be brought in the parties' "individual capacity, and not as a plaintiff or class member in any purported class or representative proceeding."[6]

The Concepcions opposed AT&T's motion to compel arbitration, contending that the prohibition on class action arbitration was unconscionable under California law, relying on the holding in *Discover Bank*.

---

"state-law principle that takes its meaning precisely from the fact that a contract to arbitrate is at issue," which is preempted by section 2 of the FAA, and a state law that "govern[s] issues concerning the validity, revocability, and enforceability of contracts generally," which is not. (*Perry* [*v. Thomas* (1987)], 482 U.S. at p. 493, fn. 9.).

6 563 U.S. at 336.

The District Court agreed with the Concepcions and denied AT&T's motion. Citing *Discover Bank*, the District Court stated:

> [f]aithful adherence to California's stated policy of favoring class litigation and arbitration to deter alleged fraudulent conduct in cases involving large numbers of consumers with small amounts of damages, compels the Court to invalidate [the] class waiver provision. A class waiver provision may "serve[ ] as a disincentive for [a party with superior bargaining power] to avoid the type of conduct that might lead to class action litigation in the first place." *Discover Bank*, 36 Cal.4th at 159, 30 Cal.Rptr.3d 76, 113 P.3d 1100 (quoting *Szetela*, 97 Cal.App.4th at 1101, 118 Cal.Rptr.2d 862). "By imposing [a class waiver] clause on its customers, [a party with superior bargaining power] has essentially granted itself a license to push the boundaries of good business practices to their furthest limits. ..." *Id.* This overarching policy concern of deterring corporate wrongdoing is not sufficiently addressed by [the] arbitration provision.[7]

The Ninth Circuit Court of Appeals affirmed the District Court decision, stating that the class action waiver was unconscionable and that the *Discover Bank* rule was not preempted by the FAA. The Court stated:

> The Federal Arbitration Act does not expressly or impliedly preempt California law governing the unconscionability of class action waivers in consumer contracts of adhesion. The FAA "does not bar federal or state courts from applying generally applicable state contract law principles and refusing to enforce an unconscionable class action waiver in an arbitration clause." *Shroyer*, 498 F.3d at 987.[8]

AT&T filed a *writ of certiorari* with the U.S. Supreme Court, which was granted in 2010.

---

7 *Laster v. T-Mobile USA, Inc.*, No. 05CV1167DMS AJB, 2008 WL 5216255, at *14 (S.D. Cal. Aug. 11, 2008), aff'd sub nom. *Laster v. AT & T Mobility LLC*, 584 F.3d 849 (9th Cir. 2009), rev'd sub nom. *AT&T Mobility LLC v. Concepcion*, 563 U.S. 333, 131 S. Ct. 1740, 179 L. Ed. 2d 742 (2011), and amended in part, No. 05CV1167 DMS WVG, 2012 WL 1681762 (S.D. Cal. May 9, 2012).

8 *Laster v. AT & T Mobility LLC*, 584 F.3d 849, 856–57 (9th Cir. 2009), *rev'd sub nom. AT&T Mobility LLC v. Concepcion*, 563 U.S. 333, 131 S. Ct. 1740, 179 L. Ed. 2d 742 (2011).

### 3.2 *Issue and Parties' Allegations*

The issue in this case was whether the California unconscionability rule as applied in *Discover Bank* was preempted by section 2 of the FAA—specifically, whether state law prohibiting the waiver of class-proceedings in consumer adhesion contracts is among "such grounds as exist at law or in equity for the revocation of any contract"[9] under section 2 and thus a valid ground to decline to enforce an arbitration agreement.

California's unconscionability standard is codified at section 1670.5(a) of the California Civil Code, which provides:

> If the court as a matter of law finds the contract or any clause of the contract to have been unconscionable at the time it was made the court may refuse to enforce the contract, or it may enforce the remainder of the contract without the unconscionable clause, or it may so limit the application of any unconscionable clause as to avoid any unconscionable result.[10]

California courts have stated that unconscionability requires proof of: (i) a procedural element: oppression or surprise due to the unequal bargaining power of the contractual parties;[11] and (ii) a substantive element: an overly harsh and one-sided result in favor of the dominant party.[12]

In *Discover Bank*, the California Supreme Court applied this unconscionability framework to a waiver of class-actions in a consumer contract of adhesion.

9 9 U.S.C. § 2.

10 Cal. Civ. Code § 1670.5 (West).

11 The Supreme Court of California stated in *Armendariz v. Found. Health Psychcare Servs., Inc.*, 24 Cal. 4th 83, 114, 6 P.3d 669, 690 (2000): As explained in *A & M Produce Co.*, supra, 135 Cal.App.3d 473, 186 Cal.Rptr. 114, "unconscionability has both a 'procedural' and a 'substantive' element," the former focusing on "oppression" or "surprise" due to unequal bargaining power, the latter on "overly harsh" or "one-sided" results. (*Id.* at pp. 486–487, 186 Cal.Rptr. 114.) "The prevailing view is that [procedural and substantive unconscionability] must both be present in order for a court to exercise its discretion to refuse to enforce a contract or clause under the doctrine of unconscionability." (*Stirlen v. Supercuts, Inc.*, supra, 51 Cal.App.4th at p. 1533, 60 Cal.Rptr.2d 138 (*Stirlen*).) But they need not be present in the same degree. "Essentially a sliding scale is invoked which disregards the regularity of the procedural process of the contract formation, that creates the terms, in proportion to the greater harshness or unreasonableness of the substantive terms themselves." (15 Williston on Contracts (3d ed. 1972) § 1763A, pp. 226–227; see also *A & M Produce Co.*, supra, 135 Cal.App.3d at p. 487, 186 Cal.Rptr. 114.) In other words, the more substantively oppressive the contract term, the less evidence of procedural unconscionability is required to come to the conclusion that the term is unenforceable, and vice versa.

12 *Id.*

For the procedural element, the court limited its rule to consumer contracts of adhesion. For the substantive element, the court required that the consumer allege a relatively small amount of damages and a scheme to defraud or cheat consumers. The court explained that:

> [W]hen [a class-action] waiver is found in a consumer contract of adhesion in a setting in which disputes between the contracting parties predictably involve small amounts of damages, and when it is alleged that the party with the superior bargaining power has carried out a scheme to deliberately cheat large numbers of consumers out of individually small sums of money, then … the waiver becomes in practice the exemption of the party 'from responsibility for [its] own fraud, or willful injury to the person or property of another.' Under these circumstances, such waivers are unconscionable under California law and should not be enforced.[13]

The Concepcions argued that the *Discover Bank* rule was a valid ground to invalidate the arbitration agreement of their cell phone contract. The Concepcions added that, even if construed as a prohibition on collective-action waiver under California law, the *Discover Bank* rule is not preempted by section 2 of the FAA because the rule prohibits waivers of class proceedings in all dispute resolution contracts, and does not single out arbitration agreements for special treatment.

AT&T argued that the Concepcion's interpretation of California law discriminated against arbitration, and emphasized that "class proceedings would hinder a speedy resolution, place extra burdens on the arbitral process, and lead to companies abandoning arbitration altogether."[14]

### 3.3 *The Supreme Court's Opinion*

The U.S. Supreme Court decided by a majority of five to four, with an opinion by Justice Scalia, joined by Chief Justice Roberts and Justices Kennedy, Thomas, and Alito, that the *Discovery Bank* rule was preempted by section 2 of the FAA. Justice Thomas wrote a concurring opinion. Justice Bryer wrote a dissenting opinion, joined by Justices Ginsburg, Sotomayor, and Kagan.

In deciding that the *Discover Bank* rule was inconsistent with the intent of the FAA to promote arbitration, Justice Scalia stated that:

---

13 *Discover Bank* at 36 Cal.4th at 162–163.

14 *Laster and Concepcion v. AT & T Mobility LLC*, 584 F.3d 849 (2009), at 858.

> [t]his saving clause [of section 2 of the FAA] permits agreements to arbitrate to be invalidated by "generally applicable contract defenses, such as fraud, duress, or unconscionability," but not by defenses that apply only to arbitration or that derive their meaning from the fact that an agreement to arbitrate is at issue. *Doctor's Associates, Inc. v. Casarotto*, 517 U.S. 681, 687, 116 S.Ct. 1652, 134 L.Ed.2d 902 (1996); *see also Perry v. Thomas*, 482 U.S. 483, 492–493, n. 9, 107 S.Ct. 2520, 96 L.Ed.2d 426 (1987).[15]

Applying this principle to the present facts, the majority held that a state cannot apply any rule that permits revocation of contracts generally "in a fashion that disfavors arbitration."[16]

Justice Scalia stated that "a court may not rely on the uniqueness of an agreement to arbitrate as a basis for a state-law holding that enforcement would be unconscionable, for this would enable the court to effect what ... the state legislature cannot."[17]

Justice Scalia then gave illustrations of "grounds traditionally thought to exist at law or in equity for the revocation of any contract" that are preempted by the FAA.[18] These included determinations that a consumer arbitration agreement was unconscionable because it failed to provide for jury trials, judicially-monitored discovery or application of the Federal Rules of Evidence. Such rules, said Justice Scalia, would have a disproportionate impact on arbitration, as a streamlined system designed to avoid jury trials, judicial discovery, and formal rules of evidence.

Justice Scalia went on to explain that:

> Although § 2's saving clause preserves generally applicable contract defenses, nothing in it suggests an intent to preserve state-law rules that stand as an obstacle to the accomplishment of the FAA's objectives. Cf. *Geier v. American Honda Motor Co.*, 529 U.S. 861, 872, 120 S.Ct. 1913, 146 L.Ed.2d 914 (2000); *Crosby v. National Foreign Trade Council*, 530 U.S. 363, 372–373, 120 S.Ct. 2288, 147 L.Ed.2d 352 (2000).
>
> ...
>
> ... a federal statute's saving clause "'cannot in reason be construed as [allowing] a common law right, the continued existence of which would be absolutely inconsistent with the provisions of the act. In other words,

15 *AT&T Mobility*, at 340.

16 *Id.*

17 *Id.*, at 341, *citing Perry v. Thomas*, at 493, n. 9, (internal quotations omitted).

18 *Id.*, at 341–342.

> the act cannot be held to destroy itself.'" *American Telephone & Telegraph Co. v. Central Office Telephone, Inc.*, 524 U.S. 214, 227–228, 118 S.Ct. 1956, 141 L.Ed.2d 222 (1998) (quoting *Texas & Pacific R. Co. v. Abilene Cotton Oil Co.*, 204 U.S. 426, 446, 27 S.Ct. 350, 51 L.Ed. 553 (1907)).[19]

Justice Scalia continued:

> The overarching purpose of the FAA, evident in the text of §§ 2, 3, and 4, is to ensure the enforcement of arbitration agreements according to their terms so as to facilitate streamlined proceedings. Requiring the availability of classwide arbitration interferes with fundamental attributes of arbitration and thus creates a scheme inconsistent with the FAA.[20]

Justice Scalia cited the Supreme Court's decision in 2010 (the previous term) in *Stolt-Nielsen S.A. v. Animal Feeds Int'l Corp, in* which the court majority stated that class arbitration is a "fundamental" departure from bilateral arbitration.[21] In *Stolt-Nielsen*, the Court majority stated that "class-action arbitration changes the nature of arbitration to such a degree that it cannot be presumed the parties consented to it by simply agreeing to submit their disputes to an arbitrator."[22]

Justice Scalia stated that bilateral arbitration is intended "to allow for efficient, streamlined procedures tailored to the type of dispute",[23] but class arbitration is a costlier, slower, and less adaptable process, for the following reasons:

(i) the speed, procedural efficiency and cost-saving aspect of the arbitral procedure are voided by the necessity to certify the class, ensure adequate representation, determine the proper conduct of discovery etc.;[24]

(ii) class-arbitration requires additional procedural formality (usually adapting the Federal Rules of Civil Procedure for Class Arbitrations) to ensure that absent parties are also bound by the result of the arbitration;[25] and

---

19 *Id.*, at 343.

20 *Id.*, at 344.

21 *Id.*, at 347, citing *Stolt–Nielsen S.A. v. Animal Feeds Int'l Corp.*, 559 U.S. 662 (2010).

22 559 U.S. at 685.

23 *AT&T Mobility*, at 344.

24 *Id.*, at 348–349.

25 *Id.*, at 349–350.

(iii) class-arbitration increases the risk to the respondents: its outcome impacts the dispute with the entire class of claimants, not only an individual, but still cannot be reviewed by a higher court.[26]

Justice Scalia stated that "arbitration is poorly suited to the higher stakes of class litigation,"[27] and that class arbitration "is not arbitration as envisioned by the FAA, lacks its benefits, and therefore may not be required by state law."[28] Justice Scalia concluded that "[b]ecause it stands as an obstacle to the accomplishment and execution of the full purposes and objectives of Congress, California's *Discover Bank* rule is pre-empted by the FAA."[29]

The court majority rejected the argument that class actions are necessary to deter corporate wrongdoing, stating that individual arbitration can provide effective relief for consumers, and that federal and state agencies can pursue public enforcement actions.[30]

In his concurrence, Justice Thomas focused on the literal interpretation of the FAA. He stated that the wording of section 2 suggests that the only exception to the enforcement of arbitration clauses would be in case of "revocability" of such clause, omitting the "invalidation" and "nonenforcement" defenses available with respect to other contracts. Reading sections 2 and 4[31] of the FAA together, Justice Thomas considered that "the grounds for the revocation preserved in § 2 would mean grounds related to the making of the agreement."[32] Therefore, he argued that "the FAA requires that an agreement to arbitrate be enforced unless a party successfully challenges the formation of the arbitration agreement, such as by proving fraud or duress. 9 U.S.C. §§ 2, 4."[33]

Justice Thomas stated that California 's *Discover Bank* rule does not relate to the making of an agreement,[34] but was based on public-policy reasons.[35] Accordingly, Justice Thomas concluded that the *Discover Bank* rule was not a

26 *Id.*, at 350.

27 *Id.*, at 350.

28 *Id.*, at 350.

29 *Id.*, at 352 (internal quotations omitted).

30 *Id.*, at 350.

31 Section 4 of the FAA requires "upon being satisfied that the making of the agreement for arbitration or the failure to comply therewith is not an issue," the court must order arbitration "in accordance with the terms of the agreement." Justice Thomas stated that §4 can be read to clarify the scope of §2's exception to the enforcement of arbitration agreements. *AT&T Mobility*, at 353.

32 *Id.*, at 355.

33 *Id.*, at 353.

34 *Id.*, at 356.

35 *Id.*, at 357.

ground for the revocation of any contract under §2 of the FAA, "dictat[ing] that the arbitration agreement here be enforced and the *Discover Bank* rule [be] pre-empted."[36]

The dissenting opinion, written by Justice Breyer and joined by Justices Ginsburg, Sotomayor, and Kagan, opined that the *Discover Bank* rule—by which some class action waivers in consumer contracts are exculpatory, unconscionable, and unenforceable under California law—does not conflict with the FAA, and therefore should not be preempted.

First, Justice Breyer emphasized that the *Discover Bank* rule does not generally prevent California courts from enforcing "all" class-action waivers, but only applied to "some" arbitration agreements.[37] Second, he argued that the *Discover Bank* rule "falls directly within the scope of the [FAA]'s exception permitting courts to refuse to enforce arbitration agreements on grounds that exist 'for the revocation of *any* contract.'"[38] Third, Justice Breyer found that the *Discover Bank* rule is consistent with the Congressional "purpose behind" section 2 of the FAA: ensuring the enforcement of arbitration agreements, "save upon such grounds as exist at law or in equity for the revocation of any contract."[39]

Finally, Justice Breyer disagreed with the majority's view that the rule in *Discover Bank* presents an "obstacle" to the accomplishment of the FAA's federal law's objective by increasing the complexity of arbitration procedures.[40] Opposing the majority's opinion that class-arbitration is incompatible with arbitration itself, Justice Breyer cited the rules of several arbitral institutions and the number of class cases decided and existing under such rules.[41] He emphasized that class-arbitrations, under the circumstances set forth by *Discover Bank*, allow claimants to bring claims when they would otherwise be discouraged from doing so by the small amount at issue in their individual claims (USD 30.22 in this case), therefore preventing a party engaging in fraudulent conduct from evading liability.[42]

36 *Id.*, at 357.

37 *Id.*, at 358. (emphasis added).

38 *Id.*, at 359.

39 *Id.*, at 359, 360, citing, *inter alia*, *Dean Witter Reynolds Inc. v. Byrd*, 470 U.S. 213, 219, 105 S.Ct. 1238, 84 L.Ed.2d 158 (1985), *Marine Transit Corp. v. Dreyfus*, 284 U.S. 263, 274, n. 2, 52 S.Ct. 166, 76 L.Ed. 282 (1932), *Mitsubishi Motors Corp. v. Soler Chrysler–Plymouth, Inc.*, 473 U.S. 614, 628, 105 S.Ct. 3346, 87 L.Ed.2d 444 (1985).

40 *Id.*, at 362.

41 *Id.*, at 362, 363.

42 *Id.*, at 365.

### 3.4 *Key Takeaways*

While the saving clause of Section 2 of the FAA allows courts to invalidate arbitration agreements upon grounds that exist for the revocation of any contract—*e.g.*, fraud, duress, mutual mistake—in *AT&T Mobility*, the Court majority held that it would be inconsistent with the FAA if the savings clause permitted courts to apply such doctrines to (1) prohibit arbitration outright or (2) adversely affect the parties' agreement to arbitrate. In both such cases, the Court held that FAA preempts application of such grounds for revocation. Applying this rule to the present case, the Court decided that the FAA preempted a state rule deeming waiver of class-arbitration in consumer contract arbitration agreements unconscionable.

In the view of the Court majority, such an application of the doctrine of unconscionability is incompatible with the FAA because it impedes accomplishment of the objectives of the FAA. In the Court's view, when Congress adopted the FAA in 1925, it intended to promote streamlined dispute resolution, and class-arbitration is fundamentally different from bilateral arbitration, requiring costlier, lengthier, and more formal procedures. Thus, the Court majority held that imposing a class mechanism in arbitration agreements when the parties did not expressly agree to it interferes with parties' freedom to agree to arbitration, as envisioned by the drafters of the FAA.

## 4 Critical Analysis of the Opinion and How It Impacted the U.S. Arbitration Law and Practice

The Supreme Court majority in *AT&T Mobility* appeared sensitive to concerns that its decision would lead businesses to impose arbitration clauses that would disincentivize consumers from bringing small value disputes.

Justice Scalia's opinion began by referencing the arbitration provision of the Concepcions' contract, which he described as follows:[43]

The revised agreement provides that customers may initiate dispute proceedings by completing a one-page Notice of Dispute form available on AT&T's Web site. AT&T may then offer to settle the claim; if it does not, or if the dispute is not resolved within 30 days, the customer may invoke arbitration by filing a separate Demand for Arbitration, also available on AT&T's Web site. In the event the parties proceed to arbitration, the agreement specifies that AT&T must pay all costs for nonfrivolous claims; that arbitration must take place

43 *Id.*, at 338.

in the county in which the customer is billed; that, for claims of $10,000 or less, the customer may choose whether the arbitration proceeds in person, by telephone, or based only on submissions; that either party may bring a claim in small claims court in lieu of arbitration; and that the arbitrator may award any form of individual relief, including injunctions and presumably punitive damages. The agreement, moreover, denies AT&T any ability to seek reimbursement of its attorneys' fees, and, in the event that a customer receives an arbitration award greater than AT&T's last written settlement offer, requires AT&T to pay a $7,500 minimum recovery and twice the amount of the claimant's attorney's fees.[44]

At the end of the Court's opinion, Justice Scalia stated that "the claim here was most unlikely to go unresolved" and "the District Court concluded that the Concepcion's were *better off* under their arbitration agreement with AT&T than they would have been as participants in a class action."[45] This emphasis on the particular arbitration provision at issue may have suggested that the *AT&T Mobility* decision was a fact-specific ruling, to be narrowly applied.

However, subsequent decisions confirmed the Court majority's view not only that waivers of class-action litigation or arbitration generally under bilateral arbitration agreements were enforceable under the FAA, and but that parties must explicitly agree to class arbitration.

In *American Express Co. v. Italian Colors Restaurant* (2013),[46] the Court held that an arbitration agreement with a class action waiver was enforceable even if were economically impracticable for plaintiffs to pursue their antitrust claims individually, and in *Epic Systems Corp. v. Lewis* (2018),[47] the Court stated that an arbitration agreement with a class action waiver was enforceable even if it violated the National Labor Relations Act's protection of employees' collective action.

In *Lamps Plus, Inc. v. Varela*,[48] decided by the Supreme Court in 2019, an employee filed a class arbitration action alleging that his employer unlawfully released the employee's private information. Relying on the parties' employment agreement, the employer moved to compel bilateral arbitration. The Supreme Court stated that:

44 *Id.*, at 336–337.

45 *Id.*, at 351–352 (emphasis in original).

46 *American Exp. Co. v. Italian Colors Restaurant*, 570 U.S. 228, 133 S.Ct. 2304, 186 L.Ed.2d 417 (2013).

47 *Epic Systems Corp. v. Lewis*, 584 U.S. ___, 138 S.Ct. 1612, 200 L.Ed.2d 889 (2018).

48 *Lamps Plus, Inc. v. Varela*, 587 U.S. ___, 139 S.Ct. 1407 203 L.Ed.2d 636 (2019).

> Class arbitration "sacrifices the principal advantage of arbitration—its informality—and makes the process slower, more costly, and more likely to generate procedural morass than final judgment." *Concepcion*, 563 U.S. at 348, 131 S.Ct. 1740. Because of such "crucial differences," *Stolt-Nielsen*, 559 U.S. at 687, 130 S.Ct. 1758, this Court has held that courts may not infer consent to participate in class arbitration absent an affirmative "contractual basis for concluding that the party *agreed* to do so," *id.*, at 684, 130 S.Ct. 1758. Silence is not enough. *Id.*, at 687, 130 S.Ct. 1758. That reasoning controls here. Like silence, ambiguity does not provide a sufficient basis to conclude that parties to an arbitration agreement agreed to "sacrifice[ ] the principal advantage of arbitration." *Concepcion*, 563 U.S. at 348, 131 S.Ct. 1740. This conclusion aligns with the Court's refusal to infer consent when it comes to other fundamental arbitration questions. See, *e.g.*, *First Options of Chicago, Inc. v. Kaplan*, 514 U.S. 938, 945, 115 S.Ct. 1920, 131 L.Ed.2d 985.[49]

*Lamps Plus* made clear what was implicit in *AT&T Mobility*: differences between bilateral arbitration and class-arbitration were so fundamental that consent to the former cannot be presumed to be consent to the latter. The *Discover Bank* rule not only impeded the objectives of the FAA, but it imposed on respondents a mode of dispute resolution to which they did not consent.

This was confirmed in the Supreme Court's decision in 2022, *Viking River Cruises, Inc. v. Moriana*,[50] in which an employee filed an action against her employer on behalf of her coworkers under California's Labor Code Private Attorneys General Act of 2004. The employer moved to dismiss the action arguing that the employee's arbitration agreement required all employment disputes to be arbitrated. The Court stated that:

> Section 2's mandate protects a right to enforce arbitration agreements. That right would not be a right to *arbitrate* in any meaningful sense if generally applicable principles of state law could be used to transform "traditiona[l] individualized ... arbitration" into the "litigation it was meant to displace" through the imposition of procedures at odds with arbitration's informal nature. *Epic Systems*, 584 U.S., at 138 S.Ct., at 1623. See also *Concepcion*, 563 U.S. at 351, 131 S.Ct. 1740. And that right would not be a right to arbitrate based on an *agreement* if generally applicable

49 *Id.*, at 1410.

50 *Viking River Cruises, Inc. v. Moriana*, 596 U.S. 639, 142 S. Ct. 1906, 213 L.Ed.2d 179 (2022).

law could be used to coercively impose arbitration in contravention of the "first principle" of our FAA jurisprudence: that "[a]rbitration is strictly 'a matter of consent.' "*Granite Rock Co. v. Teamsters*, 561 U.S. 287, 299, 130 S.Ct. 2847, 177 L.Ed.2d 567 (2010) (quoting *Volt Information Sciences, Inc. v. Board of Trustees of Leland Stanford Junior Univ.*, 489 U.S. 468, 479, 109 S.Ct. 1248, 103 L.Ed.2d 488 (1989)); see also *Lamps Plus*, 587 U.S., at 139 S.Ct., at 1416; *Stolt-Nielsen S. A. v. AnimalFeeds Int'l Corp.*, 559 U.S. 662, 685, 130 S.Ct. 1758, 176 L.Ed.2d 605 (2010).

Based on these principles, we have held that "a party may not be compelled under the FAA to submit to class arbitration unless there is a contractual basis for concluding that the party *agreed* to do so." *Id.*, at 684, 130 S.Ct. 1758. See also *Lamps Plus*, 587 U.S., at 139 S.Ct., at 1412; *Epic Systems*, 584 U.S., at 138 S.Ct. at 1621–1623; *Concepcion*, 563 U.S. at 347–348, 131 S.Ct. 1740. The "shift from bilateral arbitration to class-action arbitration" mandates procedural changes that are inconsistent with the individualized and informal mode of arbitration contemplated by the FAA. *Id.*, at 347, 131 S.Ct. 1740 (quoting *Stolt-Nielsen*, 559 U.S. at 686, 130 S.Ct. 1758). As a result, class procedures cannot be imposed by state law without presenting unwilling parties with an unacceptable choice between being compelled to arbitrate using procedures at odds with arbitration's traditional form and forgoing arbitration altogether. Putting parties to that choice is inconsistent with the FAA.[51]

These cases, and others,[52] leave no doubt as to the legacy of the Supreme Court's ruling in *AT&T Mobility*: class-action waivers in arbitration agreements are valid and enforceable, not only because state law rules that would invalidate them are pre-empted by the FAA, but because the parties did not expressly consent to class arbitration.

---

51 *Id.*, at 651.

52 *See Morgan v. Sundance, Inc.* (2022), (Federal courts may not adopt an arbitration-specific rule conditioning a waiver of the right to arbitrate on a showing of prejudice); *Viking River Cruises, Inc. v. Moriana* (2022) (individual claims arising under California's Labor Code Private Attorneys General Act (PAGA) can be compelled to arbitration); *DirectTV Inc. v. Imburgia* (2015) (preempted California law invalidating class arbitration waivers did not apply to arbitration clause governed by FAA); *Epic Systems Corp. v. Lewis* (2018) (National Labor Relations Act does not displace FAA enforcement of class and collective arbitration waivers); *Kindred Nursing Centers Ltd. Partnership v. Clark* (2017) (FAA preempted state rule requiring power of attorney to clearly authorize the waiver of jury trial and court access); *CompuCredit Corp. v. Greenwood* (2012) (Credit Repair Organizations Act did not bar arbitration of claims under the FAA).

## 5 Conclusion

*AT&T Mobility LLC v. Concepcion* and its progeny has been criticized by consumer advocates, who assert that its validation of class waivers undermines the rights of consumers to seek accountability from corporations that violate the law.[53] They also argue that consumers are often unaware of the arbitration clauses in their contracts, and have no choice but to agree to the terms even if they are aware of them.[54]

Supporters of the *AT&T Mobility* decision contend that the rule promotes efficiency and reduces litigation costs, and that a bilateral arbitration agreement, properly drafted, is a fair and accessible alternative to court proceedings.[55]

Whatever one's perspective, it is inarguable that the decision substantially diminished the prospects for class action arbitration in the United States. Many well-known consumer companies have incorporated provisions to their arbitration clauses similar to the agreement at issue in *AT&T Mobility*, which provides for relatively cheap, expedited dispute resolution process in many cases.[56]

---

53 Ann M. Tracey & Shelley McGill, *Seeking a Rational Lawyer for Consumer Claims After the Supreme Court Disconnects Consumers in AT&T Mobility LLC v. Concepcion*, 45 Loy. L.A. L. Rev. 435; Sternlight, Jean R. *Tsunami: AT&T Mobility LLC v. Conception Imposed Access to Justice*, Sternlight, Jean R., 2012, Oregon Law review, *Vol. 90, No. 3, pp. 703–728;* Jonathan Gertier and Christian Shreiber, *AT&T Mobility v. Concepcion: The Death Knell For Class Actions?* Plaintiffmagazine.com (June 2011), available at https://plaintiffmagazine.com/recent-issues/item/at-t-mobility-v-concepcion-the-death-knell-for-class-actions.

54 Charles Gibbs, *Consumer Class Actions After AT&T v. Concepcion: Why the Federal Arbitration Act Should Not Be Used to deny Effective Relief to Small-Value Claimants*, University of Illinois Law Review, pp. 1345–1382 (2012); Frank Blechschmidt, *All alone in Arbitration: A&T Mobility v. Concepcion and the Substantive Impact of Class Action Waivers*, University of Pennsylvania Law Review, Vol. 160 Issue 2, pp. 541–584 (January 2012).

55 Michael Hoenig and Linda M. Brown, *Arbitration and Class Action Waivers: Reason and Reasonableness Deflect Strident Attacks*, Arkansas Law Review (2015); Eliot D. Ostrove, *Commentary: Concepcion allows companies to avoid the morass of class actions*, The National Law Journal, (Online Edition, July 2011).

56 *See* Myriam Gilles, *Killing them with Kindness: Examining Consumer—Friendly Arbitration Clauses after AT&T Mobility v. Concepcion*, Vol. 88, Notre Dame L. Rev. 825 (2012), available at: http://scholarship.law.nd.edu/ndlr/vol88/iss2/6; *See also* Peter B. Rutledge and Christopher R. Drahozal, *"Sticky" Arbitration Clauses? The Use of Arbitration Clauses After Concepcion and Amex,* Vanderbilt Law Review, Vol. 67 (Mau 2014); *See also* Josephine Lee, *California Consumer Contracts after AT&T Mobility v. Concepcion*, Vol. 15, UC Davis Business Law Journal (2015), available at https://blj.ucdavis.edu/archives/vol-15-no-2/BLJ-15.2-Lee.pdf.

However, in recent years consumer lawyers have begun to use a new collective mechanism: so-called "mass arbitration": filing hundreds, or thousands, of nearly identical demands for individual arbitration *en masse.*[57] The consequences for corporations can be massive, especially for those which provide "friendly" terms in their mandatory arbitration clauses, such as reimbursement to plaintiffs of their arbitration fees. Such mass arbitrations have led some corporations to drop mandatory arbitration clauses altogether from their adhesion contracts, and return to traditional civil litigation.[58]

---

57 Andrew B. Nissensohn, *Mass Arbitration 2.0*, Washington and Lee Law Review, Vol. 79 (2022), available at: https://scholarlycommons.law.wlu.edu/wlulr/vol79/iss3/11/.

58 J. Maria Glover, *Recent Developments in Mandatory Arbitration Warfare: Winners and Losers (So Far) in Mass Arbitration*, Washington University Law Review, Vol. 100, No. 6 (2023), available at: https://papers.ssrn.com/sol3/papers.cfm?abstract_id=4509465.

CHAPTER 24

# *Oxford Health Plans* LLC *v. Sutter* (2013)

*James Hosking, Gretta Walters and Marcel Engholm*

## 1 Introduction

> The arbitrator's construction holds, however good, bad, or ugly.[1]

In *Oxford Health Plans* LLC *v. Sutter*, the U.S. Supreme Court continued to grapple with how the field of class arbitration fits within the Federal Arbitration Act ("FAA"). The FAA itself does not expressly address class arbitrations. That is not surprising, however. Rule 23 of the Federal Rules of Civil Procedure ("FRCP"), which regulates class actions, was first enacted only in 1937,[2] twelve years after enactment of the FAA, and the modern class action regime was not created in the United States until 1966, when Rule 23 went through significant revisions.[3] Nevertheless, over the last 40 years, the U.S. Supreme Court has granted *certiorari* to no less than ten disputes dealing with class arbitration—seven of those decided between 2010 and 2019.

In *Oxford Health*, which arose in the middle of this period of heightened interest in class arbitration, the Supreme Court was asked whether an arbitrator had exceeded his powers in finding that class arbitration was permitted when the arbitration agreement was silent on the matter.[4] The *Oxford Health*

1 *Oxford Health Plans* LLC *v. Sutter*, 569 U.S. 564, 573 (2014).

2 The previous provision—Equity Rule 38 (Representatives of Class)—applied to equitable actions only and provided for a class action when the question was "one of common or general interest to many persons constituting a class so numerous as to make it impracticable to bring them all before the court." Fed. R. Civ. P. 23. *Advisory Committee Notes* (1937). Rule 23 adopted the same test, but it defined "common or general interest" and extended its application to both legal and equitable claims. *Id.*

3 For an overview of the changes enacted in 1966, see Marvin E. Frankel, *Some Preliminary Observations Concerning Civil Rule 23*, 43 F.R.D. 39 (1968).

4 Oxford Health Plans LLC's Petition for Writ of Certiorari filed July 27, 2012, 2012 WL 3109485, at *i (2012) (hereinafter "Oxford's Petition for Certiorari") ("Question Presented ... [w]hether an arbitrator acts within his powers under the Federal Arbitration Act (as the Second and Third Circuits have held) or exceeds these powers (as the Fifth Circuit has held) by determining that parties affirmatively "*agreed to authorize* class arbitration," (citations omitted) based solely on their use of broad contractual language precluding litigation and requiring arbitration of any dispute arising under their contract.").

 | DOI:10.1163/9789004715820_025

Court answered "no."[5] Interestingly, just a few years prior to *Oxford Health*, the Court had taken a similar question (i.e., whether arbitrators improperly authorized class arbitration on the basis of arbitration agreements that did not address the issue) and reached different outcomes. In one of those prior cases, the Court refused to address the merits of the issue and remanded to the arbitrators to decide in the first instance, and, in the other, the Court reached the opposite conclusion—that the arbitrators did exceed their authority in such circumstances.[6] At first these three decisions might suggest an apparent inconsistency, but a closer read reveals that each turned on the very specific facts before the Court. *Oxford Health* is significant in providing an example of a class arbitration being permitted, notwithstanding an arbitration clause that is silent on the matter.

But the case is also significant in affirming the Court's (and FAA's) steadfast deference to arbitrators' decisions on interpretation and application of the parties' contracts. As *Oxford Health* confirms, the FAA does not authorize a court to review or displace such a decision—a principle that applies equally to class arbitrations, as it does to any other category of arbitration.

## 2 Preliminary Considerations

Much debate has been had on how to read properly the trilogy of Supreme Court decisions discussing whether arbitrators can allow class arbitration when it is not addressed in the arbitration agreement.[7] *Oxford Health*—the only case involving class arbitration in which the Justices reached a unanimous decision—provides the key to the Supreme Court's position on this issue.

The Court decided the first of these three cases, *Green Tree Financial Corp. v. Bazzle*,[8] in 2003. There, the Supreme Court of South Carolina found that class

5 *Oxford Health*, 569 U.S. at 573.

6 *See Green Tree Financial Corp. v. Bazzle*, 539 U.S. 444 (2003); *Stolt-Nielsen S.A. v. AnimalFeeds Int'l Corp.*, 559 U.S. 662 (2010).

7 *See, e.g.*, B. Ted Howes & Hannan C. Banks, *A Tale of Two Arbitration Clauses: The Lessons of Oxford Health Plans LLC v. Sutter for the Future of Class-Action Arbitration in the United States*, 30 J. Int'l Arb. 727 (2013); Rachel Kent & Marik String, *Availability of Class Arbitration Under U.S. Law*, *in* Albert Jan van den Berg (ed.), ICCA Congress Series No. 2018 853 (2014); Claudia Pharaon, *The extent of arbitrators' power to order class arbitration*, *in* William W. Park (ed.), 31 Arb. Int'l 589 (2015); David M. Orta, Matthew A. Lee & Brian Rowe, *Class Action Arbitration under U.S. Jurisprudence*, *in* Laurence Shore, Tai-Heng Cheng et al. (eds.), *International Arbitration in the United States* 649 (2017).

8 *Green Tree Financial Corp. v. Bazzle*, 539 U.S. 444 (2003). Note that an argument involving class arbitration appeared briefly before the Supreme Court in a previous case also

arbitration was permitted, where the arbitration agreement did not specifically address class arbitration but stated that "all disputes" would be resolved by arbitration.[9] The U.S. Supreme Court granted *certiorari* to assess whether this decision was consistent with the FAA, specifically whether "9 U.S.C. § 1 *et seq.*, prohibits class-action procedures from being superimposed onto an arbitration agreement that does not provide for class-action arbitration."[10] At the time, this issue was relatively unexplored. Of the few prior cases in which the courts considered the topic, they generally found that class arbitrations could not be upheld where the underlying agreement was silent on the question of whether the parties had agreed to class proceedings.[11]

The Court in *Bazzle* did not reach a majority decision on the issue and remanded to the arbitrators to decide, in the first instance, whether class arbitration was permitted under the parties' contract.[12] Justice Breyer, writing for a plurality of the Court, reasoned that whether the arbitration agreement was truly silent as to the possibility of class arbitration was a matter of contract interpretation and therefore for the arbitrators to decide in the first instance.[13]

The *Bazzle* Court's reasoning was vague, yet the decision was primarily interpreted as an "implicit endorsement" of class arbitration as long as the

involving Green Tree, in which the defendant argued the arbitration agreement was unenforceable because it precluded the pursuit of claims as a class action. The issue was not dispositive and was only acknowledged in the dissent of Justice Ginsburg, who would have remanded the case for the circuit court to decide on the appropriate forum. *See Green Tree Fin. Corp.-Alabama v. Randolph*, 531 U.S. 79, 97 (2000).

9 *Bazzle v. Green Tree Financial Corp.*, 351 S.C. 244 (2002).

10 Green Tree Financial Corp.'s Petition for Writ of Certiorari filed October 23, 2002, 2002 L 32101094, at *i (2002).

11 *See, e.g.*, *Champ v. Siegel Trading Cp., Inc.* 55 F.3d 269, 274–75 (7th Cir. 1995) (stating that the court was unaware of decisions on this particular issue and relying, by analogy, on decisions concerning a district court's authority to order consolidation of arbitrations when the agreements do not address this possibility to find "section 4 of the FAA forbids federal judges from ordering class arbitration where the parties' arbitration agreement is silent on the matter").

12 Justice Stevens concurred with the plurality decision to form a controlling judgment, but he wrote that he would have simply affirmed the judgment, as he found the court's interpretation of the arbitration agreement to be correct. *Id.* at 454–55. Chief Justice Rehnquist, joined by two other justices, dissented finding that this issue of arbitrability was for the courts to decide and that the South Carolina Supreme Court's holding contravened the terms of the contract and was preempted by the FAA. *Id.* at 455–59. Lastly, Justice Thomas dissented finding the FAA did not apply to proceedings in state courts. *Id.* at 460.

13 *Id.* at 450–54.

arbitration agreement did not expressly prohibit it.[14] The decision greatly impacted the U.S. arbitration landscape in the following years, which saw a sudden increase in the number of requests for class arbitration and of arbitrators finding that arbitration agreements silent on the issue could be read to permit class proceedings.[15] Some arbitration institutions even issued class arbitration rules to deal with the influx of such cases.[16]

The Supreme Court heard the second of this line of cases, *Stolt-Nielsen S.A. v. AnimalFeeds Int'l Corp.*,[17] in 2010. The case involved circumstances similar to *Bazzle*. The arbitrators had authorized class arbitration in circumstances where the arbitration agreement was silent as to the availability of class arbitration but instead broadly provided that "any disputes" would be resolved by arbitration.[18] The arbitrators in *Stolt-Nielsen* apparently rested their decision on AnimalFeeds's public policy argument, *i.e.*, that, separate from the fact that the clause was silent as to the availability of class arbitration, it "should be construed to permit class arbitration as a matter of public policy."[19]

The Southern District of New York vacated the arbitrators' award on the grounds of "manifest disregard of the law," finding that the arbitrators had wrongly applied New York law to the question before them and that applying

14 *See, e.g., Trumper v. Travelers Indem. Co*, 2006 WL 6553086, at *1 (S.D. Tex. Jan. 9, 2006) (citing *Bazzle* for the proposition that "class arbitration is permissible under the FAA wherever the governing contract does not expressly prohibit such arbitration").

15 *See* Brief of American Arbitration Association as Amicus Curiae in Support of Neither Party filed in *Stolt-Nielsen v. AnimalFeeds Int'l Corp.*, dated September 4, 2009, at 22–23, 2009 WL 2896309 (2009) (stating that 283 class proceedings had been filed between 2003 and 2009, 102 of which had objections as to whether class arbitration was permitted, and, in 95 out of 102, the tribunal found class arbitration to be permitted).

16 *See, e.g.*, the AAA Supp. Rules for Class Arbitration, effective as of October 2003; JAMS Class Action Procedures, effective as of February 2005.

17 559 U.S. 662 (2010). The U.S. Supreme Court decided another case on class arbitration in between *Stolt-Nielsen* and *Oxford*. *AT&T Mobility LLC v. Concepcion*, 563 U.S. 333 (2011). This case did not deal with a "silent" arbitration agreement, but rather whether the FAA preempted California's *Discover Bank* rule, finding class arbitration waivers in adhesion consumer contracts were unconscionable. The case is of less impact to the Supreme Court's decision in *Oxford*, except to the extent that *Concepcion* stressed how bilateral and class arbitration are disputes of different "natures." *See Concepcion*, 563 U.S. at 347–51.

18 *Stolt-Nielsen*, 559 U.S. at 667.

19 *Id.* at 673. AnimalFeeds raised three arguments in support of construing the agreement as allowing for class arbitration: (i) that the arbitration agreement was silent and, without prohibition, class arbitration should be permitted under *Bazzle*; (ii) that class arbitration should be permitted as a matter of public policy; and (iii) that the clause would be unconscionable and unenforceable if it forbade class arbitration. *Id.* at 672. The arbitrators expressly rejected the first argument and did not address the third. *Id.* at 672–73.

the correct law (*i.e.*, maritime law, which incorporates trade customs and usages) would have led to a different result on the permissibility of class arbitrations.[20] The Second Circuit reversed the lower court, finding that the arbitrators' decision did not manifestly disregard maritime law or New York law, as neither had an applicable rule against class arbitrations.[21]

The U.S. Supreme Court granted *certiorari* to assess the same question that it had taken in *Bazzle*: "[w]hether imposing class arbitration on parties whose arbitration clauses are silent on that issue is consistent with the Federal Arbitration Act, 9 U.S.C. §§ 1 et seq."[22] In a 5–3 majority opinion, the Court reversed and remanded to the Second Circuit,[23] giving much clearer direction than it had seven years earlier in *Bazzle*. The Court acknowledged that "no single rationale commanded a majority in *Bazzle*"[24] and opined that parties and arbitrators "seem to have misunderstood *Bazzle*" as establishing a standard for deciding whether class arbitration is permitted, which the Court explained *Bazzle* had left "open."[25]

In examining the arbitrators' decision, the Court found that the arbitrators exceeded their authority under FAA § 10(a)(4) by deciding based on their own policy choices rather than by interpreting the parties' arbitration agreement.[26] This was all the more telling given that the parties had expressly stipulated that they had reached "no agreement" in drafting the arbitration agreement as to whether class arbitration would be permitted.[27]

The Court further reasoned that "class-action arbitration changes the nature of arbitration to such a degree that it cannot be presumed the parties consented to it by simply agreeing to submit their disputes to an arbitrator."[28] According to the Court, in bilateral arbitration, parties forego the procedural rigor and appellate review of the courts in exchange for the hallmark benefits

20 *Stolt-Nielsen SA v. Animalfeeds Int'l Corp.*, 435 F. Supp. 2d 382, 385–86 (S.D.N.Y. 2006) ("The court finds, therefore, that the arbitrators manifestly disregarded a well defined rule of governing maritime law that precluded class arbitration under the clauses here in issue and that their decision to the contrary must therefore be reversed.")

21 *Stolt-Nielsen SA v. AnimalFeeds Int'l Corp.,* 548 F.3d 85, 96–101 (2d Cir. 2008).

22 Stolt-Nielsen's Petition for Writ of Certiorari filed March 26, 2009, 2009 WL 797583, at *i (2009).

23 Justice Sotomayor did not take part in the decision. The Second Circuit ultimately confirmed the arbitral award's vacatur by the lower court. *See Stolt-Nielsen S.A. v. AnimalFeeds Int'l* Corp., 624 F.3d 157 (2d Cir. 2010).

24 *Stolt-Nielsen.*, 559 U.S. at 663.

25 *Id.* at 680.

26 *Id.* at 676–77.

27 *Id.* at 669.

28 *Id.* at 685.

of arbitration—"lower costs, greater efficiency and speed, and the ability to choose expert adjudicators."[29] Class arbitration, however, causes "fundamental changes" to such traits of bilateral arbitration, in particular it can broaden the scope of the issues discussed and bind absent class members (*i.e.*, parties).[30] The Court reasoned that those differences "are too great for arbitrators to presume ... that the parties' mere silence on the issue of class-action arbitration constitutes consent to resolve their disputes in class proceedings."[31] Accordingly, the Supreme Court concluded that "a party may not be compelled under the FAA to submit to class arbitration unless there is a *contractual basis* for concluding that the party agreed to do so."[32] The Court expressly refrained from deciding "what contractual basis may support a finding that the parties agreed to authorize class-action arbitration," however, perhaps unsurprisingly given that in the instant case the parties had stipulated that they had reached "no agreement" on whether class arbitration would be permitted.[33]

Following that decision, a circuit split developed as to the "contractual basis" required to authorize class arbitration under *Stolt-Nielsen.* The Second, Third, and Fifth Circuits were each seized with cases in which arbitral tribunals allowed class arbitration based on arbitration agreements silent on the issue.[34] In all three cases, the parties moving to vacate the arbitral awards argued that the tribunals had exceeded their authority and that the arbitrators' respective decisions conflicted with *Stolt-Nielsen.*[35] But the circuit courts disagreed on how to resolve the matter.

The Fifth Circuit found that a tribunal exceeds its authority in allowing class arbitration based on an arbitration agreement silent on the issue because, in its view, *Stolt-Nielsen* barred arbitrators from presuming that "mere silence constitutes consent."[36] The Second Circuit, however, found no excess of authority on the ground that *Stolt-Nielsen* only required "a contractual basis" for class arbitration but did not require the arbitration agreement to authorize it expressly.[37]

---

29 *Id.*

30 *Id.* at 686–87.

31 *Id.* at 687.

32 *Id.* at 684 (emphasis added).

33 *Id.* at 669.

34 *See Jock v. Sterling Jewelers Inc.*, 646 F.3d 113 (2d Cir. 2011); *Sutter v. Oxford Health Plans LLC*, 675 F.3d 215 (3d Cir. 2012); *Reed v. Fla. Metro. Univ., Inc.*, 681 F.3d 630 (5th Cir. 2012).

35 *Jock*, 646 F.3d at 115; *Oxford Health*, 675 F.3d at 219; *Reed*, 681 F.3d at 633.

36 *Reed*, 681 F.3d at 644.

37 *Jock*, 646 F.3d at 121.

The Third Circuit was seized with the same question in a case involving John Sutter and Oxford Health Plans[38] and joined the Second Circuit's interpretation, finding that the arbitrator did not exceed his powers by construing a broadly worded arbitration agreement to authorize class arbitration (even though it was silent on the specific issue of class arbitration).[39] Oxford Health Plans, in turn, asked the U.S. Supreme Court to weigh in on the issue.[40]

## 3 The Case

### 3.1 *Background to the Case*

Dr. John Ivan Sutter, a New Jersey pediatrician, entered a "Primary Care Physician Agreement," with Oxford Health Plans LLC, under which Sutter would provide medical care to members of Oxford's network in exchange for compensation at predetermined rates. The contract, drafted by Oxford, contained an arbitration agreement reading:

> No civil action concerning any dispute arising under this Agreement shall be instituted before any court, and all such disputes shall be submitted to final and binding arbitration in New Jersey, pursuant to the Rules of the American Arbitration Association with one arbitrator.[41]

In 2002, a dispute arose between the parties in relation to payment of various medical procedures performed by Sutter. Sutter filed a class action complaint against Oxford and other health insurers in the Superior Court of New Jersey, alleging breach of provider agreements with putative class members as to payment of claims, as well as other violations of New Jersey law.[42] Oxford moved to compel arbitration, and the Superior Court of New Jersey granted Oxford's motion.[43] Sutter then commenced arbitration before a sole arbitrator under the American Arbitration Association's ("AAA's") class arbitration rules on behalf of all physicians who provided services to any person covered by

---

38 *Oxford Health*, 675 F.3d at 215.
39 *Id.* at 224–25.
40 Oxford Petition for Writ of Certiorari filed July 27, 2012, 2012 WL 3109485 (2012).
41 *Id.* at 217.
42 *Sutter v. Oxford Health Plans LLC*, 2005 WL 6795061 at *1 (D.N.J. 2005).
43 *Oxford Health*, 569 U.S. at 566.

Oxford between 1996 and 2004 and signed agreements with a similarly worded arbitration clause.[44]

After his appointment, the sole arbitrator noted that the Supreme Court was scheduled to hear oral arguments in *Bazzle* within a month and determined that "[i]t appeared sensible to take no action on the class action issues until the determination of the *Green Tree* case had been received and analyzed."[45] Accordingly, the sole arbitrator then stayed arbitration pending the U.S. Supreme Court's ruling in *Bazzle.*

Following issuance of the *Bazzle* decision, the sole arbitrator twice determined that the arbitration agreement in the Primary Care Physician Agreement permitted class arbitration (first in a September 2003 "Clause Construction Award"[46] and again in a March 2005 "Partial Final Class Determination Award"[47]). In his decisions, the arbitrator noted that the arbitration clause was "broader even than the usual broad arbitration clause" and that its first sentence—"no civil action concerning any dispute arising under this Agreement shall be instituted before any court"—embraced "any conceivable court action concerning any dispute under the Agreement," including class actions.[48]

Oxford moved to vacate the March 2005 Partial Final Class Determination Award in the District Court for the District of New Jersey under 9 U.S.C. § 10(a)(4), arguing that the arbitrator exceeded his powers and manifestly disregarded the law by, in relevant part, ignoring *Bazzle,* which Oxford argued required the arbitrator to find the arbitration agreement did not permit class arbitration.[49] According to Oxford, the arbitrator's interpretation contradicted the terms of the arbitration agreement and therefore was impermissible under *Bazzle.*[50] The district court rejected Oxford's application, finding that the arbitrator did exactly what *Bazzle* required him to do—*i.e.*, "interpret the agreement to determine whether the contract permits class certification"[51]—and moreover that *Bazzle* "did not instruct on the method the arbitrator must use

44 AAA Case No. 18 193 20593 02, Partial Final Class Determination Award of Arbitrator dated March 24, 2005 (Oxford's Petition for Certiorari at 82a).

45 AAA Case No. 18 193 20593 02, Memorandum and Order dated September 23, 2003 (Oxford's Petition for Certiorari at 44a-45a), hereinafter "Clause Construction Award."

46 Clause Construction Award at 43a.

47 AAA Case No. 18 193 20593 02, Partial Final Class Determination Award of Arbitrator dated March 24, 2005 (Oxford's Petition for Certiorari at 79a), hereinafter "Class Determination Award."

48 Clause Construction Award at 47a–48a.

49 *Sutter v. Oxford Health Plans LLC*, 2005 WL 6795061 at *5 (D.N.J. Oct. 31, 2005).

50 *Id.*

51 *Id.*

in interpreting the contract."[52] Accordingly, the district court concluded that the arbitrator neither exceed his powers under Section 10(a)(4) of the FAA nor manifestly disregarded the law.[53]

On appeal, the Third Circuit affirmed the district court's judgment, finding that the arbitrator "individually went through each requirement for a class action set forth in Rule 4 of the AAA Rules" and his decision was "not irrational" and did not evidence a manifest disregard of the law.[54] Following these decisions, the class arbitration proceeded before the sole arbitrator.

Three years after the Third Circuit's decision, the U.S. Supreme Court issued its ruling in *Stolt-Nielsen,* and Oxford asked the sole arbitrator to reconsider his prior decisions in light of this new precedent.[55] The arbitrator issued a procedural order revisiting the issue but concluding that class arbitration was still authorized following *Stolt-Nielsen*, finding *Stolt-Nielsen* distinguishable. First, the arbitrators' decision authorizing class arbitration in *Stolt-Nielsen* had been based on their own views on public policy, while the arbitrator's determination in *Oxford Health* had been based on "the parties' intent as evidenced by the words of the arbitration clause itself."[56] In addition, the parties in *Stolt-Nielsen* specifically stipulated that they had reached "no agreement" on the issue of class arbitration.[57] Sutter and Oxford had entered into no such stipulation, and therefore the arbitrator had to investigate the parties' intention as reflected in the arbitration agreement, which he found "unambiguously evinced an intention to allow class arbitration."[58] Thus, the *Oxford Health* arbitrator reaffirmed his prior construction of the arbitration agreement that the expression "no civil action" was sufficiently broad so as to encompass class actions.[59]

Oxford moved the district court to reopen the case to either vacate the arbitrator's new procedural order or to reconsider the court's prior ruling in light of *Stolt-Nielsen.*[60] The district court again affirmed the arbitrator's decisions,

52 *Id.* at *6.

53 *Id.* at *8.

54 *Sutter v. Oxford Health Plans LLC,* 227 F. App'x 135, 138 (3d Cir. 2007). The appeal also alleged that the district court erred in the standard of review used to analyze the arbitrator's decision.

55 *See* AAA Case No. 18 193 20593 02, Procedural Order No. 18 Determining Motion dated July 6, 2010 (Oxford's Petition for Certiorari at 31a), hereinafter "Procedural Order No. 18."

56 Procedural Order no. 18 at 35a.

57 *Id.* at 35a-36a.

58 *Id.* at 36a.

59 *Id.* at 39a.

60 *Sutter v. Oxford Health Plans LLC,* 2011 WL 734933 at *1 (D.N.J. 2011). There were other motions and legal issues involved that we do not address herein.

authorizing class arbitration on two basis. First, it reasoned that questions of contract interpretation, including whether a contract is indeed silent on the issue of class arbitration, are for the arbitrators to decide and that courts should give deference to such decisions.[61] Second, the court found that *Stolt-Nielsen* did not require arbitration agreements to expressly address class arbitration in order for class proceedings to be allowed.[62]

Oxford appealed and the Third Circuit affirmed, finding "*Stolt-Nielsen* did not establish a bright line rule that class arbitration is allowed only under an arbitration agreement that incants 'class arbitration.'"[63] Instead, class arbitration is allowed when "there is a contractual basis for concluding that the party *agreed* to [it]."[64] Applying that reading to the instant case, the court found that the arbitrator endeavored to interpret the parties' agreement within the bounds of the law and his interpretation was not "totally irrational," and, accordingly, it did not warrant vacatur under 9. U.S.C. § 10(a)(4).[65]

Following this decision, Oxford filed a petition for writ of *certiorari* before the Supreme Court, citing a circuit split over what is the "contractual basis" required by *Stolt-Nielsen* for a finding that class arbitration is permissible.[66] The U.S. Supreme Court granted *certiorari*.[67]

### 3.2 *Issue and Parties' Allegations*

The sole issue before the U.S. Supreme Court was "whether [FAA] § 10(a)(4) allows a court to vacate an arbitral award" due to an arbitrator exceeding its powers in circumstances like Oxford's case.[68] As put by Oxford, the main question the Supreme Court had to answer was whether an arbitration agreement that does not specifically address the possibility of class arbitration can, without more, be construed as an affirmative agreement to authorize class arbitration.[69] Sutter framed the issue differently, arguing that the case involved

61 *Id.* at *4.

62 *Id.*

63 *Sutter v. Oxford Health Plans LLC*, 675 F.3d 215, 221–22 (3d Cir. 2012).

64 *Id.* (emphasis in the original).

65 *Id.* at 224–25.

66 Oxford's Petition for Certiorari at 13–20.

67 Oxford Health Plans LLC v. Sutter, 568 U.S. 1065 (2012).

68 *Oxford Health*, 569 U.S. at 568.

69 Oxford Health Plans LLC's Brief for Petitioner filed January 22, 2013, 2013 WL 244026, at 15 (2013).

the finality of arbitration and posed the question of whether the FAA allowed courts to review an arbitrator's construction of the contract.[70]

Among other issues,[71] the parties differed in (i) the level of review allowed by a court at the post-award stage under FAA § 10 and (ii) how to properly read *Stolt-Nielsen*'s holding that a party may not be compelled to submit to class arbitration unless there is a "contractual basis" for the arbitrator to find the party agreed to do so.[72]

In relation to the first issue, Oxford argued that the lower courts' review was deficient and that they should have considered whether the arbitrator's construction of the arbitration agreement "was correct, or even plausible."[73] According to Oxford, effective judicial checks on the exercise of arbitral authority are essential to ensure arbitrators do not take on powers the parties did not intend to delegate to them, and therefore the arbitrator's determination that class arbitration is permitted should be subject to "meaningful review" by the courts so as to not render *Stolt-Nielsen* "an insignificant precedent."[74]

As to the second issue, Oxford argued that the FAA permits class arbitration only if the parties have affirmatively agreed to it.[75] The Supreme Court held in *Stolt-Nielsen* that a party cannot be compelled to submit to class arbitration unless there is a "contractual basis" for concluding it agreed to do so, but the Court left open what that "contractual basis" could be.[76] Oxford's argument proposed class arbitration would be possible only when there is an "affirmative,"[77] "proper,"[78] "distinct and sound,"[79] "legitimate,"[80] "plausible,"[81] "adequate,"[82] or

70 *See* Oxford's Petition for Certiorari; John Ivan Sutter, M.D.'s Brief in Opposition filed November 15, 2012, 2012 WL 3838439 (2012); Oxford Health Plans LLC's Reply Brief for Petitioner filed November 20, 2012, 2012 WL 10919118 (2012).

71 Additional issues not analyzed herein include arguments on the construction of the specific language of the arbitration agreement in the Primary Care Physician Agreement, arbitrability, and estoppel.

72 *Oxford Health,* 569 U.S. at 684.

73 Oxford's Petition for Certiorari, at 33–34.

74 *Id.* at 34–35 (citing *Jock,* 646 F.3d at 129), at 35–39.

75 Oxford Health Plans LLC's Brief for Petitioner filed January 22, 2013, 2013 WL 244026, at 15 (2013).

76 *Stolt-Nielsen,* 559 U.S. at 684, 687 fn.10.

77 Oxford Health Plans LLC's Brief for Petitioner filed January 22, 2013 (hereinafter "Oxford Brief") at 13.

78 *Id.* at 14 and 38; Oxford Health Plans LLC's Reply Brief for Petitioner filed March 18, 2013 (hereinafter "Oxford Reply Brief") at 7.

79 Oxford Brief at 21.

80 *Id.* at 33.

81 *Id.* at 34.

82 *Id.* at 39; Oxford Reply Brief at 9.

"sufficient"[83] contractual basis for it. In other words, Oxford's reading of *Stolt-Nielsen* was that the absence of evidence that the parties intended to *preclude* class arbitration was not sufficient under the FAA. Instead, Oxford argued that evidence of an affirmative showing of consent to class proceedings was required.[84]

Sutter argued on the first issue that Oxford improperly sought to expand the scope of judicial review allowed under the FAA.[85] Sutter maintained that Section 10 of the FAA provides the exclusive grounds for vacatur and generally does not allow courts to review or overturn an arbitrator's decision based on an error of law or fact.[86] According to Sutter, "[t]he power to interpret a contract includes the power to interpret the contract incorrectly."[87] Sutter argued that Oxford's appeal would authorize judicial review where an arbitrator erred, adding a new vacatur ground to the FAA and hindering the finality of arbitration, which for many is the most attractive aspect of arbitration.[88] Further, Sutter protested that Oxford failed to propose a coherent standard for a "meaningful review" on the correctness of an arbitrator's decision[89] and instead was proposing a *de novo* review of "what the parties actually authorized."[90] This would, Sutter forewarned, lead to an increase in post-arbitration litigation and open the door for courts to second-guess an arbitrator's construction of an arbitration agreement in other areas, such as regarding punitive damages, discovery, or certain types of relief.[91]

As for the second issue (the meaning of *Stolt-Nielsen*), Sutter criticized Oxford's attempt to include limiting adjectives—"sufficient," "proper," "legitimate," etc.—to qualify the "contractual basis" required by the Court.[92] In addition to those qualifiers not being part of the Supreme Court's decision, Sutter identified that Oxford failed to explain how they actually would provide meaningful guidance for arbitrators.[93] Sutter further argued that the circumstances

83 Oxford Reply Brief at 2.

84 Oxford Brief at 17–18. This point, according to Oxford, was further confirmed in the Supreme Court's decision in *Concepcion,* where the Court emphasized the difference between agreeing to bilateral arbitration and class arbitration. *Id.* at 19–21.

85 John Ivan Sutter's Brief for Respondent filed February 21, 2013.

86 *Id.* at 19–25.

87 *Id.* at 22.

88 *Id.* at 38–42.

89 *Id.* at 44–45.

90 *Id.* at 46.

91 *Id.*

92 *Id.* at 45–46.

93 *Id.*

of *Stolt-Nielsen* made it distinguishable. For instance, the *Stolt-Nielsen* Court had found that the arbitral tribunal exceeded its powers because it did not interpret the contract—given that the parties stipulated that they reached "no agreement" on the issue of class arbitration—but rather attempted to develop a rule based on its own policy preferences.[94] In contrast, Sutter argued that the arbitrator in Sutter's case based his decision on his construction of the contract, and the FAA does not allow judicial review of such interpretation.[95]

In reply, Oxford argued that it did not propose to depart from the principles of limited judicial review under the FAA but rather that *Stolt-Nielsen* stands for the proposition that an arbitral tribunal exceeds its powers when it imposes class arbitration without a "sufficient contractual basis" and that such basis is not present in broadly worded arbitration agreements that do not expressly address class arbitration.[96] Further, Oxford replied that its proposed reading of *Stolt-Nielsen* would not harm the finality of arbitration but would rather best serve the principles of the FAA by requiring courts to "consider[] the rationale for an award imposing class arbitration" thereby barring arbitrators from inferring implicit agreements to authorize class arbitration based on "bare arbitration clauses."[97]

In addition to the parties' submissions, *amici* briefs were filed by the U.S. Chamber of Commerce, the DRI—Voice of the Defense Bar, Pacific Legal Foundation, New England Legal Foundation, and Equal Employment, calling for the reversal of the lower court's decision, and by the American Medical Association and The Medical Society of New Jersey, in support of affirming the decision. The arguments raised in these submissions were similar to the parties' submissions, except for an additional focus on due process concerns, particularly in relation to absent class members.[98]

---

94 *Id.* at 21.

95 *Id.* at 24–25, 33–36.

96 Oxford Reply Brief, at 5–7.

97 *Id.* at 9–13.

98 *See* Brief Amicus Curiae of Pacific Legal Foundation in Support of Petitioners filed January 23, 2013 at 6–17 2009 WL 2875370 (2009) (arguing class arbitration may not properly protect absent parties, and that the notice requirements in class proceedings run headlong into conflict with the parties' desire to confidentiality in arbitration proceedings); Brief Amicus Curiae of DRI—The Voice of the Defense Bar in Support of Petitioner filed January 29, 2013 at 20–26 (arguing class arbitration lacks the procedural safeguards present in judicial litigation, such as motions to dismiss and motions for summary judgment, and that a defendant might face additional litigation from absent class members even if an arbitrator issues an award in a class arbitration); Brief Amicus Curiae of The American Medical Association and The Medical Society of New Jersey in Support of Respondent

During oral argument, the Justices mainly focused on three issues. First, they analyzed the limits to a court's deference to arbitrators' decisions. The Court stressed its consistent jurisprudence that errors of law or fact are insufficient for vacatur under FAA § 10(a)(4)[99] and that "an arbitrator's interpretation of a contract term, wrong or right, unless it's off the wall, is ... not to be overturned."[100] Oxford argued that *Stolt-Nielsen* established a strong presumption that there can be no agreement to arbitrate as a class without a "clear statement of a meeting of the parties' minds" and that a broad "all-dispute clause" does not satisfy this showing.[101] In response, Sutter took the position that as long as an arbitrator attempts to interpret the parties' contract, *i.e.*, have a "contractual basis" for its decision, the arbitrator's finding is owed deference regardless of whether it is right or wrong.[102] The Justices posited that the arbitrator's construction needed to be plausible, a proposition with which Sutter disagreed.[103]

Second, the Justices were concerned with potential due process violations. In particular, they raised concerns that an erroneous decision—*i.e.*, a finding that parties agreed to class arbitration when in reality they did not—could

filed February 27, 2013 at 8–20 (arguing physicians would be effectively precluded from enforcing their contracts with insurers in the absence of a class device).

99 *See* Transcript of Oral Argument before the Supreme Court of the United States on March 25, 2013 (hereinafter "Tr.") at 5:24–6:1 ("JUSTICE SOTOMAYOR: More than once we have said an error of law or fact is not a basis to say that an arbitrator exceeded his or her powers."); Tr. at 6:15–6:18 ("JUSTICE KENNEDY: So your rule is that although we must defer to an arbitrator's interpretation of the contract, in this case, there is an exception because?"); Tr. at 8:11–8:14 ("JUSTICE GINSBURG: ... the ordinary rule is that—that the arbitration—arbitrator's interpretation of a contract term, wrong or right, unless it's off the wall, is—is not to be overturned."); Tr. at 13:13–13:17 ("JUSTICE KAGAN: And that we have said quite a number of times that the fact that the arbitrator committed an error and even a serious error is not enough, that he had to be doing something that was simply outside the scope of his authority.").

100 Tr. at 8:11–8:14 (Justice Ginsburg).

101 Tr. at 6:19–7:6; Tr. at 8:15–8:25; Tr. at 14:17–15:7; Tr. at 18:5–18:10.

102 Tr. at 25:7–25:14 ("JUSTICE SCALIA: And you think that standard—all that standard means is that the arbitrator has to say is, I am interpreting the contract, even though what he says is flatly, visibly, unquestionably contrary to what the contract says, and the court has to accept that, so long as he says I'm interpreting the contract. MR. KATZ [Sutter's counsel]: This Court's jurisprudence for almost 2 centuries has held just exactly that.").

103 Tr. at 33:3–33:14 ("JUSTICE SCALIA: But that's not enough. As stated by Justice Breyer, he has to have come to a plausible construction. It's not enough that he said I'm construing the contract. I have looked at the terms of the contract and what the parties said, and my construction is X. That's not enough. It has to be plausible. ... MR. KATZ [Sutter's counsel]: Well, with all due respect, Justice Scalia, I don't think plausibility comes into play.").

bind absent class members to an arbitration.[104] Relatedly, the Justices questioned the source of an arbitrator's authority in such a case[105] and whether (and how) the absent class members would be able to opt out of the class.[106] Sutter maintained, however, that, even if an arbitrator was mistaken, such mistake did not warrant a court's review and vacatur of the award under FAA § 10(a)(4).[107]

104 Tr. at 36:6–36:17 ("JUSTICE ALITO: And if we assume …that this agreement does not constitute an agreement to engage in class arbitration, where did the arbitrator get the authority to make that holding with respect to all of these absent class members? … If they didn't agree to class arbitration … [h]ow did he purport to bind them to that decision?").

105 Tr. at 37:8–37:17 ("JUSTICE ALITO: Wait a minute. Where did he get the authority to make that decision to interpret the contract with respect to them [absent class members]? … You're saying he can do it with respect to Oxford because Oxford agreed to have the arbitrator decide whether this calls for class arbitration. But these other people didn't."); Tr. at 38:11–38:17 ("JUSTICE SCALIA: Did these other people agree to this arbitrator? … They didn't agree to this arbitrator. Why should they be bound by—by whatever he says?").

106 Tr. at 38:22–39:9 ("JUSTICE KENNEDY: Could they—could they opt out? MR. KATZ [Sutter's counsel]: Well, ultimately they could… JUSTICE SCALIA: How can they opt out if they've agreed to class arbitration? … It seems to me if they've agreed to class arbitration, they've agreed to class arbitration."); Tr. at 39:18–40:3 ("JUSTICE KENNEDY: But—but how could—how could they opt out if the arbitrator said—says, as Justice Scalia and Justice Alito are suggesting, we have—I have jurisdiction to decide this case. I decide that there is a class action, all these people are in the class. MR KATZ [Sutter's counsel]: Justice Kennedy, the determination that this matter could proceed as a class arbitration was only the first issue that was decided. We then engaged in the procedural mechanism by which the matter could be certified and that they could-—"); Tr. at 40:19–41:1 ("JUSTICE ALITO: … how are these absent people bound? And it's really not an answer to say, well, they can opt out. If they didn't agree to be bound by this arbitrator's decision, then they didn't agree to be bound absent by opting out, which is an unusual procedure for being bound by an agreement. JUSTICE GINSBURG: You would never have class action arbitration if that were so.").

107 *See* Tr. at 41:7–41:19 ("MR. KATZ [Sutter's counsel]: … And even if the arbitrator was wrong, Justice Alito, I submit that under 10(a)(4) in the applicable standard, that even in *Concepcion,* this Court said 10(a)(4) is—is not an issue of mistake, it's an issue of misconduct. And that's not what we have here. If there was a mistake, that still would not be enough with respect to the courts to have vacated the arbitrator's determination on this matter."); Tr. at 46:23–46:25 ("MR KATZ: … this Court has recognized for 2 centuries that an arbitrator's error in law or fact cannot be grounds for a vacatur."); Tr. at 47:18–47:23 ("MR. KATZ: I submit we have to—if we trust arbitrators to handle such important issues as civil rights issues and other very important matters of singular importance, we have to expect that they will follow the precepts of this Court and the FAA as to what constitutes grounds for class arbitration.").

Third, the Justices referenced the Court's decision in *First Options of Chicago, Inc. v. Kaplan*[108] in questioning whether an arbitrator's decision on which parties are bound to arbitrate is subject to *de novo* review.[109] While the discussion was not fully explored, in passing, Oxford suggested that an arbitrator would exceed his or her powers by holding someone who did not agree to arbitrate bound by a class arbitration determination.[110] Sutter, on the other hand, argued that there would no excess of power in that case, given that the arbitrator still acted within the bounds of the issue submitted for determination.[111]

### 3.3 *The Court's Opinion*

In a decision dated June 10, 2013, the Supreme Court affirmed the Third Circuit's decision, concluding that the arbitrator's award should not be vacated given the limited review allowed under FAA § 10(a)(4).

Justice Kagan delivered the opinion of a unanimous court. The decision focused on two issues. First, it addressed and reaffirmed the Court's understanding of the standard of review under FAA § 10(a)(4). Second, it clarified *Stolt-Nielsen*'s holding that an arbitrator needs to have a "contractual basis" to conclude an arbitration agreement authorizes class arbitration.

In relation to the standard of review under FAA § 10(a)(4), the Court reaffirmed the high level of deference warranted to an arbitrator's construction of a contract and that an arbitrator's error—even a serious one—did not warrant vacatur for excess of power.[112] The Court explained that an arbitrator's decision must stand "regardless of a court's view of its (de)merits" unless it "reflects his

108 514 U.S. 938 (1995).

109 Tr. at 30:2–30:14 ("CHIEF JUSTICE ROBERTS: In other words, not everything an arbitrator says is subject to the deferential standard of review, even if he purports to say I'm interpreting the agreement, which I think the arbitrator in First Options did?"); Tr. at 37:24–38:4 ("CHIEF JUSTICE ROBERTS: ... The one thing First Options says is the question of who's going to be bound by arbitration is decided by the court de novo. And in the class context, you are binding 19,999 individuals who did not agree to be bound, depending upon the particular interpretation.").

110 Tr. at 21:15–22:1 ("MR. WAXMAN [Oxford's counsel]: ... [an arbitrator] exceeds—he or she exceeds his or her power if they—if he or she decides, as this Court stated in Stolt-Nielsen, that you agreed to arbitrate with someone with whom you didn't agree to arbitrate. That is this case.").

111 Tr. at 30:15–30:18 ("MR. KATZ [Sutter's counsel]: Here, Mr. Chief Justice, the arbitrator did exactly what the parties had asked him to do, though. He did not venture and do something outside of what the parties had asked him."); Tr. 38:18–38:21 ("MR. KATZ: Well, for one thing, Justice Scalia, that's exactly what Oxford wanted. Oxford argued that the class action should go into arbitration.").

112 *Oxford Health*, 569 U.S. at 569.

own notions of economic justice rather than drawing its essence from the contract."[113] Therefore, the sole question for courts entertaining vacatur for excess of power is "whether the arbitrator (even arguably) interpreted the parties' contract, not whether he got its meaning right or wrong."[114] In the instant case, the Court found that the arbitrator's decision was indeed based on contract interpretation, rather than his own policy views, and therefore survived the limited scrutiny allowed under FAA § 10(a)(4).[115]

As to the second issue, the Court clarified what it meant by "contractual basis" in *Stolt-Nielsen.*[116] It rejected Oxford's argument that the arbitration agreement had to provide a "sufficient" contractual basis for finding class arbitration permissible and explained that what *Stolt-Nielsen* required was, rather, "any" contractual basis.[117] This put Oxford's case in stark contrast with *Stolt-Nielsen.*[118] In *Stolt-Nielsen,* the arbitral tribunal's decision could only have been based on the tribunal's own policy choice, given that the parties stipulated there that they had not agreed to class arbitration.[119] That is to say, in *Stolt-Nielsen,* there was not "any" basis for the arbitrator to find that the parties agreed to class arbitration. Meanwhile, the arbitrator in *Oxford Health* interpreted the contract language, finding that it revealed the parties' intent to permit class arbitration.[120] The Court explained that an arbitrator's interpretation of the parties' contract is not subject to judicial review.[121]

That is so, the Court expounded, regardless of how incorrect a court might find the arbitrator's interpretation.[122] While the Court made clear that it did not endorse the arbitrator's decision, it affirmed that it was barred from reviewing the substance of that decision given the limits imposed by the FAA:

> Nothing we say in this opinion should be taken to reflect any agreement with the arbitrator's contract interpretation, or any quarrel with Oxford's

113 *Id.* (citations omitted).

114 *Id.*

115 *Id.* at 570.

116 *Id.* at 570–71.

117 *Id.* at 571.

118 *Id.* at 572 ("*Stolt-Nielsen* and this case thus fall on opposite sides of the line that § 10(a)(4) draws to delimit judicial review of arbitral decisions.").

119 *Id.* at 571–72.

120 *Id.*

121 *Id.* at 572.

122 *Id.* at 573 ("He provided an interpretation of the contract resolving that disputed issue. His interpretation went against Oxford, maybe mistakenly so. But still, Oxford does not get to rerun the matter in a court. Under § 10(a)(4), the question for a judge is not whether the arbitrator construed the parties' contract correctly, but whether he construed it at all.").

> contrary reading. All we say is that convincing a court of an arbitrator's error—even his grave error—is not enough. So long as the arbitrator was 'arguably construing' the contract—which this one was—a court may not correct his mistakes under §10(a)(4). The potential for those mistakes is the price of agreeing to arbitration. ... The arbitrator's construction holds, however good, bad, or ugly.[123]

Justice Alito's concurring opinion, with which Justice Thomas joined, went further, making the disagreement with the arbitrator's construction abundantly clear.[124] In particular, Justice Alito picked up on the concerns raised during oral arguments related to absent class members, stating that "an arbitrator's erroneous interpretation that an agreement authorizes class arbitration cannot bind someone who did not authorize him to make that determination,"[125] an issue that he considered could not be cured simply by opt-out notices.[126]

Justice Alito ultimately concurred with the decision, however, because he agreed that FAA § 10(a)(4) does not allow a *de novo* review of an arbitrator's contract interpretation.[127] In other words, courts cannot reverse an arbitrator's decision that "arguably construct[s]"[128] the contract, however wrong they believe that interpretation might be.[129] Having to live with an unreviewable decision is the bargain the parties strike when opting for arbitration.[130]

Notwithstanding these holdings, the Court potentially left open a basis for further debate on the issues. In a footnote, the Court recorded that its decision does not address whether an arbitration agreement's authorization of class arbitration raises a question of arbitrability, *i.e.*, the arbitrator's jurisdiction.[131]

---

123 *Id.* at 572–73 (citations omitted).

124 *Id.* at 573 ("If we were reviewing the arbitrator's interpretation of the contract *de novo*, we would have little trouble concluding that he improperly inferred 'an implicit agreement to authorize class-action arbitration ... from the fact of the parties' agreement to arbitrate.").

125 *Id.* at 574.

126 *Id.* at 574–75 ("Arbitration is simply a matter of contract between the parties, and an offeree's silence does not normally modify the terms of a contract. Accordingly, at least where absent class members have not been required to opt in, it is difficult to see how an arbitrator's decision to conduct class proceedings could bind absent class members who have not authorized the arbitrator to decide on a classwide basis which arbitration procedures are to be used.") (citations omitted).

127 *Id.* at 573–74.

128 *Id.* at 572.

129 *Id.* at 573.

130 *Id.*

131 *Id.* at 569 n. 2.

Raising the question *sua sponte*, the Court noted that its decision might have been different had Oxford argued the point.[132] The Court explained that, unlike questions of pure contract interpretation, an arbitrator's determination on questions of arbitrability are subject to *de novo* review by the courts, making it within a court's authority to correct an arbitrator's erroneous interpretation of a contract where it leads to a wrong decision on arbitrability (*i.e.*, the arbitrator's jurisdiction).[133] The Court found that the case was inapposite to resolve this matter, however, because Oxford had agreed that the arbitrator had the authority to determine the matter.[134]

### 3.4 *Key Takeaways*

*Oxford Health* builds on the long-standing body of law in the United States that a court's review at the post-award stage is severely limited. The decision reaffirms the significant deference that courts must give to arbitrators' decisions, which U.S. courts will not review except on very limited grounds and in narrow circumstances. The case also makes plain that the high level of deference afforded to the arbitrators in a review under Section 10 of the FAA is the same, regardless of whether the underlying dispute is a bilateral or class arbitration.

As the Court previously held, petitioners seeking vacatur based on an excess of authority under FAA § 10(a)(4) face an extremely "high hurdle,"[135] which is rarely met. A party cannot merely show that the arbitrator erred in exercising his or her authority—even seriously or gravely so—to meet this burden. Instead, a petitioner must show that the arbitrator did not have the authority to make the decision at all.

In the specific context of class arbitration, an arbitrator's decision premised on construction of an arbitration agreement to permit class proceedings will not be subject to vacatur unless such decision is shown to have been based on something other than his or her interpretation of the contract (such as the arbitrator's policy views, as was the case in *Stolt-Nielsen*).[136] That is an exceedingly high threshold for a petitioner to meet, meaning that an arbitrator's decision should be expected to stand as long as the arbitrator *arguably* attempted to construct the contract.[137]

---

132 *Id.*

133 *Id.*

134 *Id.* ("Indeed, Oxford submitted that issue to the arbitrator not once, but twice—and the second time after *Stolt-Nielsen* flagged that it might be a question of arbitrability.")

135 *Stolt-Nielsen,* 559 U.S. at 671.

136 *Oxford Health,* 569 U.S. at 571–72.

137 *Id.* at 572.

In addition, the Supreme Court's passing mention in a footnote of the possibility that judicial review of arbitrability may still be available cannot be overlooked.[138] The Court had already raised this issue in *Stolt-Nielsen,* saying "the parties appear to have believed that the judgment in *Bazzle* requires an arbitrator, not a court, to decide whether a contract permits class arbitration[,] [but] [w]hat *Bazzle* says is that the *contract interpretation* issue is left up to the arbitrator."[139] Yet neither *Stolt-Nielsen* nor *Oxford Health* provided an appropriate vehicle to explore arbitrability, as in both cases the parties had agreed to submit the decision on class arbitration to the arbitrators.[140]

Judicial review of class action arbitration awards based on arbitrability could open up a significant avenue for challenge. Under *Stolt-Nielsen* and *Oxford Health,* the arbitrator only has to have "arguably" constructed the parties' contract for his or her decision to be granted deference and affirmed.[141] Were the Supreme Court to find in an appropriate case that this still leaves open a question of arbitrability, which would therefore be subject to *de novo* review, an arbitrator's decision authorizing class arbitration on the basis of a silent agreement would be vulnerable to challenge on a much lower standard than would apply to defending the decision merely on an arguable "contractual basis."

Certain Circuit courts have anticipated that the Supreme Court, when seized with a pertinent case on appeal, will find this is a gateway issue and therefore subject to review, failing clear and unmistakable evidence that the parties wished the arbitrators to decide it.[142] Indeed, harking back to Chief Justice Rehnquist's dissent in *Bazzle,* it was clear that he would have reversed because "this determination is one for the courts, not for the arbitrator."[143] However, the two Court members who joined his dissent—Justices O'Connor

138 *Id.* at 569, n.2 (noting the Supreme Court has "not *yet*" decided whether the availability of class arbitration is a question of arbitrability).

139 *Stolt-Nielsen,* 559 U.S. at 680. (emphasis added).

140 *Id; Oxford Health,* 569 U.S. at 569, n. 2.

141 *Oxford Health,* 569 U.S. at 572.

142 *See Del Webb Communities, Inc. v. Carlson,* 817 F.3d 867, 875 (4th Cir. 2016) ("The evolution of the [Supreme] Court's cases are but a short step away from the conclusion that whether an arbitration agreement authorizes class arbitration presents a question as to the arbitrator's inherent power, which requires judicial review."); *Reed Elsevier, Inc. ex rel. LexisNexis Div. v. Crockett,* 734 F.3d 594, 598 (6th Cir. 2013) ("[R]ecently the Court has given every indication, short of an outright holding, that classwide arbitrability is a gateway question rather than a subsidiary one.")

143 *Bazzle,* 539 U.S. at 455.

and Kennedy—have since retired, and the position of the current Court is less clear.

## 4 Critical Analysis of the Opinion and How It Impacted U.S. Arbitration Law and Practice

Are *Oxford Health*, *Bazzle*, and *Stolt-Nielsen* decisions on how to interpret silent arbitration agreements? Can they be read to create a standard for the interpretation of whether class arbitration is permitted when the arbitration agreement does not address the matter? If so, what is that standard?

The answers to these questions remain unclear. A high-level reading might suggest that the outcome should depend on the language of the arbitration agreement—while a default clause providing that "any disputes" are subject to arbitration may not allow for class arbitration, broader clauses like the one in *Oxford Health* could be read to authorize it. However, while the language of the clause remains important, such a conclusion would be overly simplistic.

First, not all silent arbitration agreements are created equal. The distinguishing factor between the arbitration agreements in *Stolt-Nielsen* and *Oxford Health* was not their different language, but the parties' stipulation in the former case that they had not reached an agreement on the issue. Accordingly, the focus should be on the broader question of the parties' manifested intent. In *Stolt-Nielsen,* the clause did not reflect an agreement one way or the other on whether the parties intended to permit class arbitration, so the arbitrator exceeded his powers as he could not possibly have found evidence of the parties' intent to authorize class proceedings. No similar evidence existed in *Oxford Health,* so the arbitrator was within his powers to interpret the arbitration agreement as reflecting the parties' intent to use class arbitration. Absent a stipulation of the sort found in *Stolt-Nielsen,* arbitrators might want to look more broadly for evidence of the parties' intent.

Second, and perhaps most importantly, in none of the three cases did the Supreme Court actually articulate a standard that should be applied in interpreting the contracts. On the contrary, the decisions were carefully drafted to focus on the limits of judicial review under FAA § 10(a)(4). As Justice Kagan stated during oral arguments:

> you're saying that [the arbitrator] exceeded his authority because he didn't apply a kind of clear statement presumption. But I don't think that we've ever suggested that there is such a clear presumption. ... we've not said [in Stolt-Nielsen] that in the process of construing an agreement

> there is a clear statement rule. Now, maybe we should have said that, but—you know, it's—it's no place in our case law now.[144]

It is unsurprising that the Supreme Court—in keeping with its long-held avoidance of dictating rules for interpreting arbitration agreements—has eschewed establishing a brightline rule for finding consent to class arbitration. Without derogating from this conclusion, *obiter dicta* suggests that the Supreme Court remains wary of finding class arbitration to be authorized based only on a broad arbitration clause that is silent on class proceedings. This wariness is manifested in at least three places in *Oxford Health*. First, Justice Alito's concurrence stated that "[i]f we were reviewing the arbitrator's interpretation of the contract *de novo*, we would have little trouble concluding that he improperly inferred 'an implicit agreement to authorize class-action arbitration from the fact of the parties' agreement to arbitrate."[145] Second, Chief Justice Roberts remarked during oral arguments that the arbitrator's interpretation of the contract was "inconsistent with the law that's developed ... which is that if you have something that just says 'disputes' and doesn't address the issue of class arbitration at all, that you can't have class arbitration."[146] And third, between the lines of Justice Kagan's opinion, there is reference to the "(de)merits"[147] of the arbitrator's reading and "his grave error."[148]

Ultimately, however, *Oxford Health* is best read not as a case on how to interpret silent arbitration agreements but rather as a reaffirmation of the Supreme Court's longstanding deference to an arbitrator's construction of the parties' agreement. Indeed, that seems to be how most courts have applied *Oxford Health* in the 10 years since it was issued, finding that it provides guidance on such deference in cases beyond class arbitrations. For example, in *Spirit of the East, LLC v. Yale Products, Inc.*,[149] the Eleventh Circuit enforced an arbitral award over the petitioner's argument that it called for the "criminal" transfer of a vessel when the parties had not completed various legal formalities required by Florida law for such transfer.[150] The Eleventh Circuit relied on *Oxford Health* for the proposition that "an arbitral decision even arguably

144 Tr. at 15:8–15:19.

145 *Oxford*, 569 U.S. at 573.

146 Tr. at 28:23–29:4.

147 *Oxford*, 569 U.S. at 569.

148 *Id.* at 572.

149 2023 WL 2890013, at *3 (11th Cir. Apr. 11, 2023), cert. denied, 144 S. Ct. 485, 217 L. Ed. 2d 254 (2023).

150 *Id.* at *3–4.

construing or applying the contract must stand, regardless of a court's view of its (de)merits."[151] Likewise, in *Ross Dress for Less Inc v. VIWP, L.P.*,[152] the Third Circuit confirmed an arbitral award over a party's objection that the tribunal had exceeded its power by granting relief on a time-barred claim.[153] The court found, citing *Oxford Health,* that "an arbitrator's error—even his grave error," did not warrant vacatur, as "the potential for those mistakes is the price of agreeing to arbitration."[154]

The foregoing observations should not detract from the fact that *Oxford Health* has been used to support an arbitrator's class certification based on an underlying silent arbitration agreement. However, in those cases *Oxford Health* does not seem to be relied on as setting forth a standard for contract interpretation—nor should it. Rather, it is more often quoted as establishing a high hurdle for a party seeking to vacate an award on the basis of the arbitrator having allegedly exceeded his or her authority.[155]

*Oxford Health* has also contributed to jurisprudence that continues to chart a very narrow course for those Circuits that still consider manifest disregard of law to be a valid ground for vacatur of an award. Courts have cited *Oxford Health* in affirming the high bar for vacatur on the basis of alleged manifest disregard of the law by the arbitrator. That is true in the context of challenges to decisions authorizing class arbitration over silent agreements,[156] as well as in other broader contexts.[157]

151 *Id.* (quoting *Oxford Health,* 569 U.S. at 569).

152 750 F. App'x 141 (3d Cir. 2018).

153 *Id.* at 145.

154 *Id.* (quoting *Oxford Health,* 569 U.S. at 572–73). *See also Am. Postal Workers Union, AFL-CIO v. U.S. Postal Serv.,* 754 F.3d 109, 113 (2d Cir. 2014) (arbitrator did not exceed authority by rejecting the claim on the basis of collateral estoppel given prior administrative decision on the same matter); *BNSF R. Co. v. Alstom Transp., Inc.,* 777 F.3d 785, 789 (5th Cir. 2015) (arbitrator did not exceed authority by, among other conduct, granting a remedy that was arguably not provided for in the parties' contract).

155 *See, e.g., S. Commc'ns Servs., Inc. v. Thomas,* 720 F.3d 1352, 1359 (11th Cir. 2013) (arbitrator did not exceed authority in finding that a silent arbitration agreement that adopted the AAA rules authorized class arbitration) (citing *Oxford Health,* 569 U.S. at 569); *DIRECTV, LLC v. Arndt,* 546 F. App'x 836, 839–40 (11th Cir. 2013) (finding "[t]he Supreme Court allows federal courts little leeway in determining whether an arbitrator exceeded her powers within the meaning of § 10(a)(4)" and enforcing the arbitrator's decision authorizing class arbitration even if that decision could "have been ugly, … mistaken, incorrect or in manifest disregard of the law.") (citing *Oxford Health,* 569 U.S. at 573).

156 *See, e.g., Dish Network L.L.C. v. Ray,* 900 F.3d 1240, 1252 (10th Cir. 2018) (arbitrator did not manifestly disregard Colorado law in concluding that a broadly worded arbitration agreement adopting the AAA rules authorized class arbitration).

157 *See, e.g., THI of New Mexico at Vida Encantada, LLC v. Lovato,* 864 F.3d 1080, 1088 (10th Cir. 2017) (arbitrator did not exceed authority nor manifestly disregard the law in granting cost-shifting that was not expressly authorized by the arbitration agreement).

The *Oxford Health* decision also continues to have an impact on two related issues that were not at the forefront of the Court's reason but were at least alluded to in the opinions, namely, an arbitrator's authority over absent class members (i.e., the due process concerns this raises) and the question of whether the arbitration agreement authorizes the arbitrator to determine his or her own jurisdiction to determine there is a class arbitration (i.e., arbitrability).

First, the issue of absent class members was front and center in the Second Circuit's decision in *Jock v. Sterling Jewelers Inc.*[158] In that case, 250 of defendant's employees had opted into the subject arbitration, but the arbitrator's class certification also purported to bind over 44,000 other employees who had not opted in but merely had signed identical employment agreements with defendant.[159] The Southern District of New York vacated the arbitrator's class determination finding that, even if the arbitrator's "erroneous interpretation" of the arbitration agreement could bind the employees who opted in, she did not have the authority to bind absent class members.[160] The Second Circuit reversed, finding that the absent class members had agreed to submit the question of class arbitrability to an arbitrator by signing the agreement with defendant.[161] Importantly, the agreement called for the application of the AAA rules, and the AAA Supplementary Rules for Class Arbitration provide "the arbitrator shall determine as a threshold matter ... whether the applicable arbitration clause permits the arbitration to proceed on behalf of ... a class."[162] Relying on *Oxford Health,* the court found that the arbitrator acted within her authority because "the parties 'bargained for the arbitrator's construction of their agreement' with respect to class arbitrability."[163] And the arbitrator's interpretation of the arbitration agreement stood, regardless of whether the court thought it was erroneous.[164]

Second, in the wake of *Oxford Health,* it remains highly contentious whether the determination of whether an arbitration agreement authorizes class arbitration should be considered a gateway issue, presumptively for courts to decide.

---

158 942 F.3d 617 (2d Cir. 2019).

159 *Id.* at 621.

160 *Id.* at 622.

161 *Id.* at 623–24.

162 *Id.* at 623 (quoting the AAA Supplementary Rule 1(a)).

163 *Id.* at 624 (quoting *Oxford Health,* 569 U.S. at 569).

164 *Id.* at 625 ("It is not for us, as a court, to decide whether the arbitrator's class certification decision was correct on the merits of issues such as commonality and typicality. We merely decide that the arbitrator had the authority to reach such issues even with respect to the absent class members.")

Eight Circuits so far—the Third,[165] Fourth,[166] Fifth,[167] Sixth,[168] Seventh,[169] Eighth,[170] Ninth,[171] and Eleventh[172]—have concluded in the affirmative. The Eighth Circuit has even go so far as to say that the incorporation of institutional rules covering class arbitration—in that case, the AAA rules—is not "clear and unmistakable" evidence that the parties delegated this decision to an arbitrator.[173] Although not ultimately ruling on whether this is a gateway issue, the Second and Tenth Circuits have both issued decisions contrary to the Eighth Circuit, i.e., finding that the incorporation of institutional rules governing class arbitration is indeed "clear and unmistakable" evidence of an agreement to arbitrate arbitrability.[174]

Given this debate, it is perhaps not surprising that the only occasion on which the Supreme Court has itself cited *Oxford Health* was to raise directly whether this issue raised a question of judicially reviewable arbitrability, but once again—teasingly—to conclude that it was an issue to be resolved on another day in another case.[175] Given the degree of attention the arbitrability dilemma continues to garner and the apparent Circuit split, it seems only a matter of time before the Supreme Court steps in to provide some much-needed clarification.

---

165 *Opalinski v. Robert Half Int'l Inc.*, 761 F.3d 326, 334–35 (3d Cir. 2014).

166 *Del Webb Communities, Inc. v. Carlson*, 817 F.3d 867, 873 (4th Cir. 2016).

167 *20/20 Commc'ns, Inc. v. Crawford*, 930 F.3d 715, 718–19 (5th Cir. 2019).

168 *Reed Elsevier, Inc. ex rel. LexisNexis Div. v. Crockett*, 734 F.3d 594, 598 (6th Cir. 2013).

169 *Herrington v. Waterstone Mortg. Corp.*, 907 F.3d 502, 506–07 (7th Cir. 2018).

170 *Catamaran Corp. v. Towncrest Pharmacy*, 864 F.3d 966, 971 (8th Cir. 2017).

171 *Shivkov v. Artex Risk Sols., Inc.*, 974 F.3d 1051, 1065 (9th Cir. 2020).

172 *JPay, Inc. v. Kobel*, 904 F.3d 923, 931 (11th Cir. 2018).

173 *Catamaran*, 864 F.3d at 973 ("incorporation of AAA Rules by reference is insufficient evidence that the parties intended for an arbitrator to decide the substantive question of class arbitration."). *But compare Brennan v. Opus Bank*, 796 F.3d 1125, 1131–32 (9th Cir. 2015) (finding incorporation of AAA rules "clearly and unmistakably delegates arbitrability questions to the arbitrator"); *Cooper v. WestEnd Cap. Mgmt., L.L.C.*, 832 F.3d 534, 546 (5th Cir. 2016) (finding "[t]he express adoption of these [JAMS] rules presents clear and unmistakable evidence that the parties agreed to arbitrate arbitrability.").

174 *Wells Fargo Advisors, LLC v. Sappington*, 884 F.3d 392, 396 (2d Cir. 2018) (finding the incorporation of the 1993 Securities Arbitration Rules of the AAA in the arbitration agreement "serves as clear and unmistakable evidence of the parties' intent to delegate [issues of arbitrability] to an arbitrator."); *Belnap v. Iasis Healthcare*, 844 F.3d 1272, 1284 (10th Cir. 2017) ("we conclude that by incorporating the JAMS Rules into the Agreement, Dr. Belnap and SLRMC clearly and unmistakably agreed to submit arbitrability issues to an arbitrator.")

175 *Lamps Plus, Inc. v. Varela*, 587 U.S. 176, 186 (2019) ("This Court has not decided whether the availability of class arbitration is a so-called "question of arbitrability," which includes these gateway matters. *Oxford Health Plans LLC v. Sutter*, 569 U.S. 564, 569, n. 2, 133 S.Ct.

## 5 Conclusions

The U.S. Supreme Court has shown a remarkable willingness to wade into the class arbitration debate, commandeering an outsize portion of the highest court's limited docket. The Court's decisions between 2010 and 2019 have established the basic parameters for the use—or avoidance—of class arbitration in the United States. *Oxford Health* stands at the half-way point of the Supreme Court's jurisprudence in this era. But far from merely being a stepping stone, the decision—properly read—discloses the core of the Court's thinking on the issue,[176] and establishes the conceptual framework for the position it would take in future cases. Moreover, the case's influence extends beyond the narrow issue of class arbitration and has contributed to the development of arbitration law in a broad range of applications, none less so than Justice Kagan's evocative reaffirmation of deference to the arbitrator's construction, "however good, bad, or ugly."[177]

---

2064, 186 L.Ed.2d 113 (2013). We have no occasion to address that question here because the parties agreed that a court, not an arbitrator, should resolve the question about class arbitration"); BG *Grp.*, PLC *v. Republic of Argentina*, 572 U.S. 25, 33, 134 S. Ct. 1198, 1206, 188 L. Ed. 2d 220 (2014) (addressing question of arbitrability in a case not involving class arbitration).

176 Including a policy concern that restricting class arbitration would effectively strip parties with low value claims of an available forum assuming that class litigation remained unavailable, which debate will continue to play out in the U.S. Supreme Court's ongoing jurisprudence, *American Exp. Co. v. Italian Colors*, 570 U.S. 228, 235–38 (2013) (discussing whether the "effective vindication" exception invalidates a bar to class arbitration when the value of the individual claim was too small compared to the costs of individual arbitration). *See* Tr. at 22:12–22:23 ("JUSTICE GINSBURG: Well, of course, this was—this was an adhesion contract, so there's no—it was drafted by Oxford. And you made a point about betting the house, that the company wouldn't have agreed to it. But on the side of the doctor, he has a $10,000—a $1,000 claim, and he is saying that without a class proceeding, there is—there is essentially no means to enforce the contract against Oxford, that none of these parties, none of the, what was it, 13,000 doctors, none of them could enforce the contract because the expense would be much greater than the $1,000 they could get at the end.")

177 *Oxford*, 569 U.S. at 573.

CHAPTER 25

# *American Express Co. v. Italian Colors Restaurant* (2013)

*Fabiano Robalinho, Caetano Berenguer and João Lucas Bevilacqua*

## 1 Summary of the Facts

Class-action damages lawsuits are a source of potentially huge costs to U.S. corporations. In order to reduce exposure, many have resorted to the insertion into contracts of arbitration clauses containing class-action waivers, meaning that in the event of a dispute, plaintiffs are obliged to engage in individual arbitration proceedings to seek redress and enforce their rights.

This trend has caused concern amongst legal practitioners, and in wider society, as to the risk of individual claimants being effectively denied the right to redress, due to the difficulties and costs of pursuing individual arbitration claims.

In *American Express Co. v. Italian Colors Restaurant*,[1] the U.S. Supreme Court reinforced its support for the contractual freedom of parties and upheld an arbitration clause that included waiver of recourse to class-action arbitration. The Court held that the clause was consistent with the provisions of the Federal Arbitration Act, which Congress had enacted "*in response to widespread judicial hostility to arbitration*".[2]

On a majority vote (5x3),[3] the Supreme Court held that claims for redress under contracts that contained arbitration clauses with class-action waivers were to be dealt with as individual bilateral (arbitration) proceedings. They could not be referred to the judiciary on a class-wide basis. The Court upheld the waiver even though it meant that, in practice, the plaintiffs ("*Italian Colors*") would incur costs that were vastly in excess of any potential credit judgment in their favor against American Express Company and its subsidiary ("*American Express*").

1 *American Express Co. v. Italian Colors Restaurant*, 570 U.S. 228 (2013).

2 *Id.* at 232.

3 Justice Sotomayor took no part in the consideration or decision of this specific case as a Justice of the Supreme Court. She was originally a member of the Second Circuit panel but was elevated from the Second Circuit to the Supreme Court in August 2009.

 | DOI:10.1163/9789004715820_026

This position was in line with earlier Supreme Court rulings that reinforced the presumption of enforceability of arbitration agreements. The Court again interpreted the provisions of the Federal Arbitration Act in such a way as to uphold class action waivers.

In the earlier case of *AT&T Mobility LLC v. Concepcion*, 563 U.S. 333 (2011), a majority of the Supreme Court Justices held that the FAA preempted state laws from prohibiting waivers of class-wide arbitration. In *Nielsen SA v AnimalFeeds International Corp*, the majority of the Bench held that a class arbitration was not possible in the absence of specific provision in the agreement that permitted it.

Despite this trend, some arbitration practitioners and commentators considered that the Supreme Court might invalidate a class waiver in circumstances in which the waiver would constitute a bar to effective vindication of federal statutory rights. This view was based on *dicta* from the *Mitsubishi* case.[4]

The plaintiffs in *American Express Co. v. Italian Colors Restaurant* argued before the judiciary that if, in accordance with the dispute resolution provision inserted into their contract with *American Express*, they were to be compelled to file individual bilateral arbitration proceedings, the cost they would incur would be prohibitive and disproportionate to any amounts they might expect to recover. As such, upholding the class action waiver would be tantamount to denying their right to enforce statutory rights under federal legislation.

The Supreme Court, however, upheld the class waiver. The Court[5] dismissed the arguments advanced on behalf of the plaintiffs that enforcing the waiver would prevent them from bringing a federal antitrust claim under the Sherman Act (the U.S. federal statute of 1890 that prohibits actual or attempted monopolization of any aspect of interstate trade or commerce and which was amended by the Clayton Act in 1914).

## 2 The Background to the Dispute

American Express obtained significant revenue from charging merchants for card-support services. Merchants that wish to accept payment via Amex cards must sign a commercial agreement with American Express in which they agree

4 *Mitsubishi Motors Corp. v. Soler Chrysler-Plymouyth, Inc*, 473 U.S. 614.

5 "We consider whether a contractual waiver of class arbitration is enforceable under the Federal Arbitration Act when the plaintiff's cost of individually arbitrating a federal statutory claim exceeds the potential recovery" (*American Express Co. v. Italian Colors Restaurant*, 570 U.S. 228 (2013) at 231).

to pay stipulated fees for payments received from customers using individual and corporate credit or charge cards.[6]

In the lawsuit that led to the Supreme Court ruling, the plaintiff merchants challenged an "Honor All Cards" clause contained in their contract with American Express and American Express Travel Related Services Company, Inc (a wholly owned subsidiary of the American Express Company). The clause was worded as follows: "your acceptance of American Express© Cards (...) American Express Card(s) (...) shall mean any card or other account access device issued by American Express Travel Related Services Company, Inc., or its subsidiaries or affiliates or its or their licensees bearing the American Express name or an American Express trademark, service mark or logo".[7]

Italian Colors argued that through this clause, American Express was effectively exercising a monopoly over the sector and was forcing merchants to pay exorbitant fees on a wide range of credit and charge cards *"which [fees] vastly exceeded the rate for comparable Visa, MasterCard or Discover products".* This conduct, according to Italian Colors, amounted to a 'tying arrangement', and was unlawful under the Sherman Act.[8]

The contracts in question contained an arbitration clause which stipulated that there "shall be no right or authority for any Claims to be arbitrated on a class action basis",[9] i.e. "a provision which forbids the parties to the contract from pursuing anything other than individual claims in the arbitral forum".[10]

## 3 The Dispute

Notwithstanding the existence of the arbitration clause, a group of merchants filed a lawsuit before the judiciary arguing violation by American Express of Section I of the Sherman Act through imposition of an unlawful *tying arrangement.*

Plaintiffs argued that entering into individual bilateral arbitration with American Express was not economically viable. They produced evidence

6 The District Court noted that "a charge card requires its holder to pay the full outstanding balance at the end of a standard billing cycle. A credit card, by contrast, allows the cardholder to pay a portion of the amount owing at the close of a billing cycle, subject to interest charges. In plain terms, the credit card is a means of financing purchases, the charge card is a method of payment" (Amex I, 554 F.3d at 304).

7 *American Express Co. v. Italian Colors Restaurant,* 570 U.S. 228 (2013) at 231.

8 *Id.*

9 *Id.*

10 In re American Express Merchants' Litigation, 554 F.3d 300 (2d Cir. 2009).

demonstrating that the maximum that Italian Colors could effectively recover in individual arbitration would be US$ 12,850 (or US$ 38,549 if the award were to be trebled in line with the provisions of the Sherman Act). They also demonstrated that in order to prove their case before the tribunal they would need expert reports at a cost of hundreds of thousands of dollars. Therefore, filing individual arbitrations would not be economically feasible. Even if American Express were to concede that all merchants could rely on one single report for the multiple arbitrations, the maximum award and individual claimant in bilateral arbitration might recover would still not cover their costs of prosecuting the case.[11]

The merchants asserted the 'effective vindication rule', relying on dicta from the Supreme Court ruling in the *Mitsubishi* case, to the effect that Courts were entitled to set aside an arbitration agreement if its terms would prevent a party from enforcing federal statutory rights. In the case of the Amex merchants, the federal rights in question were the protections afforded by the antitrust provisions of the Sherman and Clayton Acts.

The merchants also relied on *Green Tree Financial Corp.—Alabama v. Randolph*, 531 U.S. 79 (2000), in which the Supreme Court considered that an arbitration agreement could be held unenforceable if its terms posed a risk that the plaintiff's ability to vindicate statutory rights would be undone by "steep" arbitration costs, albeit that on the specific facts of the case the majority of the justices found that Randolph would not in fact have incurred unduly onerous arbitration costs.[12]

## 4 The Proceedings

In response to the lawsuit filed by the plaintiffs/merchants, American Express moved to compel arbitration.

On March 16, 2006, the District Court accepted American Express' argument that the arbitration clause in the contracts was sufficiently broad to cover the dispute that had arisen between the parties and that therefore the Judiciary was obliged to decline jurisdiction in favor of an arbitral tribunal. The District Court also found that "[t]he enforceability of the collective action waivers is a

11 In reply to questions put by Justice Ginsburg and Chief Justice Roberts, counsel for American Express' stated that this client would agree to the filing one antitrust report on behalf of all of the plaintiffs: "Our position is that multiple claimants in arbitration could share the costs of an expert for preparation of a report".

12 *Green Tree Financial Corp.-Ala. v. Randolph* 531 U.S. 79 at 91–92.

claim for the arbitrator to resolve. Issues relating to the enforceability of the contract and its specific provisions are for the arbitrator, once arbitrability is established".[13] On that basis, the District Court held that the antitrust claims and the validity of the "class action waiver" were issues to be dealt with by arbitration.

The merchants (Italian Colors) appealed against this ruling. The Second Circuit held, as a preliminary matter, that the "class action waiver" was an issue to be resolved by the Court and not the arbitration tribunal.[14]

On the substantive issue of effective vindication, the Second Circuit cited the Supreme Court ruling on *Green Tree Financial Corp.-Alabama v. Randolph*, that "[when] a party seeks to invalidate an arbitration agreement on the ground that arbitration would be prohibitively expensive, that party bears the burden of showing the likelihood of incurring such costs".[15]

The Second Circuit court held that the appellant Italian Colors had satisfied this requirement and that the District Court was wrong to "ignore the statutory protections provided by the Clayton Act".

The Second Circuit also found that the appellant (Italian Colors) would incur prohibitive costs if forced to submit the conflict to bilateral arbitration as a consequence of the waiver of recourse to a class action. The Court referred to the expert economic evidence produced by Italian Colors in which the expert concluded that: "[since] Amex has brought no serious challenge to the plaintiffs' demonstration that their claims cannot reasonably be pursued as individual actions, whether in federal court or in arbitration, we find ourselves in agreement with the plaintiffs' contention that enforcement of the class action waiver in the Card Acceptance Agreement 'flatly ensures that no small merchant may challenge American Express's tying arrangements under the federal antitrust laws'".[16]

The Second Circuit held, citing *Reiter v. Sonotone Corp., 442 U.S. 330, 344, 99 S.Ct. 2326, 60 L.Ed.2d 931 (1979)*, and based on all the documentation provided to it, that: "the effective negation of a private suit under the antitrust laws is troubling because such private suits provide a significant supplement to the limited resources available to the Department of Justice for enforcing the antitrust laws and deterring violations".

The Bench held that "the record abundantly supports the plaintiffs' argument that they would incur prohibitive costs if compelled to arbitrate under

13 In re Am. Express Merchs. Litig., 2006 WL 662341, at 6.

14 Amex I, 554 F.3d em 310.

15 531 U.S. at 92, 121 S. Ct. 513.

16 In re Am. Express, 554 F.3d at 315–16.

the class action waiver. The Card Acceptance Agreement therefore entails more than a speculative risk that enforcement of the ban will deprive them of substantive rights under the federal antitrust statutes".[17] The Court, on that basis, held that the "class action waiver" was unenforceable and that the arbitration was not the adequate means of resolving the conflict.

American Express then filed a petition for a writ of certiorari. The Supreme Court granted the petition and vacated the Second Circuit ruling, directing the Court to review its decision in the light of the Supreme Court ruling on the *Stolt-Nielsen*[18] case. In that case, the Supreme Court Justices had held that "a party may not be compelled under the FAA to submit to class arbitration unless there is a contractual basis for concluding that the party agreed to do so".[19]

Having reviewed its earlier decision, as directed, the Second Circuit initially reaffirmed its earlier position. Then, when *American Express* filed a second writ for certiorari and in the light of the subsequent Supreme Court ruling on *AT&T Mobility LCC v. Concepcion,* the Second Circuit decided *sua sponte* to reexamine the case.

Having analyzed the Stolt-Nielsen decision and the Supreme Court ruling on *AT&T Mobility LCC v. Concepcion,* the Second Circuit held that "a careful reading of the cases demonstrates that neither one addresses the issue presented here: whether a class-action arbitration waiver clause is enforceable even if the plaintiffs are able to demonstrate that the practical effect of enforcement would be to preclude their ability to vindicate their federal statutory rights".

In *AT&T Mobility LCC v. Concepcion,* the Supreme Court had declared the illegality of a state law that invalidated the use of "class action waivers" in consumer contracts. The Supreme Court held that the legislation was inconsistent with the pro-arbitration provisions of the FAA.

The Second Circuit considered that *AT&T Mobility LCC v. Concepcion* did not constitute grounds for alteration of its earlier ruling on the case in hand, because AT&T dealt with issues of state contract law in the light of the Federal Arbitration Act whereas the present case of *American Express v. Italian Colors Restaurant* involved issues of direct violation of federal legislation.[20]

The Second Circuit, in a majority ruling, denied American Express' request for an *en banc* review of this judgment.[21] American Express then filed another writ of certiorari to the Supreme Court.

17 In Re: American Express Merchants' Litigation. (2011).

18 *Stolt Nielsen S.A. v AnimalFeeds International Corp.*, 130 S. Ct. 1758 (2010).

19 *Id.* at 1773, 1775.

20 *In re Am. Exp. Merchants' Litig.*, 667 F.3d 204, 218 (2d Cir. 2012).

21 *In re Am. Exp. Merchants' Litig.*, 681 F. 3d 139 (2d Cir. 2012).

## 5 The Petition for a Writ of Certiorari

The question raised by American Express in its third Petition for a Writ of Certiorari was: "Whether the Federal Arbitration Act permits courts, invoking the "federal substantive law of arbitrability", to invalidate arbitration agreements on the grounds that they do not permit class arbitration of a federal law claim".

American Express argued that: "In Stolt-Nielsen S.A. v. AnimalFeeds International Corp., 130 S. Ct. 1758 (2010), this Court [SCOTUS] held that the Federal Arbitration Act ("FAA") prohibits arbitrators from imposing class arbitration on parties that have not agreed to such procedures. Then, in AT&T Mobility LLC v. Concepcion, 131 S. Ct. 1740 (2011), this Court held that the FAA preempts state laws invalidating commercial arbitration agreements on the ground that they forbid class arbitration".

Furthermore: "These cases embody a straightforward principle: the FAA's overarching purpose is to require enforcement of arbitration agreements" *in accordance with the terms of the agreement. 9 U.S.C. § 4.* Accordingly, "class arbitration, to the extent it is manufactured by force of law rather than the product of voluntary agreement, is inconsistent with the FAA". *Concepcion, 131 S. Ct. at 1750–51.* Likewise, "conditioning the enforceability of arbitration agreements on the availability of class wide arbitration procedures" also "creates a scheme inconsistent with the FAA, because it overrides the terms of agreements calling for bilateral rather than class arbitration. Id. At 1744, 1748, 1753".

According to American Express, the Second Circuit had "ignored this Court's order vacating and remanding the panel's original decision for reconsideration in light of Stolt-Nielsen", and that "Four times in three years, this Court has instructed lower courts to enforce arbitration agreements according to their terms. See CompuCredit Corp. v. Greenwood, 132 S. Ct. 665, 671–73 (2012); Concepcion, 131 S. Ct. at 1745–46; Rent-A-Center, West, Inc. v. Jackson, 130 S. Ct. 2772, 2776 (2010); Stolt-Nielsen, 130 S. Ct. at 1773–76".

American Express also referred to judgments by appeal-judges from the Ninth Circuit, as well as the Third and Fifth Circuits that had reached the opposite conclusion to that of the Second Circuit.

## 6 Briefs Filed by *amici curiae* in Support of Petitioners and Defendants

Given the significance of the issue that was before the Supreme Court, several entities, professors, institutions, States of the Union and the United States filed *amici curia* briefs. These detailed statements are essential reading in order to fully comprehend the repercussions of the case. We have selected key passages from some of them, which we transcribe below.

The Solicitor General filed a brief on behalf of the United States asserting "substantial interest [of the United States] in ensuring that arbitration agreements are not used to prevent private parties from obtaining redress for violations of their federal statutory rights".

In the words of the Solicitor-General, "[t]he effective-vindication rule harmonizes the FAA with the various rights-conferring federal statutes under which private claims are brought". As such, "[t]he [effective vindication] rule allows contracting parties to agree that their disputes will be resolved by an alternative adjudicator (an arbitrator rather than a court), while denying enforcement in circumstances where an arbitration agreement functions in practical effect as a prospective waiver of substantive rights".

Furthermore, in relation to case in hand, the Solicitor General stated that "[the] petitioners' [American Express] approach would impede not only the assertion of federal antitrust claims, but the vindication of numerous other federal statutory rights as well", because "rather than encourage the adoption of arbitration procedures that can feasibly be used even for small-value cases, petitioners' approach would legitimize the use of arbitration agreements to extract what are in substance prospective waivers of substantive federal rights".

According to the Solicitor General, "private actions are a vital supplement to government enforcement not only under the antitrust laws, but also under a wide range of other federal statutes".[22] Furthermore, they "confer important protection from practices that are broadly harmful even if they do not result in a large monetary damages to particular affected individuals", and "reflect a congressional judgement that private enforcement, even of small-value claims, is an important component of the statutory scheme".

Finally, the Solicitor General concluded that the approach suggested by American Express "would subvert the purposes of the relevant rights-conferring statutes, without furthering the FAA's purpose of encouraging actual arbitration", because "companies could use a combination of class-action and joinder prohibitions, confidentiality requirements, and other procedural restrictions

---

22 The brief mentions the following statutes as examples of consumer-protection statutes that are covered by private actions: "Servicemembers Civil Relief Act, 50 U.S.C. App. 501 et seq.; antidiscrimination statutes such as Title VII of the Civil Rights Act of 1964, 42 U.S.C. 2000e et seq., and the Equal Credit Opportunity Act, 15 U.S.C. 1691 et seq.; and labor and employment statutes such as the FLSA, and the Uniformed Services Employment and Reemployment Rights Act of 1994, 38 U.S.C. 4301 et seq".

to increase the likelihood that a plaintiff's cost of arbitration will exceed its projected recovery". The consequence of that would, the institution of a mechanism that could be [mis]used to block federal claims, rather than the desired result of promoting arbitration as a means of dispute resolution.

Twenty-two States of the Union filed a brief in support of the respondent merchants, in which they stated that "the unique status of antitrust claims can and should have a role in evaluation of effective vindication claims", this being a "vital principle", because "every "private" [antitrust] case is designed to protect a broader public interest".

Whilst acknowledging the importance of arbitration—and stressing that they did not consider that antitrust claims should not be automatically exempt from arbitration *per se*—the twenty-two States argued that "courts should consider whether the relief available in the arbitral forum would benefit competition, and thus the market as a whole", for which reason if the "effective vindication of a claim is impossible in arbitration, a clause nevertheless demanding arbitration would amount to a prospective waiver of a party's right to pursue statutory remedies". That, according to those States, should not be acceptable by the Supreme Court under the approach adopted in the Mitsubishi case.[23]

On the other hand, several organizations, including the United States Chamber of Commerce and Business Roundtable, filed *amici curiae* briefs in support of Petitioners American Express.

These institutions claimed that the Second Circuit's ruling unduly undermined the enforceability of the arbitration agreements without legitimate grounds for doing so, in that "neither the FAA itself nor any other federal statute authorizes such an exception". Invoking the *Concepcion* case, these *amici curiae* argued that Congress had not envisioned class arbitration when enacting the FAA. They further stated that there was no provision in federal antitrust statutes to indicate that "Congress intended to require that antitrust arbitrations proceed on a class-wide basis".

The *amici curiae* statement in support of *American Express* asserted that the Second Circuit had incorrectly applied the *Green Tree Financial Corp.–Alabama v. Randolph, 531 U.S. 79 (2000)* ruling to the case at hand. In their view, the Supreme Court had merely indicated in *Randolph* that a party could resist arbitration if the costs involved were prohibitive, with 'costs', in that sense, being limited to those strictly and directly related to the arbitration process itself (i.e. filing fees and related panel costs).

---

23 *Mitsubishi*, 473 U.S. at 637, n.19.

They considered that the position taken by the Second Circuit would in effect institute a procedural step in which Courts would be required to predict the outcome of the litigation (including the total cost that a party would incur to pursue a claim, and the likely quantum of the award the party could expect). This approach would, in turn, undermine the FAA's policy of promoting arbitration by empowering arbitration-hostile judges to rule against the arbitrability of certain disputes.

This pro-AMEX *amicus curiae* brief touched on the possibility of potential claimants pooling resources and sharing the costs of pursuing the claim (such as the fees of expert-witnesses). The conclusions they advanced were that (i) the vast majority of the disputes arising from arbitration agreements could not be brought as a collective action on a class basis; (ii) arbitration enables claimants to bring small claims; and (iii) Second Circuit's ruling would cause undue uncertainty regarding the enforceability of the arbitration clauses.

## 7 The Final Ruling by the Supreme Court

The case then returned to the Supreme Court, which overruled the Second Circuit.

Justice Scalia delivered the majority opinion. First, he observed that the FAA required courts to uphold arbitration clauses that had been freely entered into by parties. As such, a Court was not legally entitled to override a class arbitration waiver unless Congress required otherwise. Furthermore, antitrust laws did not guarantee parties a right to financially accessible proceedings. Financial burden could not therefore be relied upon as grounds for disregarding the waiver contained in the arbitration clause, or for requiring that the dispute be dealt with on a class basis.

Turning to the specific legislation in issue, Justice Scalia highlighted the fact that the Sherman and Clayton Acts were silent as to the possibility of filing class actions and furthermore, that the approval by Congress of Rule 23 of the Federal Rules of Civil Procedure—governing how class actions are to be handle before the U.S. Courts—did not establish any right to collective litigation on statutory rights.

The Supreme Court considered the "effective vindication" argument and the extent to which it might be considered an exception to the general rule. Justice Scalia held that "effective vindication" could be relied upon when an arbitration clause rendered impossible the exercise of statutory rights. However, he found that in the case of *American Express v. Italian Colors Restaurant,* that circumstance did not arise. The expense in obtaining relief did not amount to denial of redress. The class-action waiver merely limited the manner in which parties to the contract could seek relief and they were fully entitled to pursue claims through the established procedure.

Justice Scalia considered that the position taken by the Second Circuit Court of Appeals would be excessively laborious to implement and would undermine the fundamental purpose of arbitration, which was greater time efficiency.

Justice Thomas concurred in full with Justice Scalia. He added that the majority Supreme Court position was consistent with the Federal Arbitration Act and that it was not open to parties to seek to avoid complying with their contractual duties on the basis that doing so would be economically burdensome.

In adopting Justice Scalia's opinion, the Supreme Court restricted even further the grounds on which a class action waiver inserted in arbitration clauses may be challenged before the U.S. Courts. In effect, such challenges can only be made in circumstances in which "filing and administrative fees attached to arbitration (…) are so high as to make access to the forum impracticable".[24]

## 8 The Dissent

Justice Kagan, joined by Justice Ginsburg and Justice Breyer, dissented. At the beginning of her opinion, Justice Kagan stated that by considering a class arbitration waiver to be enforceable, the Supreme Court would in effect enable companies that held a monopoly to prevent clients/customers from vindicating federal statutory rights.

Justice Kagan pointed out that the position being taken by the Supreme Court ran contrary to its own precedent rulings and the provisions of antitrust law. She stated that Congress had introduced the Sherman Act not only for purpose of redressing individuals for their loss but also to promote "*the public interest in vigilante enforcement of the antitrust laws*" as held in *Lawlor v. National Screen Service Corp*, 349 U.S. 322, 329 (1955).

She referred to precedent rulings in which the Supreme Court had held that an arbitration clause was not to be enforced if it prevented 'effective vindication' of federal statutory rights ("Our decision in Green Tree Financial Corp.— Ala v. Randolph, 531 U.S. 79 (2000), confirmed that this principle applies when an agreement thwarts federal law by making arbitration prohibitively expensive").[25]

24 *Am. Express Co. v. Italian Colors Rest.*, 570 U.S. 228 (U.S. S.Ct. 2013) at 236.

25 *Id.* at 243.

Addressing the facts of the case, Justice Kagan stated that if *Italian Colors* were to pursue the case individually, in bilateral arbitration, it would need to spend ten times the amount of the maximum award that might be issued against *American Express*. That, she held, was prohibitive. Furthermore, the arbitration clause in question prevented not only class arbitration, but several other forms of collective defense of rights, thereby barring the parties from effectively vindicating their federal rights.

Justice Kagan closed by stating that the Supreme Court ruling in *AT&T Mobility LLC v. Concepcion* did not apply to the case in hand because the *Concepcion* case was not a ruling on the effective vindication doctrine as such, and in any event involved state, rather than federal, legislation.

## 9 Final Remarks

The Supreme Court ruling on the *American Express Co. v. Italian Colors Restaurant* case did not come as a complete surprise to the dispute resolution community. Earlier Supreme Court rulings, as we saw above, created a presumption in favor of the enforcement of class waivers contained in arbitration agreements. It was clear which way the wind was blowing.

The majority of the Bench took the view that, in the absence of measures by Congress clearly establishing the circumstances in which courts could depart from the provisions of the FAA, the general rule upholding the freedom of the parties of parties to a contract should prevail.

The Supreme Court's pro-contractual freedom stance has bolstered recourse by corporations to arbitration clauses featuring class action waivers as a means of reducing exposure to litigation and the related costs (including both frivolous and no-frivolous litigation).

On the other hand, given that the 'effective vindication' doctrine was one of very last remaining lines of challenge to the enforcement of clauses containing class action waivers, the ruling has caused considerable disquiet in some quarters amongst academics, legal practitioners, and professionals from certain sectors of society.

The concern is that unfettered use of class action waivers will aggravate the perceived imbalance in power between major corporations and smaller business entities and consumers. Increased use of the mechanism by a greater number of companies may, hinder effective enforcement of antitrust legislation and other federal laws when the only available means of recourse, individual arbitration proceedings, are not economically viable for plaintiffs. That opens the door to corporations using arbitration clauses with class-action waivers as a means of effectively avoiding liability for harm caused to individuals and entities.

Critics of the Supreme Court ruling have demanded intervention by Congress in the form of legislative amendment specifying the circumstances in which a class-action waiver in an arbitration clause is legally permissible.

The *American Express Co. v. Italian Colors Restaurant* ruling has certainly provided corporations with a greater degree of legal security and predictability of outcome. It continues, however, to be the target of criticism based on the perception of some society sectors of an ever-widening discrepancy between the bargaining power of monopolistic companies and that of consumers, small businesses, and workers.

CHAPTER 26

# BG *Group, Plc v. Republic of Argentina*, 572 U.S. 25 (2014)

*Elliot Friedman and Cameron Russell*

## 1 Introduction

BG *Group* is the first case in which the Supreme Court considered an arbitration arising out of a bilateral investment treaty (*BIT*). A BIT is a treaty between two states designed to encourage nationals or companies of one state to invest in the territory of the other state. BITs typically protect foreign investors against discrimination and uncompensated expropriation, and guarantee "fair and equitable" treatment of investments. A key aspect of many BITs is the sovereigns' agreement to resolve disputes with qualifying investors through international arbitration seated outside the sovereigns' territory. Thousands of BITs have been concluded between states, and over a thousand investor-state arbitrations have been filed.

While BG *Group* was the first case of its kind to be considered by the Supreme Court, the Court resolved the dispute in a traditional way, grounding its decision in the settled principles developed in its prior arbitration cases—principles highly deferential to arbitral decision-making. The Court made clear that the strong policy of deference to arbitration awards applies equally to awards involving foreign sovereigns and decided under international law.

## 2 The Case

### 2.1 *Background of the Case*

BG Group's dispute with Argentina arose in the context of the Argentine financial crisis at the start of the millennium. Argentina's response to the crisis undermined the value of a substantial number of foreign investments, ultimately leading to dozens of arbitrations between Argentina and foreign investors.

Many of those foreign investors had invested in Argentina in the early 1990s following, and in reliance on, a series of economic reforms enacted by Argentina in response to a previous financial crisis, hyperinflation in the 1980s.

 | DOI:10.1163/9789004715820_027

Those reforms included the deregulation and privatization of state-owned industries, including public utilities, and laws designed to protect foreign investors' returns.

One of the industries privatized by Argentina was the natural gas industry. Argentina restructured its state-owned gas utility, Gas del Estado, into several gas transmission and distribution companies, which were then sold off to private companies. As part of that privatization process, and as an additional incentive for foreign investors concerned about the country's history of hyperinflation, Argentina provided that the tariffs for gas distribution (*i.e.*, the revenues earned by the gas distribution companies) would be calculated in U.S. dollars (rather than Argentine pesos). Argentina further promised to set those tariffs at a level that would give foreign investors a reasonable return on their investment.

BG Group, a British company, was part of a consortium that had bought a majority stake in MetroGAS, one of the gas distribution companies spun off from Gas del Estado. When Argentina's economic crisis hit, however, the State eliminated the U.S. dollar peg for gas distribution tariffs, amongst other measures. This "pesification" of tariffs undermined many profitable investments, including that of BG Group.

BG Group responded by initiating arbitration against Argentina under the terms of the Argentina–United Kingdom BIT (the *Argentina–UK Treaty*). The three-member tribunal, which was seated in Washington, D.C., ultimately awarded BG Group US$185 million for, *inter alia*, Argentina's breach of the treaty's "fair and equitable treatment" clause, calculated as the difference between the value of BG Group's investment with and without the application of the "pesification" measures.

Argentina sought to vacate the award in U.S. federal court in Washington, D.C., under the Federal Arbitration Act, section 10(a). BG Group cross-moved to confirm the award.

### 2.2 *Issue and Parties' Allegations*

A preliminary issue in the arbitration, which later came to dominate the U.S. court proceedings, concerned the effects of BG Group's decision not to undertake the pre-arbitration steps set out in Article 8 of the Argentina–UK Treaty. Article 8 requires foreign investors to litigate in local courts for eighteen months prior to initiating international arbitration proceedings, which BG Group did not do. Importantly, Article 8 also provided that only the decision of the arbitral tribunal, and not any decision rendered by the local court, would be final and binding on the parties.

ARTICLE 8: Settlement of Disputes Between an Investor and the Host State

(1) Disputes with regard to an investment which arise within the terms of this Agreement between an investor of one Contracting Party and the other Contracting Party, which have not been amicably settled shall be submitted, at the request of one of the Parties to the dispute, to the decision of the competent tribunal of the Contracting Party in whose territory the investment was made.

(2) The aforementioned disputes shall be submitted to international arbitration in the following cases:

(a) if one of the Parties so requests, in any of the following circumstances:

(i) where, after a period of eighteen months has elapsed from the moment when the dispute was submitted to the competent tribunal of the Contracting Party in whose territory the investment was made, the said tribunal has not given its final decision;

(ii) where the final decision of the afore-mentioned tribunal has been made but the Parties are still in dispute; …

(4) The arbitration decision shall be final and binding on both Parties.
Agreement for the Promotion and Protection of Investments, Arg.-U.K., art. 8, Dec. 11, 1990, 1765 U.N.T.S. 38.

Because BG Group had initiated arbitration proceedings under the Argentina–UK Treaty without first litigating in a local Argentine court for eighteen months, Argentina argued to the arbitral tribunal that it lacked jurisdiction over the dispute.

The tribunal disagreed, holding that BG Group was excused from complying with the eighteen-month local litigation requirement because Argentina had hindered foreign investors' access to Argentine courts. Specifically, the tribunal found that Argentina had (*i*) placed an automatic six month stay on judgments in cases where investors claimed harm from the economic measures taken in response to the financial crisis, and (*ii*) excluded those foreign investors who had brought domestic litigation against the State from participating in a process of renegotiating public service contracts. The tribunal decided that while these acts had not rendered compliance with the local litigation requirement technically impossible, the impediments imposed by Argentina were significant enough to excuse BG Group's obligation to litigate domestically before filing for arbitration:

> As a matter of treaty interpretation … Article 8(2)(a)(i) cannot be construed as an absolute impediment to arbitration. Where recourse to the domestic judiciary is unilaterally prevented or hindered by the host State, any such interpretation would lead to the kind of absurd and unreasonable result … allowing the State to unilaterally elude arbitration. *BG Group Plc v. Republic of Argentina*, UNCITRAL, Final Award, ¶ 147 (Dec. 24, 2007).

In a U.S. federal district court located in Washington, D.C., Argentina sought vacatur under 9 U.S.C. § 10(a)(4) on the basis that (*inter alia*) the tribunal had exceeded its authority when it decided to exercise jurisdiction over the dispute notwithstanding BG Group's non-compliance with Article 8's local litigation requirement. The district court rejected Argentina's argument and confirmed BG Group's award, finding that deference was owed to the arbitration tribunal's own determination of its jurisdiction, and that the tribunal's reasoning on this issue was reasonable.

The Court of Appeals for the D.C. Circuit reversed, finding that the district court should have considered the local litigation requirement without deference to the tribunal's own views. And in conducting that *de novo* review, the D.C. Circuit held that the Argentina–UK Treaty required BG Group to comply with the local litigation requirement in Article 8 before commencing arbitration, and that BG Group's failure to do so deprived the tribunal of jurisdiction. As a result, the D.C. Circuit vacated BG Group's award.

BG Group then filed for certiorari.

### 2.3 *The Court's Opinion*

The question before the Supreme Court was whether "a United States court [should] review the arbitrators' interpretation and application of [Article 8's local litigation] provision *de novo*, or with the deference that courts ordinarily show arbitral decisions on matters the parties have committed to arbitration." *BG Group, PLC v. Republic of Argentina*, 572 U.S. 25, 32–33 (2014).

To answer this question, the Court engaged in a two-step analysis. First, the Court considered whether the interpretation and application of Article 8's local litigation requirement would be a matter for the tribunal or the courts to decide, if the Argentina–UK Treaty were an ordinary contract. The Court decided that, under its longstanding arbitration precedents, the matter would be for the tribunal. The Court then considered whether the analysis changed because the Argentina–UK Treaty was not an ordinary contract but a treaty between states. The Court found that the analysis did not change in that international context. The Court therefore decided that the tribunal's interpretation of Article 8's local litigation requirement should not be reviewed *de novo* by a court, but rather was due the significant deference afforded to matters properly submitted to arbitration for resolution. Applying that deferential standard of review, the Court held that the tribunal had committed no excess of powers when deciding that BG Group was excused from strict compliance with Article 8's local litigation requirement.

### 2.3.1 Interpretation and Application of Article 8 Is Presumptively for the Arbitrator

Because arbitration is a creature of contract, the scope of an arbitrator's powers is determined by the parties' intent. *Id.* at 33–34. Where the parties' intent is unstated or unclear, however, courts will apply certain presumptions to decide questions relating to an arbitrator's powers.

Absent indications to the contrary, courts will presume that the parties intended a *court* to decide disputes about "arbitrability"—*e.g.*, disputes as to whether a kind of claim can properly be sent to arbitration under the contract's arbitration clause, or whether certain parties are bound by an arbitration agreement. *Id.* at 34. These types of issues are often termed questions of "substantive arbitrability." On the other hand, courts presume that the parties intend for *arbitrators* to decide disputes about the interpretation and application of procedural preconditions to arbitration—*e.g.*, whether a party has waived (or is estopped from asserting) a defense to arbitration, and whether a party has satisfied a time limit, notice requirement, or other condition precedent to arbitration. *Id.* at 34–35. These issues are often termed questions of "procedural arbitrability."

The Supreme Court decided that the eighteen-month local litigation requirement in Article 8 was a question of procedural, not substantive, arbitrability: it was a procedural precondition to arbitration that is presumptively left for arbitrators to interpret and apply. According to the Court, the language of Article 8 indicates that the local litigation requirement "determines *when* the contractual duty to arbitrate arises, not *whether* there is a contractual duty to arbitrate at all." *Id.* at 35. The Court relied on the specific wording of Article 8, which states that disputes "*shall* be submitted to international arbitration" "*if* one of the Parties so requests," and that the tribunal's decision, not that of the local court, will be final and binding on the parties. *Id.* (emphasis added). In the Court's view, the text and structure of Article 8 therefore demonstrated that the local litigation requirement is "a purely procedural requirement—a claims-processing rule that governs when the arbitration may begin, but not whether it may occur." *Id.* at 35–36.

### 2.3.2 Nothing in the Argentina–UK Treaty Rebuts the Presumption

Having concluded that the interpretation and application of the local litigation requirement presumptively would have been for the tribunal to decide, were the Argentina–UK Treaty an ordinary contract, the Court then considered whether the fact that the treaty is an international legal instrument between two states changed the Court's analysis. Specifically, the Court considered whether there was evidence in the Argentina–UK Treaty that Argentina (and the United Kingdom) intended courts, not arbitrators, to decide questions regarding the local litigation requirement.

The Court began by noting that treaty interpretation is, "like a contract's interpretation, a matter of determining the parties' intent." *Id.* at 37. On that basis, the Court held that "in the absence of explicit language in a treaty demonstrating that the parties intended a different delegation of authority, [the] ordinary interpretive framework [*i.e.*, that the interpretation of procedural preconditions to arbitration is presumptively for arbitrators to decide] applies." *Id.* at 39.

The Court considered whether anything in the Argentina–UK Treaty manifested an intention that courts, not arbitrators, should interpret and apply Article 8's local litigation provision. It found no evidence in the Argentina–UK Treaty that the parties intended for procedural preconditions to arbitration to be determined by courts rather than arbitrators:

> [T]he text and structure of the litigation requirement set forth in Article 8 make clear that it is a procedural condition precedent to arbitration—a sequential step that a party must follow before giving notice of arbitration. The [Argentina–UK] Treaty nowhere says that the provision is to operate as a substantive condition on the formation of the arbitration contract, or that it is a matter of such elevated importance that it is to be decided by courts. … The upshot is that our ordinary presumption applies and it is not overcome. The interpretation and application of the local litigation provision is primarily for the arbitrators. Reviewing courts cannot review their decision *de novo*. Rather, they must do so with considerable deference.
>
> *Id.* at 40–41.

The Court also considered whether the tribunal's decision regarding BG Group's non-compliance with the local litigation requirement should be reviewed *de novo* because Argentina's consent to arbitrate may have been premised on the foreign investor's compliance with the local litigation provision, such that a failure to satisfy that condition meant that the sovereign's consent to arbitrate never came into effect. The Court rejected that reading of the Article 8. In the Court's view, there was no authority for the proposition that "the use of the 'consent' label in a treaty should make a critical difference in discerning the parties' intent about whether courts or arbitrators should interpret and apply the relevant provision." *Id.* at 38. In any event, because the Argentina–UK Treaty did not explicitly label the local litigation requirement as a condition of Argentina's consent to arbitrate with a foreign investor, the Court chose not to decide whether such a "'consent' label" might require courts to conduct *de novo* review of an arbitrator's determination of a dispute over whether a state had consented to arbitrate. The Court did note, however, that such a label "is unlikely to be conclusive" because the Court did "not … see why the presence of the term 'consent' in a treaty warrants abandoning, or increasing the complexity of, [the] ordinary intent-determining framework." *Id.* at 38–39.

#### 2.3.3 The Court Upheld the Tribunal's Decision

The final step in the Court's analysis was to review, with "considerable deference," the tribunal's decision not to hold BG Group to a strict application of Article 8. While the Court did not agree with the tribunal that it would be "absurd and unreasonable" to have held BG Group to the eighteen-month local litigation requirement, the Court nevertheless found that the tribunal's conclusions were not barred by the Argentina–UK Treaty and that the arbitrators had not "dispensed their own brand of justice." *Id.* at 45 (citing *Stolt–Nielsen S.A.* v. *AnimalFeeds Int'l Corp.*, 559 U.S. 662, 671 (2010) (cleaned up)). Accordingly, the Court reversed the decision of the D.C. Circuit.

### 2.4 *The Dissent*

In many respects, the *BG Group* decision reflects a straightforward application of principles the Supreme Court developed in other seminal arbitration cases, such as *First Options of Chicago, Inc. v. Kaplan*, 514 U.S. 938 (1995) and *Howsam v. Dean Witter Reynolds, Inc.*, 537 U.S. 79 (2002). *BG Group* is nevertheless an important addition to the Supreme Court's arbitration precedents because it shows, for the first (and so far only) time, that the Court's pro-arbitration jurisprudence applies equally in the context of an arbitration involving a sovereign state and governed by international law.

The significance of this was not lost on the Chief Justice and Justice Kennedy, whose dissent finds fault in the majority's treatment of the Argentina–UK Treaty as simply "a contract, though between nations":

> The Court begins by deciding a different case, "initially treat[ing] the document before us as if it were an ordinary contract between private parties." The "document before us," of course, is nothing of the sort. It is instead a treaty between two sovereign nations: the United Kingdom and Argentina. No investor is a party to the agreement. … It should come as no surprise that, after starting down the wrong road, the majority ends up at the wrong place. BG *Group*, 572 U.S. at 49 (Roberts, C.J., dissenting)

In the dissent's view, the majority wrongly underplayed the significance of a sovereign state's consent to resolving disputes with foreign investors through international arbitration:

> The nature of the obligations a sovereign incurs in agreeing to arbitrate with a private party confirms that the local litigation requirement is a condition on a signatory country's consent to arbitrate, and not merely a condition on performance of a pre-existing arbitration agreement. … It is no trifling matter for a sovereign nation to subject itself to suit by private parties; we do not presume that any country—including our own—takes that step lightly. But even where a sovereign nation has subjected itself to suit in its own courts, it is quite another thing for it to subject itself to international arbitration. *Id.* at 57; *see also id.* at 51 (describing the majority's approach as "trivializ[ing] the significance to a sovereign nation of subjecting itself to arbitration anywhere in the world, solely at the option of private parties").

The dissent focused on the fact that, because BG Group was not a party to the Argentina–UK Treaty, the only way for BG Group to form an agreement to arbitrate with Argentina was through compliance with one of the avenues laid out in Article 8. *Id.* at 50. According to the dissent, "[s]ubmitting the dispute to [Argentina's] courts [as required by Article 8(2)(a)] is … a condition to the formation of an agreement, not simply a matter of performing an existing agreement. Article 8(2)(a) constitutes in effect a unilateral *offer* to arbitrate, which an investor may accept by complying with its terms." *Id.* (emphasis in original). In the dissent's view, since there is no arbitration agreement between state and foreign investor except through one of the avenues outlined in Article 8, the question of compliance with Article 8 is a question of the existence of an arbitration agreement. *Id.* at 50–51. Unlike procedural preconditions to arbitration, questions about the formation and existence of agreements to arbitrate are presumptively for courts, not arbitrators, to decide. *See id.* at 62 ("[O]ur precedents presume that parties do not submit to arbitration the most important matter of all: whether they are subject to an agreement to arbitrate in the first place.") (Roberts, C.J., dissenting).

The majority rejected the dissent's criticism. According to the majority, there was no material difference between the local litigation requirement in the Argentina–UK Treaty and the many claims processing requirements found in ordinary commercial contracts, all of which are presumptively for the arbitrators, not the courts, to decide. Indeed, compliance with any procedural precondition to arbitration can be recast as a condition on a party's consent to arbitrate, but consistent Supreme Court precedent holds that disputes concerning compliance with procedural preconditions are for the arbitrators to decide. And the majority found nothing in the Argentina–UK Treaty to compel a different answer here:

> [The Dissent's interpretation of the Argentina–UK Treaty is] not consistent with [Supreme Court] case law interpreting similar provisions appearing in ordinary arbitration contracts. ... [I]nterpreting the [local litigation] provision in such a manner would require us to treat treaties as warranting a different kind of analysis [from ordinary contracts]. And the dissent does so without supplying any different set of general principles that might guide that analysis. That is a matter of some concern in a world where foreign investment and related arbitration treaties increasingly matter. ... [W]e agree with the dissent that a sovereign's consent to arbitration is important. We also agree that sovereigns can condition their consent to arbitrate by writing various terms into their bilateral investment treaties. But that is not the issue. The question is whether the parties intended to give courts or arbitrators primary authority to interpret and apply a threshold provision in an arbitration contract—when the contract is silent as to the delegation of authority. We have already explained why we believe that where, as here, the provision resembles a claims-processing requirement and is not a requirement that affects the arbitration contract's validity or scope, we presume that the parties (even if they are sovereigns) intended to give that authority to the arbitrators.
>
> *Id.* at 41–43

## 3 Comment

There may be some superficial appeal in the dissent's argument that compliance with the terms of Article 8 affected the existence of an agreement to arbitrate, and was not a procedural precondition to an already-existing arbitration agreement. But that position may be difficult to reconcile with the fact, pointed out by the majority, that the text of Article 8 describes *when* the parties may proceed to arbitration, not *whether* they may do so. *See id.* at 42. Further, Article 8's provision that only the tribunal's decision will bind the parties may make it more difficult to conclude that the local litigation condition had a substantive role to play in determining Argentina's consent to arbitrate.

There is also the conceptual problem that many procedural preconditions could be recast as a condition on a party's consent to arbitrate. Take, for example, an arbitration clause that requires a meeting between executives before arbitration can be initiated, and assume that party X does not engage in that step before commencing arbitration. Party Y could argue that it has not consented to arbitrate this dispute—it has only consented to arbitrate disputes that have first been submitted to executives for discussion—and therefore that its jurisdictional objection raises an issue of substantive arbitrability for the courts, and not the arbitrators, to resolve. That argument would fail under clear Supreme Court precedent, but it still highlights the mischief that can be made when the procedural steps in an arbitration agreement are viewed as conditions on the existence of an agreement to arbitrate.

There are also policy considerations supporting the Court's decision. As recognized in *Mitsubishi Motors Corp. v. Soler Chrysler-Plymouth, Inc.*, the United States has an "emphatic federal policy in favor of arbitral dispute resolution," which "applies with special force in the field of international commerce." 473 U.S. 614, 631 (1985). The Court's decision that the local litigation requirement in Article 8 functions as a procedural precondition to arbitration and was thus presumptively for arbitrators to decide was likely influenced by the Court's desire not to "'set United States courts on a collision course with the international regime embodied in thousands of [bilateral investment treaties].'" *BG Group*, 572 U.S. at 43 (quoting Brief for Professors and Practitioners of Arbitration Law as *Amici Curiae* 12–16). The U.S. courts had vacatur power in this case only because the parties chose, once the dispute had arisen, to seat their arbitration in Washington, D.C. The Supreme Court may have been guided by a desire not to become involved in questions of international law—like whether the local litigation requirement in the Argentina–UK Treaty must be exhausted before proceeding to arbitration—in circumstances where the United States has no (or a limited) connection to the underlying dispute.

Finally, it is also worth noting what the Court did not decide. Following *First Options*, courts presume that the parties intended for courts to resolve disputes concerning questions of substantive arbitrability (such as the existence and scope of an arbitration clause) unless there is "clear and unmistakable evidence" that the parties intended for an arbitrator to resolve those disputes. *First Options*, 514 U.S. at 944. Most circuit courts have found that sophisticated parties' incorporation of arbitration rules that give arbitrators the power to rule on questions of their own jurisdiction constitutes "clear and unmistakable evidence" that the parties intended an arbitrator, not a court, to decide those issues. *See, e.g., Schneider v. Kingdom of Thailand*, 688 F.3d 68, 72–73 (2d Cir. 2012) (incorporation of UNCITRAL rules was clear and unmistakable evidence that the parties agreed that the arbitrator would decide arbitrability); *Apollo Computer, Inc. v. Berg*, 886 F.2d 469, 473 (1st Cir. 1989) (incorporation of ICC Rules was clear and unmistakable evidence that arbitrator could determine her own jurisdiction); *cf.* Restatement (Third) U.S. Law of Int'l Comm. Arb. § 2.8, Reporter's Note (b)(iii).

BG Group made that argument in its brief to the Court. BG Group argued that even if the local litigation requirement were an issue of substantive arbitrability, affecting the existence of an agreement to arbitrate, the Argentina–UK Treaty's specification that UNCITRAL or ICSID rules (both of which permit arbitrators to rule on their own jurisdiction) would apply to any arbitration under the treaty constituted clear and unmistakable evidence that the parties intended for arbitrators, not courts, to interpret and apply Article 8. The Court did not address this argument, and explicitly declined to decide the question in another case. *See Henry Schein, Inc. v. Archer & White Sales, Inc.*, 139 S. Ct. 524, 531 (2019).

## 4 Conclusion

Almost three decades after *Mitsubishi Motors*, *BG Group* confirmed that the United States' strong policy in favor of arbitration continues to "appl[y] with special force in the field of international commerce." 473 U.S. at 631.

CHAPTER 27

# *Lamps Plus, Inc. v. Varela* (2019): The Supreme Court Limits Class Arbitration

*John Fellas*

In its April 24, 2019 decision in *Lamps Plus, Inc. v. Varela,* 139 S.Ct. 1407 (2019), the Supreme Court held that an ambiguous arbitration agreement cannot provide a basis for class arbitration. In doing so, it added to a series of mostly 5–4 decisions making it harder for parties to bring an arbitration on behalf of a class. Together with *Lamps Plus*, the net effect of these decisions appears to be that class arbitration is permitted only under two conditions: (i) the arbitration clause explicitly authorizes it; and (ii) there is no class action waiver in the arbitration agreement.

## 1 The Rise and Fall of Class Arbitration

Before getting to the specifics of *Lamps Plus*, it is worth putting it in context. For that, we have to go back 16 years to the Supreme Court's plurality decision in *Green Tree Financial Corp. v. Bazzle*, 539 U.S. 444 (2003). While there were rare sightings of class arbitration in the U.S. prior to *Bazzle*, for a few years after that decision, class arbitration was all the rage.

*Bazzle* arose out of a standard form contract by which a bank gave loans to homeowners in the state of South Carolina. The contract had an arbitration clause. Under a South Carolina Consumer Protection law, the bank was required it to provide the homeowner with a form that would have told the homeowner of its right to name its own lawyer and insurance agent. But here, Green Tree, the bank did not provide that form. One homeowner, Bazzle, brought a class action in court on behalf itself and similarly situated homeowners, claiming damages for itself and other homeowners who borrowed money from Green Tree. Relying on the arbitration clause in the underlying contract, Green Tree said asked the court compel arbitration.

The court granted the motion to compel arbitration, but required that the arbitration go forward as a class action, since Bazzle had brought a class action in court.

 | DOI:10.1163/9789004715820_028

The arbitrator heard the case as a class action, and awarded about $10 million in damages to the class based on the South Carolina Consumer Protection statute. After the award was rendered, Green Tree challenged the arbitration award claiming that class arbitration was forbidden by the contract on the ground that the contract was silent as to class arbitration.

The case ultimately reached the United States Supreme Court. The Supreme Court, with some Justices dissenting, held that where a contract is silent on the issue of whether it allows a class action, the question of whether a contract permits class arbitration was one for arbitrators to determine. This point is worth emphasizing. The Court itself did not decide the question of whether a class arbitration was or was not consistent with the terms of the underlying arbitration clause or consistent with the Federal Arbitration Act (FAA). Rather, the Court took it as a given that class arbitration is consistent with the FAA. Bazzle, in fact, addressed a narrow question: Given that class arbitration is permitted under the FAA, the fundamental question is who, as between a court and an arbitrator, has the authority to determine whether a particular arbitration clause permits class arbitration. The Court held that it is for an arbitrator to decide.

In reaching this conclusion, Justice Breyer began by noting that there was a narrow category of arbitration-related issues that courts, rather than arbitrators, are expected to resolve: "They include certain gateway matters, such as whether the parties have a valid arbitration agreement at all or whether a concededly binding arbitration clause applies to a certain type of controversy." 539 U.S. at 452. Breyer was careful to stress that "[t]he question here—whether the contracts forbid class arbitration—does not fall into this narrow exception." Rather, it was for an arbitrator rather than a court to decide the class arbitration question because "[i]t concerns contract interpretation and arbitration procedures. Arbitrators are well situated to answer that question." 539 U.S. at 453.

This decision put class arbitration on the map. Less than four months after *Bazzle*, the American Arbitration Association (AAA) issued a set of rules designed for class arbitration—the Supplementary Rules for Class Arbitration—that became effective on October 8, 2003. Within a few years, the AAA was administering hundreds of class arbitrations.

Having begotten class arbitration in 2003, a few years later, a Court majority began a two-pronged attack designed to drain the life out of it. The two prongs were driven by a common theme: despite the underlying assumption in *Bazzle* that class arbitration is consistent with the FAA, in fact it isn't.

One prong of the Court's attack was to uphold the validity of provisions in arbitration agreements under which a party waived the right to pursue a claim on behalf of a class. Thus, in *AT&T Mobility LLC v. Concepcion*, 131 S.Ct. 1740 (2011), the Court (5–4) rejected a challenge to the enforceability of a class action waiver on grounds of unconscionability under California state law. In *Discover Bank v. Superior Court*, 36 Cal. 4th 148 (2005), the California Supreme Court held class actions waivers to be unconscionable under two conditions: (i) when found in a consumer contract of adhesion that were likely to involve small damages claims; and (ii) when the party with the superior bargaining power was alleged to have carried out a scheme to deliberately cheat many consumers out of small sums of money.

In *Concepcion*, Justice Scalia, writing for the majority, stated "that class arbitration, to the extent it is manufactured by *Discover Bank* rather than consensual, is inconsistent with the FAA" for two primary reasons. 131 S.Ct. at 1750–1751. First, he noted that "the switch from bilateral to class arbitration sacrifices the principal advantage of arbitration—its informality—and makes the process slower, more costly, and more likely to generate procedural morass than final judgment." *Id.* Second, noting the similarity between the AAA's Supplementary Rules for Class Arbitration and the Federal Rules of Civil Procedure governing class action litigation, Justice Scalia bemoaned the fact that "class arbitration *requires* procedural formality" (emphasis in original).

The second prong of the Court's attack related to the construction of arbitration clauses. While, in *Bazzle*, the Court had held that it was for arbitrators to decide whether a contract properly construed permitted class arbitration, seven years later in *Stolt-Nielsen SA v. Animal Feeds*, 130 S.Ct. 1758 (2010), the Court began to backpedal. In that case, it held that an arbitration tribunal's decision that class arbitration was authorized by an arbitration agreement that was "silent" on the issue was inconsistent with the FAA. The reason advanced by Justice Alito echoed the one later given in *Concepcion*: "the differences between bilateral arbitration and class arbitration are too great for arbitrators to presume, consistent with their limited powers under the FAA, that the parties *mere silence* on the issue of class-action arbitration constitutes consent to resolve their disputes in class proceedings." 130 S.Ct. at 1776(emphasis in original). *Lamps Plus* took *Stolt-Nielsen* one step further: where *Stolt Nielsen* held that a silent contract could not, consistent with the FAA, authorize class arbitration, *Lamps Plus* held that an ambiguous contract could not either.

## 2 Lamps Plus

In *Lamps Plus*, Frank Varela, an employee sought to bring a class action lawsuit against his employer on behalf of 1,300 employees affected by an allegedly negligent data breach. Lamps Plus moved to compel individual (rather than class) arbitration based upon the arbitration clause in Varela's employment agreement. The Ninth Circuit affirmed the district court's decision to compel class arbitration. Central to the Ninth Circuit's decision was a finding that the arbitration clause was ambiguous. Applying the *contra proferentem* rule—that ambiguities are construed against the drafter of a contract—the Ninth Circuit resolved the ambiguity against Lamps Plus.

On appeal, the Supreme Court majority framed the issue before it as whether "an ambiguous agreement can provide the necessary 'contractual basis' for compelling class arbitration." 139 S.Ct. at 1415. Relying on *Stolt Nielsen*, the Court held that the FAA requires "more than ambiguity to ensure that the parties actually agreed to arbitrate on a class wide basis." *Id.*

Underlying the Supreme Court's post-*Bazzle* decisions, are differing views regarding the merits of the class action. In *Lamp Plus*, Chief Justice Roberts, writing for the majority, expressed solicitude for its targets—noting that a class action "greatly increases risks to defendants." 139 S.Ct. at 1414. By contrast, Justice Ginsburg, in dissent, expressed concern for those who might bring them, noting that, through its post-*Bazzle* decisions, "the Court has hobbled the capacity of employees and consumers to band together in a judicial or arbitral forum." 139 S.Ct. at 1421.

Regardless of one's personal view of the merits of class arbitration, in the opinion of this author, the majority's reasoning in *Lamps Plus* is fundamentally flawed.

## 3 The Majority's Reasoning

There were two independent, but related, bases for the majority's decision. The first is a theme common to many of the Court's post-*Bazzle* decisions: class arbitration is inconsistent with the FAA because it makes the "process slower, more costly, and more likely to generate procedural morass than final judgment" and, thus, "undermine[s] the central benefits of arbitration itself." 139 S.Ct. at 1416. The second is that the majority's decision "aligns with our refusal to infer consent when it comes to fundamental arbitration questions." 139 S.Ct. at 1416.

The first basis for the majority's decision confuses the practices typical of arbitration for those essential to it. While arbitration typically is quicker, cheaper and procedurally simpler than litigation in the U.S. courts, nothing mandates that it must be. The FAA does not apply solely to speedy, quick and procedurally straightforward arbitration. Rather, as the Court affirmed in

*Lamps Plus*, the core principle of the FAA requires courts to "enforce arbitration agreement according to their terms." 139 S.Ct. at 1415. Parties could theoretically enter into a bilateral arbitration agreement that required a lengthy, complex and costly process, including appellate review by a new arbitration panel. Such a cumbersome process might be criticized by some as "undermining the benefits of arbitration." But this does not change the fact that such a process is consistent with the FAA.

The majority misses the point by focusing on whether the inevitable procedurally complexity of class arbitration undermines the "benefits of arbitration." What matters is not whether parties agreed to a process that secures the typical benefits of arbitration, but whether they agreed to a process that entitles them to *the benefits of the FAA*. This is because, when an arbitration agreement falls under the FAA, the parties to it are entitled to certain benefits, most notably, the right to go to court to enforce their arbitration agreement and any ensuing award. Since the FAA's cardinal principle is that "arbitration agreements should be enforced according to their terms," it follows that an arbitration agreement must be enforced even if the process contemplated by the parties does not secure the benefits of speed and efficiency typical of many arbitration proceedings. This point can be illustrated by imagining that two parties agree to resolve their disputes by appointing an arbitrator to flip a coin. Even though that process would be quick, cheap and simple, it would surely be inconsistent with, and denied the benefits of, the FAA because it is arbitrary and unreasoned.

But if parties to a bilateral arbitration agreement who agreed to costly, slow and complex procedures must be accorded the benefits of the FAA, there is no logical reason why parties who agree to class arbitration should be denied them. It is important to note in this context that the majority accept that an *explicit* agreement to class arbitration *is* consistent with the FAA. As Roberts noted in *Lamps Plus* (quoting *Concepcion*): "[C]lass arbitration, to the extent it is manufactured by [state law] *rather than consen[t]*, is inconsistent with the FAA." 139 S.Ct. at 1417–1418. (emphasis added). If that is true of an explicit agreement to class arbitration, then surely the same result follows when an ambiguous agreement, properly construed in accordance its governing state law that applies equally to all contracts, requires class arbitration. This is especially the case given that the *contra proferentem* rule is so well-established in each of the 50 states that, if the parties to a contract do not intend it to apply, they can exclude it.

The second basis for the majority's decision is that it aligns with precedent regarding the Court's "refusal to infer consent when it comes to other fundamental arbitration questions." 139 S.Ct. at 1416. Roberts quotes Breyer's opinion in *Bazzle* to identify "fundamental arbitration questions": "we presume that parties have not authorized arbitrators to resolve certain 'gateway' questions such as 'whether the parties have a valid arbitration agreement at all or whether a concededly binding arbitration agreement applies to a certain type of controversy." 139 S.Ct. at 1416–1417. But if, as Roberts's suggests, class arbitration raises a "fundamental arbitration question[]," it is important to be clear about precisely what that question is. In *Lamps Plus*, it was undisputed that the parties had agreed to arbitrate—that, after all, was the basis of Lamps Plus's motion to compel—so the question raised there was not "whether the parties have a valid arbitration agreement at all." Rather, the question raised in *Lamps Plus* arose out of the ambiguity that the Court accepted characterized the arbitration agreement, i.e., "whether a concededly binding arbitration agreement applies to a certain type of controversy." But, as Roberts acknowledged, there is a well-established rule to address ambiguities about the scope of an arbitration clause (i.e., does an arbitration clause permit only individual claims or extend to claims on behalf of a class?): "we have repeatedly held that ambiguities about the scope of an arbitration agreement must be resolved in favor of arbitration." 139 S.Ct. at 1418. Yet the Court never addressed the application of that rule to the question before it.

In a separate dissent, Justice Kagan criticized the majority's decision, stating that "the FAA does not empower a court to halt the operation of such a garden-variety principle of state law" as California's *contra proferentem* rule. 139 S.Ct. at 1434. Kagan pointedly asked "[h]ow could the majority go so wrong?" 139 S.Ct. at 1432. She went on to answer her own question by suggesting that the majority was driven more by the desire for a particular outcome than the requirements of the FAA: its decision "would never have graced in pages of the U.S. Reports save that this case involves … class arbitration" (ellipsis in original). 139 S.Ct. at 1435.

## 4 The Future of Class Arbitration

The Court's post-*Bazzle* decisions raise a concern that goes beyond the majority's flawed reasoning. Regardless of one's personal view of the merits of the class action, it is clear that the effect of the Court's post *Bazzle* decisions has been to severely limit the ability of consumers and employees to seek relief in small value cases. As Justice Breyer put it in his dissent in *Concepcion*, "[t]he *realistic* alternative to class action is not 17 million individual suits, but zero individual suits, as only a lunatic or a fanatic sues for $30" (emphasis in original), quoting *Carnegie v. Household Int'l Inc.*, 376 F.3d 656, 661 (9th Cir. 2004). 563 U.S. at 365.

It is, likely, therefore, that there will be continued attempts to address this issue through legislation, such the proposed Arbitration Fairness Act of 2017, which proposed to invalidate pre-dispute arbitration agreements for certain types of disputes, including those involving employment and consumers. In fact, Ginsburg ends here dissent by stating: "Congressional correction of the Court's elevation of the FAA over the rights of employees and consumers to act in concert remains urgently in order." 139 S.Ct. at 1422. The concern is that the legislation—if and when it comes—might be so vaguely drafted (as it has been in the past) that it applies not just claims by employees or consumers, but also to domestic business-to-business agreements and international agreements, as to which, in both cases, there are compelling reasons in favor of arbitration.

CHAPTER 28

# *New Prime Inc. v. Oliveira*, 139 S. Ct. 532 (2019)

*Michael A. Fernández*

## 1 Introduction

The Federal Arbitration Act (FAA) allows employers in the United States to include binding arbitration language in their employment contracts that require employees to agree to use designated arbitration methods to resolve disputes with the company rather than seeking action in the court system. Section 1 of the FAA sets out exemptions for employees involved in foreign or interstate commerce activities providing, in pertinent part, that "nothing herein contained [within the Statute] shall apply to contracts of employment of seamen, railroad employees, or any other class of workers engaged in foreign or interstate commerce."

In *Circuit City Stores, Inc. v. Adams*, 532 U.S. 105 (2001), the Supreme Court "acknowledged that 'Section 1 exempts from the [Act] … contracts of employment of transportation workers.'" That case left open the question of whether the FAA's Section 1 exemption, which applies on its face only to "contracts of employment," is inapplicable to independent contractor agreements and, as a corollary, whether a dispute involving such an arrangement could be delegated to an arbitrator. *New Prime Inc. v. Oliveira*, 139 S. Ct. 532 (2019) resolved both of those open issues.

## 2 Preliminary/General Considerations on the Major Topic Decided by SCOTUS in the Case in Question

*New Prime Inc. v. Oliveira*, 139 S. Ct. 532 (2019) case turns on whether Dominic Oliveira was properly categorized as an independent contractor, and, if so, whether he was required to submit to arbitration or could have his claims heard in court as part of a class action. Whether claims by purported independent contracts could be compelled into arbitration was an issue of great importance for the trucking industry. When the case was heard, for example,

 | DOI:10.1163/9789004715820_029

some analysts were predicting that a result in favor of truckers would result in higher consumer prices.[1]

## 3 The Case

### 3.1 *Background of the Case*

The case arises from New Prime's policies vis-à-vis its putative independent contractors.

New Prime operates a "Paid Apprenticeship" training program, which is advertised as an on-the-job training program for new truck drivers. As explained by the District Court, the program operates as follows:

> Apprentices first obtain a Missouri Commercial Driver's License (CDL) permit. They next shadow New Prime drivers for three to four weeks and drive 10,000 miles under supervision. During this time, apprentices receive an advance of $200 per week, which is subtracted from their future earnings, but otherwise receive no remuneration. As a result, apprentices are essentially free labor while they train with New Prime. Under Department of Transportation regulations, trucks can be on the road for longer periods of time when a New Prime driver switches off with an apprentice.
>
> After completion of this on-the-road instruction, apprentices take a CDL exam and then work as a 'B2' company driver trainee for 30,000 miles. During this period, the trainees earn fourteen cents per mile driven, but are not paid for time spent loading and unloading cargo or protecting company property. The company also regularly deducts money from paychecks, including the $200 weekly advance from the apprenticeship program.
>
> …
>
> Finally, after completing the 30,000 miles as a B2 company driver trainee, the truck drivers complete additional orientation classes, which last for about a week. They are then classified as either company drivers or independent contractors. The truck drivers are not paid for the time spent in the orientation classes, and receive a $100 bonus if they opt to become independent contractors.[2]

1 Tucker Higgins, *Supreme Court, missing a justice, considers a trucking case that could rattle the economy*, CNBC (Wed, Oct 3 2018, 3:34 PM ED), available at https://www.cnbc.com/2018/10/03/supreme-court-considers-trucking-case-that-could-rattle-the-economy.html.

2 *Oliveira v. New Prime, Inc.*, 141 F. Supp. 3d 125, 128 (D. Mass. 2015).

As relevant here, Dominic Oliveira entered New Prime's "Paid Apprenticeship" training program in March 2013.[3] He alleged that his pay was often reduced with deductions during his training.[4]

After returning from his trainee driving, Oliveira was allegedly told by "representatives of New Prime ... that he could make more money driving as an independent contractor than he could as an employee driver."[5] In that regard, Oliveira alleged that New Prime "walked him through the process of becoming an independent contractor driver."[6] Specifically, New Prime directed him to a company on the second floor of New Prime's building called Abacus Accounting.[7] Abacus Accounting told Oliveira to provide suggested names for a limited liability company (LLC), and then created Hallmark Trucking LLC on his behalf.[8]

Oliveira alleged that he was then "instructed to go to Success Leasing on the first floor of New Prime's building to look for a truck."[9] At Success Leasing, Oliveira was given a document entitled "INDEPENDENT CONTRACTOR OPERATING AGREEMENT," which repeatedly states that the intent of the agreement is to establish an independent contractor relationship between New Prime and Hallmark Trucking LLC.[10] The agreement also contains the following arbitration clause:

> GOVERNING LAW AND ARBITRATION. THIS AGREEMENT SHALL BE GOVERNED BY THE LAWS OF MISSOURI. ANY DISPUTES ARISING UNDER, ARISING OUT OF OR RELATING TO THIS AGREEMENT, INCLUDING AN ALLEGATION OF BREACH THEREOF, AND ANY DISPUTES ARISING OUT OF OR RELATING TO THE RELATIONSHIP CREATED BY THE AGREEMENT, AND ANY DISPUTES AS TO THE RIGHTS AND OBLIGATIONS OF THE PARTIES, INCLUDING THE ARBITRABILITY

3 First Amended Complaint at ¶8, *Oliveira v. New Prime, Inc.*, 141 F. Supp. 3d 125 (D. Mass. 2015) (Case No. 1:15-CV-10603).

4 First Amended Complaint at ¶35, *Oliveira v. New Prime, Inc.*, 141 F. Supp. 3d 125 (D. Mass. 2015) (Case No. 1:15-CV-10603).

5 First Amended Complaint at ¶41, *Oliveira v. New Prime, Inc.*, 141 F. Supp. 3d 125 (D. Mass. 2015) (Case No. 1:15-CV-10603).

6 First Amended Complaint at ¶42, *Oliveira v. New Prime, Inc.*, 141 F. Supp. 3d 125 (D. Mass. 2015) (Case No. 1:15-CV-10603).

7 First Amended Complaint at ¶43, *Oliveira v. New Prime, Inc.*, 141 F. Supp. 3d 125 (D. Mass. 2015) (Case No. 1:15-CV-10603).

8 *Id.*

9 First Amended Complaint at ¶44, *Oliveira v. New Prime, Inc.*, 141 F. Supp. 3d 125 (D. Mass. 2015) (Case No. 1:15-CV-10603).

10 *Oliveira v. New Prime, Inc.*, 141 F. Supp. 3d 125, 128 (D. Mass. 2015).

> OF DISPUTES BETWEEN THE PARTIES, SHALL BE FULLY RESOLVED BY ARBITRATION IN ACCORDANCE WITH MISSOURI'S ARBITRATION ACT AND/OR THE FEDERAL ARBITRATION ACT ... THE PARTIES SPECIFICALLY AGREE THAT NO DISPUTE MAY BE JOINED WITH THE DISPUTE OF ANOTHER AND AGREE THAT CLASS ACTIONS UNDER THIS ARBITRATION PROVISION ARE PROHIBITED ... THE PLACE OF THE ARBITRATION HEREIN SHALL BE SPRINGFIELD, MISSOURI.

Although New Prime labeled Oliveira an independent contractor in the operating agreement, he alleged that his responsibilities "were substantially identical to his job responsibilities as a New Prime employee driver."[11] As set forth in the Complaint:

> New Prime exercised operational and actual control over Plaintiff Oliveira and others similarly situated under similar, if not substantially identical, agreements through, among other things, either directly or indirectly controlling drivers' scheduling, vacations, home time, requiring drivers to take New Prime training courses and follow New Prime procedures, effectively requiring that drivers take certain shipments, and rendering drivers unable to work for other trucking and/or shipping companies. Because of the structure of lease payments, the drivers have no choice but to take shipments as directed by New Prime or they would quickly fall into default. The drivers bought insurance through a New Prime affiliated company.[12]

While working for New Prime, the company allegedly continued to make regular deductions from Oliveira's paycheck, ostensibly because of lease payments on the truck and payments for the other tools that New Prime instructed him to buy.[13] On several occasions, his weekly pay was negative after spending dozens of hours on the road.[14]

In March 2014, Oliveira signed a second contract titled "INDEPENDENT CONTRACTOR OPERATING AGREEMENT" on behalf of Hallmark Trucking LLC, which contains an identical arbitration clause to that in the first agreement.[15]

---

11 First Amended Complaint at ¶48, *Oliveira v. New Prime, Inc.*, 141 F. Supp. 3d 125 (D. Mass. 2015) (Case No. 1:15-CV-10603).

12 First Amended Complaint at ¶50, *Oliveira v. New Prime, Inc.*, 141 F. Supp. 3d 125 (D. Mass. 2015) (Case No. 1:15-CV-10603).

13 *Oliveira v. New Prime, Inc.*, 141 F. Supp. 3d 125, 128 (D. Mass. 2015).

14 *Oliveira v. New Prime, Inc.*, 141 F. Supp. 3d 125, 128 (D. Mass. 2015).

15 *Oliveira v. New Prime, Inc.*, 141 F. Supp. 3d 125, 128 (D. Mass. 2015).

The second contract also repeatedly states that the agreement establishes an independent contractor relationship between New Prime and Hallmark Trucking LLC.[16]

In late September 2014, Oliveira terminated his relationship with New Prime.[17] "In October of 2014 New Prime rehired Plaintiff Oliveira as a company driver. As a condition of employment, he agreed that New Prime could deduct money from his checks to pay an alleged debt to Success Leasing."[18]

In March of 2015, Oliveira filed a four-count complaint in the District of Massachusetts seeking certification of a class action and alleging, inter alia, that he and other New Prime drivers were not paid the minimum wage under federal and state law.[19] On July 6, 2015, Oliveira filed his Amended Complaint in this Court, raising the same claims, but alleging new facts. After withdrawing a pending motion to compel, New Prime filed a Motion to, among other things, Compel Arbitration pursuant to the arbitration provisions in Oliveira's Contract Agreements and § 2 of the FAA.

On October 27, 2015, the district court entered its Memorandum and Order denying New Prime's Motion without prejudice.[20] The court concluded that although the delegation clause was valid, the applicability of the Section 1 exemption could not be adjudicated by an arbitrator. In pertinent part, the district court explained that:

> Neither the First Circuit nor Supreme Court has answered the central question in this case: does a district court have to determine the applicability of the FAA § 1 exemption itself, or is the exemption issue just another gateway question of arbitrability that contracting parties may validly delegate to an arbitrator? The Ninth Circuit has held that the "district court must make an antecedent determination that a contract is arbitrable under Section 1 of the FAA before ordering arbitration pursuant to Section 4." *In re Van Dusen*, 654 F.3d 838, 843 (9th Cir.2011). Meanwhile, the Eighth Circuit has adopted the opposite viewpoint: it characterizes the applicability of the § 1 exemption as a "threshold question of

16 *Oliveira v. New Prime, Inc.*, 141 F. Supp. 3d 125, 128 (D. Mass. 2015).

17 First Amended Complaint at ¶55, *Oliveira v. New Prime, Inc.*, 141 F. Supp. 3d 125 (D. Mass. 2015) (Case No. 1:15-CV-10603).

18 First Amended Complaint at ¶56, *Oliveira v. New Prime, Inc.*, 141 F. Supp. 3d 125 (D. Mass. 2015) (Case No. 1:15-CV-10603).

19 Complaint, *Oliveira v. New Prime, Inc.*, 141 F. Supp. 3d 125 (D. Mass. 2015) (Case No. 1:15-CV-10603), 2015 WL 13875684.

20 *Oliveira v. New Prime, Inc.*, 141 F. Supp. 3d 125 (D. Mass. 2015).

> arbitrability" that parties "can agree to have arbitrators decide." *Green v. SuperShuttle Int'l, Inc.*, 653 F.3d 766, 769 (8th Cir.2011). This Court finds the Ninth Circuit's analysis more persuasive and adopts its approach for the reasons that follow.[21]

Because the contract terms and factual record did not, in the district court's view, make clear whether New Prime and respondent were engaged in an employer-employee or independent-contractor relationship, the district court ordered discovery.[22]

New Prime appealed the district court's order denying its motion to compel arbitration. The First Circuit affirmed, observing that:

> This case raises two questions of first impression in this circuit. First, when a federal district court is confronted with a motion to compel arbitration under the Federal Arbitration Act (FAA or Act), 9 U.S.C. §§ 1–16, in a case where the parties have delegated questions of arbitrability to the arbitrator, must the court first determine whether the FAA applies or must it grant the motion and let the arbitrator determine the applicability of the Act? We hold that the applicability of the FAA is a threshold question for the court to determine before compelling arbitration under the Act. Second, we must decide whether a provision of the FAA that exempts contracts of employment of transportation workers from the Act's coverage, see id. § 1 (the § 1 exemption), applies to a transportation-worker agreement that establishes or purports to establish an independent-contractor relationship. We answer this question in the affirmative.[23]

New Prime filed a petition for writ of certiorari, which was granted.[24]

### 3.2 *Issue and Parties' Allegations*

On February 26, 2018, the Supreme Court granted certiorari to consider the following questions:

1. Whether a dispute over applicability of the FAA's Section 1 exemption is an arbitrability issue that must be resolved in arbitration pursuant to a valid delegation clause.

---

21 *Oliveira v. New Prime, Inc.*, 141 F. Supp. 3d 125, 133 (D. Mass. 2015).
22 *Oliveira v. New Prime, Inc.*, 141 F. Supp. 3d 125, 135 (D. Mass. 2015).
23 *Oliveira v. New Prime, Inc.*, 857 F.3d 7, 9 (1st Cir. 2017).
24 *New Prime Inc. v. Oliveira*, 138 S. Ct. 1164 (2018).

2. Whether the FAA's Section 1 exemption, which applies on its face only to "contracts of employment," is inapplicable to independent contractor agreements.[25]

On May 14, 2018, New Prime filed its opening brief arguing that:

I. Where, as here, a contract contains a valid delegation clause, the question whether the contract is a 'contract of employment' within the meaning of Section 1 of the FAA is an arbitrability issue that must be submitted to arbitration. This Court has explained that delegation clauses are simply 'additional, antecedent agreement[s]' to arbitrate that must be enforced the same as any other arbitration agreement. *Rent-A-Center, W., Inc. v. Jackson*, 561 U.S. 63, 70 (2010).
The FAA must be interpreted against the background principle that a bargained-for arbitration agreement is enforceable so long as the agreement is 'susceptible of an interpretation that covers the asserted dispute.' AT&T *Techs., Inc. v. Commc'ns Workers of Am.*, 475 U.S. 643, 650 (1986). ... The First Circuit's refusal to enforce the parties' bargained-for delegation clause in this case flouts this Court's commands, usurping the authority to decide an important arbitrability issue notwithstanding the parties' express agreement that an arbitrator should resolve the issue.

II. The text, historical context, and purpose of the FAA leave no doubt that 'contracts of employment' exempted from arbitration under Section 1 include only those agreements that purport to establish an employer-employee relationship under common-law agency principles, and not independent-contractor agreements.
   A. At the time the FAA was enacted, just as today, the plain meaning of the term 'contracts of employment' encompassed only contracts between an employer and an employee that stated the terms and conditions of employment. The distinction between employees and independent contractors goes back centuries and was well understood when Congress enacted the FAA. In fact, Congress used terms such as 'employer,' 'employee,' and 'employment' in numerous contemporaneous statutes for the express purpose of distinguishing common-law employees from

25 Questions Presented, *New Prime Inc. v. Oliveira,* 139 S.Ct. 532 (U.S. 2018) (Case No. 17–340), *available at*: https://www.supremecourt.gov/docket/docketfiles/html/qp/17-00340qp.pdf.

independent contractors. Reading 'contracts of employment' to include independent contractor agreements contradicts the plain language of the statute, frustrates the statute's purpose, and violates the Court's admonition that the Section 1 exemption be given a narrow and precise reading.

B. The determination of whether a contract is a 'contract of employment' or something else (such as an independent-contractor agreement) for purposes of Section 1 of the FAA must be made by looking only at the relationship described within the four corners of the contract. No discovery or mini-trial into the nature of the parties' interactions is necessary or appropriate under the FAA.

C. The Independent Contractor Operator Agreements executed between New Prime and respondent plainly are not contracts of employment—not only by virtue of their express declaration of intent 'to establish an independent contractor relationship at all times,' ..., but also because they grant respondent the authority to choose the method and manner in which he performs his work, to refuse any work at his discretion, to hire others to perform his work for him, and to work for other trucking companies. In fact, respondent entered into the agreements as proprietor of his own limited liability company, Hallmark Trucking LLC. Because the Section 1 exemption is inapplicable to the contracts between New Prime and respondent, the court below should have compelled arbitration of the parties' dispute under the FAA.[26]

On July 18, 2018, Oliveira filed his brief arguing that:

> The FAA is emphatic: '[N]othing herein contained shall apply to contracts of employment of seamen, railroad employees, or any other class of workers engaged in foreign or interstate commerce.' 9 U.S.C. § 1 (emphasis added).
>
> Courts, of course, may not rely on laws that don't apply. A court, therefore, must determine whether a contract is a transportation worker's 'contract of employment'—and thus whether the FAA applies to it—before

26 Brief for Petitioner, *New Prime Inc. v. Oliveira,* 139 S.Ct. 532 (U.S. 2018) (Case No. 17–340), 2018 WL 2278112.

relying on the statute to enforce any arbitration provision the contract contains.

Prime attempts to evade this requirement by asking this Court to enforce its delegation clause—an agreement to arbitrate disputes about arbitrability—rather than its substantive arbitration provision. But a delegation clause is nothing more than a specific kind of arbitration clause. And the FAA prohibits courts from using the statute to enforce any arbitration clause contained in a transportation worker's contract of employment. There is no exception for delegation clauses. Thus, Prime's contention that courts must rely on the FAA to enforce a delegation clause before determining whether the statute even applies not only defies logic—it defies the plain text of the FAA. Like any other statute, courts must decide whether the FAA applies before they apply it.

The FAA does not apply here. The fundamental principle of statutory interpretation is that a statute must be given its 'ordinary, contemporary, common meaning at the time Congress enacted' it. *Wis. Cent. Ltd. v. United States*, 138 S. Ct. 2067, 2074 (2018) (quotation marks and alteration omitted). The FAA does not apply to transportation workers 'contracts of employment.' 9 U.S.C. § 1. In 1925, when the statute was passed, the ordinary meaning of the phrase 'contracts of employment' was agreements to perform work. Case law, statutes, administrative decisions, treatises, and even actual contracts, contemporary with the passage of the statute, all used 'contracts of employment' as a general term to refer to all work agreements—including those of independent contractors.

Prime does not cite a single source contemporary with the FAA that says otherwise. Instead of looking to the ordinary meaning of the statutory text when the FAA was enacted in 1925, Prime relies on a dictionary published in 2014. And rather than the actual phrase Congress used—'contracts of employment'—Prime relies on a different term—the word 'employee.' But statutes are interpreted according to their ordinary meaning at the time they were enacted—not a century later. And they are interpreted in accordance with the meaning of the words Congress actually used, not similar-sounding words it didn't. While the word 'employee' in 1925 had multiple common meanings, the phrase 'contracts of employment' had only one: agreements to perform work. The employment status of the worker was irrelevant.

The history, purpose, and statutory context of the transportation-worker exemption all support the conclusion that the FAA incorporates this ordinary meaning. By the time Congress passed the FAA, it had—for years—been trying to rein in the oftentimes violent and destructive labor unrest that plagued the transportation industry. To do so, Congress passed a series of dispute resolution statutes governing maritime and railroad workers. These statutes applied to all workers in the regulated industries, regardless of their employment status—after all, independent contractors can disrupt commerce just as well as common-law servants can. Congress exempted transportation workers from the FAA to avoid unsettling these dispute resolution schemes and to reserve for itself the ability to regulate other transportation workers' disputes in the future. Given this purpose, it makes perfect sense that Congress exempted all transportation workers' agreements to perform work—not just those of common-law servants. If it hadn't, it would have disrupted the preexisting dispute resolution schemes it had worked so hard to enact—and limited its ability to regulate future disputes.

Prime recites an imaginary parade of horrible it claims will result if this Court does not limit the transportation-worker exemption to agreements that describe on their face a common-law master-servant relationship. But there's no reason to believe that enforcing the FAA's narrow exemption for transportation workers' employment agreements as written will have any negative impact whatsoever. Prime's countertextual interpretation, on the other hand, will cause a host of problems that the ordinary meaning avoids. For example, Prime's reading would require courts to apply the test for common-law servitude—ordinarily applied to the actual employment relationship—to the employment contract itself. This would be a difficult and, in many cases, impossible task. It would also allow employers who illegally misclassify their workers as independent contractors to circumvent the transportation-worker exemption, while companies that obey the law must abide by it. The plain meaning of the statute avoids these problems.

And, in any event, this Court's role is to enforce the text of statutes as written. If Prime believes it would be good policy to rewrite the FAA, it must direct its arguments to Congress, not this Court. The FAA means what it says: It does not apply to transportation workers' agreements to perform work. Prime's Operating Agreement is indisputably a transportation worker's agreement to perform work. The FAA, therefore, does not apply.[27]

27 Brief for Respondent, *New Prime Inc. v. Oliveira*, 139 S.Ct. 532 (U.S. 2018) (Case No. 17–340), 2018 WL 3523975.

On August 22, 2018, New Prime filed its reply brief.[28]

### 3.3 *The Court's Opinion*

In a unanimous opinion authored by Justice Neil Gorsuch, the Supreme Court held that a court should determine whether the FAA applies, and that "contracts of employment" include those that purport to establish an independent-contractor relationship.[29]

Looking to the language and structure of the FAA, the Court reasoned that, notwithstanding any delegation clause, courts must make the threshold determination whether the FAA applies to the contract at issue. The Supreme Court explained that:

> If two parties agree to arbitrate future disputes between them and one side later seeks to evade the deal, §§ 3 and 4 of the Act often require a court to stay litigation and compel arbitration 'accord[ing to] the terms' of the parties' agreement. But this authority doesn't extend to all private contracts, no matter how emphatically they may express a preference for arbitration.
>
> Instead, antecedent statutory provisions limit the scope of the court's powers under §§ 3 and 4. Section 2 provides that the Act applies only when the parties' agreement to arbitrate is set forth as a 'written provision in any maritime transaction or a contract evidencing a transaction involving commerce.' And § 1 helps define § 2's terms. Most relevant for our purposes, § 1 warns that 'nothing' in the Act 'shall apply' to 'contracts of employment of seamen, railroad employees, or any other class of workers engaged in foreign or interstate commerce.'
>
> Given the statute's terms and sequencing, we agree with the First Circuit that a court should decide for itself whether § 1's 'contracts of employment' exclusion applies before ordering arbitration. After all, to invoke its statutory powers under §§ 3 and 4 to stay litigation and compel arbitration according to a contract's terms, a court must first know whether the contract itself falls within or beyond the boundaries of §§ 1 and 2. The parties' private agreement may be crystal clear and require arbitration of every question under the sun, but that does not necessarily

---

28 Reply Brief for Petitioner, *New Prime Inc. v. Oliveira,* 139 S.Ct. 532 (U.S. 2018) (Case No. 17–340), 2018 WL 4859377.

29 Justice Brett Kavanaugh took no part in the consideration or decision of the case. Justice Ruth Bader Ginsburg filed a concurring opinion noting her agreement with the result while suggesting that a flexible approach to interpretation would be appropriate.

> mean the Act authorizes a court to stay litigation and send the parties to an arbitral forum.[30]

In analyzing the meaning of "contracts of employment" in Section 1 of the FAA, the Supreme Court looked to the original meaning and evolution of the phrase, finding that it was not a term of art that referred only to contracts that created an employer-employee relationship, but instead broadly meant "work agreements."[31] Because Oliveira's agreement with New Prime fell within § 1's exception, the Supreme Court held that the court of appeals was correct that it lacked authority to order arbitration.

### 3.4 *Key Takeaways*

*New Prime Inc. v. Oliveira*, 139 S. Ct. 532 (2019) is important to employers in the interstate transportation industry and companies that contract with transportation workers because it places limits on their ability to channel employment disputes to arbitration. Specifically, an employer with transportation workers—whether they are employees or independent contractors—who are involved in interstate work may no longer be able to compel such workers to arbitrate their dispute(s) under the FAA.

## 4 Critical Analysis of the Opinion and How It Impacted the U.S. Arbitration Law and Practice

*New Prime Inc. v. Oliveira*, 139 S. Ct. 532 (2019) was the first of three cases the Court agreed to hear during the 2018 Term related to arbitration.[32] Empirically, its impact on arbitration practice has been significantly more limited than the *Henry Schein, Inc. v. Archer & White Sales, Inc.*, 139 S. Ct. 524 (2019) case and somewhat less limited than the *Lamps Plus, Inc. v. Varela*, 139 S. Ct. 1407 (2019) case, both decided in the same term.[33] However, *New Prime*'s impact on labor and employment arraignments has been significant for transportation and

---

30 *New Prime Inc. v. Oliveira*, 139 S. Ct. 532, 537–538 (2019).

31 *New Prime Inc. v. Oliveira*, 139 S. Ct. 532, 539–540 (2019).

32 October 2018 Term, SCOTUSBLOG, https://www.scotusblog.com/case-files/terms/ot2018/.

33 As of October 22, 2023, a Westlaw search of the citing references of the three cases decided in the Supreme Court's 2018 Term indicates that: *Henry Schein* has been cited in 1204 opinions, *Lamps Plus* have been cited in 390 opinions; and *New Prime* has been cited in 352 opinions.

logistics companies who want to work around the restrictions on arbitration and class action waivers in their services contracts.[34]

While *New Prime* resolved several important questions about certain aspects of the Section 1 exemption, the Supreme Court left open several questions. Specifically, "the Court did not determine who qualifies as a 'transportation worker.' Additionally, [the] case [did not] elaborate[] how closely related a worker's employment industry must be to a transportation sector or how closely related the employee's responsibilities must be to interstate commerce."[35] Lower courts have thus continued grappling with the scope of the exemption, particularly in the "gig industry" where companies often contract with drivers to transport persons and parcels locally but not across state lines.[36] As anticipated by commentators,[37] there has been litigation over whether a local driver who does not cross state lines (or does not often do so) is engaged in interstate commerce within the meaning of Section 1 simply because the transported person or parcel crosses state lines. This litigation has been percolating across circuits with divergent results to date.[38]

34 *See, e.g.*, Kyle Petersen, *Keep On Truckin': Strategies for Managing Wage and Hour Risks with Transportation Contractors After New Prime, Inc. v. Oliveira* (Mar. 20, 2019), https://www.seyfarth.com/news-insights/keep-on-truckin-strategies-for-managing-wage-and-hour-risks-with-transportation-contractors-after-new-prime-inc-v-oliveira.html.

35 Emina Sadic Herzberger, The Gig Economy's Short Reach: An Analysis of the Scope of the Federal Arbitration Act's "Transportation Worker" Exemption, 56 Ga. L. Rev. 299, 317 (2021).

36 Janice L. Sperow, Arbitrating Gig Economy Mass Claims, Disp. Resol. J., 2023, at 1, 59 (2023).

37 Richard G. Rosenblatt, et al., *US Supreme Court: Interstate Independent Contractor Transportation Workers Exempt from FAA* (Jan. 18, 2019), https://www.jdsupra.com/legalnews/us-supreme-court-interstate-independent-40052/

38 Janice L. Sperow, Arbitrating Gig Economy Mass Claims, Disp. Resol. J., 2023, at 1, 59 (2023) ("For example, the First and Ninth Circuits ruled that drivers who drove intrastate routes but delivered out-of-state goods fell under Section 1's exemption. Conversely, the Seventh Circuit ruled that a driver who drove intrastate routes but delivered meals with out-of-state ingredients did not. The difference in these rulings dictated which forum would adjudicate the worker's claims because, if a court finds a class of workers exempt, then the FAA falls away, and the workers become free to challenge arbitration agreements containing class waivers on the basis that they violate state public policy. By contrast, if a court finds that the exemption does not include the class of workers, the FAA governs, and the workers must pursue their claims in arbitration.")

## 5 Conclusions

While having limited impact on the practice of arbitration itself, *New Prime's* has had a significant impact on how companies—particularly those in the gig economy—can structure their relationships with workers. While *New Prime's* impact is difficult to quantify,[39] the open issues it has left will continue to percolate. It is very likely that the Supreme Court may resolve some of those issues in the coming years.

---

39 Some commentators anticipated that "[t]he transportation industry is likely to see an increase in class action litigation in the wake of this decision," *See, e.g., New Prime v. Oliveira: Independent Contractor Truck Drivers Exempt From Arbitration Under The* FAA (Mar. 2019), https://lewisbrisbois.com/newsroom/articles/new-prime-v-oliveira-independent-contractor-truck-drivers-exempt-from-arbi The author located no empirical studies analyzing such outcomes.

CHAPTER 29

# *Henry Schein, Inc. v. Archer & White Sales, Inc.* (2019): The *Henry Schein* Dispute—Uncertainty Regarding Arbitral Jurisdiction and the End of the Wholly Groundless Exception

*Mark Kantor*

## 1 Introduction

*Henry Schein, Inc. v. Archer & White Sales, Inc.* (*Henry Schein*),[1] is a case decided by the Supreme Court of the United States on January 8, 2019. The underlying controversy in *Henry Schein* involved a dispute over the applicability of an arbitration agreement to an antitrust lawsuit. The primary issue before the U.S. Supreme Court was whether a court may disregard an otherwise valid delegation of arbitrability to the arbitrator—a contract provision stating that an arbitrator should decide whether a dispute is subject to arbitration—when the argument in favor of arbitration is "wholly groundless." The U.S. Courts of Appeals for the Fifth, Sixth, and Federal Circuits had previously recognized this "wholly groundless" exception to an otherwise valid delegation of arbitrability. In a unanimous (9–0) opinion written by Justice Brett Kavanaugh, the U.S. Supreme Court sided with petitioner Henry Schein, Inc., holding that the "wholly groundless" exception to arbitrability was inconsistent with the Federal Arbitration Act (FAA)[2] and Supreme Court precedent. Therefore, a valid delegation of arbitrability should be honored even if a court believes the argument for arbitration to be "wholly groundless."

The Court remanded the case to the Fifth Circuit to determine whether the arbitration agreement in this case in fact delegated the arbitrability question to an arbitrator. On remand, the Fifth Circuit relied on a carve-out in the arbitration clause for injunctive relief to deny Henry Schein's motion to compel arbitration.

1 586 U.S. 63, 139 S.Ct. 524 (2019).

2 9 U.S. C. Sec. 1 et seq.

 | DOI:10.1163/9789004715820_030

The Supreme Court decision therefore reinforces previous Court precedent barring a court from reviewing merits or jurisdiction at the "front-end" before compelling arbitration under a valid arbitration agreement. The subsequent Fifth Circuit opinion on remand, though, creates uncertainty about the impact on arbitral jurisdiction of common clauses in arbitration agreements excluding certain intellectual property matters or permitting recourse to the courts for injunctive relief.

## 2 Arbitration Agreement

The dispute in this matter arose out of a contract between Henry Schein, Inc., a dental equipment manufacturer, and Archer and White Sales, Inc., a dental equipment distributor. The contract provided for arbitration of any dispute arising under or related to the agreement, except for, among other things, actions seeking injunctive relief and disputes related to Henry Schein's intellectual property.

> Disputes. This Agreement shall be governed by the laws of the State of North Carolina. Any dispute arising under or related to this Agreement (except for actions seeking injunctive relief and disputes related to trademarks, trade secrets, or other intellectual property of [Pelton & Crane [the predecessor to Henry Schein]), shall be resolved by binding arbitration in accordance with the arbitration rules of the American Arbitration Association [(AAA)]. The place of arbitration shall be in Charlotte, North Carolina.[3]

## 3 Preliminary Matters

In 2012, Archer and White, Inc. sued Henry Schein, Inc. and other defendants, alleging Henry Schein had violated the Sherman Antitrust Act and the Texas Free Enterprise and Antitrust Act. Importantly, Archer and White's complaint sought both money damages and injunctive relief. Henry Schein moved to compel arbitration, arguing that the parties had delegated the question of arbitrability to an arbitrator by incorporating the rules of the American Arbitration Association (AAA), which empower arbitrators to resolve arbitrability questions. Archer and White opposed the motion, contending that the arbitration

3 *Henry Schein*, 139 S.Ct. at 528.

agreement did not apply to this dispute because it expressly excluded actions seeking injunctive relief.

The U.S. District Court for the Eastern District of Texas denied Henry Schein's motion to compel arbitration. The District Court found that the argument for arbitration was "wholly groundless" because the plain language of the contract excluded actions seeking injunctive relief from arbitration.[4] The U.S. Court of Appeals for the Fifth Circuit affirmed, agreeing that the "wholly groundless" exception to arbitrability applied and that the contract did not delegate arbitrability to an arbitrator.[5] The U.S. Supreme Court granted *certiorari* in June 2018 to review that decision and heard oral argument in October 2018.

## 4 Description of Legal Issues

The legal issues in this case were:

- Whether the FAA permits a court to disregard a valid delegation of arbitrability when the court believes that the argument for arbitration is "wholly groundless."
- Whether the contract between Henry Schein and Archer and White delegated arbitrability to an arbitrator.

Readers should be aware that jurisprudence in the United States refers interchangeably to arbitrability and jurisdiction without distinction. Elsewhere, the term "arbitrability" commonly refers to a public measure to exclude a particular subject matter from arbitration. Readers are cautioned to recognize this difference between U.S. Supreme Court terminology and terminology in the international community.[6]

---

4 *Archer & White Sales, Inc. v. Henry Schein, Inc.*, Civ. Act. No. 2:12-cv-572-JRG (E.D. Tex. Dec. 7, 2016).

5 *Archer & White Sales, Inc. v. Henry Schein, Inc.*, 935 F.3d 274 (5th Cir. 2019).

6 According to the Reporters of the Restatement of the U.S. Law of International Commercial and Investor-State Arbitration, the Supreme Court's "use of the term "arbitrability" in this connection is regrettable. In the international arbitration literature, the term "arbitrability" connotes the narrow, if important, notion that enforcement of an arbitration agreement may be precluded if the claim or dispute in question is not legally capable of being arbitrated (i.e., if the relevant law declares the resolution of such claims or disputes is exclusively reserved to courts of law). See 2.22. By contrast, the Supreme Court uses the term "arbitrability" much more loosely to encompass the entire range of grounds on which an agreement might be denied enforcement (including such questions as whether an arbitration agreement is valid, whether the dispute at issue falls within the scope of the agreement or whether conditions precedent to arbitration have been met)." American Law

## 5 The Supreme Court Decision

The U.S. Supreme Court reversed the Fifth Circuit. The January 8, 2019 opinion in the case, written by Justice Brett Kavanaugh, was unanimous. That decision was Justice Kavanaugh's first opinion from the Supreme Court bench. In ruling that there was no basis for a "wholly groundless" exception to the FAA, Justice Kavanaugh based the analysis on a series of previous Supreme Court decisions. In *AT&T Technologies, Inc. v. Communications Workers of America*,[7] the Court had stated that parties could delegate arbitrability, but held that the arbitrability determination should typically be made by a court absent clear and unmistakable provision by the parties otherwise. In the *AT&T* case, the Court wrote: "the question of arbitrability ... is undeniably an issue for judicial determination. Unless the parties clearly and unmistakably provide otherwise, the question of whether the parties agreed to arbitrate is to be decided by the court, not the arbitrator."[8] Justice Kavanaugh reminded readers that the principle from *AT&T Technologies* applied even if the argument appeared frivolous:[9]

> We have held that a court may not "rule on the potential merits of the underlying" claim that is assigned by contract to an arbitrator, "even if it appears to the court to be frivolous." *AT&T Technologies, Inc. v. Communications Workers*, 475 U.S. 643, 649–650, 106 S.Ct. 1415, 89 L.Ed.2d 648 (1986). A court has "'no business weighing the merits of the grievance'" because the "'agreement is to submit all grievances to arbitration, not merely those which the court will deem meritorious.'" *Id.*, at 650, 106 S.Ct. 1415 (*quoting Steelworkers v. American Mfg. Co.*, 363 U.S. 564, 568, 80 S.Ct. 1343, 4 L.Ed.2d 1403 (1960)).

The *Henry Schein* opinion made clear that the *AT&T Technologies* principle applied equally to merits questions and arbitrability questions.[10]

> That *AT&T Technologies* principle applies with equal force to the threshold issue of arbitrability. Just as a court may not decide a merits question

---

Institute, Restatement of the Law, The U.S. Law of International Commercial and Investor-State Arbitration, Chapter 2, § 2.8, Reporters' Notes (b) (i) (hereinafter, the "*Restatement*").

7 475 U.S. 643 (1986).

8 Id., 475 U.S. at 649.

9 *Henry Schein*, supra at 530–531.

10 *Henry Schein*, supra at 531.

> that the parties have delegated to an arbitrator, a court may not decide an arbitrability question that the parties have delegated to an arbitrator.

In *First Options of Chicago, Inc. v. Kaplan*[11] the Court reiterated that "clear and unmistakable" standard.

Then, in *Rent-A-Center v. Jackson*,[12] the Court yet again held that parties could agree to delegate decisions on specific issues to arbitrators, and that courts must respect those delegations. The *Henry Schein* opinion quoted from *Rent-A-Center*, 'Applying the Act, we have held that parties may agree to have an arbitrator decide not only the merits of a particular dispute but also "'gateway' questions of 'arbitrability,' such as whether the parties have agreed to arbitrate or whether their agreement covers a particular controversy."'[13]

Reaffirming these cases, the Supreme Court reversed the Fifth Circuit's decision and held that the ""wholly groundless" exception is inconsistent with the text of the Act and with our precedent." The unanimous Court explained that, under the FAA, arbitration is a matter of contract, and courts must enforce arbitration contracts according to their terms.

The Court rejected several arguments in favor of the "wholly groundless" exception. First, the Court found no textual basis for the exception in the FAA, which contains no such carve-out.

> First, Archer and White points to §§ 3 and 4 of the Federal Arbitration Act. Section 3 provides that a court must stay litigation "upon being satisfied that the issue "is "referable to arbitration" under the "agreement." Section 4 says that a court, in response to a motion by an aggrieved party, must compel arbitration "in accordance with the terms of the agreement" when the court is "satisfied that the making of the agreement for arbitration or the failure to comply therewith is not in issue."
>
> Archer and White interprets those provisions to mean, in essence, that a court must always resolve questions of arbitrability and that an arbitrator never may do so.

The Supreme Court was not impressed by that argument, asserting "But that ship has sailed," referring to *First Options* and *Rent–A–Center*. "To be sure," wrote Justice Kavanaugh, "before referring a dispute to an arbitrator, the court determines whether a valid arbitration agreement exists. See 9 U.S.C. § 2. But if

11 514 U.S. 938, 944 (1995).

12 561 U.S. 63 (2010).

13 *Henry Schein*, supra at 530, quoting *Renta-Center v. Jackson*, 561 U.S. at 70.

a valid agreement exists, and if the agreement delegates the arbitrability issue to an arbitrator, a court may not decide the arbitrability issue."[14]

The Court also rejected Archer and White's argument that, since § 10 of the FAA called for judicial review of arbitrability questions at the "back-end," so too a court should be able to address arbitrability at the "front-end" before the arbitration has commenced.

> Archer and White cites § 10 of the Act, which provides for back-end judicial review of an arbitrator's decision if an arbitrator has "exceeded" his or her "powers." § 10(a)(4). According to Archer and White, if a court at the back end can say that the underlying issue was not arbitrable, the court at the front end should also be able to say that the underlying issue is not arbitrable.

The Supreme Court viewed that as an argument to redesign the FAA based on policy considerations or judicial efficiency. The Court's opinion stated that Congress had already balanced those factors when enacting the FAA, and it was not the Court's "proper role to redesign the statute."[15]

> The dispositive answer to Archer and White's § 10 argument is that Congress designed the Act in a specific way, and it is not our proper role to redesign the statute.

Further, accepting Archer and White's argument would, said Justice Kavanaugh, presumably call for its application to merits decisions as well. Again, that would contravene Supreme Court precedent.[16]

> Archer and White's § 10 argument would mean, moreover, that courts presumably also should decide frivolous merits questions that have been delegated to an arbitrator. Yet we have already rejected that argument: When the parties' contract assigns a matter to arbitration, a court may not resolve the merits of the dispute even if the court thinks that a party's claim on the merits is frivolous. *AT&T Technologies*, 475 U.S., at 649–650, 106 S.Ct. 1415. So, too, with arbitrability.

---

14 *Id.*
15 *Id.*
16 *Id.*

Arguments based on convenience and efficiency also did not deter the Court. Archer and White had contended that:[17]

> it would be a waste of the parties' time and money to send the arbitrability question to an arbitrator if the argument for arbitration is wholly groundless. In cases like this, as Archer and White sees it, the arbitrator will inevitably conclude that the dispute is not arbitrable and then send the case back to the district court. So why waste the time and money?

The Court quickly disposed of this argument. "The short answer is that the Act contains no "wholly groundless" exception, and we may not engraft our own exceptions onto the statutory text."[18] Further, the Court was "dubious" that the "wholly groundless" exception would in fact save time and money "systemically" even if it might do so in individual matters. Rather, the Court was concerned to avoid creating a basis for a "time-consuming sideshow" in "collateral litigation (with briefing, argument, and opinion writing)" over whether or not the arbitrability argument was "wholly groundless" or merely "groundless."[19]

> Archer and White assumes that it is easy to tell when an argument for arbitration of a particular dispute is wholly groundless. We are dubious. The exception would inevitably spark collateral litigation (with briefing, argument, and opinion writing) over whether a seemingly unmeritorious argument for arbitration is wholly groundless, as opposed to groundless. We see no reason to create such a time-consuming sideshow.

Lastly, the Supreme Court dismissed the argument that arbitrators might lack competence to decide arbitrability questions. The Court observed that arbitrators are capable of efficiently disposing of frivolous cases and deterring frivolous motions. After all, "We are not aware that frivolous motions to compel arbitration have caused a substantial problem in those Circuits that have not recognized a "wholly groundless" exception."[20]

While the Supreme Court roundly rejected the "wholly groundless" exception, it declined to address the subsidiary question of whether a

---

17 *Id.*

18 *Id.*

19 *Id.*, at 530–531.

20 *Id.*, at 531.

"competence-competence" provision in the chosen arbitration rules was sufficient to satisfy the "clear and unmistakable" test of *First Options* and progeny.[21]

> We express no view about whether the contract at issue in this case in fact delegated the arbitrability question to an arbitrator. The Court of Appeals did not decide that issue. Under our cases, courts "should not assume that the parties agreed to arbitrate arbitrability unless there is clear and unmistakable evidence that they did so." *First Options*, 514 U.S., at 944, 115 S.Ct. 1920 (alterations omitted). On remand, the Court of Appeals may address that issue in the first instance, as well as other arguments that Archer and White has properly preserved.

The Court accordingly remanded the case to the Fifth Circuit Court of Appeals to address whether this contract actually delegated the arbitrability question to an arbitrator.

## 6 Consequences of the Supreme Court Decision

*Henry Schein* clarified a split in the U.S. Federal Courts of Appeals about the arbitrability of disputes. Only the Courts of Appeals for the Fifth, Sixth, and Federal Circuits had previously recognized the "wholly groundless" exception to an otherwise valid delegation of arbitrability. These appellate courts believed it would be wasteful to send a dispute to an arbitrator only to have the arbitrator send the parties back to court because the arbitrator lacked jurisdiction. In *Henry Schein*, though, the Court stressed that courts must first determine the "who decides" question, who is authorized to determine arbitrability, as set out in *AT&T Technologies* and *First Options*. After the Supreme Court's unanimous decision rejecting the exception, courts may not skip that step by looking first at the merits of the arbitrability question and deciding that the claim in favor of arbitration is "wholly groundless."

The *Henry Schein* decision reinforces the fundamental principle that, under the FAA, arbitration is a matter of consent. By eliminating the "wholly groundless" exception, the Supreme Court concluded in effect that courts applying the FAA must respect the parties' intent to delegate arbitrability questions to an arbitrator. That approach may move the burden of resolving arbitrability disputes from courts to arbitrators, potentially reducing judicial workload and

21 *Id.*

increasing arbitration efficiency. However, it may also increase the costs and risks for parties faced with frivolous claims that a matter must be arbitrated rather than being resolved in court.

## 7 Description of Issues Not Addressed

By referring the question of whether the *Henry Schein* arbitration agreement actually delegated the arbitrability question to an arbitrator, the Supreme Court left untouched the proper interpretation of the arbitration clause in the contract, given that it expressly excluded actions seeking injunctive relief and that Archer and White sought both money damages and injunctive relief.

Arbitration clauses regularly incorporate the rules of an arbitration organization (like AAA or the ICC) that include a competence-competence clause. Many Federal courts have determined that these types of clauses qualify as "clear and unmistakable" delegations of authority under *First Options*. However, some observers, including the Reporters of the American Law Institute's Restatement of the U.S. Law of International Commercial and Investor-State Arbitration,[22] have argued that although these types of clauses do not exclude or disclaim the authority of courts to rule on the question, and therefore courts may still rule on arbitrability. In the *Henry Schein* case, this question was addressed by the district court and the Fifth Circuit, but the Fifth Circuit originally declined to make a ruling on the question.

### 7.1 *Description of Subsequent Fifth Circuit Court of Appeals Decision*

On remand, the Fifth Circuit Court of Appeals again affirmed the district court's denial of Henry Schein's motion to compel arbitration.[23] The carve-out in the arbitration clause for injunctive relief proved decisive for the Court of Appeals. Archer and White asserted that the effect of that carve-out was to eliminate the argument that the choice of the AAA rules constituted clear and unmistakable evidence that arbitrability decisions in cases involving injunctive relief had been delegated to the arbitrator.[24]

> Archer contends that there is no clear and unmistakable evidence that the parties delegated arbitrability disputes to an arbitrator. The way the

22 *Restatement*, supra, Ch. 2. Enforcement of the Arbitration Agreement, § 2.8 Reporter's Notes (b)(iii).

23 *Archer and White, Inc. v. Henry Schein, Inc.*, 935 F.3d 274 (5th Cir. 2019).

24 Id., at 279.

> agreement is written, Archer asserts that the AAA rules (and resulting delegation) only apply to disputes that fall outside of the arbitration clause's carve-out for actions seeking injunctive relief.

The Fifth Circuit agreed with Archer and White, holding that the contract did not delegate arbitrability to an arbitrator because the plain language of the arbitration clause excluded actions seeking injunctive relief from arbitration, and Archer and White's complaint sought injunctive relief. The Fifth Circuit reasoned that the parties' intent to arbitrate only certain types of disputes was evident from the express carve-out provision in the arbitration clause.[25]

The Fifth Circuit confirmed its precedent that the incorporation into an arbitration agreement of arbitration rules that contain a "competence-competence" clause is sufficient to satisfy the "clear and unmistakable" standard of First Options. However, in the circumstances where the arbitration clause also contained an express carve-out of certain matters, the existence of a "competence-competence" clause was not itself enough to resolve the "who decides" issue when that carve-out is applicable.[26]

### 7.2 *Description of Dismissal of Second Certiorari Petition*

Henry Schein thereupon filed a second petition for *certiorari* to the Supreme Court, raising two questions: (1) whether a provision in an arbitration agreement that exempts certain claims from arbitration negates an otherwise clear and unmistakable delegation of questions of arbitrability to an arbitrator; and (2) whether a party waives its right to arbitrate by participating in litigation before seeking arbitration. The Supreme Court granted *certiorari* on June 15, 2020, but dismissed it as improvidently granted on January 25, 2021, without providing any explanation.

While the question of the impact of the incorporation of arbitration rules was consequently not addressed by the Supreme Court, of the 12 U.S. Circuit Courts of Appeal, the First, Second, Third, Fourth, Fifth, Sixth, Eighth, Ninth, Tenth, Eleventh and Federal Circuit Courts of Appeal have all held that agreeing to arbitrate under arbitration rules that permit arbitrators to rule on their own jurisdiction constitutes "clear and unmistakable evidence" allocating that authority to the arbitral tribunal under the First Options test. Only the Seventh Circuit has not yet addressed the issue.[27] Also, in January 2021 the Supreme

25 Id., at 283.

26 Id., at 283–284.

27 See *Blanton v. Domino's Pizza Franchising LLC*, Case No. 19–2388, 2020 U.S. App. LEXIS 18975 at *7 (6th Cir. June 17, 2020). "And the one remaining circuit has precedent suggesting

Court denied *certiorari* in *Piersing v. Domino's Pizza Franchising LLC*,[28] yet another case in which the courts have held that a "competence-competence" provision in the chosen arbitration rules satisfies the "clear and unmistakable" standard set out in *First Options* for determining if the contract parties had allocated "who decides" authority over arbitrability issues to the arbitrator. In light of the virtual unanimity among the U.S. Circuit Courts of Appeal on this question, many critics of the incorporation doctrine have lost considerable hope that the U.S. Supreme Court will intervene to overturn those Courts of Appeals.

It is noteworthy that the Fifth Circuit court did not consider severing Archer and White's remedial request for injunctive relief from its remedial request for damages, which might have resulted in sending the latter to arbitration but keeping the former in court.

The appellate panel's decision on remand in *Henry Schein* is of particular importance to intellectual property practitioners. It is common in the marketplace for patent licensing and similar agreements to contain arbitration clauses. However, those clauses often expressly exclude from arbitration a dispute, for example, "concerning the validity, scope, infringement and essentiality of a patent or a patent claim." Moreover, it is also extremely common in all sorts of contracts for an arbitration clause to include as well an express authorization for a disputing party to seek injunctive relief from the courts. The Fifth Circuit remand opinion in *Henry Schein* raises significant questions about arbitral jurisdiction under contracts that contain carve-outs for certain intellectual property disputes from arbitration, as well as equally significant questions for arbitration agreements that permit disputing parties to seek injunctive relief in the courts. Contract drafters beware.

## 8 Conclusion

The decisions in *Henry Schein, Inc. v. Archer and White Sales, Inc.* illustrate the complex and evolving legal landscape of arbitration law in the United States. The Supreme Court's first decision reaffirmed the principle that courts must enforce arbitration contracts according to their terms and rejected the "wholly groundless" exception to arbitrability. The Fifth Circuit's decision on remand

that it would join this consensus. See *Commonwealth Edison Co. v. Gulf Oil Corp.*, 541 F.2d 1263, 1272–73 (7th Cir. 1976) (relying on the incorporation of the AAA Rules to find that the parties had agreed to binding arbitration)."

28 Case No. 20–695.

favored a narrow interpretation of the arbitration agreement and gave effect to the parties' intent to exclude actions seeking injunctive relief from arbitration. These cases have significant implications for parties who enter into or seek to enforce arbitration agreements that contain carve-out or delegation provisions.

CHAPTER 30

# GE *Energy Power Conversion France* SAS *Corp v. Outokumpu Stainless USA,* LLC (2020): Application of U.S. Domestic Arbitration Law to Non-Signatory Enforcement of International Arbitration Agreements, and Other Potential Impacts of Domestic Arbitration Doctrines in International Contexts

*Ari D. MacKinnon, Jonathan I. Blackman and Katie L. Gonzalez*

## 1 Introduction

Because arbitration is rooted in the consent of the parties to arbitrate their disputes, there is a presumption that generally only the signatories to a contract with an arbitration clause are bound by, or may invoke, the agreement to arbitrate.[1] In 2009, the U.S. Supreme Court held that under Chapter 1 of the Federal Arbitration Act ("FAA"), which applies to domestic arbitration agreements, "background principles of state contract law" may govern whether non-signatories have also agreed to arbitrate despite not having signed the contract containing the arbitration agreement.[2] Those principles include "'assumption, piercing the corporate veil, alter ego, incorporation by reference, third-party beneficiary theories, waiver and estoppel.'"[3]

1 This presumption is reflected in the Restatement of U.S. Law of International Commercial and Investor-State Arbitration. *See* Comment a to Restatement Section 2.3 ("Ordinarily, only persons who have formally executed an international arbitration agreement or otherwise expressly assented to it are bound by or may invoke such an agreement.").

2 *Arthur Andersen* LLP *v. Carlisle*, 556 U.S. 624, 630 (2009). The Supreme Court considered whether Chapter 1 of the FAA categorically prohibited "those who are not parties to a written arbitration agreement" from invoking the FAA's provisions under state contract law principles entitling a non-signatory to enforce such agreements. The Supreme Court held that Chapter 1's provisions concerning the validity and enforcement of arbitration agreements did not "alter background principles of state contract law regarding the scope of agreements (including the question of who is bound by them)." *Id.*

3 *Id.* at 631 (internal citation omitted).

 | DOI:10.1163/9789004715820_031

Until GE *Energy Power Conversion France* SAS *Corp. v. Outokumpu Stainless USA,* LLC, however, courts of appeals were split over whether those principles also apply to determining whether non-signatories may be considered as having agreed to arbitrate under *international* arbitration agreements. In this 2020 decision, the Supreme Court resolved the split in a unanimous decision authored by Justice Thomas and held that the 1958 Convention on the Recognition and Enforcement of Foreign Arbitral Awards ("New York Convention"), as implemented in Chapter 2 of the FAA, does not preclude a non-signatory from seeking to enforce an international arbitration agreement by invoking common law principles routinely relied on in domestic arbitration proceedings.[4] Under that holding, it is now clear that United States courts will apply domestic law principles to determine questions of who may enforce (and presumably, who is bound by) an agreement to arbitrate beyond its actual signatories, although the Court did not reach the important question of *whose* domestic law should govern that issue.

## 2 The Case

### 2.1 *Background of the Case*

The dispute at issue in GE *Energy Power Conversion France* SAS *Corp. v. Outokumpu Stainless USA,* LLC arose after the motors of an Alabama cold-rolling mill, used to produce stainless steel, failed and allegedly caused substantial damage to the owner. At the time of the incident in the summer of 2015,[5] the mill was owned by Outokumpu Stainless USA, LLC ("Outokumpu"), a U.S. company with a Finnish parent.[6] Eight years earlier, ThyssenKrupp Stainless USA, LLC ("ThyssenKrupp"), the then-owner of the plant, had entered into three contracts with F.L. Industries, Inc. ("F.L. Industries") for the construction of the cold rolling mills at issue.[7] F.L. Industries had in turn entered into a subcontractor agreement with the French company GE Energy Power

4 *See generally*, GE *Energy Power Conversion Fr.* SAS, *Corp. v. Outokumpu Stainless USA,* LLC, 140 S. Ct. 1637 (2020). The same reasoning would apply to international arbitration agreements governed by the Inter-American Convention on International Commercial Arbitration of 1975 (the "Panama Convention"), implemented in Chapter 3 of the FAA, and throughout this chapter references to the New York Convention should be understood to apply to both the New York Convention and the Panama Convention.

5 *Id.* at 1642.

6 *Id.*

7 *Id.*

Conversion SAS Corporation ("GE Energy"), then known as Converteam SAS, to design, manufacture, and supply the motors of the cold rolling mills.[8]

Each of the contracts between ThyssenKrupp and F.L. Industries contained an identical arbitration clause providing that "[a]ll disputes arising between both parties in connection with or in the performances of the Contract" would be settled by an International Chamber of Commerce ("ICC") arbitration seated in Germany and applying German law.[9] The contracts defined ThyssenKrupp as the "Buyer" and F.L. Industries as the "Seller," and stated that "Buyer and Seller [are] also referred to individually as 'Party' and collectively as 'Parties.'"[10] Critically, the contracts specified that "[w]hen Seller is mentioned it shall be understood as Sub-contractors included, except if expressly stated otherwise."[11] The contracts also imposed a list of mandatory subcontractors, which included Converteam SAS.[12] However, Converteam SAS had never signed any of these contracts.

In the wake of the motor failures, Outokumpu and its insurers asserted tort and warranty claims in Alabama state court against Converteam SAS, now GE Energy, as well as its insurers.[13] GE Energy removed the case to the federal district court and moved to compel arbitration based on Chapter 2 of the FAA.[14] In support, GE Energy argued that Outokumpu's and its insurers' claims were subject to the arbitration agreement contained in the three contracts between ThyssenKrupp and F.L. Industries.[15]

The district court granted GE Energy's motion to compel arbitration. The court ruled that a motion to compel must be granted under Chapter 2 of the FAA "'so long as (1) the four jurisdictional prerequisites [of the New York Convention and Chapter 2] are met and (2) no available affirmative defense under the Convention applies.'"[16] With respect to the first prong, the district court noted that (1) there must be an agreement in writing within the meaning of the New York Convention; (2) the agreement must provide for arbitration in the territory of a signatory of the Convention; (3) the agreement must arise out of a legal relationship, whether contractual or not, which is considered

---

8 *Id.*

9 *Outokumpu Stainless USA, LLC v. Converteam SAS*, No. 16-00378-KD-C, 2017 WL 401951, at *2 (S.D. Ala. Jan. 30, 2017) (internal citations omitted).

10 *Id.* at *3–4.

11 *Id.* (internal citations omitted).

12 *Id.* at *1, 4–5.

13 *Id.* at *5.

14 *Id.* at *2.

15 *Id.* at *3–4.

16 *Id.* at *3 (quoting *Suazo v. NCL (Bahamas), Ltd.*, 822 F.3d 543, 546 (11th Cir. 2016)).

commercial; and (4) either a party to the agreement must be a non-American citizen, or the commercial relationship must have some reasonable relation with one or more foreign states.[17]

Outokumpu, in opposing the motion, argued that the term "parties" in the contracts excluded subcontractors such as GE Energy and that, in any event, neither GE Energy nor Outokumpu had signed the contracts.[18] The district court rejected this argument, pointing out that the contract provided that "[w]hen Seller is mentioned it shall be understood as Sub-contractors included, except if expressly stated otherwise," and concluded that GE Energy as a subcontractor qualified as a party to the contract by virtue of the contractual definition of "Seller."[19] Based on this conclusion, the court declined to address the alternative argument GE Energy also sought to raise that it was entitled to enforce the agreement under principles of equitable estoppel, which would allow a non-signatory to enforce an agreement when the signatory must rely on the terms of that agreement to assert its own claims against the non-signatory.

Outokumpu appealed, and the U.S. Court of Appeals for the Eleventh Circuit reversed.[20] The Eleventh Circuit held that GE Energy could not invoke the arbitration agreement because it was not a signatory to the underlying contracts.[21] In so holding, the Eleventh Circuit relied on the four jurisdictional prerequisites for a party to compel arbitration that the lower court had identified, but found that the inquiry ended with the first prerequisite because there was no agreement in writing within the meaning of the New York Convention.[22] The Eleventh Circuit read Article II(2) of the New York Convention – which states that "[t]he term 'agreement in writing' shall include an arbitral clause in a contract or an arbitration agreement, signed by the parties or contained in an exchange of letters or telegrams"[23] – as requiring a signature by the parties or their privies and therefore disagreed with the district court's conclusion that GE Energy qualified as a signatory.[24]

The Eleventh Circuit also addressed and rejected the equitable estoppel argument that the district court had declined to reach. In so doing, the Eleventh Circuit recognized that the U.S. Supreme Court's precedent in *Arthur*

---

17 *Id.*

18 *Id.* at *5.

19 *Id.* at *4.

20 *See generally Outokumpu Stainless USA, LLC v. Converteam SAS*, 902 F.3d 1316 (11th Cir. 2018).

21 *Id.* at 1325–27.

22 *Id.* at 1325.

23 *Id.*

24 *Id.* at 1325–26.

*Andersen* LLP *v. Carlisle*[25] made equitable estoppel available under Chapter 1 of the FAA to compel arbitration in domestic settings.[26] The Eleventh Circuit found, however, that "estoppel is only available under Chapter 1 because Chapter 1 does not expressly restrict arbitration to the specific parties to an agreement."[27] The Eleventh Circuit held that, by contrast, Chapter 2 of the FAA requires the application of the New York Convention where there is a conflict with Chapter 1, and the New York Convention expressly requires that the parties have signed an arbitration agreement in order to compel arbitration. This requirement, according to the Eleventh Circuit, prevents the use of equitable estoppel to compel arbitration by a non-signatory under Chapter 2. GE Energy sought *certiorari* review.

### 2.2 *Issues and the Parties' Allegations before the Supreme Court*

Although equitable estoppel was a secondary issue in the Eleventh Circuit proceedings – and was not addressed at all by the district court – the question that GE Energy presented to the U.S. Supreme Court was "whether the [New York Convention] permits a non-signatory to an arbitration agreement to compel arbitration based on the doctrine of equitable estoppel."[28] Framing the case around that issue permitted GE Energy to point to the existence of a circuit split, usually a critical element for a successful *certiorari* petition. The First and Fourth Circuits had previously held that non-signatories may compel a signatory to arbitrate under the Convention based on the doctrine of equitable estoppel.[29] By contrast, the Ninth Circuit and now the Eleventh Circuit had read the New York Convention's requirement that an agreement to arbitrate be in writing as precluding non-signatories from enforcing an arbitration agreement governed by the New York Convention.[30] GE Energy's strategy worked, and review was granted.

On the merits before the Supreme Court, GE Energy stressed that Chapter 2 of the FAA requires courts to apply Chapter 1 unless doing so would conflict

---

25 *Arthur Andersen* LLP *v. Carlisle*, 556 U.S. 624 (2009).

26 *Converteam* SAS, 902 F.3d at 1327 (citing *Arthur Andersen* LLP *v. Carlisle*, 556 U.S. 624 (2009)).

27 *Id.* at 1326–27.

28 Brief of Petitioner at i, *GE Energy Power Conversion Fr.* SAS, *Corp. v. Outokumpu Stainless USA,* LLC, 140 S. Ct. 1637 (2020) (No. 18–1048) ("Brief of Petitioner").

29 *See generally Sourcing Unlimited, Inc. v. Asimco Int'l, Inc.*, 526 F.3d 38 (1st Cir. 2008); *Aggarao v.* MOL *Ship Mgmt. Co.*, 675 F.3d 355 (4th Cir. 2012).

30 *See generally Int'l Paper Co. v. Schwabedissen Maschinen & Anlagen* GMBH, 206 F.3d 411 (4th Cir. 2000); *Yang v. Majestic Blue Fisheries,* LLC, 876 F.3d 996 (9th Cir. 2017); *Outokumpu Stainless USA,* LLC *v. Converteam* SAS, 902 F.3d 1316 (11th Cir. 2018).

with Chapter 2 or the New York Convention,[31] and pointed to traditional tools of treaty interpretation to show the absence of any conflict.[32] GE Energy reasoned that Chapter 2 therefore permitted common law contract principles such as equitable estoppel to apply, just as Chapter 1 did.[33]

Outukumpo, by contrast, focused on a textualist argument. It primarily contended that the New York Convention limited the enforcement of arbitration agreements to the "parties" to the agreement, arguing that Article II(3) – read as a whole and together with Article II(1) and Article II(2) – can be understood as authorizing judicial enforcement only when "one of the parties to the written agreement requests enforcement of the agreement."[34] It recognized that within the New York Convention concept of "parties," enforcement by non-signatories through "privity-based" theories like agency, assignment, succession, or alter ego would be consistent with "the . . . consent principle foundational to the Convention."[35] By contrast, it claimed that equitable estoppel was based "on vague, ill-defined concepts of 'equity' and 'fairness.'"[36] In any case, it argued that determining whether equitable estoppel was consistent with this "privity" limitation was unnecessary because German law, as the law of the seat, did not recognize the estoppel doctrine.[37]

The issue before the Court garnered significant interest from the legal community, and specifically international arbitration practitioners, as demonstrated by the submission of nearly 10 *amicus curiae* briefs. The United States asked the Court to reverse the "categorical" rule adopted by the Eleventh Circuit barring the application of *all* domestic law contract and agency principles to determine whether a non-signatory may enforce a valid arbitration agreement.[38] Rather, since the New York Convention does not purport to define who might be deemed a "party" to an arbitration agreement, the United States argued that the question of whether someone could enforce or be bound by an arbitration agreement should generally be determined by the consent of the

31 Brief of Petitioner at 28–35 (citing 9 U.S.C. § 208, which provides that Chapter 1 "applies 'to the extent that chapter is not in conflict with [Chapter 2] or the Convention.'").

32 *Id.* at 36–44.

33 *Id.* at 23–28.

34 Brief of Respondent at 15, *GE Energy Power Conversion Fr. SAS, Corp. v. Outokumpu Stainless USA, LLC*, 140 S. Ct. 1637 (2020) (No. 18–1048) ("Brief of Respondent").

35 *Id.* at 2.

36 *Id.*; *see also id.* at 44–45.

37 *Id.* at 39–40.

38 Brief for the United States as *Amicus Curiae* Supporting Petitioner, *GE Energy Power Conversion Fr. SAS, Corp. v. Outokumpu Stainless USA, LLC*, 140 S. Ct. 1637 (2020) (No. 18–1048) ("U.S. Brief").

relevant persons.[39] As a gloss on this view, the United States warned that binding a non-signatory *sovereign* to an arbitration agreement would raise "special concerns" arising from principles of sovereign immunity.[40]

Columbia Law School Professor George Bermann, along with other Reporters and Advisers to the Restatement of the U.S. Law of International Commercial and Investor-State Arbitration, provided further bases for the proposition that the New York Convention permits non-signatories to be bound by or to enforce international arbitration agreements.[41] In particular, the *amici* posited that the Eleventh Circuit interpretation of the New York Convention, and in particular Article II(2), overlooked the post-ratification understanding of the New York Convention by its Contracting States. *Amici* pointed to a UNCITRAL 2006 recommendation which had clarified that Article II(2) was not an exhaustive statement of the agreements meant to be covered by the New York Convention, and suggested that Article VII(1) – allowing a party to rely on a more favorable domestic law to enforce an arbitration award – also applied to the enforcement of arbitration agreements.[42] *Amici* further noted that whereas the Restatement recognized the general rule that parties must expressly consent to arbitration, the Restatement also recognized exceptions based on implied *and*, in some instances, imputed consent.[43]

### 2.3 *The Supreme Court's Opinion*

In a unanimous opinion by Justice Thomas, the U.S. Supreme Court resolved the circuit split regarding the application of state law principles to determine whether non-signatories may be bound by or invoke arbitration agreements.[44] The Court accepted GE Energy's narrow framing of the issue as being

---

39 *Id.* at 31–35.

40 *Id.* at 32–34 (citing to non-arbitration precedents in which equitable estoppel and third-party beneficiary theories were held not to apply when asserted against the United States). Because of these concerns, the U.S. argued that doctrines such as equitable estoppel and third-party beneficiary status should *not* provide a basis to compel arbitration against a sovereign absent a clear expression of consent. *GE Power* obviously did not involve a foreign sovereign, but the United States clearly wished to signal the Court to be careful in the way it framed its decision to avoid later misunderstanding on this point.

41 *See generally* Brief of *Amici Curiae* Professor George A. Bermann, R. Doak Bishop, Professor Andrea A. Bjorklund, Douglas Earl McLaren, Professor Alan S. Rau, Professor W. Michael Reisman and John M. Townsend, *GE Energy Power Conversion Fr. SAS, Corp. v. Outokumpu Stainless USA, LLC*, 140 S. Ct. 1637 (2020) (No. 18–1048).

42 *Id.*

43 *Id.* at 34.

44 *See generally GE Energy Power Conversion Fr. SAS, Corp. v. Outokumpu Stainless USA, LLC*, 140 S. Ct. 1637 (2020).

whether the New York Convention conflicts with domestic equitable estoppel doctrines.[45] It held that the New York Convention does not preclude a non-signatory – in this case, GE Energy – from seeking to enforce an international arbitration agreement by invoking state law principles routinely relied on in domestic arbitration proceedings.[46] The Court applied familiar tools of treaty interpretation and reasoned that the silence of the New York Convention on whether non-signatories may enforce arbitration agreements under domestic doctrines was dispositive of the issue.[47]

At the outset, the Court explained that the question before the Court could be resolved by determining whether the doctrine of equitable estoppel "'conflict[ed] with . . . the Convention,'"[48] noting that Section 208 of the FAA provides that "'Chapter 1 applies to actions and proceedings brought under this chapter [Chapter 2] to the extent that [Chapter 1] is not in conflict with this chapter or the Convention.'"[49] Based on this framing of the inquiry, the Court looked to "familiar tools of treaty interpretation" and concluded that the text of the New York Convention did "not address whether non-signatories may enforce arbitration agreements under domestic doctrines such as equitable estoppel."[50]

The Court first determined that Article II(3) is the only provision to address the enforcement of arbitration agreements and found that while Article II(3) requires courts of Convention States to enforce written arbitration agreements at the request of a party, it does not expressly preclude the application of domestic law principles that are more generous in enforcing arbitration agreements in other circumstances.[51] In support of this textualist reading of Article II(3), the Court pointed out that the New York Convention was drafted against the backdrop of domestic law and contemplated that there would be a place for domestic law in international arbitration.[52] As a result, the Court explained that it would be unnatural to displace domestic law doctrines absent explicit exclusionary language.[53] Examining Article II(3), the Court concluded that the provision did not contain any such exclusionary language and that instead, the provision left many concepts undefined – such as disputes "'capable of

45 *Id.* at 1642.
46 *Id.* at 1642.
47 *Id.* at 1645.
48 *Id.* at 1644–45 (citing 9 U.S.C. § 208).
49 *Id.* at 1644 (citing 9 U.S.C. § 206).
50 *Id.* at 1645.
51 *Id.*
52 *Id.*
53 *Id.*

settlement by arbitration'" or agreements "null and void, inoperative or incapable of being performed" – thereby requiring courts to rely on domestic law to fill the gaps.[54]

This textual analysis was reinforced by the Court's consideration of the New York Convention's context.[55] The Court concluded that the drafting history showed that the drafters only sought to impose baseline requirements on State parties and did not suggest that the New York Convention drafters sought to prevent Contracting States from applying domestic law.[56] As to the post-ratification understanding of other Contracting States, as evidenced by their court decisions, and their post-ratification conduct, the Court found again that these aids merely indicated that the New York Convention does not prohibit the application of domestic law addressing the enforcement of arbitration agreements.[57] In particular, the Court pointed out that numerous Contracting States permit enforcement of arbitration agreements by non-signatories and noted that, consistent with such view, a recommendation issued by the United Nations Commission on International Trade Law had adopted a non-exclusive interpretation of the requirement in Article II(2) that the agreement be signed.[58] Consistent with the "originalist" views of its author in other contexts, the Court's opinion downplayed the weight to be given to these sources because they dated from decades after the New York Convention's finalization and therefore did not reflect the "original shared understanding of the treaty's meaning."[59] It nonetheless noted that they "confirm our interpretation of the Convention's text."[60]

Based, therefore, on both the text and States parties' understanding of the New York Convention, the Court concluded that the Eleventh Circuit had erred. Critically, the Court of Appeals had failed to distinguish between Articles II(1) and II(2), which deal with "the recognition of arbitration agreements," and Article II(3), which alone "speaks to who may request" arbitration, and does not prohibit the application of domestic law in answering the latter question. Noting that the Court of Appeals had not reached the issue of whether GE Energy could actually enforce the arbitration clauses under principles of equitable estoppel under domestic law, or "which body of law governs that

54 *Id.* (citation omitted).
55 *Id.* at 1645–46.
56 *Id.*
57 *Id.* at 1656–47.
58 *Id.*
59 *Id.*
60 *Id.* at 1647.

determination," the Supreme Court remanded for the lower courts to address these issues.[61]

In a concurrence, Justice Sotomayor emphasized that, in all cases, the application of state law principles to permit non-signatories to enforce arbitration agreements was subject to the "important limitation" that such "domestic doctrines must be rooted in the principle of consent to arbitrate" which "governs the FAA on the whole."[62] Acknowledging the lack of any "bright-line test for determining whether a particular domestic non-signatory doctrine reflects consent to arbitrate," Justice Sotomayor advised lower courts that they "must . . . determine, on a case-by-case basis, whether applying a domestic non-signatory doctrine would violate the FAA's inherent consent restriction."[63]

On remand, the district court again did not address whether Outokumpu could be compelled to arbitrate on equitable estoppel grounds. Instead, largely following its initial decision, it held that "GE Energy is a defined party covered by the arbitration clause" such that "Outokumpu simply agreed to arbitrate with GE Energy per the contract's plain terms."[64]

## 3 Critical Analysis

The Supreme Court's opinion in *GE Energy* is important but narrow, and it leaves many issues undecided, and indeed unaddressed. The decision clearly holds that under U.S. law there is no distinction between domestic arbitration agreements governed by Chapter 1 of the FAA and international arbitration agreements governed by the New York Convention in Chapter 2 of the FAA in terms of *who* may enforce them, and that domestic contract law principles may be invoked in either situation by parties seeking enforcement. The opinion, however, leaves at least two key questions unanswered.

*First*, while domestic law is clearly available to decide who may enforce an agreement to arbitrate, the Court's opinion is absolutely silent about which jurisdiction's domestic law should govern this question. In particular, while there are references throughout its opinion to domestic law, and less frequently to "state law," as gap-fillers in deciding questions of *who* can enforce arbitration agreements, there is no reference to *which* state's domestic law should apply;

61 *Id.* at 1648.

62 *Id.* at 1648–49.

63 *Id.* at 1649.

64 *Outokumpu Stainless USA, LLC v. GE Energy Power Conversion Fr. SAS, Corp.*, No. 1:16-cv-00378-KD-C, 2022 WL 2643936, at *3 (S.D. Ala. Jul. 8, 2022).

indeed, the Supreme Court's opinion does not even mention the seat of the arbitration, the governing law of the contracts, or *lex arbitri*, although these sources of law would be likely relevant to this unanswered question. *A fortiori* there is no discussion of whether it is the *lex arbitri* or the substantive law governing the contract in which the arbitration agreement is contained, or some other law in the place where the relevant conduct may have occurred, that should govern the "who can enforce" question.

This lack of guidance is especially striking because it is far from clear that equitable estoppel, an essentially common law concept, even exists under German law, which would seem to have been the most likely domestic law to govern the issue of non-signatory enforcement under the facts of *GE Energy*. The Supreme Court was clear that nothing in the FAA or New York Convention precludes a non-signatory from enforcing an arbitration agreement, but there is no reason to think that U.S. law would otherwise play any role in deciding the underlying question of whether, or under what circumstances, a non-signatory can enforce an arbitration agreement in any particular case.[65]

*Second*, the Supreme Court did not discuss whether there is any difference between who may *enforce* an arbitration agreement, and who is bound by it. The issue in *GE Energy* was only the former, not the latter. It would seem that the Court would expect "domestic law" to provide the answer as to who is bound by an arbitration agreement, but there may conceivably be differences in what that answer is, depending on the domestic law that governs. As Justice Sotomayor's concurrence emphasized, the notion of consent underpins all U.S. arbitration law, and the same is true of most if not all other domestic legal systems. It may be conceptually easier to find that a non-signatory can enforce an agreement to arbitrate against someone who clearly signed it and thereby consented to arbitrate, than to require a non-signatory to arbitrate based on someone else's consent.

What if, for example, the relevant domestic law required a non-signatory to arbitrate based on a ground that did not satisfy U.S. notions of consent, and the U.S. court were asked to compel arbitration on that foreign domestic law ground? The logic of *GE Energy* suggests that if the governing domestic law indeed requires arbitration under these circumstances, nothing in the FAA or New York Convention would permit the U.S. court to refuse to order it. Nonetheless, one can imagine a court feeling uneasy about compelling a non-consenting non-signatory to arbitrate in such a case. Like other situations

65 Indeed, U.S. courts only entered the picture in *GE Energy* because an action was brought in the United States on claims that the defendant asserted were covered by an arbitration agreement.

left unaddressed by *GE Energy*, the law on this fact pattern, if it ever emerges, would require further development.

## 4 Conclusion

*GE Energy* definitively holds as a matter of U.S. law that there is nothing in the New York Convention or Chapter 2 of the FAA implementing it that precludes resorting to principles of domestic law to determine who may enforce an international arbitration agreement in United States courts. However, the Supreme Court did not address which domestic law applies or how that question is to be answered. In short, on the non-signatory enforcement issue itself, it is a narrow opinion leaving much to be explored by future decisions.

Interestingly, though, *GE Energy* is already being applied to answer other questions of interpretation of Chapter 2 of the FAA and its interplay with Chapter 1. In *Day v. Orrick, Herrington & Sutcliffe LLP*, for example, it was invoked by the Ninth Circuit in a case where an arbitrator in an international arbitration seated in Washington, D.C. issued a non-party subpoena to a witness in California under Section 7 of the FAA, which is part of Chapter 1. In rejecting the non-party's challenge to the subject matter jurisdiction of the California federal district court to enforce the subpoena, the Ninth Circuit relied on the Supreme Court's reasoning in *GE Energy* that "rejected the notion that the New York Convention must list every 'judicial tool' for it to 'fall under the Convention,'" and concluded that "[n]either the Convention nor Chapter 2 contains any language excluding the use of petitions to enforce arbitral summonses."[66] In another decision, *Corporación AIC, SA v. Hidroeléctrica Santa Rita S.A.*, the Court of Appeals for the Eleventh Circuit recently reversed its prior precedent and joined the Second, Third, Fifth, Sixth, Ninth, Tenth, and D.C. Circuits in finding that the grounds for vacatur under Chapter 1 of the FAA may also apply to non-domestic awards (that is, arbitration awards with a seat in the United States but involving a non-U.S. party).[67] The Eleventh Circuit reached this conclusion "based on the Supreme Court's discussion in [*GE Energy v.*] *Outokumpu* and the New York Convention's binary framework," holding that "the primary jurisdiction's domestic law acts as a gap-filler that provides the vacatur grounds for an arbitral award."[68]

---

66 *Day v. Orrick, Herrington & Sutcliffe, LLP*, 42 F.4th 1131, 1135–36 (9th Cir. 2022).

67 *Corporación AIC, SA v. Hidroeléctrica Santa Rita S.A.*, 66 F.4th 876, 886 (11th Cir. 2023).

68 *Id.*

GE *Energy* is thus being read to reinforce the idea that both the U.S. domestic procedures of Chapter 1 of the FAA, and more important, relevant substantive domestic arbitration law principles, must be applied by U.S. courts in international/non-domestic arbitrations, unless there is an explicit conflict between those principles and the New York Convention. GE *Energy* leaves open the question of *how* the relevant domestic arbitration law principles should be chosen but makes clear that it should be domestic law principles that fill in the gaps where procedural or substantive provisions of the New York Convention are silent.

CHAPTER 31

# *ZF Automotive, Inc. v. Luxshare, Ltd.* and *Alixpartners, LLP v. Fund for Protection of Investors' Rights in Foreign States* (2022)

*Flávio Luiz Yarshell and Rafael Stefanini Auilo*

## 1 Introduction

This article will examine the cases *ZF Automotive, Inc. v. Luxshare, Ltd.* and *AlixPartners, LLP v. Fund for Protection of Investors' Rights In Foreign States*, jointly ruled by the Supreme Court of the United States. At the judgment in question, the Supreme Court had to decide on the application of Section 1782 of Title 28 of the U.S. Code to international commercial arbitrations.

The analysis of the opinion is divided into three main topics. In the first, general and introductory considerations are made about the legal issue discussed; in the second, the object of the debate and the opinion, including the allegations of the parties and the conclusion reached, are examined in the respective factual-legal context; in the third, the opinion was critically analyzed, with possible projections of potential effects on arbitration practice in the United States and, eventually, outside it.

## 2 Preliminary Considerations on the Major Topic Decided by the Supreme Court of the United States in the Case in Question

Section 1782 is inserted in Title 28 of the U.S. Code, which provides for the assistance of U.S. courts to foreign and international courts and their respective litigants. Section 1782 is the primary discovery mechanism for the production of evidence in the United States, to be eventually used in proceedings abroad.[1]

Section 1782(a) states that "The district court of the district in which a person resides or is found may order him to give his testimony or statement or to produce a document or other thing for use in a proceeding in a foreign or

1 See George A. Bermann; William Dodge; Donald Childress III. *Transnational Litigation in a Nutshell*, 2nd ed, Saint Paul, West Academic Publishing, 2021, p. 429.

 | DOI:10.1163/9789004715820_032

international tribunal, including criminal investigations conducted before formal accusation." That is, "a party to foreign or international legal proceedings, or indeed any party having an interest in them, may petition a court for assistance in obtaining evidence for use in those proceedings."[2]

Before the present case, the Supreme Court had the opportunity to rule on the application and interpretation of Section 1782(a), particularly on what would be the requirements for the discovery order to be granted. This case became known as *Intel*.[3] Among other things, the Supreme Court concluded that the meaning of "litigants" contained in the statute should not be interpreted restrictively, as only one who asks or against whom something is asked (i.e., claimant or respondent). Instead, a "litigant" could be anyone interested and who develops or has developed an important role in the foreign proceeding. Furthermore, as in such case the foreign proceeding was filed with the Directorate-General for Competition of the European Commission, the Supreme Court also had to decide whether such body would be qualified as a "foreign or international tribunal". Considering that the European Commission acted as a "first-instance decisionmaker", the Supreme Court understood that there would be no way to exclude the body from the scope of Section 1782(a), even if that proceeding had not passed the initial stage of investigation. The Supreme Court also ruled that "nothing in the text of §1782 limits a district court's production-order authority to materials that could be discovered in the foreign jurisdiction if the materials were located there."[4]

While the Supreme Court has not decided on the possibility of using Section 1782 in the context of international commercial arbitrations, the reasoning has included observations made by Professor Hans Smit, one of the creators of the draft bill that resulted in the amendment of the statute in 1964. Among others, Professor Smit's article maintained that the term "tribunal" was thought to include "investigating magistrates, administrative and arbitral tribunals, and quasi-judicial agencies, as well as conventional civil, commercial, criminal, and administrative courts."[5]

As previously stated by one of the authors of this commentary, "The reference to Professor Hans Smit's article and international arbitration triggered

---

2 *Id. Ibid.*, p. 148.

3 *Intel Corp. v. Advanced Micro Devices, Inc.*, 542 U.S. 241 (2004).

4 *Ibid.*

5 *Ibid.* See also Hans Smit. "International Litigation under the United States Code", in *Columbia Law Review*, v. 65, n. 6, June 1965, p. 1.026, note 71. For a brief examination of *Intel*, see Gustavo Favero Vaughn; Flávio Luiz Yarshell. "Two reasons why Section 18792 is pro-arbitration", in *Revista Brasileira de Arbitragem*, v. XIX, n. 75, July-Sept./2022, pp. 71–73.

a wave of conflicting decisions on the matter in the U.S. There has been no consensus on the availability of Section 1782 applications in the context of international commercial arbitration – this statement seems to remain true even after the U.S. Supreme Court decision in the consolidated case. At least two federal circuits (Fourth and Sixth Circuits) allowed foreign parties to issue subpoenas to obtain discovery in assistance of private international arbitral tribunals, while at least three federal circuits did not (Second, Fifth, and Seventh Circuits). The circuit split on the scope of Section 1782 discovery led the Supreme Court to first grant certiorari in *Servotronics, Inc. v. Rolls-Royce PLC*. Despite the expectations this case created in the international arbitration realm, the parties presented a joint stipulation to dismiss under Rule 46.1 of the Rules of the U.S. Supreme Court. Accordingly, the case was dismissed and removed from the Supreme Court's oral argument schedule."[6]

The issue was brought again to the Supreme Court from the cases *ZF Automotive U.S., Inc. v. Luxshare, Ltd.* and *AlixPartners, LLC v. Fund for Protection of Investors' Rights in Foreign States*, which were eventually consolidated. Although relatively diverse in their factual aspects, both involved "a party seeking discovery in the United States for use in arbitration proceedings abroad. In both, the party seeking discovery invoked §1782, which permits a district court to order the production of certain evidence 'for use in a proceeding in a foreign or international tribunal.' And in both, the party resisting discovery argued that the arbitral panel at issue did not qualify as a 'foreign or international tribunal' under the statute".[7]

## 3 The Case

### 3.1 *Background of the Case*

The *ZF Automotive U.S., Inc. v. Luxshare, Ltd.* case involved an allegation of fraud in a business transaction. ZF Automotive U.S., Inc., a Michigan-based North American subsidiary of a German automotive parts company, sold two of its operating units to Luxshare, Ltd., a Hong Kong-based company, for nearly $1 billion. After the execution, Luxshare claimed to have discovered that ZF had concealed relevant information regarding the operations so that there was a relevant overpricing.

6 See Gustavo Favero Vaughn; Flávio Luiz Yarshell. "Two reasons why Section 18792 is pro-arbitration", in *Revista Brasileira de Arbitragem*, v. XIX, n. 75, July-Sept./2022, pp. 73–74.

7 *ZF Automotive, Inc. v. Luxshare, Ltd.* and *AlixPartners, LLP v. Fund for Protection of Investors' Rights In Foreign States*, 596 U.S. __ (2022).

The contract executed by the parties was governed by an arbitration clause, according to which three arbitrators should decide any dispute under the Arbitration Rules of the German Institute of Arbitration (DIS[8]), a private dispute resolution organization based in Berlin, Germany. The contract also provided that German laws would govern it, that the seat of arbitration would be Munich, and that the panel[9] would be formed by arbitrators appointed by the parties, who would appoint the president.

In order to initiate an arbitration against ZF, Luxshare filed a Section 1782 Application with the U.S. District Court for the Eastern District of Michigan. Its goal was to obtain information about ZF and two ZF senior officers. District Court granted the request, and ZF moved to quash, arguing that the DIS arbitration panel was not, under Section 1782, a "foreign or international tribunal". The claim was rejected, and a request for a stay was submitted to the Sixth Circuit, also denied.

Then, the Supreme Court "granted a stay and certiorari before judgment to resolve a split among the Courts of Appeals over whether the phrase 'foreign or international tribunal' in §1782 includes private arbitral panels. Compare *Servotronics, Inc.* v. *Boeing Co.*, 954 F. 3d 209 (CA4 2020); *Abdul Latif*, 939 F. 3d 710, with *National Broadcasting Co.* v. *Bear Stearns & Co.*, 165 F. 3d 184 (CA2 1999); *Republic of Kazakhstan* v. *Biedermann Int'l*, 168 F. 3d 880 (CA5 1999); *Servotronics, Inc.* v. *Rolls-Royce PLC*, 975 F. 3d 689 (CA7 2020)".[10]

The *AlixPartners, LLC v. Fund for Protection of Investors' Rights in Foreign States* case was initiated from a dispute between Lithuania and a Russian investor in AB bankas SNORAS (Snoras), a Lithuanian bank. After discovering that Snoras would not be able to fulfil its obligations, the Central Bank of Lithuania nationalized it and appointed as provisional administrator the CEO of a New York-based consulting firm, AlixPartners. Following the submission of a report by the provisional administrator, the Lithuanian authorities authorized the initiation of bankruptcy proceedings and declared Snoras insolvent. The Fund for Protection of Investors' Rights in Foreign States, "a Russian corporation and the assignee of the Russian Investor"[11] alleged that Lithuania had expropriated investments from Snoras during the proceeding.

---

8 In German, Deutsche Institution für Schiedsgerichtsbarkeit.

9 The terms "panel" and "arbitral tribunal" are used as synonyms in this text.

10 *ZF Automotive, Inc. v. Luxshare, Ltd.* and *AlixPartners, LLP v. Fund for Protection of Investors' Rights in Foreign States*, 596 U.S. __ (2022).

11 Cf. *Ibid.*

The Fund initiated a proceeding against Lithuania under a bilateral investment treaty (BIT) between the State and Russia.[12] A clause of the BIT provided that any dispute between the contracting parties and an investor could be resolved in four separate *fora* (bodies). The dispute resolution method chosen was an *ad hoc* arbitration under the Arbitration Rules of the United Nations Commission on International Trade Law (UNCITRAL).

Before the arbitrators were appointed, the Fund filed a Section 1782 Application with the U.S. District Court for the Southern District of New York. The purpose of the Fund was to obtain information from the administrator and AlixPartners during their work on the Snoras bankruptcy proceedings. The company objected to the request, arguing that an *ad hoc* arbitral tribunal would not, under Section 1782, be considered a "foreign or international tribunal" but a private adjudicatory body. The objection was rejected, and the District Court ordered the discovery. The Second Circuit upheld the decision.

In this context, it should be remembered that the Second Circuit had already decided on another occasion that a private arbitral tribunal would not constitute, under Section 1782, a "foreign or international tribunal."[13] However, the Second Circuit had not yet faced the specific case of an *ad hoc* arbitral tribunal constituted from a BIT. So, "After employing a multifactor test to determine 'whether the body in question possesses the functional attributes most commonly associated with private arbitration,' it concluded that the *ad hoc* panel was 'foreign or international' rather than private. 5 F. 4th 216, 225, 228 (2021)."[14]

The Supreme Court also granted *certiorari* to this case and then consolidated both.

### 3.2 *Issue and Parties' Allegations*

Notwithstanding the differences, applicants for both discovery measures argued that Section 1782(a) provides that a district court may order discovery for use in a proceeding in an international arbitration tribunal.

The respondents argued that any discovery would be admissible if the evidence to be produced were for use before a governmental or intergovernmental adjudicatory body and neither an arbitration panel constituted under the rules of a private arbitral institution, nor an *ad hoc* panel constituted under the UNCITRAL rules could be qualified in this manner. Moreover, the interpretation

12 The BIT's goal was to create conditions for foreign investments by nationals of one country in the other.

13 *National Broadcasting Co. v. Bear Staerms Co*, 165 F.3d 184 (2d. Cir. 1999).

14 *ZF Automotive, Inc. v. Luxshare, Ltd.* and *AlixPartners, LLP v. Fund for Protection of Investors' Rights In Foreign States*, 596 U.S. __ (2022).

of the statute would not be limited to the literalism of the expressions "foreign tribunal" and "international tribunal". Nevertheless, one should consider the context and the moment it was promulgated, mainly because the statute's structure, history and objectives would confirm its focus on governmental entities.

In this context, the Supreme Court had to resolve two main issues. First, whether the terms "foreign tribunal" or "international tribunal" provided for in Section 1782 would refer to a private adjudicatory body or a body with governmental authority. Second, whether the adjudicatory bodies involved in the cases (an arbitral tribunal constituted under the DIS rules and a BIT *ad hoc* arbitral tribunal constituted under the UNCITRAL rules) would be covered by the statute.

### 3.3 *The Supreme Court's Opinion*

The central issue to be resolved by the Supreme Court concerned the interpretation of the expression "foreign or international tribunal" contained in Section 1782. According to the opinion, if considered individually, the word "tribunal" would not be of great use since, depending on the case, it could carry different meanings. It may or may not be synonymous with a governmental body. To illustrate the equivalence of the term, a passage from the Black's Law Dictionary 1677 (4th ed. rev. 1968) is cited, in which it is stated that court is "'[t]he Seat of a Judge' or 'a judicial court; the jurisdiction which the judges exercise'" on the one hand; and the American Heritage Dictionary 1369 (1969), in which it is stated that "tribunal" could mean "'[a]nything having the power of determining or judging'", on the other hand.

Accordingly, "A prior version of §1782 covered 'any judicial proceeding' in 'any court in a foreign country,' 28 U.S.C.§1782 (1958 ed.), but in 1964, Congress expanded the provision to cover proceedings in a 'foreign or international tribunal.' As we have previously observed, that shift created 'the possibility of U.S. judicial assistance in connection with administrative and quasi-judicial proceedings abroad.' *Intel*, 542 U.S., at 258 (alterations omitted). So a §1782 'tribunal' need not be a formal 'court,' and the broad meaning of 'tribunal' does not itself exclude private adjudicatory bodies. If we had nothing but this single word to go on, there would be a good case for including private arbitral panels."[15]

Nevertheless, considering that the word "tribunal" would belong to a broader expression, in which the words "foreign" and "international" are mentioned,

---

15 *Ibid.*

the Supreme Court concluded that a joint examination of the terms would be indispensable. In this frame, the Supreme Court recalled that in another case, it had already been decided that "two words together may assume a more particular meaning than those words in isolation."[16]

Then, the Supreme Court concluded that "The word 'foreign' takes on its more governmental meaning when modifying a word with potential governmental or sovereign connotations. (...) 'Tribunal' is a word with potential governmental or sovereign connotations, so 'foreign tribunal' more naturally refers to a tribunal belonging to a foreign nation than to a tribunal that is simply located in a foreign nation. And for a tribunal to belong to a foreign nation, the tribunal must possess sovereign authority conferred by that nation."[17]

Furthermore, according to the Supreme Court, the proposed interpretation would be reinforced by the full reading of the rule. In addition to authorizing district courts to hear witnesses or produce other evidence, Section 1782, "permits them to 'prescribe the practice and procedure, which may be in whole or part *the practice and procedure of the foreign country or the international tribunal*, for taking the testimony or statement or producing the document or other thing.' §1782(a) (emphasis added)." Reference to procedural rules "of 'the foreign country or the international tribunal' parallels the authorization for district courts to grant discovery for use in a 'foreign or international tribunal' mentioned just before in §1782." This means that the rule "presumes that a 'foreign tribunal' follows 'the practice and procedure of the foreign country.' It is unremarkable for the statute to presume that a foreign court, quasi-judicial body, or any other governmental adjudicatory body follows the practice and procedures prescribed by the government that conferred authority on it. But that would be an odd assumption to make about a private adjudicatory body, which is typically the creature of an agreement between private parties who prescribe their own rules. See *Stolt-Nielsen S. A.* v. *AnimalFeeds Int'l Corp.*, 559 U.S. 662, 683 (2010). That the default discovery procedures for a 'foreign tribunal' are governmental suggests that the body is governmental too."[18]

In examining the term "international tribunal", the Supreme Court stated that the word "international" could refer to something involving two or more nations or nationalities. However, this "definition is unlikely in this context because an adjudicative body would be 'international' if it had adjudicators of different nationalities – and it would be strange for the availability of discovery

16 *FCC v. AT&T Inc.*, 562 U.S. 397, 406 (2011).

17 *ZF Automotive, Inc. v. Luxshare, Ltd.* and *AlixPartners, LLP v. Fund for Protection of Investors' Rights in Foreign States*, 596 U.S. __ (2022).

18 *Ibid.*

to turn on the national origin of the adjudicators. So no party argues that 'international' carries that meaning here. A tribunal is 'international' when it involves or is of two or more nations, meaning that those nations have imbued the tribunal with official power to adjudicate disputes. See Tr. of Oral Arg. 77 (the United States arguing that 'the touch-stone' is whether the body is 'exercising official power on behalf of the two governments')."[19]

Thus, on the premise that the terms "foreign tribunal" and "international tribunal" would complement each other, the Supreme Court concluded that the former concerns a tribunal vested with sovereign governmental authority and that the latter refers to a tribunal vested with governmental authority from different nations.

In a confirmation exercise, the Supreme Court also conducted both historical and comparative examinations of Section 1782 and the Federal Arbitration Act (FAA), 9 U.S. Code, Section 1 *et. seq.*

Regarding the historical examination, the Supreme Court stated that, since the beginning of its creation, the institute considered the respect given to foreign nations and their respective governmental and intergovernmental bodies. Thus, "From 1855 until 1964, §1782 and its antecedents covered assistance only to foreign 'courts.' (…). And before 1964, a separate strand of law covered assistance to 'any international tribunal or commission … in which the United States participate[d] as a party.' Act of June 7, 1933, ch. 50, 48 Stat. 117. The process of combining these two statutory lines began when Congress established the Commission on International Rules of Judicial Procedure. See Act of Sept. 2, 1958, Pub. L. 85–906, §§1–2, 72 Stat. 1743. It charged the Commission with improving the process of judicial assistance, specifying that the 'assistance and cooperation' was '*between the United States and foreign countries*' and that 'the rendering of assistance *to foreign courts and quasi-judicial agencies*' should be improved. *Ibid.* (emphasis added). In 1964, Congress adopted the Commission's proposed legislation, which became the modern version of § 1782."[20]

Even concerning the statute amendment in 1964, the Supreme Court concluded that the changes did not expand its scope to private bodies. In its view, the amendment sought to reach other government bodies since Congress aimed to strengthen ties of assistance and cooperation between the United States and other nations. That is, "the animating purpose of §1782 is comity: Permitting federal courts to assist foreign and international governmental bodies promotes respect for foreign governments and encourages

19 *Ibid.*

20 *Ibid.*

reciprocal assistance. It is difficult to see how enlisting district courts to help private bodies would serve that end. Such a broad reading of §1782 would open district court doors to any interested person seeking assistance for proceedings before any private adjudicative body – a category broad enough to include everything from a commercial arbitration panel to a university's student disciplinary tribunal. See Brief for Petitioners in No. 21–401, at 19. Why would Congress lend the resources of district courts to aid purely private bodies adjudicating purely private disputes abroad?"[21]

Furthermore, according to the Supreme Court, an extensive interpretation of the statute could contradict the Federal Arbitration Act (FAA), which regulates domestic arbitrations. Under this approach, taking discovery under Section 1782 would have greater scope than that in force in domestic arbitrations without any reason for such distinction. In this sense, the opinion stated that "Among other differences, the FAA permits only the arbitration panel to request discovery, see 9 U.S.C. §7, while district courts can entertain §1782 requests from foreign or international tribunals or any 'interested person,' 28 U.S.C. §1782(a). In addition, pre-arbitration discovery is off the table under the FAA but broadly available under §1782. See *Intel*, 542 U.S., at 259 (holding that discovery is available for use in proceedings 'within reasonable contemplation')."[22]

Finally, the Supreme Court examined the issue of the qualification of the adjudicatory bodies in the cases under examination.

Regarding arbitration involving ZF and Luxshare, the Supreme Court held that the parties had entered into a private contract and that the arbitral tribunal was constituted under the rules of a private dispute resolution body – which occurs with any panels operating under the rules created by private institutions. According to the Supreme Court, "The panels are formed by the parties – with each party selecting one arbitrator and those two arbitrators choosing a third. No government is involved in creating the DIS panel or prescribing its procedures. This adjudicative body therefore does not qualify as a governmental body".[23]

The Supreme Court also rejected the argument that an arbitral tribunal could be qualified as governmental if the law of the country regulates aspects of the arbitration process and the judicial courts exercise a relevant function in effecting arbitration agreements – as it would happen in the case of the DIS tribunal. To the Supreme Court, "private entities do not become governmental

21 *Ibid.*

22 *Ibid.*

23 *Ibid.*

because laws govern them, and courts enforce their contracts – that would erase any distinction between private and governmental adjudicative bodies. Luxshare's implausibly broad definition of a governmental adjudicative body is nothing but an attempted end run around §1782's limit".[24]

As regards the *ad hoc* arbitration panel, the Supreme Court concluded that the dispute involving the Fund and Lithuania would have two relevant characteristics to qualify it as an intergovernmental body: the sovereignty of a State in relation to one of the parties to the dispute and the fact that the arbitration agreement was contained in an international treaty and not in a private contract. Still, "neither Lithuania's presence nor the treaty's existence is dispositive, because Russia and Lithuania are free to structure investor-state dispute resolution as they see fit."[25]

According to the opinion, the main point was to define whether the two nations intended to confer on the *ad hoc* arbitral tribunal a status of governmental authority. In consonance with the Supreme Court's interpretation, this would not have been the intention since the dispute resolution clause provided for different ways to resolve any potential dispute, one of them by means of proceedings before the courts of one of the contracting parties. That is: "The inclusion of courts on the list reflects Russia and Lithuania's intent to give investors the choice of bringing their disputes before a pre-existing governmental body. An ad hoc arbitration panel, by contrast, is not a pre-existing body, but one formed for the purpose of adjudicating investor-state disputes. And nothing in the treaty reflects Russia and Lithuania's intent that an ad hoc panel exercise governmental authority. For instance, the treaty does not itself create the panel; instead, it simply references the set of rules that govern the panel's formation and procedure if an investor chooses that forum. In addition, the ad hoc panel 'functions independently' of and is not affiliated with either Lithuania or Russia. 5 F. 4th, at 226. It consists of individuals chosen by the parties and lacking any 'official affiliation with Lithuania, Russia, or any other governmental or intergovernmental entity.' *Ibid.* And it lacks other possible indicia of a governmental nature. See *ibid.* ('[T]he panel receives zero government funding,' 'the proceedings ... maintain confidentiality,' and the 'award may be made public only with the consent of both parties')."[26]

Regarding form and function, the *ad hoc* tribunal of the case involving Lithuania and the arbitral tribunal constituted under the DIS rules would be materially identical: the authority of both panels would derive from the

---

24 *Ibid.*
25 *Ibid.*
26 *Ibid.*

parties' consent to arbitrate. Indeed, "inclusion in the treaty does not, as the Fund suggests, automatically render ad hoc arbitration governmental. Instead, it reflects the countries' choice to offer investors the potentially appealing option of bringing their disputes to a private arbitration panel that operates like commercial arbitration panels do."[27] Therefore, none of the two panels would be imbued with official authority, although governmental and intergovernmental bodies can take various forms.

In comparative terms, the Supreme Court also stated that the *ad hoc* panel would not be confused with other adjudicatory bodies created in the past, such as those cited by Luxshare (i.e., a derivative of a treaty between the U.S. and Britain following the sinking of the Canadian ship "I'm Alone" or another of the "United States-Germany Mixed Claims Commission"), although some similarities could be drawn from those hypotheses. Unlike the treaty under review involving Lithuania and Russia, "those treaties specified that each sovereign would be involved in the formation of the bodies, and, with respect to the treaty creating the Mixed Claims Commission in particular, it also specified where the commission would initially meet, the method of funding, and that the commissioners could appoint other officers to assist in the proceedings."[28]

### 3.4 *Key Takeaways*

Until ZF and AlixPartners' cases, Section 1782 was a relevant instrument through which a broader discovery was admitted than that usually granted by tribunals in international arbitrations. The Supreme Court opinion now makes it clear the assistance cannot take place in the context of international arbitral tribunals not imbued with governmental power. In these terms, the decision can be divided into two main chapters.

In the first, the Supreme Court examined the scope of the expression "foreign or international tribunal" from the following perspective: would it include private adjudicatory bodies or only those considered governmental or intergovernmental?

Unanimously, the Supreme Court understood that the word "tribunal", read in a decontextualized way, would be ambiguous and, therefore, less useful in the interpretation of the rule. Thus, it recognized that it would be essential to examine the word in the context in which it was found, with the words "foreign" and "international".

27 *Ibid.*
28 *Ibid.*

Thus, a "tribunal" would be better understood as a body exercising governmental authority. It is worth saying that the word "tribunal", allied to the other terms, would mean sovereign, state or interstate power of a sovereign nation or an international body invested with governmental power by two or more nations. Then, the Supreme Court concluded that Section 1782 would only apply to cases related to adjudicatory bodies of a governmental or intergovernmental nature, although not necessarily courts in a narrow sense.

The Supreme Court also understood that the history of the statute and its comparison with Section 7 of the FAA would confirm the conclusion reached. Regarding the historical aspect, it stated "After all, the animating purpose of §1782 is comity", that is, "respecting foreign nations and the governmental and intergovernmental bodies they create. (…) Permitting federal courts to assist foreign and international governmental bodies promotes respect for foreign governments and encourages reciprocal assistance."[29] As for the comparative aspect, it was recognized that a broad interpretation of Section 1782 would lead to an eventual and unwanted contradiction between it and the Section 7 of the FAA, since it would allow a much broader discovery than this, with no apparent reason.

In the second, given the delimitation made, the Supreme Court examined whether the arbitral tribunals of the consolidated case would fit into the concept of governmental or intergovernmental adjudicatory bodies, concluding negatively. Regarding the dispute involving Luxshare and ZF, it was understood that there would be no governmental power involved in the creation of the arbitral tribunal nor the definition of the procedural rules. Concerning the other dispute, the solution was considered more complex, given that intergovernmental and sovereignty aspects would also be involved in a dispute arising from an investment treaty between two states. However, even considering this, the Supreme Court concluded that the parties to the treaty did not intend to confer on that *ad hoc* panel governmental or intergovernmental power.

The Supreme Court held that "only a governmental or intergovernmental adjudicative body constitutes a 'foreign or international tribunal' under § 1782. Such bodies are those that exercise governmental authority conferred by one nation or multiple nations. Neither the private commercial arbitral panel in the first case nor the ad hoc arbitration panel in the second case qualifies."[30]

---

29 *Ibid.*

30 *Ibid.*

## 4 Critical Analysis of the Opinion and How It Impacted the U.S. Arbitration Law and Practice

As stated in the *Intel* case, Section 1782 reflects an almost one hundred and fifty (150) year policy of "federal-court assistance in gathering evidence for use in foreign tribunals."[31] While this policy was originally "limited to proceedings in which a foreign sovereign was a party or had an interest", it subsequently underwent some changes, increasing the scope of assistance in producing evidence according to the statute. For instance, in 1958, "having recognized '[t]he extensive increase in … international, commercial, and financial transactions … and the resultant disputes' that 'involv[ed] both individuals and governments,' (…), Congress further expanded the scope of section 1782(a) to 'improve the assistance that it had previously afforded.' *Servotronics, Inc. v. The Boeing Co.*, 954 F.3d 209, 213 (4th Cir. 2020). That process – led by Professor Hans Smit and the Commission on International Rules of Judicial Procedure – lasted six years and resulted in a 'complete revision of § 1782.' *Intel*, 542 U.S. at 248. Ultimately, the 1964 amendments to section 1782(a) 'increas[ed] international cooperation by providing U.S. assistance in resolving disputes before not only foreign *courts* but before all foreign and international *tribunals*.' *Servotronics*, 954 F.3d at 213 (emphasis in original); S. Rep. No. 88–1580, at 3782 (1964), as reprinted in 1964 U.S.C.C.A.N. 3782 ('1964 Senate Report') (explaining that the amendments' purpose was to 'improve U.S. judicial procedures for … [o]btaining evidence in the United States in connection with proceedings before foreign and international tribunals.')". And all that led to the statement in one of the briefs introduced by *amici curiae*, that "the revised section 1782(a) gave U.S. federal courts the broad authority to provide evidentiary assistance to any 'foreign or international tribunal.' Such 'tribunals' undoubtedly include commercial arbitral tribunals."[32]

Accordingly, legal scholars argued, as *amici curiae*, that "Section 1782 permits, but does not require, U.S. federal district courts to order discovery 'for use in a proceeding in a foreign or international tribunal.' 28 U.S.C. § 1782(a)." Since the 1964 amendment, the U.S. Congress has deliberately used terms of great vagueness without making any distinction or creating any exception concerning arbitral tribunals. Indeed, "The text shows that Congress chose the capacious term 'tribunal,' which unambiguously encompasses adjudicatory bodies. The history shows that Congress removed a previous statutory requirement that a tribunal be established by a government when it amended Section 1782

31 *Intel Corp. v. Advanced Micro Devices, Inc.*, 542 U.S. 241 (2004).

32 See Brief of Federal Arbitration, Inc. (FEDARB) as *amicus curiae* in support of Respondent, pp. 4–5.

in 1964. Nor have those courts that distinguish between international commercial arbitral tribunals and international investor-State tribunals advanced any principled policy justification for doing so." Moreover, it was argued that when ruling *Intel* case, the Supreme Court would have concluded that the term "foreign or international court" should be interpreted broadly.[33]

It is interesting to note that the Supreme Court did not address the argument raised by the International Court of Arbitration of the International Chamber of Commerce (ICC Court) and the United States Council for International Business,[34] according to which the use of Section 1782 in international commercial arbitrations could impair the autonomy enjoyed by those tribunals, which would have the power to determine which evidence should be produced, and would be the most appropriate forum to assess any discovery request.[35] However, there would be no risk of such undue interference because the admissibility and especially the assessment of evidence fall to the arbitral tribunal. Furthermore, in any case, the parties may ask the arbitral tribunal to decide on the possibility of direct production of evidence by means of Section 1782 – in the same way as in a case before a state or federal court, which autonomy is not in doubt when it comes to the application for discovery based on Section 1782. In these scenarios, producing evidence based on the American statute could seem unnecessary, either because the arbitral tribunal would have already denied the production request or the evidence could be obtained directly by the arbitral tribunal, by itself or by the assistance of some other authority, anticipating the possible examination of needlessness or uselessness that would be made by a U.S. Court to which discovery was required.

In this regard, it was already stated that "There is no doubt that arbitrators are the masters of arbitration proceedings. Their adjudicatory authority stems

33 See Brief *amici curiae* of George A. Bermann, Robert H. Smit, D. Brian King, Ruth Teitelbaum, and Lucas Bento in support of Respondents Luxshare, Ltd. and the Fund for the Protection of Investors' Rights in Foreign States, pp. 4–7.

34 One of the authors of this commentary had the opportunity to affirm, together with another legal scholar, that "After reading Justice Barrett's opinion in the consolidated case, one can easily say that the Court did not address all the issues related to Section 1782, at least not all the issues presented by the parties and *amici curiae*. It targeted the plain language and the history of the statute, and also comity. Not a word was directed to policy concerns. Because of that, we believe that these concerns remain of practical and academic interest." (see Gustavo Favero Vaughn; Flávio Luiz Yarshell. "Two reasons why Section 18792 is pro-arbitration", in *Revista Brasileira de Arbitragem*, v. XIX, n. 75, July-Sept./2022, pp. 73–74).

35 See Brief of the International Court of Arbitration of the International Chamber of Commerce (ICC Court) and the United States Council for International Business *amici curiae* in support of neither party, pp. 12–17.

from the parties' autonomy, who agree to arbitrate certain disputes in a contract (commonly referred to as an arbitration agreement). Arbitrators are not only entitled to adjudicate disputes, but they are also responsible for conducting and managing the arbitration as per the procedure the parties agree upon. In fact, arbitrators must prepare the case for their award, and of course this preparation entails the taking of evidence. Like any adjudicator, arbitrators decide whether a piece of evidence is admissible and material to the case. In assessing the admissibility and materiality of the evidence, arbitrators consider the arbitration rules and laws applicable to the dispute, as well as any procedural arrangements parties may have agreed upon in advance. Entertaining a Section 1782 application available to international commercial arbitration should not change anything in this regard. There is no such a thing as 'compulsory disclosure of evidence' under Section 1782. The statute does not compel a U.S. district court to grant every discovery application. As the Supreme Court observed in Intel, '§1782(a) authorizes, but does not require, discovery assistance'. U.S. district courts can, but not necessarily have to, grant Section 1782 applications, be it in aid of international litigation or arbitration. Courts have wide discretion to accept, deny, or even limit the scope of evidence gathering under Section 1782."[36]

From a different angle, the rejection of the production of evidence via Section 1782 is that it may, even if reflexively, negatively interfere in an arbitration. Imagine the example of an arbitral tribunal that is aware and in accordance with the request made by one of the parties before a U.S. Court precisely because the arbitrators believe that the evidence to be produced is admissible and may be useful. In this case, the rejection of the request by an American judge, if it does not make it impossible to obtain the proof, will bring a considerable additional burden of time and costs for this result to be obtained. Arbitrators will need to ask for U.S. courts to cooperate by a rogatory letter. In this case, the autonomy of the arbitral tribunal is not affronted because the request was granted but precisely because the evidence that the arbitral tribunal understood should be produced was rejected.

The argument that discovery obtained via Section 1782 could be broader than that allowed for domestic arbitrations, given the limits of FAA regulation, does not seem logical: domestic arbitrations are not being discussed. Therefore, unless the parties had chosen the FAA as the applicable law, it would not apply in any way. Ultimately, the decision equates international and domestic

36 See Gustavo Favero Vaughn; Flávio Luiz Yarshell. "Two reasons why Section 18792 is pro-arbitration", in *Revista Brasileira de Arbitragem*, v. XIX, n. 75, 2022, pp. 81–82.

arbitrations, as if those were subject to a limit that the law imposes – as far as we know, in a valid way – on these. As it has already been said, when deciding a claim found in Section 1782, a U.S. court has the power to assess whether the request should be granted. However, this control does not go through the extent that discovery may have in the arbitration related to the request – for which, once again, the acquiescence of the arbitral tribunal may be a relevant fact in order to allow the cooperation of the U.S. courts.

Ultimately, despite the criticism that can be made, given to what has been decided, it remains to determine to what extent the arbitration practice is or can be affected in the U.S. On this, some topics can be raised.

Indeed, the Supreme Court's decision ended any possibility of using Section 1782 to obtain, through discovery, evidence that could be used before private (or commercial) arbitration tribunals. This conclusion should be especially relevant for cases that fall under the competence of the Fourth and Sixth Circuits, which have been granting the requests made in this regard. Otherwise, nothing should change regarding the Second, Fifth and Seventh Circuits as such courts had not been granting discovery orders under the statute.

Nevertheless, there still seems to be doubt as to whether a commercial arbitral tribunal could be constituted under laws that guarantee some governmental or intergovernmental authority – a premise adopted by the Supreme Court to deny assistance.[37] In the context of the opinion, it is unclear to what extent the U.S. courts would be free to interpret – differently – the rules of another sovereign State.

In other words, on the one hand, the Supreme Court denied that an arbitral tribunal could be qualified as governmental if the laws of the country provided for the arbitration proceedings or for the effectiveness of the arbitration agreements. On the other hand, the opinion said nothing about cases in which the local law expressly equates the authority of state or federal courts and arbitration tribunals, to the point of establishing that the decisions of one and the other have the same effectiveness and authority.

This can be illustrated by the Brazilian Arbitration Act, according to which, "By performing their service, or as a result thereof, the arbitrators shall be considered comparable to public officials for the purpose of criminal law" (Article

37 "In sum, we hold that §1782 requires a 'foreign or international tribunal' to be governmental or intergovernmental. Thus, a 'foreign tribunal' is one that exercises governmental authority conferred by a single nation, and an 'international tribunal' is one that exercises governmental authority conferred by two or more nations. Private adjudicatory bodies do not fall within § 1782" (*ZF Automotive, Inc. v. Luxshare, Ltd.* and *AlixPartners, LLP v. Fund for Protection of Investors' Rights in Foreign States*, 596 U.S. __ (2022)).

17); and, "An arbitrator is the judge in fact and in law, and his award is not subject to appeal or recognition by judicial court" (Article 18).

In this case, it is not just about legal regulation of the arbitration proceedings or the implementation of arbitration agreements but about equality between state courts and arbitral tribunals[38] – of course, without prejudice to the elements that distinguish them. All this, finally, suggests that the assistance founded in Section 1782 could be possible in relation to a private arbitral tribunal constituted under Brazilian law.

In this same context, it may be possible to admit assistance founded in Section 1782 by indirect means – without confronting the grounds of the Supreme Court opinion – when an arbitral tribunal requests a state or federal court to cooperate in obtaining evidence situated in a foreign country, and in particular in the United States. In such cases, although the initiative to produce evidence originates in a private body, the acquiescence of the court to give its governmental authority causes the request to be covered by the latter as if it were for any judicial process (litigation). Once again, Brazilian law could illustrate this possibility in cases where the arbitral tribunal requested, via "arbitral letter", the support of a state court to obtain evidence outside the scope of the power of the arbitrators.[39]

Regarding arbitrations related to arbitral tribunals involving different sovereign States, the Supreme Court does not seem to have resolved another relevant question. That is, although the Supreme Court has held that the *ad hoc* arbitral tribunal of AlixPartners case does not qualify as a "foreign or international tribunal", the decision did not address the possibility of other investment arbitral tribunals being qualified as governmental or intergovernmental, that is, imbued with governmental authority.[40]

---

38 On equality between judges and arbitrators under Brazilian law, see: Carlos Alberto Carmona. *Arbitragem e processo: um comentário à Lei n. 9.307/96*, 4th ed., São Paulo, Atlas, 2023, pp. 20–21 e 270–282; Cândido Rangel Dinamarco. *O processo arbitral*, 2nd ed., Curitiba, EDC, 2022, pp. 45–48 e 55–60; Flávio Luiz Yarshell. *Curso de direito processual civil*, 2nd ed., São Paulo, Marcial Pons, 2020, pp. 197–198.

39 In this sense, see the provisions of Article 22-C of the Brazilian Arbitration Act: "Art. 22-C. An arbitrator or the arbitral tribunal may issue an arbitration letter so that the judicial court offers assistance or imposes compliance, in the area of their territorial jurisdiction, of an act requested by the arbitrator. Sole paragraph. In compliance with the arbitration letter, the respective court proceedings will be under seal, as long as the confidentiality set forth in the arbitration is verified."

40 Some authorities have already expressed their opposition to the reasoning adopted (see George A. Bermann "*ZF Automotive*: Predictable Outcome, Lackluster Reasoning", in *Trasnational Litigation Blog*, published on June 14, 2022. Available in: https://tlblog.org/zf-automotive-predictable-outcome-lackluster-reasoning/. Accessed on September 10,

As it was already stated, "Because the Court declined to adopt a bright-line rule that arbitral tribunals in public international law arbitrations cannot constitute a 'foreign or international tribunal' under Section 1782, and instead found that 'the inquiry is whether those [governmental] features and other evidence establish the intent of the relevant nations to imbue the body in question with governmental authority,' parties in investor-State cases may still pursue Section 1782 discovery in the United States if there are cognizable arguments that the arbitral tribunal exercises governmental authority conferred by one or multiple nations."[41]

This can be illustrated by the hypothesis that arbitration is constituted under the rules of the Convention on the Settlement of Investment Disputes Between States and Nationals of Other States (ICSID Convention), of which one hundred and sixty-five (165) States are signatories or contractors.[42]

Article 21 of the ICSID Convention provides that, "The Chairman, the members of the Administrative Council, persons acting as conciliators or arbitrators or members of a Committee appointed pursuant to paragraph (3) of Article 52, and the officers and employees of the Secretariat (a) shall enjoy immunity from legal process with respect to acts performed by them in the exercise of their functions, except when the Centre waives this immunity; (b) not being local nationals, shall enjoy the same immunities from immigration restrictions, alien registration requirements and national service obligations, the same facilities as regards exchange restrictions and the same treatment in respect of travelling facilities as are accorded by Contracting States to the representatives, officials and employees of comparable rank of other Contracting States". It is a typical right usually granted only to sovereign states and their representatives.

---

2023), as well as to the lack of clarity of the scope of the opinion in relation to investment arbitrations (see Michael Feit; Louis Christe. "The U.S. Supreme Court closes the door on discovery in support of international commercial arbitration", in *Lexology*, published on June 20, 2022. Available in: https://www.lexology.com/library/detail.aspx?g=9d2e2d38-459d-4645-ae38-cb20a906f65a. Accessed on September 10, 2023).

41 See Ari D. MacKinnon; Rüdiger Harms; Katie L. Gonzalez; Till Hackstein. "ZF Automotive v. Luxshare – Opinion of the Supreme Court of the United States, 13 June 2022", in *JusMundi*, published on July 1, 2022, p. 10. Available in: https://jusmundi.com/en/document/pdf/publication/en-zf-automotive-v-luxshare-opinion-of-the-supreme-court-of-the-united-states-13-june-2022. Accessed on September 10, 2023.

42 For further information on signatory or contracting States, see: https://icsid.worldbank.org/about/member-states/database-of-member-states. Accessed on September 10, 2023.

Similarly, ICSID Convention had created "a self-contained system whereby resulting awards are not subject to any remedies except those provided for in the Convention and are automatically enforceable within contracting states as if they were final judgments of the courts in those states. Further, the ICSID system is the result of a multilateral treaty creating a permanent institution for investor-state dispute resolution in which contracting states play a significant role, including by participating in an Administrative Council that meets annually and by designating people to serve on ICSID panels of arbitrators and conciliators"[43] – characteristics that could be typically attributed to governmental or intergovernmental bodies.

In this context of a potential gap, the Supreme Court may have to rule on whether arbitral tribunals constituted under other investment arbitration rules, such as ICSID Convention, might be qualified as international and imbued with governmental or intergovernmental authority under Section 1782.[44]

## 5 Conclusions

As one of the authors of this comment had the opportunity to, in co-authorship, state, "Arbitration and litigation proceedings are different creatures in many ways. However, they do have one critical feature in common: in both arbitration and litigation, adjudicators aim to resolve the dispute before them in a fair and just manner according to the applicable law, and to that end, they rely on the facts and evidence presented by the parties. Evidence production is thus fundamental to resolving any sort of dispute, and this remains true for arbitration, regardless of cultural differences. In this sense, the possibility of discovery under Section 1782 should not necessarily be seen as a burdensome tool for international arbitration practitioners, including in private disputes. Rather, it

43 See Ed Mullins; William W. Russel; James P. Duffy IV; Steven Cooper; Rebeca E. Mosquera. "Section 1782 no longer a discovery tool in aid of private international arbitrations; ICSID in play?", published on June 28, 2022. Available in: https://www.reedsmith.com/de/perspectives/2022/06/section-1782-no-longer-a-discovery-tool. Accessed on September 10, 2023.

44 At the time this article was written, at least two decisions, one from the Eastern District of New York and the other from the Southern District of New York, considered that Section 1782 application would not be admissible in relation to investment arbitration (investor-state) conducted under the ICSID Convention rules (cf. *In re Alpene* 2022 WL 15497008 (Oct. 27, 2022) e *In Re: Application of Webuild S.p.A. and Sacyr S.A.* 2022 WL 17807321 (Dec. 19, 2022), respectively).

should be seen as an additional and important tool for fact-finding".[45] For no other reason, experience shows that Section 1782 has been used as a relevant tool in the production of evidence based in the United States for the benefit of international arbitrations.

However, the examination of the use of this measure in connection with international arbitration seems to be at least partially overcome. The Supreme Court had concluded that the request for discovery would not be admissible when the adjudicatory body is not considered a governmental or intergovernmental authority, especially those relating to international commercial arbitrations.

Nevertheless, it is not clear to what extent the decision will reach arbitration courts constituted under foreign laws or international treaties that qualify them as bodies imbued with governmental or intergovernmental power or authority, as could be said with regard to arbitration panels created under the Brazilian Arbitration Law or the ICSID Convention; or in cases where the request for assistance, although arising in an arbitration process, is also determined by a state court.

---

45 See Gustavo Favero Vaughn; Flávio Luiz Yarshell. "Two reasons why Section 18792 is pro-arbitration", in *Revista Brasileira de Arbitragem*, v. XIX, n. 75, 2022, p. 93.

CHAPTER 32

# *Morgan v Sundance, Inc.* (2022)

*Liz Snodgrass and Laura França Pereira*

## 1 Introduction

*Morgan v. Sundance, Inc.* arose out of a dispute regarding the requirements adopted by federal courts to find a waiver of a party's arbitration rights. Over the years, federal courts had disagreed on whether a showing that a party "prejudiced the other party by its inconsistent actions"—such as litigating the underlying merits of a dispute—was a condition for finding that its right to stay litigation or compel arbitration under the Federal Arbitration Act (FAA) had been waived.[1] Until *Morgan v. Sundance, Inc.*, nine out of the twelve U.S. circuit courts applied an Eighth Circuit precedent enforcing that prejudice requirement based on a "federal policy favoring arbitration,"[2] while two circuits rejected such a requirement.[3]

In *Morgan v. Sundance, Inc.*, the Supreme Court granted certiorari to resolve that circuit split. In its May 2022 ruling, the Court sided with the minority of the circuits in finding that the federal rule of waiver does not include a prejudice requirement and that courts may not fabricate a new procedural rule based on the FAA's policy favoring arbitration. In doing so, the Supreme Court made clear that federal courts may not create "arbitration-preferring procedural rules"[4] premised on a "'liberal national policy favoring arbitration'"[5]—which, according to the Court, was devised essentially "to make 'arbitration agreements as enforceable as other contracts, but not more so.'"[6]

1 Morgan v. Sundance, Inc., 596 U.S. 411 (2022) (citing Erdman Co. v. Phoenix Land & Acquisition, LLC, 650 F.3d 1115, 1117 (8th Cir. 2011)).

2 *Morgan*, 596 U.S. at 416 (citing *Erdman*, 650 F.3d at 1120).

3 *Morgan*, 596 U.S. at 416.

4 *Morgan*, 596 U.S. at 418.

5 *Morgan*, 596 U.S. at 418 (citing Carolina Throwing Co. v. S & E Novelty Corp., 442 F.2d 329, 331 (4th Cir. 1971) (*per curiam*)).

6 *Morgan*, 596 U.S. at 418 (citing Prima Paint Corp. v. Flood & Conklin Mfg. Co., 388 U.S. 395, 404, n.12 (1967)).

 | DOI:10.1163/9789004715820_033

## 2 The Case

### 2.1 *Background of the Case*

The petitioner, Robyn Morgan, worked as an hourly employee at a Taco Bell franchise owed by Sundance, Inc., a company holding more than 150 Taco Bell's franchises in the U.S. When entering an employment relationship with Taco Bell, Morgan agreed to "'use confidential binding arbitration" to resolve any employment-related dispute.[7]

Notwithstanding her consent to arbitration, in September 2018, Morgan filed a nationwide collective action in federal court (on behalf of herself and all similarly situated hourly employees of other Taco Bell franchises) against Sundance alleging violations of the Fair Labor Standards Act.[8] Under that statute, employees working more than 40 hours in a week must receive overtime payment.[9] According to Morgan, Sundance had a policy of recording hours worked in one week as having been worked in another, so that the total number of hours in any given week would never exceed 40 hours.[10] For employees who generally worked 40 hours a week, Sundance's policy meant that they were simply never paid for any overtime hours, as those could not be registered in another week.[11] Morgan also alleged that, sometimes, Sundance would instruct its employees to work overtime off the clock so that the hours were never recorded and they were never paid for them.[12] Morgan claimed that, by enforcing such policies, Sundance was routinely violating the Fair Labor Standards Act.[13]

Upon receiving notice of Morgan's collective action, Sundance began to defend itself in the courts as if no arbitration agreement existed.[14] First, Sundance filed a motion to dismiss claiming that Morgan's lawsuit was duplicative of a collective action previously filed by another Taco Bell employee.[15] After Sundance's motion to dismiss was denied, the company answered Morgan's complaint by asserting various affirmative defenses, none of which

---

7 *Morgan*, 596 U.S. at 414.

8 *Morgan*, 596 U.S. at 414; Brief for Petitioner at 8, Morgan v. Sundance, Inc., 596 U.S. 411 (2022) (No. 21–328).

9 29 U.S.C. § 207(a).

10 *Morgan*, 596 U.S. at 414; Brief for Petitioner at 8, Morgan v. Sundance, Inc., 596 U.S. 411 (2022) (No. 21–328).

11 Brief for Petitioner at 8, Morgan v. Sundance, Inc., 596 U.S. 411 (2022) (No. 21–328).

12 Brief for Petitioner at 8–9, Morgan v. Sundance, Inc., 596 U.S. 411 (2022) (No. 21–328).

13 Brief for Petitioner at 9, Morgan v. Sundance, Inc., 596 U.S. 411 (2022) (No. 21–328).

14 *Morgan*, 596 U.S. at 414.

15 *Morgan*, 596 U.S. at 414.

ever invoked the existence of an arbitration agreement.[16] Subsequently, in April 2019, Sundance and the plaintiffs in both collective actions attempted to settle the dispute through a class-wide mediation, which was ultimately successful in relation to the other collective action, but failed as to Morgan's.[17]

It was only after this failed mediation attempt that, in May 2019, Sundance first invoked the arbitration agreement, moving to stay litigation and compel arbitration under Sections 3 and 4 of the FAA.[18] Given that Sundance first invoked the arbitration agreement almost eight months after Morgan's action had been filed, Morgan opposed Sundance's motion arguing that any right that Sundance might have had to compel arbitration had been waived because it had engaged in litigation for too long.[19] In response, Sundance argued that it asserted its rights to arbitrate as soon as it became clear that arbitration would proceed on a bilateral (rather than collective) basis, consistent with the 2019 Supreme Court decision in *Lamps Plus, Inc. v. Varela*.[20]

In deciding whether Sundance had waived its right to arbitration, the district court applied the Eighth Circuit's tripartite test, under which a party waives such a right if (i) it knew of an existing right to arbitrate; (ii) acted inconsistently with that right; and (iii) prejudiced the other party by its inconsistent actions—the latter being a waiver requirement that the Eighth Circuit applied in the arbitration context because of the "federal policy favoring arbitration."[21] The district court found all three requirements to be met, given that (i) it was undisputed that Sundance knew of an existing right to arbitrate; (ii) Sundance acted inconsistently with such right by waiting for eight months to assert it for the first time while litigating on the merits with Morgan; and (iii) Morgan was prejudiced by spending time and resources litigating against Sundance, including by defending against Sundance's motion to dismiss and later preparing for a class-wide mediation.[22]

---

16 *Morgan*, 596 U.S. at 414.

17 *Morgan*, 596 U.S. at 414; Brief for Petitioner at 10, Morgan v. Sundance, Inc., 596 U.S. 411 (2022) (No. 21–328).

18 *Morgan*, 596 U.S. at 415; Brief for Petitioner at 10, Morgan v. Sundance, Inc., 596 U.S. 411 (2022) (No. 21–328).

19 *Morgan*, 596 U.S. at 415; Brief for Petitioner at 11, Morgan v. Sundance, Inc., 596 U.S. 411 (2022) (No. 21–328).

20 *Morgan*, 596 U.S. at 415.

21 *Morgan*, 596 U.S. at 415 (citing *Erdman*, 650 F.3d at 1120); Brief for Petitioner at 11, Morgan v. Sundance, Inc., 596 U.S. 411 (2022) (No. 21–328) (citing Lewallen v. Green Tree Servicing, LLC, 487 F.3d 1085 (8th Cir. 2007)).

22 Brief for Petitioner at 11, Morgan v. Sundance, Inc., 596 U.S. 411 (2022) (No. 21–328).

Sundance appealed from the district court's decision and the Eighth Circuit reversed it, with the majority finding that a waiver of Sundance's arbitration rights had not been established and sending Morgan's case to arbitration.[23] According to the majority, even if Sundance's conduct was inconsistent with its right to arbitrate, it did not materially prejudice Morgan because the parties had not yet begun formal discovery nor engaged in discussing the merits of Morgan's claims, meaning that she would not have to duplicate efforts in arbitral proceedings.[24] Judge Colloton dissented, raising doubts about the adoption of the Eighth Circuit's prejudice requirement—a "debatable prerequisite," in his words—in the arbitration context, including because in ordinary contract law a showing of prejudice is not required for a waiver to be established.[25]

The dissent reflected the approach to waiver of the right to arbitrate taken by the D.C. Circuit and the Seventh Circuit. In imposing a prejudice requirement, the Eighth Circuit majority reflected the approach taken in all of the remaining circuit courts.

The Supreme Court granted certiorari to resolve that circuit split and decide whether, in the arbitration context and on the basis of a federal policy favoring arbitration, federal courts may apply an arbitration-specific waiver rule demanding a showing of prejudice.

### 2.2 *Issues and Parties' Allegations*

The Supreme Court made clear that, although in their briefs the parties disagreed about a myriad of issues—including the role of state law in determining when a party's litigation conduct leads to a loss of a right to arbitrate, and whether the inquiry applied to rules of waiver, forfeiture, estoppel, laches, or procedural timeliness—it would limit its ruling in *Morgan v. Sundance, Inc.* to a single issue, responsive to the predominant analysis of the Eighth Circuit.[26] Given that the Eighth Circuit had generally resolved similar cases as a matter of federal law and using the "waiver" terminology, the Court assumed for purposes of its ruling that the Eighth Circuit was right in doing so (without deciding on this point), and considered in its decision the following single issue arising from the Eighth Circuit's reasoning: whether federal courts are entitled

23 *Morgan*, 596 U.S. at 415; Brief for Petitioner at 11–12, Morgan v. Sundance, Inc., 596 U.S. 411 (2022) (No. 21–328).

24 *Morgan*, 596 U.S. at 415; Brief for Petitioner at 12, Morgan v. Sundance, Inc., 596 U.S. 411 (2022) (No. 21–328).

25 *Morgan*, 596 U.S. at 415–416; Brief for Petitioner at 12–13, Morgan v. Sundance, Inc., 596 U.S. 411 (2022) (No. 21–328).

26 *Morgan*, 596 U.S. at 416–417.

to "create arbitration-specific variants of federal procedural rules, like those concerning waiver, based on the FAA's 'policy favoring arbitration.'"[27]

Regarding this specific issue, Morgan argued that prejudice was not required for waivers of contractual rights outside the arbitration context and, as such, federal courts needed to justify such a departure from ordinary contract law on the basis of the FAA and federal rulings interpreting it.[28] However, according to Morgan, the imposition of a prejudice requirement for establishing a waiver of arbitration rights was supported by neither the plain text nor the structure of the FAA.[29] To the contrary, Morgan claimed, *inter alia*, that the imposition of a prejudice requirement was opposed to the FAA's equal-treatment principle, set out in its Section 2, which required courts to place arbitration agreements on an equal footing with other types of contracts.[30] In arguing that the FAA did not raise arbitration agreements above other types of contracts, and did not authorize applying a more rigorous standard for arbitration rights in comparison to other contractual rights, Morgan also noted that the Supreme Court itself had already ruled that courts should apply generally-applicable contract law to arbitration agreements, being prohibited from creating rules only applicable to arbitration agreements.[31] Finally, Morgan claimed that the prejudice requirement also had an impact on some of arbitration's key advantages, such as speed and efficiency, given that, by raising the burden of proof for the party asserting waiver, federal courts incentivized "the same sort of gamesmanship that Congress enacted the FAA to prevent" (such as "pre-arbitration judicial skirmishes" and litigation-related delays "by allowing parties to test judicial water before seeking to arbitrate").[32]

Sundance, on the other hand, argued that the issue was governed by Section 3 of the FAA, not Section 2, as the former specifically governs motions to stay

27 *Morgan*, 596 U.S. at 417.

28 Brief for Petitioner at 31–32, Morgan v. Sundance, Inc., 596 U.S. 411 (2022) (No. 21–328).

29 Brief for Petitioner at 32–45, Morgan v. Sundance, Inc., 596 U.S. 411 (2022) (No. 21–328).

30 Brief for Petitioner at 33–37, Morgan v. Sundance, Inc., 596 U.S. 411 (2022) (No. 21–328) (citing AT&T Mobility LLC v. Concepcion, 563 U.S. 333, 339 (2011)). Section 2 of the FAA provides that "[a] written provision in any maritime transaction or a contract evidencing a transaction involving commerce to settle by arbitration a controversy thereafter arising out of such contract or transaction, or the refusal to perform the whole or any part thereof, or an agreement in writing to submit to arbitration an existing controversy arising out of such a contract, transaction, or refusal, shall be valid, irrevocable, and enforceable, save upon such grounds as exist at law or in equity for the revocation of any contract or as otherwise provided in chapter 4."

31 Brief for Petitioner at 35–36, Morgan v. Sundance, Inc., 596 U.S. 411 (2022) (No. 21–328) (citing, e.g., DIRECTV, Inc. v. Imburgia, 577 U.S. 47, 54–58 (2015)).

32 Brief for Petitioner at 47, Morgan v. Sundance, Inc., 596 U.S. 411 (2022) (No. 21–328).

litigation and compel arbitration.[33] According to Sundance, FAA's Section 3 provides a pro-arbitration direction to courts, mandating them to stay litigation ("shall") unless the party seeking to enforce the arbitration agreement is "in default"[34] (which, in the absence of a definition in the FAA's text, Sundance defined as a violation of a clear deadline or legal rule or, at least, as causing prejudice to the other side).[35] Sundance argued that it was clear that it was not "in default" within the meaning of Section 3—also given that Morgan did not even claim a default under the parties' arbitration agreement or the applicable arbitration rules—and, therefore, Section 3 was sufficient for the Court to affirm the Eighth Circuit's ruling.[36] Sundance also noted that the same conclusion should be reached under Section 2 of the FAA, which, differently from what Morgan suggested, does not impose a strict equal-treatment rule and, like the rest of the FAA, embodies a pro-arbitration approach strongly favoring the enforcement of arbitration agreements.[37] In other words, Sundance's position was that "[a]s long as arbitration agreements are enforced at least as favorably as other contracts, Section 2 is not offended,"[38] meaning that Section 2 sets a floor, not a ceiling, which allows arbitration agreements to be treated more favorably than other types of contracts—consistently with the Court's reference to the "liberal policy favoring arbitration" in *AT&T Mobility LLC v. Concepcion*.[39] Finally, Sundance also refuted Morgan's argument that the prejudice requirement created perverse incentives against the FAA's purposes by encouraging tactical gamesmanship and delay.[40] Sundance argued not only that federal courts have incorporated anti-gamesmanship components into their prejudice inquiry (e.g., finding prejudice when parties have litigated for years, expending judicial resources while aiming to obtain information out

33 Brief for Respondent at 14–27, Morgan v. Sundance, Inc., 596 U.S. 411 (2022) (No. 21–328). Section 3 of the FAA provides that "[i]f any suit or proceeding be brought in any of the courts of the United States upon any issue referable to arbitration under an agreement in writing for such arbitration, the court in which such suit is pending, upon being satisfied that the issue involved in such suit or proceeding is referable to arbitration under such an agreement, shall on application of one of the parties stay the trial of the action until such arbitration has been had in accordance with the terms of the agreement, providing the applicant for the stay is not in default in proceeding with such arbitration."

34 Brief for Respondent at 15–18, Morgan v. Sundance, Inc., 596 U.S. 411 (2022) (No. 21–328).

35 Brief for Respondent at 19–27, Morgan v. Sundance, Inc., 596 U.S. 411 (2022) (No. 21–328).

36 Brief for Respondent at 14, 27, Morgan v. Sundance, Inc., 596 U.S. 411 (2022) (No. 21–328).

37 Brief for Respondent at 27–31, Morgan v. Sundance, Inc., 596 U.S. 411 (2022) (No. 21–328).

38 Brief for Respondent at 29, Morgan v. Sundance, Inc., 596 U.S. 411 (2022) (No. 21–328).

39 Brief for Respondent at 12, 29 Morgan v. Sundance, Inc., 596 U.S. 411 (2022) (No. 21–328) (citing *Concepcion*, 563 U.S. at 339).

40 Brief for Respondent at 41–49, Morgan v. Sundance, Inc., 596 U.S. 411 (2022) (No. 21–328).

the opposing party) but also that Morgan's argument was "vastly overinclusive as a means of combatting gamesmanship,"[41] as it denied arbitration rights to defendants who attempted to initially resolve disputes amicably or without expending material judicial or arbitral resources.[42]

### 2.3 *The Court's Opinion*

Justice Kagan delivered the unanimous opinion of the Court, ruling that federal courts cannot create arbitration-specific variants of federal procedural rules—like those concerning waiver—based on the FAA's policy favoring arbitration. The Court therefore found that the Eighth Circuit was "wrong to condition a waiver of the right to arbitrate on a showing of prejudice."[43]

The Court first analyzed the origins of that arbitration-specific waiver rule and its spread amongst circuit courts. According to the Court, in assessing waivers outside the arbitration context, federal courts are focused on the actions of the person holding the right that had been allegedly waived, and not on the effects that such actions had on the opposing party.[44] Therefore, in demanding proof of prejudice to the opposing party in order to find a waiver of arbitration rights, the Court confirmed that the Eighth Circuit applied a "rule found nowhere else," *i.e.*, a "bespoke rule of waiver for arbitration."[45] That arbitration-specific rule, according to the Court, traces back to a Second Circuit decision that (i) referred to "'an overriding federal policy favoring arbitration;'" and (ii) held that a waiver to arbitration rights was "not to be lightly inferred," so that a "mere delay" in seeking to stay litigation and compel arbitration was not enough "without some resultant prejudice."[46] This explains why over the years circuit courts have justified the adoption of that prejudice requirement based on a "'liberal national policy favoring arbitration.'"[47]

In clarifying the contents of "the FAA's 'policy favoring arbitration,'" however, the Court ruled that such a policy does not authorize federal courts to create arbitration-specific procedural rules.[48] According to the Court—and consistently with its previous decisions—the FAA's federal policy is "to make

41 Brief for Respondent at 45, Morgan v. Sundance, Inc., 596 U.S. 411 (2022) (No. 21–328).

42 Brief for Respondent at 41–49, Morgan v. Sundance, Inc., 596 U.S. 411 (2022) (No. 21-328).

43 *Morgan*, 596 U.S. at 417.

44 *Morgan*, 596 U.S. at 417.

45 *Morgan*, 596 U.S. at 417.

46 *Morgan*, 596 U.S. at 417 (citing Carcich v. Rederi A/B Nordie, 389 F.2d 692, 696 (C.A.2 1968)).

47 *Morgan*, 596 U.S. at 418.

48 *Morgan*, 596 U.S. at 418.

'arbitration agreements as enforceable as other contracts, *but not more so*.'"[49] This meant that the core of such policy is not to foster arbitration as such, but simply to neutralize hostility to it. And a court "may not devise novel rules to favor arbitration over litigation."[50] The Court also identified support for such a finding in the FAA's text, which in Section 6 gives a clear command to federal courts to apply "usual federal procedural rules" in applications under the statute—including motions to stay litigation or compel arbitration—and, consequently, bars the adoption of arbitration-specific procedural rules "to tilt the playing field in favor of (or against) arbitration."[51]

As a result, given that federal rules applicable to waiver do not include a prejudice requirement, the Court concluded that federal courts should not consider prejudice as a condition of finding that a party waived its arbitration rights by litigating for too long. In the case at hand, the Eighth Circuit's waiver inquiry should have focused on Sundance's conduct and whether it "knowingly relinquish[ed] the right to arbitrate by acting inconsistently with that right."[52] The Court, thus, vacated the court of appeals' judgment and remanded the case for the court to resolve that question (while also determining, if need be, whether a different procedural framework, such as forfeiture, would be appropriate).[53] The Court also made clear that its sole holding in *Morgan v. Sundance, Inc.* was that federal courts "may not make up a new procedural rule based on the FAA's 'policy favoring arbitration.'"[54] Nothing more, nothing less.

### 2.4 *Key Takeaways*

The practical effect of the decision is to lower the threshold for waiving the right to arbitrate: this can now be established without a showing that the other party was prejudiced by the conduct said to amount to a waiver. The decision does not speak to the question of whether Sundance's conduct constituted waiver—that issue was remanded—or otherwise change the test that is to be applied to show waiver.

The holding in *Morgan v. Sundance, Inc.* is notably narrow, but it signals the limit of the FAA's oft-invoked "policy favoring arbitration." This case establishes

---

49 *Morgan*, 596 U.S. at 418 (citing *Prima Paint*, 388 U.S. at 404, n.12) (emphasis added).

50 *Morgan*, 596 U.S. at 418.

51 *Morgan*, 596 U.S. at 419. Section 6 of the FAA provides that "[a]ny application to the court hereunder shall be made and heard in the manner provided by law for the making and hearing of motions, except as otherwise herein expressly provided."

52 *Morgan*, 596 U.S. at 419.

53 *Morgan*, 596 U.S. at 419.

54 *Morgan*, 596 U.S. at 419.

that this policy trumps both rules that uniquely disfavor arbitration agreements and also rules that subject arbitration agreements to uniquely favorable or protective treatment. In fact, it violates the FAA and its pro-arbitration policy for agreements to arbitrate to be subjected to special rules, whether those rules tend to promote arbitration or not. What the federal policy dictates is even-handed treatment of arbitration agreements.

## 3 Critical Analysis of the Opinion and How It Impacted the U.S. Arbitration Law and Practice

Outside the waiver context, this judgment may have little direct impact. Indirectly, it would rein in arguments that the federal pro-arbitration policy goes beyond ensuring that arbitration agreements are not subjected to uniquely unfavorable or onerous rules.

## 4 Conclusion

One can read *Morgan v. Sundance, Inc.* as restricting the scope of the federal policy favoring arbitration. The ruling is, however, perhaps better understood as confirming that the purpose and effect of this policy is not to favor arbitration as such over other methods of dispute resolution, but to invalidate rules that would uniquely disfavor arbitration agreements and make them harder to enforce than other contracts. That is continuous with the authorities that recognized the policy in the first place, and no more than a juridical "level playing field" is required to allow the effective enforcement of arbitration agreements.

CHAPTER 33

# *Viking River Cruises, Inc. v. Moriana* (2022)

*Eduardo Damião Gonçalves, Arthur Gonzalez Cronemberger Parente and Laura Lambert da Costa*

## 1 Introduction

The Supreme Court has consistently upheld the enforceability of arbitration agreements even when doing so would mean that consumers and employees waive their right to participate in class action lawsuits or class arbitrations. In *AT&T Mobility LLC v. Concepcion*, for example, the Court stressed that state laws denying enforcement to arbitration agreements with class arbitration waivers are preempted by the Federal Arbitration Act ("FAA") and its substantive federal policy in favor of arbitration.[1]

As the following Sections will show, the Supreme Court's decision in *Viking River Cruises, Inc. v. Moriana* has reinforced the Court's preference to individualized arbitration over not only class actions and class arbitrations, but also over other types of high-stakes multi-claim proceedings.

## 2 Case Overview

### 2.1 *Background of the Case*

The California legislature enacted the Labor Code Private Attorneys General Act ("PAGA") to address a perceived deficit in the enforcement of the State's Labor Code.[2] Because enforcement agencies did not have enough resources to adequately enforce California's labor laws, PAGA authorized any "aggrieved employee" to initiate an action against a former employer to obtain civil penalties that previously could have been recovered only by the State.[3]

PAGA liability can be predicated on labor law violations not suffered by the employee plaintiff, since a plaintiff "who alleges he or she suffered a single violation is entitled to use that violation as a gateway to assert a potentially

1 *AT&T Mobility LLC v. Concepcion*, 563 U.S. 333 (2011).
2 *Viking River Cruises, Inc. v. Moriana*, 596 U.S. _, 142 S. Ct. 1906, 1913 (2022).
3 *Id.* at 1913–1914.

 DOI:10.1163/9789004715820_034

limitless number of other violations as predicates for liability."[4] If the PAGA action is successful, California's Labor and Workforce Development Agency ("LWDA") is entitled to 75 percent of the award, while the remaining 25 percent is distributed among the employees affected by the violations at issue.[5]

Thus, as the Supreme Court noted, California precedents hold that a PAGA suit is a "representative action" in which the employee plaintiff sues as an "agent or proxy" of the State[6] and is allowed to join multiple claims against the employer defendant in a single action.[7] And according to the California Supreme Court's decision in *Iskanian v. CLS Transportation Los Angeles, LLC*: (i) categorical waivers of PAGA standing to bring PAGA claims in a judicial or arbitral forum are contrary to state policy; and (ii) agreements to separately arbitrate or litigate only the "individual" PAGA claims arising from the Labor Code violations allegedly suffered by the employee plaintiff are invalid, since resolving victim-specific claims in separate proceedings does not serve the deterrent purpose of PAGA.[8]

In the case at hand, Angie Moriana was a former sales representative employed by Viking River Cruises, Inc. ("Viking"), a company that offers ocean and river cruises around the world.[9] When Moriana was hired, the parties executed an agreement to arbitrate any dispute arising out of her employment.[10] According to the Supreme Court:

> The [arbitration] agreement contained a 'Class Action Waiver' providing that in any arbitral proceeding, the parties could not bring any dispute as a class, collective, or representative PAGA action. It also contained a severability clause specifying that if the waiver was found invalid, any class, collective, representative, or PAGA action would presumptively be litigated in Court. But under that severability clause, if any 'portion' of the waiver remained valid, it would be 'enforced in arbitration.'[11]

After leaving her position with Viking, Moriana filed a PAGA action against Viking in California Court, claiming a wide array of labor law violations

4 *Id.* at 1915.
5 *Id.* at 1914.
6 *Id.*
7 *Id.* at 1915.
8 *Id.* at 1916–1917.
9 *Id.* at 1915–1916.
10 *Id.* at 1916.
11 *Id.*

allegedly sustained either by her or by other employees.[12] Viking moved to compel arbitration of Moriana's individual PAGA claim – i.e., the claim arising from the Labor Code violation allegedly suffered by Moriana – and dismiss the claims based on violations allegedly suffered by other employees.[13]

Relying on *Iskanian,* the trial Court denied Viking's motion, and the California Court of Appeals affirmed,[14] holding that: (i) the representative action waiver in the arbitration agreement between Moriana and Viking is invalid insofar as it is construed as a wholesale waiver of PAGA standing; and (ii) even if the waiver is construed as applying only to Moriana's ability to arbitrate PAGA claims arising from violations not suffered by her, the severability clause does not allow arbitration of Moriana's individual PAGA claim alone because *Iskanian* prohibits dividing a PAGA action into constituent claims.[15]

On Viking's appeal, the Supreme Court reversed the California Court of Appeals' judgment and remanded the case for further proceedings.[16]

### 2.2 *Issue and Parties' Allegations*

The Supreme Court granted certiorari to decide "whether the Federal Arbitration Act (FAA), 9 U.S.C. §1 *et seq*., preempts a rule of California law [*Iskanian*] that invalidates contractual waivers of the right to assert representative claims under California's Labor Code Private Attorneys General Act of 2004."[17]

Petitioner Viking argued that the *Iskanian* rule is preempted because the *Concepcion* line of cases invalidating prohibitions on class arbitration waivers should also apply to PAGA waivers.[18] In *Concepcion,* the Court had held that "[t]he "'shift from bilateral arbitration to class-action arbitration'" mandates procedural changes that are inconsistent with the individualized and informal mode of arbitration contemplated by the FAA."[19] According to Viking, PAGA actions also deviate from the individualized and informal mode of arbitration prototype protected by the FAA because they involve litigation or arbitration on behalf of an absent principal and, thus, are not "bilateral."[20] Consequently, Viking contended that *Iskanian*'s prohibition on PAGA waivers – like the state

12 *Id.*
13 *Id.*
14 *Id.*
15 *Id.* at 1916–1917.
16 *Id.* at 1925.
17 *Id.* at 1913.
18 *Id.* at 1918.
19 *Id.*
20 *Id.* at 1921–1922.

law prohibitions on class arbitration waivers – is inconsistent with the FAA because it requires parties either to arbitrate in a format at odds with arbitration's traditional form or forego arbitration altogether.[21]

Respondent Moriana, on the other hand, argued that the *Iskanian* rule is not preempted for the following reasons: (i) PAGA creates a substantive cause of action and the Supreme Court's FAA precedents do not invalidate state laws prohibiting waivers of substantive rights; and (ii) the *Concepcion* line of cases does not apply because PAGA actions are different from class proceedings, since the multiple predicate violations for PAGA liability do not constitute distinct claims belonging to distinct individuals.[22]

### 2.3 *The Court's Opinion*

In an 8-1 ruling,[23] the Supreme Court held that the FAA does preempt *Iskanian* insofar as *Iskanian* precludes division of PAGA claims through an arbitration agreement.[24] Thus, while the Court found no issue with *Iskanian*'s prohibition on wholesale waivers of PAGA standing, the majority opinion stated that the separability clause in the parties' arbitration agreement allowed Viking to compel arbitration of Moriana's "individual" PAGA claim alone.[25] Moreover, since "PAGA provides no mechanism to enable a Court to adjudicate non-individual PAGA claims once an individual claim has been committed to a separate proceeding," the Court concluded that Moriana's remaining "non-individual" PAGA claims should be dismissed for lack of standing.[26]

In reaching this decision, the Supreme Court rejected both parties' characterizations of the nature of PAGA actions. The Court ruled that Moriana's arguments are incorrect because (i) PAGA does not create substantive rights and (ii) the multiple predicate violations for PAGA liability do constitute multiple claims, since such violations arise from different "transaction" or "nucleus of operative facts."[27]

---

21 *Id.*

22 *Id.* at 1918–1919.

23 Justice Samuel Alito authored the majority opinion. Justice Sonia Sotomayor filed a concurring opinion. Justice Amy Coney Barrett filed an opinion concurring in part and concurring in the judgment, joined in full by Justice Brett Kavanaugh, and joined as to all but the footnote by Chief Justice John Roberts. Justice Clarence Thomas filed a dissenting opinion.

24 *Id.* at 1924.

25 *Id.* at 1924–1925.

26 *Id.* at 1925.

27 *Id.* at 1919–1920.

Viking's arguments, on the other hand, were rejected on the theory that "important structural differences between PAGA actions and class actions [...] preclude any straightforward application of [the] precedents invalidating prohibitions on class-action waivers."[28] As the Court explained, class actions adjudicate individual claims of multiple absent third parties; in PAGA actions, in contrast, a single plaintiff raises multiple claims belonging to a single absent principal (the LWDA).[29] In the Court's opinion, the degree of deviation from bilateral norms that "single-principal, single-agent representative actions" entail is not alien to traditional arbitral practice,[30] nor does it present the same "problems of notice, due process, and adequacy of representation that render class arbitration inconsistent with arbitration's traditionally individualized form."[31]

Instead, the Supreme Court reasoned that the conflict between PAGA's procedural structure and the FAA arises from PAGA's built-in mechanism of claim joinder.[32] As the Court stated, "the most basic corollary of the principle that arbitration is a matter of consent is that 'a party can be forced to arbitrate only those issues it specifically has agreed to submit to arbitration.'"[33] According to the Court, *Iskanian*'s rule prohibiting the parties from contracting around PAGA's claim joinder mechanism conflicts with that fundamental principle because it unduly circumscribes the parties' freedom to determine the issues subject to arbitration.[34] As the majority opinion stated:

> [S]tate law cannot condition the enforceability of an arbitration agreement on the availability of a procedural mechanism that would permit a party to expand the scope of the arbitration by introducing claims that the parties did not jointly agree to arbitrate.
>
> [...]
>
> A state rule imposing an expansive rule of joinder in the arbitral context would defeat the ability of parties to control which claims are subject to arbitration. Such a rule would permit parties to superadd new claims to the proceeding, regardless of whether the agreement between them committed those claims to arbitration. Requiring arbitration procedures

28 *Id.* at 1920.
29 *Id.* at 1920–1921.
30 *Id.* at 1922.
31 *Id.* at 1921.
32 *Id.* at 1923.
33 *Id.*
34 *Id.*

> to include a joinder rule of that kind compels parties to either go along with an arbitration in which the range of issues under consideration is determined by coercion rather than consent, or else forgo arbitration altogether. Either way, the parties are coerced into giving up a right they enjoy under the FAA.[35]

Moreover, despite the noted differences between class proceedings and PAGA actions, the Supreme Court further stressed that – like state law prohibitions on class arbitration waivers – *Iskanian*'s indivisibility rule effectively coerces parties to opt for a judicial forum rather than risk arbitrating high-stakes disputes.[36] Borrowing language from *Concepcion* and *Stolt-Nielsen*, the Court reinforced that "[a]rbitration is poorly suited to the higher stakes" of massive-scale disputes because the absence of "multilayered review" in arbitral proceedings "makes it more likely that errors will go uncorrected," increasing the "risk of 'in terrorem' settlements."[37] And, unlike other types of proceedings with more limited claim joinder mechanisms, the Court concluded that PAGA actions entail higher litigation risks insofar as every employee in California is allowed to act on behalf of a sovereign and unite "a massive number of claims in a single-package suit" to enforce a subset of California public laws.[38]

## 3 Key Takeaways

Although the Court rejected a "straightforward application of [the] precedents invalidating prohibitions on class-action waivers"[39] to the facts in *Viking River*, the Court's reasoning to invalidate *Iskanian*'s claim indivisibility rule heavily relied on such precedents. Thus, as Justice Barrett noted in her partially concurrent opinion, the Supreme Court's decision in *Viking River* effectively expanded the reach of the Court's precedents on class-wide proceedings to "other aggregation devices that cannot be imposed on a party to an arbitration agreement."[40]

Nonetheless, despite this expansion to PAGA's aggregation device, the Supreme Court's opinion contains important language suggesting that the

35 *Id.* at 1923–1924.
36 *Id.* at 1924.
37 *Id.*
38 *Id.*
39 *Id.* at 1920.
40 *Id.* at 1926.

FAA's preemptive effect does not extend to all types of multi-claim or representative proceedings. The Court distinguishes PAGA actions from other "non-class representative actions"[41] – such as shareholder-derivative suits, wrongful-death actions, trustee actions, and suits on behalf of infants or incompetent persons – in the following terms:

> Liberal rules of claim joinder presuppose a backdrop in which litigants assert their own claims and those of a limited class of other parties who are usually connected with the plaintiff by virtue of a distinctive legal relationship – such as that between shareholders and a corporation or between a parent and a minor child. PAGA departs from that norm by granting the power to enforce a subset of California public law to every employee in the State. This combination of standing to act on behalf of a sovereign and mandatory freeform joinder allows plaintiffs to unite a massive number of claims in a single-package suit.[42]

Thus, *Viking River* seems to suggest that the FAA mandates "enforcement of waivers of standing to assert claims on behalf of absent principals"[43] only insofar as the joinder of those claims in a single suit would create high stakes for defendants akin to those entailed by class-wide proceedings.

## 4 Critical Analysis of the Opinion and How It Impacted the U.S. Arbitration Law and Practice

*Viking River* was clearly a victory for California employers. Arbitration agreements encompassing only "individual" PAGA claims are enforceable, so employees that are parties to such agreements cannot pursue claims based on violations allegedly suffered by other employees in the arbitration. Worse: according to the majority opinion's interpretation of PAGA, once an employee's "individual" PAGA claim is subject to arbitration, the employee does not have standing to bring the other PAGA claims in Court either.

The practical result is that employers were allowed to hide behind arbitration agreements to completely insulate themselves from PAGA liability. After all, once deprived of the ability to bring "non-individual" PAGA claims, it is

41 *Id.* at 1922.
42 *Id.* at 1924.
43 *Id.* at 1922.

likely that the low cost-benefit of arbitrating "individual" claims alone would discourage employees from pursuing any claims at all.[44]

This is not the first time that the Supreme Court has condoned the use of arbitration agreements as shields against liability by corporate defendants. In the highly criticized *American Express Co. v. Italian Colors Restaurant* precedent, Justice Kagan noted in her dissenting opinion that:

> Here is the nutshell version of this case, unfortunately obscured in the Court's decision. The owner of a small restaurant (Italian Colors) thinks that American Express (Amex) has used its monopoly power to force merchants to accept a form contract violating the antitrust laws. The restaurateur wants to challenge the allegedly unlawful provision (imposing a tying arrangement), but the same contract's arbitration clause prevents him from doing so. That term imposes a variety of procedural bars that would make pursuit of the antitrust claim a fool's errand. So if the arbitration clause is enforceable, Amex has insulated itself from antitrust liability – even if it has in fact violated the law. The monopolist gets to use its monopoly power to insist on a contract effectively depriving its victims of all legal recourse.
>
> And here is the nutshell version of today's opinion, admirably flaunted rather than camouflaged: Too darn bad.[45]

However, as Justice Sotomayor noted in her concurrent opinion, the Supreme Court did leave the door open for California courts or the state legislature "to modify the scope of statutory standing under PAGA" to allow employees to bring "non-individual" PAGA claims in Court even if their "individual" claims are subject to an arbitration agreement.[46]

And as predicted by Justice Sotomayor, one year after the ruling in *Viking River*, the California Supreme Court ruled that "[w]here a plaintiff has brought a PAGA action comprising individual and non-individual claims, an order compelling arbitration of the individual claims does not strip the plaintiff of

44 As the Supreme Court recognized, "[t]he default penalties set by PAGA are $100 for each aggrieved employee per pay period for the initial violation and $200 for each aggrieved employee per pay period for each subsequent violation. Cal. Lab. Code Ann. §2699(f)(2). Individually, these penalties are modest; but given PAGA's additive dimension, low-value claims may easily be welded together into high-value suits." *Id.* at 1915.

45 *American Express Co. v. Italian Colors Restaurant*, 570 U.S. 228, 240 (2013).

46 *Viking River*, supra note 2, at 1925–1926.

standing as an aggrieved employee to litigate claims on behalf of other employees under PAGA."[47]

## 5 Conclusion

Notwithstanding California's neutralization of the extreme practical effects of the Supreme Court's interpretation of PAGA, *Viking River* stands as a reminder of the Court's commitment to enforce arbitration agreements requiring individualized arbitration even when doing so might leave vulnerable parties without any legal recourse to pursue high-stake claims against corporate defendants.

47 *Adolph v. Uber Technologies Inc.*, No. S274671, --- P.3d ---, 2023 WL 4553702 at 2–3 (July 17, 2023).

CHAPTER 34

# *Coinbase v. Bielski* (2023): Shift from Judicial Discretion to a Mandatory Stay of Proceedings Pending Resolution of an Interlocutory Appeal from the Denial of a Motion to Compel Arbitration

*Boaz S. Morag and Peter E. Carzis*

## 1 Introduction

The plaintiff sues the defendant in court because she believes her claim is subject to judicial determination. The defendant maintains that the claim asserted is subject to an agreement to arbitrate and moves to compel arbitration and to dismiss the litigation. The trial court hears the motion to compel; if it is granted, the parties are ordered to proceed with arbitration and the plaintiff has no right to an immediate appeal from that interlocutory decision; if the motion to compel is denied, Congress has afforded the defendant the exceptional right of an immediate (interlocutory) appeal from that decision if the case was initially filed in, or removed to, federal court.

Does such an appeal "oust a district court's jurisdiction to proceed with litigation pending appeal,"[1] such that proceedings are mandatorily stayed pending resolution of the appeal? Or alternatively, "does the district court retain discretion to proceed with litigation while the appeal is pending,"[2] affording it the authority to tailor proceedings before it as appropriate given the facts and circumstances of the dispute? In 2023, following a decades-long circuit split among the federal Courts of Appeal, the Supreme Court resolved this question in *Coinbase v. Bielski*, ruling that as a matter of federal common law, district court proceedings must be stayed pending the resolution of an appeal from the denial of a motion to compel arbitration.

Looking forward, the practical consequences of *Coinbase* are far-reaching. For parties resisting a motion to compel arbitration, the shift to a universal mandatory stay in federal courts threatens to reshape the dynamics of litigation

1 Joint Pet. Writ Cert. at (i), *Coinbase, Inc. v. Bielski*, No. 22–105, 2022 WL 3107708 (U.S. July 29, 2022).

2 *Id.*

 | DOI:10.1163/9789004715820_035

over arbitrability by adding an inevitable two year or longer delay before being able to reach the merits of the dispute in litigation (or arbitration). For the proponents of arbitration, the automatic stay rule provides the assurance that the parties will engage in no litigation activities in court unless and until the Court of Appeals (or the U.S. Supreme Court were it to grant review) has decided that the dispute is *not* subject to arbitration.

## 2 Background to the Case

### 2.1 *Doctrinal Background*

The question of what, if anything, may occur with respect to further resolution of the dispute in the trial court while an appeal from the denial of arbitrability is pending has its origin in a 1988 amendment to the Federal Arbitration Act (FAA) by which Congress confirmed that a district court's denial of a motion to compel arbitration is immediately appealable as of right.[3] Prior to this amendment, the FAA did not explicitly grant any right to an interlocutory appeal; nevertheless, litigants would sometimes seek to appeal denials of motions to compel arbitration by invoking related statutory provisions.[4] The 1988 amendment also clarified that absent discretionary review permitted by both the district court and the court of appeals, "an appeal may *not* be taken from an interlocutory order" directing arbitration to proceed or compelling arbitration.[5]

3 9 U.S.C. § 16(a)(1) (codifying the rule that "[a]n appeal may be taken from … an order … (B) denying a petition under section 4 of this title to order arbitration to proceed [or] (C) denying an application under section 206 of this title to compel arbitration"). Section 16(a)(1)(B) refers to "domestic" agreements to arbitrate subject only to Chapter 1 of the FAA and Section 16(a)(1)(C) refers to "international" agreements to arbitrate subject to the New York Convention and Panama Convention and thus subject to Chapter 2 or 3 of the FAA, respectively.

4 See, e.g., *Nesslage v. York Secs., Inc.*, 823 F.2d 231, 232 (8th Cir. 1987) (invoking 28 U.S.C. § 1292(a)(1)); *Int'l Ass'n of Machinists & Aerospace Workers, AFL-CIO v. Aloha Airlines, Inc.*, 776 F.2d 812, 814–15 (9th Cir. 1985) (similar); *Langley v. Colonial Leasing Co.*, 707 F.2d 1, 3 (1st Cir. 1983) (similar). 28 U.S.C. § 1292(a)(1) provides, in relevant part, that "the courts of appeals shall have jurisdiction of appeals from … [i]nterlocutory orders of the district courts of the United States … granting, continuing, modifying, refusing or dissolving injunctions, or refusing to dissolve or modify injunctions, except where a direct review may be had in the Supreme Court."

5 9 U.S.C. § 16(b) (emphasis added). If, however, the district court issues a final order and dismisses the entire proceeding, that final order is appealable even if the court has granted the motion to compel arbitration. See *Green Tree Fin. Corp.-Alabama v. Randolph*, 531 U.S. 79, 121 S. Ct. 513, 148 L. Ed. 2d 373 (2000) (the FAA "preserves immediate appeal of any 'final decision with respect to an arbitration,' regardless of whether the decision is

It should be noted that the legal issue underlying the question whether to compel arbitration is not a monolithic question; rather, the underlying issue can vary widely and include whether: a contract containing the allegedly applicable arbitration agreement was ever formed;[6] the arbitration agreement is either procedurally or substantively unconscionable;[7] an agreement to arbitrate accompanied by a delegation agreement giving arbitrators the power to determine arbitrability was later superseded by an agreement to litigate;[8] an agreement to arbitrate *not* accompanied by such a delegation agreement was later superseded by an agreement to litigate;[9] non-signatories to the arbitration agreement are bound to arbitrate or entitled to invoke the arbitration agreement;[10] and arbitration was waived by litigating the claims or delaying in asserting a right to arbitrate.[11]

To place in context the statutory right of immediate appeal from the denial of a motion to compel arbitration, it is important to note that the overarching principle of federal appellate jurisdiction is, with only certain limited exceptions, to provide for an appeal as of right only from final decisions entirely disposing of the action, rather than to permit piecemeal appeals of interim rulings along the way.[12] Thus, for example, the district court's rejection to other

---

favorable or hostile to arbitration," and moreover, that such dismissals constitute "final decision[s] with respect to an arbitration" under the FAA). If the court compels arbitration of less than all of the claims or of the claims of less than all of the plaintiffs, such order would be interlocutory and not be immediately appealable as of right.

6 See generally, *e.g.*, *Will-Drill Res., Inc. v. Samson Res. Co.*, 352 F.3d 211 (5th Cir. 2003); *Grosvenor v. Qwest Corp.*, 733 F.3d 990 (10th Cir. 2013); *Zachman v. Hudson Valley Fed. Credit Union*, 49 F.4th 95 (2d Cir. 2022); *Edmundson v. Klarna Inc.*, No. 22–557-cv, 2023 WL 723871 (2d Cir., Nov. 3, 2023).

7 See generally, *e.g.*, *Coinbase, Inc. v. Bielski*, 599 U.S. 736, 143 S. Ct. 1915, 1916 216 L. Ed. 2d 671 (2023).

8 See generally, *e.g.*, *Suski v. Coinbase, Inc.*, No. 22–15209, 2022 WL 3099846 (9th Cir. May 27, 2022), cert. granted *sub nom. Coinbase Inc. v. Bielski*, 143 S. Ct. 521, 214 L. Ed. 2d 298 (2022), and *cert. dismissed as improvidently granted sub nom. Coinbase, Inc. v. Bielski*, 599 U.S. 736, 143 S. Ct. 1915, 216 L. Ed. 2d 671 (2023). *Goldman, Sachs & Co. v. City of Reno*, 747 F.3d 733 (9th Cir. 2014); *Sanchez v. Clipper Realty, Inc.*, No. 22–2917 (2d Cir., Nov. 3, 2023).

9 See generally, *e.g.*, *Goldman, Sachs & Co. v. City of Reno*, 747 F.3d 733 (9th Cir. 2014); *Sanchez v. Clipper Realty, Inc.*, No. 22–2917 (2d Cir., Nov. 3, 2023).

10 See generally, *e.g.*, *Al Rushaid v. Nat'l Oilwell Varco, Inc.*, 814 F.3d 300 (5th Cir. 2016); *Janvey v. Alguire*, 847 F.3d 231 (5th Cir. 2017); *In re Rotavirus Vaccines Antitrust Litig.*, 789 F. App'x 934 (3d Cir. 2019); *GE Energy Power Conversion France SAS, Corp. v. Outokumpu Stainless USA, LLC*, 140 S. Ct. 1637, 207 L. Ed. 2d 1 (2020).

11 See generally, *e.g.*, *Sweater Bee by Banff, Ltd. v. Manhattan Indus., Inc.*, 754 F.2d 457 (2d Cir. 1985); *Hurst v. Prudential Sec. Inc.*, 21 F.3d 1113 (9th Cir. 1994); *Dasher v. RBC Bank (USA)*, 745 F.3d 1111 (11th Cir. 2014).

12 See, *e.g.*, *Mohawk Indus., Inc. v. Carpenter*, 558 U.S. 100 (2009).

types of challenges to the propriety of the judicial forum selected by the plaintiff are not eligible for immediate appellate review. Accordingly, a defendant bringing and losing a challenge based upon (i) a claimed exclusive forum selection clause providing for litigation in another judicial forum; (ii) the lack of subject matter jurisdiction of the federal court; (iii) the absence of personal jurisdiction over the defendant; (iv) improper venue in the judicial district; (v) *forum non conveniens* in favor of litigation in the courts of another country; (vi) the doctrine of abstention in favor of state court, rather than federal court proceedings; or (vii) transfer to another U.S. judicial district for the convenience of the parties or due to the absence of venue, has no right to an immediate appeal of that denial.[13] Naturally, in these litigation contexts, the absence of immediate appellate review also necessarily means there is no possibility of obtaining a stay or suspension of the litigation, as the case proceeds on the assumption of the correctness of the district court's denial of the defendant's challenge to the forum.

Although Congress created an exceptional right of immediate appeal in the context of the rejection of arbitrability, it was silent, both in the text of the FAA amendment and in its legislative history, as to whether the court proceeding should be stayed pending resolution of that appeal. This legislative silence engendered a split in the courts over whether the district court was (i) required to suspend all proceedings while the Court of Appeals considered the arbitrability issue or (ii) retained the discretion either to (a) hear and administer the merits of the dispute unless and until its denial of arbitrability was reversed, or, (b) even more modestly, permit the parties to conduct limited document discovery or engage in other actions that would also transpire in any arbitration, as a means of advancing resolution of the underlying dispute while the appeal was pending.

By the time this issue reached the Supreme Court in 2022, nine of thirteen federal appellate courts had already weighed in. Six adopted a mandatory stay rule, requiring that district court proceedings be suspended for the duration of an appeal from the denial of a motion to compel arbitration.[14] Three other

---

13 15A Charles Alan Wright & Arthur R. Miller, *Federal Practice and Procedure* §§ 3914.6, 3914.12 (3d ed. 2023).

14 See *Ehleiter v. Grapetree Shores, Inc.*, 482 F.3d 207, 215, n. 6 (3d Cir. 2007); *Levin v. Alms & Assoc., Inc.*, 634 F.3d 260, 266 (4th Cir. 2011); *Bradford-Scott Data Corp., Inc. v. Physician Comput. Network, Inc.*, 128 F.3d 504, 505–507 (7th Cir. 1997); *McCauley v. Halliburton Energy Servs., Inc.*, 413 F.3d 1158, 1162–1163 (10th Cir. 2005); *Blinco v. Green Tree Servicing, LLC*, 366 F.3d 1249, 1253 (11th Cir. 2004); *Bombardier Corp. v. Nat'l R.R. Passenger Corp.*, 333 F.3d 250, 252 (DC Cir. 2003).

circuits, however, authorized district courts to exercise their discretion to stay the litigation or tailor what transpired in the proceeding during the pendency of the appeal to the particularities of the case before them.[15]

The six Circuits comprising the majority position drew substantially from the Supreme Court's 1982 decision in *Griggs v. Provident Consumer Discount, Co.*[16] *Griggs* did not involve an interlocutory appeal, but rather the interplay between the Court of Appeals and the district court in the circumstances where the district court renders a final decision, the losing party applies to the district court to alter or amend the judgment, but while that motion is still pending also files a notice of appeal invoking the jurisdiction of the appellate court. The issue in that circumstance (and at that time)[17] was the effectiveness of the notice of appeal to oust the district court of jurisdiction to consider the post-judgment motions before it.[18] In deciding that the subsequent notice of appeal was a nullity, so as to avoid the untenable situation of simultaneous jurisdiction by multiple courts,[19] the Supreme Court articulated the general rule that an appeal necessarily "divests the district court of its control over those aspects of the case involved in the appeal."[20]

As noted, *Griggs* dealt with the issue potentially applicable in all federal court litigation of when the proceedings in the district court are in fact concluded, and when all activity moves to the Court of Appeals. That is different from the situation in all *interlocutory* appeals, where the case is "pending" in both the district court and the court of appeals simultaneously. In the most frequent interlocutory appeal in the federal system—the immediate appeal from either the grant or the denial of a preliminary injunction—the general rule is that "[o]rdinarily an interlocutory injunction appeal ... does not defeat the

15 See *Motorola Credit Corp. v. Uzan*, 388 F.3d 39, 53–54 (2d Cir. 2004); *Weingarten Realty Invs. v. Miller*, 661 F.3d 904, 910 (5th Cir. 2011); *Britton v. Co-op Banking Grp.*, 916 F.2d 1405, 1412 (9th Cir. 1990).

16 459 U.S. 56 (1982).

17 The legal issue that animated *Griggs* emerged from language in the Federal Rules of Appellate Procedure, Rule 4(a)(4), that required litigants to file a new notice of appeal after the disposition of a post-trial motion, even where notice had already been filed before such motion.

18 *Id.* at 57–58.

19 *Id.* at 57–59.

20 *Id.* at 58. The specific issue in *Griggs* has now been addressed via an amendment to the Federal Rules of Appellate Procedure ("FRAP"). In short, any notice of appeal filed before or during the pendency of a timely made post-judgment motion "becomes effective to appeal a judgment or order, in whole or in part, when the order disposing of the last such remaining motion is entered." FRAP 4(a)(4)(B)(i).

power of the trial court to proceed further with the case"[21] on the theory that the issues underlying the propriety of the decision to grant or deny the preliminary injunction are sufficiently distinct from the merits of the dispute to require the district court to continue administering the case while the appeal is pending.

Despite the differences between the procedural posture of the appeal from a final decision in *Griggs* and the interlocutory appeal from the denial of a motion to compel arbitration, the six Circuits in the majority were persuaded that under *Griggs*, district courts are divested of jurisdiction over the action because there were no elements of the proceeding not "involved in the appeal" since the issue on appeal was whether the case belonged in court in the first instance.[22]

In accepting an alternative to a mandatory stay, the Second, Fifth, and Ninth Circuits[23] looked similarly to the law of federal appellate jurisdiction, ultimately reaching the opposite conclusion from the majority of Circuits. These courts each concluded that appeals from the denial of a motion to compel arbitration do not present the degree of overlap between the issue on appeal and the underlying dispute necessary to require a stay.[24] These courts were also motivated by the concern that staying district court proceedings automatically "would allow a defendant to stall a trial simply by bringing a frivolous motion to compel arbitration."[25] These courts ruled that in exercising their discretion whether to stay the proceeding pending appeal, district courts should apply the general four-factor balancing test adopted by the Supreme Court whenever a request to suspend litigation is presented outside the arbitration context: specifically, trial courts were instructed to weigh "(1) whether the stay applicant has made a strong showing that he is likely to succeed on the merits; (2) whether the applicant will be irreparably injured absent a stay; (3) whether issuance of a stay will substantially injure other parties interested in the proceedings; and (4) whether public interest favors a stay."[26]

21 16 Charles Alan Wright & Arthur R. Miller, *Federal Practice and Procedure* § 3921.2 (3d ed. 2023).

22 See, *e.g.*, *Bradford-Scott Data Corp.*, 128 F.3d at 505 (quoting *Griggs*, 459 U.S. at 58).

23 These three Circuits include the federal courts in New York, Texas and California, three U.S. States where many arbitrations are seated and where much litigation about arbitration is heard.

24 *Motorola Credit Corp.*, 388 F.3d at 53 (quoting *Griggs*, 459 U.S. at 58 (1982)).

25 *Britton*, 916 F.2d at 1412.

26 *Weingarten Realty Invs.*, 661 F.3d at 910 (quoting *Hilton v. Braunskill*, 481 U.S. 770 (1987)).

## 2.2 *Factual Background of the* Coinbase *Case*

Such was the doctrinal landscape when Abraham Bielski opened his Coinbase account. In 2021, California investor Bielski registered with the trading platform Coinbase, an exchange that allows users to trade a wide variety of traditional fiat currencies alongside more novel cryptocurrencies.[27] Shortly after creating his account, Bielski fell victim to an online confidence trick, and his Coinbase account was robbed by an unidentified third party; after he was unable to reach a non-automated customer service representative at Coinbase, Bielski filed a putative class action lawsuit against the trading platform at the United States District Court for the Northern District of California, alleging violations of the Electronic Funds Transfer Act.[28] In response to the complaint, Coinbase moved to compel arbitration pursuant to the account agreement's terms.[29]

Before the district court, Bielski conceded that a valid arbitration agreement existed, and that the dispute he had sued over fell within its scope; however, he sought to avoid the agreement to arbitrate by contending that it was unconscionable by reason of its substantive unilaterality.[30] In effect, Coinbase's contract bound users to a dispute resolution system under which they were required to contact customer service and subsequently pursue Coinbase's formal complaint process in order to be permitted to seek arbitration.[31] Crucially, however, this process applied only to Coinbase users; since the contract's arbitration clause related only to Coinbase's formal complaint process, only users were bound by its terms—thus, "the arbitration provision impose[d] no obligation on Coinbase itself to submit its disputes with users to binding arbitration."[32] In the narrow circumstances under which users were permitted to pursue any claims against Coinbase in court, moreover, such claims were restricted to small claims courts, sharply limiting users' capacity to seek substantial compensatory damages outside of arbitration.[33] Focusing on these features, the district court determined the arbitration agreement as a whole was unconscionable, and in turn, unenforceable; this conclusion rested largely on the agreement's imposition of "a burdensome and unfair pre-arbitration dispute process on users" that "sends their complaints, but not Coinbase's complaints, to binding arbitration."[34]

27 *Bielski v. Coinbase, Inc.*, No. C 21-07478 WHA, 2022 WL 1062049, at *1 (N.D. Cal. Apr. 8, 2022).
28 *Id.*
29 *Id.*
30 *Id.* at *2.
31 *Id.* at *3–4.
32 *Id.* at *4.
33 *Id.* at *5.
34 *Id.* at *2–6.

Coinbase invoked its right under Section 16 of the FAA to an immediate appeal to the United States Court of Appeals for the Ninth Circuit and also moved to stay proceedings in the district court pending that appeal. In denying Coinbase's motion to stay, the district court applied the four-part balancing test quoted above.[35] Although the court noted that "reasonable minds may differ" as to unconscionability, lending some support for a stay, it determined that all remaining factors weighed in Bielski's favor, stressing the imbalance of litigation resources as well as the public interest in efficient and speedy "determination of civil actions" as important considerations in reaching this decision.[36]

Coinbase renewed its stay application before the Court of Appeals,[37] claiming an entitlement to a stay as of right under *Griggs*.[38] That application was summarily denied without a written opinion,[39] presumably on the basis of the earlier Ninth Circuit case, *Britton v. Co-op Banking Group*, rejecting an entitlement to a stay as of right. Seizing on the split in the Circuits that had emerged, Coinbase filed a petition for a writ of certiorari with the United States Supreme Court,[40] and the Court granted the petition to decide "whether the district court must stay its pre-trial and trial proceedings while the interlocutory appeal is ongoing"[41] from the denial of a motion to compel arbitration.

## 2.3 *Briefing before the Supreme Court*

### 2.3.1 Coinbase's Arguments

In its brief before the Supreme Court, Coinbase echoed the arguments that had become commonplace among the majority-rule circuits. Coinbase began by contending that when it amended the FAA to provide for an appeal as of right from the denial of a motion to compel arbitration, "Congress legislated against the backdrop" of *Griggs*, and its holding that an appeal "divests the district court of its control over those aspects of the case involved in the

35 *Bielski v. Coinbase, Inc.*, No. C 21-07478, at 2 (N.D. Cal. June 7, 2022).

36 *Id.* at 2–3.

37 As a general rule, "[a] party must ordinarily move first in the district court for ... a stay of the judgment or order of a district court pending appeal," and may renew that application before the Court of Appeals only if "the district court denied the motion or failed to afford the relief requested." FRAP 8(a)(1)(A); 8(a)(2)(A)(ii).

38 Brief for Coinbase, Inc. at 1–2, *Coinbase, Inc. v. Bielski*, No. C 21-07478 (N.D. Cal. June 7, 2022).

39 *Bielski v. Coinbase, Inc.*, No. 22-15566, 2022 WL 3095991 (9th Cir. July 11, 2022), *cert. granted*, 143 S. Ct. 521, 214 L. Ed. 2d 298 (2022), and *rev'd and remanded*, 599 U.S. 736, 143 S. Ct. 1915, 216 L. Ed. 2d 671 (2023).

40 See generally, Petition for Writ of Certiorari.

41 *Coinbase, Inc. v. Bielski*, 143 S. Ct. 1915, 1918 (2023).

appeal."[42] Thus, "[i]n conferring the right to immediately appeal orders hostile to arbitration," Congress "understood that divestiture principles would prohibit district courts from proceeding to the merits during the appeal."[43] This reading is further supported, Coinbase argued, by the structure of the FAA: in departing from the default final-judgment rule asymmetrically—by authorizing appeals from interlocutory orders *denying*, but not *granting*, a motion to compel arbitration—Congress "reflect[ed] a strong preference for arbitration over continued district court litigation."[44]

Coinbase next argued that a mandatory stay furthers the overarching purpose of promoting the efficiency and speed with which arbitration is associated.[45] "By amending the FAA in 1988 to strengthen protections for arbitration, Congress cannot reasonably be understood to have given district courts an easy mechanism to flout the FAA's central purpose."[46] Looking beyond the amendment itself, moreover, Coinbase posited that "[w]here Congress seeks to depart from the presumption of divestiture, it does so expressly," citing to a series of federal procedural provisions authorizing interlocutory appeals and expressly clarifying that trial courts were *not* to be divested of jurisdiction during the appeal.[47] Finally, Coinbase concluded its argument by responding to a handful of rationales for the discretionary-stay approach.[48]

### 2.3.2 Bielski's Arguments

In response, Bielski made the overarching argument that a mandatory-stay model had "no basis in the law," as "[n]one of the … sources understood to give rise to automatic stays in other contexts … provide justification for an automatic stay for Section 16(a) appeals."[49] Bielski began by focusing on the text, structure, and history of the FAA itself, casting the dispute as a typical "statutory interpretation case[]" that must first be assessed by "analyzing the statute's 'text and structure.'"[50] Establishing as a threshold matter that "[t]he

42 Br. Pet. Coinbase, Inc. at *16, Coinbase, Inc. v. Bielski, No. 22–105, 2023 WL 425097 (U.S. Jan. 20, 2023) (quoting *Griggs* 459 U.S. at 58).

43 *Id.* at *25.

44 *Id.* at *27, *29–30.

45 *Id.* at *31–32.

46 *Id.* at *34.

47 *Id.* at *34–28.

48 *Id.* at *43–52.

49 Br. Resp't Abraham Bielski at *5, *Coinbase, Inc., v. Bielski*, No. 22–105, 2023 WL 2209764 (U.S. Feb. 21, 2023).

50 *Id.* at *9 (quoting *Oklahoma v. Castro-Huerta*, 142 S. Ct. 2486, 2497 (2022) (cleaned up in brief)).

text does not require a district court to stay its proceedings if a Section 16(a) appeal is taken," Bielski further contended that Congressional intent to permit stays discretionarily is suggested by the FAA's structure, inasmuch as other, similar provisions of the Act grant automatic stays *explicitly*.[51] If Congressional silence indicates an intention to stay automatically, these explicit grants would be rendered surplusage.[52]

Rather, Bielski argued that the appropriate background rule to be applied absent any direction from Congress is a presumption in favor of discretionary stays.[53] The more recent *Griggs* principle, on the other hand, was characterized as insufficient to demand an automatic stay: since "arbitrability" is "easily severable from the merits of the underlying disputes,"[54] simultaneous district court proceedings during an appeal of a denied motion to compel arbitration do not pose any "danger [that] a district court and a court of appeals would be simultaneously analyzing the same judgment."[55]

In concluding its argument, Bielski contended that the discretionary analysis typically followed by district courts represents an appropriate means of balancing these competing interests while simultaneously arguing that the problem of frivolous appeals would be exacerbated by a mandatory stay rule, since "[t]he frivolity standard is too toothless" to effectively dissuade the pursuit of non-meritorious appeals.[56]

### 2.3.3 Input of Amici

A number of organizations filed amicus curiae briefs with the Supreme Court, including commercial lobbying organizations, think tanks, and plaintiff-side nonprofit litigation organizations.[57] By and large, the amici supporting Coinbase expressed a concern that the difficulty associated with obtaining a stay while appealing a denial of a motion to compel arbitration would frustrate the purposes that make arbitration attractive in the first place.[58] The U.S.

---

51 *Id.* at *10.

52 *Id.*

53 *Id.* at *16–19.

54 *Id.* at *30 (quoting *Moses H. Cone Mem'l Hosp. v. Mercury Constr. Corp.*, 460 U.S. 1, 20–21 (1983)).

55 *Id.* at *32 (quoting *Griggs v. Provident Consumer Discount, Co.*, 459 U.S. 56, 58 (1982)).

56 *Id.* at *41.

57 SUPREME COURT OF THE UNITED STATES, Docket, *Coinbase v. Bielski*, No. 22–105 (last visited Oct. 4, 2023), https://www.supremecourt.gov/search.aspx?filename=/docket/docketfiles/html/public/22-105.html.

58 See, *e.g.*, Br. Nat'l Retail Federation as Amicus Curiae at *5, *Coinbase, Inc., v. Bielski*, No. 22–105 (Jan. 27, 2023) (suggesting that "[f]orcing parties to litigate in court during an appeal from an order denying arbitration necessarily deprives them of the substantive

Chamber of Commerce and the National Federation of Independent Business echoed this theme in their jointly-filed brief, noting that in the past year, while only twelve percent of private civil appeals had been reversed in federal court, the reversal rate for denials of motions to compel stood at an impressive fifty-two percent.[59]

The amici writing in support of Bielski were similarly concerned with the practical consequences of the resolution of the issue; Public Justice, for example, suggested that adopting a mandatory-stay rule would ultimately have a *negative* effect on judicial economy, inasmuch as such an outcome "would cause delay and prejudice and create incentives for serial, court-clogging interlocutory appeals."[60] This rule, moreover, was characterized as bereft of the flexibility required to manage complex disputes, as "the universe of litigation around arbitration contains far more nuance and complexity than Coinbase's simplified picture suggests."[61]

## 3 The Supreme Court's Decision

The Supreme Court heard oral arguments on March 21 and rendered its decision on June 23, 2023, finding for Coinbase. In a narrow victory, a five-justice majority consisting of Chief Justice Roberts, and Justices Alito, Gorsuch, Kavanaugh, and Barrett, accepted Coinbase's reading of the FAA, with Justice Kavanaugh writing for the Court.[62] Justice Jackson filed a dissent, joined by Justices Sotomayor and Kagan, and in part, by Justice Thomas as well.[63]

---

protections of the FAA."); Br. Civ. Just. Assoc. of Cal. as Amicus Curiae at *8–9, *Coinbase, Inc., v. Bielski*, No. 22–105 (Jan. 27, 2023) (contending that "[t]he [p]urpose of the FAA [f]avors an [a]utomatic [s]tay," given that the Act's "'overarching purpose is to ensure the enforcement of arbitration agreements according to their terms so as to facilitate informal, streamlined proceedings'") (quoting *AT&T Mobility LLC v. Concepcion*, 563 U.S. 333, 344 (2011) (citations omitted by amicus brief)); Br. Atl. Legal Found. as Amicus Curiae at *9, *Coinbase, Inc., v. Bielski*, No. 22–105 (Jan. 27, 2023) (proposing that "[a] defendant forced to litigate in the district court while an appeal from an order denying its motion to compel arbitration is pending suffers the very harm it contracted to avoid—litigation in court, with its attendant expenses and inefficiencies").

59 Br. Chamber Com. U.S.A. & Nat'l Federation of Indep. Bus. Small Bus. Legal Ctr. as Amici Curiae at *17–18, *Coinbase, Inc., v. Bielski*, No. 22–105 (Jan. 27, 2023).

60 Br. Pub. Just. as Amicus Curiae at *3, *Coinbase, Inc., v. Bielski*, No. 22–105 (Feb. 28, 2023).

61 *Id.* at *2.

62 *Coinbase, Inc. v. Bielski*, 599 U.S. 736 (2023).

63 *Id.* Justice Thomas joined except as to parts I (analyzing the statutory text vis-à-vis similar provisions) and V (addressing the potential consequences of the majority's holding). *Id.* at 1916, 1924–26, 1931.

### 3.1 *The Majority Opinion*

In finding for Coinbase, the majority looked principally to the federal common law, reasoning that the 1988 amendment to the FAA had been drafted in the shadow of Supreme Court precedent establishing mandatory stays as the default rule. For the majority, the *Griggs* rule that an appeal necessarily "divests the district court of its control over those aspects of the case involved in the appeal,"[64] "resolves this case."[65] Justice Kavanaugh reasoned that "[b]ecause the question on appeal is whether the case belongs in arbitration or instead in the district court, the entire case is essentially 'involved in the appeal.'"[66] While the Court acknowledged that the FAA amendment did not provide any affirmative direction to stay proceedings, this, it determined, was of no moment given the strength of the *Griggs* default rule. Congressional silence on the stay question did not indicate a lack of intent to provide an automatic stay, because "absent contrary indications, the background *Griggs* principle already requires an automatic stay of district court proceedings;" this conclusion was premised on the notion that, inasmuch as an appeal as to arbitrability determines the very permissibility of those proceedings, anything the district court might do is involved in the appeal, and as such, must be stayed absent a clear statement otherwise.[67]

The majority also identified a number of ancillary factors that it viewed as buttressing its core holding. Drawing on notions of internal consistency and jurisdictional orderliness, the Court invoked "common sense," observing that "[a]bsent an automatic stay of district court proceedings, Congress's decision in § 16(a) to afford a right to an interlocutory appeal would be largely nullified."[68] The Court also provided a functionalist justification for this outcome, noting that were it to adopt the discretionary stay rule, "many of the asserted benefits of arbitration (efficiency, less expense, less intrusive discovery, and the like) would be irretrievably lost," and that parties could be more easily "coerc[ed]" into the very "blackmail settlements" that arbitration is intended to limit.[69] The Court concluded that the mandatory approach also furthers an interest in judicial economy, as permitting cases plausibly bound for arbitration to languish unnecessarily in district court would threaten to "waste scarce judicial resources."[70]

---

64 *Id.* at 1916 (quoting *Griggs*, 459 U.S. at 58 (1982)).
65 *Id.*
66 *Id.* (quoting *Griggs*, 459 U.S. at 58 (1982)).
67 *Id.* at 1921.
68 *Id.*
69 *Id.*
70 *Id.*

Finally, the majority addressed Bielski's counterarguments. In response to Bielski's objection "that an automatic stay would encourage frivolous appeals that would improperly delay district court proceedings,"[71] the Court countered that he had not adequately established the persistence and seriousness of this problem, and that in any case, other countermeasures are available (*e.g.*, dismissal on grounds of frivolity, certification by the trial court as frivolous, sanctions).[72] Bielski's concern that automatic stays are unnecessary because the discretionary approach "would adequately protect parties' rights to an interlocutory appellate determination of arbitrability,"[73] moreover, was rejected as empirically inaccurate, and—even if accepted as true *arguendo*—insufficient to overcome the force of the *Griggs* principle.[74]

### 3.2 *Justice Jackson's Dissenting Opinion*

While Justice Jackson's dissent was primarily focused on the same set of considerations as the majority opinion, it offered a trenchant critique of the majority opinion's basis in existing law: the Court, it contended, had broken with the "traditional approach" to staying proceedings to "invent[] a new stay rule perpetually favoring one class of litigants—defendants seeking arbitration," and had announced a rule that "comes out of nowhere."[75] Invoking the traditional rule against surplusage, the dissent highlighted Congress's decision not to explicitly impose mandatory stays for interlocutory appeals of arbitrability, arguing that this "underscores that § 16 does not mandate a stay."[76] In particular, the dissent highlighted a number of statutory provisions enacted as part of the same 1988 law, which provided specifically that in the case of an interlocutory appeal, "proceedings shall be ... stayed until the appeal has been decided,"[77] as well as a provision of the FAA dictating that where the trial court is "satisfied" that an issue should be referred to arbitration, it "*shall* on application of one of the parties stay the trial of the action until such arbitration has been had."[78] Criticizing the majority's reliance on the "background principle" announced in *Griggs*, the dissent countered that "on the contrary, the

71 *Id.* at 1922.
72 *Id.*
73 *Id.* at 1923.
74 *Id.*
75 *Id.* at 1923–24 (Jackson, J., dissenting).
76 *Id.* at 1924–25.
77 *Id.* at 1924 (quoting 28 U.S.C. §1292(d)(4)(B)).
78 *Id.* at 1925 (quoting 9 U.S.C. §3 (emphasis original to dissent)).

background rule is that courts have case-by-case discretion regarding whether or not to issue a stay."[79]

The dissent further distinguished *Griggs* as "stand[ing] for a modest proposition: Two courts should avoid exercising control over the same order or judgment simultaneously."[80] Whereas the majority treated all elements of the dispute before the Court as insufficiently extricable to warrant simultaneous proceedings during the interlocutory appeal, the dissent characterized the issues as "easily severable," and contended that there is no "danger a district court and a court of appeals would be simultaneously analyzing the same judgment."[81] Per the dissent, merely being 'involved in the appeal' was insufficient under *Griggs* to demand a stay; rather, it suggested, so long as the issues are conceptually severable so as to obviate any danger of redundant analysis, a stay is not required.

Turning next to the functionalist arguments, Justice Jackson wrote that a mandatory stay rule suffers from its own inflexibility: while the discretionary approach allows courts to tailor proceedings to the particularities of the matters before them, under the mandatory approach, courts are locked into the potential benefits of a stay (*e.g.*, conservation of resources if the dispute is ultimately arbitrated) even when those benefits are unlikely to be reaped (*e.g.*, the party appealing the denial is unlikely to succeed)—or more pressingly, where the benefits of simultaneous proceedings are rendered permanently out of reach by a stay.[82] Rather than permitting courts to balance considerations as appropriate to the specific cases before them, the dissent complained that the majority "categorically resolv[es] these conflicts in favor of the pro-arbitration party," permitting, if not encouraging, the appealing party to "press pause on the case—leaving plaintiffs to suffer harm, lose evidence, and bleed dry their patience and funding in the meantime."[83]

## 4 Conclusion

*Coinbase* represents a further strengthening of the federal courts' and federal laws' solicitude for arbitration as a dispute resolution mechanism whose possible application in a given case must be preserved unimpaired by litigation

---

79 *Id.* at 1926.

80 *Id.*

81 *Id.* at 1927 (quoting *Griggs*, 459 U.S. at 59 (1982)).

82 *Id.* at 1929–30.

83 *Id.* at 1930.

activity during an appeal, even though a trial court has already decided that the claim is not subject to arbitration.[84] Even crediting and extrapolating from the snapshot statistics of the amicus who asserted a 50% reversal rate on appeals from the rejection of a motion to compel arbitration, in at least half the cases, the appeal will not change the outcome and not lead to the dispute being resolved in arbitration.

It seems unavoidable that the *Coinbase* decision will further encourage defendants to scour their documents looking for some potentially applicable arbitration clause and then pursue an appeal if the district court is not persuaded. The instances of appeals being dismissed as frivolous are so rare as to not be a significant deterrent to pursuing a weak or even meritless appeal, unless perhaps the defendant were contractually or statutorily exposed to paying the plaintiff's legal fees should the plaintiff prevail.

The expansion of the automatic stay position means that the two or more years it will take, on average, to litigate arbitrability before the trial court and then the appellate court, may create strong incentives for a plaintiff facing such delay before being able to pursue the merits of their claims to acquiesce to the arbitration agreement the defendant contends is applicable or negotiate terms by which the plaintiff will agree to pursue its claims in an arbitration in exchange for concessions by the defendant as to the arbitral rules, discovery, timetable or other issues that may mitigate the advantages to court litigation the plaintiff believed it was entitled to in selecting a judicial forum in the first instance.

---

84 Because the *Coinbase* rule is premised on federal common law explicating the provisions of the Federal Arbitration Act, state courts in the United States applying the FAA to any agreement to arbitrate touching on interstate commerce will also be bound by the mandatory stay rule.

CHAPTER 35

# CMB *Monaco v Smagin* (2023)

*Katharine Menéndez de la Cuesta and Rafael Francisco Alves*

On June 22, 2023, the U.S. Supreme Court opened the door to foreign plaintiffs seeking civil liability under the Racketeer Influenced and Corrupt Organizations Act ("RICO") against debtors who made fraudulent domestic efforts to avoid the enforcement of an international arbitration award.

The Court held that in determining whether a plaintiff has sustained a domestic injury for purposes of a private civil suit under RICO, courts should look to the circumstances surrounding the alleged injury to assess whether it arose in the U.S. Although it is still unclear how lower courts will interpret the context-specific approach the Court adopted, this avenue will probably remain the exception rather than the rule.

## 1 Introduction

CMB *Monaco v. Smagin* and *Yegiazaryan v. Smagin*, the two consolidated cases the U.S. Supreme Court decided on June 22, 2023, involve the use of RICO in the context of the enforcement of a foreign arbitral award. RICO is a 1970 United States federal statute providing for criminal penalties to any person involved in an enterprise of racketeering activity in violation of certain federal and state criminal laws, known as "predicate acts." RICO also provides a civil cause of action to any person injured by reason of a violation of RICO substantive provisions.

The issue is deceptively straightforward: does an injury to "intangible property" of a foreign citizen constitute a "domestic injury" for purposes of a RICO civil action?

The "intangible property" here was a multimillion-dollar arbitral award rendered under the auspices of the London Court of International Arbitration ("LCIA Award") against Ashot Yegiazaryan. When Yegiazaryan failed to voluntarily comply with the LCIA Award, the creditor, Vitaly Smagin, initiated a lawsuit to confirm and enforce the LCIA Award in the Central District of California

 | DOI:10.1163/9789004715820_036

pursuant to the New York Convention.[1] The LCIA Award was confirmed, but Yegiazaryan engaged in a pattern of wire fraud and other RICO predicate acts to frustrate Smagin's collection efforts.

The Supreme Court precedent the Court discussed and interpreted in *CMB Monaco v. Smagin* was *RJR Nabisco, Inc. v. European Community* (2016),[2] a case which reinforced a strong presumption against the extraterritorial applicability of RICO and established a "domestic injury" requirement for a civil RICO cause of action to be available to a plaintiff. The *CMB Monaco* Court applied the "domestic injury" test established in *RJR Nabisco* and gave further guidance on how courts should determine whether a plaintiff has alleged a domestic injury for purposes of a private RICO cause of action.

## 2 The Case

### 2.1 *Background*

The case involves three separate (but related) proceedings.

First, in 2014, an LCIA arbitral tribunal seated in London issued the LCIA Award, awarding USD 84 million to Smagin, a Russian citizen, against Yegiazaryan, another Russian citizen. The tribunal found that Yegiazaryan misappropriated Smagin's "shares in a joint real estate venture in Moscow"[3] between 2003 and 2009. In 2010, to avoid criminal indictment, Yegiazaryan moved from Russia to California, refusing to satisfy the LCIA Award.

Second, Smagin started an enforcement action in the Central District of California to confirm and enforce the LCIA Award under the New York Convention. Meanwhile, Smagin learned that Yegiazaryan was granted an arbitration award issued against Suleymon Kerimov in an unrelated matter ("Kerimov Award"). Smagin immediately applied for injunctive relief in California, concerned that Yegiazaryan would take steps to keep any funds paid in satisfaction of the Kerimov Award out of Smagin's reach.

In such context, the U.S. District Court for the Central District of California ("District Court") issued a temporary protective order and a preliminary injunction freezing Yegiazaryan's assets. Yegiazaryan then obtained a $198 million settlement in satisfaction of the Kerimov Award, and engaged in a pattern of wire fraud and other criminal activities, through a complex web of

1 Convention on the Recognition and Enforcement of Foreign Arbitral Awards, made in New York on 10 June 1958 ("New York Convention").

2 *RJR Nabisco, Inc. v. Eur. Cmty.*, 579 U.S. 325, 136 S. Ct. 2090, 195 L. Ed. 2d 476 (2016).

3 *Yegiazaryan v. Smagin*, 599 U.S. 533, 537, 143 S. Ct. 1900, 1905, 216 L. Ed. 2d 521 (2023).

companies, to prevent Smagin from reaching the Kerimov Award to satisfy the LCIA Award, in violation of the District Court's asset freeze. In particular, as the Court in *CMB Monaco* explained:

> Yegiazaryan accepted the money through the London office of an American law firm headquartered in Los Angeles. Yegiazaryan then created "a complex web of offshore entities to conceal the funds," ... and ultimately transferred the funds to a bank account with petitioner CMB Monaco. Yegiazaryan also directed those in his inner circle to file fraudulent claims against him in foreign jurisdictions, which he would not oppose, in an attempt to obtain sham judgments that would encumber the $198 million, thereby blocking Smagin's access to it.[4]

Shortly after, the District Court granted Smagin's motion for summary judgment and entered judgment against Yegiazaryan for U.S. $92 million.

The District Court also eventually found Yegiazaryan in contempt of court for failing to comply with the asset freeze. To avoid compliance with the contempt order, however:

> Yegiazaryan falsely claimed he was too ill, and submitted a forged doctor's note to the District Court. When Smagin notified Yegiazaryan that he would be seeking to depose the doctor in question, who resides in California, Yegiazaryan used "intimidation, threats, or corrupt persuasion" ... to get the doctor to avoid service of the subpoena.[5]

Third, in 2020, Smagin filed a civil lawsuit under RICO ("RICO Complaint") against Yegiazaryan, CMB Bank and others in California. Invoking the private cause of action provided under 18 U.S.C. § 1964(c), Smagin advanced two separate claims: (i) a substantive RICO violation—18 U.S.C. §1962(c); and (ii) a RICO conspiracy claim—18 U.S.C. §1962(d). Smagin argued that defendants worked together to frustrate the enforcement and collection of the LCIA Award, and he sought not only actual damages, but also attorney's fees and treble damages as authorized under 18 U.S.C. § 1964(c).

The District Court dismissed the RICO Complaint on the basis that Smagin failed to prove a "domestic injury" as required under *RJR Nabisco*. The District Court adopted a bright-line "residence-based" approach: if Smagin is a resident

4 *Id.* at 538.
5 *Id.* at 539.

of Russia, the injury must have occurred (and can only occur) in Russia. This was in line with Seventh Circuit precedent on this issue. The Ninth Circuit reversed the District Court decision, adopting the opposite approach, that is, a context-specific approach, which would be consistent with Second and Third Circuits precedent. The Ninth Circuit found that Smagin had pleaded a "domestic injury" because his efforts to enforce the LCIA Award occurred in California, that is, Smagin tried to enforce a Californian judgment against a Californian resident (Yegiazaryan) in California.

Given the Circuit split (Seventh versus Second, Third and Ninth Circuits), the Supreme Court granted certiorari.

## 2.2 *Issue and Summary of Parties' Allegations*

The issue is the following: does Smagin, a Russian citizen and resident, have the right to bring a civil RICO action against Yegiazaryan, a Russian citizen who moved to California in 2010, based on actions related to interfering with the enforcement of a foreign arbitral award?

Because *RJR Nabisco* established a "domestic injury" requirement for a civil cause of action under RICO, the Court had to determine whether Smagin had met this requirement.

As stated in *Yegiazaryan*:

> The "domestic-injury" requirement for private civil RICO suits stems from this Court's decision in *RJR Nabisco*. There, the question before the Court was whether RICO applies extraterritorially. To answer that question, the Court employed the presumption against extraterritoriality, which "represents a canon of construction, or a presumption about a statute's meaning, rather than a limit upon Congress's power to legislate." *Morrison v. National Australia Bank Ltd.*, 561 U.S. 247, 255 (2010). The presumption provides that "[a]bsent clearly expressed congressional intent to the contrary, federal laws will be construed to have only domestic application."[6]

As for the parties' allegations, on the one hand, Yegiazaryan and CMB Monaco ("Petitioners") asked the Court to follow a bright-line rule, locating Smagin's injuries at his country of residence, that is, Russia. They further pled two versions of this rule: (i) first, they argued that RICO private cause of action only remedies economic injuries, which, in their view, necessarily occur at the plaintiff's place of residence; (ii) second, in the alternative, at least when the alleged

6 *RJR Nabisco*, 579 U.S. at 335.

injury is related to "intangible property," as in the case of an enforcement of a foreign arbitral award, some common law principles refer, once again, to the plaintiff's place of residence.

On the other hand, Smagin argued for a context-specific approach that would require considering the specific facts of each case. Here, all such facts occurred in California, which would make Smagin the victim of a "domestic injury." In particular, Smagin argued that a California resident (Yegiazaryan) engaged in criminal activity, including the creation of U.S. shell companies to hide U.S. assets, in an attempt to avoid compliance with a California judgment (confirming the award) in California. As will be addressed below, these and other facts arising in California, were the basis for the Court's holding that domestic injury occurred.

### 2.3 *The Court's Opinion*

Justice Sotomayor delivered the opinion of the Court, agreeing with Smagin and the Ninth Circuit and adopting a context-specific approach. This approach means, "looking to the nature of the alleged injury, the racketeering activity that directly caused it and the injurious aims and effects of that activity."[7]

The Court further explained:

> This approach to the domestic-injury requirement is most consistent with *RJR Nabisco*. There, the Court clarified that its domestic-injury requirement 'does not mean that foreign plaintiffs may not sue under RICO'.[8]

Accordingly, the Court found that Petitioners' approach would be inconsistent with *RJR Nabisco,* as it would exclude all foreign plaintiffs from advancing civil claims under RICO:

> Petitioners' bright-line rule, in contrast, […] makes the location of the plaintiff's residence determinative, thus barring all foreign plaintiffs, exactly as *RJR Nabisco* said it was not doing.[9]

In *RJR Nabisco,* the Court had established a two-step test to overcome the presumption against the extraterritorial applicability of RICO. In the words of the *CMB Monaco* Court:

---

7 *Yegiazaryan*, 599 U.S. at 544.

8 *Id.*

9 *Id.*

> The first [step] asks 'whether the statute gives a clear, affirmative indication that it applies extraterritorially.' If the answer is 'yes,' the presumption is rebutted, and the test ends. If the answer is 'no,' the inquiry proceeds, and step two asks whether the case involves a domestic application of the statute, which is assessed 'by looking to the statute's 'focus."' (…) Proceeding to step two, the Court held that " [a] private RICO plaintiff … must allege and prove a domestic injury to its business or property.[10]

So, in *RJR Nabisco,* step two of the test established the referred "domestic injury" requirement for a civil RICO cause of action.

In applying such test in *Yegiazaryan,* the Court now clarified that:

> § 1964(c)'s focus is on the injury, not in isolation, but as the product of racketeering activity. Thus, in assessing whether there is a domestic injury, courts should engage in a case-specific analysis that looks to the circumstances surrounding the injury. If those circumstances sufficiently ground the injury in the United States, such that it is clear the injury arose domestically, then the plaintiff has alleged a domestic injury.[11]

Finally, the Court concluded that the "central features of the alleged injury" occurred in the United States, more specifically in California:

> Much of the alleged racketeering activity that caused the injury occurred in the United States. Yegiazaryan took domestic actions to avoid collection, including allegedly creating U.S. shell companies to hide his U.S. assets, submitting a forged doctor's note to a California District Court, and intimidating a U.S.-based witness. It is true that other components of the scheme occurred abroad. As Smagin alleges, however, even those 'wrongful acts and plans were devised, initiated, and carried out … through acts and communications initiated in and directed towards Los Angeles County, California,' with the 'central purpose of frustrating enforcement of [the] California judgment.' (…) In sum, Smagin's interests in his California judgment against Yegiazaryan, a California resident, were directly injured by racketeering activity either taken in California or directed from California, with the aim and effect of subverting Smagin's rights to execute on that

10 *Id.* at 534.

11 *Id.* at 545.

> judgment in California. On the Court's contextual approach, those allegations suffice to state a domestic injury in this suit.[12]

Moreover, the Court also dismissed Petitioners' arguments relying on "some common law principles": as to economic injuries, Petitioners argued on the basis of the Restatement (First) of Conflict of Laws; as to intangible injuries, Petitioners argued on the principle *mobilia sequuntur personam*. The Court rejected both arguments:

> The core problem with petitioners' approach is that it is unmoored from the presumption against extraterritoriality. While legal fictions regarding the situs of economic injuries and intangible property have their justifications in other areas of law, those justifications do not necessarily translate to the presumption against extraterritoriality, with its distinctive concerns for comity and discerning congressional meaning.[13]

### 2.4 *Key Takeaways*

*Yegiazaryan* opened the door to foreign plaintiffs seeking civil liability under RICO against debtors who made fraudulent domestic efforts to avoid the enforcement of an international arbitration award. Civil RICO claims are a powerful litigation tool because they allow the victim to recover treble damages and attorney's fees. This remedy is unavailable in most other jurisdictions around the word.

Successful RICO claims in this context, however, are likely to be the exception and not the rule, given the difficulty of proving civil RICO claims. Key takeaways of *Yegiazaryan* may be:

- A private cause of action under RICO is only available to victims of "domestic injury" under *RJR Nabisco*. *Yegiazaryan* clarified that a foreign plaintiff may have sustained domestic injury within the meaning of RICO if the circumstances surrounding the injury "sufficiently ground the injury in the United States, such that it is clear the injury arose domestically."[14]
- Plaintiff's injury in *Yegiazaryan* involved Smagin's inability to collect on intangible property, namely, a foreign arbitral award (converted into a California judgment).

12 *Id.* at 546.

13 *Id.* at 547–548.

14 *Id.* at 545.

- The approach the Supreme Court adopted in *Yegiazaryan*, the so-called context specific approach, is very fact specific. The Court even refused to adopt a set of factors because "no set of factors can capture the relevant considerations for all cases."[15] As a result, each case will be different, and the outcome will depend on the circumstances.
- Substantial uncertainty remains as to how courts will apply this approach, precisely because the Supreme Court refused to provide guidance to lower courts. For example, it is unclear whether the analysis only applies to intangible property like in *Yegiazaryan* or to tangible property as well. This distinction may be, or not, a circumstance to consider under the approach the Court adopted.
- The Court in *Yegiazaryan* only held that Smagin had sufficiently pled a colorable RICO claim and allowed the case to proceed. Smagin must now establish his RICO claim which requires showing a "pattern of racketeering activity" within the meaning of RICO. These cases are extremely difficult to prove, due in part to the punishment that comes with it—treble damages and attorney's fees.
- Smagin alleged that CMB Monaco assisted Yegiazaryan in his plan to thwart Smagin's efforts to collect on the LCIA Award, and the Court allowed the case to proceed against the bank, too. The London office of a U.S. law firm allegedly assisted Yegiazaryan to avoid the District Court's asset freeze, collect on the Karimov Award and prevent Smagin from using the funds to satisfy the LCIA Award. This is a stark warning to third parties, including law firms, who assist debtors to hide and remove assets to avoid payment of an award. They could be held jointly and severally liable for three times the amount of the award if the plaintiff shows they knew about and participated in the pattern of racketeering activity.

## 3 Critical Analysis

RICO is a U.S. federal statute that makes it a crime for any person to invest income derived from "a pattern of racketeering activity" in an enterprise engaged in interstate or foreign commerce;[16] to acquire or maintain an interest in an enterprise through a pattern of racketeering activity;[17] to conduct an

15 *Id.*
16 18 U.S. Code § 1962(a).
17 *Id.* § 1962(b).

enterprise's affairs through a pattern of racketeering activity;[18] and to conspire to violate any of these prohibitions.[19] The statute requires a "pattern" of racketeering activity, a single act is not enough, and defines "racketeering activity" broadly to include a myriad of criminal activities, from murder or kidnapping to mail fraud, wire fraud, financial institution fraud, or extortion.[20] A pattern of activity requires "a series of related predicates that together demonstrate the existence or threat of continued criminal activity."[21]

Section 1964(c) of the RICO statute provides a private right of action for injuries sustained as a result of violations of section 1962's substantive provisions, as follows:

> Any person injured in his business or property by reason of a violation of section 1962 of this chapter may sue therefor in any appropriate United States district court and shall recover threefold the damages he sustains and the cost of the suit, including a reasonable attorney's fee.[22]

In *RJR Nabisco Inc*, the U.S. Supreme Court held that section 1964(c) "requires a civil RICO plaintiff to allege and prove a domestic injury to business or property and does not allow recovery for foreign injuries."[23] But because the *RJR Nabisco* plaintiffs had waived their domestic injury damages claims and were only seeking redress for injury suffered abroad, their claims were dismissed and the Court could not address what constitutes a "domestic injury."

As a result of this uncertainty, prior to *Yegiazaryan*, the U.S. Courts of Appeals applied different tests to determine if a domestic injury to intangible property had occurred for purposes of RICO. The Seventh Circuit adopted a "bright-line rule," locating the injury at plaintiff's place of residence. *See Armada (Singapore) PTE Ltd. v. Amcol Int'l Corp.*, 885 F.3d 1090, 1094 (7th Cir. 2018). Under this theory, only residents in the U.S. could claim civil liability under RICO for injuries sustained as a result of violations of RICO substantive provisions. The Second and Third Circuits applied a multifactor approach that considered the specific circumstances surrounding the dispute. *See Bascunan v. Elsaca*, 874 F. 3d 806, 809 (2d Cir. 2017); *Humphrey v. GlaxoSmithKline PLC*, 905 F.3d 694, 707 (3d Cir. 2018). Under this approach a non-resident in the

18 *Id.* § 1962(c).

19 *Id.* § 1962(d).

20 *Id.* 1961(1).

21 *RJR Nabisco, Inc. v. Eur. Cmty.*, 579 U.S. at 330.

22 18 U.S. Code § 1964(c).

23 *RJR Nabisco, Inc.*, 579 U.S. at 354. (emphasis added).

U.S. could, in some circumstances, have sustained 'domestic injury" for RICO purposes.

For example, in *Bascunan*, a case involving a Chilean national and resident who stole $54 million dollars from another Chilean national and resident through four separate schemes, the Second Circuit reversed the district court and held that "where the injury is to tangible property, ... absent some extraordinary circumstance, the injury is domestic if the plaintiff's property was located in the United States when it was stolen or harmed, even if the plaintiff himself resides abroad."[24] The Second Circuit's holding in *Bascunan* was limited to tangible property, and the question of when an injury to intangible property may be domestic was left open.[25]

On the contrary, in *Humphrey*, the Third Circuit affirmed the district court's dismissal of the case applying also a test which considered a myriad of factors, and not only the plaintiffs' place of residence. *Humphrey* involved two plaintiffs residing in China who accused a multinational company with offices in the U.S. (and other places, like England) of corrupt dealings. The district court dismissed the RICO claims because the plaintiffs failed to allege a domestic injury: "Plaintiffs' business was in China, their only offices were in China, no work was done outside of China, Plaintiffs resided in China, and ... any destruction of Plaintiffs' business occurred while Plaintiffs were imprisoned in China by Chinese authorities."[26] The Third Circuit affirmed and explained the approach as follows:

> Whether an alleged injury to an intangible interest was suffered domestically is a particularly fact-sensitive question requiring consideration of multiple factors. These include, but are not limited to, where the injury itself arose; the location of the plaintiff's residence or principal place of business; where any alleged services were provided; where the plaintiff received or expected to receive the benefits associated with providing such services; where any relevant business agreements were entered into and the laws binding such agreements; and the location of the activities giving rise to the underlying dispute.[27]

---

24 *Bascunan v. Elsaca*, 874 F.3d at 820–21.

25 *Id.* at 814 ("At a minimum, when a foreign plaintiff maintains tangible property in the United States, the misappropriation of that property constitutes a domestic injury.").

26 *Humphrey v. GlaxoSmithKline PLC*, 905 F.3d 694, 697–98 (3d Cir. 2018).

27 *Id.* at 707.

Here, in *Yegiazaryan*, the Ninth Circuit reversed the District Court and adopted the context-specific approach, joining the Second and Third Circuits. The Ninth Circuit focused, first, on the fact that Smagin had obtained a California judgment (enforcing the LCIA Award) and it made no sense to consider that property is in Russia, because the judgment confers Smagin rights in California, not in Russia.[28] The Ninth Circuit additionally considered other factors, and in particular the fact that much of Yegiazaryan's conduct occurred in, or targeted, California. The analysis of the Ninth Circuit was, too, intensively fact specific:

> Our conclusion is bolstered by the fact that much of the conduct underlying the alleged injury also occurred in, or was targeted at, California. As noted, Plaintiff alleges that Defendants corruptly and illegally prevented him from executing the judgment by, among other things, filing false documents in the California court; intimidating a witness who resides in California; and directing, from California, a scheme to funnel millions of dollars into the United States through various companies, including a U.S.-based company that Ashot effectively controlled. Plaintiff also alleges that Ashot had associates file fraudulent claims against him in various jurisdictions in order to obtain sham judgments that were designed to compete with the California Judgment. Those alleged illegal acts were designed to subvert Plaintiff's rights that are executable in California. Accordingly, the alleged harm to Plaintiff's rights under the California Judgment constitutes a domestic injury.[29]

By adopting the context-specific approach, the Ninth Circuit parted ways with the Seventh Circuit's "rigid, residency-based test for domestic injuries involving intangible property."[30] The Ninth Circuit considered that such test "does not align with *RJR Nabisco*" for two separate reasons:

> First, the test makes the location of the plaintiff dispositive, when the Supreme Court stated that it is the location of the injury that is relevant to standing. *RJR Nabisco*, 579 U.S. at 346, 136 S.Ct. 2090. Second, the

28 *See Smagin v. Yegiazaryan*, 37 F.4th 562, 567 (9th Cir. 2022), *cert. granted*, 143 S. Ct. 645 (2023), and *cert. granted sub nom. CMB Monaco v. Smagin*, 143 S. Ct. 646, 214 L. Ed. 2d 382 (2023), and *aff'd and remanded*, 599 U.S. 533, 143 S. Ct. 1900, 216 L. Ed. 2d 521 (2023).

29 *Id.* at 567–68.

30 *Id.* at 568.

> Seventh Circuit's test effectively truncates the standing requirement set forth in *RJR Nabisco* if the harm is to intangible property. Rather than asking whether a plaintiff alleges "a domestic injury to its business or property," as the Supreme Court described, *id.* (emphasis omitted and added), the Seventh Circuit requires that a plaintiff allege a domestic injury to its business only, with the location of that business defined by the plaintiff's residence.[31]

The U.S. Supreme Court granted certiorari to resolve the split. In *Yegiazaryan*, the Court was able to conduct the analysis that it did not get to conduct in *RJR Nabisco* on what domestic injury to intangible property means, and held that in determining whether a plaintiff has pled "domestic injury" under RICO, courts must look to "the circumstances surrounding the alleged injury to assess whether it arose in the United States."[32] That means looking to "the nature of the alleged injury, the racketeering activity that directly caused it, and the injurious aims and effects of that activity."

The Court did not modify the substantive elements of RICO, and simply addressed what a plaintiff must pled to survive a motion to dismiss. Several questions remain open, as addressed above, in particular, what is the test to tangible property and how the test will be applied by lower courts, which did not receive guidance on the specific circumstances or factors to consider making the determination.

## 4 Conclusions

A RICO claim is a significant tool in U.S. civil litigation because of the severe consequences it may have for the defendant.

Under *Yegiazaryan*, if a foreign international arbitral award is converted into a U.S. judgment, by having it enforced by a U.S. court, and the defendant engages in a pattern of criminal conduct within the meaning of RICO to thwart plaintiff's efforts to collect on the judgment, then it is possible that a RICO claim is available to that plaintiff. Critically, the circumstances must "sufficiently ground the injury in the United States, such that it is clear the injury

31 *Id.* at 570.

32 *Yegiazaryan*, 599 U.S. at 543–44.

arose domestically," then the plaintiff would have 'alleged a domestic injury" and plaintiff's RICO claim would be allowed to proceed.

Each case will be different under the context-specific approach the U.S. Supreme Court adopted in *Yegiazaryan*, and uncertainty remains on how lower courts will apply this approach.

CHAPTER 36

# *Coinbase, Inc. v. Suski et al.* (2024): Delegation *versus* Forum Selection Clause, Contradictory Contracts, and Kompetenz-Kompetenz Doctrine

*Peter C. Sester*

## 1 Introduction

In the present case the Supreme Court ruled for the first time on an arbitration that emerged in the aftermath of a cryptocurrency deal. However, the issues at the heart of the dispute are not new at all. Instead, the decision depended on addressing some of the most classic issues in domestic and international arbitration, in other words the Court was served old wine in new barrels.

The essence of the dispute was a competence conflict between an arbitral tribunal and a federal court. The parties had executed two contradictory contracts regarding the same deal – one of the contracts contained an arbitration clause, the other one a forum selection clause in favor of California courts (state and federal). Who decides in such a case on the competence issue? Is it the arbitral tribunal or the court? The answer to the question requires drawing a borderline between the co-called Kompetenz-Kompetenz principle and the Supreme Court's consolidated stance that "consent is essential under the FAA because arbitrators wield only the authority they are given".[1]

In the Court's view arbitration is essentially a matter of consent, not coercion; to put it differently: the parties' will, or intentions determine the scope of an arbitration agreement.[2] Hence, that scope is ultimately a matter of contract interpretation.[3]

1 Lamps Plus, Inc. v. Varela, 587 U.S. __, 139 S. Ct. 1407, 1416, 203 L. Ed. 2d 636, 646 (2019).

2 *See* Mitsubishi Motors Corp. v. Soler Chrysler-Plymouth, Inc., 473 U.S. 614, 626, 105 S. Ct. 3346, 3354, 87 L. Ed. 2d 444, 455 (1985) ("[A]s with any other contract, the parties' intentions control"); Mastrobuono v. Shearson Lehman Hutton, Inc., 514 U.S. 52, 57, 115 S. Ct. 1212, 1216, 131 L. Ed. 2d 76, 84 (1995) ("[T]he FAA's pro-arbitration policy does not operate without regard to the wishes of the contracting parties"); Stolt-Nielsen S. A. v. AnimalFeeds Int'l Corp., 559 U.S. 662, 684, 130 S. Ct. 1758, 1775, 176 L. Ed. 2d 605, 624 (2010) (highlighting the "foundational FAA principle that arbitration is a matter of consent").

3 Peter Sester, *Contract Law in International Commercial Arbitration* (Kluwer, IALL Vol. 66, 2023).

 | DOI:10.1163/9789004715820_037

Importantly, the issue decided by the Supreme Court in Coinbase, Inc. *v.* Suski et al. is very different from the question under which circumstances non-signatories are bound by an arbitration agreement that was signed by only some but not all of the parties involved in the dispute. The non-signatory issue arises in multi-party arbitrations (e.g. construction projects) or where one of the signatories is part of a holding structure. Instead, Coinbase, Inc. *v.* Suski et al. was a classical bilateral dispute: the operator of a trading platform, the Petitioner, against the users of the platform, Respondents, acting as a bloc by means of a class action filed in California.

## 2 A Primer on the Kompetenz-Kompetenz Doctrine and the Nature of Arbitration

Kompetenz-Kompetenz is a German word. The origin explains the spelling that is weird from an English language perspective. However, the expression became over the decades a globally used technical term in international arbitration. It was originally created by the German Federal Constitutional Court (*Bundesverfassungsgericht*) in a completely different context.

The German Constitutional Court was established 75 years ago when the Fundamental Law (*Grundgesetz*, the German post war constitution) entered into force. That Law regulates not only the basic structure of the Constitutional Court (e.g. appointment of judges) but also its competences. The Court is the guardian of the Fundamental Law and has the authority to interpret the wording of the constitutional text. In the light of this function and authority it was only logical that the Court established the rule that it also enjoys the competence to interpret the articles of the Fundamental Law on the Court's competence, hence, to determine its own jurisdiction, in other words rule on the Kompetenz-Kompetenz.

That idea was transposed to (international) arbitration in the following form: the arbitral tribunal is competent to rule on its own jurisdiction, including challenges to the scope and validity of the arbitration agreement, which may be a clause of the main contract or established in a separate legal document. As far as the doctrine applies, the arbitral tribunal can not only decide issues relating to the main contract (merits)—the contract that underlies the deal that gave rise to the dispute. It also has the authority to decide issues concerning the scope and validity of an arbitration clause (included in the main contract) or of an arbitration agreement that was separately executed.

Where the doctrine applies, state or federal courts can neither rule on a suit brought by one of the parties that signed the arbitration clause (or agreement), nor may such a court issue a so-called anti-arbitration injunction deemed to stop the commencement or continuation of an arbitration. Notably, once the arbitration proceeding is terminated, the parties may challenge the arbitral award before a court. The Kompetenz-Kompetenz doctrine poses, in principle, no obstacle to seek vacation of the award. Thus, *ex post* control by the courts is possible, if the arbitral tribunal erroneously held it had jurisdiction. The Kompetenz-Kompetenz doctrine only poses an obstacle to *ex ante* control by the courts.

However, in Coinbase, Inc. *v.* Suski et al. the Supreme Court did not apply the doctrine. Instead, the Court highlighted the fact that the same parties had agreed on two contracts—one sending arbitrability disputes to arbitration, and the other either explicitly or implicitly sending arbitrability disputes to the courts.[4] Both contracts referred to the same transaction that gave rise to the dispute. The Supreme Court's approach is consistent with its prior case law. Since the enactment of the FAA, the Court has held, that the nature of arbitration is fundamentally a matter of contract and that arbitrators derive their authority solely from the parties' mutual agreement.[5]

There is indeed a broad international consensus that "the arbitration agreement is the basis for and the cornerstone of every arbitration: there can be no

---

4 602 U.S. ___ (2024), Opinion of the Court, p. 8.

5 *See* United Steelworkers v. Warrior & Gulf Navigation Co., 363 U.S. 574, 582, 80 S. Ct. 1347, 1353, 4 L. Ed. 2d 1409, 1417 (1960). ("[A]rbitration is a matter of contract and a party cannot be required to submit to arbitration any dispute which he has not agreed so to submit"); Gateway Coal Co. v. United Mine Workers, 414 U.S. 368, 374, 94 S. Ct. 629, 635, 38 L. Ed. 2d 583, 590 (1974) ("The law compels a party to submit his grievance to arbitration only if he has contracted to do so"); Nolde Bros., Inc. v. Local No. 358, Bakery & Confectionery Workers Union, 430 U.S. 243, 250, 97 S. Ct. 1067, 1071, 51 L. Ed. 2d 300, 308 (1977) ("[T]he arbitration duty is a creature of the collective-bargaining agreement and ... a party cannot be compelled to arbitrate any matter in the absence of a contractual obligation to do so"); First Options of Chicago, Inc. v. Kaplan, 514 U.S. 938, 943, 115 S. Ct. 1920, 1924, 131 L. Ed. 2d 985, 992 (1995) ("[A]rbitration is simply a matter of contract between the parties; it is a way to resolve those disputes—but only those disputes—that the parties have agreed to submit to arbitration"); Buckeye Check Cashing, Inc. v. Cardegna, 546 U.S. 440, 443, 126 S. Ct. 1204, 1207, 163 L. Ed. 2d 1038, 1042 (2006) ("Section 2 [of the FAA] embodies the national policy favoring arbitration and places arbitration agreements on equal footing with all other contracts"); Rent-A-Center, West, Inc. v. Jackson, 561 U.S. 63, 67, 130 S. Ct. 2772, 2776, 177 L. Ed. 2d 403, 410 (2010) ("The FAA reflects the fundamental principle that arbitration is a matter of contract"); AT&T Mobility LLC v. Concepcion, 563 U.S. 333, 351, 131 S. Ct. 1740, 1752, 179 L. Ed. 2d 742, 758 (2011) ("Arbitration is a matter of contract, and the FAA requires courts to honor parties' expectations"); Am. Express Co. v. Italian Colors Rest., 570 U.S. 228, 233, 133 S. Ct. 2304, 2309, 186 L. Ed. 2d 417, 424 (2013) (Describing "the overarching principle that arbitration is a matter of contract").

arbitration without an arbitration agreement. The arbitration agreement also determines the scope of the arbitration. Thus, there can be no arbitration outside the limits set by the parties' agreement to arbitrate".[6]

Hence, arbitration certainly has a strong contractual element. As previously said, in the view of the Supreme Court the contractual component is dominant and thus determines the nature of arbitration. However, in other jurisdictions the courts and legal doctrine emphasize that the nature of arbitration also entails a quasi-judicial or adjudicative component. Some jurisdictions put arbitrators explicitly on equal footprint with the judges (e.g., article 18 Brazilian Arbitration Act); almost equal for, at the end of the day, courts may set an award aside or vacate it provided extraordinary circumstances are proven (e.g., violation of due process or public policy). Nowhere in the world this works the other way round.

Gabrielle Kaufmann-Kohler, a leading authority in international arbitration, summarized the non-contractual element of arbitration in clear words: "Arbitration also has a quasi-judicial or adjudicative component. To the extent they (the arbitrators) are called upon to administer justice *in lieu* of the courts, the arbitrators render a decision (the arbitral award), which is equivalent to a court judgement and produces the same effect (in particular, the *res judicata* effect and enforceability)".[7]

Although the existence of the quasi-judicial or adjudicative component is recognized in many legal orders, there is no consensus on its impact and relative strength. Where the emphasize of the quasi-judicial component is strong (e.g. Brazil), the Kompetenz-Kompetenz principal has gained force, and consequently courts are more reluctant to claim competence vis-à-vis an arbitral tribunal. This is especially true if the arbitral proceeding was already set in motion before the dispute is somehow brought before a court. From a comparative law perspective, the U.S. Supreme Court's stance is at the lower end of a sliding scale that illustrates the quasi-judicial nature of arbitration.

Yet, even in jurisdictions where the courts value the Kompetenz-Kompetenz doctrine high, it is in practice very difficult to draw the exact borderline between the competence of arbitral tribunals and the courts. In Brazil, for instance, the wording of the Brazilian Arbitration Act (article 18) highlights the judicial character of arbitrator's decision-making "arbitrators are judges of the

---

6 Gabrielle Kaufmann-Kohler and Antonio Rigozzi. *International Arbitration: Law and Practice in Switzerland* (Oxford University Press 2015), p. 6.

7 Gabrielle Kaufmann-Kohler and Antonio Rigozzi. *International Arbitration: Law and Practice in Switzerland* (Oxford University Press 2015), p. 6–7.

facts and the law". Consequently, Brazilian courts have consistently emphasized the importance of the Kompetenz-Kompetenz doctrine.[8]

Nevertheless, the Superior Court of Justice (*Superior Tribunal de Justiça*) created a special suit that limits the scope of the doctrine. Whenever an arbitral tribunal and a court (first or second instance) claim jurisdiction regarding the same dispute, it falls within the competence of the Superior Court of Justice to rule on that conflict. The respective lawsuit is called conflict of competence (*conflito de competência*). It can be brought by the interested party directly before the Superior Court of Justice (hereinafter STJ), which is according to the Brazilian Federal Constitution the one and only Court that can rule on a conflict of competence. This rule applies, according to the STJ, to conflicts between two courts but also to conflicts between a court and an arbitral tribunal, and even to a competence conflict between two arbitral tribunals.

The suit can be filed before the end of the arbitration proceeding,[9] hence it is a form of *ex ante* control of decisions on jurisdiction made by arbitral tribunals. After an arbitral award is rendered, the interested party may anyway request vacation of the arbitral award if the arbitral tribunal had no jurisdiction (*ex post* control). That suit starts in Brazil before a judge of first instance.

## 3 The Case

### 3.1 *Background of the Case*

The root cause of the dispute is a contradiction between two contracts that were both executed by the same parties that now dispute over a certain issue. Petitioner is Coinbase, Inc. which operates a cryptocurrency exchange platform. Respondents are users of Coinbase. To buy and sell cryptocurrency on the platform, users create accounts which obviously require them to accept the standard or adhesion contract offered by Coinbase. According to the Supreme Court[10]:

---

8 Peter Sester. *International Arbitration: Law and Practice in Brazil* (Oxford University Press 2020), p. 12.

9 See the landmark ruling of the Superior Court of Justice (STJ) on a competence conflict between an arbitral tribunal and a federal court, CC No. 151.130—SP (2017/0043173–8). On the discussion prior to the ruling see Peter Sester. *Business and Investment in Brazil: Law and Practice* (Oxford University Press 2022), p. 66–77.

10 602 U.S. ___ (2024), Opinion of the Court, p. 2.

The first relevant contract is the Coinbase User Agreement that respondents agreed to when they created their accounts. The User Agreement contains a provision that the contract calls the Arbitration Agreement. 1 App. 218. The Arbitration Agreement includes a delegation clause:

> This Arbitration Agreement includes, without limitation, disputes arising out of or related to the interpretation or application of the Arbitration Agreement, including the enforceability, revocability, scope, or validity of the Arbitration Agreement or any portion of the Arbitration Agreement. All such matters shall be decided by an arbitrator and not by a court or judge.

Respondents each agreed to the User Agreement, complete with the above-quoted arbitration language. If that were the only contract at issue, we would not be deciding this case, since the Arbitration Agreement quite clearly sends to arbitration disputes between Coinbase and its users, including disputes about arbitrability. These parties, though, agreed to a second contract. Coinbase offered a sweepstakes that users could enter for a chance to win a cryptocurrency called Dogecoin. Respondents each submitted entries in June 2021, and in doing so, agreed to the Official Rules of the sweepstakes. Unlike the User Agreement, the Official Rules contained a forum selection clause, which provided:

> The California courts (state and federal) shall have sole jurisdiction of any controversies regarding the [sweepstakes] promotion and the laws of the state of California shall govern the promotion. Each entrant waives any and all objections to jurisdiction and venue in those courts for any reason and hereby submits to the jurisdiction of those courts. ... Thus, after respondents entered the sweepstakes, the parties had executed two contracts: the User Agreement, which sent disputes about arbitrability to arbitration, and the Official Rules, which appeared to send disputes to California courts.
>
> Once the sweepstakes concluded, the conflict between these contracts came to a head. Respondents filed a class action complaint in the U.S. District Court for the Northern District of California, alleging that the sweepstakes violated California's False Advertising Law, Unfair Competition Law, and Consumer Legal Remedies Act. Invoking the User Agreement and its delegation clause, Coinbase moved to compel arbitration. The District Court denied Coinbase's motion. It reasoned that

deciding which contract governed was a question for the court; that the User Agreement's arbitration provision conflicted with the forum selection clause in the Official Rules; and that, under California contract law, the Official Rules superseded the User Agreement. The District Court therefore determined that the Official Rules' forum selection clause controlled, so the parties' sweepstakes-related dispute was not subject to arbitration. The Ninth Circuit affirmed. 55 F. 4th 1227 (2022)".

### 3.2 *Issue and Parties' Contentions*

The Supreme Court "granted certiorari to answer the question of who—a judge or an arbitrator—should decide whether a subsequent contract supersedes an earlier arbitration agreement that contains a delegation clause".[11] This type of clause empowers an arbitral tribunal to decide all disputes under the contract, including whether a specific dispute is arbitrable.[12]

According to the Supreme Court the central issue in Coinbase, Inc. *v.* Suski et al. was the question[13]:

> whether the parties agreed to arbitrate arbitrability can be answered only by determining which contract applies. In other words, the substance of the parties' supersession dispute is whether there is an agreement to arbitrate. Field Intelligence Inc. v. Xylem Dewatering Solutions Inc., 49 F. 4th 351, 356 (CA3 2022). When homing in on the conflict between the delegation clause in the first contract and the forum selection clause in the second, the question is whether the parties agreed to send the given dispute to arbitration—and, per usual—so the Supreme Court—that question must be answered by a court.

After having distilled the central issue of the case the Supreme Court summarized and addressed the key contentions of the petitioner[14]:

> First, Coinbase invoked the so-called severability principle. Under the severability principle, an arbitration [or delegation] provision is severable from the remainder of the contract, and unless the challenge is to the arbitration [or delegation] clause itself, the issue of the contract's validity is considered by the arbitrator in the first instance. Buckeye Check

11 602 U.S. ___ (2024), Opinion of the Court, p. 3.
12 602 U.S. ___ (2024), Opinion of the Court, p. 1.
13 602 U.S. ___ (2024), Syllabus p. 2.
14 602 U.S. ___ (2024), Opinion of the Court, p. 6–7.

> Cashing, Inc. v. Cardegna, 546 U.S. 440, 445–446 (2006). Coinbase argues that, pursuant to this principle, the Ninth Circuit should have isolated the User Agreement's delegation provision and considered only arguments specific to that provision.

The Supreme Court did not find this argument of the Petitioner convincing and countered it as follows[15]:

> Assuming without deciding that the severability principle is implicated here, it is nonetheless satisfied. The severability principle establishes that a party seeking to avoid arbitration must directly challenge the arbitration or delegation clause, not just the contract as a whole. But this rule does not require that a party challenges only the arbitration or delegation provision. Rather, where a challenge applies equally to the whole contract and to an arbitration or delegation provision, a court must address that challenge. Rent-A-Center, 561 U.S., at 71. Again, basic principles of contract and consent require that result. Arbitration and delegation agreements are simply contracts, and, normally, if a party says that a contract is invalid, the court must address that argument before deciding the merits of the contract dispute. So too here. If a party challenges the validity ... of the precise agreement to arbitrate at issue, the federal court must consider the challenge before ordering compliance with that [arbitration] agreement.

Second, "Coinbase contended that, as a matter of California Law, the Ninth Circuit was wrong to hold that the Official Rules' forum selection clause superseded the User Agreement's delegation provision".[16] The Supreme Court considered the issue to be outside the scope of the question presented, and, consequently did not address it. The Court justified this holding as follows:[17]

> "We took this case to decide whether, under the FAA, a court or an arbitrator decides which of the two contractual provisions controls. We decline to consider auxiliary questions about whether the Ninth Circuit properly applied state law."

---

15 602 U.S. ___ (2024), Opinion of the Court, p. 7.
16 602 U.S. ___ (2024) p. 10.
17 602 U.S. ___ (2024 p. 8.

Lastly, so the Supreme Court, "Coinbase contended that the Supreme Court's approach will invite chaos by facilitating challenges to delegation clauses".[18] The Court rejected this last resort argument as follows:[19]

> "We do not believe that such chaos will follow. In cases where parties have agreed to only one contract, and that contract contains an arbitration clause with a delegation provision, then, absent a successful challenge to the delegation provision, courts must send all arbitrability disputes to arbitration. But, where, as here, parties have agreed to two contracts—one sending arbitrability disputes to arbitration, and the other either explicitly or implicitly sending arbitrability disputes to the courts—a court must decide which contract governs. To hold otherwise would be to impermissibly elevate [a delegation provision] over other forms of contract."

### 3.3 *The Supreme Court's Opinion*

#### 3.3.1 Building on Existing Rulings of the Supreme Court

The first part of the Supreme Court's reasoning builds on its prior rulings which Justice Jackson, who wrote the Court's opinion, brilliantly summarized. The summary leaves no room for doubt: in the Court's view arbitration agreements and arbitration are essentially a matter of contract (law) where party autonomy prevails. According to the Supreme Court's opinion delivered by Justice Jackson

> "the Federal Arbitration Act (FAA) reflects the fundamental principle that arbitration is a matter of contract. Rent-A Center, West, Inc. v. Jackson, 561 U.S. 63, 67 (2010). As a result, arbitration agreements are valid, irrevocable, and enforceable, save upon such grounds as exist at law or in equity for the revocation of any contract. 9 U.S.C. §2. If a court is satisfied that the making of the agreement for arbitration ... is not in issue, it must send the dispute to an arbitrator. §4. The FAA thereby places arbitration agreements on an equal footing with other contracts. Rent-A-Center, 561 U.S., at 67. Given that arbitration agreements are simply contracts, [t]he first principle that underscores all of our arbitration decisions' is that arbitration is strictly a matter of consent. Lamps Plus, Inc. v. Varela, 587 U.S. 176, 184 (2019) (quoting Granite Rock Co. v. Teamsters, 561 U.S. 287,

18 602 U.S. ___ (2024) p. 10.

19 See Prima Paint Corp. v. Flood & Conklin Mfg. Co., 388 U.S. 395, 404, n. 12 (1967).

299 (2010); some alterations in original). Arbitration is a way to resolve those disputes—but only those disputes—that the parties have agreed to submit to arbitration. First Options of Chicago, Inc. v. Kaplan, 514 U.S. 938, 943 (1995). Consequently, the first question in any arbitration dispute must be: What have these parties agreed to?

As relevant here, parties can form multiple levels of agreements concerning arbitration. At a basic level, parties can agree to send the merits of a dispute to an arbitrator. They can also agree by contract that an arbitrator, rather than a court, will resolve threshold arbitrability questions as well as underlying merits disputes.[20] Henry Schein, Inc. v. Archer & White Sales, Inc., 586 U.S. 63, 65 (2019). An agreement to allow an arbitrator to decide whether a dispute is subject to arbitration—i.e., its arbitrability—is simply an additional, antecedent agreement ..., and the FAA operates on this additional arbitration agreement just as it does on any other. Rent-A-Center, 561 U.S., at 70.

A contest over the merits of the dispute is a first-order disagreement, First Options, 514 U.S., at 942, the resolution of which depends on the applicable law and relevant facts. The parties may also have a second-order dispute—whether they agreed to arbitrate the merits—as well as a third-order dispute—who should have the primary power to decide the second matter. ... Under contract principles, these second- and third-order questions are also matters of consent. Just as the arbitrability of the merits of a dispute depends upon whether the parties agreed to arbitrate that dispute, so the question who has the primary power to decide arbitrability' turns upon what the parties agreed about that matter.

We ask who has the power to decide arbitrability because a party who has not agreed to arbitrate will normally have a right to the court's decision about the merits of its dispute.[21] ... Thus, we have explained that courts should not assume that the parties agreed to arbitrate arbitrability unless there is clear and unmistakable evidence that they did so.[22] Before referring a dispute to an arbitrator, therefore, the court determines whether a valid arbitration agreement exists. Henry Schein, 586 U.S., at 69."

20 That is actually the standard scenario in (international) commercial arbitration.

21 Notably, in Coinbase, Inc. *v.* Suski et al. the party, Respondent, that refused to resolve the dispute before an arbitral tribunal, had already filed a class action in California. In the light of Lamps Plus that party would not have been able to file a class arbitration because none of the contracts in Coinbase, Inc. *v.* Suski et al. provided for class arbitration.

22 See AT&T Technologies, Inc. v. Communications Workers, 475 U.S. 643, 649 (1986).

### 3.3.2 Amending the Existing Three Layers Approach

Thus far the quoted opinion of the Supreme Court in Coinbase, Inc. *v.* Suski et al. builds on prior rulings of the Court. In the last step the author of the opinion, Justice Jackson, resumes the three layers of arbitration disputes and adds a fourth layer that fits the central issue of the present case:

> In prior cases, we have addressed three layers of arbitration disputes: (1) merits, (2) arbitrability, and (3) who decides arbitrability. This case involves a fourth: What happens if parties have multiple agreements that conflict as to the third-order question of who decides arbitrability? As always, traditional contract principles apply. Coinbase says the User Agreement's delegation clause controls. Respondents counter that the Official Rules' forum selection clause superseded that agreement. If Coinbase is right that the User Agreement's delegation clause was meant to govern all agreements moving forward, then the parties agreed to arbitrate all subsequent arbitrability disputes. If respondents are correct that the Official Rules' forum selection clause superseded the User Agreement's delegation clause, then the parties meant to send sweepstakes disputes—including those over arbitrability—to California courts.
>
> Thus, the question whether these parties agreed to arbitrate arbitrability can be answered only by determining which contract applies. In other words, the substance of the parties' supersession dispute is whether there is an agreement to arbitrate. Field Intelligence Inc. v. Xylem Dewatering Solutions Inc., 49 F. 4th 351, 356 (CA3 2022). When we home in on the conflict between the delegation clause in the first contract and forum selection clause in the second, the question is whether the parties agreed to send the given dispute to arbitration—and, per usual, that question must be answered by a court.

The Supreme Court concluded that a court, not an arbitrator, must decide whether the parties' first agreement was superseded by their second agreement. Consequently, the Ninth Circuit's judgment was affirmed.

## 3.4 *Concurring Opinion*

Justice Gorsuch wrote a short concurring opinion with a slightly different emphasis. He highlights that the Supreme Court "did not endorse the reasoning in the Ninth Circuit's opinion, let alone its state contract law analysis of the parties' agreements".[23] According to Justice Gorsuch

> parties choose to send disputes arising from their contracts to an arbitrator instead of a court. Ante, at 4; see 9 U.S.C. §2. Just as often, it seems, parties later wind up disagreeing about whether a particular dispute is subject to that arbitration agreement. Sometimes a court can resolve their disagreement about the "arbitrability" of a particular dispute. But sometimes not. For parties can agree to send arbitrability questions to an arbitrator too, through what this Court calls a delegation clause. Ante, at 4–5; Henry Schein, Inc. v. Archer & White Sales, Inc., 586 U.S. 63, 65 (2019).
>
> What happens when (as in this case) the parties have two contracts, one with a delegation clause, a second without, and a dispute later arises? Like everything else in this area, it depends on what the parties have agreed. Ante, at 4. Sometimes, a court may conclude that the parties' agreements are best read as leaving for the court the task of resolving the arbitrability of the dispute at hand. But sometimes, the parties' agreements may be best read as vesting that power in an arbitrator. Just imagine a master contract providing that all disputes arising out of or related to this or future agreements between the parties, including questions concerning whether a dispute should be routed to arbitration, shall be decided by an arbitrator. Absent some later amendment, a provision like that would seem to require a court to step aside.
>
> It is not clear to me whether the Ninth Circuit appreciated this point. But nor does that matter. Our decision today recognizes—and stresses—that arbitration is a matter of contract ... and parties can agree by contract that an arbitrator, rather than a court, will resolve threshold arbitrability questions as well as underlying merits disputes.[24] Notably, too, the Court does not endorse the reasoning in the Ninth Circuit's opinion, let alone its state contract law analysis of the parties' agreements. ... Instead, the Court simply reaffirms well-established principles about the primacy of the parties' agreements when it comes to arbitration ... and the Ninth Circuit's bottom-line conclusion that a court had to decide whether and to what extent the parties here reached an agreement to have an arbitrator resolve the question of arbitrability.

23 602 U.S. ___ (2024), concurring opinion by Justice Gorsuch, p. 2.

24 See Henry Schein, 586 U.S., at 65.

After having outlined his understanding of the case Justice Gorsuch declared that he is pleased to concur.

## 4 Key Takeaways

In prior cases, the Supreme Court had addressed three layers of arbitration disputes: (1) the merits, (2) arbitrability, and (3) who decides arbitrability. In Coinbase, Inc. *v.* Suski et al. the Court decided that there is a fourth layer: What happens if parties have multiple agreements that conflict as to the third-order question of who decides arbitrability?

According to the Court traditional contract principles apply because arbitration is essentially a matter of contract (law). Hence, without a valid agreement that sends each of the disputes on each of the four layers to arbitration the missing layer(s) is (are) decided by the courts. The fundamental question of whether such an agreement exists does not fall—in the Supreme Court's view—within the competence of an arbitral tribunal. Thus far—so the Court implicitly—the Kompetenz-Kompetenz doctrine does not apply.

Consequently, the Court held unanimously: where parties have agreed to two contracts—one sending arbitrability disputes to arbitration, and the other either explicitly or implicitly sending arbitrability disputes to the courts—a court must decide which contract governs.

## 5 The Impact of Coinbase, Inc. *v.* Suski et al. on U.S. Arbitration Law and Practice

Coinbase, Inc. *v.* Suski et al. was decided by the Supreme Court on May 23, 2024. Ten days later I sent this piece to the publisher. Hence, when writing the piece, it was far too early to make a robust statement on the impact of the decision on U.S. arbitration law and practice. I do not have a crystal ball.

However, in the light of the Supreme Court's previous rulings on arbitration one can, at least, state that the holdings of the Court in Coinbase, Inc. *v.* Suski et al. are no surprise. Remarkably, none of the Justices dissented. This is perfectly understandable for the decision is consistent with the Court's longstanding contractual approach to arbitration. Hence, one can expect that no major changes will occur, certainly not in U.S. statutory law on arbitration. The Supreme Court added only another piece to its consolidated approach to arbitration; the Court names this piece the "fourth layer" of arbitration disputes: What happens if parties have multiple agreements that conflict as to the third-order question of who decides arbitrability? According to the Court's holding in Coinbase, Inc. *v.* Suski et al. the decision is up to the courts.

As far as U.S. arbitration practice is concerned some voices say that the decision might have a negative impact on seating arbitrations in the USA, for courts of other countries value the Kompetenz-Kompetenz doctrine higher and would have ruled differently. I do not share this point of view, at least not as far as international arbitration in the USA is concerned. First and foremost, you never know how another court would rule.

Second, the facts of the case (a trading platform operator *versus* various platform users that filed a class action in the courts) are very different from the typical scenario of international commercial arbitration: a dispute that arises in the context of a transaction specific contract (or a set of contracts) that was executed by equally sophisticated enterprises with a more or less similar bargaining power.

Third, New York City (not California, the origin of *Coinbase*) is the predominant seat of international arbitration in the USA. There is also a clear market preference to combine seat New York with a choice of law clause in favor of New York contract law. New York courts are famous to uphold commercial contracts and enforce them literally.[25] This is widely considered a competitive advantage of the seat New York for, whoever seeks to challenge the validity of an arbitration (delegation) clause before a New York judge or court will face an uphill battle. The challenge will not be much different in Miami or Houston, the main alternatives to New York when negotiating a seat for international arbitration in the USA.

## 6 Conclusions

In the Supreme Court's view arbitration is essentially a matter of contract. Thus, *in dubio* the courts and not the arbitrator(s) decide on whether there is a valid arbitration agreement that sends a specific dispute to arbitration. Hence drafting clear delegation clauses and avoiding contradictions when amending or adding contracts to an existing agreement is crucial. These are obviously very basic recommendations that always apply. However, the Supreme Court's holding in Coinbase, Inc. *v.* Suski et al. gives us arbitration lawyers munition

25 Peter Sester, *Contract Law in International Commercial Arbitration* (Kluwer, IALL Vol. 66, 2023).

to alert once again clients and transaction lawyers that arbitration clauses require the same diligence as price and payment clauses.

The bottom-line result in Coinbase, Inc. *v.* Suski et al. is: the party that brought a class action before the courts in California won. Hence, not only the reasoning of the Supreme Court (arbitration is essentially a matter of contract) is consistent with previous decisions handed down by the Court, but also the policy implication. At least since *Lamps Plus* it is clear that the Supreme Court prefers class action over class arbitration.[26] Although this was not the question in Coinbase, Inc. *v.* Suski et al. the outcome of the case—the class action in California may continue—fits the Supreme Court's preference as expressed in *Lamps Plus*.

---

26 See William H. Baker, "Class Action Arbitration" in James H. Carter and John Fellas, *International Commercial Arbitration in New York*, 2nd edn (OUP, 2016) 373–420.

# Index